The Politics of the Administrative Process

The Politics of the Administrative Process

Second Edition

JAMES W. FESLER
Yale University

and

DONALD F. KETTL
University of Wisconsin — Madison

CHATHAM HOUSE PUBLISHERS, INC.
Chatham, New Jersey

THE POLITICS OF THE ADMINISTRATIVE PROCESS
SECOND EDITION

CHATHAM HOUSE PUBLISHERS, INC.
Post Office Box One
Chatham, New Jersey 07928

PUBLISHERS: Edward Artinian
COVER DESIGN: Lawrence Ratzkin
PRODUCTION SUPERVISOR: Katharine Miller
COMPOSITION: Bang, Motley, Olufsen
PRINTING AND BINDING: R.R. Donnelley & Sons Company

LIBRARY OF CONGRESS CATALOGING-IN-PUBLICATION DATA

Fesler, James William, 1911–
        The politics of the administrative process / James W. Fesler
    and Donald F. Kettl. — 2nd ed.
        p.   cm. —
        Includes bibilographical references and index.
        ISBN 1-56643-025-9 (pbk.)
        1. Public administration.   I. Kettl, Donald F.   II. Title.
JF1351.F46   1996
350—dc20   95-50155
                                                            CIP

Manufactured in the United States of America
10   9   8   7   6   5   4   3   2

Acknowledgments

Authors of a book of this scope are indebted to the many scholars in academic and governmental careers whose writings inform, analyze, and stimulate. Our reference notes reveal this debt and suggest other opportunities for scholars and students to explore further the issues identified in the text. Rosslyn S. Kleeman of the General Accounting Office and Jerry Mashaw of the Yale Law School have kindly read and commented on chapters touching their fields of knowledge.

This book, though a thorough revision, builds on the first edition of *Public Administration* to which many colleagues contributed comments on drafts of the whole or of particular chapters. It is appropriate to express again our indebtedness to them: William I. Bacchus, Bruce Buchanan, Geoffrey C. Hazard, Jr., Hugh Heclo, Charles E. Lindblom, Edward W. Pauly, Harold W. Stanley, and Douglas T. Yates.

The authors are also grateful to Patricia W. Ingraham, Michael D. Reagan, and Aaron Wildavsky, who reviewed the manuscript for Chatham House. They read the manuscript with great care and raised numerous issues that forced us to rethink and recast our treatment of several topics. All of our colleagues who generously commented on the text deserve our deep thanks for the improvements they helped us make. Of course, none of them bears any responsibility for the final results.

Our work was greatly facilitated by the librarians at Yale University, the University of Virginia, Vanderbilt University, and the University of Wisconsin—Madison. We are especially grateful to the government documents librarians at these institutions for helping guide us through the great mass of remarkably informative materials that the federal government publishes. In addition, we are grateful for the generous support of the University of Wisconsin—Madison's Robert M. La Follette Institute of Public Affairs.

Finally, we thank our students, whose thoughtful questions over the years have kept our eyes on the important issues. We hope the text conveys some of the enthusiasm and excitement for public administration they have engendered in us.

Contents

Part I: What Government Does— And How It Does It

Part II: Organizations and the Role of Government's Structure

Part III. People in Government Organizations

Part IV. Government Decisions— Making and Implementing Them

Part V. Administration in a Democracy

Figures and Tables

1

Introduction

Our subject is large, complex, and important. It embraces a significant part of government in action. So pervasive has government's role in society become and so much of government is administrative that some see the arrival of "the administrative state." Some fear the bureaucratization of our lives as a consequence of the many ways in which we encounter administrative constraints and even beneficial programs wrapped in administrative red tape. Some plead for "businesslike" public administration and doubt that public administration and private administration are, or should be, different in character. If they are different, and we think they are, then we face the problem of how to study public administration. Because both its central features and ways of studying it are variously perceived, we set forth a smorgasbord from which readers may make choices. Though the aspects of our subject are many and the approaches to its study vary, one issue remains dominant: administrative responsibility within the American constitutional system. If that issue is resolved satisfactorily, the issues about big government, bureaucracy, administrative discretion, and modeling of public administration on business practice will lend themselves to more accurate analysis than now prevails in public debate.

An "Administrative State"?

The marked increase in what citizens demand of government has led to a multiplicity of administrative agencies, a large number of civil servants, and swelling governmental budgets to pay for what citizens want and for the administrative work by which such expectations are met. This has brought us, it is said, into a new era, one characterized by "the administrative state."[1] The term is meant to emphasize bigness and to suggest that administrators now exercise so much discretion that constitutional arrangements have been disrupted.

The phenomenon of bigness needs to be put in perspective lest a parochial view of the American scene distort our assessment. As figure 1.1 reveals, the combined dollar outlays of all American governments—national, state, and local—amount to little over a third of the society's gross domestic product. In twelve of the listed nations the governmental sectors spend over half of their countries' GDPs.[2] Ranking eighteenth among the nineteen nations, the United States seems less likely than most others to have achieved the status of an "administrative state," if such a status is a consequence of the size of government.

A separate issue is whether and how far administrative decision making has superseded decision making by the constitutionally empowered branches of government. Unquestionably, administrators exercise discretionary judgments to a greater degree than in eras of more restricted governmental responsibilities. Yet legislative bodies, courts, chief executives, and political appointees exercise so detailed a control of administrators' discretion that "the administrative state," with its large connotations, does not accurately characterize the present situation.

Citizens may not agree. Their principal contacts with government are with administrative agencies and their employees. They find the complexities of administrative structure so great that they often do not know which agency to turn to with their problems. They are dissatisfied with budgetary, regulatory, and subsidy policies and programs, and they vent their animus on the administrative agencies charged with execution. This is true despite the fact that legislative bodies, often prompted by chief executives, enact the policies and programs and could change them. We all complain of *red tape*, a term attributed to the ribbon used to tie up English legal documents.

"Bureaucracy," in fact, has become an epithet almost universally. "Unelected bureaucrat" is even worse. Citizens often complain about bureaucracy in dealing with government. Yet we count on firefighters to extinguish fires, police officers to arrest criminals, snow-plow operators to clear the roads, social security officials to process checks for senior citizens, and guards to maintain order in prisons. At all levels of American government, elected officials shape ambitious policies and rely on "unelected bureaucrats" to transform the ambition into reality. Bureaucracy thus is about much deeper issues: the connection between government and the services it provides to citizens; and how those services can be made as effective, efficient, and fair as possible. The connections between democracy and bureaucracy are intimate and, indeed, lie at the core of the politics of the administrative process. Probing them is the mission of this book.

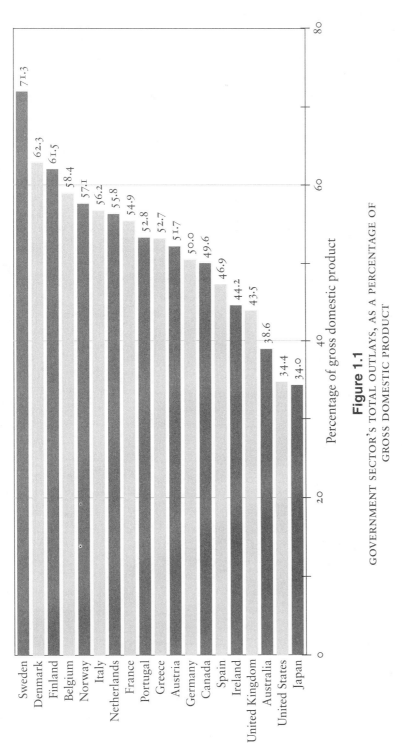

Figure 1.1

GOVERNMENT SECTOR'S TOTAL OUTLAYS, AS A PERCENTAGE OF
GROSS DOMESTIC PRODUCT

Percentage of gross domestic product

SOURCE: Organisation for Economic Cooperation and Development, *OECD Economic Outlook* 55 (June 1994): table A29. Data presented for 1993.

The Bureaucracy Problem

Public administration is bureaucracy. The word *bureau* originated in four-teenth-century France.[3] The word *bureaucracy* carries both favorable and unfavorable meanings. In an 1836 novel Balzac characterized the bureaucracy as "a gigantic power manipulated by dwarfs," and again as "that heavy curtain hung between the good to be done and him who commands it."[4]

Even in its derogatory sense, bureaucracy has had two contradictory meanings.[5] On the one hand, bureaucracy refers to a red-tape-bound set of civil servants, inefficient, negative, bored, impolite, and unhelpful to citizens seeking services. On the other hand, it conjures up visions of a body of all-too-efficient exercisers, and often abusers, of power arbitrarily deciding matters without due process.

Bureaucracy has also a neutral, or even a favorable, meaning in the study of administration. We use it in this book to refer to the formal, rational organization of relations among persons vested with administrative authority and the staffing of administration with qualified, full-time, sala-ried civil servants. In chapter 3 we examine this interpretation of bureaucracy more fully. Red tape has a place in this neutral meaning. Much red tape exists to assure rational decision making, consultation with affected interests, protection of individual rights, and effective review and control of administrative actions by auditors, prosecutors, courts, the chief executive, and the legislature.[6]

Yet the pejorative meanings of bureaucracy should never be far from our consciousness, for contradictory though they are, they point to real problems of large-scale administration and figure in the rhetoric of political contests (both Jimmy Carter and Ronald Reagan campaigned with "bureaucracy bashing" themes). They are also not peculiar to the United States. Two foreign prime ministers have complained, the first saying, "Creating the appearance of work, taking cover behind hollow rhetoric, bureaucracy may hold back the improvement of the economic mechanism, dampen independence and initiative, and erect barriers to innovation." The second said, "Bureaucratism remains a serious problem in the political life of our party and state. The overstaffing, overlapping and unwieldiness of Government organs, confusion of their responsibilities and buck-passing are ... major causes of bureaucratism. We must therefore reform these organs from top to bottom." The first speaker was the prime minister of the USSR, the second the acting prime minister of the People's Republic of China.[7]

If bureaucracy and red tape are perceived as evils by political leaders and other opinion formers here and abroad, one wonders why those who attain powerful positions do not rid us of these evils. The answer is that they are inherent in large organizations, serve important values in governments, and, reflecting both explanations, are most typical of governments whose policies embrace a wide range of regulatory and compassionate objectives.[8] The complaints are of a kind with those against a large budget, a numerous body of civil servants, and a multiplicity of departments and agencies. Any substantial reduction of these, as of bureaucracy and red tape, would require a reversal of the currently accepted role of government in society. Attempts at such reversal, as by the Reagan administration in the 1980s, have achieved only marginal changes.

Bureaucracy and Size

Given the scope of governmental activities in our era, public administration is mostly large-scale administration. How very large that scale can be is one of the most remarkable of its attributes.

The federal government's total outlays are a third of the total sales of the 500 largest-selling companies.[9] By these measures, the largest such company, General Motors, is about a tenth as large as the federal government. Its sales are much smaller than the outlays of the Department of Health and Human Services, the Defense Department, or the Treasury Department. The number of employees provides another measure. The results are comparable. The federal government's executive branch personnel, civilian and military, total 5 million. General Motors, the largest private employer, has about one-sixth as many employees, fewer than the *civilian* employees of the Defense Department. Tables 1.1 and 1.2 (pages 6, 7) rank the country's largest companies and governmental organizations.

The federal government has as its "customers" the over 250 million American people (not to add, as one might, the people in other countries who are beneficiaries of foreign-aid programs). Every decade, the Census Bureau tries to get information from *all* of them. The only roughly comparable private enterprise was the Bell System, before its dissolution, which had 150 million telephones in service. But the U.S. Postal Service annually moves 160 billion pieces of mail, the Internal Revenue Service receives 200 million tax returns in a year, and the workers in employment covered by the government's Old-Age, Survivors, and Disability Insurance program number 160 million.

It is important to have a sense of the great scale of administration that characterizes the U.S. government, and with it, a sense of the number, complexity, and variety of its programs. The complexity of the whole is manifested in the possibilities that a set of programs or agencies may have distinct, identical, or overlapping groups of "customers" and may have contradictory objectives.[10] Furthermore, the programs call for different mixes

Table 1.1

LARGE ORGANIZATIONS RANKED BY SALES OR OUTLAYS

Rank	Organization	Sales or outlays (in billions)
1	Department of Defense	$307.8
2	Department of the Treasury	298.8
3	Department of Health and Human Services: Social Security	298.3
4	Department of Health and Human Services, except Social Security	282.8
5	General Motors	138.2
6	Ford Motor	108.5
7	Exxon	97.8
8	California State Government	97.1
9	New York State Government	73.2
10	Wal-Mart Stores	67.3
11	American Telephone & Telegraph	67.2
12	Department of Agriculture	63.1
13	IBM	62.7
14	General Electric	60.6
15	Mobil	56.6

SOURCES: "Sales," *Forbes* 25 April 1994, 199; Executive Office of the President, *Budget of the United States Government: Fiscal Year 1995* (Washington, D.C.: Government Printing Office, 1994), 62; U.S. Bureau of the Census, *Statistical Abstract of the United States: 1994* (Washington, D.C.: Government Printing Office, 1994), 306.

of administrative, professional, technical, and clerical skills and require different kinds of procedures for effective operation. The scale and complexity of programs contrast sharply with those found in even the largest private corporations. More important, they are striking measures of how far we have advanced in designing social institutions of remarkable capacity.

All this said, it remains possible for public administration to be small in scale. The governments of the 9,000 municipalities with fewer than a thousand inhabitants to serve are clearly engaged in small-scale administration. Within a large bureaucracy it is of course possible to study a single subunit of a bureau and even a face-to-face working group within that subunit. Though choice of such a focus is feasible, analysis may be distorted

Table 1.2

LARGE ORGANIZATIONS RANKED BY NUMBER OF EMPLOYEES

Rank	Organization	Employment (in thousands)
1	Department of Defense	982.8
2	U.S. Postal Service	792.0
3	General Motors	710.8
4	Wal-Mart Stores	472.5
5	New York City Government	441.9
6	PepsiCo	397.5
7	California State Government	386.5
8	Sears, Roebuck	382.5
9	Ford Motor	322.2
10	Kmart	320.0
11	American Telephone & Telegraph	310.7
12	New York State Government	291.2
13	IBM	278.9
14	Texas State Government	266.7
15	General Electric	226.5

SOURCES: "Where Did All the People Go?" *Forbes* 25 April 1994, 242–56; U.S. Bureau of the Census, *Statistical Abstract of the United States: 1994* (Washington, D.C.: Government Printing Office, 1994), 346.

if this "small-scale" administration is perceived as complete in itself rather than as a fragment of large-scale administration.

"Public" and "Administration"

Public administration has never achieved a definition that commands general assent.[11] Examples of public administration abound, from the prosaic delivery of mail, collection of trash, and licensing of motor vehicles to the dramatic putting of a man on the moon, the dispatching of Peace Corps volunteers to scores of countries, and the development and control of nuclear energy. But examples do not add up to a definition. To define a subject is to fix its boundaries or, if those turn out to be fuzzy, to identify its essence, its core character. But for public administration this has proved so intractable a problem that its scholarly study is said to be suffering a "crisis of identity."

A two-step approach, defining first *administration* and then *public* seems promising but fails. Both dictionary editors and scholars have stumbled over the first step. Some use other words that themselves need definition or are too confining, as in "administration is executing." Other writers say that administration is cooperative human action that has a high degree of rationality, which means that the cooperative action is intended to maximize the realization of certain goals.[12] But this seems to embrace even a child's persuading two friends to play a game of marbles. Still other writers, operating at a less abstract level, say that administration is concerned with how, not what; with means, not ends; with process, not substance; with efficiency, not other values—a set of dichotomies that provoke debate rather than settle the definition.

As *administration* is so elusive a term, we should not be surprised that *public administration* has yet to be satisfactorily defined. Here, though, we can at least explain the failure. Public administration in all modern nations is identified with the executive branch.[13] That branch itself eludes definition. As Anthony King persuasively demonstrates, this is because the early monolithic, sovereign governments were transformed into modern three-branch governments by pressure from powerful interests demanding a legislature and courts, both vested with independent powers. Quite simply, "with the passage of time legislative and judicial institutions broke off, so to speak, from the central core of government." This historical explanation "says nothing about the emergence of executives precisely because executives did not emerge; being the central core of government, they were already there. The executive alone, on this account, does not need to be explained: it is neither more nor less than what is left of government . . . when legislatures and courts are removed."[14]

Although the historical explanation affords grounds for escaping definitional precision, we need an initial sense of what public administration is and what it is not. With that behind us, we can then consider the question of how to go about studying the subject.

The starting point for understanding the meaning of public administration is clarification of its distinctness from private administration. We start by considering the argument that administration is administration wherever it exists, whether in the public or the private sector. Next we probe the involvement of public administrators in policy formation as well as policy execution, though the latter is conventionally treated as the whole of administration. Finally, we emphasize the transcendent importance of administrative responsibility in a democratic government, a feature far more spacious and differently shaped than its analog in private enterprises.

Public versus Private Administration

Public administration is *public:* It is the administration of *governmental* affairs. Yet it is also administration, a kind of activity found in all large organizations. For years a debate has brewed about how to treat public administration. Are its basic features the same as administration of all sorts (and, therefore, is it but a subset of more generic management issues)? Or does it have special elements that make it distinctly *public* and thus require separate attention?

Leading the movement to include public administration with generic administration are sociologists who specialize in organization theory and many business school students of management:

□ At the broadest level, some organizational theorists contend that administration is administration, whatever its setting, and that the problems of organizing people, leading them, and supplying them with resources to do their jobs are the same regardless of setting.[15]

□ More practically oriented thinkers have argued that politics is about conflict and that "political conflict is at the center of management life." Management is fundamentally about managing that conflict. While the organizational setting may vary, the argument goes, the basic problem does not.[16]

□ Most broadly, Barry Bozeman has cast an argument that "all organizations are public because public authority affects some of the behavior or processes of all organizations." Thus, organizations are neither purely public nor private, but all organizations, he contends, share "public" and "private" features independent of their legal or formal status.[17]

In fact, a leading British political scientist, William A. Robson, has noted that "modern American theory is heavily committed to the view that one can discuss every kind of administration in a generalized manner." This effort, he explains, is like "an effort to produce a treatise on ball games, as distinct from studies of golf, or tennis, or football, or polo, or baseball."[18] Indeed, the distinction between the public and private sectors has gradually become more blurred. As Dwight Waldo has pointed out, "in the United States—and I believe much more widely—there is a movement away from a sharp distinction between *public* and *private,* and *toward* a blurring and mingling of the two."[19] As government becomes more involved in business, and as more businesslike approaches are incorporated into government, such blurring is unmistakable, but our central question remains: Is there something distinctly *public* about public administration?

The response of private-sector managers who move into top public-sector positions is a solid yes. They have universally underlined crucial differences between the two.[20] Scholars have emphasized other differences as well.[21] We can distinguish public agencies in two ways. First, the crucial distinction: public organizations do the public's business; they administer law. Second, the characteristic differences: public organizations have characteristically different processes from those of private organizations and work in a different environment.

The Critical Role of Public Authority. The most fundamental distinction between public and private organizations is the rule of law. Public organizations exist to administer the law, and every element of their being —their structure, staffing, budget, and purpose—is the product of legal authority. Every action taken by a public administrator ultimately "must be traceable to a legal grant of authority; those of private firms need not be," as Gortner, Mahler, and Nicholson argue. In fact, they point out:

> Managers of private firms can generally take any action, establish any policy, or use any means of operation not specifically prohibited. Public managers, in contrast, may not do so in the absence of specific grants of authority. Private organizations can act unless proscribed or forbidden; public ones may act *only* if the authority is granted. As a veteran public manager remarked ... "For the private organization, it is a matter of 'go until I say stop'; but to the public manager the message is 'don't go unless I tell you to.' "[22]

Public administration thus exists to implement law. In the American system, authority flows from the people to those they elect to govern them. When a legislature passes a law and an executive signs it, the law does not implement itself. That is the task the legislature delegates to the administrator, and it is this chain of authority, flowing from the people through elected institutions to the public administrator, that makes public administration distinctively public. Faithful execution of these laws is the highest calling of public administrators and the core of administrative responsibility. Public and private administration thus differ sharply on the core that shapes every administrative action.

Characteristic Public Processes. In addition to this fundamental legal distinction, there typically are important differences between public and private organizational processes. Although they are not fixed in law—and although some private-sector organizations share these public-sector characteristics—there tend to be regular differences in the way public-sector organizations do business.[23]

1. *Time perspective.* While private-sector organizations tend to be led by individuals who devote their careers to the organization, public bureaucracies tend to be headed by relative amateurs whose tenure is of short duration. Assistant secretaries in federal departments, for example, typically serve only eighteen months and spend much of their time simply learning their jobs.

2. *Measuring performance.* The private sector has the market in which to test its performance. Few public-sector organizations, by contrast, have any "direct way of evaluating their outputs in relation to the cost of the inputs used to make them," as Anthony Downs puts it.[24] For public administrators, compliance with the law is the ultimate measure of performance, but laws often are vague and give little guidance.

3. *Competing standards.* Whereas efficiency is the ultimate private standard, public administrators are expected to manage both efficiently and equitably. These two standards often compete—what is fair often is not the most efficient, and vice versa.

4. *Public scrutiny.* To a far greater degree than in the private sector, public administrators work under public scrutiny. Public administrators labor under laws whose very titles, such as "Government in the Sunshine," underline the role of public oversight, covering both internal and external operations. This "goldfish-bowl effect" is in stark contrast with the much more limited public scrutiny that private organizations receive. Dealing with the media has long been a feature of public administrative activity.[25]

5. *Persuasion.* In the private sector, managers manage far more by authority; they give orders and expect them to be obeyed. In the public sector, by contrast, administration depends far more on persuasion and the balancing of conflicting political demands.

6. *Oversight.* Public administrators must also answer not only to their superiors but also to legislators and the courts. Administrators must appear before legislative committees to explain their activities and must answer complaints raised in court. If the private sector has *the* bottom line, the public sector has several: accountability to higher-level administrative officials, to the chief executive, to legislators, to the courts, and ultimately to the public.

We tend sometimes to separate public and private activities by the profit motive. To be sure, this is an important difference, but it does not clearly distinguish the two sectors. Private organizations sometimes submerge profit making to other goals, and some private organizations are nonprofit; they exist to perform services, not to make a profit. Some public organizations, furthermore, simulate the market by imposing fees and charges. Such strategies are on the rise as reformers attempt to make public organizations more efficient.

Most fundamentally, however, public organizations are public because they administer the law and because their very being springs from the law. Moreover, public organizations typically operate in a different environment from that of private organizations. Wallace Sayre once commented that "business and public administration are alike only in all unimportant respects."[26] This statement is more than just the product of a clever wit. As Elmer B. Staats, former comptroller general of the United States and long-time observer of business persons in Washington, pointed out, "many businessmen who come to Washington are not notable successes. . . . They average less than two years. They bring experience and capability, but they lack an understanding of the environment of Government." And of executives who succeed in Washington, he observes, many find on returning to industry that their "work lacks the same scope, challenge, and public service satisfaction."[27] It is this challenge of public service that distinguishes public from private administration.

Policy Execution versus Policy Formation

What a government accomplishes for a society depends on what policies it formulates and adopts and on how effectively they are put into practice. Public administration contributes to both the shaping and the execution of policies. We look first at the more familiar function—that of execution.

Policy Execution. Consider what it means when we say that the government has adopted a policy. In our system, this normally means that the elected policymakers have enacted a law forbidding, directing, or permitting members of the society to behave in specified ways. Then what happens? The law is merely printed paper. The task of public administration is to translate the print of statute books into changed behavior by individual members of society, to convert words into action, form into substance.

This is a complex task. It means expanding some individuals' opportunities by extending governmental services and protections to them. It means regulating some individuals' freedom by drawing taxes from them, discovering and prosecuting those who engage in forbidden kinds of behavior, granting or denying permission to engage in certain activities (e.g., licensing radio stations), and manipulating the environment of subsidies and interest rates. The government administers some enterprises itself, either as monopolies or as competitors of private enterprises; the postal service, TVA, social security, and the public schools and universities are illustrative. It also administers the defense establishment and foreign affairs and their hundreds of outposts over the world. The range is immense and the pattern is a mixture of old and new concerns.

The authorization of these governmental activities, the giving of a policy direction to them, and the provision of resources for their accomplishment are among the central tasks of the elective legislature and chief executive. But all this merely permits something to happen; it does not make it happen. Administration is what translates these paper declarations of intent into reality—altering the behavior of citizens toward conformity with the statutory mandates and delivering promised benefits to the intended beneficiaries.

Administration as execution cannot be taken for granted. Its weakness or unresponsiveness enfeebles the political system itself. For example, in many a developing country the critical problem seems not so much political instability of the government or inability to devise rational programs for development as it is administrative incapacity to get the government's decisions and programs carried out. In the United States the role of the state governments depends heavily on their possession of substantial administrative capability, a need now satisfied more than in past decades. More immediately, administrative complexity imperils coordinated attack by many agencies and many programs on the problems of the cities and their poor.

Policy Formation. Administration's second role is in the policy-formation process. This role is played at two stages of the process: (1) before the constitutionally empowered legislature and chief executive have made their policy decisions, and (2) after they have enacted statutes or issued executive orders and passed on to administration the job of making sense of them. In the first stage, proposals for statutes and for amendments of statutes flow from many sources, but administrative agencies are among the most important of them. The general reasons for this are apparent. An agency in a given program field is likely to possess much factual information about needs and trends in that field, to have an expert staff for the analysis of such data, to have discovered the defects that existing statutes have when tested by the experience of trying to apply them, and to have a strong devotion to the program's objectives and so to their fuller realization. Often, though not always, the agency is trusted as a less biased source of information than other available sources, such as organized interest groups.

In our time, two developments have enhanced the role that administrative agencies play at this initiating and preparatory stage of policymaking. One is the increased technicality of subjects with which legislation deals, a phenomenon paralleled by a growth in the specialized competence of administrative agency staffs. Economic stabilization policies, for example, must be guided by sophisticated information, analysis, and advice by professional economists, as well as by the value preferences and political sense of the elected president and members of Congress. Expert knowledge and advice are essential to policy development for national defense weaponry, space exploration, public health, research and development, education, poverty, urban renewal, energy, air and water pollution, and a host of other program areas. And most of the government's experts are in the administrative agencies.

The second development is the marked expansion of the chief executive's role as a major policy-agenda setter of the government. He initiates many of the principal measures given legislative attention. Typically his legislative program is shaped through consultation with the agencies of the executive branch. Although they are not the only sources of his ideas, they are strategically situated to initiate and counsel on policy proposals that may win his influential sponsorship. And, of course (to complete the circle), his need for expert help has mounted as public policy problems have become increasingly technical.

A second stage of the policy-formation process occurs after statutes are on the books. Often, and particularly in important and complex fields, the statutes are not clear enough for us to regard what happens afterward as execution in the narrow sense. Legislative behavior follows no very consistent pattern, sometimes yielding statutory measures in the greatest detail and other times resulting in only the identification of a problem that the administrator is directed to wrestle with. In effect, then, the administrator must make policy.

The reasons for deliberate or inadvertent delegation of policymaking power are various. In a new policy field in which there is little or no accumulated experience to build on, the legislature wants something done but can make only a vague gesture as to the direction that action should take. In a field whose technology or other features are expected to change rapidly, the statute must permit flexible action by the agency, rather than require frequent returns to the legislature for enactment of new language. Some subjects (e.g., liquor store and taxi licensing) simply do not lend themselves to specification of criteria to confine administrative discretion.[28] Also, in some areas the ingenuity of business people can be depended on to generate clever ways of evading any highly specific prohibitions in a statute;

hence, Congress broadly forbids "unfair methods of competition ... and unfair or deceptive acts in commerce," leaving the administrative agency and the courts to give content to those vague terms *unfair* and *deceptive.*

At times, the legislative process itself is so stormy and full of crosscurrents that the statute passed incorporates a number of contradictory policy guidelines, and the agency has to use its own judgment in making sense out of the mishmash. Sometimes, too, the necessity of reaching a compromise solution leads the legislature to use language that papers over disagreement but whose deliberate ambiguity leaves the agency great scope for interpretation. Most agencies, furthermore, administer a multiplicity of statutes, passed by different Congresses with differing majority preferences, so that the need to reconcile the accumulated set of legislative instructions forces some exercise of agency discretion. Finally, the legislature may appropriate insufficient funds for an agency's exercise of its statutory responsibilities. Unless the legislature itself gives specific direction, the agency must decide whether to spread the money thinly or, more commonly, decide which of its objectives it will pursue with vigor and which it will slight.

In essence, then, public administration includes the shaping of policy on the way up, execution of policy after it has been made, and—as a necessary part of the execution—decision making about policy matters on the way down.

The Policy/Administration Dichotomy. In the early period of the study of public administration, a prevalent theme was the separation of policy from administration. This resulted both from the need to identify a distinctive field of study and, probably more, from the efforts to reform city government and then state and national governments in the late nineteenth and early twentieth centuries. The reform movement was directed against political corruption, often the mother's milk of local political machines. Establishing a neutral realm for administration, protected by civil service laws and governed by a drive for businesslike efficiency, would both dry up patronage resources of machines and leave policymaking organs of government as the proper realm for democratic politics.

The goals of assuring a nonpartisan body of civil servants, one that can loyally serve a succession of superiors of varying political party affiliations, and of achieving efficient administration remain. Nevertheless, the obvious fact that administrative staffs share in the policy-formation function has led many students to reject the policy/administration dichotomy. A confusion is introduced by relabeling the formula the "politics/administration" dichotomy, again for rejection as unsound. In all advanced countries, permanent staffs assist in policy formation. The line is drawn when it comes to politics, but the line may waver. The civil servant needs to be respectful of the policy goals of the elected administration and sensitive to political implications of his or her policy suggestions. But the civil servant has other obligations as well—to long-range goals, continuity and consistency, effective administration, and resistance to corruption. Furthermore, he or she must balance the administration's preferences against the mandates of the legislative body and the courts.[29] In sum, the civil servant has a kind of responsibility that is distinguishable from that of politically chosen officials. Policy and administration are certainly intertwined. But to conceive of the permanent staff as indistinguishable from politicians in motivation and behavior is to meld two sets of people with very different roles in our society.

Administrative Responsibility

Every well-developed organization has some system of holding subordinates accountable to their superiors. Nowhere is the system so complex and confining as in government.[30] Statutes and regulations specify elaborate procedures that seriously limit administrators' discretionary authority. Congressional committees and subcommittees call administrators to testify, often on the same matter before a variety of such bodies and often to answer criticisms of actions and proposed actions. Members of the large congressional staff closely monitor administrative actions in agencies of interest to their superiors. The Office of Management and Budget, acting for the president or under congressional instruction, reviews proposed regulations and information-gathering proposals in addition to reviewing budgetary requests and setting personnel ceilings. Political appointees at cabinet and subcabinet levels direct bureaus and clusters of bureaus and have much to say about the rewards and penalties visited on senior career civil servants.

From the career administrators' side, this is a formidable control system. Yet, as we have earlier suggested, administrative responsibility goes beyond these external controls on behavior. There are internalized guides to conduct—internalized, that is, by administrators themselves. They know, to begin with, that they serve in government. Knowing that, they are sensitive to the legitimate roles of other elements of the government, roles that include control of administrative behavior. Second, they have a loyalty to their agencies and the programs entrusted to them. Third, in a civil service now markedly populated by professional experts, they are loyal to their professions' standards and are motivated to win the regard of members of the profession who are outside the government. All these commitments build administrative responsibility, even though at times they do not all point in the same direction.

A major problem is how to maximize what we have called internalized controls so that the burdensome red tape resulting from elaborate external controls can be reduced. For that problem to be solved requires an enhanced degree of trust between the political strata and the civil service strata of the government.

The Study of Public Administration

How, then, should we think about and study public administration? There is no lack of conflicting responses.[31] Dwight Waldo has suggested that we face a difficult task, that of reconciling the political ideas of the small Greek city-state (the *polis*) with the large-scale administrative example of the Roman Empire, both of which are inherited by the American system.[32] One way of addressing this task, as we have earlier indicated, is to claim that administration and policy (or politics) are separate spheres. This was substantially the view of Woodrow Wilson and Frank J. Goodnow, writing in the late nineteenth century and early twentieth century.[33] Nicholas Henry identifies 1900 to 1926 as the period when the politics/administration dichotomy reigned. Later periods he traces as follows: 1927–37, when students affirmed the existence of clear principles of public administration; 1938–50, marked by rejection of the politics/administration dichotomy and loss of confidence in principles, along with reactions leading to the next period; 1950–70, years of reorientation to public administration as political science; and, overlapping and contradicting that, a 1956–70 emphasis on management, often borrowing from business management, together with the rise of public policy studies (focused on effective achievement of policy objectives); and finally the post-1970 reversion to a self-aware orientation, often lodged in distinct schools of public administration hospitable to management methods but also sensitive to the public-interest commitment of administrators of governmental affairs.[34]

For our own study, three questions need to be confronted. First, is public administration something that we can generalize about regardless of time? Second, is it generalizable regardless of place and circumstance? Third, if we are to make a start toward even limited generalizations, how shall we proceed? To such questions, candor requires these perplexing answers:

1. Public administration is timeless but is time-bound.[35]
2. It is universal but is culture-bound and varies with situations.
3. It is complex but is intelligible only by a simplified model or a step-by-step combining of such models.

We consider the first two puzzling answers together, for time and space are related variables.

Time and Space: Critical or Noncritical Variables?

Public administration has a longer history and a wider geographic range than almost any other aspect of government. It has been the instrument of ancient empires, of monarchies, of both democracies and dictatorships, of both developed and developing countries. Carl J. Friedrich has cogently argued that the achievement of representative government in Western Europe depended on the prior development of effective bureaucracies by undemocratic regimes.[36] Indeed, revolutions that seek to transform the structure of political authority are at the same time struggles for control of the bureaucracy.

In the United States, though public administration was mentioned in *The Federalist Papers,* it received little or no deliberate attention in the century that followed. In 1835 Alexis de Tocqueville remarked with amazement, the greater because of his familiarity with French administration, on the neglect of the subject in the United States.

> The public administration is, so to speak, oral and traditional. But little is committed to writing and that little is soon wafted away forever, like the leaves of the Sibyl, by the smallest breeze.... The instability of administration has penetrated into the habits of the people ... and no one cares for what occurred before his time: no methodical system is pursued, no archives are formed, and no documents are brought together when it would be very easy to do so.... Nevertheless, the art of administration is undoubtedly a science, and no science can be improved if the discoveries and observations of successive generations are not connected together in the order in which they occur.... But the persons who conduct the administration in America can seldom afford any instruction to one another.... Democracy, pushed to its furthest limits, is therefore prejudicial to the art of government; and for this reason it is better adapted to a people already versed in the conduct of administration than to a nation that is uninitiated in public affairs.[37]

Woodrow Wilson and Comparative Administration. In 1887, early in his scholarly career, Woodrow Wilson wrote, "the poisonous atmosphere of city government, the crooked secrets of state administration, the confusion, sinecurism, and corruption ever and again discovered in the bureaux at Washington forbid us to believe that any clear conceptions of what constitutes good administration are as yet very widely current in the United

States."[38] Noting that "the functions of government are every day becoming more complex and difficult" and "are also vastly multiplying in number," Wilson pleaded for "a science of administration which shall seek to straighten the paths of government, to make its business less unbusiness-like, to strengthen and purify its organization, and to crown its duties with dutifulness." Such a science, he noted, existed on the European continent and was to be found reflected in, for example, Prussian and French practice. He anticipated that comparative study would yield "one rule of good administration for all governments alike. So far as administrative functions are concerned, all governments have a strong structural likeness; more than that, if they are to be uniformly useful and efficient, they *must* have a strong structural likeness."

From one point of view, then, public administration has universal elements, independent of time, place, and political system. The many individuals who serve in any public bureaucracy must be selected, compensated, given specific assignments, controlled, disciplined when necessary, and so on. To pay them and to support other governmental activities (minimally, provision for military forces and construction of roads), a revenue system must be devised, the receipts allocated by some kind of budgetary system, and accounting and other recordkeeping methods worked out.

To say that there are such universal elements implies that governments' accumulated experience in dealing with these elements constitutes a rich fund of knowledge requiring only skillful analysis to save wasteful repetition of errors. As Wilson put it, "the object of administrative study is to rescue executive methods from the confusion and costliness of empirical experiment and set them upon foundations laid deep in stable principle."

Despite the reasonableness of expectations that the study of public administration should by now have yielded stable principles, the fact is that governments' administrative experiences have not been funded and sorted out in a way that permits confident generalization about the wide range of problems encountered in public administration. Some of the reasons for this are to be found in Wilson's essay itself, which contains a central contradiction. Basic to much of his analysis is his perception of administration as a neutral instrument, distinct from policy, politics, and particular regime. Such a perception seemed essential to define a distinct field of study, separate from the study of policy and politics. It may also have sprung from the neutrality doctrine of civil service reformers, who had succeeded in getting the Pendleton Civil Service Act passed just four years before Wilson's essay appeared in the *Political Science Quarterly*.

But it was an especially critical assumption for Wilson's thesis that "nowhere else in the whole field of politics, it would seem, can we make use of the historical, comparative method more safely than in this province of administration." That is, we can learn administration from the Prussian and French (Napoleonic) autocracies without being infected by their political principles. "If I see a murderous fellow sharpening a knife cleverly, I can borrow his way of sharpening the knife without borrowing his probable intention to commit murder with it; and so, if I see a monarchist dyed in the wool managing a public bureau well, I can learn his business methods without changing one of my republican spots."

Over against this line of argument are two contradictory themes. One is that administration must be fitted to the particular nation's political ideas and constitutional system. The science of administration, Wilson wrote,

> is not of our making; it is a foreign science, speaking very little of the language of English or American principles.... It has been developed by French and German professors, and is consequently in all parts adapted to the needs of a compact state, and made to fit highly centralized forms of government.... If we would employ it, we must Americanize it, and that not formally, in language merely, but radically, in thought, principle, and aim as well. It must learn our constitutions by heart; must get the bureaucratic fever out of its veins; must inhale much free American air.

Wilson advanced a second theme that blurs the distinction he elsewhere makes between policy and administration. The distinction, to be sure, can be made by the fully initiated, but the "lines of demarcation, setting apart administrative from nonadministrative functions ... run up hill and down dale, over dizzy heights of distinction and through dense jungles of statutory enactment, hither and thither around 'ifs' and 'buts,' 'whens,' and 'however,' until they become altogether lost to the common eye... ." Wilson, it is true, suggests "some roughly definite criteria": "public administration is detailed and systematic execution of public law," "every particular application of general law," "the detailed execution" of "the broad plans of governmental action," the "special means" as distinguished from the "general plans." Yet he goes on to plead for the vesting of "large powers and unhampered discretion" as the indispensable conditions of administrative responsibility.

If, then, public administration needs to be interpreted in the light of a particular country's political ideas and kind of government, if it is not merely a neutral instrument as is a knife or "as machinery is part of the manufactured product" but includes administrators with large powers and discretion, and if what is administration cannot readily be distinguished from the nonadministrative aspects of government, the search for universal principles of public administration is unlikely to yield Wilson's goal of "one rule of good administration for all governments alike."

Much of the literature on administration since Wilson's time has been troubled by the same contradictions that he inadvertently set forth. The reason is that each of the positions he embraced has its contribution to make to the whole truth. A number of problems are common to all or most public bureaucracies. It is possible to consider many of these in terms of a simple criterion, which Wilson put in language closely paralleled in the administrative literature of our own time: how government can do things "with the utmost possible efficiency and at the least possible cost either of money or of energy." Yet there are also problems, some of them among the most critical for administration, that require different criteria and different answers in dissimilar social and political systems, at the several stages of national development, and even in the individual agencies of a single government.

That such problems exist has been most vividly demonstrated in efforts by developed countries' administrators and scholars to counsel or study about administration in developing countries. Western models have proven not very suitable points of departure for the understanding of the role of the bureaucracy in non-Western political systems. And, insofar as developing countries have looked to the West for models, their need to choose which Western model to follow has sharpened awareness that there are significant and inadequately understood differences among the administrative systems of the developed countries of the West.

A substantial comparative administration movement appeared in the 1960s, but is characterized by its leading exponent as "plateauing at a relatively low level in recent years."[39] Time and space are interlinked in the recent and growing literature on the history of governmental administration.[40]

Complexity and Simplicity

Any actual organizational system is extremely complex. So much is this true that we can assume that no one can describe such a system fully. But it is a reasonable assumption that the main features of the system can be described—for example, by a single model that simplifies *total* reality in order to clarify *essential* reality. Even this assumption is wrong. The reasons are three.

First, the complexity of any large-scale organization seems not to be one of the kinds of puzzles that a single key will unlock. Instead, there are so many ways of looking at an organization that no single model can be expected to embrace them all. Consider the following:[41]

1. An organization (as we have seen) is both a policy-program-decision-making set of processes and a policy-program-decision-executing set of processes, and they intertwine.

2. It is both a way of dividing up work and a way of coordinating work.

3. It is both a formal, prescribed structure of relations among offices and organization units and an arena for the dynamic conflict of ambitious persons and units intent on expanding or at least maintaining their status and power.

4. It both persists over time despite changes in its personnel (*complete* change in the case of long-lived organizations), and at any single point in time is a particular group of individuals each with his or her special set of psychological needs and frustrations.

5. It is both a top-down system of authority, conformity, and compliance, and a down-up system for the flow to the top of innovative ideas, proposed solutions to problems, claims on resources, and reports of trouble signs in program execution and content.

6. It is an information storage and retrieval system and a communication network, subject to "overloads" of information, misreading of signals, and supplementations and wire crossing by informal "grapevines."

7. It usually includes both a headquarters staff and a far-flung field service, the former organized by functions and the latter by geographical areas—a feature that hinders their effective linkage.

8. Its decision-making process must embrace the broad choices in which the personal value preferences and educated guesses of officials play a large part; it must provide for other major choices for which quantified data and other scientific evidence can clarify the options and reduce the role of mere hunches; and it must "program" the narrow choices capable of routine handling by clerks and automatic data-processing machines.

9. It looks both inward and outward, having to maintain internal effectiveness and to adapt to the external environment in which it encounters the pressures of other organizations, the sea changes and temporary crises of the society and the economy, and the often poorly articulated needs of the customers of its service.

10. It can be likened to a physical system such as a machine, or it can be likened to the system of a biological organism such as an animal or a living plant.

11. It can be judged successful if it simply survives, or instead it can be so judged only if it achieves the purpose that justifies its existence.

Second, a single reality-based model is unavailable because most writers on organization happen to have sought not to describe a particular organization but to describe organizations in general—that is, organization in the abstract. Theorizing has outrun concrete experience and is the poorer for it. Available models, therefore, though often intellectually attractive, have not been demonstrated to fit the facts.[42]

Third, organization theorists do not agree on a single theory or model. Theories and models of organization abound, each usually intended as the way of seeing what an organization essentially is but, in fact, each selecting only one or a very few of the characteristic features of organizations (usually from those identified above). The complexity of an organization can be accurately portrayed only by a combination of the partial truths that most models have expressed. We can imagine each model's bit of truth being mapped on a transparent sheet of paper; put one on top of another, the series of overlays comes closer to the real organization than any single sheet does.[43]

With these difficulties in our way, how shall we proceed? We develop the book in five parts.

In part I we start with what government does and how it does it. The business of public administration is directly tied to the missions that government undertakes. A careful study of government administration must begin with *what* government must administer.

In part II we move to the way that government organizes the *structure* of administration. We consider the traditional building blocks for organizations[44] and the many strategies and tactics developed, both in the United States and around the world, to reform government management. This section concludes with a careful look at how the executive branch of government is organized and the problems that tend to accompany organizational structure.

Once we have built government's basic structure, in part III we put people in the organizations. This section first examines the civil service system that applies to most civilian members of the executive branch's staff. It then moves on to consider the higher civil service, whose political appointees and top career civil servants set the tone for the whole national administration, not least because they are in important decision-making positions.

In part IV we then move to the decision-making processes themselves. Government managers face the tasks of shaping their programs and obtaining the money needed to run them. Indeed, budgeting is the most important instance of decision making in government, for through society it allocates resources between the public and private sectors of the economy and among public programs and agencies. Few decisions are self-executing; they require implementation. In this section we try to discover why policies and programs succeed or fail at the implementation stage.

Finally, in part V, we directly confront the question of how administrative organizations, people, and processes are meant to operate in a government of democracy and of law. We therefore examine the effectiveness of legislative control, administrators' use of delegated regulatory powers, and the role of the judiciary in controlling the exercise of those and other discretionary powers by administrators. We conclude by focusing again on the questions with which we began this book: the central problem of assuring bureaucratic accountability for the faithful execution of the laws, responsiveness to the public will, and ethical behavior by public administrators.

Part I

What Government Does—And How It Does It

Public administration does not exist as a separate entity. It is intimately connected with the job to be done. Put differently, separate kinds of programs require separate approaches to administration. We move, therefore, to charting the different approaches that government uses to do the public's business.

2

What Government Does

The loss of confidence in governmental institutions since the mid-1960s has been palpable. The share of the population believing that "people in the government waste a lot of money we pay in taxes" rose from 47 to 75 percent from 1964 to 1991.[1] At the same time, most of us continue to call on government for a remarkable range of services. We expect government to keep the environment clean and to provide the elderly with adequate health care. We expect it to research cures for diseases and provide for the national defense. In fact, when major problems and disasters arise, from plane crashes to oil spills, our first reaction often is, "Why didn't the government keep the problem from occurring?" And our second reaction? "What can government do to keep the problem from happening again?"

There is another paradox. Americans continue to believe that their political system offers the best possible means of governance. They treasure basic principles such as the separation of powers and access to government. As each branch of government checks the other, as each one stops to listen to citizens' views, efficiency often suffers. Government responsiveness is not free; its cost typically is slower progress toward fuzzier goals.

At the same time, however, citizens have developed deep suspicions about government's effectiveness. We fret over tales of overpriced hammers and coffee makers purchased by the Pentagon, of waste in federal housing grants, of problems in performance throughout government. Sometimes these problems are the direct result of our endless search for responsiveness in government, and sometimes they *are* the product of mismanagement (although it is often very hard even for experienced observers to tell the difference). Since the 1960s, Americans have tended to think that "the system is good, but it is not performing well because the people in charge are inept and untrustworthy." Indeed, "the public suspects that unchecked power will be abused by self-interested power-holders."[2]

At the center of these swirling problems have been public administrators. For political candidates, running against Washington and its bureaucrats became a can't-miss campaign strategy. Nevertheless, while running against government and its bureaucracy was an easy way to build public support, once officials were elected they had to work with the very institutions they had campaigned against. It then became attractive for new candidates to campaign against *them,* in an endless cycle of disparagement that only deepened citizens' cynicism.

All these problems have deep implications for our study of public administration. The self-interested power of faceless bureaucrats is one of the strongest, most negative images in American political culture. Furthermore, there is a strong sense that government is getting bigger and that, as its size grows, problems magnify. In the public's mind, "bigness" and "badness" are inextricably linked in the public's fear of concentrated governmental power.[3] At the same time, we want bureaucracy to be open and responsive, even if administration takes longer and effectiveness suffers.

Many of these images and debates are based on profound misunderstandings about the nature of governmental activity. Quoting from the Gospel according to St. John, two students of American public administration have warned: "Judge not according to the appearance."[4] In examining American public administration, the advice is sound indeed. Our search for understanding about the responsiveness and effectiveness of American public administration depends, first, on carefully probing two important questions:

1. What does government do?
2. How does government do it?

The Functions of Government

Consider the following:

☐ The Social Security Administration monthly mails 42 million checks, mostly to retirees. A study by the Census Bureau estimated that, in 1986, these checks raised 15.1 million people above the poverty line.[5]

☐ In 1989, the Federal Deposit Insurance Corporation (FDIC), best known for its bank-window stickers promising $100,000 insurance for each account, took over the management of 200 financially troubled savings and loan institutions. As part of this process, the FDIC found itself the owner of 12 percent of the Dallas Cowboys football team.[6]

☐ Inspectors for the Food and Drug Administration (FDA), alerted in

March 1989 to the possibility that terrorists might attempt to poison imported fruit, managed to find two grapes—in a shipment of 364,000 *crates* of grapes—that had been injected with cyanide.

☐ The federal government is, by far, the biggest lender in the country. Its portfolio of direct loans alone amounted to $222 billion in 1989, 61 percent larger than the loan assets of the largest commercial bank in the United States.[7]

The scope of the American government's activities is nothing short of remarkable. From controlling air safety to researching AIDS, from protecting the food supply to protecting the nation's finances, government agencies oversee an amazing variety of services. Public administration is central to all these operations.

The Growth of Government

Any discussion of what government does, and how public administrators help do it, must begin with a look at how government has changed. No matter how measured, government has grown dramatically during the twentieth century. The federal, state, and local governments combined spent $1.6 billion in 1902. That amount rose to $70.3 billion in 1950 and $2.5 *trillion* in 1992.

The changes in government over the years, however, have varied greatly by the level of government.

What the Federal Government Does

The unmistakable trend in federal spending has been the growing dominance of the budget by just a few categories. In just over thirty years, from 1962 to 1993, spending for entitlements grew from 30 to 54 percent. (Entitlements are programs such as social security and Medicare to which individuals are "entitled" by law. The law defines who is eligible for the programs and how much they receive.) Defense is the second-largest piece of federal spending, though it has gone in the opposite direction from entitlements: from 49 percent to all federal spending in 1962 to just 21 percent in 1993. Interest on the national debt has more than doubled from 6 to 14 percent of federal spending as the national debt has grown. Just these three categories account for 89 percent of all federal spending. Everything else —from federal grants to building highways to foreign aid, federal prisons to AIDS research— accounts for the rest. Indeed, as figure 2.1 shows, the recent history of federal spending is the story of much more money concentrated in far fewer categories, led by the huge increase in entitlement spending.

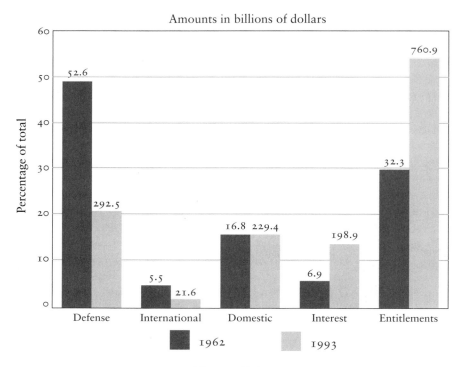

Figure 2.1

FEDERAL GOVERNMENT SPENDING

SOURCE: Congressional Budget Office, *The Economic and Budget Outlook: Fiscal Years 1995–1999* (Washington, D.C.: Government Printing Office, 1994), 92, 94.

Such figures surprise most Americans. In fact, a public opinion poll conducted on election night 1994 revealed that 30 percent of citizens responding thought that defense was the largest category of spending, 27 percent said foreign aid (it is actually only 1.5 percent of all spending), and 15 percent said social security (which is the government's single largest program—$302 billion in 1994, or 21 percent of the total).[8]

These sweeping changes in the federal budget have had two important implications for administration of its programs. First, a large part of the federal budget (more than two-thirds) goes simply to writing checks for entitlement programs and interest on the national debt (most of which comes back to American citizens). A relatively small share of federal employees, however, work on these programs. Second, more than two-thirds of federal employees work to administer the remaining third of the federal budget.

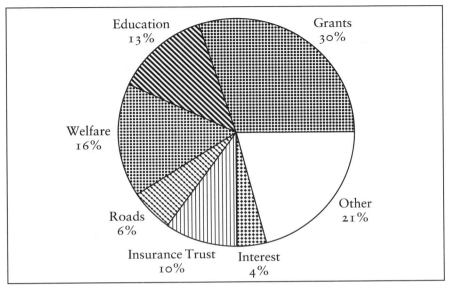

Figure 2.2

STATE GOVERNMENT SPENDING

SOURCE: U.S. Bureau of the Census, *Government Finances in 1990–91* (Washington, D.C.: Government Printing Office, 1992).

They are the prison guards, FBI agents, passport officers, virus researchers, national park managers, and the millions of other workers who make federal programs work. The federal budget describes what the government does but not how it does it. It certainly does not describe well at all what most federal employees do.

What State Governments Do

In comparing what the federal and state governments do, two conclusions are immediately obvious. First, state governments' direct functions are very different from the federal government's. State governments concentrate on education, welfare, road construction, and trust funds (especially for retired state employees). See figure 2.2 above.

Second, state governments occupy the middle role in the nation's federal system, and that role is reflected in their spending. The states, in fact, play a major banking role in the federal system. They receive federal grants and administer them, for services ranging from highway construction and social services to Medicaid and welfare. They also raise revenues and give

Table 2.1

NUMBER OF GOVERNMENTAL UNITS BY TYPE

	1942	1962	1982	1992
Total	155,116	91,237	81,831	86,743
Federal government	1	1	1	1
State governments	48	50	50	50
Local governments	155,067	91,186	81,780	86,692
County	3,050	3,043	3,041	3,043
Municipal	16,220	18,000	19,076	19,296
Township/town	18,919	17,142	16,734	16,666
School district	108,579	34,678	14,851	14,556
Special district	8,299	18,323	28,078	33,131

SOURCE: U.S. Bureau of the Census, *Statistical Abstract of the United States: 1994* (Washington, D.C.: Government Printing Office, 1994).

them to local governments for education. In fact, nearly one-third of all state spending goes for such education grants. In 1992, state governments raised $211 billion for education, but spent only 40 percent themselves (principally for colleges and universities). The rest went to local governments to support primary and secondary schools.[9]

Third, state spending patterns, especially when compared with federal spending, have stayed relatively constant over time. As the interstate highway system was built during the 1950s and 1960s, highway construction grew. Then, as highway spending shrank in the late 1970s, welfare spending grew to replace it. Since World War II, however, the patterns of state spending have been much more stable. And while state governments make some payments to individuals—principally for welfare—they play in general a much smaller redistributive role than does the federal government.

What Local Governments Do

The first thing any observer of local administrative patterns notices is their incredible variety. Most states are subdivided into counties, and the counties are subdivided in turn into cities, towns, and townships. (Connecticut, however, has no county governments, and in Virginia the counties and cities are completely separate.) Moreover, there is an amazing variety of special-district governments, from local school and water-quality districts to airport and transportation authorities.

If it is hard to characterize local governments, it is at least possible to

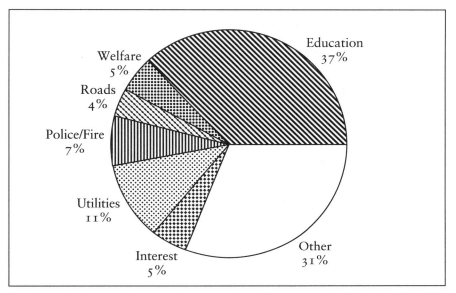

Figure 2.3

LOCAL GOVERNMENT SPENDING

SOURCE: U.S. Bureau of the Census, *Government Finances in 1990–91* (Washington, D.C.: Government Printing Office, 1992).

count them: more than 86,000 local governments in 1992, more than half of which were school and special districts. The number of local governments is down substantially since before World War II, largely because of a huge drop in the number of school districts. Other special districts, however, have quickly grown in number, more than tripling from 1942 to 1992 (see table 2.1).

Despite their remarkable number and variety, local governments share a common purpose: compared with other levels of government in the United States, they are singularly devoted to providing goods and services (see figure 2.3). Of the $622 billion local governments spent in 1991, education—mostly for elementary and secondary schools—accounted for 37 percent. Local governments also concentrated on building roads; protecting citizens with police and fire services; and providing utilities, from water and public transportation to gas and electric power in some jurisdictions. In addition, local governments administered a broad range of other services, including health and hospitals, natural resources, parks and recreation, and employee retirement.

The pattern of local government spending varies tremendously. In

THE POLITICS OF THE ADMINISTRATIVE PROCESS

some states, such as Alaska, Delaware, Hawaii, Rhode Island, and Vermont, state governments conduct most governmental activities; local governments account for less than 40 percent of all state-local spending. In other states, local governments account for more than 60 percent of the total: Arizona, California, Colorado, Florida, Georgia, Kansas, Minnesota, Nevada, New York, and Texas.[10] Some state governments fund most local education, while others allow local governments to raise most of the money.

Thus, local governments around the country share one distinctive feature: compared with governments at other levels, they concentrate far more on direct delivery of services. This common characteristic masks remarkable variation in how this happens, however, and what role the states play in financing it. These variations are part of the rich texture of federalism and American political tradition.

Appearances versus Reality

"Judge not according to the appearance" thus is sage advice. The federal government's outlays have grown, but growth has come principally through transfer payments. Judged by tax dollars collected, the federal government has taken a larger share of the national economy. When judged by the goods and services it purchases, however, the federal government's share of the economy has actually gotten smaller. State and local governments, finally, account for a large share of government spending, but state governments engage in many intermediary functions, while local governments concentrate on delivery of services.

Each level's functions vary significantly as well. The traditional way of viewing the American federal system was as a "layer cake" of compartmentalized functions. Other analysts argued that the division of functions was not cleanly separated but was intricately mixed, like a marble cake.[11] American government, however, is really neither a layer cake nor a marble cake—or any kind of cake at all. Instead, different levels of government concentrate on different kinds of services. The levels of American government do not share these functions equally but specialize in performing different functions, as table 2.2 shows. The federal government, for example, is solely responsible for defense, the postal service, and space exploration, and it spends more than the other two levels of government put together on veterans' services, protection of natural resources, and trust programs (such as social security). State governments have primary responsibility for higher education, welfare, highways, correction (including jails), and public safety inspections and liquor stores (in states where the sale of liquor is a government-owned monopoly). Finally, local governments carry primary responsi-

Table 2.2

CONCENTRATION OF GOVERNMENT SPENDING

Level of government with the primary responsibility[a]

Federal	*State*	*Local*	*Mixed responsibility*
Defense	Higher education	Elementary	Health
Postal service	Welfare	Libraries	Hospitals
Space	Highways	Police	
Veterans' services	Corrections	Fire	
Natural resources	Inspections	Parks	
Retirement	Liquor stores	Housing and community development	
		Sanitation	
		Utilities	

a. The level of government accounts for more than 50 percent of direct government spending for the function.

bility for basic services such as fire protection, police, and elementary and secondary education. On just a few services—health and hospitals—are governmental responsibilities balanced among the levels of government.

The administrative tasks of different levels of government vary accordingly. Administrators at all levels are charged with the task of effectively, efficiently, and responsively implementing public programs. But the programs they implement often differ greatly. The diversity of public administration not surprisingly matches the diversity of the American republic.

The Tools of Government

Doing the work of government requires a wide array of administrative tools. In fact, one helpful way of understanding the work of government is to see public administration not just as a collection of departments, bureaus, and agencies but as a collection of basic instruments. As Christopher C. Hood puts it:

> We can imagine government as a set of administrative tools—such as tools for carpentry or gardening, or anything else you like. Government administration is about social control, not carpentry or gardening. But

there is a tool-kit for that, just like anything else. What government does to *us*—its subjects or citizens—is to try to shape our lives by applying a set of administrative tools, in many different combinations and contexts, to suit a variety of purposes.[12]

Within government's tool kit is a remarkable array of instruments, which we examine in turn: direct administration, grants, contracts, regulations, tax expenditures, and loan programs.

Direct Administration

Direct administration is what most people think of when they think of public administration. From police and fire protection to air-traffic control and inspection of food safety, administrators provide a remarkable range of government services. As we have seen, however, such services represent only a part—at the federal level, a small part—of governmental activity. In fact, federal spending can be broken down into three categories: entitlements (54 percent), programs such as social security and Medicare to which individuals are legally entitled if they meet eligibility criteria; interest on the national debt (14 percent), most of which is owed to American citizens; and discretionary spending (38 percent), over which the president and members of Congress have more control (see figure 2.4). Most citizens are surprised to find that entitlements is such a large share of spending and that discretionary spending is so small. International programs, including foreign aid, account for just 1 percent of all federal spending. Defense is just 21 percent, while discretionary domestic spending is only 16 percent of all spending. The whole range of federal welfare programs (including food stamps, supplemental security income, family support, and child nutrition) totaled just $69 billion in fiscal year 1993, or less than 5 percent of all federal spending.[13]

The other surprise is that most of what the federal government spends it spends indirectly, through contracts, grants, and transfer payments to individuals. In fact, only about 12 percent (in fiscal 1993) of all federal spending went to activities the federal government itself performs, and much of that went to fielding the armed forces.[14]

Similar statistics for state and local governments are not available, but it is a reasonable guess that local governments are much more heavily dominated by direct-service programs. They spend most of their money on education, police, and fire protection, in which local government employees themselves provide the services. The state governments fall between the federal and the local governments. Hence, the lower the level of government,

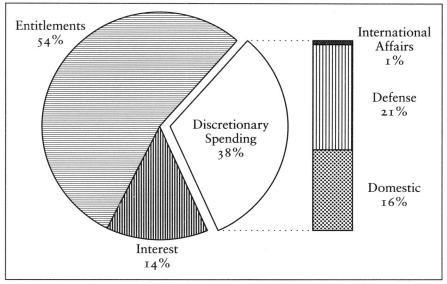

Figure 2.4

FEDERAL SPENDING

SOURCE: Congressional Budget Office, *The Economic and Budget Outlook: Fiscal Years 1995–1999* (Washington, D.C.: Government Printing Office, 1994), 92, 94.

NOTE: The total adds to more than 100 percent because of offsetting receipts and net deposit insurance inflows.

the more government administrators will be involved in direct provision of services. And, by extension, the higher the level of government, the more public administrators will be involved in managing other governmental tools. The nature of public administration thus varies markedly by level of government.

Grants

Much governmental activity, moreover, is *between* levels of government. Sometimes one level of government wishes to provide financial assistance to another level. Many state governments, as we have seen, provide a large share of the cost of local schools. Sometimes one level of government wants to induce another level to perform a certain service a particular way. For example, the federal government created the interstate highway system to encourage state governments to build modern high-speed roads. Federal grants date from the Ordinance of 1787—before the drafting of the Constitution—which provided land grants to the states for education. As Donald Haider argues, "federal grants are the oldest, most widely used, and probably the best-understood tool that the federal government has available to carry out public policy."[15]

We return to the role of grants in implementing public programs in chapter 11. In the meantime, we can note that the administration of grants differs significantly from direct administration. Administrators at one level must supervise administrators at another, whose behavior they cannot directly control but must attempt to influence through the grant system. That requires substantially different administrative skills.

Contracts

While governments have always relied on contracts—to feed and supply armies, for example—their use has increased markedly since World War II. As we see in chapter 11, the growing complexity of government has led government to rely more on private-sector experts and outside organizations. In a contract, government administrators sign a formal agreement with private parties, and the agreement embodies a quid pro quo: the government agrees to pay a certain amount of money in exchange for a good or a service.

Contract administration thus requires the government to employ officials to set the standards for contracts, to negotiate effective programs at low prices, and to oversee the results that contractors produce. While newspaper stories about Pentagon contracting scandals remind us about both the scope of federal contracting and how difficult it can be to administer contracts well, they disguise how reliant government at all levels is on contracting. From the management of cafeterias in federal office buildings to the construction of roads by local governments, contractors play an important role in many parts of government. The effective management of contracts poses a growing challenge for public administrators.

Regulations

Budgetary spending gauges only one part of governmental activity. Regulatory programs can significantly expand government's power while spending relatively little money, since only a handful of government regulators can promulgate extensive and costly rules. Even the volume of regulations —more than 200 volumes in the *Code of Federal Regulations,* the federal government's compendium of rules—does not really provide a good gauge of their size or scope. The rules are wide ranging: 20 volumes of rules on agriculture, 18 covering the Internal Revenue Service's tax regulations, and one on the Panama Canal.

Even a casual look around us shows how widespread and important regulation by all levels of government is. Federal food experts found the tainted grapes. State regulators check the management of many banks and insurance companies. Local inspectors ensure that the scales grocery stores use to measure and charge for our food are accurate. Everything from the cars we drive, the clothes we wear, the banks we use, the air we breathe, the food we eat, to the airplanes in which we fly is covered by regulations—and by public administrators who write and enforce them. We return to a discussion of regulatory agencies in chapters 5 and 13.

Tax Expenditures

Governments at all levels use a wide variety of features in their tax codes to give individuals and taxpayers special advantages in paying their taxes. These features do more than ease taxpayers' burdens. They are also incentives to promote many different social and economic policies, to encourage taxpayers to do some things and avoid doing others. The tax advantages are called by a variety of names—tax breaks, tax loopholes, and tax expenditures (which we will use to emphasize their relationship to regular spending). Tax expenditures reduce the cost of homeownership and thus encourage taxpayers to buy rather than rent their homes. The federal tax deduction for mortgage interest and local property taxes makes family homes much cheaper to own, for example. It is the equivalent of a federal subsidy program costing $55 billion per year.[16] Other tax expenditures exempt from income taxes the interest taxpayers earn on state and local borrowing and thereby reduce the cost of state and local governments' borrowing. They allow special tax breaks for oil and gas exploration and thus encourage more exploration. State governments, and even local governments that administer income taxes, also employ tax expenditures, but it is the federal government that makes the most use of this tool.[17] Many local economic growth programs, including "enterprise zones," require special tax abatements to make investment in depressed areas more attractive.[18]

Proponents of tax expenditures often promote them as "free" programs. The government does not have to appropriate any money to the programs, yet they can provide substantial assistance. Such programs, of course, are not free.

In calculating the deficit, as we see in chapter 10, it makes little difference if a program adds to expenditures or takes away from revenues. Even if the cost is the same, though, the administrative consequences are very different. Tax expenditures require tax administrators to write and enforce rules, which often are complex.[19]

Loan Programs

As we saw at the beginning of this chapter, the federal government has become the largest lender in the country. From guaranteeing student loans to

making loans to farmers, the federal government provides financial assistance through a broad range of programs. While other levels of government
conduct much more modest lending programs, the federal government
plays the most important role in government lending programs. Federal
lending began during the Great Depression, but it grew dramatically during
the late 1970s and early 1980s. As budget deficits swelled, members of
Congress sought new ways of funding federal programs, and loans provided
an easy answer. As Representative Willis D. Gradison, Jr. (R-Ohio) put it,
federal loans are "a technique used during a period of budget stringency to
do good things where the cost doesn't show up until later."

Although the federal government dominates government credit policy,
lending programs are administered in a highly decentralized fashion. Loans
for college students and home mortgages, for example, are administered by
local banks under the supervision of state and federal agencies. Government
lending programs thus are part of the subtle and complex public/private
mixture of administrative strategies that have grown in the American system, especially since 1945.

Implications for Public Administration

The many threads winding through this discussion on what government
does and how it does it combine to suggest three broad implications.

1. *The job of government varies by level.* Local governments tend to
concentrate on directly providing goods and services. State governments
also directly provide many goods and services, but they play a crucial intermediary role in the American federal system: transferring money to local
governments (especially for local schools); and administering money from
the federal government (especially for welfare and Medicaid—grants to
provide medical care for the poor). The federal government, by contrast,
devotes most of its administrative energy to national defense and the transfer function.

2. *The job of government varies by function.* The growth of transfer
functions emphasizes as well that different kinds of governmental programs
require different administrative approaches. Providing goods and services,
from education to national defense, requires sharp technical skills. Administrators work to develop the best techniques: the best way to train teachers,
the right kind of audiovisual aids, textbooks that do not promote stereotypes or advance the "wrong" values, tests that most appropriately measure
students' achievements. In direct provision of goods and services, most administrative action is *internal* to the government's bureaucracy.

By contrast, administering transfer programs involves extensive action *external* to the government bureaucracy. Instead of mailing checks for welfare and social security, government could directly provide services: government-run shelters for those who could not afford their own homes, government-run kitchens for those who could not afford food, and so on. Transfers both make the government's administrative task easier and preserve dignity and free choice for the recipients. They also fundamentally change the administrative task. Instead of providing services, the government seeks to determine the size of check to which the law entitles a recipient. That is a very different kind of government-citizen interaction than in direct services, and it requires a different collection of administrative skills.

3. *The job of government varies by who finally provides the goods and services.* In a related point, even services that formerly were directly provided by government are now being provided instead through contracts, intergovernmental grants, tax expenditures, and loan programs. Just as in transfer programs, much of the administrative work is external to the governmental bureaucracy. When contractors manufacture weapons for defense or collect local garbage, governmental officials are "in the uncomfortable position of being held responsible for programs they do not really control."[20]

There is, in short, a difference between who *provides* a service, by creating a program and paying for it, and who *produces* it by actually administering the service.[21] As government has grown bigger, more and more of its growth has come by providing more services but by relying on nongovernmental persons and organizations—or sometimes governments at other levels—to produce them.

Such "government by proxy"—the use of third-party agents to deliver programs that the government funds—is thus different from transfer programs because the responsibility of government officials extends far past simply ensuring that checks are mailed out correctly, and different from directly administered programs because government officials do not control those who finally provide the service. Each kind of program requires a different approach to administration, tailored to the special problems and needs that the program presents. We explore this problem in more depth in chapter 12.

Conclusion

If there truly is a "crisis of confidence" in American government, its roots are not necessarily in "big government." While government unquestionably has gotten bigger, it has not become more concentrated. Instead, the problems that lie at the heart of the "crisis of confidence" stem from government's growing complexity. More and more, government programs rely on intricate relationships among levels of government or between government and private contractors or other agents. There has, moreover, been a growing disconnection between the raising and spending of governmental money. Those responsible for the performance of governmental programs are not always within the same level of government, so accountability is predictably harder to ensure.

Indeed, from filling out income tax forms to borrowing money through student loans to working as government contractors, the performance of government programs has come to depend more and more on all of us. Public functions are more intricately interwoven with the private sector, and this interweaving brings new complexities into the administration of government. If government depends both on public and private values, whose values are to prevail in the inevitable conflicts, and who will work out solutions to these conflicts?

These fundamental issues underline the crucial problems of accountability and performance in public administration. These issues will follow us through the book as we explore the value of traditional theories of management, both public and private; and as we examine the challenges of the new approaches, both to existing notions of public administration and to lasting values of American democracy.

Part II

Organizations and the Role of Government's Structure

The structure of organizations has for centuries been the basic building block of government administration. There is a long history of thinking about how best to structure organizations. There is an equally long history of efforts to reform organizational structure. Every structural choice represents an emphasis on some values over others. No value choice has ever proven very stable and, as values shift, so too do the ways we arrange organizational structures. We examine here the basic foundations of organization theory, recent efforts to improve it, the effects of organizational structure on executive branch behavior, and the enduring problems with which reformers have long struggled.

3

Organization Theory: Foundations

Large-scale administration has structure—a patterned arrangement of the relations among the persons and groups engaged in the administrative enterprise. This is both obvious and problematic, for it hides a number of disagreements among organization theorists. Some theorists start with the whole organization and the patterns by which its principal units and their subunits are related to one another. Particularly if their interest focuses on public administration, they must wrestle with the classic problem of authority and its delegation to department heads and, in turn, to their subordinates. In other words, their model is *hierarchical*. The implications of the concept of authority appear more fully in two models, the classical and the bureaucratic, whose principal proponents were Luther Gulick and Max Weber. Systems theorists choose a different starting point. They attempt to generalize about all organizations, whether public or private. Nonetheless, systems theory shares some key features of the whole-organization approach.

Three major theories challenge the hierarchical authority model. One, rooted in the dynamics of human relations, condemns the impersonality of bureaucratic hierarchies and so pleads for the humanizing of organizations. The second, rooted in the realities of political life, yields a pluralistic model. The third, noting how extensively a government delegates authority to other governments, to private organizations, and to mixed public-private enterprises, calls for a third-party administration model.

We examine each of these varied approaches to the development of organization theory.

The Structural Approach to Large Organizations

Suppose one wishes to study the general pattern of a large administrative enterprise—the executive branch of a government, a major executive department, or a large bureau. Because the social scientist is here examining the relational pattern among millions or thousands of persons, his or her concern cannot be with each individual staff member or each small group of day-to-day co-workers. Instead, the social scientist either works from the whole to its major parts and their subparts or starts with the subparts as building blocks and constructs from them a patterned aggregate that is the whole. The approach can therefore be termed formal and impersonal. And so the analyst designing a major reorganization is often charged with "just moving boxes around on the organization chart."

We need to make a clear distinction between *positions* and the *persons* who occupy them. Anyone using the structural approach to an organization is indeed concerned with the relations among the chief executive, the department heads, the bureau chiefs, the division directors, and the section chiefs. But, knowing that structural patterns tend to persist at and among these levels, despite changes of persons, the analyst usually speaks in terms of positions rather than their temporary incumbents.[1] Although no one in the U.S. government puts a personal stamp on a position as much as does the person who is the president, we do not hesitate to speak of the presidency or the president as an office with certain powers and a reasonably determinate scope of expected behavior, independent of the incumbent.

The concept of an administrative position abstracted from its current human occupant has a close kinship with the concept of role as it is used in sociology and psychology. Though these scholarly disciplines expect a person's role to be defined by the expectations of "adjacent" fellow workers (including peers, superiors, and subordinates), those expectations in turn derive substantially from the person's formal position in the organization.

The relation of role to organizational position is captured by the social psychologists Daniel Katz and Robert L. Kahn, who write:

> [I]n any organization we can locate each individual in the total set of ongoing relationships and behaviors comprised by the organization. The key concept for this is *office* [i.e., position], by which is meant a particular point in organizational space; space in turn is defined in terms of a structure of interrelated offices and the patterns of activities associated with them. . . . Associated with each office is a set of *activities* or expected behaviors. These activities constitute the *role* to be performed, at least approximately, by any person who occupies that office. . . .
>
> To a considerable extent the role expectations . . . are determined by the broader organizational context. The technology of the organization, the structure of its subsystems, its formal policies, and its rewards and

penalties dictate in large degree the content of a given office.... The structural properties of organization are sufficiently stable so that they can be treated as independent of the particular persons in the role-set.[2]

Formal organization, then, accounts for a large part of the behavioral pattern of the people in administration and thus for the ways in which the human beings manning public agencies relate to one another. In governments, the formalization of structural arrangements has always had a special importance, for the arrangements derive from the political society's basic philosophical and juristic ideas. We need to appreciate this if we are to be ready for the leap from a democratic electorate and a multimember, representative, legislative body to what seems an authoritarian structuring of the administrative bureaucracy. To those following the structural approach, that is no great leap. We see why in the following section.

Authority and Hierarchy

The central problem of political societies is the distribution and structuring of power. In constitutional systems the government is accorded power that, within the stated limits, is *legitimate* power—that is, constitutionally conferred, rather than naked, power. Clothed thus with legitimacy, the government has a "right" to expect citizens to comply with its decisions. This means that most citizens voluntarily comply regardless of their personal agreement or disagreement with the decisions' specific content, and regardless of the severity or lightness of punishment for noncompliance. In sum, a government having legitimacy is said to have *authority*—that is, rightful power to make decisions within constitutionally defined limits, with the expectation of widespread compliance.[3]

A government's authority is exercised through institutions and people, and particular elements of authority are therefore vested in designated major bodies and offices (e.g., legislature, courts, chief executive). A constitution that distributes authority limits the kind and scope of authority allotted to each body or office. Compliance by major bodies and officials with the constitutionally prescribed conditions is requisite to the legitimacy of their decisions.

We have briefly reviewed the concept of legitimacy of the power of a government and its major institutional segments because the authority exercised by administrative agencies derives from and is defined by these higher power holders. Administrative authority is therefore a further extension of the idea of legitimacy; it is delegated authority. Note, though, that by this point the idea has two applications. An administrative agency can expect most citizens to comply with its administrative decisions because, within its field of activity, the agency is vested with the government's legitimacy. In addition, the legislature, the courts, and the chief executive expect compliance with *their* decisions because they bear a *higher* legitimacy. Now, put these two applications together and the outcome is that citizens owe obedience to an administrative agency only insofar as its demands on citizens comply with the relevant constitutional, legislative, judicial, and executive limitations and instructions.

It should be apparent that the structuring of authority in administration, with its emphasis on linking power and legitimacy, has theoretical and historical roots in such great political questions as the nature of "the State," the legitimacy of governments themselves, the limits to their powers, and the rights of revolution and civil disobedience. The answers reached provide premises for elaborate bodies of doctrine about the delegation of power, the legal liability of government executives and their agencies for wrongs done private citizens, and the "right" of public servants individually to expose wrongdoing and collectively to strike. Public administration, being government in action, cannot be understood without an appreciation of its relation to these great political, doctrinal, and moral issues.

Administrative Implications. At the risk of being somewhat elementary, let us list six basic propositions that flow from the view of public administration as a structuring of authority:

1. A public administrative "agency" is formally established by law —usually by specific action of a legislative body, though sometimes by a constitutional provision and sometimes by the chief executive under a constitutional or statutory grant of power. As the term suggests, the agency is the agent of the principal who created it, serving the principal's instructions and interests.

2. Such an agency is assigned by law a particular field of activity and a set of responsibilities (e.g., execution of particular statutes).

3. The agency has an internal structure that divides responsibilities among bureaus (or whatever its principal units are called) and, further down, among individual positions.

4. The agency has a set of procedures that identify which units and position holders do what in what sequence during the flow of business through the agency.

5. The agency has a staff of officials and employees who are expected to contribute to performance of the kind of activity and the specific responsibilities assigned to the agency. Though the staff is constantly losing and

gaining members, this by itself does not alter the stable expectations about the nature of the members' contributions.

6. Other parts of the government (e.g., the legislature, chief executive, and judiciary) have authority to abolish the agency, to continue, add to, or contract the scope of its field of activity and its responsibilities, to fix the amount of funds it can use, to appoint some staff members and specify how others shall be chosen, and to impose structural and procedural requirements on its organization and operation.

These statements exclude or seriously qualify some notions found in organization theories that slight the issue of legitimacy of power. The agency does not spontaneously spring into being, but is formally created by a constitutionally legitimized body or official. The agency is not free to choose its own objectives, but is expected to operate in a limited range of subject matter and to fulfill responsibilities assigned to it by an outside authority. The agency is not simply a social pattern developed out of who likes whom or who can seize and hold power, but has a formal organizational structure intended to specify who is meant to do what and who is meant to have authority over whom. Its officials and employees are not supposed to serve private groups' interests that are incompatible with their official responsibilities, to mobilize colleagues to subvert the agency's objectives, or to use their power for personal gain. Instead, they will be judged by their service to the agency and its assigned objectives. The agency is not set up and left to proceed on its own as an autonomous "closed organization" or to wrestle with a vague set of forces called "the environment," but remains part of a very specific environment, the government, whose major legitimate power holders have authority to appraise its performance, determine the input of resources to it, and alter its mission and activities.

These statements, based on the structure of authority, do not say that any of the indicated procedures or behaviors will be well performed or will be free of problems. The lawmaking body may establish an agency that is not needed. The assignments of fields of activities and sets of responsibilities may be vague and may overlap those of other agencies. The internal structure of an agency may be poorly designed. And any feature of the legitimate power model may be subverted by developments not taken into account by the model itself. Thus, aggressive individuals or groups in an agency may seize or gradually accumulate power so that the formal structure of authority is undermined. An agency may generate such internal dynamics and so powerful a set of allies that superior holders of authority will hesitate to challenge its independent actions. Or a superior holder of authority may induce an agency to make decisions that serve private economic, political, or personal interests that are incompatible with the larger public purpose. Though these and other practical possibilities need our attention, they do not destroy the usefulness of our starting with theories based on the structuring of authority.

Two Models

The premise that legitimate power is the starting point for developing the structure of public administration is also the premise of two schools of administrative thought that developed in the first half of the twentieth century. They assume a higher source of authority for the agency's existence and powers, and they see the organizational problem as one of setting up internal units and subunits each with a specified portion of the agency's activities supportive of its assigned responsibilities. This is a top-down approach, easily criticized as "authoritarian," for it of course assumes a subordination of lower units to higher units—often unfortunately called a "chain of command"—and a conformity by officials and employees that can as well be called "obedience" or "submissiveness."

Both the classical and bureaucratic schools of thought make explicit certain values additional to legitimacy. Among them *rationality* is preeminent. This is partly because both schools view organizations as simply neutral instruments for achieving whatever policy objectives (i.e., values) a modern state's rulers may choose. The models are therefore meant to be value free, save for the value of rationality, which is equated with efficiency.

The Classical Model. The classical theory of organization reached its peak in the 1930s when Luther Gulick published its most persuasive exposition.[4] It still has wide currency. The theory stresses the establishment of definitely bounded jurisdictions of authority and responsibility among top positions, and, in turn, division and subdivision of these jurisdictions among the positions immediately under the top positions and so on down through all administrative levels. Efficiency is the prime value, differentiation of functions (i.e., specialization) and coordination of them are the twin elements in efficiency, and "objective principles" of organization provide guides on how to organize.

Specific doctrines of the classical school include the following six:

1. The bases of organization are four:
    a. *Purpose* (e.g., defense, education, crime control)
    b. *Process* (e.g., accounting, engineering, typing, purchasing)
    c. *Clientele* (e.g., Indians, children, veterans, the aged)
    d. *Place* (e.g., the Tennessee Valley, New England, Mississippi, Latin America).

2. For each specific choice of mode of organization, these bases are mutually exclusive alternatives; one must be given precedence. But if an organization is erected on one base, "it becomes immediately necessary to recognize the other[s] in constructing the secondary and tertiary divisions of work."[5]

3. The executive branch of a government should be organized at its top level by major purposes (not by any of the other three bases or by a mixture), and each department should include all activities contributory to its purpose.

4. Because any executive can effectively oversee only a limited number of immediate subordinates, the number of departments under the chief executive, of bureaus under a department head, and so on, should not exceed the executive's "span of control" (i.e., the number of subordinates he or she can effectively supervise).

5. Administrative authority and responsibility should be vested in single administrators, not in plural-membership ("collegial") bodies such as boards and commissions—because under the latter arrangement the fixing of individual responsibility for mistakes is difficult, and clear-cut decisions are less likely than fuzzy compromises among the members.

6. Line activities and staff activities should be sharply distinguished. Line activities are operations *directly* related to the major purpose of the agency—that is, the achievement of a public objective through service to or regulation of the public or particular segments of it. Staff activities, in contrast, are assisting functions to facilitate the work of the line officials—for example, research, policy and program analysis, planning, budgeting, personnel administration, and procurement of supplies. Essentially, line executives exercise powers of decision and command, whereas staff officials are —or should be—restricted to advising.

The classical organization theory has been closely associated with such nonstructural administrative ideals as a civil service of qualified persons selected by merit, a budget system for the whole executive branch, and a rational decision-making process through which higher officials draw on the specialized knowledge at lower levels and decision makers at lower levels are furnished criteria and subjected to controls that assure conformity with higher policy.

The Bureaucratic Model. Max Weber (1864–1920), a German sociologist, is the intellectual father of the bureaucratic model, and sociologists are its contemporary exponents and refiners. Bureaucratic theory is remarkably similar to classical theory, though it is reached by a different path of study, attained prominence in the United States only after World War II,[6] and was elaborated by a quite different group of scholars. Weber focused an important part of his studies on why people feel an obligation to obey commands without assessing their own attitudes as to the value of the content of each command. He suggested that a stable system of authority cannot depend on appeals to subordinates' purely material interests and calculation of personal advantage, or on affectual motives (e.g., liking or admiration of the superior), or on ideal motives. Instead, a stable pattern of obedience must rest on a belief in the *legitimacy of the system of authority* and so on deference to the source of command in that system.

Weber found it useful to think in terms of three "pure" types or models of legitimate authority: (1) traditional, (2) charismatic, and (3) legal-rational. *Traditional* authority rests on wide belief in the sacredness of immemorial traditions ("what actually, allegedly, or presumably has always existed"), and so on the obligation of personal loyalty to the individual who has attained chiefship in the traditional way. *Charismatic* authority rests on personal devotion to an individual because of the exceptional sanctity, heroism, or exemplary character of this person. Because in both of these types authority may legitimately be exercised arbitrarily or by revelations and inspirations, both types of authority lack rationality.

By contrast, *rational-legal* authority (Weber sometimes used "rational" and sometimes "legal" in characterizing the type) rests in "the legally established impersonal order." Obedience is due "the persons exercising the authority of office under it only by virtue of the formal legality of their commands and only within the scope of authority of the office."[7] "The official duty ... is fixed by *rationally established* norms, by enactments, decrees, and regulations, in such a manner that the legitimacy of the authority becomes the legality of the general rule, which is purposely thought out, enacted, and announced with formal correctness."[8] Persons in a corporate body, "in so far as they obey a person in authority, do not owe this obedience to him as an individual, but to the impersonal order."[9] Weber was talking about a government of laws and not of men, and he carried the concept over to administrative organization, its staffing, and methods: "the purest type of exercise of legal authority is that which employs a bureaucratic administrative staff."[10]

To Weber, rationality implies efficiency (an assumption also basic to the classical theory described earlier). He wrote:

Experience tends universally to show that the purely bureaucratic type of administrative organization ... is ... from a purely technical point of view, capable of attaining the highest degree of efficiency and is in this sense formally the most rational known means of carrying out imperative control over human beings. It is superior to any other form in precision, in stability, in the stringency of its discipline, and in its reliability. It thus makes possible a particularly high degree of calculability of results for the heads of the organization and for those acting in relation to it.[11]

The organizational requisites of a bureaucracy, as set forth by Weber, are simple and largely parallel the requisites stated by the classical theory of organization. First, laws and administrative regulations establish "fixed and official jurisdictional areas" as part of a systematic division of labor, each area being assigned "regular activities ... as official duties" and "the authority to give the commands required for the discharge of these duties" (subject to rules delimiting the use of coercive means for obtaining compliance). Second, "the principles of office hierarchy and of levels of graded authority mean a firmly ordered system of super- and subordination in which there is supervision of the lower offices by the higher ones."[12]

Weber, like the classical theorists, complements the organizational requisites with other characteristics of a full-fledged rational bureaucracy. He specifies particularly that officials should be full-time, salaried, and selected on the basis of technical qualifications. But, again as with the classical theory, the human beings who constitute "the bureaucratic machine" seem stripped of their human differences. "The individual cannot squirm out of the apparatus in which he is harnessed ... the professional bureaucrat is chained to his activity by his entire material and ideal existence. In the great majority of cases he is only a single cog in an ever-moving mechanism which prescribes to him an essentially fixed route of march."[13]

It is an oddity of the history of administrative study that, despite the similarities of the two theories, classical organization theory has been scathingly attacked by many modern students of administration, whereas bureaucratic organization theory continues to command their profound respect. Weber is criticized, to be sure, but his concepts remain central to modern sociological analyses of bureaucratic organization.[14]

Systems Theory

Systems theory is the most ambitious effort to generalize about *all* organizations, public and private, large and small. Indeed, the theory has far larger scope than that, for a "system" can be any set of related parts, whether the universe, the solar system, or a molecule. Its application to organizations, therefore, draws on analogies to physical and biological phenomena.[15]

A system can be either closed or open. Closed-system theorists analogize an organization to a physical system, such as a machine, whose own operation is substantially unaffected by its environment. A common example is the heating system of a house: the thermostat is set for a given room temperature; when the room temperature falls, the thermostat triggers the furnace to restore it, and when the restoration is effected, the thermostat turns off the furnace. (Room temperature is an environmental factor affecting the timing of the thermostatic system's activity. But the system's own efficiency of operation is self-contained; once set, it "reads" the temperature changes and performs its function.)

Open-system theorists analogize an organization to a biological organism, such as an animal or a plant living in and exchanging with the environment. A common example is the human body's normal temperature of 98.6 degrees, which may rise by contraction of a disease from others and which the individual's own reflexes or a physician must try to restore. One consequence of system theorists' fascination with nature's processes for mechanically and homeostatically restoring equilibrium or normalcy is that their models tend to have a conservative bias, making them static, rather than dynamic, models.

Most organizational theory using the systems approach treats an organization as an open system—that is, one that interacts with its environment. The essentials can be briefly stated. An organization is a system that receives *inputs* of resources (equipment, supplies, the energies of employees) that it *throughputs* and transforms to yield *outputs* (products or services). (Some of the input resources, however, are spirited off for use in maintaining the organization itself as a system—that is, for overhead costs.) Such a system also operates a *feedback loop,* which provides negative feedback that flags back to the input stage the system's output mistakes or its departures from the normal so that they can be corrected. The usual graphic representation is shown in figure 3.1.

Though the organization is usually seen as an open system, the closed

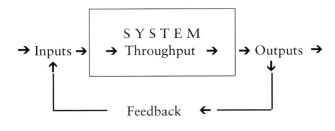

Figure 3.1

SYSTEMS THEORY

system is not irrelevant. A common tendency of a large organization is to try to reduce dependence on an uncertain environment by, in effect, bringing much of the environment within its own system. Manufacturing corporations absorb competitors, and they integrate vertically by developing or acquiring sources of their inputs and wholesale and retail distribution outlets. Government departments and bureaus seek autonomy in selecting employees, purchasing supplies, and evaluating their own program outputs. In sum, open systems try to reduce risks by evolving toward closed systems.

Two elements that are explicit or implicit in the classical and bureaucratic theories receive their clearest expression in systems theory. In the former theories, they are stated as agency jurisdiction and agency purpose. In the latter, they appear as system boundaries and system purpose.

System Boundaries

Both classical and bureaucratic theories emphasize the need for defined jurisdictions so that the authority and responsibility of each department and each bureau will be clear. A system, too, must have boundaries so that one can tell what is within the system and what is outside it. This inside-outside distinction is vital for two reasons: (1) systems theorists need to identify inputs to the system from "the environment" and the system's outputs to the environment, and these transactions occur at the system's boundaries; and (2) the theory distinguishes two requisites for the survival of a system—its capacity to manipulate or adapt to its external environment and its capacity to suppress or moderate internal threats.

However easy it may be to identify a business corporation as a neatly bounded organizational system, the analyst will encounter difficulties in the public sector. Formalistically, of course, one can simply assert that the Department of Agriculture is a distinct system with precise boundaries, everything else in the government and outside it being merely the department's environment.[16] Nevertheless, legal, political, and organizational realities allow the department far less autonomy and clarity of boundaries than the corporate analogy would require. The Department of Agriculture is a part of the executive branch.[17] Many of its important decisions require concurrence of other departments, the president, and central agencies (such as the Office of Management and Budget). Indeed, decisions directly affecting agriculture may actually lie with other agencies or with the president. These active sharers of decision-making authority cannot realistically be analogized to a business corporation's competitors, suppliers, and customers. To be sure, the Department of Agriculture does have a distinctive identity within the executive branch. But its identity rests in its core of concerns, not in the sharpness of its boundaries.

System Purpose

Classical theory, you will recall, proposes that the executive branch *should* be organized at the top by major purpose. Systems theory goes much further. It asserts that every organizational system *has* a purpose, goal, or objective. Talcott Parsons, the leading systems theorist among social scientists, wrote that "primacy of orientation to the attainment of a specific goal is used as the defining characteristic of an organization which distinguishes it from other types of social systems."[18]

Such statements fortunately carry us beyond the commonly encountered view that a system's objective is simply to survive.[19] This view is closely tied to the analogy of a biological organism, though it also fits nicely the assumption that a business corporation's objective is to make profits, the absence of which spells its doom. Long life, therefore, is the measure of a system's success. The counterview is that, unlike most biological organisms but like that subtype, humans as moral beings, an organizational system seeks to serve a purpose beyond itself, even if the pursuit or achievement of that purpose may lead to the organization's death. Lord Ashby, writing about universities as organizations, has put the point clearly:

> Among living organisms it is assumed that the prime function is to survive.... Among social institutions one cannot make so simple an assumption. The biological analogy breaks down. It is not enough to say that the function of a university is to survive. It has functions over and above survival: in other words, it has purpose.... Unlike the biologist, the university administrator cannot eschew teleology; he must squarely face the fact that universities do not exist simply for their own sakes, as daffodils and sparrows and mice do; they have a purpose.[20]

But to *define* a system or an organization as having a purpose is to beg a number of questions that need analysis. The principal difficulty is that an organization's purpose is elusive, and if there are several purposes, the difficulty is compounded. Certainly, this is the case with government agencies.

Is it the purpose of the Department of Agriculture to advocate the American farmer's interests or is it to assure that the agricultural sector contributes to stability and growth of the national economy, serves consumer needs, adjusts to world trade conditions and American foreign policy, and forgoes products and practices that endanger public health? Is its purpose to serve the interests of large-scale, commercial farm corporations, or is it to reduce the poverty of small-scale farmers and migratory farm workers, or is it both, and, if so, in what proportions? Congress does not provide the answers, for Congress has assigned the department a multiplicity of purposes, which are often at odds with one another and carry no indications of relative weight. The president does not provide the answers. President Nixon said (1) that he wanted his secretary of agriculture "to speak for the farmers to the president" rather than to speak "for the president to the farmers,"[21] and, contrarily, (2) that "when any department or agency begins to represent a parochial interest, then its advice and support inevitably become less useful to the man who must serve *all* of the people as their president."[22]

A set of purposes appropriate to systems theory also cannot be derived from examination of what the department itself states as its purposes.[23] These are parts of the department's *performance,* often rhetorical flourishes to enlist external and internal support. Systems theory needs a clear statement of an organization's objectives so that the organization's performance can be measured against the stated objectives. Circular reasoning will not help.

It appears, then, that the absence of a specific goal or of explicit objectives does not define away an organization. At least, that is true of governmental agencies. What we can assume is that an agency operates in a field of activity, such as agriculture, national defense, transportation, or public health. The agency may not monopolize the field, and the field's boundaries may be imprecise. The objectives pursued by the agency, and the priorities among them, may shift with changes in political control of the executive and legislative branches (to name only the most obvious of many factors). These features of the real world are compatible with locating an organization in a field of activity and attributing to it a core of concerns, while they require relaxation of system theory's demand that every organizational system have exactly described boundaries and purposes.

The Humanist Challenge

The models and theories described so far have much in common. All offer a rather formal, abstract view of an organization as itself sharply bounded and one ideally composed of clearly bounded units and subunits that are so arranged as to provide a hierarchical structuring of authority, often pictured as a pyramid.[24] This "textbook model" has been attacked from three directions. The humanist charge is that the model is authoritarian, stifling the creativity and full development of the human beings who are employees of the bureaucratic organization. The two others argue that the model (except for the systems-theory version) ignores the environment of governmental organizations. The pluralist charge is that the classical and bureaucratic models ignore the political system, give an unreal portrayal of the executive branch, and conflict with democratic values. The indirect administration challenge is that those models ignore the extent to which any American government relies on other governments and on private and mixed public-private organizations for administration of public functions.

The humanist challenge to the formal, structural model is internally oriented. Its concern is with the life of individual workers within the organization. As the theorizing and research relevant to this have dealt mostly with industrial and other business enterprises, our discussion reflects that fact.

Jobs, Productivity, and Happiness

Industrial management has long recognized that the business organization's performance depends on the productivity of its individual workers. Among the major factors in a worker's productivity are the design of the job and the procedures that all workers follow. The "scientific management" movement, which developed the profession of industrial engineering, dates back to the early 1900s, when Frederick W. Taylor undertook time-and-motion studies of individual workers, created patterns for specialization and standardization of jobs, and designed procedures to guide the flow of work from job to job.[25] This single-minded pursuit of efficiency was even then perceived as dehumanizing.[26] Well before the humanist approach reached full flower, psychologists sought to clarify the motivations that lead an individual to join a particular organization, to stay with it, to perform well, and to leave.[27] Money helps. But it does not adequately explain variations among companies or among a single company's work groups.

The "human relations" movement, which peaked in the 1950s and again in the antiestablishment mood of the late 1960s, had a connective link to the managerial approach. Both were concerned with workers' productivity and such related matters as absenteeism and turnover.[28] The humanists argued that happy workers were more productive and unhappy workers less productive, and their early research studies confirmed this. Happiness, or satisfaction, as it was usually called, was not a matter of monetary and promotional rewards but of the interpersonal relations in the small face-to-face group of fellow workers and their immediate supervisor. According to the humanists, a satisfaction-generating and presumably productive atmosphere is not bureaucratically structured but one that fosters democratic participation by the workers in the reaching of decisions for the group; the supervisor is not autocratic and directive, but informal, consultative, trusting, and concerned for the team members' welfare.

The only trouble is that the accumulated evidence now indicates that (1) these conditions make some workers happy and some unhappy, and (2) happy workers are not necessarily more productive workers.[29] Though the many research studies on job satisfaction consistently show that "job satisfaction is related to absences and turnover, they have been equally consistent in showing negligible relationships between satisfaction and level of performance or productivity."[30] This broke the link to the managerial approach, the shared concern for ways to improve productivity.

Ideology

What remained was a normative commitment to the individual's opportunity for "self-actualization" (creativity, self-direction, the realization of one's full potential as a human being) and to the equality of persons (and thus minimal subordination to a leader's direction and maximal participation in decision making). Members of the human relations movement made clear their conviction that the large, formal organization with its hierarchical authority structure is repressive. Chris Argyris wrote that organization planners

> assume that efficiency is increased by a fixed hierarchy of authority. The man at the top is given formal power to hire and fire, reward and penalize, so that employees will work for the organization's objectives.
>
> The impact of this design-feature on human personality is clearly to make the individuals dependent on, passive and subordinate to the leader. The results are obviously to lessen their self-control and shorten their time-perspective ... pushing individuals back from active toward passive, from being aware of long time-perspectives toward having only a short time-perspective. In all these four ways, the result is to move employees back from adulthood toward immaturity.[31]

The human relations school has been severely attacked. Four grounds of criticism are illustrative.[32] First, most of the early research presenting empirical proof of the doctrines was conducted by "true believers," and other scholars found it seriously flawed. Second, the sweeping contrast of the bad hierarchical organization with the ideal humanist organization was overdrawn and rested on assertion rather than scientific study of organizations. Many writers simply adopted Douglas McGregor's contrast of Theory X (hierarchical authority) organizations and Theory Y (humanist) organizations.[33] Recent studies have rejected this simple contrast. Instead, a multitude of situational variables, occurring in diverse combinations and with different weights, call for a tailoring of leadership and participatory styles to the particular circumstances.[34] This welcome discovery, however, thwarts the search for generalizing propositions, which is the essence of theory. Third, though the school was committed to development of "the whole person," the job was treated as if it were the whole life. Critics made the obvious point that in societies with limited workdays and workweeks most people obtain important satisfactions off the job; a high overall level of happiness is often achieved despite only moderate satisfaction with the job's sociopsychological attributes. Fourth, the school's normative commitments blocked out awareness that a qualified leader needs to lead and not just be "one of the boys." Curiously, it is Abraham Maslow, a psychologist much admired by humanists, who makes the point most sharply:

> The writers on the new style of management have a tendency to indulge in certain pieties and dogmas of democratic management that are sometimes in striking contrast to the realities of the situation.
>
> With dogma occupying this front-rank position, it is not surprising that human relations theory has evaded the problem of the very superior boss. The participative kind of management, where subordinates work toward a good solution to a problem, is often an inappropriate setting for the superior boss. He is apt to get restless and irritated.... The less intelligent subordinates are also affected adversely. Why should they sweat for three days to work toward the solution of a particular problem when they know all the time that the superior can see the solution in three minutes....
>
> The relationship of the boss to the people whom he might have to order around or fire or punish is, if we are realistic about it, not a friendly relation among equals.... This hard reality ought to have some impact on the theories of participative, democratic management.[35]

Sensitivity Training and Organization Development

Many members of the human relations school concluded that change toward their ideal could come only if the large organization and its high- and mid-level officials changed their behavioral patterns. If higher executives were more "authentic" in their own interpersonal relations—letting down the guards associated with their hierarchical and competitive positions in the authority structure and clarifying their own identities as human beings interacting with other human beings—the psychological atmosphere of the whole organization would be transformed. To achieve this, the executives needed to be trained in new attitudes. Business corporations embraced the approach, and selected executives were sent off for one or two weeks to participate in "sensitivity training," "T-groups" (the "T" is for "training"), or "laboratory training," as the approach is variously known. Typically, participants in a group were strangers to one another. The group leader or trainer was a member of the human relations school and took a nondirective role, the intent being for group members to engage in interpersonal dynamics characterized by extreme candor. It is no accident that two studies appraising sensitivity training incorporated as well an appraisal of "encounter groups," which also flourished in the troubled 1960s.[36]

Objective assessments of the approach report a paucity of reliable evidence to support its claims.[37] Though many participants value the experience and alter their behavior back on the job, the new behavior may either improve or lessen their effectiveness in their organizations. The effects of the experience usually fade after a few months. The participants' organizations are not changed.[38]

A response to these problems was attempted by the movement labeled Organization Development (OD), which specifically seeks to change organizations.[39] Instead of attempting to train individuals in new behaviors by assembling "pick-up groups" of strangers, who then return to their set of untrained colleagues, OD tries to change a whole organization by bringing together the executives who are joint actors in operating the enterprise. The sensitivity-training approach is used, but a team of OD consultants continues to monitor behavior in the organization and intervenes to provide "reinforcement experiences" when the old ways threaten to reestablish themselves.

The antibureaucratic thrust of the human relations school, in theory directed toward all large organizations but at first concentrated on corporate settings, had a substantial impact on public administration. The State Department launched "the first major OD effort undertaken in the federal government," which provided sensitivity training and team development workshops for high-level department officials, including ambassadors.[40] Twenty of the most prestigious T-group trainers were employed in the program. The program was terminated after only two years and its stated objectives "were, at best, achieved only to a marginal extent."[41] Nevertheless, many bureaus and agencies of the federal government initiated OD programs, and sensitivity training was until 1989 part of the curriculum of the Federal Executive Institute, the government's training center for its senior officials.[42] In the late 1980s, organization development faded away as total quality management (TQM) infiltrated government from the private sector. The TQM movement gained many zealous advocates and generated a broader movement through the 1990s for "continuous improvement" of public programs, which we explore more in the next chapter.

The Pluralist Challenge

The pluralist challenge to the formal, structural model is externally oriented, for its emphasis is on a government organization's responsiveness to society's politically active interest groups.

The pluralist model assumes a society characterized by the political war of groups seeking to have their interests prevail, and it regards administration as a set of battlegrounds to which the interest groups carry their struggles from the electoral and legislative arenas.[43] It perceives a fragmented administrative structure linked with a fragmented Congress. Overhead direction is weak. The president is so occupied with policy and political leadership, international affairs, and other demands on his energies that he can give only partial and discontinuous attention to maximizing the administrative authority of his position as the chief executive. And the department heads he appoints, birds of passage as they are, only rarely achieve effective control of the bureaus in their charge. Far from being a symmetrical pyramid, the executive branch is but a jumble of stones, haphazardly disposed as their specific gravity (and perhaps congressional levity) may have dictated. The task of administration, at least at its highest levels, is the same as the task of politics—to facilitate the peaceful resolution of conflicts of interests compatibly with the distribution of power among groups in our society.

Administrative organizations, according to the pluralistic model, are themselves the products of this conflict and accommodation of interests.[44] Their survival as individual agencies depends upon their command of sufficient outside support to withstand assault by disadvantaged interests. Their top officials can retain their power only as they adjust their use of power to the preferences of the supporting groups or succeed in winning sufficient support from other groups to break free from the original supporters. The president himself appears in this model not as spokesman for the nation in the sense of "all the people." Instead, he is the spokesman for that combination of forces that enabled him to attain power and that makes it possible for him to retain and exercise the substance of power. He is, in a sense, just another player, more a man with influence than a man with effective authority. To survive, administrative agencies must be responsive to Congress, and especially to congressional committees and their leaders, as both substantive power and appropriations derive from Congress. This has a sobering influence on administrators inclined to look to the president for their sole guidance.

Organization Culture

A variant of the pluralistic approach emphasizes the variety of organization cultures.[45] Agencies differ in many ways, a fact that makes suspect any generalizations about the structure of authority. Some have such strong interest-group support that they enjoy substantial autonomy within the executive branch; some enjoy such support without creating and mobilizing it; others foster the birth of sympathetic organizations. Some have such records of devotion to the public interest or to professional standards that they can resist interest-group and politically motivated efforts to intervene; others are orphans in the storm, the easy victims of unsympathetic interest groups, politicians, and sister agencies. An agency physically consolidated in one building differs from one whose headquarters units and staff members are scattered among many buildings or among capital suburbs and distant cities.[46]

The concept of organization culture stresses these and many other differences among agencies. One can enter a state liquor-control agency or an athletics-regulating agency and sense a different atmosphere from that in, say, a banking or insurance department or a labor department. In Washington, "one has only to walk into the ancient Treasury Department building ... to sense the atmosphere of a conservative financial institution."[47] Even more is this the case with the independent Federal Reserve, which additionally illustrates the possibility of a culture in which one "subordinate" (the New York Federal Reserve Bank) at various times dominates the system.[48] The Forest Service and the National Park Service, in different departments, will probably never be merged because they cannot forget a bitter controversy early in this century. The Forest Service, too, has a professional esprit de corps, a decentralization practice, and a systematic socialization of its rangers to the agency's norms that substitutes for centralization.[49] Other agencies often have difficulty maintaining morale and effective control of their field-office employees.

The hierarchic and pluralistic models perform different functions for us. The pluralistic model yields a more realistic description and explanation of what goes on in administration and politics. But the fragmentation it describes and even celebrates as part of the genius of the American political system affords little or no guidance as to what direction we should move in if we have the opportunity to express a preference or exert influence. Thus, even though this model, by applauding pluralism, slides across the line dividing description from prescription, what *is* from what *ought to be,* it does not help those confronted by opportunities to change organizations. The organization-culture variation of pluralist theory even suggests that change may be a will-o'-the-wisp, for cultures are deep-seated, rooted in particular functions and histories that alter only slowly and incrementally.

The hierarchic model, in contrast, has the operational significance of a belief widely subscribed to. It is implicitly or explicitly the pattern advocated by every reorganization commission that surveys the whole sweep of federal administration. Much of what are widely regarded as advances in national administration in the last several decades can best be understood as attempts to apply to a pluralistic government the arrangements implied by the hierarchic administrative model. Nevertheless, such proposals must be acted on by political people. The power-group forces and the organization cultures identified by the pluralistic model often block reforms designed to strengthen hierarchical administration.

The tension between the two models is by no means simply that between reality and unsubstantiated belief. For the very multiplicity of social forces and interest groups and the intensity of their competition for governmental favor underline the unacceptability of anarchy and the need for administrative institutions and processes that contribute rationality and order rather than happenstance and confusion; that are designed to seek the general interest rather than merely reflect particular private, often selfish, interests; that take the long view of policy goals rather than the short view of tactical maneuvers. The role of government in a democracy has always been to combine energies for widely shared objectives, whether for national security against foreign enemies, for maintenance of the legal system, or for the affirmative promotion of economic and social welfare. We should not be surprised that efforts to improve government and its administration should often emphasize the coordination, rationality, and legitimacy found in the hierarchic model and that such efforts need to be accommodated to the variety of interest groups, congressional committees, and government agencies whose competing interests are the central fact of the pluralistic model.

The Challenge of Third-Party Administration

All the theories reviewed assume that a government's programs are carried out by the government's own employees. What if that is not substantially true? Suppose that much of the government's work is farmed out to other governments and to private organizations, or to entities whose mix of public and private control puts them outside the administrative hierarchy. The supposition is true. Frederick Mosher estimates that "only between 15 and 20 percent of federal spending is directed to activities that the federal government performs itself (other than making and superintending payments to others)" and that less than half of that is allotted to domestic (rather than armed services) activities that the federal government performs itself. The rest of the money goes for direct transfers of funds (e.g., for social security and interest on the public debt), for grants-in-aid to state and local governments, and for grants and contracts to private institutions and individuals, all for carrying out federally sponsored and supported programs.[50]

This calls for reconsideration of organization theory. First, federal agencies are more than ever operating in a complex environment, which is populated by a host of candidates for funding or more generous funding.

This phenomenon is new, not in kind, but surely in degree. Second, much federal administration is third-party administration, "government by proxy."[51] This means that the classical and bureaucratic models no longer fit the real world (except within the government proper). Hiring, firing, and direct management of work are hierarchical powers that are no longer available to a government official when dealing with state and local governments and private organizations. Third, when government lets contracts or makes grants, it can attach conditions. The rationalization is that the government would expect such conditions to apply to its own agencies and employees, and that compliance is "voluntary" because no one need accept a grant or contract carrying unwelcome conditions. Conditional grants and contracts, however, do not amount to hierarchical direction of programs. Furthermore, the government cannot readily monitor all these outside agents, nor can it cancel large grants and contracts for violation of the prescribed conditions without damaging its programs and the public served.

Some scholars have suggested that an approach built on organizational networks might help explain these problems better.[52] Such networks, Eugene Bardach explains, consist of "a set of working relationships among actors such that any relationship has the potential both to elicit action and to communicate information in an efficient manner."[53] The approach is pragmatic; it explores how organizations that share common ground—missions, clients, and goals—coordinate their work. The approach has grown from work by administrative scholars who sought to explain the management of public programs and who found existing theory lacking. For example, they have discovered that most social service programs work through complex networks: a chain of federal grant money, frequently supplemented by state grant funds, passed on to local governments, and administered through government organizations as well as for-profit and nonprofit contractors. These programs, in turn, connect with local schools, police departments, antidrug programs, programs managed through churches and volunteer organizations, among others.

Network analysis revolves around two issues. On one level, the network approach is important for what it is not: it is based on neither traditional, hierarchical control of organizations nor on market-based transactions among them. Organizations help one another because they discover cooperation advances their own goals as well. On another level, such interdependence has come to define more governmental programs. Traditional administration begins by assuming that Congress delegates to government agencies the job of managing programs. Network analysis begins with the discovery of interconnections among programs, of the way government agencies share both programs and recipients, and of how the interconnections among them determine how well the programs work. Some networks connect different agencies within a single department; the performance of a state's human services department typically depends on the network connecting its child welfare, health, and social service agencies. Some networks, especially for federal grant programs, connect different departments at different levels of government. Finally, the performance of many government organizations depends on their connections with private and nonprofit contractors.

Network analysis is in its relative infancy. Its proponents argue whether it is a broad-based theory or simply a useful approach. But in moving past the traditional theories of hierarchy and in exploring the pragmatic tactics that managers develop to tackle the problems of third-party administration, network analysis offers fresh insights for government's emerging issues.

Conclusion

At first it seems improbable that theorists could look at the organizational phenomenon and arrive at such disparate interpretations.[54] Contradictions there certainly are. But three strategies can be considered by those seeking to escape defeatism. First, we can reasonably conclude that each approach embodies a significant truth about government organizations. Second, we can conclude, as a mere matter of common sense, that the error of these approaches lies in overgeneralization. Not all organizations are the same; not all small groups are the same; not all jobs are the same; therefore, situational variables need to be taken into account. Saying that suggests an agenda for research, though its pursuit risks losing the capacity for generalization, which is the essence of theory.

Third, and not unrelated to the point just made, we can turn aside from grand-scale theorizing in favor of two more modest, but possibly more productive, undertakings. One is the direct study of reality—in this case the actual structuring and environmental contexts of public administrative agencies. The other is the formulation of "middle-range" theories—that is, theories that attempt to explain only a limited range of phenomena (e.g., Which organizational arrangements appear most likely to save a regulatory agency from being dominated by those it is meant to regulate? Is coordination of the elements of a complex program more likely under a hierarchical authority arrangement or under an interagency committee? What are the major frustrations of government executives, of civil servants, and of clients? Can they be significantly reduced, and how?).

If, as we have suggested, each of the approaches reviewed in the chapter contributes something that is true, then together they may be viewed as enriching our understanding.

☐ The growth of third-party administration is a fact, one that forces a shift from reliance on hierarchical authority to honing of bargaining and negotiation skills. Yet, because the execution of farmed-out work by contractors and grant-receiving organizations is susceptible to corruption and other abuses, governmental officials need to devise incentives for faithful performance, to monitor behavior, and to apply sanctions.

☐ The pluralist approach soundly emphasizes the societal and political environment in which powerful interest groups intervene in administration to achieve their objectives. How such groups' often narrow interests can receive due attention without sacrifice of the larger public interest is an issue that tends to redirect attention to the role of hierarchical responsibility.

☐ The humanist approach, though flawed in several ways, usefully reminds us that individual workers' incentives and teamwork matter to the effectiveness of administration.

☐ A systems approach, however simple to portray, is in fact complex in application. Its contribution is, as with pluralism, its emphasis on interplay between an administrative system and its environment; in addition, its attention to "feedback" reminds us that organizations learn from experience over time.

☐ The structural approach, with which we started, goes back to first principles about government, viewing authority—legitimate power —as the heart of the matter. Executive branch departments are agents that hold authority delegated and restricted by other elements of the constitutional system—Congress, the president, and the courts. In turn, each such agency organizes a hierarchy for further delegating and restricting authority and for holding subordinates accountable for their use of such authority.

These first principles oriented to authority are, we believe, the building blocks for understanding organizational structure, staffing, the making and implementing of decisions, budgeting, and the enforcement of bureaucratic responsibility. The other approaches are complementary to this one, variously reinforcing or modifying its thrusts.

We should find it possible to tolerate the ambiguities of organizational theory. Physical scientists have long lived with both the wave theory of light and the particle theory of light, despite their contradiction. Our problem seems less troublesome.

4

Organization Theory: Strategies and Tactics for Administrative Reform

In the administrative world, nothing has become more constant than change.[1] A 1993 survey by the Organization for Economic Cooperation and Development, a group representing the industrialized world, found that every one of its twenty-four members was in the midst of some major administrative reform.[2] The reforms, however, were very different and often had multiple personalities. They carried inherent conflicts, usually buried deeply under the frenzy of the tough political realities that provoked the reforms in the first place.

Public administrative reform in industrialized nations typically has had three faces: reengineering, formed from private-sector efforts to rebuild organizational processes and structures; continuous improvement, formed from the quality movement; and downsizing, formed from the worldwide effort to shrink the size of government. Major administrative initiatives in many countries have often taken on several—and sometimes all—of these faces. Indeed, there is a powerful and irresistible lure in redesigning the work of government so that it is simultaneously cheaper and more responsive. These bold promises, however, are extremely difficult to achieve. In part, this is because the job itself is tough. It is also because the personalities of administrative reform often drive in conflicting directions.

Reform in America

Three important truths characterize public management reform in the United States. First, many other industrialized nations—notably Great Britain, Sweden, Australia, and New Zealand—are many years ahead of the

United States. They encountered tight budgets, taxpayer revolts, and demands for better services many years before America did. As a result, there is a decade of foreign experience to guide American actions. Second, in the United States, much of the most innovative administrative thinking has occurred in the private sector. Public managers anxious to save money and improve service delivery have looked for solutions wherever they could find them, and that search has often led them to corporate strategies and tactics. The match between private solutions and public problems has often not been a good one, but that has scarcely deterred public officials from trying to borrow anything that might prove a good idea. Finally, most American governmental reforms have tended to bubble up from the experiments of state and local governments, rather than move from the federal government down. The federal government has often been the last link in the chain. In playing catch-up, however, the very different programs that the federal government manages—programs such as food stamps and social security—have often proved poor matches for innovative solutions developed for such state and local programs as garbage collection and park maintenance.

Conflicting Theories

Despite the peculiar problems that government officials at different levels must tackle, there has been surprising convergence around three basic approaches. Terms such as *downsizing, reengineering,* and *continuous improvement* have quickly entered the administrative vocabulary of managers around the world. The terms themselves are appealing; they speak to the aspirations of managers and citizens alike. Hardly anyone wants to make the public sector bigger, so "downsizing," or shrinking government, gains quick support. There is little support for the status quo, so "reengineering" organizations is attractive. And no one thinks that the incentives in traditional bureaucracy produce the right incentives to help government bureaucrats adapt easily to a quickly changing world, so "continuous improvement" seems an attractive reform.

Behind these three faces of reform, however, are deceptively complex ideas. The old bureaucratic orthodoxy, founded on traditional authority and hierarchy, promised a clear, straightforward, and universal set of principles: delegation of authority on the basis of expertise, and democratic accountability through hierarchical control. The new ideas driving bureaucratic reform are neither orthodox, clear, nor universal. Moreover, at their core are important but often unrecognized contradictions that threaten the success of administrative reform, as recent American experience illustrates.

Downsizing

Downsizing is quite simple. Its strategy has a simple goal—shrink the public sector—and a straightforward set of tactics—do whatever is politically feasible to reduce the number of agencies, the level of government spending, and the number of government employees. Rarely is there anything more sophisticated underlying the movement, nor indeed need there be. The theory is nothing more than this: do what can be politically done. Set arbitrary ceilings on taxes or personnel, promise across-the-board cuts, or pledge to trim the middle of the bureaucracy. Angry taxpayers have often proved willing to wield blunt axes in making cuts, even if good programs or key managers are eliminated, if that what it takes to get their message across.

In the United States, such blunt-edge downsizing originated at the state level, although reducing property taxes imposed by local government has most often been the target of angry state voters. The movement started in the mid-1970s, as inflation fueled real estate prices and spiraling real estate values drove up property taxes. New Jersey legislators began in 1976 by limiting the growth of expenditures to the growth of per capita personal income. California voters fired the loudest shot by approving in 1978 an amendment to the state constitution, Proposition 13, which reduced property taxes to 1 percent of market value and limited future property tax growth to a 2 percent annual increase over the amount calculated from the 1975–76 base. Massachusetts voters followed with "Proposition 2½," which reduced property taxes by 15 percent per year until they reached 2½ percent of full market value, where they had to remain (hence the name applied to the vote).[3] State legislators passed scores of other tax limitations or special tax breaks in the following decade.[4] From just 1976 to 1982, legislators and voters in nineteen states agreed to limit revenues or expenditures.[5]

In 1994 two states launched a novel reform. Michigan voters agreed to shift a substantial amount of local property tax revenues for education to state taxes, while Wisconsin legislators voted to replace most local property taxes for schools with state aid, to be financed by state government spending cuts. In both cases, state officials first committed themselves to the broad reform—property tax relief—without deciding how they would produce it. In both cases, the strategy provoked wild bargaining in the state legislatures to produce the promised aid.

The problem, several surveys at the time revealed, was not that citizens were unhappy with the services they were receiving. Instead, they believed that the public sector was fundamentally inefficient and could easily provide the same service with less money.[6] Elected officials discovered that the mantra of cutting the unholy trinity of "waste, fraud, and abuse" resonated well with voters. For better or worse, both elected officials and voters came

to believe that public inefficiency was so great that expenditures and revenues could be slashed without hurting the quality of public services. Tax
and spending limits would force government bureaucrats to wring waste
out of the system. E.S. Savas argued that the public, "despairing of the ability or will of its elected government to reduce expenditures, has taken the
matter directly into its hands and reduced revenue, like a parent rebuking
his spendthrift child by cutting its allowance."[7]

The downsizing movement spilled over to the federal government in
the mid-1980s, but with far more uneven results. In 1984, the President's
Private Sector Survey on Cost Control, better known as the Grace Commission, after its chairman, J. Peter Grace, produced 2,478 recommendations
that its report said would save $424.4 billion over three years. The commis-
sion concluded that the federal government was "suffering from a critical
case of inefficient and ineffective management." Only more businesslike
practices and, in particular, huge cuts in government programs could reduce
the deficit hemorrhage.[8] Academic critics argued that the report built largely
on an ideological, probusiness, antigovernment base. They contended that
the report contained misrepresentations and that following the report's recommendations could actually hurt the work of the federal government.[9]
Suspicious Democrats, who controlled Congress, saw it as a partisan maneuver by Republican President Ronald Reagan, and the battles doomed
most of the report's recommendations.

The Grace Commission report did, however, fuel a downsizing movement at the federal level. It helped promote in 1985 the Balanced Budget
and Emergency Deficit Control Act, better known as Gramm-Rudman, after two of its key sponsors. (We explore the features of Gramm-Rudman
more fully in chapter 10.) Among the many important effects of Gramm-
Rudman, it forced both Congress and the president, Democrats and Republicans alike, to begin bringing the burgeoning federal deficit under control.
Downsizing became an inescapable part of politics at all levels of American
government.

By the early 1990s, the tax and spending limitation movement helped
fuel the presidential campaign of independent H. Ross Perot. Perot's surprising support forced President Bill Clinton to attack the issue head-on, so
soon after taking office he put Vice-President Al Gore to work on "reinventing" the federal government, to make it work better and cost less. The
phrase came from a best-selling 1993 book, *Reinventing Government*, by
David Osborne and Ted Gaebler.[10] Gore's campaign, the National Performance Review, promised voters $108 billion in savings by fiscal year 1999.
Some of the savings were to come from reforms already under way, while
other projected cuts were to come from proposed policy changes and

elimination of field offices of federal agencies. Most of the cuts, however, were to come from reducing the federal workforce by 12 percent over five years, a total cut of 252,000 positions to leave the workforce at under 2 million for the first time since 1967. The vice-president's report promised that the cuts would come from pruning away unnecessary layers of the federal bureaucracy:

> Most of the personnel reductions will be concentrated in the structures of over-control and micromanagement that now bind the federal government: supervisors, headquarters staffs, personnel specialists, budget analysts, procurement specialists, accountants, and auditors. These central control structures not only stifle the creativity of line managers and workers, they consume billions per year in salary, benefits, and administrative costs. Additional personnel cuts will result as each agency reengineers its basic work processes to achieve higher productivity at lower costs—eliminating unnecessary layers of management and nonessential staff.[11]

The report promised that the many reforms it proposed, from streamlining the procurement process to giving managers more flexibility to make decisions without endless cross-checking, would streamline the government. That efficiency, it argued, would make it possible to eliminate functions and layers of the federal bureaucracy and, therefore, save billions of dollars. In theory, new efficiencies would produce the savings. In practice, the savings were almost totally separate from the administrative reforms. The report promised that strategic planning within the bureaucracy was to determine where the cuts could be made. When department heads began working to deliver the promised reductions, the cuts had little if anything to do with the plans. In fact, most departments planned to meet their targets by offering employees a "buyout" package that offered them financial inducements if they took early retirement.[12]

As a political maneuver, the promise to "reinvent government" by shrinking the workforce seemed a no-lose issue for Clinton and a handy way to appeal to many voters, especially those who angrily voted for independent industrialist H. Ross Perot in the 1992 presidential election, whose support the Clintonites believed would determine the outcome of the next presidential election.[13] A Gallup poll conducted for CNN/*USA Today* credited Clinton with a sincere effort to cut government waste. By a margin of 68 percent to 21 percent, respondents said that they would be willing to support cuts in federal spending, even if the cuts came in their own area. Respondents also overwhelmingly said, perhaps surprisingly, that "making sure government programs accomplish what they're supposed to" was more important than "saving money for taxpayers," by a margin of 66 percent to 26 percent.[14]

The state and local tax limitation movement, coupled with the Clinton administration's effort to reinvent the federal government, underlined a series of important points about the downsizing movement. First, although from time to time it built on such wildly different theoretical bases as "reinventing government"[15] and utility maximizing behavior of bureaucrats,[16] the movement itself is largely atheoretical. A pragmatic principle has guided it: the only way to force greater governmental efficiency is to put a cocked gun, in the form of tax and spending limits, to the heads of public managers. Taxpayer anger fueled a movement to cut wherever possible. Indeed, when President Bill Clinton struggled to resuscitate his presidency in early 1995 by promising a middle-class tax cut, he promised to fund it by cutting government bureaucracy even further.

Second, although there often has been bold talk about planning carefully to determine where cuts can be made, planning has tended to come after the fact, if at all. Elected officials and managers alike struggled to cope in the short-term; long-term planning was a luxury that the quickly moving political system did not allow. Downsizing focused the attention of government officials on coping with immediate pressures over charting strategies for lasting performance.

Third, while downsizing has in fact limited the growth of government spending and tax revenues in the United States, its effect on the quality of services and the efficiency of administration is anything but clear. Government at all levels in the United States, in fact, has increasingly underinvested in the capacity to understand the quality of what it buys.[17] In appealing to the deep-seated anger of the voters, elected officials became bolder in proclaiming the pathologies of the governments they led while promoting the very policies that have helped create the pathologies.

Downsizing has thus largely become a symbolic tactic. It has given elected officials a way to resonate with the concerns of the voters without directly attacking the problem of making government work better. Public officials, both elected and appointed, have turned instead to reengineering and culture change for that purpose.

Reengineering

Few management books make it onto the best-seller list, but Hammer and Champy's *Reengineering the Corporation* sat there for months.[18] They tell a tale of corporations faced not only with new challenges but with threats to their very existence. To succeed, even to survive, they argue, business leaders must jump past incremental improvements to a fundamental reexamination of their operations. Completely new work processes and organizational structures can produce, they contend, quantum leaps in performance. That argument has proven powerful in the private sector, and its influence has spilled over into government.[19]

Reengineering, Hammer and Champy argue, begins by putting everything on the table. It "means starting all over, starting from scratch," through "discontinuous thinking."[20] Too often, they believe, managers tinker at the edges when they need to start over. The process begins by having managers consider the "three-Cs": customers, competition, and change. The foundation for the new reality builds on customers "who know what they want, what they want to pay for it, and how to get it on the terms that they demand." The successful companies will be those that build their operations to serve customers' needs. More intense competition means that companies that do not incorporate cutting-edge technology into their operations will not survive. And as change becomes constant, only organizations light on their feet, quick to adapt, will prosper.

Reengineering requires fundamental and radical redesign of work processes. Indeed, *process* is the fundamental building block of reengineering. Effective managers redesign the processes within their organizations to ensure that customers' needs are met. They incorporate the latest technology, especially information technology, to wring extra efficiency out of their operations. Hammer and Champy emphatically argue that reengineering is not the same as downsizing, which is not driven by the need to improve performance. It is not the same as administrative reorganization because reengineers view process as far more important than structure. It is not the same as total quality management (TQM), which seeks to improve quality within existing processes through continuous improvement. Reengineers, by contrast, search for breakthrough strategies instead of incremental improvements. Rather than try to do a job 10 percent better, reengineers look for strategies that can make work ten, or a hundred, times better.[21]

As private managers have popularized reengineering, public managers have found the movement irresistible. Massachusetts, for example, reengineered its child-support collection system. Previously, collection rested on complaints by the caregiving spouse against the nonsupporting spouse. Caseworkers, through a labor-intensive system, tried to track down scofflaws and intervene to try to win support. The state instead began relying on computers to find cases with similar characteristics, to search the database for parents who owed support, and to launch letters insisting on payment. After two years, according to one report, 85 percent of collections occurred without the caseworker's intervention. The number of cases in which payments were collected increased 30 percent, and the compliance rate jumped from 59 to 76 percent. In Merced County, California, new software designed for individual work stations replaced mainframe-based programs for processing welfare eligibility claims. In the process, the time from initial application to interview decreased from four weeks to three days or less.[22] Texas, meanwhile, launched several major initiatives to improve the state's tax administration system that supporters believed could produce an additional $51 million in revenues per year.[23]

Not all students of public administration agree that the customer service approach is valid. H. George Frederickson, for example, contends that "governments are not markets" and that "citizens are not the customers. They are the owners."[24] Critics add that the broader movement to make government more entrepreneurial is dangerous. Even if entrepreneurial behavior were a good idea, they argue, the concept could never be applied to government. There frequently is little private competition in most public functions.[25] Nevertheless, the reinventers counter that energetic, problem-solving managers would perform far better than more traditional bureaucrats rooted in standard operating procedures and organizational structures.

Moreover, even though citizens quite clearly own their government, many reformers argued that citizens could be treated far more responsively—as "customers" of government programs—without violating the fundamental premises of democratic government. Wisconsin's Department of Motor Vehicles, for example, installed new systems to make it much easier to obtain driver licenses: take-a-number machines that told citizens how long they could expect to wait; new systems to minimize those waits, and satellite offices located in shopping malls, open evenings and weekends, that gave citizens new options. The state's Department of Revenue developed a new quick-refund system that got taxpayers their income tax refund checks within two weeks. In Oregon, the state's driver license bureau surveyed citizens to determine what problem they most wanted solved. The response was the poor quality of driver license photographs that citizens had to carry around for years. The state installed a new electronic system that allowed citizens to choose the photo that would grace the license, and citizens were much happier with their services.

The customer service movement in government is in its infancy. Substantial problems need to be worked out, from the tough problem of identifying customers to developing fresh incentives for government employees to serve citizens better. The very strategies and tactics of government further complicate the problem. As we saw in chapter 2, many government programs operate indirectly, through transfers, grants, and contracts. Most government employees are far from the front lines and the ultimate customers of their programs. That does not mean that a customer service approach is invalid; it does mean, however, that government's managers must work far more creatively to ensure that managers throughout the system remain focused on the ultimate goals of public programs. The growth of performance management, in states like Oregon and at the federal level, has proven important in reshaping incentives throughout the system.

As for the reengineers, they aggressively present their arguments as fresh and novel, all the better, of course, to promote book sales and consultancy contracts. In fact, their focus on customers, radical change, nimble organizations, and information technology represents a creative combination. As we saw in the last chapter, however, organization theory traditionally focused on an organization's purpose and how to maximize its efficiency. Process, in fact, was central to much organizational thinking in the 1930s, especially to the work of Henri Fayol.[26] So, too, was information. As L. Urwick argued, "the underlying principle of any form of administration which aims at scientific precision and integrity must be investigation or research yielding information."[27] Indeed, Luther Gulick's famous paper, "The Theory of Organization," written for the Brownlow Committee, which advised President Franklin Roosevelt on reorganization of his office, explicitly tackled the issue of "organization by major process." Along the way, he noted the critical problem of process-based organization: "while organization by process thus puts great efficiency within our reach, this efficiency cannot be realized unless the compensating structure of co-ordination is developed."[28]

In the decades that followed World War II, the interest of organizational theorists, especially *public* organizational theorists, in organizational process diminished considerably. Most discussion of process revolved around *due process* and the guarantee of fair treatment for citizens.[29] James Q. Wilson's brilliant book *Bureaucracy,* however, talks about "procedural organizations" as ones where "managers can observe what their subordinates are doing but not the outcome (if any) that results from those efforts."[30] This creates a stark tension. Wilson posits a situation where managers cannot determine what results subordinates produce; for him, government managers often cannot understand, let alone control, the results of their programs. The reengineers, in contrast, contend that controlling process to improve results is essential to better administration. Indeed, organizational process is implicit in the work of most modern public organization theorists, but it is central to almost nothing (except, as noted earlier, in securing fair treatment).[31] Reengineering seeks to reestablish organizational process in the minds of managers, and to elevate it above even the level it enjoyed in the pre–World War II period.

The very single-mindedness of the reengineers is their greatest virtue but also their biggest weakness. Hammer and Champy un-self-consciously point to a single book as the predecessor to theirs: Adam Smith's 1776 classic, *The Wealth of Nations*. "We believe that the application of the principles of business reengineering will have effects as significant and dramatic as those created by Smith's principles of industrial organization," they write.[32] Like most modern organizational reform best-sellers, Hammer and Champy are unabashed in their enthusiasm for their idea and unreserved in touting its promise. They strongly argue, moreover, that halfway measures will always prove inadequate. (That, of course, provides the perfect excuse. Any failure can be traced to a failure to reengineer thoroughly enough.) Such advice, however, provides scant guidance for coping in an environment full of competing expectations. It gives fuzzy advice about what to do when problems emerge except try even harder, or how to sustain the revolutionary change over the long haul after the revolution has ended and routine has set in.

Nevertheless, the bold advice had widespread effect, especially in Vice-President Gore's reinventing government task force. Indeed, the report promised that the Clinton administration would "reengineer government activities, making full use of computer systems and telecommunications to revolutionize how we deliver services."[33] The vice-president's reinventers argued the need to eliminate or consolidate obsolete and duplicate organizational structures, replacing governmental units with improved technology to link them together better. The vice-president's task force, however, dropped into the usual dilemma of reengineers within government. Reengineering theorists argue unequivocally that strategy has to drive tactics, and especially that downsizing has to be a result rather than a goal of administrative reform. The process of framing the report, however, put downsizing as a central goal, and everything else became secondary.

This contradiction became more than theoretical. Reengineers promised sweeping results, but they also argued that the process needs great maneuvering room and some time to achieve those results. They strongly contended that they could not have their hands tied by arbitrary targets. The vice-president's task force thus caught itself in a dilemma: by first committing the federal government to arbitrary downsizing targets, the reinventers subverted the reengineering process that was to produce them. The political rationale for the move was inescapable. In the short term, the big headline was the downsizing. The long-run cost of the short-run gain, however, was to undermine the process that was to achieve the bold reforms.

This dilemma scarcely diminished enthusiasm for reengineering in government, however. Reformers everywhere have embraced it, at least at the rhetorical level. But even its most ardent fans admit that process reengineering is a high-risk venture. Some reports suggest that up to 70 percent of private-sector reengineering projects fail. "In the public sector," writes one expert, "there's less motivation to change, and many more structured impediments," so the odds might not be even that good.[34] Nevertheless, the pressures on government to reduce costs and improve services is so severe that managers, public and private, are often willing to risk the odds. Although reengineering has barely entered the public administration landscape as more than a slogan, its promise has proved alluring. More important, it has provided a battle flag under which armies of reformers have marched.

Continuous Improvement

Other administrative reformers have pursued a very different tack. In the place of the discontinuous, top-down, revolutionary change that the reengineers recommend, they have advocated a more gradual, continuous, bottom-up movement. In the past decade, the movement has been most strongly associated with total quality management (TQM) launched by W. Edwards Deming, but its roots in fact go far deeper.[35] Other theorists have adapted TQM to drive a broader movement toward continuous organizational improvement.

TQM builds on the notion that the quality of the product matters most. Deming contends that costs decline as quality increases. "Better quality leads to lower costs and higher productivity," one admirer explains. "The consequences for an individual company are that increasing quality leads to higher productivity, lower costs, higher profits, higher share price, and greater security for everyone in the company—the managers, the workers, and the owners."[36] Instead of looking backward into an organization to determine how to squeeze out more profit, industry should look forward to improve quality, and profit will take care of itself. Workers dominated by the profit motive tend to be unhappy, while employees pursuing quality take more satisfaction in what they do, feel more secure, and work more productively. Thus, according to the TQM movement, a total commitment to continuous effort to achieve quality in everything the organization does is the keystone to everything that managers must worry about.

On one level, this might sound little different than the strategy of the reengineers, who care deeply about quality. The reengineers, however, believe that fundamental organizational processes too often get in the way of achieving quality and that only radical change in those processes can improve results. TQMers, by contrast, argue the need to "think small," to build from the bottom to the top of an organization.[37] In TQM, whether in government or the private sector, workers themselves are the experts who know best how to solve problems, serve customers, and improve the work.[38]

TQM, moreover, views reengineering as only one part of administrative improvement. Changing the process alone is not enough, in the view of the movement's supporters. One of its foremost advocates, in fact, argued that process is but one of the five pillars supporting management improvement (along with product, organization, leadership, and commitment). The reengineers contend that only large-scale, fundamental change can work; TQMers, on the other hand, urge managers to win big by organizing small and improving continuously.[39]

Total quality management, in part because of its precepts and in part because as an idea it has been around longer, has been far more broadly deployed in American government. The Environmental Protection Agency used the technique to improve its management of a program dealing with leaking underground storage tanks, while the Air Force Logistics Command improved the readiness rate of its fighter planes from 40 to 76 percent. In the New York City sanitation department, TQM helped resolve labor union problems. The U.S. Department of Veterans' Affairs Philadelphia Regional Office used TQM to improve service to veterans applying for loans.[40] In fact, two students of the process concluded, that "quality improvement projects have resulted in significant cost savings, improved services to agency customers and clients, and measurable improvements in employee morale and productivity."[41]

The quality movement has bred a broader range of progeny than reengineering. Some advocates delete "total" from the label to distance themselves from the zealotry that alienated some managers from TQM. Other writers have advocated a broader approach to quality improvement based on shaping continuous improvement to help organizations learn and on having individuals assume personal responsibility for organizational results. TQM and its progeny focus far more on people than on organizations.[42] They tend to be more holistic than reengineering and its cousins, more driven by a concern for operating-level workers than top leadership, and more convinced in the ability of workers to improve organizational results as they improve their own work.

Indeed, this approach builds on a long tradition of organization theory, beginning with Mary Parker Follett[43] and continuing through Abraham H. Maslow[44] to more modern motivation-based theorists. This tradition has argued that personal factors, from motivation to personal satisfaction, matter as much as structure and process in determining organizational results. The tradition has always been influential, but it has never been central to organization theory. It does not promise quite the same magic in such a short period of time as reengineering. Indeed, its basic precept is that the movement toward quality, once launched, is never finished. No level of quality is ever enough, and only the constant search for quality can keep an organization and its workers sharp.

These ideas, not surprisingly, found deep resonance in American administrative reform, from Vice-President Gore's reinventing government task force to state and local government efforts. Gore's report promised to "give customers a voice—and a choice" and to "put citizens first." Employees were to be "empowered to get results." Indeed, the footnotes at the back of the report are littered with references to TQM. More than any other set of ideas, the continuous improvement movement drove the Gore report. Similar customer-based, continuous processes have driven reforms at state and local levels as well, from state-based reinvention efforts in Minnesota to sweeping strategic planning in Oregon.[45] The discussion of continuous improvement, however, sits side by side the argument for downsizing and reengineering. The advocates of continuous improvement would argue quite vigorously that managers cannot be expected to take risks when their jobs are on the line. Nor, in their view, can reengineering comprehend the full range of reform needed to make any organization work better. The result, from Gore's task force to other reform efforts around the country, was an uneasy alliance among competing ideas.

Assessing the Reforms

A side-by-side comparison of the defining ideas of these three major administrative reforms—downsizing, reengineering, and continuous improvement —reveals stark differences. Figure 4.1 arrays the reforms according to the goal they seek, the direction in which they are implemented, the method that drives them, the central focus of managers following them, and the action that drives them. In brief,

- □ *Downsizing*, enforced from the outside in by angry citizens, seeks lower government expenditures. Its methods are blunt targets, driven by the assumption that there is ample waste in government to accommodate the cuts. Downsizers seek to shrink the size of government through strategic intervention, indeed, by firing a weapon of sufficient size to signal their fundamental disdain for existing policymakers and managers.
- □ *Reengineering* seeks greater organizational efficiency by seeking a radical change in organizational process. Top leaders, with the broad strategic sense of where the organization needs to go, attempt to har-

	Downsizing	Reengineering	Continuous improvement
Goal	Lower expenditures	Efficiency	Responsiveness
Direction	Outside-in	Top-down	Bottom-up
Method	Blunt targets	Competition	Cooperation
Central focus	Size	Process	Interpersonal relations
Action	Discontinuous	Discontinuous	Continuous

Figure 4.1

MAJOR ADMINISTRATIVE REFORMS IN THE UNITED STATES

ness competition and the urge to serve customers and thereby transform their organizations.

□ *Continuous improvement* seeks greater responsiveness to the needs of customers by launching an ongoing process to improve the quality of an organization's products. Advocates of continuous improvement believe that workers know best how to solve an organization's problems, so, unlike reengineering, continuous improvement builds from the bottom up. Cooperation among workers replaces the competition imperative, and stronger relations among employees is more important than organizational structure and process.

The fundamental precepts of each movement directly conflict with the other two. Downsizing begins with the assumption that dramatic action is required to get the attention of public managers and policymakers; reengineers and continuous improvers, in contrast, believe that greater efficiency and smaller organizations ought to be the result, not the cause, of administrative action. Reengineering seeks to transform the behavior of lower-level workers by dramatic policy change at the top; continuous improvement contends that the job of top managers is to promote the conditions that will allow lower-level workers themselves to define the organization's transformation. Downsizers seek simply smaller government; reengineers focus on process, while continuous improvers concentrate on people. Reengineers promote competition to drive behavior change, while continuous improvers argue that competition can undercut the interpersonal cooperation required to achieve quality.

Assessing the conflicts among the driving ideas of these administrative reform approaches is itself an important problem. We simply do not know which one works best. Finding out is impossible, not only because governments tend grossly to underinvest in program evaluation but also because no organization adopts any reform in its pure form. Elected officials and managers shop around among the reform ideas elements that most attract them. As a result, managers often find themselves attempting to cope with externally imposed downsizing targets by reengineering their processes from the top down while encouraging their employees to improve quality from the bottom up. The advocates of each approach often are aghast at such hybrids. The push for competition and cooperation, for top-down and bottom-up leadership, for process versus interpersonal approaches, for discontinuous change and continuous improvement, rarely mesh well. They send out contradictory signals to workers and create conflicting expectations about results.

These contradictions, however, have scarcely prevented both public managers and policymakers from embracing the basic ideas. The labels themselves have strong symbolic appeal. The overall goals of each technique, moreover, are unassailable. Citizens and elected officials alike find alluring the promise of a smaller government, engineered with better processes and devoted to greater responsiveness to citizens and quality. The contradictions of administrative reform ideas were both fundamentally unresolvable and politically unavoidable.

All the World's a Stage

Around the globe, there are two undeniable truths about public administration.[46] One is that administrative reform is a fixture of government everywhere. Indeed, it might be the issue that governments share more than any other. Nations that have just broken out of a generation of domination by the Soviet Union are struggling to catch up. They face tasks ranging from inventing a system of public law from which a new private sector can grow to revising a tax system to fund public programs better. Developing nations are rushing to modernize their economies; reconstructing their governments is a critical part of that strategy. More-developed nations are seeking to reinvent themselves by wringing waste out of the public sector and making government programs more efficient. Administrative reform has the spotlight on the world stage.

The other truth is that, despite the universality of reform, no single set of ideas is driving it. Reform of public administration is as varied as the nations attempting it. As in the colored squares on Rubik's famous cube, only a small number of basic ideas have contributed to each picture, but they come together in a remarkable array of combinations.

The Strategies of Administrative Reform

The Organization of Economic Cooperation and Development's 1993 survey of public administration developments among in its twenty-four members, the world's most developed nations, underlines these two points. Its member nations were struggling to wring greater economies from their public sectors while trying to make their public services more responsive.[47] Their strategies can be separated into three broad categories.

First, many members were relying on *downsizing* to shrink their public sectors. Most members were relying more on such market-type mechanisms as user charges, vouchers, and contracting out. Some nations, notably the Netherlands, Portugal, the United Kingdom, and New Zealand, were selling public enterprises to new private owners. When public enterprises were not sold off, nations ranging from Belgium and Finland to Canada and Sweden were reorganizing them to introduce private-sector incentives. Taxpayer revolts have led to limits on the size of the public sector, especially on the number of government employees and their pay. In Italy, for example, only 25 percent of local government workers who retire can be replaced. Finland, Japan, and the Netherlands have imposed goals for a smaller civil service.

Second, almost as many members were *reengineering* their public sectors by radically transforming the way public organizations did their work. Most OECD members were changing their central management bodies. A fresh focus on performance measurement and strategic planning was replacing detailed control of administrative activities. France and Japan, in particular, have actively sought to spin power out of the hands of central administrators and vest more responsibility in local governments. Several nations, particularly the United Kingdom, Canada, and Denmark, are experimenting with a new definition of a government "agency" by giving managers more operating flexibility in exchange for greater accountability to performance standards.

Finally, many nations are employing *continuous improvement* strategies by distributing more power *within* government bureaucracies to lower-level officials. Too much power for too long, government officials came to believe, rested in the hands of top officials. More responsive public services required giving more power to government officials on the front lines to make decisions.

Although each nation's approach to administrative reform has been unique, the near-universal sweep of reform strategies is remarkable. So, too, is the reappearance of common themes. That is scarcely surprising. Public officials, as well as critics who follow government operations closely, are increasingly in touch with each other and with fresh ideas that guide public actions. Indeed, the Australian and New Zealand administrative reforms of the late 1980s—or, more precisely, *perceptions* of those reforms—fueled much of Vice-President Gore's "reinventing government" initiative and other reforms at state and local levels in America.[48]

The Tactics of Administrative Reform

On Rubik's cube, the same colors tend to appear regularly, but they frequently come together in combinations that make sorting out the puzzle difficult. Downsizing carries a simple goal: shrink the public sector as much as possible, whether by selling off public enterprises, contracting out services that remain publicly provided, or imposing limits to limit future growth. While simple, this goal has driven a remarkable movement around the world.

The reengineering approaches employ both procedural and analytical tactics. Many countries have developed new processes to link operating units together better. For example, New Zealand is training top managers to develop new skills in administering programs that cut across agency boundaries. The French decentralization movement aims, in part, to bring together at the local level all those concerned with similar problems. Meanwhile, the deregulation movement of the 1980s is continuing. Countries are relying as well on information and analysis to increase leverage over administrators' actions. Spain is relying more on information technology as a linkage among governmental units. The cutting-edge reform in the 1990s has been the development of performance management systems, in which operating managers are given greater discretion in return for accountability to top officials for performance against agreed-upon indicators. Many nations are linking such performance measurement with reform of financial management systems to promote planning and cost control. Australia, Finland, Iceland, New Zealand, the United Kingdom, and the United States all have moved (some much further and more eagerly than others) from cost toward accrual accounting to improve accountability.

At the same time, many nations are relying on better measurement and training systems as they seek to change the culture of bureaucrats. Performance measurement systems are designed to focus managers on results and outputs instead of budgets and inputs. Countries are working to change expectations about career paths and to enhance managers' leadership ability.

Both the Netherlands and the United States have committed themselves to pushing decisions down to the lowest possible level. Many nations are working as well to make public services more "customer-centered." In Canada, for example, public officials are working to "co-locate" related services so that citizens needing public services can come to one place instead of having to run from government office to office. Japan has launched a major movement to make its programs more consumer oriented and transparent to citizens.

All the world unquestionably is a stage for administrative reform. Indeed, both the scope and variety of reform are unprecedented in the last generation. Not since the immediate post–World War II years have so many governments attempted so dramatic a reshaping of the way they do business. The last round of reforms focused principally on establishing the right structures, organized according to existing administrative orthodoxy to help governments manage their programs most efficiently. Those reforms proved remarkably long lasting. By the late 1970s, however, it was clear that they had sowed the seeds of their own undoing. Earlier strategies to create strong bureaucracies for solving post–World War II problems evolved into bureaucracies that too often seemed oversized, overbearing, and overcontrolling. Citizens around the world complained that the taxes they paid governments were far higher than the benefits they received. Meanwhile, governments in less-developed countries and in newly independent countries struggled to catch up.

Conclusion

One overarching conclusion stands out sharply in this review of administrative reform in industrialized countries. Even though many different ideas have driven administrative reform and even though these ideas have contradictory ideas built within them, reformers have indiscriminately mixed and matched them with little regard for the contradictions. Moreover, the mixtures tend to come together in very different forms, so that patterns rarely repeat themselves. That makes it hard to determine whether the administrative reforms work, whether some ideas work better than others, or which work best where. Reformers can and do take credit for any positive change that happens on their watch. Reform theorists do likewise, and quickly point to inadequate application of their theories to explain any problems.

It would, in fact, be possible to use this explanation to drive a broader, cynical conclusion that administrative reform is nothing but symbolic politics practiced cleverly. Is there, under it all, anything real going on? The cynical explanation has merit, for it recognizes one important feature of administrative reform. Quite apart from whatever else it accomplishes, administrative reform has developed a powerful and attractive vocabulary for understanding bureaucratic pathologies and for prescribing solutions. Administrative reform theories have an important symbolic value for galvanizing action. It would, however, be far too cynical to suggest that things stop there. The American reinventing government effort is too young to give a clear picture of its results.[49] Efforts elsewhere, however, have produced clear results: administrative reforms have produced both more efficient and more effective government. Quite simply, management matters. It provides a symbolic language for understanding government activity and both strategies and tactics for improving results. This might not seem a very bold claim. But it is one that often is underestimated.

An equally important second conclusion is that management matters only to the degree to which it matters politically. It is unrealistic to expect that public administration can live a life independent of politics, or that its most fundamental meaning will be administrative rather than political The internal theoretical contradictions of most administrative reform efforts matter far less than the fact that the contradictions themselves seem so often to have important political value.

This suggests two important implications. First, public managers themselves must be ready to accommodate such conflicting and contradictory demands. Their lives would unquestionably be far simpler if they were allowed to pursue a single administrative approach. For that matter their lives would be simpler yet if they were free to follow their own ideas independently of the policies established by elected officials or the needs of citizens. But that was not what they were hired to do. In democratic societies, the fundamental mission of public managers is to reconcile such fundamentally irreconcilable demands. The job in the late twentieth century has become harder because expectations have grown even as resources have shrunk. That means that the challenges for public mangers have never been greater, nor has the need for good public managers ever been larger.

Second, administrative theorists have perhaps an even greater challenge. To a significant degree, the central ideas of *public* administration reform have tended to come from *private* managers. Administrative theory has significantly lagged behind these startling changes. The tasks and environment of public administration are so fundamentally different, however, that no matter how suggestive private reforms may be, they are unlikely to provide very sure guides for the public sector. For example, the "customer service" movement has swept the Western world, but there simply has been little careful thought about who government's customers are, how government activities can be restructured to advance customer service, how to balance the often conflicting expectations of government's multiple customers, and what other important goals might be sacrificed in the process.

Moreover, administrative theorists face an equally imposing job of reconciling the contradictions that political realities impose on neat organizational theories. Too often, like public managers who complain that their jobs would be much easier if elected officials would stop interfering in their work, theorists complain about elected officials whose contradictory messages muddy neat theories. The problem is far more with the theory than with the practice. And the pace of administrative reform around the world demonstrates just how important tackling these issues is.

5

The Executive Branch

Organization matters. Some "realists" say it doesn't matter. They dismiss organization with a wave of the hand, saying, "It's people that count. The right people can make any organization work; the wrong people can make any organization fail." Or they say, "all administration is politics—persuasion, advocacy, conflict, negotiation, compromise." We need belittle neither people nor politics to appreciate organization's importance. Individuals' personal qualities and their adeptness at the politics of inducement do indeed affect decision making. Yet their roles are shaped substantially by their positions in the organizational design. According to Miles's Law, "where you stand depends on where you sit."[1] It is in the nature of bureaucratic politics that the secretary of defense will not advocate a drastic cut in military outlays, that the secretary of agriculture will be more concerned with farmers' income than with consumers' cost of living, and that the secretary of the treasury will be a defender of fiscal prudence.

Organization does not make things happen. It provides patterns of relations within the executive branch that increase or decrease the probabilities that policies will be well designed and well implemented.[2] When, as before 1966, the government's concern with transportation is fragmented among a number of separate agencies each concerned with a single mode of transportation—rail, air, highway, water, subway—the probabilities of an integrated national transportation policy are sharply reduced. If, as since 1966, this concern is focused in a national Department of Transportation, those probabilities are increased. In turn, though, achievement of the integrative potential depends on how the department's internal organization distributes power and on how well the department manages its relations with specific industries and with Congress.

Organization is not simple. It is remarkably complex. Perhaps all transportation concerns of the government should not be brought under a single department. It can be argued that urban mass transit should be in the department concerned with cities, the Department of Housing and Urban Development, and that regulation of transportation companies' routes, rates, and safety should be left with independent regulatory commissions rather than be under a political cabinet member. And, as some have argued, intervention by the secretary of transportation in the work of the single-industry units may be excessive and ill serve the public interest.[3]

To convey a sense of the national government's organizational complexity we begin with an overview of the executive branch. In chapter 6 we focus on critical and persistent organizational problems.

Executive Branch Components

Bureaus

The principal operating organizations of the government are bureaus. This is a generic term, embracing many organizations within departments despite the variety of titles—for example, Bureau of Mines, Internal Revenue Service, Geological Survey, Antitrust Division, Federal Highway Administration, Office of Energy Research. These operating units are so important in federal administration that one might regard the executive branch as literally a "bureaucracy"—that is, a government by bureaus—and could dismiss the departmental and presidential levels merely as superstructure. This, of course, is an inaccurate view. Bureaus are subordinate units of larger organizations, the building blocks of departments and other major agencies.

Bureaus vary dramatically. Table 5.1 shows the size of the fourteen cabinet departments and the largest executive branch agencies and bureaus. Some bureaus have long historical roots—longer, often, than those of the departments in which they are currently located. The Public Health Service system traces its origins to 1798 when Congress authorized marine hospitals to care for merchant seamen. Four years later, Congress established the Army Corps of Engineers and soon charged it with improving the navigability of rivers and harbors for civilian as well as military purposes. The Bureau of the Census in the Commerce Department finds its raison d'être in the Constitution's 1789 provision requiring a decennial population census, though the bureau itself dates only from 1902; before that, the census was taken by U.S. marshals under supervision of the State Department and, after 1850, the Interior Department. The Bureau of Land Management is successor to the General Land Office, established in 1812. Some of the bureau's land records bear the signatures of George Washington and Thomas Jefferson.[4] Many other bureaus are old enough to have developed a distinctive culture—a sense of organic institutional life and a doctrine and tradition to which their staffs are dedicated. Bureaus do not quickly abandon

Table 5.1

FEDERAL CIVILIAN EMPLOYMENT, BY AGENCY, 1993

Department or agency	Employment (in thousands)	
Total	2,134	
Executive departments	1,931	
Defense		931.8
Veterans Affairs		234.4
Treasury		161.1
Health and Human Services		129.0
Agriculture		113.4
Justice		95.4
Interior		76.7
Transportation		69.6
Commerce		36.1
State		25.6
Energy		20.3
Labor		19.6
Housing and Urban Development		13.3
Education		4.9
Other agencies	203	
Corps of Engineers		28.4
National Aeronautics and Space Administration		24.9
Federal Deposit Insurance Corp./Resolution Trust Corp.		21.6
General Services Administration		20.2

these commitments at the behest of temporary incumbents of the presidency and the cabinet.

Bureaus, then, whatever they may be called, conduct most of the operations of the executive branch, subject to departmental oversight; they vary in size and significance; many are a century or two old; and partly because of that, many have institutional cultures that are valued and that resist change by department heads and presidents.

Departments and Major Agencies

Above and embracing bureaus are departments and so-called independent establishments, the latter term simply meaning agencies independent of de-

Table 5.1 — continued

Department or agency	Employment (in thousands)
Other agencies — *continued*	
Environmental Protection Agency	18.3
Tennessee Valley Authority	17.3
Other small agencies	16.4
Panama Canal Commission	8.5
United States Information Agency	8.3
Office of Personnel Management	5.9
Smithsonian Institution	4.5
Agency for International Development	4.1
Small Business Administration	3.9
Nuclear Regulatory Commission	3.4
Equal Employment Opportunity Commission	2.8
Securities and Exchange Commission	2.7
Federal Emergency Management Agency	2.6
National Archives and Records Administration	2.6
National Labor Relations Board	2.1
Railroad Retirement Board	1.8
National Science Foundation	1.2
Peace Corps	1.2

SOURCE: Executive Office of the President, *Budget of the United States Government: Fiscal Year 1995* (Washington, D.C.: Government Printing Office, 1994), 178.

NOTE: In 1994, Congress passed legislation splitting the Social Security Administration from the Department of Health and Human Services.

partments. The departments have about 90 percent of the executive branch's civilian employees. (The total does not include the U.S. Postal Service, which is a government corporation separate from regular civilian government employment.)

If measured by dollar outlays, as in table 5.2 (page 92), we find that the fourteen cabinet departments spend virtually all of the total. Over three-fourths is spent by just three departments: Health and Human Services, Defense, and Treasury.

By either test—employees or outlays—the executive branch is not, as often portrayed, a sprawling mass of departments and agencies whose great

Table 5.2

OUTLAYS BY DEPARTMENT AND AGENCY,

FISCAL YEAR 1993

Department or agency		Outlays (in millions)
Total	$1,408,205	
Executive departments	$1,462,932	
Defense		$307,840
Treasury		298,804
Health and Human Services: Social Security		298,349
Health and Human Services, except Social Security		282,779
Agriculture		63,144
Labor		44,651
Veterans' Affairs		35,487
Transportation		34,457
Education		30,290
Housing and Urban Development		25,181
Energy		16,942
Justice		10,170
Interior		6,796
State		5,244
Commerce		2,798
Other agencies	$69,996	
Office of Personnel Management		$36,794
National Aeronautics and Space Administration		14,305
Funds appropriated to the president		11,245
Environmental Protection Agency		5,930
Small Business Administration		785
General Services Administration		743
Executive Office of the President		194
Other branches of government	$5,034	
Judicial branch		$2,628
Legislative branch		2,406

SOURCE: Executive Office of the President, *Budget of the United States Government: Fiscal Year 1995* (Washington, D.C.: Government Printing Office, 1994), 62.

NOTE: Totals do not add because of unallocated offsetting receipts.

number condemns the president to ineffective performance of his role as chief executive. On the contrary, through only the fourteen cabinet departments and the Postal Service he can have a potential impact on activities involving 95 percent of the civilian employees and outlays. Even more strikingly, through just five cabinet members—the secretaries of defense, veterans' affairs, treasury, agriculture, and health and human services—over three-fourths of the nonpostal employees and total budget outlays can be brought under his review. The president is not without leadership opportunities.

Until the 1950s, the general outline of the national government's executive branch had been remarkably stable. Of the fourteen executive departments now operating, three date from 1789 (State, Defense,[5] and Treasury), and a fourth (Justice) was established then as a separate office, though it did not achieve full departmental status until eighty years later. The heads of those four departments are still regarded as "the inner cabinet" and, as such, counselors of the president on broad issues extending beyond their departments' jurisdictions. In "the outer cabinet" the Interior and Agriculture departments are over a hundred years old, and the Commerce and Labor departments date from 1913.

The six newer "outer" departments have appeared only since 1950: Health, Education, and Welfare in 1953 (changed to Health and Human Services in 1979), Housing and Urban Development in 1965, Transportation in 1966, Energy in 1977, Education in 1979, and Veterans' Affairs in 1989.[6]

The United States and other modern nations passed through the same four stages of administrative development. Certain functions are basic to any nation. In the first historical stage, therefore, departmental status was generally accorded to (1) revenue collection, expenditures, and debt management (as with a Treasury or Finance Ministry); (2) maintenance of internal law and order (at first through the court system, later with a Justice Department or, in centralized countries, a Ministry of the Interior); (3) defense (or, separately, military and naval defense); and (4) foreign affairs. A postal service and an engineering construction service (for roads, bridges, waterways, and public buildings) also appeared early, though not necessarily with departmental status.

At a second historical stage, most modern nations built departments around agriculture and commerce (or "trade"); at the same time, they placed other developing functions that did not fit the established pattern into a catchall department (often the Ministry of the Interior). In a third stage, dating from the latter part of the nineteenth century, previously subordinated functions burst out of the catchall departments and the older functional departments to achieve departmental status in their own right. These generally reflected governmental assumption of human welfare responsibilities in such areas as labor conditions, social security, education, public health, and housing. A fourth stage appears to be developing as organizational recognition is accorded science and technology, energy, the environment, and economic planning.

Independent Regulatory Commissions. The relative significance of agencies is only roughly indicated by the number of employees and the amount of expenditures. Power, if it could be measured, might yield a ranking of agencies startlingly different.

The independent regulatory commissions are a major example. Congress intended to assure the substantial independence of these commissions from presidential control.[7] It requires most of them to be bipartisan in membership, with members having overlapping terms that are longer than that of a presidential administration, and it permits presidential removal of commissioners only for "inefficiency, neglect of duty, or malfeasance in office" (i.e., not on grounds of policy differences with the president).[8] These requirements give "independent" a meaning different from that applied to agencies independent of departments but not of presidential control.

The commissions average only about 1,200 employees and $70 million of expenditures.[9] Yet they have broadly discretionary powers over important sectors of the American economy. By various methods (licensing, rate fixing, cease-and-desist orders, and safety regulations, for example), the eleven commissions[10] regulate major features of transportation, communication, power production and distribution, banking, the issuing of corporate securities, commodities and securities exchanges, unfair and deceptive business practices, the safety of consumer products, and labor-management relations. The commissions are not unique in possession of regulatory power in economic sectors. Such power is exercised as well by "independent agencies" (i.e., not in departments, but not independent of the president). And many bureaus in regular departments—for example, the Food and Drug Administration (HHS) and the Occupational Safety and Health Administration (Labor)—also regulate the private sector. The deregulation movement, from 1975 into the 1980s, stripped some commissions of much regulatory authority over truck and airline transportation and over telephone communication.[11] But most commissions remain powerful regulators. The chairman of the Federal Reserve Board has been rated the second most influential person in the nation, second only to the president.[12]

In recent decades, the supposed guarantees of independence from the president have collapsed.[13] During his term, a president can usually appoint a commission's majority that shares his policy goals. Most important, he designates the chairperson of each commission, who often dominates the commission.[14] The president's Office of Management and Budget reviews commissions' budgets, the Justice Department controls commissions' proposed appeals of cases to the Supreme Court, and the commissions often depend on the president's support in dealing with Congress.

The result is that commissions are responsive to presidential policy concerns.[15] Nearly every president has considered asking Congress to change the structure of the Federal Reserve, whose Board of Governors, with its Open Market Committee, is regarded as probably the most independent of all regulatory commissions. Yet, "when Presidents have known what mix of monetary and fiscal policies they wanted, they usually have gotten it.... The history of the Fed is that of an agency rarely far out of step with the President's policies."[16]

What remains of the distinction between dependence and independence surfaces when commissions make case-to-case decisions. As the process is courtlike, intervention by the president or his aides is deemed inappropriate. To be sure, a commission's decisions, even though quasi-judicial in nature, may establish a policy line at odds with that of the president. Even here, though, the president's choice of commissioners and especially the chair is bound to have an impact.

Government Corporations. A miscellaneous set of federal agencies, numbering somewhere between thirty-one and forty-seven,[17] are government corporations, mostly engaged in lending, insurance, and other business-type operations. Familiar examples are the Corporation for Public Broadcasting, Federal Deposit Insurance Corporation, Legal Services Corporation, National Railroad Passenger Corporation (Amtrak), Tennessee Valley Authority, and U.S. Postal Service. The number of government corporations has about doubled since 1960.[18] They vary greatly. Some are wholly government owned, others are mixed enterprises with both government and private investments, and yet others have only private funding. Some are meant to be profit making, others are nonprofit organizations. Some support themselves from their revenues; others are wholly or partly dependent on appropriations. Some are integrated into the regular departments; others float freely. And they vary in conformity to standard personnel, budgetary, and auditing practices and controls.

Congress tried to impose some order on this motley collection by passage of the Government Corporation Control Act of 1945, most importantly by budgetary and auditing controls hitching the corporations to the government that created them. But Congress has often exempted new corporations from various provisions of the act. The debate on the merits turns on conflict between the view that every government agency needs to be integrated into the structure of responsibility and accountability of the executive branch and the view that business-type operations need to be conducted with substantial autonomy and flexibility. In this regard, they are said to differ in kind from regular agencies that depend wholly or mostly on appropriations. The debate is not resolved.[19] Meantime, nonbusiness-type agencies, if named "corporations," lay claim to an autonomy unrelated to the debate.

In sum, in contrast to popular impressions, through just five of his cabinet members the chief executive commands three-fourths of the executive branch's resources (employees and appropriated money) outside the postal service. Even the regulatory commissions' independence of presidential control has largely evaporated. Only government corporations can claim some degree of independence. As we note later, state governors usually have far less control than that of the president over administrative agencies.

Field Offices

To this point we have been concerned with the executive branch's "headquarters" organization at Washington. The bulk of federal operations are performed in the field. Only about 13 percent of federal civilian employees are in the Washington, D.C., metropolitan area; the rest are overseas and in 22,000 field offices in the fifty states.[20] The tasks of field agents are to apply laws and regulations in their assigned geographical areas, adapt them to local circumstances, and collect information and provide advice to their Washington headquarter agencies.

For most of our history, each department or agency has been free to establish its own field organization and procedures. This has meant that a department can independently decide on the number of its administrative regions and subregional districts, their boundaries, and the cities that serve as regional and district headquarters. More commonly, a department forgoes a uniform departmental system, letting each bureau set up its own field-administration system. Even the few departments that have uniform regions and departmental regional directors grant those directors little or no authority over the operation of the bureaus' programs.

These characteristics mark ours as a *functional* system of field administration. That is, the functionally specialized departments and bureaus can choose the geographical and authority patterns they deem appropriate for their particular responsibilities. This contrasts sharply with the *areal*, or, as it is often called, *prefectoral* field-administration system that many other nations have adopted. In such a system the country is divided into a single set of administrative regions or districts in each of which a single national official (in some countries called a *prefect*) represents the whole executive branch and is meant to exercise directive authority over all national field agents in the area, regardless of their departmental and bureau affiliations.[21] The French prefectoral system, originated by Napoleon, is the model widely copied.[22]

In our national government we have lacked ways of achieving effective governmentwide coordination among the many departmental, agency, and bureau field staffs operating in the same region or metropolitan area, though they serve the same general population, deal with the same state and local governments, and administer complementary or overlapping programs. The difficulty is matched in state and local governments themselves.[23] Attempted remedies have proved disappointing, or, if successful, have been aborted.[24] The latter case is true of regional coordination by several field offices of the Bureau of the Budget from 1943 to 1953, when Congress banned continuation of the field offices. An example of disappointing results is the Nixon administration's establishment of ten standard federal administrative regions and regional headquarter cities, with a Federal Regional Council in each, comprising the regional representatives of most domestic departments. The councils, weakly structured, were abolished in 1983.[25]

We are left, then, with extension of Washington's functional fragmentation into the field and without effective interagency coordination in the regions and local communities. One of many consequences is that a major undertaking, the war on narcotics, suffers from lack of cooperation about drug smuggling among the Drug Enforcement Administration (in Justice), the Customs Service (Treasury), the Coast Guard (Transportation), and the State Department.[26]

Several students of the problem propose that the president have a presidential representative in each region, whose Washington attachment would be the Office of Management and Budget or a parallel agency in the executive office.[27] President Johnson's Task Force on Government Organization described the role this way:

> As Presidential representatives, they would have authority to enter interdepartmental and intergovernmental disputes on their own initiative. Through persuasion and mediation they would be expected to resolve program conflicts in the field whenever possible, referring to Washington those issues which require arbitration by the [Executive Office agency] Director or those which have sensitive political implications for the President personally.[28]

This is no prefectoral system; *enter, persuade, mediate,* and *refer* are not the verbs of power. Yet full-time presidential representatives could improve interdepartmental coordination in the field.

The president, his White House aides, and the organizations in his Executive Office attempt to impose some order on the activities of the bureaus, departments, and other major agencies and to promote their responsiveness to the president's policy objectives. How well they succeed and what the costs of success may be are the focus of the balance of this chapter.

Direction of the Executive Branch

Congress creates all executive departments and most of the agencies outside departments. Control of them is exercised by Congress and the courts, as well as by the president. This is amply demonstrated in later parts of this book. Yet, just as we are apt to underrate Congress by forgetting that it is generally judged the most powerful legislative body in the world, we can be so impressed by the centrifugal forces drawing agencies away from the president that we underrate his comparative advantage in controlling agencies. His advantage eclipses that of many governors and mayors. In some state and local governments, the executive branch is less a branch than a heap of twigs. In most state governments, the governor is only one of five of six popularly elected executive officials, and departments' and agencies' executive heads are often chosen by the legislature or by boards and commissions (whose members have overlapping terms), rather than by the governor. On the average, governors appoint less than half their states' administrative officials (whether with or without legislative confirmation).[29] Some mayors in so-called weak-mayor systems have similar handicaps. More strikingly, as we noted in chapter 2, even those in strong-mayor systems (and city managers, too) find that many functions are vested in other local governments —single-function special districts such as those for schools.

Against this background, "the executive branch" can be seen to be a term of considerable substance in the federal government. The president and vice-president are the only elected executive officials. The president is vested by the Constitution with "the Executive power," is directed to "take Care that the Laws be faithfully executed," and is authorized to "require the Opinion in writing, of the principal Officer in each of the executive Departments, upon any subject relating to the Duties of their respective Offices." He is constitutionally empowered to nominate and, by and with the advice and consent of the Senate, to appoint all higher "Officers of the United States" whose appointments are not otherwise constitutionally provided for. The Congress can vest appointments of inferior officers only "in the president alone, in the Courts of Law, or in the Heads of Departments." The president can remove executive officers.[30]

His formal powers, of course, are only the beginning, but they suffice to distinguish him from most chief executives of American governments, to legitimize his resistance to excessive congressional incursions, and to guide courts in their interpretations of his powers.

Given the scope of his appointive and removal powers and his general mandate to see to the faithful execution of the laws, the president might be expected to assure effective management of the executive branch. That this expectation is rarely fulfilled can be explained by four facts.

First, presidents are not chosen for managerial ability, rarely have a lively interest in administrative matters, and properly devote their main energies to foreign and domestic policy decisions, the meeting of crises, and the influencing of Congress, major interest groups, and public opinion. Presidents know that administrative achievements are not what history will judge them by. Administration captures a president's interest mostly when he perceives its instrumental value for attainment of his policy and power objectives.[31]

Second, presidents are often disappointed when they count on cabinet members (and heads of noncabinet agencies) to assure a record of administrative effectiveness. Of course, the real work of administration is performed in the departments and agencies. But problems arise. Presidential appointees, including department heads, their undersecretaries, and their assistant secretaries, have short tenures: two years is the median; a third are in their positions for eighteen months or less and only a third stay as long as three years.[32] Furthermore, department heads rarely have a free hand in assembling their teams of subordinates. The presidential appointment system is centralized in the White House so that a department's undersecretary, assistant secretaries, and even lesser officials are appointed independently of the secretary or after intense negotiations. Such negotiations often pit the secretary's wish for managerial competence and prior knowledge of the subject the office deals with against the White House's quite different goals. These include the wish to staff offices with those personally loyal to the president and his ideology, to reward political service in his presidential campaign, to oblige an important senator, and to console a defeated candidate for public office. The result is that, despite notable exceptions, secretaries have difficulty in becoming effective executives—and thus in refuting an old charge that they are the weakest links in the chain of authority.

Third, interdepartmental friction points have multiplied. Departments, being specialized by function, have long disputed with other departments over issues that cut across established jurisdictions. What is new is the increase in such crosscutting issues. This increase occurred because (1) governmental involvement in economic and social problems expanded, (2) domestic and foreign policy problems multiplied their interactions, and (3) the interdependence of factors bearing on solution of each such problem became more widely recognized. This has two consequences. Because a department has relatively fewer "whole subjects" to itself, it is more difficult to hold the single department head responsible for results; and what the several departments sharing a subject cannot settle among themselves must be settled, if at all, by coordination at the presidential level.

The fourth reason that presidents do not assure effective management is that, given the president's time constraints and disinterest in administrative problems, the burden of top-level coordination falls on presidential aides and staff agencies. In practice, though, they tend to undermine department and agency heads, they have little interest in improving administrative management,[33] and presidential responsibilities get dispersed among scores of aides inexperienced in government, infrequently in direct touch with the president, and poorly coordinated among themselves.

The various and disputed roles of all three major kinds of participants in overall management of the executive branch—the president, the president's aides and staff agencies, and the department and agency heads—become clearer as we examine the growing institutionalization of the presidency.

The Executive Office and White House

As long ago as 1937, in transmitting to Congress the report of the President's Committee on Administrative Management (the Brownlow Committee), Franklin D. Roosevelt wrote,

> The Committee has not spared me; they say what has been common knowledge for 20 years, that the President cannot adequately handle his responsibilities; that he is overworked; that it is humanly impossible, under the system which we have, for him fully to carry out his constitutional duty as Chief Executive.... With my predecessors who have said the same thing over and over again, I plead guilty.
>
> The plain fact is that the present organization and equipment of the executive branch of the Government defeats the constitutional intent that there be a single responsible Chief Executive to coordinate and manage the departments and activities in accordance with the laws enacted by the Congress.[34]

Immediately after passage of the Reorganization Act of 1939, Roosevelt established the Executive Office of the President, transferred to it the Bureau of the Budget (from the Treasury Department), and set up its other units, among them the White House Office.

From its relatively modest beginnings with 570 employees in 1939, the Executive Office had expanded by 1992 to include about 1,800 employees, of whom 390 were in the White House Office.[35] In addition, the White House had about 110 persons detailed to it from executive departments, many of them appointed to department rolls specifically for White House service.[36] "The swelling of the Presidency," as Thomas Cronin has called it,[37] was not only quantitative. A qualitative change occurred in the behavior of presidential assistants in the White House Office. The Brownlow Committee proposed in 1937 that six presidential assistants be added to the three White House "secretaries" (who dealt with Congress, the public, and the media). Contrast the powerful position of recent presidents' aides to the committee's stipulation of the role of the proposed assistants:

> These assistants, probably not exceeding six in number ... would have no power to make decisions or issue instructions in their own right. They would not be interposed between the President and the heads of his departments. They would not be assistant presidents in any sense.... They would remain in the background, issue no orders, make no decisions, emit no public statements.... They should be men in whom the President has personal confidence and whose character and attitude is such that they would not attempt to exercise power on their own account. They should be possessed of high competence, great physical vigor, and a passion for anonymity.[38]

Surprisingly, eight former chiefs of staff to presidents from Eisenhower to Carter emphatically endorse this description of the role of presidential assistants.[39]

The White House staff is now so large, multitiered, and specialized that it itself is hard to coordinate.[40] One result of the long-term trend, says a Carter aide, is that "even those at the highest levels—assistants, deputy assistants, special assistants—don't see the President once a week or speak to him in any substantive way once a month."[41] Infighting among staff members to gain the president's ear has plagued every modern president.

In recent administrations, order-issuing presidential assistants and their subordinates weakened the roles of department heads by preempting their decision-making authority and by denigrating them in the eyes of departmental staff and the constituencies served by the departments. Cabinet members complain of receiving contradictory instructions on the same day from different members of the central staff, each purporting to speak for the president. The president's chief assistants, far from being anonymous, are more prominent in the news than some cabinet members. Far from providing only "staff assistance" (a role discussed later in this chapter), his assistants engage in operational activities. Given their confused role, their numbers, the White House bureaucracy's complexity, and the priority given to meeting each day's crises, a president needs a chief of staff from the start of his administration, a lesson learned tardily by some presidents.[42] The chief of staff in turn would benefit if he found already in place at the start, a small, permanent secretariat of career civil servants able to bridge the transition from one administration to another, "provide an institutional memory, advise ... on standard operating procedures and administrative processes, and coordinate the flow of papers ... to and from the Oval Office, ... insure that materials intended for the President are in the proper format, that they are seen by the appropriate people, that they are presented in a timely manner, and that presidential decisions or actions are effectively transmitted to those who are responsible for their implementation."[43]

Whether malfunctioning of the White House staff could be remedied by reducing its size is a matter of dispute. A panel of the National Academy of Public Administration urges a reduction.[44] Others see the staff's growth as the inevitable result of growth of the president's leadership responsibilities, which are attributed to weakening of congressional leadership and of political parties, the rise of presidential use of public relations technologies, and other factors. "Instead of trying to wish it away," says Samuel Kernell, "the presence of a large, complex staff must be accepted as a given and its problems addressed forthrightly. ... The President must give the staff clear direction and vigilantly oversee its performance."[45]

The pattern of White House relations with department heads tends to follow a familiar course. Presidents Nixon, Carter, Reagan, and Clinton initially committed themselves to a strong role for cabinet members in direction of their departments, partly because presidents sought better control of the departments and partly because White House staff members were more personally devoted to the president. Reagan highly centralized the appointment of cabinet members' principal departmental subordinates and lesser noncareer employees and expanded Executive Office review of departments' and agencies' proposed policy-implementation actions.

Apart from the White House Office and the Executive Residence staff, the Executive Office of the President (EOP) includes the following agencies. Their numbers of employees are indicated in parentheses.[46]

Office of the Vice-President (20)
Office of Management and Budget (586)
Office of Administration (247)
Council of Economic Advisers (34)

Except for the minor Office of Administration, these are all agencies with primarily policy concerns that cut across the whole government or a major segment of it and that, in most cases, must regularly occupy the president's attention. Their presence substantially conforms to the concept that the Executive Office agencies should provide institutional support to the president by gathering information for him, advising him, monitoring the execution of his decisions by the operating departments, and facilitating interagency coordination.[47] It was not always thus. Operating agencies and others with narrow coordinative assignments in the past were placed in the Executive Office, but are now gone.

Of the major EOP agencies, three warrant our special attention: the Office of Management and Budget, the National Security Council, and the Office of Policy Development.

Office of Management and Budget

The Bureau of the Budget, established in the Treasury Department in 1921, became a part of the new Executive Office of the President in 1939. In 1970 President Nixon renamed it the Office of Management and Budget (OMB); the intent was to emphasize its administrative management concerns, but OMB failed to effect this aim. It has long been the largest unit of the Executive Office, accounting now for over a third of the employees.

Power is the critical factor in the OMB's (as in the earlier Budget Bureau's) value to the president and in its relations with departments and agencies.[48] At the heart of its power is its function of annually reviewing all agencies' proposed expenditures in order to draft the government's budget for the president's review and transmittal to Congress. Later we look closely at the budgetary process. Here we need note only three facts. One, quite obvious, is that because money is the lifeblood of agency programs, agencies care greatly about OMB's treatment of their expenditure proposals. The second, and less obvious, is that budgeting is virtually the only comprehensive decision-forcing process in the executive branch; most other decision making is fragmented, episodic, and fluctuating in scope and intensity. The third is that through its review of budgets, the OMB is the only presidential agency commanding a comprehensive body of information about all the nooks and crannies of the executive branch. Together these facts mean that budgeting is a major instrument of policy. OMB's powerful role in the process is derivative. The formal powers it has are the president's, which he has delegated to it. The annual budget is his budget: OMB designs it to express his known policy views, and the tough decisions are his to make.[49]

The same close identification with the president characterizes OMB's nonbudgetary functions:

1. Agencies are required to submit to OMB their proposals for new legislation and amendments before transmitting them to Congress; OMB's "legislative clearance" role is to determine and inform the agencies and Congress whether the proposals are "in accord with the president's program."

2. OMB is in charge of the time-pressured review of each bill passed by Congress and sent to the president for his approval or veto. It rapidly canvasses the views of all concerned agencies about the appropriate action, assures that the president is aware of those views when he makes his decision, and often recommends what action he should take.

3. It reviews the principal regulations affecting the public that agencies propose to issue, a recent and powerful policy and management tool (which we discuss in chapter 13).

4. Its efforts to improve administrative organization, management, and coordination in the executive branch are meant to help meet the president's responsibilities as the chief executive.

5. Incidental to their other functions, OMB staff members range the corridors of the principal agencies and deal with them daily by telephone and memorandum; OMB can therefore be a rich source of intelligence to the president on what is going on "out there" at all levels of policy generation and program management.

In the course of its half century of life, the Bureau of the Budget (BOB) developed a tradition of using its resources to serve both the long-term institution of the presidency and the short-term, incumbent president. This is a difficult combination. Hugh Heclo has come closest to reconciling the two by stressing "neutral competence" as the essential qualitative factor.[50] Staffing most positions with career civil servants and capitalizing on its prestige to attract the ablest of these goes far to account for the dominance of this factor in the bureau. Higher positions were mostly filled by promotion, so that incumbents were experienced in the bureau's work and had been socialized to the bureau's standard of neutral competence. Often they had served under several presidents. Their time horizons were such that they could look back on the road traveled, thus providing an institutional memory otherwise lacking in those around a president,[51] and could look down the road ahead with a longer view than the four-year political calendar that tends to circumscribe the White House staff's vision.

The BOB's and OMB's service of both the incumbent president and the presidency declined in the 1960s and later. The growth, specialization, and assertiveness of the White House staff in the 1960s lessened presidential dependence on the large and capable career staff of BOB. White House aides had both the time and the inclination to bypass the bureau in dealing with the executive departments. As political factors came to weigh more heavily in presidential decision making, White House aides absorbed shares of advisory functions previously lodged with the nonpolitical bureau, leaving the bureau to handle procedural mechanics and to advise on only noncontroversial legislative proposals of agencies and enactments of Congress.

In the 1970s the Nixon OMB interpreted service of the incumbent president simplistically and so undid much that had been achieved in the tradition of neutral competence and service to the longer-range institutional interests of the presidency. Nixon's OMB directors and deputy directors were political activists, making political speeches, advocating Nixon policies at congressional hearings, and defending massive impoundments of appropriated funds until a number of courts ruled them illegal. A new layer of political appointees was inserted between the director and the career civil servants. In 1974 nearly two-thirds of the heads of OMB's major offices and examining divisions had one year's experience or less in their posts (compared to one-tenth in 1960).[52]

In the 1980s OMB enjoyed a surge of power. Reagan's first director of the budget, David Stockman, led the administration's top-priority policy of cutting spending on domestic programs; he centralized decision making in the bureau with little input from the agencies.[53] In other functions as well, some of them enhanced by legislation and executive orders, the bureau has become so fully in tune with the president's political objectives that it has recaptured roles earlier yielded to White House staff members. The dozen or so high-level political appointees in OMB, serving for one to three years, assure that the political orientation will prevail.

OMB's responsibility for improvement of administrative management has been a victim of OMB's primary interest in budgeting and its growing political orientation. In one view, "Management has become largely ad hoc, short-term responses to immediate political problems. The management 'initiatives' have been geared principally toward those activities which promise a quick political pay-off or have the potential for a salutary impact on budgetary 'spending.'"[54] Despairing of invigorating OMB's management work, a panel of the National Academy of Public Administration urged transfer of that work to a new Office of Federal Management, in the Executive Office.[55] When budgeting and management improvement are in a single agency, budgeting is sure to predominate; it more directly involves policy, it provides greater leverage over agencies, and its results are easier to see.

In 1994, then Budget Director Leon Panetta (and later President Clinton's chief of staff) launched a major reorganization effort within OMB christened "OMB 2000." In many ways, the reorganization was the most important change in OMB since its creation. Panetta argued that OMB needed to escape routine budget reviews that, with more of the federal budget on automatic pilot, were increasingly meaningless. Instead, he said, OMB should "better integrate our budget analysis, management review and policy development roles."[56] The reorganization virtually eliminated the agency's existing management side. It integrated these functions with budget reviews in new "resource management offices." The new offices were responsible for formulating and reviewing the federal budget, assessing program effectiveness and efficiency, conducting long-range policy analysis, and implementing governmentwide policy in areas ranging from procurement to financial management.

Some critics, long in favor of establishing a separate Office of Federal Management, condemned the merger and argued that it threatened to weaken central management review even further.[57] OMB officials, however, really had only two options. They could try to organize OMB to integrate budget and management reviews, but risk having short-term budget concerns drive out attention to long-range management problems; or they could create a separate federal management office, but risk having the separate management review be rendered impotent because of the power of budgetary questions. Panetta and his successor, Alice Rivlin, chose the former option. They planned to use powerful new performance measurement tools (discussed in chapter 10) to couple management more effectively with budgeting. The success of that effort in many ways would shape both OMB's future role. The reorganization and the criticisms of its opponents, however, demonstrated the sharp dilemmas in which central budget offices such as OMB always find themselves: the tension between long and short term, between management and budgeting, between inputs and performance.

National Security Council

The National Security Council (NSC), established by statute in 1947, is "to advise the President with respect to the integration of domestic, foreign, and military policies relating to the national security...."[58] Its statutory members are the president, vice-president, secretary of state, and secretary of defense. Also attending the meetings as statutory advisers are the chairman of the Joint Chiefs of Staff and the director of the Central Intelligence Agency; the president may add others to attend.[59] An elaborate structure of interagency committees reviews foreign, defense, international economic, and intelligence policy issues and anticipates and manages crisis situations.[60] Recommendations on policy issues are submitted to the NSC. Its role being advisory, the president retains the decision-making responsibility.

Though the formalized committee structure and procedures matter, they can mislead us. More important have been the growth of the NSC staff since 1947 and the dominant role achieved by its director, the assistant to the president for national security affairs, more commonly referred to as the national security adviser. The staff has had 190 members (including 85 on the payrolls of agencies outside the Executive Office).[61] The staff is organized in about ten regional and functional sections, similar to those of the State Department. About a third of the members are professionals from the military services, the CIA, the State Department, and universities and think tanks. It is no wonder that some perceive that the United States has two State Departments.[62]

The national security adviser has achieved a dominant role for several reasons. The NSC staff is a unit in the Executive Office. The adviser, however, is inside the White House as assistant to the president.[63] He has access, briefing the president every morning and being immediately available for counsel. With his staff members serving on all NSC interagency committees and monitoring cable traffic from abroad, he has a more comprehensive knowledge of developing issues and impending crises than anyone in the departments and agencies. Interagency conflicts, common between the State and Defense departments, make him the only arbiter short of the president. Free of departmental loyalties, he is well placed to claim primary commitment to the national interest and to loyal service to the incumbent president. And, with a staff of short-term, personally selected appointees, he can move with greater dispatch and attentiveness to the president's short-term goals than the State Department with its experienced Foreign Service officers and civil servants and its long-term goals of foreign policy. Too, he has greater freedom than the secretary of state for, unlike the secretary, he is appointed by the president without Senate confirmation and is normally not subject to reporting to or questioning by congressional committees. In several administrations, the president has lacked full confidence in the person serving as secretary of state or has disdained the State Department and its Foreign Service as unadventurous. In such circumstances, the secretary is unlikely to have the influence of the adviser, who typically commands the president's confidence and has no permanent bureaucracy to restrain him.

If these factors explain the national security adviser's and his staff's rise in power, they do not establish its wisdom. In the eight years of the Reagan administration there were six national security advisers (but only two secretaries of state, the second one serving over six years). With substantial turnover of the staff's members, institutional memory was weak.[64] In 1985 and 1986 some staff members engaged in covert, operational activities. They supplied Iran with arms in exchange for hostages (a violation of both a statutory ban on military assistance to Iran and a national policy against dealing with terrorists), arranged for private supplying of arms to Nicaraguan rebels when a statute forbade governmental shipments, and routed profits from the Iran arms sales to finance the Nicaraguan rebels' military equipment.[65]

Proposed remedies interlock. One is to restrict the national security adviser's role to serving as an "honest broker," charged with inviting and coordinating the policy views of the relevant departments and agencies, summing up the areas of consensus and dissensus, and presenting the president with the pros and cons of the options together with indication of the positions of the departments and agencies. His honest-broker role would reasonably extend to monitoring of agencies' progress in implementing presidential decisions. This prescription conforms to the classic definition of the role of presidential assistants and, more generally, of the role of all staff assistants in the government. It excludes direct engagement in operations.

A second remedy, consistent with the first, is to reestablish the secretary of state as the principal foreign policy official of the government. Some would do more, substituting him in effect for the present NSC adviser, with oversight of defense, intelligence, and international economics, as well as political affairs. A third, consistent with both of these, is to shrink the size of the NSC staff; the consequence presumably would be greater reliance on the State Department's regional and functional specialists, whose responsibilities are now duplicated by NSC staff members. Finally, few dissent from the view that operational activities belong outside the White House, in the departments and agencies, accountable to the Congress as well as to the president; dissenters are likely to include the president and his entourage, who assume that the president's staff aides will move more speedily and loyally than departments' "cumbersome" bureaucracies.

Office of Policy Development

Presidents have experimented with various arrangements for the formulation and coordination of domestic policy. Nixon began the effort to formalize matters by establishing a cabinet-level Domestic Council, "to coordinate policy formulation in the domestic area. This . . . to a considerable degree would be a domestic counterpart to the National Security Council."[66] Its staff was headed by one of the two principal assistants to the president. Since then, presidents have retained a staff for domestic policy, most recently called the Office of Policy Development, but they have varied the patterns of cabinet-level involvement. Carter relied on the staff, abolishing the council. Ford and Reagan in his first term relied heavily on smaller interagency cabinet-level bodies concerned with particular policy domains.[67] Reagan in his second term did without such bodies, as did Bush and Clinton, both depending instead on two cabinet-level councils with exceptionally broad jurisdictions, an Economic Policy Council and a Domestic Policy Council.

The Office of Policy Development never achieved a strong role, partly because of rapid turnover of directors (four in Reagan's eight years), partly because of OMB's strong policy role, and especially because other White House aides compete with the OPD's director for influence on domestic policy.[68] The system is not fully disciplined. Many initiatives are taken by other actors without clearance through the councils or the office.

The domestic policy field differs from the NSC's national security field, for its environment is more political, complex, and constraining. Domestic constituencies are more troublesome than those in the foreign affairs and military areas; several domestic constituencies even have designated advocates in the White House's Office of Public Liaison.[69] Members of the policy development staff have too much "firefighting" to do, meeting day-to-day crises and rapidly responding to requests from the president and his aides. The result is neglect of the long- and middle-range planning of governmental policies that is peculiarly a responsibility of institutionalized staff agencies, for it cannot be performed by individual aides in the White House itself.

The formal organization of the presidential decision-making process sets up distinct channels for, on the one hand, foreign, defense, intelligence, and international economic policy analysis and, on the other hand, domestic policy analysis. Increasingly, though, foreign and domestic affairs are interactive. The most obvious of many examples is the foreign trade problem—a mixture of foreign policy toward individual nations, the dollar's international exchange rate, our government's budgetary deficit, the productivity of American industry and agriculture, the comparative quality of domestic and foreign products, and American and foreign governments' import restrictions, export controls, and domestic subsidies. The organizational means for accommodating this interaction are not clear. It is no solution, though seized on by Reagan and Bush, to set up an Economic Policy Council alongside the Domestic Policy Council and the National Security

Council; overlaps among councils and staffs are merely multiplied. These were moderated by Bush's assigning economic (including international aspects) and domestic policy concerns to one aide, though a coequal aide oversees the councils. The Clinton administration followed a model more inspired by the NSC in establishing a National Economic Council.

The top of the executive branch poses two dilemmas that trouble all our discussion of organization. One is the interconnectedness of everything and the need to break down the whole into manageable parts. This afflicts the White House and Executive Office, as we have seen; it also extends to the executive branch as a whole. The other dilemma is the decision-making role of "line" officials and the advice-giving role of staff officials and units; here, too, the White House provides a microcosm of a governmentwide problem. The next chapter focuses on these dilemmas.

6

Organization Problems

Basic problems of organization attract different styles of analysis. Several of these are rooted in theories explored in chapter 3. The connection is apparent in two examinations of American administrative history that suggest analytical approaches directly relevant to the structuring of the executive branch. Jack Knott and Gary Miller challenge the classical administrative reform doctrine, arguing that "institutional choice is inherently political; we must ask 'who gets what?' from any institutional arrangement."[1] Herbert Kaufman identifies three core values that individually or in various combinations have been dominant historically and that continue to vie for organizational expression. These values are neutral competence, executive leadership, and representativeness.[2] Applied to this chapter's subject, the values imply the following: The quest for neutral competence calls for application of what we have learned about effective administration, presumptively with concern for minimizing political inroads on competent agencies and their expert staffs. The quest for executive leadership calls for a strong president and strong and loyal department heads, all politically chosen, and a strict hierarchy that assures subordination of lesser organization units to the president's direction and, so, to his policy priorities. The quest for representativeness calls for organizational arrangements responsive to congressional interests and as well responsive, once established, to the particular clienteles most affected by agency decisions. These implications obviously conflict.

We first focus on problems that fall in the neutral competence category, that is, problems that confound the search for effective organization and that are addressed largely in "neutral competence" modes familiar to classical administrative theory. Some problems, we need to keep in mind, stem from organizational, political decisions by the president and Congress, often urged on by clientele groups concerned with "who gets what." Later we focus on reorganization efforts by presidents and Congress, the president often seeking to enhance his executive leadership role (a search made evident in chapter 5) and Congress often seeking a stronger role in shaping and controlling the bureaucracy. Here again, organizational arrangements may be politically chosen, the product of institutional rivalry over the respective powers of president and Congress.

The Search for Effective Organization

Fundamental organizational problems recur over time, in most agencies, and at a variety of governmental and administrative levels. Because the problems have been frequently confronted before, alternative responses and their consequences are often known. In some cases, however, the administrator will learn that no solution has been found, that the best available alternative leads to other problems, or that two alternatives are so balanced that choice is difficult. These possibilities, of course, help to explain why such problems recur; if lasting solutions had been found, the problems would cease to be problems. Meantime, administrators will benefit from knowing that what they confront is a widely experienced organizational problem. They will also benefit from knowing that an insoluble problem and the tensions it generates may simply have to be lived with. Those who do not know when these consoling truths are applicable will be troubled by the emergence of a problem they suppose unique to their own way of administering and will be guilt-ridden at their incapability of devising a solution.

We consider four kinds of persistent organizational problems that occur largely in the neutral competence framework: (1) the choice among criteria of good organization, (2) interagency conflict, (3) interagency coordination, and (4) the role of staff in supporting and controlling operating activities.

Organizational Criteria

Anyone can make up a checklist of the criteria that should guide choices among alternative organizational structures. A good example is the checklist developed by an interagency task force:

- □ *Public Acceptance:* The amount of trust the public places in the integrity, fairness, and judiciousness of the information and decisions a system generates.
- □ *Adaptability:* The ability of a system to react quickly and positively to changes in (*a*) technology, (*b*) major public policies, (*c*) interna-

tional developments, (*d*) state-federal relationships, and (*e*) economic conditions.

☐ *Consistency of Decisions:* The degree to which a system promotes consistent policy decisions.

☐ *Professional Competence:* The degree to which a system makes it easy to recruit high-caliber professionals and makes effective use of their talents.

☐ *Participation, Representation, and Diversity:* The degree to which a system provides for diverse public inputs to governmental decision making.

☐ *Effective Database:* The capacity of the system to generate, verify, and use reliable and complete data.

☐ *Cost and Timeliness:* The reasonableness of the expense and time required by a system to yield decisions.

☐ *Promotion of Private Efficiency:* The extent to which a system avoids unintended pressures on private decision makers in their choices of technology, markets . . . , and other decisions.

☐ *Accountability to the President:* The extent to which a system provides clear lines of executive authority.

☐ *Accountability to Congress:* The extent to which a system provides clear data for congressional review and clear charters of responsibility for carrying out congressional mandates.

☐ *Compatibility with State Regulation:* The extent to which a system . . . fosters effective state-federal relationships.[3]

Whether we start with this checklist or with one of our own devising, the crucial point, as the task force declared, is that "each criterion is important, but all cannot be satisfied at the same time. For example, it is unlikely that a system that yields the fastest decision and also entails the least administrative cost would rank among the best systems with respect to public credibility or public participation. In short, the design of any . . . [organizational] system requires compromises and tradeoffs among desirable attributes."[4]

As there is no formula to guide these compromises and tradeoffs, either in general or in specific situations, we appear to be set adrift on a sea of uncertainty. This, however, exaggerates the difficulties. It invites us to minimize rationality because we cannot maximize it. Many bad decisions about organizational structure (even in the absence of political pressures) are made by hunch or by simplistic analogy. The grossest errors by analogy are usually committed by appointees without governmental experience who propose to duplicate in government their corporation's or university's organizational arrangements. The president of the United States is unlike a corporation president, the Congress unlike a corporate board of directors, and the departments and bureaus unlike profit centers that manufacture products and are judged by short-run profitability. Scholarly writing about organization by members of college faculties may have an unconscious bias favoring collegial relations among associates, autonomy for the individual, and administrators who behave more as chairpersons than as executive heads.[5] In the absence of a well-articulated set of criteria, important considerations are likely to be ignored and the oversights to result in an organization ill adapted for its task. Decision making is more rational when all significant factors are consciously taken into account, even though some must be rejected as less salient than others or as incapable of accommodation in a particular situation.

Interagency Conflict

The criteria we have quoted from a task force omit any concern with how an organization fits with other organizations at the same level. Yet conflict among agencies is often rooted in the structural patterns chosen. Clean windows were a rarity in Queen Victoria's palace because their outside cleaning was under the control of the Woods and Forests department, their inside cleaning was the responsibility of the Lord Chamberlain's department, and the work schedules of the two departments did not necessarily coincide.[6]

Interagency conflict puts a heavy burden on higher officials, particularly the president and department and agency heads, who must attempt to coordinate the agencies under their charge. One set of conflicts stems from a mismatch of organization bases identified by classical organization theory: purpose, process, clientele, and place. An organization built on one such base will not fit well with organizations built on other bases. This is the case when some are purpose based and others clientele based, as it is when some are area based and others differently based (whether on purpose, clientele, or process). Another set of conflicts arises when all relevant organizations have the same base, that of purpose.

Purpose versus Clientele. The Department of Health and Human Services (HHS) is basically a purpose-based organization, serving the general population through health research and health system financing, welfare programs, and food and drug regulation, among other functions. The Department of Veterans' Affairs and the Bureau of Indian Affairs (in the Interior Department) are clientele based. In effect, these single-clientele agencies perform or arrange for many services for their special groups that HHS would otherwise provide for them under its general, national programs.

If some agencies are purpose based and others are clientele based, certain consequences follow. HHS cannot claim to speak for a unified health or welfare policy, nor can it assert coordinative authority to assure equity and consistency in policy execution. Many of the horror stories of administration—two or three agencies building hospitals in a locality that needs only one, agents of the purpose-based FBI being killed while serving warrants on an Indian reservation that is under the clientele-based Bureau of Indian Affairs—are results of the crisscrossing of jurisdictions of purpose agencies and clientele agencies.

A reverse situation occurs when a clientele agency embraces purposes that prove incompatible. An agency with an industry as its clientele may be charged with both promoting and regulating the industry.[7] Promotion tends to be emphasized at the cost of regulation, as was true of both the Atomic Energy Commission and the Bureau of Mines. Because the AEC neglected protection of the public's health and safety, Congress placed this regulatory function in a new Nuclear Regulatory Commission and then placed nuclear energy promotion in the new Department of Energy.[8] The goal of the Bureau of Mines in the Interior Department was "to stimulate private industry to produce a substantial share of the nation's mineral needs in ways that best protect the public interest,"[9] but it also was the agency charged with protection of the health and safety of miners through mine inspections and enforcement actions. Mine disasters and the resulting public outcry led Congress to transfer the protective function from Interior to a new Mine Safety and Health Administration in the Department of Labor. In both the nuclear energy case and the coal mining case, the fostering of an industry and the constraining of it by enforcement of health and safety standards proved incompatible tasks for a single agency.

Function versus Area. Within departments, the conflicting bases of organization by *function* (whether purpose, clientele, or process) and *area* (i.e., place) create tensions that are rarely resolved. The State Department's traditional organization is by region and country. But alongside it are functional bureaus focused on politico-military affairs (e.g., arms control), human rights and humanitarian affairs, oceans and environmental and scientific affairs, economic and business affairs, refugee programs, and international organizations.

In chapter 5 we saw that, in contrast to some other countries, the U.S. government has no one in the country's various regions to coordinate the field activities of the various departments and agencies. The problem, though, runs deeper. Beyond the lack of any governmentwide regional coordination lies what appears to be the easier problem of a department's coordination of the field activities of its bureaus. The functional (bureau dominant) organization's elements are identical in the two cases: noncongruence of regional boundaries and regional headquarters-cities, lack or weakness of an overall regional coordinator, and variance in degrees of decentralization—in sum, the dominance of function-based over area-based authority. Figure 6.1 shows lines of authority of the two principal alternative systems. These lines, of course, do not preclude nonauthoritative communication (information, technical advice, counsel) flowing along different lines. The figure also shows the compromise often resorted to, a system of dual supervision, where bureaus' field offices are directed by and responsible both to their bureaus and to the areal coordinator. On its face, this compromise breeds confusion. In practice, though, the functional line to the central bureaus dominates, with the area coordinator reduced to handling public relations and tending to administrative procedural details.

President Johnson's task force recommended that the president "direct cabinet secretaries to unify operations in the field under strengthened departmental regional executives of higher rank and calibre who owe clear allegiance to department heads and the President."[10] But unification has not happened. Regional directorships, though, have been substantially switched from civil service to political appointment. Within domestic departments, functional bureaus claim direct control of their field agents, while regional directors insist that coordinating the department's field activities in an area and adapting them to the local situation require that they control the agents. In both the State Department and the domestic departments, these rival claims of function and area create friction and require frequent arbitration by the secretaries.

Conflicts among Purpose-Based Agencies. Conflicts, as is well known, also occur between purpose-based departments. To understand such conflict we need to recall some points made in an earlier chapter. The names of departments more commonly identify a field of activity than assure a constancy of purpose. When the most purpose-named domestic department was young, a wag christened its first head "the Secretary of Not-Too-Much Health, Education, and Welfare." The oldest executive departments express a commitment less to a clear purpose than to assurance of an organization-in-being for pursuit, within a roughly defined field of activity, of such purposes as policymakers may from time to time determine. The departments of State, Treasury, Defense, and Justice are not departments of clear, consistent, single purposes. Cold war or détente, inflation or deflation, offense or defense, vigorous or mild enforcement of antitrust and civil rights laws will

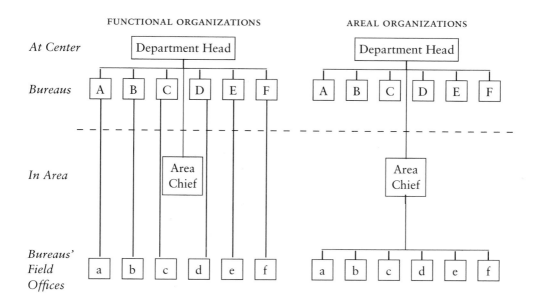

FUNCTIONAL ORGANIZATIONS

AREAL ORGANIZATIONS

At Center — Department Head

Bureaus — A B C D E F

In Area — Area Chief

Bureaus' Field Offices — a b c d e f

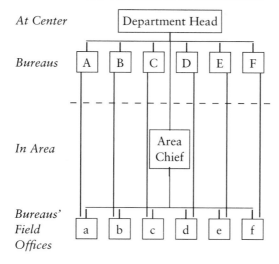

DUAL-SUPERVISION ORGANIZATIONS

At Center — Department Head

Bureaus — A B C D E F

In Area — Area Chief

Bureaus' Field Offices — a b c d e f

Figure 6.1

FIELD ADMINISTRATION PATTERNS

be pursued by these departments without much, if any, structural adaptation to the reversal of purpose.

In addition to regarding departments as having assigned fields of activity and concern, rather than clear and constant purposes, we can further relax our expectations of harmony by emphasizing that they have *core activities* instead of firm jurisdictional boundaries.[11] Border warfare occurs because borders are not and cannot be precise. A large-scale reorganization of the executive branch can remap the terrain, but border marches, new or old, will invite interagency strife. For the agencies involved, jurisdictional boundaries are of more than peripheral interest.

In 1988 the New York City police and fire commissioners nearly came to blows in the mayor's presence because of their departments' long rivalry over handling of emergencies and rescues, most recently evidenced by the police blocking scuba divers of the fire department from joining the search for survivors of a helicopter crash in a river. The police value an image as saviors, not just arresters. The city's firefighters, underemployed by a decade's 40 percent decrease in fires and fearing loss of jobs, seek emergency responsibilities comparable to those of other cities' fire departments and, with time on their hands, promise faster response to emergencies than prevails in the police department. Finally, in 1990, a detailed jurisdictional treaty was negotiated between commissioners appointed by a new mayor.[12]

Interagency Coordination

Executives resort to a variety of methods to moderate conflict among agencies. Strictly speaking, coordination requires a coordinator and, so, a vertical relation. The term, though, is used more loosely, embracing cooperation among agencies, which operates on a horizontal plane.

Horizontal Cooperation. Most cooperative approaches depend for success on agencies' willingness to negotiate and come to agreement with one another. Four methods stand out:

1. Thousands of *interagency agreements* ("treaties") have been negotiated between the concerned agencies to establish specific boundaries and so clarify which agency will do what without interference from the other.

2. Hundreds of *interagency committees* at the cabinet, subcabinet, and bureau levels exist to promote collaboration in jointly occupied areas.

3. Under the *lead agency* formula, one agency is designated to lead and attempt to coordinate all agencies' activities in a particular area.[13]

4. A *clearance procedure* links agencies horizontally by requiring that an agency's proposed decisions in a subject-matter area be reviewed,

whether for comment or for formal approval or veto, by other interested agencies.[14]

Experience with these devices is not reassuring. Numerous minor matters can be disposed of by such consensual arrangements. But matters of real moment to the agencies do not yield readily to negotiation among equals. The hard decisions do not get made.

The Joint Chiefs of Staff of the Defense Department was until 1986 simply an interagency committee, suffering all the disabilities of such committees despite its critical responsibilities. It is made up of a chairman and (since 1986) a vice-chairman, the Army and Air Force Chiefs of Staff, the Chief of Naval Operations, and the Marine Corps commandant. Four studies initiated by presidents (Kennedy, Nixon, Carter, and Reagan) have roundly assailed the Joint Chiefs as appallingly deficient as an adviser to the secretary of defense, the National Security Council, and the president,[15] and as the supervisor of the regional Unified Commands that execute military operations.[16] The key problem was that the Armed Services' chiefs were more attentive to their services' interests than to the common defense. In 1978 the study for President Carter reported:

> [T]he nature of the organization precludes effective addressal of those issues involving allocation of resources among the Services ... except to agree that they should be increased without consideration of resource constraints....
>
> Other contentious issues in which important Service interests or prerogatives are at stake tend to be resolved only slowly, if at all. These include basic approaches to strategy, roles and missions of the Services, the organization of Unified Commands, joint doctrine, and JCS decision-making procedures and documents.... Changes in these contentious areas are approached reluctantly and deferred to the extent possible.[17]

As long as the members were coequal and unanimity normally sought (common features of an interagency committee), no solution was possible, despite the high stakes involved. One comic-opera example: because the services had incompatible communication systems at the time of the 1983 invasion of Grenada, American land forces could not call in air support from the navy's nearby ships until an army officer used his AT&T credit card to telephone Fort Campbell, Kentucky, which in turn asked for air support.

Finally, in 1986, Congress reformed the system, following closely the recommendations of the President's Commission on Defense Management.[18] A new member, designated as vice-chairman, was added to represent views of the Unified Commands. The chairman was named, in place of the Joint Chiefs, as the principal military adviser to the president and the secretary of defense. And the Joint Staff, composed of specially chosen and trained officers, was placed firmly under the chairman.

Narcotics-control efforts illustrate the common situation when neither horizontal cooperation nor vertical coordination seems a likely solution. With the efforts split among many agencies, the Reagan administration's principal recourse in its "war on drugs" was creation of multiagency committees.[19] Congress, disenchanted with this weak response, provided in the Anti–Drug Abuse Act of 1988 a "czar" for coordination of narcotics-control efforts, and President Bush appointed the first such officer.[20] If largely voluntary cooperation is no answer, neither is a major shift to vertical coordination through a high-level antidrug director. Such directive power as the czar has over bureaus concerned with narcotics will conflict with department heads' authority over the same bureaus. Most of such bureaus have core functions unrelated to narcotics control (e.g., the Customs Service, Coast Guard, FBI, Immigration and Naturalization Service, and Central Intelligence Agency). The czar idea is a popular one, advanced, for example, as the cure for the bureaucratic fragmentation that has impeded response to the AIDS crisis.[21]

Vertical Coordination. A principal function of hierarchy is to provide vertical coordination of agencies or of subordinate units having substantial, shared interests. It stands in strong contrast to reliance on the weak reed of horizontal cooperation. The two patterns are quite different. In the vertical coordination model, two warring agencies are brought to book by the organizational superior of both (not a specialized "czar"), a person with formal authority to impose a decision and to monitor the agencies' compliance with it. Although this superior's disposition to use authority may be attenuated by many influences, the motivation to settle the dispute is strengthened by the incentive to see that the programs under his responsibility proceed effectively.

The vertical dimension involves far more than arbitration of jurisdictional controversies. The appropriate concern of a president or department head is as much in the core activities that a subordinate agency pursues without jurisdictional challenge by other agencies as it is in challenged and possibly more peripheral activities. The two types of involvement of the superior take different forms, however. Conflicts that cannot be resolved by horizontal cooperation bubble up to a common superior rather automatically. But there is no easy way to assure that a subordinate unit sends up those issues that should be decided or guided at a higher level, even though they are formally within the subordinate's jurisdiction. Such assurance, though never perfect, is more likely to follow from carefully hedged delegations of authority and prescribed review procedures than it is from organizational structure. Review procedures, for example, enable the OMB to examine, question, delay, and effectively veto agencies' information-gathering and regulatory initiatives.

The horizontal and vertical dimensions of a hierarchy interact. If the executive branch had a hundred departments of roughly equal scope, three consequences would be predictable: border disputes would multiply beyond the president's capacity to arbitrate; individual department and agency heads' access to the president would be curtailed; and cabinet and subcabinet committees would be too large for effective discussion and decision (or advice to the president). Hence the tendency of governments everywhere to hold the number of major departments and agencies to a range of about ten to thirty.[22] This helps. Additionally, though, each department needs to be more than an assemblage of bureaus having slight reason for interaction among themselves but having strong reason for interaction with bureaus in other departments. If the bureaus in a department do belong together, most jurisdictional battles and policy disputes among bureaus can be kept "within the family," with the department head serving as arbitrator. This explains the search for an organizing principle for each department and is the stated rationale for most efforts to reorganize the executive branch or to transfer particular bureaus from one department to another.

Restricting the number of departments or, within a department, the number of units immediately below the department head, so as to keep the president's or department head's "span of control" reasonably short, exacts a price. The fewer the number of units at each level of the hierarchy, the greater must be the number of hierarchical levels. The steeper the hierarchical pyramid, the more layers it has; the flatter the pyramid, the fewer the layers. The State Department has a steep pyramid. A deputy foreign minister for United States and Canadian affairs reports through a deputy foreign minister to the foreign minister.[23] Multiplication of levels increases the distance between the operating levels that "do the work" and the top-level decision makers. One consequence is that there are more points at which upward-flowing proposals may be blocked and information get distorted, and at which downward-flowing instructions may be drained of clarity and force. Another consequence is delay, simply because transmission and consideration of messages through a long series of offices takes longer than their passage through a short series. Here again, we confront a a tradeoff situation for which no general formula provides a solution.

Reorganization plans for both the national and the state governments have tended recently toward "superdepartments." In Washington, the Defense Department set this pattern, bringing under one cabinet member the departments of war, navy, and air; in 1986 their uniformed services were subordinated, more firmly than before, to the reformed Joint Chiefs of Staff. The superdepartment concept took shape in the Department of Health, Education, and Welfare (now slightly reduced to the Department of Health and Human Services), and this was the model (minus Education) chosen for a number of actual or proposed state governments' departments of human resources. Johnson sought unsuccessfully to merge the departments of Commerce and Labor, and Nixon's ambitious plan would, among other changes, have created a huge Department of Economic Affairs. Proponents of such moves argue from familiar premises: (1) bring related activities together for hierarchical coordination by a common superior, a cabinet member; (2) thus greatly reduce the problems that must be settled by the otherwise only common superior, the president or governor; and (3) consequently shrink opportunities for intervention by presidential or gubernatorial aides and the need for large staffs of such aides. A significant consideration in the national government is that the department head would be answerable to the Congress, as well as the president, for his decisions, a responsibility that presidential aides escape.

However attractive these advantages appear, they are often not realized in practice. The secretary of defense is weak vis-à-vis the army, navy, and air "departments" under him, as, we have seen, has been the chairman of the Joint Chiefs of Staff. The heads of state governments' departments of human resources have generally failed to overcome the autonomy claimed by their several specialized staffs (e.g., public health and social work professionals) and the constituency-oriented subgroups within those staffs.[24] Such experience reminds us that organizational structure can open possibilities that would not otherwise exist, but often needs nonstructural measures to realize the promise initially perceived.

The Role of Staff

So far in this section we have focused mainly on *operating* agencies and bureaus and their heads. That is, we have dealt with people and units that are in the direct line of command in the hierarchy of authority, those responsible for the achievement of programs that directly serve or regulate the public. Other kinds of administrative work support an agency's functioning. The standard term for these is *staff* activities, which are contrasted with *line* or *operating* activities.[25] Staff-line conflict is a persistent organizational problem. ("Staff" here should not be confused with the same word's use to refer to an agency's employees.)

We shall speak of *staff* (sometimes called "pure-staff"), *auxiliary,* and *control* activities because they differ too much to be bundled together under the single term *staff.* The first two, the pure-staff and the auxiliary activities, are meant to facilitate operations. Because persons performing these activities are thus cast in an assisting role, classical theory prescribes that they should have no power to command the line officials. The third activity is quite different, for control involves imposition of restraints on the freedom of line officials. Note that we have spoken analytically of *activities* and not organizationally of administrative *units.* One phase of our problem is that facilitative staff and auxiliary units tend to acquire control activities.

Pure-Staff Role. Aides giving staff assistance (in the pure-staff sense) to an official serve as his eyes, ears, and auxiliary brain and as the economizer of his time. They assist him by originating ideas; gathering, screening, and appraising ideas from others; giving him orderly information for his decision making; and keeping track of the pace of execution of his decisions by the relevant agencies. The nature of staff assistance is well captured by the report of the Commission on Organization of the Government for the Conduct of Foreign Policy. The president's staff, it says, must

- ☐ Identify issues likely to require presidential attention.
- ☐ Structure those issues for efficient presidential understanding and decision—ensuring that the relevant facts are available, a full set of alternatives are presented, agency positions are placed in perspective.
- ☐ Assure due process, permitting each interested department an opportunity to state its case.
- ☐ Ensure that affected parties are clearly informed of decisions once taken, and that their own responsibilities respecting those decisions are specified.
- ☐ Monitor the implementation of presidential decisions.
- ☐ Assess the results of decisions taken, drawing from those assessments implications for future action.

The defining characteristic of these tasks is that they embody staff responsibilities rather than line authority. They provide assistance to the president, not direction to department officials other than to convey presidential instructions. There should be only one official with line responsibility in the White House, and that is the president himself.[26]

Staff assistance is needed by all principal line officials, certainly by department heads and bureau chiefs as well as by the president, for such assistance extends their capacity to gather information, anticipate issues, make considered decisions, and follow the progress of implementation of those decisions.

The staff function can be institutionalized as an administrative organization rather than be solely identified with individuals. As we have seen earlier, in addition to his immediate aides in the White House, the president has in the Executive Office a number of staff agencies, all of them charged with informing, assisting, and advising the president. Department heads and bureau chiefs have not only "assistants to" themselves, but also organization units concerned with program analysis, planning, and research. At least at the departmental level, staff units abound, with such assignments as legislative affairs, international affairs, intergovernmental affairs, public affairs (media relations), civil rights and minority affairs, small business, and consumers. In some departments, all or most of the assistant secretaries have primarily staff roles cutting across the bureaus, instead of, as in other departments, being line officials, each supervising a group of bureaus.

Higher officials, of course, receive information and recommendations directly from their subordinate operating officials, not just from staff aides and staff units. The differences are two: (1) heads of subordinate operating units tend to speak for only their fraction of the organization and so may be parochial advocates, whereas staff aides and units are expected to share their line superior's organizationwide viewpoint; (2) subordinate operating officials tend to be immersed in day-to-day operational problems and so have a foreshortened time perspective, whereas staff units—especially those for program analysis, planning, and research—are free to, and are expected to, take a longer-range view.[27]

Auxiliary and Control Roles. Auxiliary activities are such common services as those of governmentwide or departmental central purchasing offices, accounting offices, procedures-designing staffs, libraries, news-release-issuance offices, and publications units. Their special character is captured by characterization as "administrative-support," "institutional," or "housekeeping" services.

Control activities focus on monitoring performance and enforcing compliance with governmentwide, departmentwide, and bureauwide standards and procedures. Most departments now have an inspector general, who has broad authority to investigate and report to the secretary and Congress on suspected fraud, waste, and other mismanagement. Additionally, personnel and budget divisions enforce civil service laws and regulations and appropriations acts and other restrictions on expenditures and programs. Technically it can be argued that control activities are not the exercise of line authority, for controllers simply apply the already prescribed constraints. But, technicalities aside, operating officials resent the "meddling" of controllers, particularly when the latter divert operators' energies from vigorous pursuit of public programs to undue absorption in compliance with red-tape requirements.

Power-Building Propensities. Individuals and units assigned "non-operating" or "non-line-of-command" activities tend in practice to acquire a kind of power that is difficult to distinguish from command authority. All such persons and units control a scarce resource.[28] A staff assistant's access to the chief of the unit is such a resource, and with this may go considerable influence on the chief's decision making. So lower operating officials seek the staff assistant's views and simply do not send the top official any proposals likely to get adverse recommendations from the assistant. Often, too, a top official will tell a staff assistant to handle a problem involving line subordinates, and the latter may come to acknowledge the staff assistant as a decision-making alter ego of the top official. White House staff assistants' assumption of command roles dramatically demonstrates the ease of role transformation.

Or take auxiliary units. The volume of work flowing to such a unit is often so great that its head must decide which operating units' work should have priority.[29] This is power. Operating units assigned low priority may be severely frustrated in trying to meet their own and their superior's deadlines.

The problem is aggravated by a tendency for staff, auxiliary, control, and command functions to be formally combined in the same organization unit. A procurement office in a department not only is charged with supplying operating units' needs for a host of supply and equipment items (an auxiliary activity) but also has authority to question and revise operating officials' specifications of their requirements, both quantitative and qualitative (a control and command activity). However obvious it is that line officials cannot be left free to purchase whatever strikes their fancy, the mixing of auxiliary and control functions is a critical organizational problem. Few events annoy operating officials more than overrulings by purchasing-office employees as to what kinds of supplies are needed for operating programs.[30]

Most staff, auxiliary, and control activities recur at a number of hierarchical levels. The resulting networks enhance the power of their members. Each department has a general counsel, and all lawyers acting as lawyers (i.e., not in posts, as many are, that involve no professional legal work) are appointed by the general counsel and are members of the Legal Division, a staff agency. Most are assigned to and are physically located with bureaus and other operating units of the department. The widely distributed legal staff is, therefore, an integrated group that assures consistency in legal advice to all officials in the department. If a subordinate operating official proposes to act contrary to the advice of the assigned counsel, the latter can report this up the Legal Division's hierarchy. The appropriate legal superior can then act to block the action—usually by urging the bureau chief or department head to order the line subordinate to abandon the proposed action. Beyond this strictly legal-control function, the Legal Division constitutes a communication network that can keep all its members and the general counsel informed about policy and implementation developments throughout the department. Most substantive and procedural proposals affecting the public either have legal implications or require drafting in legal form. With such assured entrée, agency lawyers are both informed about and influential in the analysis and shaping of such proposals. This pooled information makes the general counsel a valued adviser of the department head, who greatly needs information that supplements and corrects what is reported by bureau chiefs.

Other networks exist, though with less scope and more ambivalence than characterize legal services. Ambivalence is greater because usually the dispersed staff-auxiliary-control persons are not members of a central staff but are subordinate to the line officials who are their "bosses" at each hierarchical level. Nonetheless, among each network's members is a community of interest that is spread across hierarchical levels and reinforced by frequent contacts and a shared obligation to keep operating officials from taking shortcuts that violate laws and regulations.

Staff activities, we have seen, differ from line (or operating) activities by the fact that their role is one of assistance to, not command of, line officials. But the boundary between assistance and control is often breached. "Pure-staff" roles are often adulterated by their exercisers' temptations to give orders as well as advice. Even the apparently modest roles of auxiliary units can be converted to an excuse for the exercise of power. Control roles, though based mostly on preexisting statutes and regulations, can be magnified at the expense of program managers. These tendencies are facilitated by networks that connect staff assistants and units at different administrative levels in a common cause.

Solutions? Organizational problems, such as that of staff-line conflict, would not be recurring and persistent if solutions were easy to come by.

The pure-staff activity (leaving aside auxiliary and control activities for the moment) seems to carry its own solution almost by definition. What is needed is possession by staff aides, staff units, and their operating superior of a clear sense of the role of staff. This means that staff persons are called on to practice self-restraint, resisting the temptations to go into business for themselves as decision makers and order issuers. Such restraint does not come easily to persons accustomed to starring or featured-player roles rather than to offstage roles as coaches and prompters. Though the staff-line distinction is not so simple as the difference between thinkers and doers, people well adapted to staff work are often drawn from analytical, nonexecutive occupations.

Auxiliary units, it seems, will inevitably exercise specialized control functions, largely because top executives cannot bother themselves with "housekeeping" disputes. Yet program administrators are frustrated by having to share control over the tools for their jobs with outside auxiliary units less committed to program achievement.[31] Efforts to reduce this frustration involve delegation to program administrators of authority to act, while central auxiliary units, though abandoning the right to share decision making on every transaction, retain the right to conduct general audits of the integrity of use of the delegated authority and to recentralize the authority when there is a pattern of abuse.

Reorganization

Why, some wonder, cannot the frequently encountered organizational problems be solved, or at least mitigated, by straightening out the structural arrangement of the executive branch? A major part of the answer is that executive reorganization is more than the rearranging of organizational building blocks to achieve symmetry, logical grouping of activities, reduction of the president's or secretary's span of control, and greater administrative coordination and efficiency. These fall largely in the "neutral competence" approach to organization.[32] Reorganization, though, is political. Where a program is placed matters, and many in and out of government care. If it is placed in a department unsympathetic or so indifferent to the program that the secretary will not battle for its adequate financing and staffing, the program will likely be anemic. If a program is placed far down in the hierarchy, the director's access to the secretary will be impeded and his recommendations will move through several intermediaries who may block or change them. And when those in immediate charge of a program feel like orphans in their department, they will look elsewhere for support, for funds, staff, and program autonomy that enables them to enjoy orphanhood. All these consequences are anticipated, encouraged, or fought by presidents seeking to magnify the executive leadership value and by members of Congress attentive to their own interests and those of clienteles, both of them interests that serve to achieve the value of representativeness.

Authority to reorganize the executive branch and its elements is widely distributed, and the role of a key player, the president, has been sharply circumscribed since the mid-1980s. Congress can legislate any reorganization it wishes. It can establish departments, bureaus, and even units of the Executive Office of the President. At the other extreme, the heads of departments and major agencies have substantial authority to effect internal changes.

For much of the past half-century, the president had statutory authority to propose to Congress reorganization plans creating, renaming, consolidating, and transferring whole agencies (other than cabinet departments and independent regulatory commissions) and any of their component units. By an ingenious "legislative veto" arrangement, his plans automatically went into effect in sixty days if neither house adopted a resolution of disapproval. In 1983, however, the Supreme Court ruled unconstitutional the legislative veto provisions appearing in hundreds of statutes, including the Reorganization Act (see chapter 12).[33] Now, for a president's reorganization plan to be effective, it must be approved by a joint resolution of the two houses passed within ninety days after receipt and signed by the president (or if vetoed because of amendments, overridden by Congress).[34] The odds are altered. Before 1983, the congressional engine's idling in neutral gear was to the president's advantage. Now it is to his disadvantage; he needs the House and Senate gears engaged and propelling action in his favor. Congress's inertia is no longer his ally. Even his proposal of a statute would have a better chance of success, as Congress could pass it any time over a two-year session, instead of having to approve a plan within ninety days.

A count made before curtailment of the president's role revealed a pattern reflecting the dispersion of reorganization authority. Of the almost 400 major subdivisions of the executive departments other than Defense, about 40 percent were established by statute, 10 percent by presidential reorganization plans and executive orders, and 50 percent by departmental orders.[35]

A president has a choice of tactics. He can seek comprehensive reorganization of the executive branch. Alternatively, he can target and space efforts to change only a few agencies or bureaus. The first option, comprehensive reorganization, is tempting, but it unites in opposition the interest groups happy with existing organizations or, even if not happy, fearful of the predictable and unpredictable consequences of change. The other option, separate, incremental changes, though less widely challenged and so more easily effected,[36] often fails to relate the specific actions to the president's larger strategy of executive branch organization, if indeed there is one.

Comprehensive Reorganization

Seven of the eleven presidents from Hoover through Clinton supported a general overhaul of the executive branch.[37] Why, given the odds against them, do presidents bother? Some come into office with campaign promises to "straighten out the mess in Washington." Some—Hoover and Carter —are engineers disposed to fix the machinery of government. Some seek popular credit for trying to improve administration. Credit for the apparent effort may count more politically than actual achievement, to which they may devote little energy. Some who, like former Senators Truman, Nixon, and Johnson, know Washington well, may perceive existing executive branch organization as poorly serving the national interest and propose to invest political capital in structural reform. But political capital is precious and may evaporate or be shifted to urgent policy initiatives.[38]

No president, with the exception of Truman, has obtained much of what he wanted. Of Roosevelt's far-reaching proposals, only two were initially approved by Congress.[39] Two joint congressional-presidential Commissions on Organization of the Executive Branch of the Government, each chaired by Herbert Hoover, reported in 1949 and 1955.[40] Over half of the First Hoover Commission's recommendations were adopted, mostly because of Truman's support and a massive public relations campaign. The Second Hoover Commission focused not on major reorganization but on procedural techniques and policy issues—especially how to reduce the government's competition with and regulation of private enterprise. Nevertheless, "not a single major permanent program resulting
from the years of depression, recovery, war, and reform was abolished as a result of this prodigious inquiry."[41]

In 1971 President Nixon proposed a drastic reorganization of the executive branch.[42] It would have retained unchanged only the four departments whose heads sat in George Washington's cabinet. Four departments would be abolished (Commerce, Labor, Transportation, and Agriculture), most of their work being absorbed by a wholly new Department of Economic Affairs. Three newly named and reconstituted departments—Natural Resources, Human Resources, and Community Development—were to supersede the departments of the Interior, Health, Education, and Welfare, and Housing and Urban Development. But Congress refused to act.[43]

President Carter mounted a heavily staffed reorganization study in the OMB. Results were modest compared with his ambitions. The successes were establishment of the Department of Education (fulfilling a campaign pledge) and the Department of Energy, splitting of the Civil Service Commission into two new agencies, and reorganization of the president's Executive Office.[44] President Reagan futilely sought abolition of the departments of Education and Energy inherited from Carter, but proposed no overhaul of executive branch structure.[45] He relied instead on his cabinet councils for harmonizing interagency concerns, on centralized control of agency behavior, on procedural changes, and on political appointments.[46] Congressional Republicans returned to the battle in 1995 and struggled to eliminate the Commerce Department.

Among state governments, comprehensive reorganizations have come in four waves, the most recent one centered in the 1965–78 period when twenty-one states recast their executive branches. Usually the governor initiates the enterprise, and it is achieved through constitutional amendment or statute or both.[47]

Obstacles to Reorganization

Reorganization ideas are many, but relatively few are translated into action. Those that are tend to be specifically focused, respond to perceived performance failures believed to be products of poor organization, and either have sufficient promise of benefits to command political support or are so unproblematic as to enjoy political indifference. Some eventually succeed because they have recurred so often over the years that objections lose credibility.[48]

Stability, not fluidity, characterizes the executive branch's organization.[49] How do we account for this? Most obviously, departments and bureaus resist the loss of functions; they "protect their turf." This behavior is more dominant than the change-promoting strategies pursued by the same agencies when bent on imperialistically expanding their realms.[50] The question is how such agencies muster the political support to discourage and even defeat reorganization initiatives by presidents and department heads whose own political resources are not insubstantial. The answer is that congressional committees and powerful interest groups are already there. To muster their forces against a reorganization is not difficult; often they spring to arms unbid.

Congressional committees have their own jurisdictions to protect. One reason that Congress failed to support Nixon's major reorganization effort was the impact it would have had on legislative committees. On the average, over nine existing committees would have had fragmentary jurisdiction over each of the four new departments. The alternative would have been a reorganization of committees' jurisdictions to match those of the departments. That is not a prospect to warm the hearts of the leading members of committees marked for abolition or loss of jurisdiction.

Interest groups that perceive potential harm to their members throw their lobbying strength against proposed reorganizations. They ally themselves with the affected departments or bureaus and with sympathetic congressional committees. The result in many a field of government action is an "iron triangle" or "unholy trinity" that resists reorganizations perceived as threatening to its members' shared interest.

Indeed, a major study of government reorganization by Craig W. Thomas teaches several important lessons. First, although we are very long on rhetoric about reorganization, we are very short on evidence. We simply know relatively little about whether changes in government organization improve efficiency. Second, many efforts to improve the efficiency of government through reorganization have been disappointing. Contracting out and creating government corporations can improve efficiency if the changes are well managed, but a common approach, centralizing authority, often does not improve efficiency. Third, despite the constant rhetoric about trying to reorganize government agencies to improve efficiency, "reorganizations are profoundly and unavoidably political and we should accept them as such."[51] If reformers promote reorganization to produce more efficient and more effective government, they cannot be sure of achieving the results they desire. But they can be sure of provoking deep political battles over the structure and symbols of government programs.

This largely negativist array of political forces might be more often overcome if theory and experience pointed to one best way to organize the executive branch or to organize a department or bureau. The difficulty is that when those knowledgeable about administration are asked how to organize, they are likely to answer, "It all depends." This does not mean that anything goes. It does mean, as we have seen, that there are persistent organizational problems, several alternative approaches to them, and in any given situation a set of variables that carry different weights from those they carry in another situation. It also means that the promise of a reorganization for achieving its objectives is contingent on so many factors that neither theory nor experience can assure that the promise will be fulfilled.

Conclusion

Responses to organization problems usually seek to promote the value of neutral competence, executive leadership, or representativeness. Any of these responses may be infused with the political concern for "who gets what?" This is true, we saw, even of responses in the neutral-competence mode, for administrators, including careerists, prefer arrangements that protect their units' powers and that assure their control of subordinate units.

Organization problems, we have discovered, are not chance or unique occurrences. Instead, they fall into patterns that not only persist or recur but that, more remarkably, also appear at all levels—presidential, departmental, bureau, and field service. Why conflict seems structurally embedded and things go wrong, even when neutral competence is the goal, stems from such causes as organizers' failure to take account of the salient criteria; incompatibilities among the structural bases of organization units whose activities are interrelated; the indistinctness of jurisdictional boundaries; the weakness of voluntary, horizontal cooperation; the limits of vertical, hierarchical coordination; and the frustrations that operating officials undergo because of the controls exercised by staff and auxiliary aides and units.

Though organizational structure seems passive, it should now be clear that it both results from and shapes the dynamics of organizational conflict. Those dynamics are political, reflecting the claims of president and Congress to achieve respectively the values of executive leadership and representativeness, and reflecting as well the clash of interest groups.

As later chapters show, public organizations, however passive they appear in the abstract, come to life when perceived as sets of human beings, both civil servants and political appointees, as wrestlers over policy issues and battlers for scarce budgetary resources, as agents attempting to implement service and regulatory programs that have ambitious and contradictory goals, and as bureaucrats adapting to the control efforts of executive, legislative, and judicial overseers.

Part III

People in Government Organizations

Organizational structure provides the framework for the people who work within it. Democratic governments have long relied on a civil service system to minimize political tinkering with the administrative process. Just how to adjust the system to maximize responsiveness to elected officials while minimizing the temptation to abuse the system for short-term political gain, however, has proven an ageless question. This section examines the foundations of the civil service system and the system of political leadership that guides it.

7

The Civil Service

The first man to set foot on the moon was a civil servant, an employee of the National Aeronautics and Space Administration. The president had designated the day of the moon walk a holiday for the government's employees. This meant that most employees required to work on the holiday would get premium pay (making the total twice their regular pay). But Neil Armstrong's work that day did not qualify because his position was at the GS-16 level. Congress had provided that no employee could get premium pay if his or her aggregate pay rate for the period would exceed level GS-15's top pay, which Armstrong's would. Giving him premium pay for his day on the moon would have been illegal—though $25 billion had been spent in the eight-year effort to get a man on the moon.[1]

This apparently unusual case in fact illustrates features of normal civil service systems. First, civil service positions are grouped and ranked in a *classification* system.[2] In the federal government a congressionally established General Schedule (GS) ranks most white-collar positions at multiple grade levels, and a pay range applies to each level. With B.S. and M.S. degrees in aeronautical engineering and his experience as a pilot, Armstrong qualified for the GS-16 grade. Second, with the reference points of such a system, Congress can enact laws applying to all civil servants above, below, or at specified grade levels. Similarly, it may legislate about other categories—for example, all veterans, or all members of racial minorities. Third, the application of across-the-board measures, whether laws or executive rules and regulations, tends to neglect individual differences deemed irrelevant to the classification system and other categorizations. Fourth, transformation of the government's white-collar workforce from one mostly of clerks to one of knowledge specialists—aeronautical and other engineers, scientists, economists, attorneys, physicians, accountants, computer specialists, and many more—accentuates the importance of individualized treatment.

Immediately, we face a tradeoff problem. The scale of public employment makes unavoidable the adoption of broadly applicable personnel policies and the systematization of personnel processes. If well designed, these enshrine important values, among them judgment by merit (rather than by partisan and personal favoritism), equal pay for equal work, due process in disciplinary actions, and nondiscrimination by sex or race. Yet the morale that underlies sustained, high-level performance is an individual attribute, which needs reinforcement by organizational incentives that recognize the uniqueness of each human being. To treat a person as simply an undifferentiated member of a class of thousands of employees may quench the individual's zest for superior performance. Balancing the needs of a large-scale system for generalized categories and procedures with the same system's need to evoke individuals' best efforts is a central problem of the civil service.

Our first task is to appreciate the large-scale dimensions of public employment. In doing so we not only make evident the need for general categories as the foci of legislation and civil service rules but also cast light on much-debated issues about the growth and functions of bureaucracy in the United States.

Public Employment

In 1994 American governments' employees numbered 18 million. Twenty years earlier they numbered 12 million.[3] The contrast of the two figures, striking though it seems, gives us little or no basis for judgment. For that we need to know by how much the country's labor force grew, how the American pattern compares with the patterns of other modern democracies, and how public employees are distributed among governments and among functions.

From 1946 to 1993, total employment in the United States increased by 43 percent, while the growth in government employment lagged behind at 38 percent.[4] Thus, American government—at least in terms of the number of people it employs—has not expanded disproportionately to the private sector. Among the world's major developed nations, moreover, the United States ranks about in the middle in the share of its workforce employed by government (see figure 7.1). The United States is certainly not distinctive for its proportion of government employees.

When we ask where the public employees are and what functions they perform, the answers turn out to be poor matches for widely held beliefs.

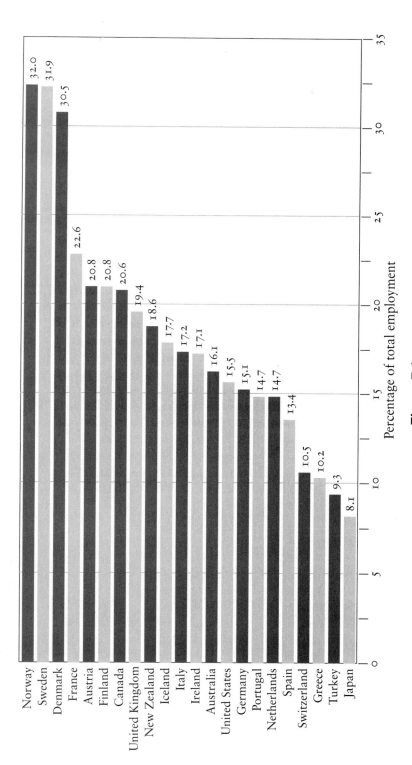

Figure 7.1

GOVERNMENT EMPLOYMENT AS A SHARE OF TOTAL EMPLOYMENT (1990)

SOURCE: Organization for Economic Cooperation and Development, *Public Management Developments: Survey 1993* (Paris: OECD, 1993), 11.

Of total public employment, 82 percent is that of state and local governments, the federal government accounting for only the remaining 18 percent. The great increase over a recent twenty-year period was at the state and local levels, which experienced a growth of 62 percent. Federal executive branch employment rose only 3 percent; in fact, yearly totals fluctuated up and down within the narrow range of 2.8 to 3.1 million (see figure 7.2).[5]

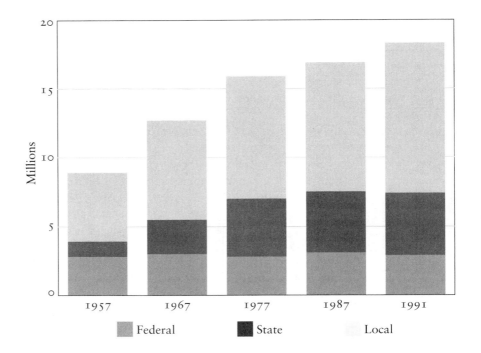

Figure 7.2

PUBLIC EMPLOYMENT

SOURCE: U.S. Bureau of the Census, *Public Employment in 1991* (Washington, D.C.: Government Printing Office, 1992), table 6.

It follows, first, that the popular tendency to attack "the swollen federal bureaucracy" needs to distinguish between swelling in relation to some concept that the federal government does too much and swelling over time, which has not occurred. Second, it follows that those distressed by the overall "swelling" of public employment should especially be concerned with state and local governments, for they have the lion's share of employ-

Table 7.1

PUBLIC EMPLOYMENT BY FUNCTION, 1992

Function	Percentage of total		
	All government	*Federal government*	*State and local governments*
Total	100.0	100.0	100.0
National defense	5.2	32.3	0
Postal service	4.1	25.4	0
Space research and technology	.1	.8	0
Education	44.0	.5	52.4
Highways	3.0	.1	3.6
Health and hospitals	9.9	10.2	9.8
Public welfare	2.7	.3	3.2
Police protection	4.6	2.9	4.9
Fire protection	1.8	0	2.2
Sanitation and sewerage	1.3	0	1.6
Parks and recreation	1.8	.9	2.0
Natural resources	2.3	7.6	1.3
Financial administration	2.6	4.5	2.3
Other administration	2.1	1.0	2.4
Judicial and legal	2.0	1.7	2.1
Other	12.3	11.8	12.4

SOURCE: U.S. Bureau of the Census, *Statistical Abstract of the United States: 1994* (Washington, D.C.: Government Printing Office, 1994), 319.

ees and have grown most rapidly. Refinement of the issue, though, requires clarification of what functions account for large groups of public employees.

Table 7.1 displays the distribution of public employees by function. Some surprises are in store for those with popular stereotypes of bureaucrats. Over half of the public employees are in two functional areas: education, and health and hospitals. Contrary to popular impressions, public welfare and administration of social insurance account for only 4 percent of state and local employees. In the federal government, over 60 percent of the civilian employees are in just two categories: national defense along with international relations, and the postal service. These are responsibilities not claimed for state and local governments by even the most ardent advocates of decentralization.

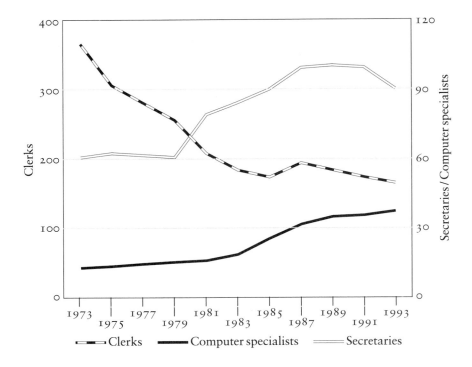

Figure 7.3

TECHNOLOGY'S EFFECTS ON FEDERAL STAFFING NEEDS
(THOUSANDS OF FEDERAL EMPLOYEES)

SOURCE: U.S. Office of Personnel Management, *Federal Staffing Digest* 6, no. 4 (September 1994): 5. Data from OPM Occupational Survey of Full-Time Employees.

NOTE: Clerks include clerical employees from all series, but exclude secretaries (GS-318) and computer assistants (GS-335). Computer specialists are in the GS-334 occupation.

In response to the changing technology and complexity of government programs, there have been subtle but important changes in government employment. Consider, for example, shifts in federal jobs. As computers have swept through the federal government, the number of clerk-typists has dropped dramatically. The number of secretaries (who spend much of their time putting documents into a final format) has grown and the number of computer specialists has increased rapidly (see figure 7.3). Moreover, as figure 7.4 shows, although the number of federal nonclerical personnel has remained relatively flat, the number of lawyers, accountants, and budget

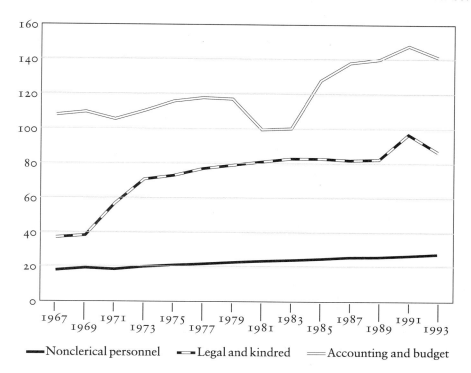

Figure 7.4

EFFECTS OF COMPLEXITY ON FEDERAL STAFFING NEEDS
(THOUSANDS OF FEDERAL EMPLOYEES)

SOURCE: See figure 7.3.

NOTE: More than half in personnel (GS-200s) work for the Department of Defense (DOD). DOD employees make up 39 percent of Accounting and Budget (GS-500s) occupations, Treasury Department employees 35 percent. Health and Human Services, Justice, Treasury, and Veterans' Affairs (in that order) together employ 68 percent of Legal and Kindred (GS-900s).

managers has grown steadily. The nature of the job can also dramatically affect employment trends. Federal spending on the elderly has grown quickly as the number of elderly citizens has increased. The number of employees managing social security, however, has grown only slightly. There the process is information and computer intensive, and the government can serve large increases in recipients with only small increases in employment. Providing medical care, in contrast, is very labor intensive. Federal employ-

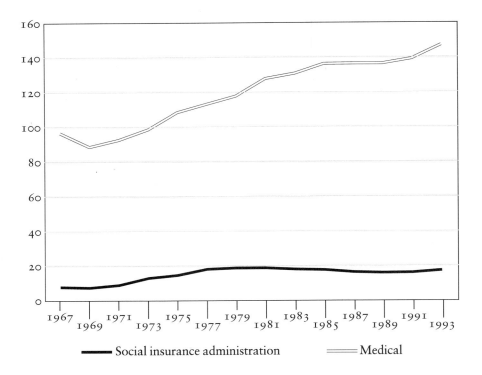

Figure 7.5

EFFECTS OF WORKLOAD ON FEDERAL STAFFING NEEDS
(THOUSANDS OF FEDERAL EMPLOYEES)

SOURCE: See figure 7.3.

NOTE: All social insurance administrators (GS-105) work for Health and Human Services. Of employees in medical occupations (GS-600s), 73 percent work for Veterans' Affairs.

ment in medical care, mostly concentrated in Department of Veterans' Affairs hospitals, has gone up much more quickly than social security employment (see figure 7.5).

The pay and benefits of public employees cost money. A popular assumption is that budgetary problems could be greatly eased, perhaps even solved, if the number of employees or their compensation were cut back. Two points might be borne in mind. First, the proposition bears more weight at the local than at the state or federal level. Of total local expenditures, 42 percent go for salaries and wages, while such payments take only 18 percent of state expenditures and 11 percent of federal expenditures.[6]

Second, given these figures, a successful drive to cut the federal or a state payroll by, say, 10 percent (whether by dismissing one of every ten employees or by cutting everyone's pay by 10 percent) would not materially improve the budgetary situation. In the federal government, for instance, a 10 percent cut would save only 1.1 percent of federal outlays.[7] This, of course, is no argument for indifference to governments' employment and pay levels. It does indicate that any who seek major reductions in expenditures must focus on eliminating or reducing government programs, rather than solely on the people charged with carrying them out.

Managing the System

A civil service system has many managers. The legislative branch has the broadest authority (subject, of course, to constitutional or city charter provisions). The chief executive often has authority to establish rules consistent with the relevant laws and to make exceptions. The budget agency has much to say about pay levels and the size of agencies' staffs. A central personnel agency—a civil service commission or a single-headed personnel office—prepares and administers examinations for entry to the civil service and is intended to be the watchdog assuring that agencies adhere to merit principles in appointments, promotions, and dismissals. It or a separate central agency concerns itself with labor relations, negotiating with civil servants' unions and administering collective bargaining agreements. Each department or sizable agency has its own personnel office.

To a bureau chief or a manager of a particular program, all of that is superstructure. Though respectful of the roles of the legislature and chief executive, the administrator chafes at laws and rules that impose a procrustean uniformity on the diversity of settings in which personnel problems must be dealt with. More often than not, the central and departmental personnel offices' staff members are perceived as abominable "no"-men, people who lack understanding of the individual program and its staffing needs, people looking for something to come up that they can turn down.

The federal government distributes central responsibilities for the civil service among a number of agencies. From 1883 to 1978, these responsibilities were mostly held by the bipartisan Civil Service Commission. The Civil Service Reform Act of 1978 abolished the commission and established three agencies in its stead.[8] The Office of Personnel Management (OPM) is charged with executing, administering, and enforcing the civil service laws, rules, and regulations. It prepares and conducts competitive examinations for positions common to federal agencies, while for positions distinctive to one or a few agencies it may (but need not) delegate examining authority to those agencies. The bipartisan Merit Systems Protection Board decides employees' appeals of adverse personnel actions, reviews OPM regulations for compliance with merit system principles, and conducts studies of the civil service system. The Federal Labor Relations Authority protects the statutory rights of government employees to join or not join labor organizations, choose collective bargaining representatives, and be protected from unfair labor practices.

The 1978 Civil Service Reform Act made more than organizational changes. It gave statutory strength to the right of federal employees to organize and bargain collectively. It reaffirmed or specifically applied many fair-employment provisions of law so that they protect federal employees against racial, sexual, and other forms of discrimination. Merit was emphasized by the requirement of performance appraisal systems generally and of merit pay for mid-level managers. We discuss these provisions later in this chapter. Most important, the act established the Senior Executive Service, a mix of political and career officials near the top of the executive branch. This is examined further in chapter 8.

The distribution of organizational responsibilities for the civil service is further provided independently of the Civil Service Reform Act. The Office of Management and Budget limits the number of agencies' employees not only by recommending dollar limits on agencies' appropriations but also by imposing personnel ceilings (which deprive agencies of discretion in moving dollars from other accounts to meet perceived personnel needs). Finally, in recent administrations the Office of Presidential Personnel, in the White House, has sought to review proposed appointments and promotions of civil servants at higher levels in the departments and agencies, either to switch the category from civil service to political, or to assure that the chosen civil servant is acceptable to the White House.

The federal government's civil service system suffers from excessive standardization, centralization, and procedural complexities. The section of the United States Code that codifies all statutory provisions about the system runs 790 pages. The codified regulations implementing the statutes take 900 pages.[9] About seven times that number appear in the more detailed *Federal Personnel Manual*. The number of personnel specialists per employee is three times that in the private sector.[10] Although authority to appoint, promote, and fire employees is vested in the heads of agencies, OPM prescribes specific procedures and often requires that proposed plans and individual actions receive its approval. A tension thus exists between OPM and agencies' program managers. Advocates of centralized operations and detailed control by OPM argue that governmentwide equity and adherence to merit principles can be achieved only by regarding the government as a single employer. The managers argue that delegation and decentralization of authority to agencies would recognize that the government is many employers, each with responsibility for the achievement of program objectives and each with distinctive staffing needs. Their intent is not just to transfer authority from OPM to agencies' personnel offices (which can be as wedded to red tape as OPM) but to move authority for human resources from personnel specialists to program managers.[11]

Haunting all such confrontations and prescriptions is the need to prevent politicizing of governmental staffing below the top level. The need is for the civil service's middle and higher levels to be occupied by persons who have professional knowledge and managerial competence and who are assured of sufficient tenure that they provide institutional memory, continuity of program administration, and smooth adaptation to newly emerging priorities. Conventionally, this need is thought best met by having one or more central agencies that serve as watchdogs over agencies' adherence to the merit system, administer most examinations for entry to the civil service, oversee the compensation system, and hear appeals from employees believing themselves unjustly dismissed. The assumption here is that departments and agencies, headed by political appointees, are not to be trusted. But the issue is not that simple. In the Nixon administration the Civil Service Commission itself neglected investigations of widespread and systematic abuses of the civil service appointment system and participated in abuses. In the first Reagan administration a campaign leader was made director of the Office of Personnel Administration, and he more than quadrupled the number of OPM's political appointees, from eight to more than thirty-two.[12] When his four-year term ended, he withdrew from Reagan's nomination for reappointment in anticipation of a Senate rejection.

The formula for establishing a proper balance between centralization and decentralization within Washington (or in state capitals or city governments) is well known. It applies to personnel administration as to most fields of activity. The first requirement, of course, is a central agency deserving of respect, a requirement increasingly met by OPM during Reagan's second term and continued under Bush. With that condition satisfied, the formula calls for central establishment of standards, delegation of operating authority to program agencies, central monitoring of agencies' application of the standards, and withdrawal of delegations from those agencies that flout the standards.

In 1989 the National Commission on the Public Service (Volcker Commission) issued a major report. The commission, a nongovernmental group of thirty-six distinguished members, was chaired by Paul A. Volcker, former chairman of the Board of Governors of the Federal Reserve System.

On the point at issue it recommended that

> OPM's current operating responsibilities ... should be decentralized to the federal departments and agencies, thereby allowing it to concentrate on five major duties: (1) providing policy guidance on personnel standards and practices, (2) overseeing implementation of those standards and practices by departments and agencies, (3) providing technical support for departments and agencies that need help, (4) undertaking research on ways to enhance government productivity and performance, and (5) anticipating future trends in the government work force.[13]

As part of its "reinventing government" initiative, the Clinton administration launched several attacks on centralized management of the civil service system. Amid much fanfare, OPM Director James King dumped the *Federal Personnel Manual* into the trash and eliminated the much-hated SF-171, the federal government's all-purpose résumé form. OPM instead delegated substantial responsibility for managing the personnel system to federal agencies. The reforms prompted much applause; virtually no one liked the complex *Manual* or the forms it generated. The move to decentralize OPM's operations to federal agencies, moreover, echoed the Volcker Commission's recommendations. King, in fact, frequently held his form up over his head to show it was longer than his own six-foot height. But many critics also worried about how OPM would manage the transition and about how it would build the capacity to perform its new mission, which, in many ways was very different from its previous operations.

Position Classification

Basic to every civil service (and to most large corporations) is a scheme that identifies and groups all positions in terms of similarities and differences in kinds of subject-matter knowledge needed, levels of difficulty and responsibility, and qualification requirements. This is the position classification system. Most other operations of personnel administration are based on this system. For example, governmentwide pay rates are tied specifically to it, and examinations are designed to fit specific classes of positions.

The federal government has over thirty pay systems to cover more than 900 occupations represented in its civilian labor force. The major ones are three: the General Schedule Classification and Pay System, for most white-collar positions (which covers 75 percent of the civilian workforce); the Federal Wage System, for blue-collar workers, mostly in the Pentagon

Table 7.2

GENERAL SCHEDULE SALARIES

GS grade	Bottom salary	Top salary	Typical roles
1	$11,903	$14,891	General entry and preprofessional
2	13,382	16,843	"
3	14,603	18,986	"
4	16,393	21,307	"
5	18,340	23,839	Senior clerical and entry-level professional or administrative
6	20,443	26,572	"
7	22,717	29,530	"
8	25,159	32,710	Senior clerical
9	27,789	36,123	Intermediate professional or administrative
10	30,603	39,783	Full professional or administrative
11	33,623	43,712	"
12	40,298	52,385	"
13	47,290	62,293	"
14	56,627	73,619	Executive
15	66,609	86,589	"

SOURCE: Office of Personnel Management, Salary Table 94-GS.

(which covers 16 percent of the civilian workforce); and the Postal Service (which covers the three-quarters of a million workers in a separate pay system).[14] A number of special pay systems, covering only about 9 percent of employees, round out the total.[15] Here our focus is on the General Schedule.

The classification system requires that the duties of every position be described by the incumbent (if any), by his or her supervisor, and finally and authoritatively by a classification specialist in a central personnel office. All like positions are then grouped in a *class*. Each class finds its place in the whole scheme according to its occupation (e.g., clerk-typist, civil engineer) and its level of qualifications and responsibility (expressed in grade level, e.g., GS-5, GS-15). There are over 400 white-collar occupations in the federal civil service and, since the 1978 reform act allowed higher ranked civil servants to join the new Senior Executive Service, there remain basically fifteen grades in the General Schedule for such occupations. Table 7.2, showing the grades, the salary range in each grade, and the various roles performed at each level, will be a useful reference for much of this chapter.

Problems. Necessary as a position classification system is, many problems inhere in its practical application. First, the system is quickly out of date, for supervisors are constantly adding to and subtracting from the actual duties and responsibilities of their staff members.

Second, the system tempts agencies to distort sound organization by multiplying high administrative positions or by shifting professional specialists to administrative roles. The object is to improve the grade level of positions, thus improving their pay and the likelihood of the agencies' retaining or recruiting able administrators or highly qualified scientists and other specialists. Classification specialists are impressed by the hierarchical level of a position and by the size of the total staff and the number of immediate subordinates supervised by the position's incumbent. When the stakes are high enough, an agency head recasts organizational relationships. Similarly, the head assigns professional and scientific specialists to managerial and supervisory positions for which they have little talent but which pay higher salaries than those for individual research.[16] Such organizational distortions and misassignments of staff members account for about 30 percent of the increase in the overall average grade from GS-5.4 to GS-8.3 between 1950 and 1983. The other 70 percent reflects the massive change from a heavily clerical workforce to one that is predominantly professional, scientific, and administrative. With the simultaneous introduction of automatic data processing and government's expansion in areas such as nuclear energy, space science, environmental protection, health research and protection, and oversight of contracting, the need for clerks declined and the need for professionally trained experts increased. Focusing on the classification system's operation ignores a major cause of the upgrading, the failure of federal white-collar pay to keep pace with private-sector pay for comparable positions.[17]

Third, the change in composition of the workforce itself intensifies a weakness of classification systems. They readily describe concretely and objectively the duties and responsibilities of the mass of easily standardized positions, such as typist, file clerk, and switchboard operator. But they do this less effectively for higher professional and policy administrative positions. Here specialization may make individual positions distinctive (e.g., not just a mining engineer, but one knowledgeable about South African mining)[18] or, on the contrary, the person may tend to make the job, not the job to define the person.

Reform? One reform proposal would drastically overhaul the classification system. The fifteen GS grades would be collapsed to just four or five broad pay bands. This would, among other things, end dependence on distinctions so refined that only experienced bureaucrats have the subtlety to master them. At present, ordinary words carry salary implications of hundreds or thousands of dollars. Thus, for positions involving "work along special technical, supervisory, or administrative lines," a federal manager drafting a job description must be alert to such gradations as the following in characterizing the work: "very" and "highly" difficult and responsible (GS-9 and -10), and of "marked," "very high," "unusual," "exceptional," and "outstanding" difficulty and responsibility (GS-11, -12, -13, -14, and -15).[19]

If the reform were adopted, each manager would prepare simple position descriptions and assign positions to broad pay bands. Individuals' pay for different levels of work in a pay band would reflect appraisal of individual performance. The proposal is based on six-year experiments in handling civilian employees at two naval research laboratories; though results from some aspects of the experiments are not clear, the changes that concern us "did produce a simpler, less burdensome, and less time-consuming classification process."[20] Broader adoption of such a pay system would enhance the responsibility of managers, while displacing detailed regulations and deemphasizing the role of personnel specialists. A major study concludes that the system is impractical outside laboratories, however, as "performance-appraisal systems tried throughout the federal sector have proven too weak to provide a basis for making financial distinctions among [most] employees."[21] Meantime, federal administration of white-collar positions remains essentially based on the fifteen-grade General Schedule.

Another proposed reform is full decentralization to agencies. A Volcker Commission task force says, "the need for flexibility and adaptability [militates] strongly against continued centralization. . . . The OPM should examine the implications of . . . allowing all classification activity to occur at the agency level."[22] We have seen, however, that even under a centrally controlled process, agencies are tempted to abuse the system.

Staffing

Staffing the civil service involves, in the broadest sense, recruiting, examining, and appointing applicants from outside the government; promoting and transferring persons already in the service; retaining those of ability; dismissing those who do poorly; and releasing from the service those whose jobs are no longer needed or financed and those who reach retirement age.

Recruitment and Appointment

Congress requires that presidentially issued rules applicable to the competitive service "shall provide, as nearly as conditions of good administration warrant, for ... open, competitive examinations for testing applicants for appointment in the competitive service which are practical in character and as far as possible relate to matters that fairly test the relative capacity and fitness of the applicants for the appointment sought.... An individual may be appointed in the competitive service only if he has passed an examination or is specifically excepted from examination."[23]

Over four-fifths of the executive branch's civilian employees are in the competitive service and comparable merit systems.[24] They are there either because of statutory requirement or because of presidential decisions made under a long-standing congressional delegation of authority.

The Process. The Office of Personnel Management conducts about three-fifths of the recruitment and examination activities of the federal government; departments and agencies conduct the rest under delegation of power from OPM.[25] Applicants for white-collar positions who meet minimum qualification requirements for the class or classes of position are given either of two kinds of examination. An *assembled* examination, a written test administered usually at a number of cities throughout the country, is used mostly for lower positions. For higher positions, those at GS-9 and up, an *unassembled* examination is more common. In this case, each candidate submits a relatively comprehensive résumé, on OPM's famous Form SF-171 or its new substitute, describing his or her relevant education, training, and experience, and identifying former employers and some teachers, whose evaluations of the candidate are then solicited. More than half the cities use this method, rather than written tests, for all college graduates.[26]

Those who pass the examination are placed on a register of eligibles for the particular class or group of positions. The federal government uses two kinds of eligible registers, one ranked and the other unranked. A ranked register lists all eligibles in the order of their examination grades, except that the earned grades of veterans who pass the examination are increased by a five- or ten-point bonus.[27] An unranked register, used for most scientific positions and for most positions at GS-9 and above, lists the eligibles without reference to numerical scores or rankings until an agency seeks to fill a specific vacancy.

Now we shift to the agency that wishes to fill a vacant position. It may decide to do so by promoting or transferring a civil servant already in the agency or elsewhere in the government. If, instead, it wishes to consider "outsiders," and has not been delegated examination authority for the position's class, it requests OPM to certify eligibles from the appropriate register. OPM certifies the names of the top three persons qualified for the position (on an already ranked register, these are the top listed persons; on an unranked register, they are the persons—up to three—that OPM selects as best fitting the position's specific requirements). Having received OPM's certification, the agency may choose one of the three candidates as its appointee. Or it can object to OPM that it needs other names because none of the original three candidates fits the particular job requirements or because one or more of them, when asked, indicated nonavailability for the job it if were offered. The latter circumstance often occurs because of the slowness of the government's appointment process or the age of the register; able persons on a register have often accepted other jobs by the time an agency is able to make an offer. Indeed, an outdated register may have so many poorly qualified candidates near the top that the agency not only rejects the certified names but leaves its position vacant, hoping that OPM will eventually hold examinations and develop a new register.

The "rule of three" exists to ensure that agency heads retain opportunity for choice corresponding to their statutory position as the appointment authorities. This would not be the case if OPM could require appointment of the top-ranked candidate, a dubious requirement anyway because distinctions of fractions of a point in examination grades are indefensible (an indefensibility ignored in some local civil service systems with a "rule of one"). But there is no magic in the number 3. One way to expand agency discretion would be to permit choice among the top five or ten persons on an eligible register. This would also recognize further the imperfections of examination methods and reduce delays inherent in agency-OPM paper-pushing. A more striking way would be for an agency to review the whole register and choose, with OPM oversight, the candidate best fitting the position's needs; but this would be incompatible with veterans' preference.

When OPM delegates examination authority to an agency, it circumscribes agency discretion by regulations calling for essentially the same methods that OPM follows in its own operations. Two key differences exist. Agencies are likely to use a rifle-shot technique in recruiting one or more persons of known quality as candidates for professional and scientific positions, rather than the shotgun method commonly used by OPM. In addition, agencies are speedier in moving from applications to examinations to appointments.[28]

The examination and appointment system currently followed is intended both to protect the merit principle and to meet agencies' needs for highly qualified staff members. Pursuit of both objectives is affected by introduction of additional objectives, however. One is favoritism to veterans. Another is affirmative action to increase representation of women and members of minority groups previously discriminated against.

Veterans' Preference.[29] We have already seen that veterans' earned examination grades are augmented by five- or ten-point bonuses. A more significant preference is that accorded veterans with service-connected disabilities. In addition to getting the ten-point bonus, all disabled veterans with passing grades are placed at the head of the eligible register (except for scientific and professional positions at GS-9 and higher). Their names, therefore, must be certified for vacancies before OPM can begin certifying nonveterans with much higher examination ratings.

The system is encumbered with a number of other preferential provisions for veterans. For example, if on the certificate of three names a veteran is listed ahead of a nonveteran, the agency cannot pass over the veteran without stating its reasons and obtaining OPM agreement with the sufficiency of the reasons (the agency's and OPM's actions are closely monitored by veterans' organizations). The federal government employs 680,000 veterans, a third of all its nonpostal employees; an eighth of them are disabled.[30] Although the federal government has only 3 percent of the country's employees, it has 9 percent of the Vietnam-era veterans, including 20 percent of those with disabilities. Because state and local governments also give preference to veterans, they and the federal government together employ a fifth of the Vietnam-era veterans, including a third of those disabled.[31]

Some think that the nation's obligation to assure employment opportunities for those who have fought its wars could be met by granting veterans' preference in governmental appointments during only the first few years after discharge from military service.[32] But veterans' organizations oppose any modification of lifelong preference, and Congress shares their view.

Affirmative Action. Federal statutes protect federal employees (and applicants for employment) against discrimination on grounds of race, color, religion, sex, national origin, age, and physical or mental impairment; some federal statutes apply to state and local governments as well as to the national government.[33] In 1971 the Civil Service Commission announced a policy going beyond "equal employment opportunity." It called for "affirmative action" by agencies; that is, they were to set numerical goals (but not binding quotas) for achievement of fairer representation and to establish schedules for achievement of the goals. Equality of opportunity, standing alone, is regarded as a passive approach to promoting nondiscrimination, one that emphasizes process. Affirmative action, in contrast, focuses on results, with emphasis on positive actions to correct underrepresentation of women and minorities. Here the goal is a "representative bureaucracy," one whose sexual and racial makeup corresponds generally to the makeup of the total population, the labor force, or (as we later see) the pool of applicants taking an examination.

To attain such goals requires preference in appointment for minority, female, disabled, and other categorized applicants over equally qualified white males. That, of course, invites dispute over whether such preference contradicts the merit principle. On the other hand, such preference implies that the conventional definition of "merit" is too narrow and should be broadened; it also takes account of the imperfections of examinations and so casts doubt on the assumption that applicants' relative merit (even narrowly defined) corresponds to their relative examination grades.

In 1978, President Carter observed, "The Civil Service Commission has in the past been lethargic in enforcing fair employment requirements within the federal government,"[34] and he vested enforcement responsibilities in the Equal Employment Opportunity Commission (EEOC). Shortly thereafter, the Civil Service Reform Act gave statutory weight to OPM's and EEOC's requirement that agencies institute affirmative action programs "to eliminate underrepresentation of minorities in the various categories of civil service employment." The act defines underrepresentation in a civil service category as a smaller proportion of a minority than its percentage in the country's labor force.[35] In 1989 a series of Supreme Court decisions, variously involving private and public employers, and often marked by 5 to 4 votes, changed the environment of employment discrimination. The court severely narrowed the grounds on which members of minorities may prove discrimination and the processes by which they may seek remedies. In 1991 Congress passed a bill to restore the scope of civil rights statutes narrowed by the court's interpretations.

The federal government in fact employs proportionately about as many women and more members of minorities than does private industry. About half of federal white-collar employees are women. Over a fourth of federal white-collar employees were members of minority groups, well above their share of the nation's labor force.

Women are disproportionately concentrated in the lower grades of the pay system, as figure 7.6 (page 154) shows. Moreover, as table 7.3 (page 155) indicates, women tend to be poorly represented at upper levels of state governments as well. Several aspects of the civil service system may play a part in this result: recruitment, examination, and appointment; classification; and promotion. In the federal government, one study concludes, the personnel system comes very close to achieving equal employment opportunity at entry. No appreciable differences exist in initial grade of similarly educated entrants of different races or genders. Advancement after entry seems unaffected by race, but women tend to fall behind. Both after entry

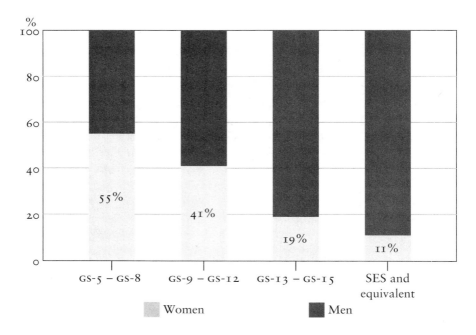

Figure 7.6
WOMEN IN THE FEDERAL WORKFORCE

SOURCE: U.S. Merit Systems Protection Board, *A Question of Equity: Women and the Glass Ceiling in the Federal Government* (Washington, D.C.: Government Printing Office, 1992), 9.

and subsequently, people with only a high school education (as in clerical occupations, predominantly staffed by women) cannot readily move up to professional and administrative positions for which a college education (and, in some cases, postgraduate school) is a relevant preparation.[36]

American governments will need to recruit heavily from such groups in the immediate future. "Non-whites, women, and immigrants will make up more than five-sixths of the net additions to the [nation's] workforce between 1985 and 2000, though they make up only about half of it today."[37]

Examinations. The fate of the Professional and Administrative Career Examination (PACE) so dramatically illustrates the impact of nondiscrimination and affirmative action mandates that it warrants review. Introduced in 1974, PACE was designed to recruit the ablest college graduates (and seniors expecting to graduate) for a third of the entry-level administrative and professional jobs. These fell in over a hundred occupational categories

Table 7.3

WOMEN IN SENIOR STATE GOVERNMENT POSITIONS

State	Percent	State	Percent	State	Percent
Alabama	33.2	Louisiana	38.5	Ohio	37.6
Alaska	30.2	Maine	23.9	Oklahoma	34.1
Arizona	25.2	Maryland	26.1	Oregon	29.5
Arkansas	33.5	Massachusetts	32.3	Pennsylvania	24.3
California	35.6	Michigan	26.2	Rhode Island	21.4
Colorado	27.4	Minnesota	27.1	South Carolina	31.8
Connecticut	29.6	Mississippi	34.4	South Dakota	29.0
Delaware	31.4	Missouri	29.3	Tennessee	31.8
Florida	32.3	Montana	27.9	Texas	29.3
Georgia	32.8	Nebraska	23.6	Utah	17.7
Hawaii	13.9	Nevada	28.8	Vermont	22.8
Idaho	27.1	New Hampshire	36.4	Virginia	29.9
Illinois	28.7	New Jersey	27.3	Washington	27.6
Indiana	35.7	New Mexico	31.1	West Virginia	36.3
Iowa	31.4	New York	35.6	Wisconsin	25.7
Kansas	30.1	North Carolina	33.4	Wyoming	31.3
Kentucky	30.3	North Dakota	27.5		

SOURCE: *New York Times,* 3 January 1992, A8.

ranging from economists, editors, and management analysts to customs in-spectors, bank examiners, and criminal investigators.[38] It turned out, given the large number of applicants (222,000 in 1976) in relation to those pass-ing (51 percent) and those appointed (7 percent of those passing), that test ratings in the high 90s were generally required for job consideration.

The results in the late 1970s appeared to favor white candidates.[39] A group of blacks and Hispanics sued, charging that PACE violated the Civil Rights Act of 1964 and should be discontinued. The expiring Carter admin-istration agreed in early 1981 to a consent decree, under which OPM undertook to phase out PACE within three years and prepare special exami-nations, free of adverse impact on minorities, for occupations previously covered by PACE.

In 1982 the Reagan administration abolished PACE, rather than phase it out gradually. For the rest of the 1980s, the recruitment of college gradu-ates for entry-level positions (GS-5 and GS-7) was chaotic. OPM had by the end of 1987 developed alternative examinations for only 16 of the 127

PACE-type occupations (though these covered about 60 percent of annual entry-level hiring under PACE). For the rest, agencies could, as usual, promote employees from clerical and other ranks below those usually requiring college graduation; this excluded competition from the country at large. As for hiring outsiders, OPM authorized agencies to make temporary appointments or, more significantly, to make entry-level appointments without open, competitive examinations. These are to Schedule B positions, defined as "positions other than those of a confidential or policy-determining character for which it is impractical to hold competitive examinations."[40] Under a 1987 court order holders of non-competitive appointments could be promoted noncompetitively to GS-9 career status. The silver lining in all this cloud was an increase in minority representation.[41]

College seniors and graduates no longer had a single governmentwide examination to apply for, nor a single examining agency to look to for information. Nor could their college advisers offer much help. Every agency did its own recruiting and selection, with its own timetable for filing of applications. Understandably this confused situation, coupled with the absence of career status and, for some years, the perception of a lack of promotional opportunity, was markedly less attractive than the superseded PACE.

Status and Prospects. For over a century, civil service systems of selection have been dogged by the conflicting claims of centralization and decentralization, personnel specialists and program managers, merit principles and the possibility of political and personal favoritism. Emphasis on the first set—centralization, personnelists, and merit—has entailed cumbersome procedures and delays. Emphasis on the second set—decentralization, program managers, and the risk of favoritism—has never gone so far as to deny a role for central personnel agencies in monitoring and enforcing adherence to merit principles. Instead, the central agency retains authority to delegate or not delegate selection responsibility to program agencies, to review those agencies' use of such responsibility (e.g., by sampling the examinations and appointments for conformity with merit standards), and to withdraw delegations from agencies found to persist in a pattern of misuse of the responsibility.

The success of this kind of arrangement depends on the central personnel agency's being, on the one hand, generous in delegating its power and, on the other hand, fully committed to the merit system. These conditions are thwarted if that agency's personnel staff cling to their expertise and disdain program managers' capability, or if that agency's top officials are themselves so political as to wink at program agencies' political and personal favoritism. Both hazards, past experience indicates, are real. Currently, in the federal government the pendulum has swung toward delegation to program agencies, with apparently satisfactory central oversight.[42]

Several special selection strategies have facilitated the entry of talented young persons into the federal government's professional and administrative occupations. Several hundred may enter each year as presidential management interns, drawn mostly from graduate schools of public administration and public affairs. Similarly, the Graduate Cooperative Program brings in subject-matter specialists. And the Cooperative Education Program enables students to serve in government during summer or while on a term's leave from their colleges; successful participants may convert non-competitively to career appointments.[43]

The public service can attract the ablest persons only by being competitive. Its competitiveness is partly a product of pay, promotional opportunities, and other conditions of work in the civil service. But it is also a product of perceptions held by members of the pool of potential recruits. Recruitment of able people (particularly college seniors and recent graduates) has been most successful in periods when the government is perceived as engaged in interesting, innovative, and exciting programs that promise to have high value for society. The New Deal, World War II, the Kennedy administration, and the Johnson administration (with its Great Society programs) were such periods for the federal government. In other periods, particularly in the 1970s and 1980s, successful presidential candidates campaigned against Washington and "the bureaucracy," with predictable effects on the morale of civil servants and on potential recruits' choices among their career options. President Bush was an exception, having expressed in his campaign "a very high regard for the overall competence of career civil servants and for the vital role they have in our democratic form of government." And, as president, he told an assembly of top careerists that he shared their "belief in public service as the highest and noblest calling."[44] President Clinton likewise did not engage in bureaucrat bashing, although his downsizing initiatives made many employees nervous.

The federal government has not been attracting the high quality of persons it needs.[45] In fact, state and local governments have been more successful, as have been nonprofit organizations and private enterprises. The Reagan administration's efforts to abandon a number of domestic programs, its reduction of domestic agencies' staffs, and its incurring of a massive debt requiring deficit reductions by succeeding administrations have discouraged college students who, in other periods, would have seriously considered public service careers. Nor were those considering such careers encouraged by a recruitment system that the OPM director characterized as "intellectually confusing, procedurally nightmarish, inaccessible to students, and very difficult to administer."[46]

In June 1990 that system yielded to a new and promising one, named Administrative Careers with America (ACWA). It comprises six OPM occupational-group examinations designed to achieve the PACE's scope and goals in a non-discriminatory way. From 300,000 to 500,000 persons take the ACWA tests annually for the 10,000 entry-level professional and administrative positions.[47]

Notwithstanding these efforts, the problem of recruiting able managers into government service remains one of the system's top problems. Despite years of experience, the impact of ACWA is not yet clear.[48] Moreover, commission after commission, at both state and federal levels, returns to recruitment as a critical issue. For example, the National Advisory Council on the Public Service found that

> the Federal government now has a confused and incomplete patchwork of recruiting programs. Potential applicants for Federal employment are discouraged by a perplexing and overly complicated process.... Too often, there is no link between the recruiting initiatives and the hiring process, especially for those people taking the Administrative Careers with America (ACWA) exam or those attending job fairs, and college recruiting events.[49]

A study conducted by Carolyn Ban and Norma Riccucci for the Winter Commission on the state and local public service likewise found that "probably the most important thing that state and local governments can do to improve the efficiency of their workforce is to improve the quality of the people they hire."[50]

Promotion

Those already holding career positions advance principally by promotion and transfer. Each year, there are almost twice as many promotions as initial recruitments to the civil service. Here the operating agencies have great discretion, subject to the promoted or transferred employee's having the *minimum* educational and experience qualifications for the higher position. The employee need not be put in competition with possibly superior talent outside the government, nor need the in-government area of competition embrace all those employees in the government, department, or bureau who might be qualified for the position. In these circumstances, an employee's ability to break out of a dead-end organization unit lacking promotional opportunities or to move from an uncongenial setting depends largely on his or her own initiative in "shopping around" to find a unit or agency to which he or she can be transferred and promoted.

The promotional system's rationality rests on four premises:

1. The initial recruitment of able candidates for entry to the public service is enhanced by prospects of long, possibly lifetime, careers with advancement by promotion. A mostly closed promotional system, without much lateral entry at higher levels by "outsiders," improves those prospects.

2. Important on-the-job characteristics, such as ability to meet and deal with others, cannot be accurately judged by initial or subsequent formal examinations. They can be accurately judged by an employee's supervisor and an agency promotional board.

3. Agency officials need to be accorded much discretion in choosing supervisory personnel and in rewarding demonstrated competence because effective supervision and the morale stemming from rewards for superior performance count so much toward program achievement—a responsibility of the agency.

4. Promotion from within builds staff morale because of its chain-reaction effect: each promotion creates a vacancy and so may set off a series of promotions.

These premises do not dispose of the concern we have encountered before—that OPM regulations trap managers in cumbersome, time-consuming procedures ill designed to assure choice of candidates who will do the best job, and, on the other hand, that the flexibility provided permits unfair and arbitrary actions tainted by favoritism. Another concern is that a largely closed promotional system will lead to bureaucratic ossification. In truly closed systems, such as those for officers of the armed services and the Foreign Service, this danger is countered by a severe "up-or-out" stage. At a certain level, officers either win promotion to a higher (and smaller) category of positions or they are "selected out" and must seek other careers. In the federal civil service such ossification as may occur is not by promotion; instead, it results when unpromoted persons stay in their current positions as long as the positions remain and their service is merely satisfactory. At the highest levels (especially in the Senior Executive Service), the infusion of new blood by outside recruitment may prevent ossification.

Separation

Separations (termination of appointments) of federal civilian employees number about 650,000 each year, but the figure reflects a massive flow of temporary, seasonal, part-time, and intermittent workers in and out of government positions. The average length of service of full-time, permanent, nonpostal employees is about thirteen years.[51] Federal rates of turnover for white-collar employees are lower than those in the private sector, but the difference shrinks when appropriate technical adjustments are made, and it virtually disappears when the peculiarities of the pre-1987 federal retirement system are taken into account.[52] Turnover can have positive or negative effects, depending on whether able or poor employees depart and on how much it costs to recruit and train new employees.

The persistent problem in discharging employees for cause has been not the removal of those who are obviously inefficient but the removal of the mediocre. In either case, a supervisor wishing to remove a subordinate must build a case carefully, whether for review within the agency or for ultimate review by the Merit Systems Protection Board if the subordinate should carry an appeal there. Even to remove a patently incompetent employee, a supervisor must assemble evidence on such matters as absenteeism and tardiness. It has been much more difficult to prove a case for removal of a faithful worker whose performance is *qualitatively* inferior to what the job requires.

The Civil Service Reform Act has eased the process of removal. Each agency is required to have a performance appraisal system that specifies the performance standards and critical elements of each employee's position. After due notice, opportunity for improvement, and opportunity for response to the charges, an agency may remove (or demote) an employee for "unacceptable performance," citing specific failures to meet the standards for critical elements of the position. If an employee appeals to the Merit Systems Protection Board, the agency's action will be upheld if it is supported by "substantial evidence."[53]

A supervisor is often reluctant to bring charges looking toward removal because if overruled in agency proceedings, he or she is then saddled with the human relations problem of a resentful and disgruntled employee whose "victory" over the supervisor may make the worker even less responsive to direction.[54] We should not be surprised that many a supervisor chooses a different strategy: encouraging the inferior employee to seek transfer to another organization unit or agency and making a favorable recommendation to anyone inquiring about the employee's qualifications for another job.

"Involuntary discharges" mostly result from "reductions in force" (RIF, or "riffing") that an agency must effect because its budget has been cut, its personnel ceilings reduced, some programs terminated or reorganized, or its existence in process of termination. Elaborate government-wide regulations govern an agency's selection of the employees to be retained or discharged.[55] Each permanent career employee in a subdivision is put in subgroup A (veterans) or B (nonveterans). Within each subgroup, employees are ranked by length of federal service (the latter enhanced by twelve to twenty years' credit for recent "fully successful" to "outstanding" performance ratings). Retention rights follow these classifications. As a result, an outstanding nonveteran with many years of service must be released ahead of a merely satisfactory veteran with three years of service. And female and minority employees recently recruited to higher-level positions, long underpopulated by members of their groups, may lose out to white males with greater length of service.

A RIF can be devastating to an agency's staff-deployment pattern and to employees' morale. Employees riffed at one grade level have the right to "bump" employees in positions at one to three grades lower; the latter in turn endure a RIF that identifies which of them must yield place to the demoted employee. Though the "bumpers" move into positions below their capabilities, they retain their earlier grades for two years and their pay for a longer period.[56] Until 1986, bumping could occur over an indefinite number of grade levels. In OPM's own RIF of 1982, the result of a 16 percent cut in its salaries-and-expenses appropriation, two GS-14 employees (a social science analyst and a personnel research psychologist) were downgraded eleven levels to GS-3 clerks. OPM's experience also reveals the wide impact of a RIF. Though only 135 full-time permanent employees were separated, over 500 others were directly affected (by downgrading, reassignment, transfer to other agencies, retirement, etc.).[57] This kind of disruption is now greatly reduced by the limit of downgrading to three GS levels.

The retirement system long reduced opportunities for federal employees to leave the government. Civil servants were not under social security and suffered penalties for early retirement. They had an incentive to stay in the federal service with its relatively generous retirement provisions tied closely to length of service and highest recent pay. On the other hand, the failure of civil service salaries to reflect cost-of-living increases in inflationary periods made early retirement attractive, as pensions automatically increased with rises in the cost of living. (A 1969 $10,000 salary increased to $28,000 in 1988, while a $10,000 pension increased to $38,000). Reform occurred in the 1980s.[58] Federal civil servants (all those hired in or after 1984, and others at their option) were brought under social security and a supplementary civil service pension plan. The "portability" of social security entitlements, plus withdrawable, tax-deferred employee savings that the government matches up to 5 percent of salary, promise to increase the ease of employees' mid-career departure for the private sector. This could eventually result in a major exodus of able civil servants, given the significant differential, especially at higher-level posts, between federal and private salary scales and some fringe benefits (especially health insurance features).[59] Should the pay and benefits contrast be remedied, of course, the departures of some civil servants would open opportunities for new blood to come into the system.

The Clinton administration took a very different approach to both RIFs and retirement in its "reinventing government" initiative. Although part of the movement was devoted to improving government performance, a dominant theme was shrinking the size of the federal government's workforce and hence reducing the size of the government. In 1993 the Clinton administration first proposed shrinking the federal workforce by 252,000; Congress later increased the total to 272,900. The reductions, which the administration said would come mostly from middle management, financed the administration's 1994 crime bill. Rather than rely on RIFs (which administration officials feared would be too disruptive) or attrition (which would not produce large enough reductions), the administration instead offered cash incentives to employees who agreed to leave government employment. The strategy risked encouraging the government's most seasoned employees, not the "checkers of checkers" targeted by the administration, to leave first. The General Accounting Office, in fact, found that although the workforce reduction had not yet harmed most departments, several agencies complained that the reductions hurt their ability to accomplish their missions. In one agency, officials said that "the buyout has 'gutted' corporate memory.... The number of key managers who left has resulted in a deleterious domino effect. Depth and coverage in certain offices has been negatively impacted."[60] The appetite of officials at all levels for further shrinking the size of government led to hosts of different strategies to downsize government employment.[61]

Pay

The government's capacity to attract and keep able people depends heavily on the salaries (and fringe benefits) it offers. Pay, to be sure, is not the only factor that people consider in seeking, accepting, or staying in a particular organization.[62] The challenge of the work, the breadth of impact one's work can have, the agreeableness of the specific setting (including physical facilities, supervisor's behavior, and stimulus and cooperativeness of one's peers), and promotional prospects all enter the scales.[63] It remains the case that government competes in the labor market for competent people. The compensation it offers significantly influences their choices of employers.

Statutes provide that federal white-collar pay rates shall be comparable with private-enterprise pay rates for the same levels of work and that the president shall annually adjust salaries to achieve comparability. Each year, the Bureau of Labor Statistics conducts a comparability survey of private firms in the professional, administrative, technical, and clerical fields. A pay agent designated by the president calculates the adjustment that would achieve comparability between government and private-sector pay rates and reports this to the president.[64] As he is supposed to observe the principle of comparability, that report might be expected to be the basis of his decision. In fact, the expectation is defeated by an escape clause in the statute.[65]

The president may submit an alternative pay-adjustment plan "if, because of national emergency or economic conditions affecting the general welfare," he deems it inappropriate to make the comparability adjustment. Presidents have so consistently used this escape clause that white-collar employees in every year since 1978 have been denied the increases reported to the president as needed to achieve comparability with pay levels in the private sector. The annual shortfalls cumulate to a need to raise federal pay nearly 30 percent.[66]

The private-sector comparability survey's coverage and techniques have continually been revised, and their soundness on a nationwide basis appears established.[67] Other studies confirm the fact of substantial pay discrepancy. One such shows that from 1981 through 1986 the increase in federal white-collar pay was 17 percent. This was less than half the rise in private salaries and wages and in those of state and local governments, and barely half the rise in military pay.[68]

Is comparability a sound goal? A former associate director of OPM (a political appointee) thinks not. He writes, "In fact, the federal government is able to hire the caliber of people it needs at current wage levels and could do so at even lower pay scales. It should be content to hire competent people, not the best and most talented people." The federal government, he argues, does not "need laboratories full of Nobel laureates, legal offices full of the top graduates of the best schools, administrative offices staffed with MBAs from Wharton, or policy shops full of the brightest whatevers." Indeed, "the brightest and most talented people should work in the private sector."[69]

Few would agree that the government's responsibilities for foreign affairs, defense, and economic and social conditions can be well administered by those left over after private employers have taken their pick. In fact, a survey of the government managers by the General Accounting Office found that "low federal pay was the factor respondents most frequently cited as a reason for employees to leave the federal government and for applicants to decline a federal job offer."[70] But there remains a doubt that the government is appropriately addressing the comparability issue.

Matching Pay Rates to Labor Markets

Two features of the approach to pay comparability conflict with the realities of the labor market. One is the reliance on national averages of private-sector pay, which ignores regional and local pay differences that reflect supply-demand variations and different costs of living. For example, government secretaries in San Francisco get about $5,000 less than private-sector secretaries, while those in Buffalo get $1,000 more than those privately employed; for computer systems analysts in Boston private pay is $8,400 more than federal pay but in Baltimore $3,000 less. The other feature is the commitment to pay equity ("equal pay for equal work") within the federal service, which calls for similar pay for employees at the same GS grade level of their varied occupations; this ignores the fact that, largely because of supply and demand differences among the country's occupations, members of some command higher salaries in the private sector than members of others. Federal pay is about 10 percent less than private pay for secretaries, but about 40, 60, and 65 percent less for, respectively, engineers, accountants, and attorneys.[71]

The Volcker Commission concluded that "the current goal of national pay comparability is unworkable." It recommended "a pay-setting system that recognizes the fact that public employees live and work in localities characterized by widely different living costs and labor market pressures, and adjusts compensation upward accordingly." It also urged "special pay rates for occupations where there are shortages or strong competitive pressure from the private sector."[72]

Comparable Worth

Key statutory principles guiding the General Schedule and related pay systems (in addition to comparability with the private sector) are that there be equal pay for jobs of comparable value and that pay distinctions be related to work and performance distinctions. Representatives of women argue that these principles are violated and, further, that sex-based discrimination blocks their rise to the higher-paying positions. They charge that the classification system has downgraded predominantly female-staffed job categories (e.g., secretaries and nurses) that are equivalent in duties, responsibilities, and qualifications to job categories usually held by men and more highly paid. They seek reform based on jobs' *comparable worth*. Many state governments have conducted comparable worth or pay equity studies, most of which found that sex-based wage differences and sex-based occupational segregation existed in their civil services. Some state and local governments have taken remedial action.[73]

Pay within a Grade

Within-grade increases for civil servants performing at a fully satisfactory level are usually based on longevity. Each GS grade has a range of pay, permitting pay increases over time, without change of position (see table 7.2, page 147). Each of grades GS-1 to GS-15 has ten "steps," and employees at lower steps normally advance one step a year and those in higher steps advance one step each two or three years until they reach the grade's pay ceiling; it takes eighteen years to get from step 1 to step 10.[74]

The Civil Service Reform Act introduced a merit-pay system for the over 100,000 supervisors and managers (but not others) in grades GS-13–GS-15.[75] The Performance Management and Recognition System (a revision of the original system) distinguishes among employees rated at five performance levels: Level 3 is "fully successful," levels 1 ("unacceptable") and 2 are lower, and 4 and 5 higher.[76] Those at the top three (fully successful or higher) get full benefit of the annual General Schedule comparability pay increase; those lower get half or none of that increase. The higher (but not the lower) group also gets a full or partial within-grade step increase.[77] An employee at the highest rating level must additionally receive a "performance award" of 2 to 10 percent (and, exceptionally, 20 percent) of his or her annual basic pay rate. Those rated at level 2 or 3 are granted performance awards at the discretion of the agency (which in practice rarely smiles on level 3, "fully successful" employees). Agencies are authorized to spend on performance awards up to 1.5 percent of GS-13 to GS-15 supervisors' and managers' aggregate salaries. Finally, for unique, highly exceptional, and unusually outstanding contributions beyond normal job responsibilities and standards, cash awards of $10,000 to $25,000 can be made.

The system's operation is far from ideal. Only 45 percent of those in the system think that better performance will result in better pay; 39 percent think this somewhat or very unlikely. And, as the system is meant to stimulate better administration, it is surprising that half the employees, half of those with ratings above fully successful, and over half of employees' supervisors believe that performance awards do not motivate better performance.

The system rests on the substantial accuracy of performance ratings, which are used throughout the civil service.[78] These, though, tend to be generous. Over two-thirds of GS-13 to GS-15 managers and supervisors were rated at the two top levels (outstanding or exceeding fully successful); three departments improbably had 89 percent at those levels. Though a measurement of the accuracy of performance ratings is unavailable, our experience with an earlier federal system indicates strong incentives to be compassionate. For careful assessments, a supervisor usually gets no reward, while he may well depress the morale of his subordinates (this is especially true if other supervisors are assigning high ratings). A succession of efforts over many decades to assure objectivity of ratings has failed to counter the incentives for generosity.[79] If nearly all managers and supervisors are "more than fully successful," rewards cannot be selective nor can they be financed.

Employee Rights and Obligations

The norm of equity calls for similar treatment of persons in substantially similar situations and for exclusion of irrelevant personal characteristics in the reaching of judgments about individuals. The norm pervades the elements of the civil service system that we have so far discussed. It is encapsulated in brief phrases: open, competitive examinations; the merit principle; equal pay for equal work within the government; comparability of civil servants' pay with private enterprise's pay rates for the same levels of work; nondiscrimination by political party, race, national origin, religion, sex, age, or physical disability.

Equity between public and private employees has dimensions that extend well beyond pay-rate comparability. Public employees should not be burdened with constraints on their public and private behavior as citizens and human beings beyond those borne by private employees *unless* such discriminatory constraints are required by the special nature of government itself. Here our concerns are the rights of government employees to organize and bargain collectively through labor unions, their rights to privacy, and their rights to engage actively in politics.

Unionization and Collective Bargaining

American governments must reckon with a major rise in unionization of public employees and the increased use of collective bargaining to determine conditions of employment.[80] While union membership fell from 23 to 18 percent of the country's total employees between 1980 and 1993, it accounts for 44 percent of government workers. Astonishingly, 38 percent of all union members work for governments.[81] These data reflect a successful effort by unions and workers in the 1960s and early 1970s to expand unionization in the public sector; since then, the situation has stabilized. "Unions" here include various professional associations, such as the National Education Association, that have switched from "passive professionalism" to collective bargaining and other practices indistinguishable from those of labor unions. Most postal workers and firefighters are organized, as are over two-thirds of public schoolteachers and two-fifths of police officers.[82] Among federal workers, 60 percent (not counting the Postal Service) are represented by unions for collective negotiation purposes; the percentage has been constant since 1977.[83]

The issues posed by unionization of public employees run deep. For over fifty years, federal statutes have assured that employees in the private sector can organize, join unions, and bargain collectively through their unions about pay, fringe benefits, promotion, hours of work, and working conditions. And the right to bargain collectively is effective only if unions have "the ultimate weapon" of the right to strike. The private-sector model is what unions seek to apply fully in the public sector. This effort is resisted by those who insist that government is different.

The Strike. Let us consider how government may be different. First, the right of government employees to strike against "the sovereign state" is not conceded by the federal government or by most state governments (whose statutes apply to local as well as state governments). Where a right to strike exists, it is legislatively, not constitutionally, conferred. Thus it may be withheld and, once conferred, may be revoked.

Denying public employees the right to strike finds its strongest rationale in the intolerable consequences of a complete cessation of police and fire protection in a community, or the grinding to a halt of the State, Treasury, or Defense Department. Almost as strong a case can be made against stoppage of the mail, abandonment of air-traffic control, closing of the schools, and refusal to collect garbage. But the rationale gets attenuated when extended to less vital and less monopolistic governmental services. A strike of public library cataloguers or of a government laboratory's assistants is not more to be feared than a strike of private telephone workers, truckers, airplane pilots, or steelworkers. Yet no simple rule can sharply distinguish among the occupations of public employees in terms of the tolerability of strikes. A strike by only 2,500 cleaners and handymen forced New York City's 960 public schools to hold only half-day sessions for their more than 1 million pupils and deprived half a million of them, mostly from poor families, of free hot lunches.[84]

Theory may not matter. Public employees do strike. Government officials usually decide that resort to the courts for aid is the least promising method of getting employees back to work and public services restored. Firing the strikers, as Reagan did the 11,000 air-traffic controllers in 1981, leads to a long process, over many years for the Federal Aviation Administration, of recruiting and training a new staff; meantime, a public function is poorly performed. Denial of the right to strike does not preclude employees' resorting to equally effective job actions that tie public administration in knots. A "sick-in" by schoolteachers can shut down the schools while the teachers continue to receive sick-leave pay. "Working to rule" (strictly adhering to prescribed procedures), when practiced by air-traffic controllers, can delay all landings and takeoffs at airports under the guise of literal enforcement of safety regulations. A "slowdown" by postal clerks can build up mountains of unsorted and undelivered mail.

Who Are the Bargainers? The second difference is in the way government is organized for decision making on conditions of employment. A number of issues are legislatively, not administratively, determined. Congress, state legislatures, and city councils prescribe the classification, appointment, and salary systems; vote appropriations; and have the last word on general pay increases.

This has two consequences. One is that no executive official can individually bargain away the legislatively fixed elements of the personnel system or commit the legislative body to make specific changes in existing pay rates. All the official can pledge the union is his or her best effort to persuade the legislative body to confirm the negotiated contract. The other consequence of the legislature's role is that organizations of public employees can lobby as do other interest groups. This has no counterpart in the private sector. Unions can lobby to get legislative approval of any agreement reached between them and the negotiator for the executive branch. But the political clout of unions goes much further: they may win in the legislative halls what they failed to win in the negotiations. The president of the largest federal union says, "We've got no choice except to try to put pressure on enough congressmen and senators to see things our way. That's our bargaining table."[85] Faced with this prospect, the executive negotiator may give in too readily to union demands. Union members and their families have substantial voting strength in many legislators' districts and wards; in local governments they may determine mayoralty elections. The head of New York City's largest union said, "There's no question about it—we have the ability to elect our own boss." He estimated that the 250,000 municipal employees living in the city accounted, with their relatives, for over 500,000 votes, a large share of the 900,000 voters in a Democratic primary and of the 1.7 million voters in a general election.[86]

The unions' voting strength, lobbying skill, and collective bargaining tactics reinforce one another. In addition, the public is often so angered by the loss of police, trash collection, or school services during a strike or slowdown that it puts pressure on government officials for a speedy settlement of the dispute. Public employee unions, of course, do not get all that they ask for. Bargainers for government know that citizens dislike settlements that substantially raise taxes or that pay public employees more than others in the community doing comparable work. For the most part, but less consistently, governmental bargainers try to protect the merit principle and civil service system and to avoid bargaining away government's right to determine public policies and to improve administrative performance.

Some governments, at all levels of the federal system, are moving away from traditionally confrontational labor-management relations to partnerships. The Clinton administration, for example, launched a "National Partnership Council" to bring union leaders into direct negotiations with top officials. In the process, however, the administration did not offer the same arrangement to organizations representing management officials, and many of them felt disenfranchised by the effort. The experience taught two important lessons. First, the civil service system and the supervisory arrangements it creates are one thing; labor-management relations often are quite different. At state and local as well as federal levels, the result frequently is a dual personnel system.[87] Second, despite the frequently large gap between top officials and front-line managers, management and labor, and supervisors and subordinates, many managers were coming to recognize the need for fresh alliances. One private executive's conclusion speaks loudly to the public sector as well: "We have lots of team efforts with union involvement. The biggest lesson we have learned is that we are all in the same boat and we need to work together."[88]

Collective Bargaining and the Civil Service System. Collective bargaining variously supports and challenges the merit principle, and it reinforces some of the least admired features of the civil service system. Unions rarely attempt to change the system of initial recruitment and appointment by merit. Because their members already hold civil service jobs, the unions concentrate on protecting civil servants' interests rather than on advancing the interests of those seeking government employment. Similarly, unions support the civil service system against patronage because patronage undermines job security, which unions value highly.

A major thrust of union policy is the limitation of management discretion in dealing with employees. Often the unions advocate seniority as the automatic criterion for determining who gets promoted, who gets the more desirable geographic locations or work shifts, and who gets retained when layoffs are necessary.[89] The seniority criterion not only departs from competition on the basis of merit but it also discriminates against members of racial minorities, women (in previously male-dominated occupations), and young employees; these usually have less seniority than most older white males.

"Papering" the civil service with lengthy, detailed bargaining agreements and operating the elaborate machinery they call for add more red tape and rigidity to a system already encumbered with these attributes. Program managers' frustrations intensify.

Both at the bargaining and contract implementation stages, the Civil Service Commission or personnel office is shunted aside or becomes only one member of the government labor-relations team. And because unions regard a Civil Service Commission or personnel office as an agent of management, the contract often provides for a grievance procedure that competes with the commission's customary appellate role. At present, then, the traditional civil service system and the new collective bargaining system operate uncomfortably side by side.

Scope of Issues. Finally, government differs from private enterprise in the scope of issues on which employees and their unions want to, or are able to, bargain. The line between employees' own conditions of work and the government's policies and programs seems a clear one—the former being the stuff of collective bargaining, the latter the responsibility of legislative bodies and political executives. But public employee unions have blurred the line. If a union blocks a mayor's effort to staff police patrol cars with one officer when the past pattern has mandated two, or if it prevents the reduction of the number of firefighters on a fire truck, that may simply parallel all unions' concern over workers' safety and the loss of jobs. But what if the mayor wants to shift firefighting companies at nighttime from the depopulated business districts to the most populous and fire-prone areas of the city? Should the size of school classes or the content of school programs be determined by government-union bargaining? Should the size of payments to welfare clients, or the location of welfare centers, be so determined? All these issues have in fact been the subject of negotiation and strikes.[90]

To this point we have tried to identify the ways in which some believe government to be so different from private enterprise as to make inappropriate the private-sector model of labor relations. These include (1) the effects of strikes on essential public services; (2) the ambiguity over who can effectively represent the government as "management" in the bargaining process, especially given the legislature's role and unions' political strength; (3) the need to protect the merit principle and to avoid entangling program administrators in a web of restrictions additional to those of the civil service system; and (4) doubts that in a democracy important issues of public policy and program administration should be settled through union-management bargaining rather than through processes that take account of all affected interests.

Collective Bargaining in the Federal Government. Since 1912, federal government employees have been free to join unions and other organizations that do not assert the right to strike. But only since 1962 has the government been committed to engage in collective bargaining. Its commitment was expressed in presidential executive orders until 1978, when the Civil Service Reform Act provided the firmer foundation of a statute.[91] The act broadly follows the private-sector model of the National Labor Relations Act and establishes an independent Federal Labor Relations Authority (FLRA) to administer the system.

Bargaining occurs within individual agencies for "units" the FLRA deems appropriate.[92] An agency accords exclusive recognition to a labor organization that wins a majority of employees' votes in a designated unit. That organization is then entitled to negotiate agreements covering all employees in the unit, whether union members or not. Overall, less than a third of the represented employees are dues-paying union members.[93]

In the federal government the scope of negotiable issues is restricted. Bargaining cannot concern matters that are the subject of any law or governmentwide rule or regulation, or any agency rule or regulation for which "a compelling need" exists (the FLRA settles disputes over compelling need). Further, the act preserves the authority of agency management officials "to determine the mission, budget, organization, number of employees, and internal security practices" of the agency; to hire, assign, lay off, and retain employees; to remove or otherwise discipline employees; and to assign work and determine the personnel by which agency operations shall be conducted. The *procedures* for exercise of such authority are negotiable, however, as are grievance procedures for adversely affected employees.[94] And, curiously, an agency may *choose* to bargain about "the numbers, types, and grades of employees or positions assigned to any organizational subdivision, work project, or tour of duty, or on the technology, methods, and means of performing work."

What, given the statutory restrictions, do agencies and unions bargain about? So far, mostly about the assignment and scheduling of work (overtime, work-week definition, temporary assignments, shift hours, work breaks, meal periods), grievance and other procedures, safety, employee counseling, technological displacement, and the color of wall paint. In comparison to the private sector and to state and local governments, the federal bargaining table is a meager one. There are many highly significant issues relating to pay, job security, promotions, and fringe benefits that are accepted as negotiable in the private sector but that are precluded from the federal bargaining table. On many issues federal statutes accord unions the right to be consulted. But consultation is not bargaining.

The Right to Privacy

The rise of drug abuse and of AIDS (acquired immune deficiency syndrome) in the 1980s provoked new confrontations between government and its employees. In 1986 President Reagan signed an Executive Order requiring federal employees to refrain from the use of illegal drugs and declaring persons who use illegal drugs unsuitable for federal employment.[95] He authorized each agency to test any applicant for his or her illegal drug use and, most important, directed it to "establish a program to test for the use of illegal drugs by employees in sensitive positions." Such positions include more than the term suggests. Included are employees in positions designated sensitive by their agency, employees with access to classified information, presidential appointees, law enforcement officers, and employees in "other positions that the agency head determines involve law enforcement, national security, the protection of life and property, public health or safety, or other functions requiring a high degree of trust and confidence." The result is that over a million employees are covered. Included by agencies as in sensitive positions are clerical assistants, mail and file clerks, auditors, cartographers, and operators of printing presses. Local governments have also instituted mandatory urinalysis for police, firefighters, schoolteachers, and other employees.

Mandatory testing of urine for evidence of illegal drug use, if inclusive or random (without, therefore, reasonable grounds for suspicion of the individual employee), is opposed by employee unions and others as an invasion of privacy and so a violation of the Fourth Amendment's protection against unreasonable searches and seizures. In 1989, by a 5 to 4 vote, the Supreme Court, while agreeing on the applicability of the Fourth Amendment, held that the U.S. Customs Service's inclusive drug testing of newly hired and transferred employees whose duties included direct interception of drugs or carrying of firearms was reasonable.[96] But, though granting the government's "compelling interest in protecting truly sensitive information," the Court deferred ruling on reasonableness of testing those handling classified information, pending a lower court's inquiry into why baggage handlers, messengers, lawyers, and accountants were included.

AIDS testing also presents the issue of privacy. The blood test identifies persons who have AIDS antibodies, but that does not mean that they have AIDS or will get it.[97] The danger of their infecting others is limited to sexual relations and intermixture of blood (as when drug users inject with needles used by others). The Foreign Service began in 1987 to test Foreign Service applicants, officers, and their dependents for the AIDS virus. Applicants testing positive for AIDS antibodies are rejected for the Foreign Service. Persons in the service and their dependents are restricted in service abroad, the concerns being both adequacy of medical facilities at some foreign posts and foreign governments' attitudes toward receiving official representatives who have or may develop AIDS.[98]

Political Activity

The right of public employees to engage in political activities resembles and intertwines with the right of such employees to join unions, bargain collectively, and strike. The word *right* gives the first clue. In both the political and labor spheres, a simple question is put: Why shouldn't citizens who are government employees enjoy the same rights as citizens who are private employees? And in both spheres the claim is made not only that they should but that, on constitutional grounds, they must. Otherwise, the argument goes, government employees are denied their First Amendment rights to freedom of speech, press, assembly, and petition. On the other side, too, the argument is consistent for both spheres: government is different; its operations would be severely compromised by strikes (and perhaps by the collective bargaining style of decision making) and by civil servants' involvement in partisan political activity.

A second factor is public employees' rising proportion of the electorate. If the 18 million public employees all voted, as they have a right to do, they would be a sixth of the voters for president and a fifth of the voters for representatives in off-year elections; this takes no account of the employees' family members. Here, too, is a body of potential precinct workers, party officers, convention delegates, and candidates for elective office. If the restrictions on such participation were removed, political parties and candidates' campaigns attracting such employees' preponderant support would receive a new infusion of strength.

The third factor closes the circle. Large-scale unionization of government employees has been a counterpoint to the decline of private-sector unionization. The union movement is eager to capitalize on its newfound source of strength by enlisting public employees in political activities directed to the movement's traditional strategy of "rewarding our friends and punishing our enemies." Not surprisingly, government unions' officers are leading advocates of bills "to restore to Federal civilian and Postal Service employees their rights to participate voluntarily, as private citizens, in the political processes of the Nation."[99]

In sum, the principled and constitutional argument that government employees should have the same civic and associational rights as other citizens, the expanded political weight of public employees in the electorate, and the scale of unionization in the public sector are all links in the chain that ties the labor movement's interests to the liberation of government employees from restrictions on their political participation.

The Hatch Act. In 1939 Congress adopted "An Act to Prevent Pernicious Political Activities," usually called the Hatch Act, after its sponsor, Senator Carl Hatch of New Mexico. The key provision applicable to federal employees reads:

> No officer or employee in the executive branch of the Federal Government, or any agency or department thereof, shall take part in political management or political campaigns. All such persons shall retain the right to vote as they may choose and to express their opinions on all political subjects.[100]

The act's restrictions extend to virtually all non-policymaking officers and employees, whether in the merit system or not.[101]

From 1940 to 1974, the Hatch Act's ban on political activity extended to state and local appointive officers and employees engaged primarily in an activity wholly or partly financed by federal loans or grants. In 1974, Congress shrank the ban to cover only candidacy for office in a partisan election and use of official authority or influence to affect others' voting or political contributions.

Constitutionality. The courts reject the claim that public employees have a constitutional right to participate actively in political management and political campaigns. In 1947 the Supreme Court upheld the Hatch Act by a 4 to 3 vote.[102] In 1973 the Court again upheld the act, this time by a 6 to 3 vote.[103] It concluded that the Hatch Act was not unconstitutionally vague and overbroad in describing what was banned[104] nor was it unconstitutional under the First Amendment. The majority opinion, supporting the government's restriction of its employees' political activities, rests largely on policy considerations. The portions of it that follow provide us with a review of the grounds for such a restriction.

> The judgment of history, a judgment made by this country over the last century [is] that it is in the best interest of the country, indeed essential, that federal service should depend upon meritorious performance rather

than political service, and that the political influence of federal employees on others and on the electoral process should be limited. . . .

It seems fundamental in the first place that employees in the Executive Branch . . . should administer the law in accordance with the will of Congress, rather than in accordance with their own or the will of a political party. They are expected to enforce the law and execute the programs of the Government without bias or favoritism for or against any political party or group or the members thereof. A major thesis of the Hatch Act is that to serve this great end of Government—the impartial execution of the laws—it is essential that federal employees not, for example, take formal positions in party politics, not undertake to play substantial roles in partisan political campaigns and not run for office on partisan political tickets. Forbidding activities like these will reduce the hazards to fair and effective government . . . .

Another major concern . . . was perhaps the immediate occasion for enactment of the Hatch Act in 1939 . . . the conviction that the rapidly expanding Government work force should not be employed to build a powerful, invincible and perhaps corrupt political machine.

A related concern . . . was to further serve the goal that employment and advancement in the Government service not depend on political performance and at the same time to make sure that Government employees would be free from pressure and from express or tacit invitation to vote in a certain way or perform political chores in order to curry favor with their superiors rather than to act out their own beliefs. . . .

Neither the right to associate nor the right to participate in political activities is absolute in any event. . . . Nor are the management, financing and conduct of political campaigns wholly free from government regulation. We agree . . . that plainly identifiable acts of political management and political campaigning may constitutionally be prohibited on the part of federal employees.

Hatch Act Revision. To say that the Hatch Act is constitutional is not to say that Congress must continue its strictures on political activity. In 1976 and 1990 Congress did pass bills to remove the ban on federal employees' active participation in partisan political management and political campaigns. Presidents Ford and Bush vetoed the bills on grounds that they would politicize the civil service, and Congress failed to override the vetoes.[105]

Had the 1990 bill become law, employees could have held office in national, state, and local political organizations, and, in their off-duty hours, could have publicly endorsed candidates, distributed campaign literature, organized phone banks and political meetings, and solicited co-workers to donate money to a political action committee representing interests of federal employees (most likely union-affiliated). Still prohibited would have been running for partisan political office and engaging in political activities while on duty in a government office building, wearing an official uniform, or driving a government vehicle. And employees could not have encouraged or discouraged political activity by any person who had pending at their agency an application for a grant, contract, or license. Still prohibited would be the use of official authority (such as promising or threatening appointment, promotion, or salary actions) to coerce or influence an employee's vote, political contribution, or participation in political activity; opponents of the bill feared that this prohibition would not prevent post-election discriminatory treatment of those who did and those who did not work for the superior official's party. Public employee unions lobbied strongly for the bill, which failed to become law over the presidential veto by only two votes in the Senate.

Congress returned to reforming the Hatch Act in 1993 and this time passed major changes. Most federal employees (notable exceptions are members of the Senior Executive Service, law enforcement officials such as members of the Secret Service and the FBI, and officials in the CIA) were permitted to take an active part in political campaigns, from making telephone calls on behalf of candidates to distributing campaign literature. They were allowed to run for office within political parties and solicit campaign contributions. The law continued to prohibit them from running for elective political office, soliciting campaign contributions from the public, openly displaying partisanship while on the job (e.g., wearing campaign buttons), or considering political recommendations in hiring or promoting employees. John Sturdivant, head of a major federal employee union, happily proclaimed the change and said, "Now federal employees can be full citizens."[106]

Patronage Restrictions. Three Supreme Court decisions have directly tested the constitutionality of party membership or support as a requirement for retention of government employment (in two cases) or for appointment, promotion, or transfer (in another case). In *Elrod* v. *Burns* (1976),[107] Elrod, a Democrat, succeeded the Republican sheriff of Cook County, Illinois (Chicago's county), and proceeded, as was the custom, to dismiss Burns and other non-civil-service employees (save those who joined the new sheriff's party or obtained sponsorship from a leader of that party). The Court's plurality opinion condemned patronage dismissals of non-civil-service employees in non-policymaking positions as violative of First Amendment rights of freedom of belief and association (which are protected against both the federal government and, through the Fourteenth Amendment, state and local governments). A concurring opinion answered no to the question "whether a non-policymaking, nonconfidential government employee can be discharged from a job that he is satisfactorily performing upon the sole ground of his political beliefs."

In *Branti* v. *Finkel* (1980),[108] Branti, a Democrat, succeeded a Republican (Finkel) as public defender in Rockland County, New York, and sought to dismiss Finkel and other Republican assistant public defenders. The Court, turning away from the question of a position's policymaking or confidential character, held that the issue is whether party affiliation is an appropriate requirement for the effective performance of the position's duties. It said that in this instance it was not and ruled against the attempted dismissal.[109]

In *Rutan* v. *Republican Party of Illinois* (1990),[110] the Republican governor of Illinois imposed a hiring freeze in 1980 for the approximately 60,000 positions under his control and permitted exceptions only with his express permission. Rutan and her fellow litigants, "low-level employees" in the Court's words, charged the governor used the freeze and exceptions to operate a political patronage system which, in their cases, denied them appointments, promotions, and transfers because they had not worked for or supported the Republican Party.[111] "Unless these patronage practices are narrowly tailored to further vital government interests," said the Court, "we must conclude that they impermissibly encroach on First Amendment freedoms." Citing the *Elrod* and *Branti* cases, it dismissed claims that the patronage practices furthered the government's interest in securing loyal and effective employees. Indeed, "A government's interest in securing employees who will loyally implement its policies can be adequately served by choosing or dismissing certain high-level employees on the basis of their political views."

The three decisions, now covering not just dismissals but also appointments, promotions, and transfers, outlaw the patronage system at all levels of government except for high-level, policymaking positions where party membership or support is an appropriate requirement for effective performance of duties. This dramatic development will mainly affect local governments and some state governments. But political bosses and officials do not lack for ways to pursue their interests even under civil service systems. Most common are choosing loyalists as civil service commissioners or underfinancing the commission so that registers of eligibles are allowed to expire and new examinations are postponed months or years. "Temporary" noncompetitive appointments are then possible and tend to go to party supporters.

Conclusion

It has been appropriate to speak of the civil service *system*, one that is composed of interlocking subsystems—one for position classification, one for staffing, and one for compensation. This has the special value of letting us appreciate better than we might how and why *any* large-scale system develops a complexity, a generalizing, impersonal style that ignores or subordinates individual differences among persons, and a formalization that breeds elaborate regulations and red tape. That such noble goals as equity and merit reinforce these tendencies should give us pause.

Now, though, we know that several major systems—and values—are in conflict. The civil service system, the collective bargaining system, and the political system start from different premises, embody different values, and are on a collision course. Governments, unions, and political parties vie for the loyalty and services of public employees. Reconciliation of these systems, their values, and their claims on citizens serving the public will not occur easily or soon.[112]

8

The Higher Public Service

The quality of national administration depends heavily on the kinds of people who fill the positions near the top of the executive branch. They number about 10,300, or about .3 percent of all federal employees. They include approximately 830 officials in the Executive Schedule (presidentially appointed and most of them senatorially confirmed), 7,100 in the Senior Executive Service (departmentally appointed, a tenth of them political appointees, and the others civil servants), and 1,260 in the Senior Foreign Service.[1] Beyond our total are almost a thousand persons in the General Schedule at slightly lower levels (GS-13 to GS-15) who, holding noncareer appointments made by the heads of executive departments and agencies, share in top-level administration.[2]

The group is far from homogeneous. It includes executives and nonexecutives (e.g., scientists and engineers without executive responsibilities), short-term political appointees and career civil servants, and persons serving under a variety of personnel systems. Yet distinctions among these types of officials are sufficiently muddied to warrant our initially treating this varied group as a whole. Although executives outnumber nonexecutives, many of the executives are themselves scientists, engineers, and other professionals by reason of training and continuing self-identification. Although top, competitive, civil service positions well outnumber political positions, some appointees to those competitive positions may be civil service careerists whose promotion to or retention in those posts was subject to political clearance; others may be "in-and-outers" who, although qualified for top civil service appointments, are not careerists, as they alternate spells of government service with other pursuits. A number of the political positions are filled by persons of high qualifications and with little or no political service to the president's party. Indeed, some political positions are filled by members of the opposite party, some by promoted career civil servants, and some, again, by in-and-outers, such as university professors, business people, labor leaders, and minority-group representatives. Finally, although several distinct personnel systems emphasize recruitment and promotion by merit, they often confusingly intersect. The State Department's Washington headquarters, for instance, has many positions that may be staffed under either the Foreign Service system or the regular civil service system; so, too, the Defense Department has the option of filling many posts with either civil servants or uniformed officers.

How Elite Is the Elite?

The American higher public service is a representative, fragmented, open elite. It *is* an elite in the three most obvious senses: (1) by definition, the men and women near the top of the executive branch of the U.S. government hold positions of great influence in the government, the society, and the world; (2) their salaries (ranging from $108,200 to $148,400) place them in the top brackets of American wage earners; and (3) recruitment to such high-level positions yields a group of people with educational attainments higher than those of the whole population or those of the whole public service.

The group, however, is not elitist by origin (i.e., by family background). It is not a close-knit group of people who, by formal organization, shared values, or informal understandings, act in a unified fashion on policy matters and protect their status, salaries, and perquisites. Instead, the American public service includes many elites built variously on educational and professional specialization, single-agency attachments, and distinctive, congressionally established career services. Finally, it is not a closed group of careerists who entered in their twenties and thereafter had their promotional opportunities protected against competition from outsiders. We examine these characteristics under the headings of representativeness, a multiplicity of elites, and outsiders and insiders.

Representativeness

The representativeness of an elite can be measured by comparing its characteristics with those of the general population. But perfect correspondence is impossible, and its substantial approximation may be undesirable. No one proposes that an eighth of the administrative elite should consist of poor people because they are an eighth of the population. Nor does anyone believe that the administrative elite should contain a proportionate number of carpenters, automobile salespersons, or bankers. Nevertheless, important groups, such as women and blacks, are underrepresented, in part because of conscious and unconscious discrimination, and in part because they have been underrepresented in graduate and professional schools from which much of the elite is initially recruited.

One way to test the representativeness of a current high-status group of persons is to examine their fathers' occupations. If the children of fathers who had modest occupations (and presumably incomes) constitute a significant proportion of a current elite, a democratic process is operative. Such intergenerational upward mobility is evident for America's higher civil servants. The fathers of a third of these officials are or were in modest walks of life—skilled and lower nonmanual workers, and skilled, semiskilled, or unskilled manual workers. The fathers of members of Congress are distributed among these callings in almost the same pattern, as are the fathers of British and German higher civil servants. Only 40 percent of American higher civil servants' fathers were in high management or professional positions, compared to 66 percent in France, and about 50 percent in Britain and Germany.[3]

College and postgraduate education is an important intervening variable. In most major Western democracies, all higher civil servants hold university degrees; in the United States, but not elsewhere, almost all of the politically appointed executives similarly qualify.[4] Among the higher civil servants, more than two-thirds have advanced degrees, with a third holding medical, law, or other doctoral degrees.[5] American higher officials have been recruited from a large number of colleges and universities, ranging from those with worldwide reputations to small colleges scarcely known outside their states. In this respect our administrative elite contrasts sharply with those of Britain and France, each of which has a narrow recruitment base. Four-fifths of the successful candidates for Britain's administrative elite in most of this century have had degrees from Oxford or Cambridge. Since 1945, three-fourths of the direct entrants to France's School of National Administration have been graduates of the Institute of Political Studies in Paris (entrance to the school confers civil service status and graduation assures entrance to the administrative elite).[6]

Whether our higher public service is sufficiently representative is arguable. In the terms of social science, the higher public service is largely an achievement elite, not an ascriptive elite. That is, most members of the administrative elite have arrived there because of their own demonstrated qualities, not because of their parents' status. Yet parents' income and race affect the opportunity to get the educational foundation for achievement, and sexual and racial discrimination have blocked the career advancement of well-qualified persons. These negative features, however, are societal characteristics, not distinctive to the public service. Perhaps the clearest verdict is a comparative one: The United States has a more nearly representative administrative elite than is to be found in other leading democracies.

A Multiplicity of Elites

America's higher officials constitute not a single elite but a variety of specialized elites. This can be demonstrated by their educational specialization, their occupational specialization within the higher public service, and their lack of mobility among agencies on their way to the top.

Educational Specialization. Of American higher civil servants, 42 percent had university majors in the fields of technology and natural science. The remarkableness of this is evidenced by foreign patterns. The corresponding figures for Britain and Germany were 26 and 14 percent.[7] Those countries recruit generalists rather than specialists. Of the successful candidates for the elite British Administrative Class in 1979, 62 percent had taken degrees in "arts subjects" (e.g., history and classics).[8] In Germany, two-thirds of the higher civil service are lawyers.[9]

Occupational Specialization. Young recruits with specialized education (in the various social sciences as well as in technology and the natural sciences) serve initially in lower civil service posts tied to their specialties. But one might suppose that the small proportion of them who rise to the top echelons of the public service would lose close identification with those specialties and become "generalist" administrators, able to apply their administrative skills to almost any program area. The supposition proves incorrect.

Over a third of the positions in the Senior Executive Service (which has absorbed most GS-16 to GS-18 positions) are occupied by scientists and engineers. They are specialized as biologists, physicians, veterinarians, engineers, physicists, and mathematicians.[10] Each of these professions in turn has subspecialties to which persons attach themselves. Most of the professionals at these high levels have administrative or supervisory posts; nonetheless, they remain specialists, not generalists, for they typically oversee work restricted to their special fields.

American top executives, then, cannot be thought of as a single pool of general administrators, for not only have most of them been educated for specialization but their career progress has been up specialized professional ladders, whether within or outside the government. Most such persons have risen because of professional distinction; some, especially government careerists, have demonstrated a capacity for administrative leadership. But few have had formal training in the economic, social, political, and administrative problems with which they must deal as public executives. Career specialization itself tends to make them unaware of gaps in their preparation for high-level responsibilities in a complex environment.

Within individual agencies, as Frederick C. Mosher has noted, professional specialization further fragments the elite.[11] In any agency staffed with members of several professions, there is likely to be a pecking order among the specialties. Engineers are the predominant elite of a highway department, psychiatrists of a mental health agency, scientists of a scientific agency. Members of other professions in these agencies (lawyers, accountants, economists, et al.) must adapt to the dominant elite, a situation that produces jealousy and tension.

Foreign practice affords a sharp contrast to the American pattern of occupational specialization within the elite. A member of the British Administrative Class is traditionally expected to be an administrative generalist, a gifted amateur, an intelligent "all-arounder" "who, moving frequently from job to job within the Service, can take a practical view of any problem irrespective of its subject matter, in the light of his knowledge and experience of the government machine."[12] He is a specialist in generalization. In France, graduates of both the Polytechnic School and the National School of Administration are persons of general culture, trained to be "polyvalent," that is, all-purpose or generalist, administrators, and their careers move among a number of ministries. German public administrators generally stay within a single ministry, but they start with a broad legal education that is meant to produce generalists.

Single-Agency Careers. The narrowing effects of educational and occupational specialization might be mitigated if American higher officials had served in several agencies during their public service. But this has not been the pattern. Ninety percent of new career appointees to the Senior Executive Service come from within the agency making the appointment. The system is not oriented to facilitate horizontal mobility, and its occurrence usually results from an individual person's taking initiative on his own.

Striking a Balance. All governments use scientists, engineers, economists, lawyers, and other professional specialists. Differences among governments turn on whether such professionals are subordinate to generalist administrators or are themselves administrators with decision-making authority. In this country, as elsewhere, the generalist-specialist conflict has long been waged. A middle position is that administrators must know something about the subjects they are administering, not least because otherwise they may become victims of subordinates claiming—and having

—superior knowledge. This means that a forester should head the Forest Service, a public health professional the Public Health Service, economist/statisticians the Bureau of the Census and the Bureau of Labor Statistics.

As the last case suggests, some mobility among agencies with related functions is possible and probably desirable. Rufus Miles, rejecting the all-purpose generalist concept, argues that "the demonstrated command of essential program knowledge is of at least as great importance in the development and selection of top-level career program managers as managerial skills." He proposes that mobility for development of future managers be confined to clusters of related program agencies (e.g., those primarily in the fields of regulation, national security and international affairs, economic stabilization and development, natural resources and the environment).[13] Note, though, that he specifies that top-level professionally specialized managers have demonstrated administrative talent. As matters stand, agencies often promote able scientists and other specialists to management positions simply because these have the higher pay levels needed to retain their services. Rising specialists need more than administrative talent. They need adequate in-service, executive-development programs to compensate for their educational gaps in understanding of the Constitution, the political system, and public administration.

Outsiders and Insiders

A fully developed elite service is "closed," which means that outsiders enter only at the lowest elite rank. With rare exceptions, all members are recruited at that rank while in their twenties, at or shortly after college graduation.[14] Higher positions are filled by promotional competition among the qualified members of the service. British, French, and German elite services substantially adhere to this model, as do the American Foreign Service and military officer corps.[15] These last exceptions aside, the American public service does not.

Next to specialization, the most striking feature of the American public service is its openness. Entry can be at any working age and at any level. Political appointees to executive-level positions (cabinet members down to some bureau chiefs), of course, enter at a high level. What is distinctive, compared to foreign patterns, is that the pattern also fits career and noncareer officials below the executive level. Just before the Senior Executive Service absorbed most GS-16 to -18 officials, almost a third of the latter category had entered at grade 13 or higher, including a tenth that entered directly at GS-16 to -18. Only a little more than a third had used the normal entry route of GS-5 to -8—normal because those are the beginning levels for recent college graduates.[16] The careerists in the Senior Executive Service (SES) in 1987 had entered at *all* levels, from GS-1 to GS-18 (half below and half above GS-9) and from the lowest to the highest SES grades.[17]

We may reasonably conclude that the American higher public service is comparatively nonelitist. It is more representative than most nations' administrative elites; it is highly fragmented by educational, occupational, and agency-career specializations; and it is open to lateral entry at all levels of the career civil service and by political appointees.

The Mix of Political and Career Officials

Every modern government's executive branch has a set of political officials at and near the top. But nations differ as to how broad this political band is, how great is the ratio of top political appointees to top civil servants, and how much the two sets of officials are distinct or commingled.

In Britain, a change of parties brings only about 120 members of Parliament into the executive part of the government, with such titles as minister, junior minister, and parliamentary secretary. In France, the government of the day has only 100 to 150 politicians, mostly ministers, secretaries of state, and their staff aides. In Germany, the strictly political echelon is thin—about 40 members, including ministers and parliamentary secretaries.

In the American executive branch there are over 3,000 political positions, of which about 1,500 are at the higher levels.[18] Alongside or under the higher political appointees are about 7,000 top careerists. There is thus about one high political appointee for every five top careerists, a ratio that strikingly contrasts with that of other Western democracies. As every democracy seeks to assure popular control of the bureaucracy, it seems odd that the United States finds so disproportionately large a number of political appointees necessary to achieve that objective. One explanation is that some presidents, notably Nixon, Carter, and Reagan, enter office from a campaign vilifying "the bureaucracy" and, believing their own rhetoric, conclude that only a small army of their own selection can assure agencies' responsiveness to presidential policy priorities.[19]

The more basic explanation runs deeper and fits presidents who avoid attacking the civil servants. The American separation of powers, in contrast to European systems, leaves the president less in command of administrative agencies than are European executives. The latter have more administrative freedom and, in parliamentary systems, can count on legislative support because their own party or coalition has the votes. The president often confronts a Congress that engages in active oversight and intervention in administrative agencies' affairs and one in which one or both houses are under the opposite party's control. Too, as Terry Moe has argued, the incongruence between the public's extravagant expectations of a president's performance and the limited resources available to him for satisfying those expectations make him seize on the tools readily at hand, namely politicization of appointments and centralization in the White House.[20]

The set of high political positions has swelled over time. "From 1933 to 1965, ... the number of cabinet and sub-cabinet officers appointed by the President and confirmed by the Senate doubled from 73 to 152. From 1965 to the present, ... that number more than tripled to 573."[21]

Even more important, as Paul Light found in an important study of senior officials in the federal government, government has steadily "thickened" as the number of political appointees has risen. There are, Light discovered, "more layers of leaders" and "more leaders at each layer." The result has been an important transformation in government:

> In the 1950s, the federal bureaucracy looked like a relatively flat bureaucratic pyramid, with few senior executives, a somewhat larger number of middle managers, and a very large number of frontline employees. By the 1970s, it was beginning to look like a circus tent, with a growing corps of senior political and career managers, a sizable "bulge" of middle managers and professionals, and a shrinking number of front-line employees.
>
> In the 1980s and 1990s, the configuration began to resemble a pentagon, with even more political and career executives at the top, and almost equal numbers of many middle-level and front-line employees.[22]

In his survey, Light found fifty-two potential managerial layers of government from top to bottom in the federal government (see table 8.1). Some positions are held by political appointees; others are occupied by careerists. Not all departments have every position. Only the Department of Energy, for example, has a principal associate deputy undersecretary. Even in recent enthusiasm for downsizing the federal government, presidents have shown little inclination to reduce the number of layers and, especially, the political appointees who fill them. Every position is an opportunity to reward a valued campaign aide or a generous contributor. But the increase of governmental layers weakens accountability by making it harder to assign clear responsibility for results.

The Foreign Service. A smaller, but surely as important, arena is that where political and career candidates seek ambassadorial appointments. In 1981, 25 percent of such appointments were held by political appointees rather than by career Foreign Service officers. In 1987 that figure had risen to 40 percent. Through the first ten months of their administrations,

Table 8.1

LAYERS OF GOVERNMENT

Secretary
  Chief of Staff to the Secretary
    Deputy Chief of Staff

Deputy Secretary
  Chief of Staff to the Deputy Secretary
  Associate Deputy Secretary

Under Secretary
  Principal Deputy Under Secretary
  Deputy Under Secretary
    Principal Associate Deputy Under
      Secretary
    Associate Deputy Under Secretary
    Assistant Deputy Under Secretary
    Associate Under Secretary

Assistant Secretary/Inspector General/
    General Counsel
  Chief of Staff to the Assistant
    Secretary
  Principal Deputy Assistant Secretary
  Deputy Assistant Secretary
    Associate Deputy Assistant
      Secretary
      Deputy Associate Deputy
      Assistant Secretary

Assistant General Counsel/Inspector
    General
  Deputy Assistant General Counsel/
    Inspector General

Administrator
  Chief of Staff to the Administrator
  Principal Deputy Administrator
  Deputy Administrator
    Associate Deputy Administrator
    Assistant Deputy Administrator

Associate Administrator
  Deputy Associate Administrator
    Assistant Administrator
      Deputy Assistant Administrator
        Associate Assistant Administrator

Principal Office Director
  Office Director
    Principal Deputy Office Director
    Deputy Office Director
      Assistant Deputy Office Director

Associate Office Director
  Deputy Associate Office Director
    Assistant Office Director
      Deputy Assistant Director

Principal Division Director
Division Director
  Deputy Division Director
    Associate Division Director
    Assistant Division Director
      Deputy Assistant Division
        Director

Sub-division Director
  Deputy Sub-division Director
    Associate Sub-division Director
    Assistant Sub-division Director

Branch Chief

SOURCE: Paul C. Light, "How Thick Is Government?" *American Enterprise* 5
(November/ December 1994): 60.

Carter, Reagan, and Bush respectively had chosen noncareerists for 37, 39, and 57 percent of their ambassadorial nominations. Our important embassies in Europe (as also in the Caribbean, and the South Pacific) are more attractive to political candidates than small, developing countries in Africa and Asia, often ill favored by climate. So twelve of Bush's early nominations to fifteen European posts went to such candidates, rather than to Foreign Service officers.[23]

Here, as in domestic departments, some noncareer appointees have served with high distinction. But the larger the number of ambassadorships to be filled politically, the more likely are the selection criteria to be lax, with too many nominees being simply rewarded for campaign contributions, ideological passion, and presidential friendship.[24]

Political Executives

No one doubts the need for having a band of political positions and, immediately below that band, for mixing political appointees and careerists. The argument runs that a president or department head needs people who share the same policy orientation, who will advocate the chosen policies to congressional committees, interest groups, and the public, who can serve as their superiors' loyal agents in bringing the permanent bureaucracy into effective service of those policies, who have their superiors' confidence, and who are expendable. Expendability means that they can readily be removed when they lose the president's or department head's confidence, resist policy directives, or become liabilities because they have antagonized relevant congressional committees or interest groups.[25]

The argument is persuasive because it merely elaborates on the conviction that in a democracy the bureaucracy must be directed and controlled by popularly elected officials. The elaboration adds politically *appointed* officials to the popularly *elected* president, vice-president, and members of Congress. Yet acceptance of the argument leaves many problems unresolved, and perhaps unresolvable. We have already said enough to pose the question of proportion: How many political executives are sufficient to accomplish the objectives stated by the argument? Beyond that question lie issues of recruitment, qualifications, and tenure, to which we turn. The problem of assuring these executives' conformity to ethical standards is treated in chapter 14.

Let us preface our discussion of those issues with a bleak comparison. Of the twenty-nine otherwise highly qualified men who in the last quarter-century served as secretaries of state or defense, national security advisers, or CIA directors, "none had prior official negotiating experience with the

Soviets. None had studied, resided or worked in the Soviet Union. None spoke fluent Russian." In the Soviet Union in 1987, the following all spoke English and all had served in Washington: the chief of state (a long-time foreign minister); the secretary of the Central Committee's International Department (a long-time ambassador to the United States) and his deputy; the chief arms negotiator; two deputy foreign ministers; and the chief of the Foreign Ministry's Department of Arms Control.[26] At the United Nations, the chief Soviet delegate had by 1984 served for seven years and some of his staff had served for fifteen years or more. From the beginning of the United Nations to 1984, the sixteen chief U.S. delegates averaged a service of nineteen months; only three remained for a full four-year presidential term.[27] It all seems an uneven match.

Recruitment and Qualifications

The number of political appointments and their many levels—from cabinet secretary to deputy assistant secretaries, bureau chiefs, and regional directors—vastly complicates the recruitment of able executives. This is most strikingly so when a new president has been elected and has only about ten weeks after the election to assemble the team that will take over the executive branch on inauguration day. He must rely heavily on his top campaign staff to handle the flood of candidacies self-generated or proposed by political and interest-group patrons. Campaign staff members are rarely qualified for the shift of focus from campaigning to governing. The qualifications needed for specific positions are poorly understood and often poorly match the chosen candidates' qualifications.[28] After inauguration the task shifts to the White House personnel office, and haste gives way to delay. By November of his first year Bush had not nominated candidates for 27 percent of departmental and other agency positions requiring Senate confirmation, a higher percentage than in the four preceding major transitions.[29]

Merely partisan service has less claim on patronage appointments now than in the past.[30] Emphasis is placed on personal and ideological commitment to the president and his goals. This reflects the decline of political parties and the rise of television's influence on the selection of presidential candidates and presidents. Candidates for nomination develop their own campaign organizations, and the winner of the nomination largely depends on his organization, rather than on national and state parties, to wage the final campaign.

The recruitment of political executives is so handicapped that one may marvel that it succeeds as well as it does. It succeeds best in the selection of cabinet members, a matter to which the president-elect gives personal attention. Many of those chosen have achieved distinction in their careers.[31] One study calculates that almost two-thirds of the cabinet appointees from the New Deal to the Carter administration belonged to the socioeconomic elite (i.e., with ties to big business, major law firms, or elite families). The range was from 55 percent under Truman to 81 percent under Eisenhower.[32] Four of Reagan's first-term cabinet members were multimillionaires (and over a fourth of the top 100 officials had net worths of $1 million or more).[33]

Most cabinet members have had federal government experience.[34] They are often generalists with prior service in other cabinet posts, at the subcabinet level, or in the White House. They are likely to be qualified for the processes of advocacy, negotiation, and compromise that dominate governmental policy making; this is true with lawyers, less so with corporate executives and academics, and not at all with ideologues.[35]

The vast number of appointments below the cabinet level poses the real problem. Because of the number, the president-elect (and later the president) rarely gives selections his personal attention, so he is dependent initially on his campaign staff and later on the White House's personnel office. An initial impulse of some incoming presidents is to delegate to cabinet members the selection of their subordinates. But this rapidly erodes after the inauguration, and subcabinet appointments are cleared or initiated in the White House personnel office. In the Reagan administration even the departments' Schedule C (noncareer) appointments at grades of GS-15 and below, including private secretaries, had to be cleared there.[36]

Most political executives have solid educational backgrounds and many have subject-matter knowledge relevant to their particular responsibilities. Over three-fourths of the presidential appointees in the 1964–84 period had at least one advanced degree.[37]

Three characteristics are less promising. One concerns prior experience in the federal government. Former political appointees who lacked such experience regret how poorly prepared they were for the Washington setting of interest groups, congressional committees, the White House staff, the goldfish-bowl exposure to the media, the budget process, and the permanent bureaucracy; a few appointees have revealed defective appreciation of the Constitution, faithful execution of the laws, and the public service code of ethics. Washington is a culture different from that of business, professional practice, or the university. An appointee unfamiliar with that environment may flounder during the initial period of his short tenure. Yet "more than half of all presidential appointees come to their positions from outside of government and almost half from outside of Washington. More than a quarter have no prior federal experience and less than half have spent as much as five years of their working lives in the federal government."[38] The contrast with Britain is striking. There the political officials are drawn from Parliament. A new cabinet typically consists of persons who in opposition were members of a "shadow cabinet," each specializing in the affairs of a particular ministry. Often the ministers have had experience in one or more governments when their party was in power.

A second concern is capability of managing large organizations or operating in them.[39] Few of the one-fourth of presidential appointees who are members of law firms, university faculties, research institute staffs, interest-group organizations, and congressional members' offices and committees are well prepared to run a bureau of 5,000 employees, let alone operate effectively in one of thirteen cabinet departments having from 13,000 to 1 million employees. Even less is this the case with the large set of noncareerists appointed by department heads with White House clearance.[40] Recruits from business are more likely to have experience in large-scale management. Nevertheless, Reagan appointed more businessmen (a fifth of all appointees) than any president since Eisenhower, without achieving notable superiority of performance.

A third concern revolves around the legitimate emphasis on appointees' commitments to the president and to his policies. The two commitments are different, though at the beginning of an administration they merge. Appointees with a personal loyalty to a president or appreciation of the president's authority adapt as the president's priorities change over time from his campaign positions. Appointees inflexibly committed to the policies enunciated in the campaign are advocates with firm agendas, stubbornly resistant to the president's shifts of policy directions.[41] Yet they are arrayed in many layers between the good to be done, as the president perceives it, and those who can do it, the career executives engaged in implementation.

Tenure and Turnover

Political appointees serve only briefly in their posts. For decades, the median length of service for presidential appointees has been barely more than two years. A third of the presidential appointees stayed a year and a half or less.[42] Between 1985 and 1987, 46 percent of the 321 top officials left the government.[43] Five problems and opportunities result.

First, so short a tenure means that many leave after they have barely learned their jobs and adapted to the Washington environment. Wide agreement exists that appointees need at least a year to become productive performers in their government posts. Some will be aware that the second year may be their last. To initiate and see results from new projects, they will prefer those that are short range, even though significant achievements in the public interest require emphasis on the long range. Those insensitive to the probability of their early departure will invest energy in substantial undertakings; these then will be passed on to their successors, who may let them proceed in their first, learning year and then scuttle or drastically re-shape them. An administration loses sustained themes when burdened by a stop-and-go or go-and-stop process. A career civil servant, who became an assistant secretary of commerce, reported his experience this way:

> I don't know how many assistant secretaries I have helped break in.... And there is always a propensity for a new guy to come in and discover the wheel all over again. And then you have the classic case of a political officer who is going to make a name for himself, and therefore he is go-ing to identify one golden chalice he is going after, and he will take the whole goddam energy of an organization to go after that golden chalice. He leaves after eighteen months, a new guy comes in, and his golden chalice is over here. "Hey guys, everybody, this way."[44]

Turnover at the cabinet level has similar costs. At the Department of Labor, the General Accounting Office reported, the then-serving secretary "has demonstrated the strong leadership needed for a well-managed organi-zation, and his management system established a sound framework for stra-tegic planning and management." Of nearly 200 Labor Department manag-ers polled about the system, "about 92 percent believed it should remain despite top-level turnover, whereas only about 35 percent believed it would."[45] Below the cabinet and assistant secretaries, the phenomenon re-peats itself. In the decade ending in 1987 the Social Security Administration had seven commissioners or acting commissioners. "These short tenures, along with commissioners' differing priorities and management approaches, resulted in frequent changes of direction, diminished accountability, and little long-term operational planning."[46]

Second, rapid turnover undermines teamwork, despite frequent talk of a president's or department head's "team." In a department, the set of top executives is constantly changing, as the timing of individual departures is usually by each official's choice. More broadly, because so many policies and programs involve interdepartmental collaboration, their shaping and constancy depend on interdepartmental networks of political executives sharing concerns with particular policy areas. For these, as Hugh Heclo has observed, there need to be "relationships of confidence and trust."[47] The chemistry of these interpersonal relations develops only over time; the sub-traction and addition of new elements can upset the developed formula.

Third, standard maxims about civil servants' obedience to political su-periors fray when those superiors, here today, are likely to be gone tomor-row. Some high careerists patiently tutor one after another political executive to speed the learning process. But others, if in charge of bureaus and programs, mount defenses to minimize damage by ill-prepared and very temporary political executives.[48]

Fourth, the high rate of turnover means that staffing the administration is far from done in the preinaugural and immediately postinaugural periods. Departures constantly create vacancies that need filling. This produces both problems and opportunities. A major problem is the many months, sometimes years, taken to recruit, nominate, and obtain Senate confirmation of successors to the vacant posts. On the eve of Reagan's second inauguration, HHS lacked three assistant secretaries, a general counsel, and two commissioners. Its Social Security Administration in early 1985 had an acting commissioner (having served thus for sixteen months) and three acting deputy commissioners (two having served nineteen months).[49] At the start of 1986, one-sixth of the 176 cabinet department positions that required presidential nomination and Senate confirmation were either vacant or occupied by persons designated as only "acting" in their positions.[50] When a position is vacant or held by a temporary designee, fresh initiatives are rarely taken, on the ground that those should be left for the properly appointed successor. So, to the red-and-green traffic lights' symbols of stop-and-go administration is added the amber light for the long pause in filling vacancies.

Departures also open a window of opportunity for the White House personnel office. It is better organized than at the start and has learned how to identify candidates and induce their acceptance of appointment offers. Most of all, the errors made by campaign staffs in initial appraisal and selection of political executives can be corrected. Further, the personnel office will have gained a good sense of which political appointees have performed well and so warrant transfer or promotion to more responsible positions.

Finally, during the last year or eighteen months of a presidency there is likely to be a substantial exodus of political appointees, many intent on capitalizing on their government experience by obtaining remunerative employment in the private sector. The primary occupation of 19 percent of the presidential appointees between 1964 and 1984 was in business and law, but, departing, over 60 percent went into those occupations.[51] Restaffing in the terminal period of a presidency is exceedingly difficult. Few qualified persons will take public office for a predictably brief period. At the start of the Reagan administration's final year, over a fifth of the 284 executive-level positions in all cabinet departments were vacant or filled by acting appointees; about half of the assistant secretaryships were vacant in the Department of Housing and Urban Development, as were about a third in the Energy and Defense departments.[52] In such a winding-down period, an administration is likely to promote subordinate political executives (leaving vacancies behind them) and career civil servants to higher positions, content itself with second-rate candidates, or leave posts unfilled. It also converts a small number of political appointees to career status.

Senate Confirmation

Article II of the Constitution provides that the president

> shall nominate, and by and with the Advice and Consent of the Senate, shall appoint Ambassadors, ... and all other Officers of the United States, whose Appointments are not herein otherwise provided for, and which shall be established by Law: but the Congress may by Law vest the Appointment of such inferior officers, as they think proper, in the President alone, in the Courts of Law, or in the Heads of Departments.[53]

Ambassadors and "superior" officers, therefore, require Senate confirmation. The Health and Human Services Department, for example, has seventeen positions whose appointees must be confirmed by the Senate.[54] Presidential nominations go to a variety of Senate committees, according to their assigned jurisdictions. Each committee may, as some do, require nominees to complete forms providing information duplicatory of that furnished the agencies and the White House, but confusingly different from the forms already completed for the executive branch. It is an unnecessary encumbrance in a confirmation process that otherwise contributes positively to the selection of top officials. Committees, though, treasure their autonomy, so reform is difficult.

More troubling, certainly, is the Senate's tradition of allowing a committee member to put a "hold" on consideration of a nomination, together with any senator's privilege of blocking the full Senate's consideration of a committee's recommendation of confirmation. The practice accounts for some lengthy vacancies in top executive positions. It has more significant consequences. In the 1980s a senior Republican member of the Senate Committee on Foreign Affairs used his position for extortion on the State Department and White House personnel office. He put "holds" on many ambassadorial and other nominations, releasing them only when embassy or State Department positions were found for persons sharing his ideology or otherwise viewed as deserving his patronage. "In most recent cases," a study reports, "holds by individual senators have been used for purposes of extortion ... in order to force some information or concession from the nominee personally or from the administration."[55] It proposes that the tradition be changed to allow a senator to delay a nomination no more than five working days.

Positions filled by presidential nomination and Senate confirmation total about 300, a tenth of the politically filled positions and a fifth of those
at the GS-16 and higher levels.[56] Most political appointments made by the
president alone or by heads of departments and agencies are not subjected
to senatorial questioning in public hearings (though they undergo conflict-
of-interest and other screening procedures). We know much less about the
quality of such appointments, as recent studies have focused on presidential
appointments requiring the Senate's consent. If senior careerists' views are
accurate, the quality of appointees in the larger group declined during the
Carter and Reagan administrations.

This, of course, is not simply because of the absence of Senate review.
Rather, the president takes little interest in these appointments, the White
House personnel office finds the large number of posts and candidates a
handicap to thorough examination of qualifications, and lesser posts are
natural nesting places for persons undistinguished save by campaign service, political endorsements, or interest-group connections. That should not
be interpreted as a wholly bleak picture. A number of appointees to subordinate positions are indeed well qualified. The problem is that one misfit in
a key post can wreak havoc with a bureau or program that is put under his
or her charge.

How Many Are Too Many?

Political appointees, we have seen, number 3,000, a figure reflecting steady
growth over several decades when the executive branch's total employment
grew scarcely at all. The rationale has not varied. The president, it is argued, needs political appointees in order to assure that the permanent civil
servants faithfully serve the chief executive, adapting to his policy priorities
however much those differ from his predecessor's. That granted, there remain two questions: (1) How many political appointees are needed to
achieve the objective? and (2) At what point does the number of such appointees become so large as to frustrate the objective? No precise answers
to these questions exist. But political appointees themselves have proposed
formulas that advance us toward resolution of the problem.

President Nixon's top political recruiter wrote:

> The solution to problems of rigidity and resistance to change in govern-
> ment is *not* to increase the number of appointive positions at the top, as
> so many politicians are wont to do.... An optimum balance between the
> number of career and noncareer appointments ... should be struck in fa-
> vor of fewer political appointees, not more. In many cases, the effective-
> ness of an agency would be improved and political appointments would

be reduced by roughly 25 percent if line positions beneath the assistant secretary level were reserved for career officials.[57]

The Volcker Commission, which included fifteen former top political appointees, recommended in 1989 that "the growth in recent years in the number of presidential appointees, whether those subject to Senate confirmation, noncareer senior executives, or personal and confidential assistants, should be curtailed.... The Commission is confident that a substantial cut is possible, and believes a cut from the current 3,000 to no more than 2,000 is a reasonable target." On our second question, the commission observed that "excessive numbers of political appointees serving relatively brief periods may undermine the president's ability to govern, insulating the administration from needed dispassionate advice and institutional memory. The mere size of the political turnover almost guarantees management gaps and discontinuities, while the best of the career professionals will leave government if they do not have challenging opportunities at the sub-cabinet level."[58]

With the answers to our questions apparently so clear, their translation into reality remains clouded. Congressional action is required to return to career status the positions now filled by the president with Senate consent or on his own. Most of those, however, have strong claims to retention as key instruments of presidential administration. The major targets for depoliticization are Senior Executive Service posts now held by political appointees—deputy assistant secretaryships and directorships of departments' and agencies' operating units (accounting, for example, for 54 of HHS's high political positions, 78 percent)—and Schedule C's GS-13–GS-15 special assistantships (85 in HHS). Department heads and OPM determine SES career and noncareer allocations and assignments. OPM determines which positions shall be in Schedule C because they are "confidential and policy-forming." Who has authority to act does not clarify when he or she will have the will to act. Interest groups, members of Congress, and other political activists cannot be expected to moderate their pressures for placement of allies in the higher public service.

The Senior Executive Service

Creation of the Senior Executive Service (SES) was the most significant accomplishment of the Civil Service Reform Act of 1978. It absorbed most of the previously GS-16 to GS-18 career and noncareer positions together with Executive Levels IV and V positions filled by the president without Senate confirmation. The SES "allocated positions" (those authorized for agencies) number about 8,000, but the positions actually filled are about 7,000. The men and women in the SES, therefore, are the critical group below the top political executives for the shaping of policy proposals and the management of the departments and agencies.

A principal objective was to give agency heads greater flexibility in assigning members of this cadre among positions and tasks. Under the old system, a GS-16 to GS-18 career official's status (tenure, grade, and salary) was an attribute of the position occupied, not of the person occupying it. So, the agency could dislodge the incumbent (apart from position abolition, firing, or forced resignation) only by promotion, demotion, or transfer to a position at the same grade and matching his qualifications. It was often difficult to find a position for which a bureau chief or other high careerist had the requisite qualifications, let alone a position that was vacant or could be made so. Substituting an SES system of rank-in-person for the old one of rank-in-position promised to remedy this.

Agency heads and their immediate subordinates seek flexibility of top career assignments for a variety of reasons, some genuinely "for the good of the service" and some not. We have said enough about specialized education, occupations, and promotional ladders to make it apparent that some careerists who rise to key positions will turn out to be narrow in outlook, inhospitable to innovations, ungifted in leadership of large staffs, insensitive to political nuances, and incapable of communicating effectively with politicians above them and in Congress. The point is easily misunderstood. Sometimes a political executive claiming that he or she wants "to eliminate deadwood" is enough of a tree surgeon to be able to distinguish a dead branch from one that might be reinvigorated, and sometimes not. Careerists who are indeed deadwood are appropriate candidates for voluntary retirement, resignation, or removal from the service, or for demotion to the GS-15 level. That deadwood category needs to be differentiated from instances where a square peg has proved too angular for the round hole it occupies. In those instances the appropriate strategy is to look around for square holes into which the square peg might be moved and, predictably, prove a good fit: the person inept in dealing with members of Congress can be placed in a position not requiring congressional contacts, the sage who is a poor leader can be shifted to a role as adviser on policy and program, without loss of status or usefulness. To facilitate this matching of officials with tasks, the new system emphasized the agency head's discretionary authority over assignments of key people.

Structure

The SES contains both careerists and political appointees. Two quotas govern their numbers. First, noncareerists cannot occupy more than 10 percent of the allocated positions on a governmentwide basis, nor more than 25 percent in any one agency.[59] The limits have been observed, even though by 1986 the Reagan administration had increased noncareer appointees by 13 percent and decreased career appointees by 5 percent. Twelve departments and agencies exceeded the governmentwide 10 percent figure, but not the 25 percent applicable to individual agencies (the departments of Education and of Housing and Urban Development, each with 24 percent noncareerists, approached the limit).[60] Their excess, of course, was balanced by agencies with less than 10 percent levels (e.g., the Treasury Department with 3.2 percent) to conform to the governmentwide limit. Note, though, that as the 25 percent limit applies to a department or major agency as a whole, subunits may exceed the figure (e.g., the International Trade Administration in the Department of Commerce had 55 percent noncareer appointees in its part of the SES).[61]

The second quota reserves for a careerist an SES position "if the filling of the position by a career appointee is necessary to ensure impartiality, or the public's confidence in the impartiality, of the Government."[62] About half of all SES positions have been "career reserved" by action of agencies and the OPM. The remaining half, called "general" positions, may be filled by either careerists or noncareerists. Practice varies among the agencies so that the same kind of positions may be career reserved in some but not in others. More generally, too few positions calling for impartiality or its appearance are career reserved, a point made especially about financial and personnel management, auditing, and investigations.[63]

The formal quotas have only slight bearing on the distribution of SES members among the six ranks. Most of the careerists, 70 percent, occupy middle-rank positions (ranks 3 and 4). Only 19 percent of them are at the two top ranks, where 39 percent of the noncareerists serve.[64] This limited access to the top rankles careerists for, while pay differences are insignificant, exclusion from higher ranks generally means exclusion from opportunities to share in the shaping and direction of programs.

A striking feature of the SES is the dominant role of individual agencies, which wars against the superficial impression that the SES is a governmentwide entity with its own esprit de corps. Partly this was intended, but a major contributing factor was the OPM's distancing itself from SES responsibilities during the first Reagan administration; it even abolished its Bureau of Executive Personnel (restored in the second Reagan term). A distinguished task force puts it simply: " . . . The OPM has left responsibility for SES development to the departments and agencies, giving them control over candidate recruitment and development, training, performance reviews, transfers, promotions, pay, and demotions. . . . This degree of decentralization is fundamentally incompatible with a high-level, cohesive senior civil service."[65] Each agency determines which of its positions should be included in the SES, subject only to light overview by the OPM. An early result was inclusion of a number of "general" positions whose noncareer incumbents were assistants to a political executive and had no executive responsibilities; later and more troubling, noncareerists were put in line positions, in charge of administering programs that previously were directed by experienced careerists.

Operation

Entry. Each agency establishes qualification standards for its SES positions. That done, it is free to choose each noncareer appointee, having only to certify that the individual meets the qualification standards for the position.

Career appointments to the SES are a different matter. A recruitment program in each agency is supposed to reach all qualified individuals both within and outside the civil service. An agency board reviews the qualifications of each candidate and, observing merit principles, makes recommendations to the agency appointing authority. OPM's own qualifications review boards determine whether the agency's candidates have executive qualifications (but not whether they have technical qualifications). In practice, the agency is the key actor, recruiting and choosing both career and noncareer members of the SES.

Reassignment, Performance Appraisal, and Removal. Politically appointed agency executives have in the past been frustrated by the difficulty of moving top careerists from positions in which they were ineffective to positions in which they would either do better or no longer be weak links in the chain of an important program's management. The SES changes this, for SES members have no right to particular assignments. A noncareerist can be reassigned to any general position in the agency for which he or she is qualified. So, too, can a career appointee, but with an important qualification. Some new political executives tend to regard most careerists as enemies or at least as hidebound bureaucrats. So disposed, they are eager to replace key careerists with politically reliable and personally valued associates. Congress, therefore, prescribes a four-month waiting period for an SES careerist's involuntary reassignment after the appointment of a new agency head or of the careerist's most immediate supervisor who is a noncareer official with authority to reassign the careerist. That is meant to afford time for new political appointees to get to know their careerists' capabilities for their current assignments, after which selective reassignments will presumably be more discriminating.

The most problematic feature of the SES is the system for evaluating the performance of the executives, particularly since the evaluations can have serious consequences for individual executives, including bonuses on the one side (discussed below) and removal from the SES on the other. Each agency is required to establish, conformably to OPM standards, one or more performance-appraisal systems, and it sets performance requirements for each senior executive in consultation with him or her. Appraisal of individual performance is by performance-review boards, which, however, have only recommendatory functions.[66]

The most novel feature is that each executive is to be judged on both his individual performance and his organization's performance. The latter includes such factors as the organization's "improvements in efficiency, productivity, and quality of work or service . . . ; cost efficiency; timeliness of performance; other indications of the effectiveness, productivity, and performance quality of the employees for whom the senior executive is responsible; and meeting affirmative action goals and achievement of equal employment opportunities."[67] Admirable goals, indeed. The question yet to be answered is whether the new agency-administered systems, which hold executives responsible for their organizations' and subordinates' performance as well as for their own, can achieve the original intent. Early experience was not reassuring. Individual, but not organizational, performance was what was appraised, partly because "it is difficult to identify individual contributions to the accomplishment of organizational objectives." Most careerists had performance plans, but most noncareerists did not. And "over half of the executives believed their agency's performance appraisal system (1) had minimal effect on performance, (2) had not improved communication between superiors and subordinates, and (3) was not worth its cost."[68]

It would not matter greatly if significant rewards and punishments were not tied to individuals' performance ratings. The rating categories are fully successful (divided into three categories by some agencies), minimally satisfactory, and unsatisfactory. An executive must be removed from the SES if rated "less than fully successful" twice in three consecutive years. A career executive may be removed if so rated at any time. The last provision, permitting *agency* termination of a careerist's membership in the governmentwide SES "at any time for less than fully successful performance" warrants comment. First, the careerist has no right to appeal to an independent agency, the Merit Systems Protection Board, in hopes of overturning the agency's decision. He is entitled to an *informal* hearing before a board official, but the board cannot overrule the agency nor delay the removal ac-

tion pending the hearing.[69] Second, on the brighter side, the careerist removed from the SES on the basis of performance rating is entitled to be
placed in a regular civil service position in any agency at GS-15 or a higher
level without reduction of the basic pay received in the SES. Alternatively, if
qualified by length of service and age, the careerist can choose retirement
on an annuity.[70] The "fallback" to a General Schedule position is important
insurance for careerists who, puzzled over the system's lack of a performance rating between "minimally satisfactory" and "fully successful," feel
vulnerable to an agency judgment that, though quite successful, they are
"less than fully successful" and so expellable from the SES at the agency's
option.

Every three years each SES careerist needs recertification of whether his
or her "overall performance over the 3 preceding years has demonstrated
the excellence expected ... in relation to the written performance requirements for the ... position." The agency head decides, after reports by the
supervisor and performance review board. Failure to be recertified means
removal from the SES.[71]

Bonuses. The base salaries of SES members fall in a range between
$92,900 and $115,700. We discuss this range and that of presidential appointees in the next major section. The political difficulty of substantially
improving base salaries is one explanation for the introduction of bonuses
for careerist members of the SES. A second explanation is the expectation
that individual financial awards recognizing excellence would motivate SES
members to perform with high distinction. And, initially, the prospect of
such rewards was a major incentive accounting for able top careerists' willingness to leave their General Schedule 16-18 positions and enlist in the
new SES despite its risks of reassignment, removal, and other insecurities
administered by political superiors.

The Civil Service Reform Act of 1978 authorized two kinds of awards
to SES careerists. *Performance awards* were to be made annually by each
agency to up to 50 percent of its career SES members, and were to amount
to up to 20 percent of a member's base pay. Selection of award winners was
to be tied to the performance appraisals described above. *Presidential rank*
awards for careerists were to be made by the president on nomination by
agencies and recommendation by the OPM. Each year, he could confer on
up to 5 percent of the SES the rank of "Meritorious Executive, for sustained accomplishment" which entitled each recipient to a lump-sum bonus
of $10,000, and on up to 1 percent of the SES the rank of "Distinguished
Executive, for sustained extraordinary accomplishment," which carried a
lump-sum bonus of $20,000.

The performance awards immediately ran into difficulties. Congress reduced the number of eligible SES members from the initial 50 percent to 25 percent, and OPM cut this to 20 percent, a figure that Congress included in the 1982 and 1983 appropriation acts. Many SES members were outraged, charging a "breach of contract" because their willingness to join the SES had stemmed partly from the prospect of bonuses spread widely enough that many could hope to supplement their base salaries. Since 1984 there has been no congressional percentage limitation on the number of awards, but an agency may not in any year make awards totaling more than 3 percent of the previous year's aggregate basic pay of its SES careerists.[72]

Although the quantitative issue has been in part resolved, there remains some concern about the distribution of bonuses and presidential rank awards. Unfair distribution (e.g., favoritism) of bonuses and presidential awards were among the ten most important reasons for careerists leaving the SES in fiscal year 1985, ranking third and sixth respectively. Yet about half of those who left thought unfairness of some, little, or no importance in their decisions to leave.[73]

In 1987, over 60 percent of SES members were "dissatisfied or very dissatisfied" with the distribution and availability of bonuses.[74] Dissatisfaction in the Internal Revenue Service was greater: "Executives approve of the concept of a bonus pay system, but have deep seated concerns about the way the current SES bonus system is administered . . . 78 percent said that the SES bonus system did not provide an effective incentive for them to meet their job objectives . . . 69 percent said the SES bonus system is not administered fairly . . . 76 percent said there is not a direct link between their performance and their likelihood of receiving an SES bonus."[75]

One factor in dissatisfaction with agencies' performance awards is that they disproportionately go to careerists in the top SES ranks; their share is about twice the share of all SES positions. This appears to reflect less quality of performance than level of responsibility and "the attitude that no subordinate should receive greater compensation than his/her superior."[76] A different and scarcely consistent complaint is that performance awards have been too widely distributed, going to two-thirds of career executives through the 1983–86 period (and to over a third in one year, 1986) with two results: (1) the amounts of awards, averaging less than $6,000 since 1984 and amounting in 1986 to only 8.4 percent of mid-level SES base pay, are too small to be strong motivators to outstanding performance; and (2) as the best performers in one year are likely to be the best performers in the next few years, they should, but do not, get the number of multiple awards to be expected (four- and five-time winners are less than 10 percent of all winners; 45 percent are one-time winners).[77]

Presidential awards of ranks carrying large bonuses may be conferred in any year on about 400 outstanding SES careerists. In fact, they have ranged from a high of 183 to a low of 70.[78] From 1980 through 1987, only about 2 percent, instead of the authorized 6 percent, received such awards.[79] Again the question is posed whether the motivational purpose of the awards system is being fully achieved.

Executive Development. Large organizations devote much attention and substantial resources to the development of executive ability. In a government, as in a large corporation, this focuses on two target sets of employees: those below the executive ranks who show promise of rising to them, and those within the top ranks who would profit from reinforcement and upgrading of their executive talents. The latter is particularly important when, as with the SES, many members are scientists, engineers, and other specialists poorly grounded in the constitutional system and ill prepared for executive roles that require not only internal management of their units but dealings with central budget and personnel agencies, interagency committees, the White House, Congress, and interest groups.

Training of such employees occurs in many fashions—one-on-one guidance by a mentor within the agency, part-time training courses within the agency or at nearby universities, week- or several-weeks-long courses at a governmentwide educational facility, sabbatical leaves of absence for full-time study at a university, exchange assignments with business firms, and so on.

Although such training opportunities for civil servants are authorized by legislation, the federal government has not fully capitalized on them. Overall the government spends .8 percent of its payroll on training (and only 5 percent of that for managerial and executive training). This contrasts with the 3.3 percent spent by corporations in the Fortune 500 (10 percent by many) and the 15 to 20 percent spent by the military.[80] In the government's military services about 20 percent of an officer's career is spent in formal training. This contrasts to an average civil servant's spending less than 5 percent of the time in such training.[81]

Some who receive training are doomed to disappointment. Careerist candidates for the SES are competitively selected and then pursue a one- to three-year executive development program of their agency. Those successful in the program are certified as qualified to enter the SES. In fact, though, such certified candidates have received only 13 percent of the appointments to the SES; over half of the certified candidates failed to get appointed, and most of them continued in their old jobs.[82]

The government operates three executive seminar centers (in New York, Tennessee, and Colorado), offering two-week courses for employees below the SES level. The flagship of the training enterprise is the Federal Executive Institute (FEI) at Charlottesville, Virginia, which trains the most senior managers. Established in 1968, the FEI suffered neglect and political intrusion during much of its second decade. It revived fully only under new OPM leadership in 1987, and with the support of an alumni association of about 2,000 members.[83]

All training activities involving absence from employees' agencies suffer from two handicaps: (1) agencies choose those to be given such training, and some choose those who can be readily spared from their jobs, are near retirement, or will be comforted erroneously by what they perceive as an agency signal that they are due for promotion; (2) candidates for training may fear that if they leave for training, they will be forgotten when advancement opportunities open. The second handicap applies especially to sabbatical leaves of up to eleven months spent at universities and other organizations. In the first six years of the leave program, only twenty-two SES members took sabbaticals.[84]

Prospects

The SES had a troubled start and remains troubled. But no critic advocates abandonment of the service and return to the old system. The most severe early trouble was cutting the number of available bonuses by more than half. For most of the 1980s, the administration's policy of curtailing domestic programs and staffs while enlarging military programs and staffs depressed morale among high careerists charged with making those domestic programs work. Those and other SES careerists also found demoralizing and unsound their exclusion from policy-formulating activities to which in other times they contributed institutional memory, technical expertise, and sophistication. Morale was further depressed by the broad-brush "bureaucrat bashing" indulged in by both the Carter and Reagan campaigns for the presidency.

Politicization of appointments to the upper levels of the Office of Personnel Management, that office's distancing itself from nurturing the new SES, and its extreme decentralization of responsibility to the noncareer leadership in the agencies led to widespread suspicions that the SES was being politically manipulated. All objective inquiries have concluded that such manipulation has rarely occurred, whether by efforts to get around the 10 percent limit on noncareerist appointments, to punitively reassign careerists on political grounds, or to convert noncareer incumbents to career status.[85]

It is true that, while only 17 percent of Nixon's supergrade careerists normally voted Republican, 45 percent of Reagan's top SES careerists and 28 percent of lower SES careerists did so; this, however, largely expressed a shift from Independent voters, for the Democrats' percentages remained in the mid-40s.[86] Such phenomena do not have pat explanations. If it is possible that the Reagan administration rewarded Republican careerists with top positions, it is also possible that careerists, as the rest of the country, became more polarized, abandoning identification as political independents, and that some shared the population's drift toward "neoconservatism." While 6 percent of Nixon's Independent top careerists and 11 percent of his Democratic top careerists held right and right-of-center views on government's role in the economy, those figures were 63 and 31 percent for Reagan's Independent and Democratic topmost careerists.[87]

Careerists who left the SES in 1985 had many reasons for doing so, and of course, their relative significance varied among individuals and agencies. Overall, among fifty-five reasons they were asked to rate, the two most important reasons were dissatisfaction with top management and dissatisfaction with their agency's political appointees. (Careerists who left between 1983 and 1988 told much the same story.)[88] This disenchantment was registered in the fifth year of the Reagan administration, late enough for careerists not to be reflecting initial feelings about an influx of untried political appointees early in an administration. The depth of discontent is revealed by the dismal fact that, although many departing careerists said they had enjoyed their careers, almost two-thirds of the total said that they would advise someone beginning a career to go into the private sector rather than the public sector.[89]

Members still in the SES in 1987 were dissatisfied most (90 percent) with perceptions of federal workers by the press, politicians, and the public. From 60 to 80 percent were dissatisfied with salaries, benefits, and bonuses. About 75 percent rated as most satisfactory their co-workers; their own job's match with their aptitudes, abilities, or interests; their supervisor; and the subordinate staff. And, again, about two-thirds would advise or strongly advise someone beginning a career to choose the private sector. Only 13 percent would recommend public-sector employment.[90]

Few of the formal reforms that have been proposed promise to remove the roots of discontent. Some would confine the SES to careerists. Others would confine it to executives by removing to another system the scientists, engineers, and related professionals (40 percent of the SES members) who, being specialists, lack the mobility among positions and agencies that the administrative-generalist concept incorporates.[91] This is advocated, too, by the Office of Science and Technology Policy and the National Institutes of Health, which hope the new system would permit higher pay than SES's to attract able scientists and engineers. Such a separation, though, would narrow the political support for the SES.[92]

The problem runs deeper than a structural change can solve. If we accept departing careerists' views at face value, we then come full circle back to the issue of how to recruit political appointees who have executive ability and other qualifications for their positions and how to keep them while they learn their jobs and achieve full effectiveness.

Twelve state governments have introduced executive personnel systems of varying comparability to the SES. But a careful assessment of them concludes that they have neither added to the attractiveness of a career in government nor been consequential in heightening mobility of executives or their executive development.[93]

Pay

The government competes with the private sector for high-level executives and professional people. As would be true of most of us, such people must consider how their acceptance of a political or career appointment will affect their incomes. But, again as with most of us, pay is only one part of the total compensation package. Many less tangible gains and deficits count in one's anticipatory assessment of an employment opportunity, as they do later in one's on-the-job assessment of the desirability of remaining or leaving the organization.

This needs to be understood because the impact of government pay levels on the quality of the higher public service is not easily measured. We have adequate data on the comparability of public and private top pay scales. We know that the higher public-service positions get filled. But we do not know how many able people have turned down offers of presidential appointments (sometimes, according to anecdotal reports, as many as a dozen for one key position) or how many able persons have declined agencies' career and noncareer appointments to the SES. We know, it will be recalled, that political appointees on the average leave after two years, and we know that in recent years SES members resigned or chose optional retirement in alarming numbers. But those departures do not seem to stem from dissatisfaction with pay, even though many of those who leave do improve their incomes.

An SES example illustrates the difficulty of sorting pay issues from other considerations affecting departures. In the fifty-five years up to mid-1989, only three persons had held the Securities and Exchange Commission's position of director of the enforcement division. Because of its vast powers to open and close investigations, says one commissioner, it is the most significant securities law enforcement post in the nation. The third incumbent, Gary C. Lynch, spent nearly all his legal career on the commission staff. In 1989, only thirty-eight years old, he resigned his position at the top of the Senior Executive Service, which paid $80,700 (about what a new law school graduate gets at a leading law firm in New York), to enter private practice, where he was likely to make three times his government salary. Many in the agency questioned whether anyone could match Lynch's legacy for solid judgment and high-profile cases.[94] But we do not know whether his departure was because his pay was so low, because he thought it wise to leave when his accomplishments were unlikely to be topped by his future performance, or because he was uncertain about whom the new president (Bush) would appoint to the chairmanship and a majority of the commissionerships.

Two pay issues are central. One is pay comparability between the higher public service and the upper reaches of the private sector. The other is the linkage of executive pay to the pay of members of Congress.

Comparability with the Private Sector

In the private sector the financial rewards for successful corporate executives, lawyers, physicians, scientists, and engineers outdistance anything that an egalitarian society would tolerate for public servants. In the public sector, in contrast, top officials have intangible rewards rarely matched in the private sector, not least the opportunity to advance the public interest and to share in the shaping and execution of the nation's foreign and domestic policies.

The testimony of officials who have come from and returned to the private sector abounds in references to the richness of their brief experience in public office, the high quality of the career officials with whom they worked, and the letdown feeling when they resumed the narrow focus of their private callings. Four-fifths of presidential appointees between 1964 and 1984 "regard their service in office as an extremely valuable and enriching experience." Three-fourths of them say that the two greatest satisfactions on the job were dealing with challenging and difficult problems and accomplishing important public objectives. A former deputy secretary of agriculture under Reagan said, "... when I left government I worked half as hard and got paid twice as much." He added, "In every case, I found career people that were absolutely splendid. Their experience was absolutely invaluable.... These people want the job done right ... all of them are nonpartisan."[95] Appointees between 1964 and 1984 rated careerists competent in a range (according to presidential administration) of 77 to 92 percent, and responsive by 78 to 89 percent, with Reagan appointees giving the lowest ratings and Johnson appointees the highest. Curiously, Nixon appointees' ratings of careerists were the second highest, 88 and 84 percent.[96]

Elliot Richardson, who has headed four cabinet departments, has summed it up this way:

> The trouble is that all too many [new] political appointees ... suspect ... that senior civil servants lie awake at night scheming to sabotage the President's agenda and devising plans to promote their own. Having worked with most of the career services under five administrations, I can attest that this is not true....
>
> Almost any job at the deputy assistant secretary level ... is more responsible and has wider impact on the national interest than most senior corporate positions....
>
> I have many friends who once held responsible but not necessarily prominent roles in government and who now occupy prestigious and well-paid positions in the private sector—some of them very prestigious and very well-paid. Not one finds his present occupation as rewarding as his government service.... Society treats public servants, together with teachers, ministers, and the practitioners of certain other honorable but low-paid callings, as the beneficiaries of a high level of psychic income. But the psychic income of public service is being steadily eroded....[97]

At the end of Reagan's term, his secretary of commerce, formerly chief executive officer of a large steel company, said,

> I had always felt that Government people were not motivated, because in industry you have various incentives where you can motivate people, and that perhaps Government people didn't work so hard because they weren't so highly motivated. Well, I was dead wrong.
>
> I find that in this department there are a tremendous cadre of professionals, highly motivated not by financial incentives but to serve their country. It's as simple as that.[98]

A proper balance between financial and psychic incomes in the higher public service varies roughly by rank. Cabinet members are not a serious problem. Most are well-off, are at an age when family responsibilities are not pressing, and welcome high public status and the prospect of posthumous life in history books as a suitable culmination of successful careers. None of these conditions applies to most of the potential candidates for noncareer, subcabinet posts. They are, in fact, a diverse group. Consider, first, the persons accepting presidential appointments. Of a large sample of them, 38 percent experienced salary decreases (for three-fourths of those a decrease of more than $10,000) and 33 percent increased their incomes.[99] We do not know whether the quality of the two groups differed. We do know that people of high quality decline presidential appointments for financial reasons, forcing the White House to turn to less-preferred candidates. We also know that of three-fifths of former presidential appointees whose inadequate salaries affected their decisions to leave, three-fourths said that a pay increase of 50 to 100 percent would have been needed to keep them.[100]

Consider, second, the SES picture. Both noncareer candidates and career members are younger, their children are likely to be at or approaching college with its high tuition costs, and for many the government positions are at a level carrying slight prestige. Yet, for political appointees, their primarily private-sector careers are still in the making. Such relatively young appointees are likely to benefit from the government experience (notably in special fields such as taxation and antitrust law), the embellishment of their biographical résumés, and improved eligibility for future, higher, governmental appointments when their party again wins the presidency. Some political SESers, of course, will in fact get higher pay in the executive branch than in the think tanks, small advocacy organizations, and congressional staffs from which many come. Yet, as one study concluded, "inadequate salaries are a barrier to recruiting from among one group of especially desirable candidates for government service: those highly trained technicians and midcareer managers whose expertise, energy, and creativity [have] been amply demonstrated in the private sector."[101]

We might suppose that those who join the government as noncareerists or are in it as careerists are tempted to leave by the assured boosts in income. Yet in 1985, only a minority of the persons leaving the SES did so on grounds of inadequacy of salary; other dissatisfactions, as we have noted, played a larger role. Nevertheless, half of those leaving obtained increased salaries in their new positions, three-fourths of such salaries being $10,000 or more above their government salaries (including a fifth with a gain of $40,000 or more).[102] When the National Institutes of Health lost a fifth of their top scientific talent in a recent period, those leaving gained salary increases of 50 to 300 percent at university medical schools and private corporations.[103] The nation's physicians' average annual income (after expenses) is $132,000, a third or more above that of NIH's key health scientists.[104] No wonder that a director of one of the institutes testified, "Over the last decade NIH has not been able to recruit a single senior research scientist from the private or academic sector to engage in the independent conduct of a clinical or basic biomedical research program."[105]

Federal salaries also offer a peculiar contrast to those in state and local governments.[106] In 1988, cabinet members were paid the same as the average salary of the sixteen city managers in cities with populations over 250,000. The deputy secretary of defense got less than the New York City fire commissioner and about the same as that city's director of the Parking Violations Bureau. The attorney general of the United States made less than the attorney general of the State of New York. The secretary of education got less than the higher education heads in six states.[107]

Since 1967, when the Federal Salary Act was adopted, seven commissions on executive, legislative, and judicial salaries have been convened. Each was composed largely of corporate chief executives, distinguished private attorneys, university presidents, and other eminent Americans. Every commission concluded that top federal officials are critically underpaid. The one reporting in December 1988 found that "the level of salaries of high federal officials are now only about 65–70 percent in constant dollars of what their 1969 salaries were for the same positions."[108]

Many citizens express dismay at the salaries paid public officials. Strongly attached to the egalitarian spirit of democracy, and sensitive to the disparity between their own incomes and those of high officials, they show little patience with arguments that government needs a fair share of the best educated and most skilled managers and professional specialists. That this fair share must come from an elite pool whose members will take some account of tangible rewards is a proposition not readily conceded.[109]

The federal government's Executive Schedule salaries improve or handicap an administration's capacity to attract and retain the ablest prospective presidential appointees, a matter of concern especially at the levels below the cabinet. They also limit the Senior Executive Service, whose salary levels interlock with the two lowest Executive Schedule levels (IV and V). Both effects are closely tied to the fact that the rate for Executive Level II cannot exceed the salary level of senators and representatives.

Executive-Congressional Pay Linkage

The Federal Salary Act of 1967 called for the president to appoint every four years a Commission on Executive, Legislative, and Judicial Salaries, whose recommendations the president considered before recommending salary changes for congressional enactment. A 1985 amendment provided that the president's recommendations automatically go into effect unless disapproved within thirty days by a joint resolution of Congress.[110] The procedure nearly collapsed in 1987 and fully collapsed in early 1989.

In late 1989 Congress abolished the commission, substituting an eleven-member Citizens' Commission on Public Service and Compensation.[111] Six members, variously appointed by the president, chief justice, president pro tem of the Senate, and Speaker of the House, "should be selected from among persons who have experience or expertise in such areas as government, personnel management, or public administration." Five members are chosen by lot from geographically diverse voter registration lists. After considering the Commission's recommendations, the president recommends salary rates, which Congress, by recorded vote, may enact into law. However, those rates are operative only if a House election has occurred between enactment and their proposed effective date.

Members of Congress are reluctant to raise their own salaries, for such raises provoke highly critical reactions from their constituents and may be capitalized on by opponents at the next election. A storm of public protest about congressional raises accounts for the 1989 debacle. The executive and judicial branches were victims, though not the prime targets of the citizenry. This problem is avoidable by treating legislative salaries wholly apart from those of the other branches. This requires not only such separation but also abandonment of existing linkages that set caps on executive and judicial salaries, caps defined in relation to legislative salaries. The salary levels for Executive Level II presidential appointees and district court judges must be identical to that of members of Congress. In turn, salary levels of members of the Senior Executive Service cannot exceed level IV of the Executive Schedule.

There is, of course, no necessity for the linkage arrangement. Many state and local governments recognize that there are different market situations for different talents. They do not quail at setting pay rates for some appointive executive and professional positions at levels higher than those of elective officials. Nor do foreign governments. In Britain, for example, "41 officials are paid a higher salary than the Prime Minister, and another 157 are paid higher salaries than leading Cabinet ministers"—and, of course, higher than members of Parliament.[112]

The Volcker Commission, reporting after the defeat of 1989 increases, recommended that the president make separate recommendations for judges and top-level executives.[113] President Bush did so in July 1989. Congress continued to require, however, that pay for Executive Level II presidential appointees be the same as that recommended for senators and representatives.[114]

Conclusion

Several matters should be clear by this time. First, the .3 percent of federal employees that constitutes the higher public service is of crucial importance. Here are the managers of major federal programs; the advisers and often the decision makers on large policy questions; the interagency negotiators; the spokespersons to and bargainers with the Executive Office of the President, congressional committees, interest groups, and the general public; and the agents of the current administration who, in trying to induce civil servants to follow the election returns, carry much of the responsibility for assuring democratic control of the bureaucracy.

Second, the American higher public service, elite though it must be, is more nearly representative of the public it serves than are the administrative elites of other major nations.

Third, the American higher service has a much larger proportion of positions open to political appointment than do other countries.

Fourth, professional specialization and single-agency careers are the standard background of career executives. An earlier hope that the United States might recruit and develop administrative generalists, as do Britain, France, and (to a lesser extent) Germany, has been abandoned. In its stead is a hope that rising professional civil servants can be converted to the broader role of executives by executive development programs and, as in the Senior Executive Service, by insistence on demonstrated managerial ability before appointment to high office and on sustained, distinguished performance for retention of their high status.

Fifth, although pay is only one element in the compensation of higher public servants, federal pay has lagged far behind increases in the cost of living. Partly for this reason, the gap between it and private-sector pay and even state and local government pay has so widened as to impair the government's recruitment and retention of a fair share of the society's executive and professional talent. This will not be easily remedied until the linkage of executive and congressional pay is broken.

Finally, political appointees' tenure is short and careerists' long. This makes for an uncomfortable relationship, one in which political superiors operate within a short time frame, initiating enterprises they will not see through to completion, or restricting themselves to short-run ventures for which they can get credit. Careerists, operating within a long time frame, have a memory of what has worked and not worked in the past, an awareness of the long lead time from genesis of a program to its maturation, and an institutional loyalty and interpersonal network within agency and government that are uncharacteristic of most of the strangers recruited for political posts. Government is like a repertory theater whose regular cast was there before and remains during and after the visit of each "personality" imported to star for a short run.

Part IV

Government Decisions— Making and Implementing Them

Organizational theorists have long argued that decision making is the central administrative act. They have also disagreed mightily about how best to go about making decisions. This section probes the competing theories of decision making and applies those theories to the most important of all administrative decisions, the budgetary process. Making good decisions, however, is not enough. Decisions are not self-executing; they require skillful management by effective managers if the bold promises embodied in public policy are not to find disappointment in poor implementation. This section concludes by looking carefully at the link between decision making and implementation.

9

Decision Making

Most early students of public administration concentrated on how to design an organization's structure so that it would function as efficiently as possible. Luther Gulick's classic formulation defined basic principles for administrators to use in organizing agencies. In 1945, however, Herbert A. Simon posed a very different approach. He contended that "a theory of administration should be concerned with the processes of decision as well as with the processes of action." In fact, Simon argued,

> The task of "deciding" pervades the entire administrative organization quite as much as does the task of "doing"—indeed, it is integrally tied up with the latter. A general theory of organization that will insure correct decision-making must include principles of organization that will include correct decision-making, just as it must include principles that will insure effective action.[1]

Decision making occurs through a seamless web, from top to bottom in an organization. The job of administering governmental policy means that, at each step along the way, administrators must determine what the "policy" is and what their role is in bringing it to life. Decision making thus is the quintessential administrative act. As Simon pointed out, "doing" is impossible without "deciding."

The study of administrative decision making, however, has often been full of conflict. Many different theories of decision making have struggled for acceptance. Moreover, each of these theories has carried with it heavy baggage: *descriptive* elements (i.e., providing characterizations of how decision making typically *does* work); and *normative* elements (i.e., prescribing how decision making *should* work). As a result of these conflicts, no decision-making approach has won predominance. Each one, however, has helped provide useful techniques for making decisions and has described the fundamental problems that theory must answer. In this chapter, we first examine the basic problems with which decision-making theories struggle. Then we probe competing approaches to decision making. We conclude by exploring the enduring problems that plague decision making and those who attempt to develop good descriptions and prescriptions.

Basic Problems

Every approach to administrative decision making must tackle two issues. First, what *information* can decision makers use in reaching their judgments? Information is the basic raw material of decisions, and decision makers must acquire, weigh, and act on the data they collect. Second, how do political *values* affect decisions? The sheer complexity of public problems and the overwhelming volume of information forces decision makers to simplify the context shaping their decisions. This inevitable simplification is the product of political values. Moreover, for a decision to stick, it must win enough support to prevent others from seeking to overturn it. Building support means finding a common base of values among those who could sustain the decision. Both information and values constantly intermingle as administrators seek to make decisions, and as theorists develop arguments about how the process does—and ought to—work.

Information

Decisions, of course, can be made on the basis of whim or bias. Strong opinions also can influence decisions. An administrator who believes that most development harms the environment or that all basic scientific research is useful, regardless of its costs, might be tempted to make decisions accordingly. Common knowledge, instinct, and bias can drive even the most complex of decisions.[2]

Public administrators, of course, are hired not for their bias but for their expertise, as Weber long ago pointed out.[3] Indeed, the presumption that specialized administrators will exercise expert judgment provides the basis for legislators' delegation of power. Legislators cannot be expected to anticipate or solve all of the often-complex problems that typically crop up in the administration of public programs. Furthermore, even when a general policy may be clear, conditions vary so around the country that administrators must often tailor programs to fit local needs. Thus, if decision making is the very life of administrative activity, it is no exaggeration to say that information is the mother's milk of decision making. Expert skills and good information form the core of administrative decisions.

The importance of good information to effective public administration can scarcely be overestimated. That very importance, however, creates a dilemma. On the one hand, it is often deceptively difficult to uncover useful information and to channel it to relevant decision makers. On the other hand, knowledge brings power, and it is hard for the inexpert to control expert authority. This is, of course, a reprise of the classic public administration struggle between neutral competence and political accountability, but nowhere in public administration is this struggle sharper.[4]

The problem is that information rarely is an abstract truth but, more typically, is a matter of interpretation. No one ever knows everything, and never does everyone know the same things. Acquiring information is often an expensive activity, and some participants have a greater advantage over others because they have greater resources. Moreover, sometimes participants have a vested interest in keeping information hidden from others so that the secrecy benefits them. In short, as Deborah A. Stone points out, "Because politics is driven by how people interpret information, much political activity is an effort to control interpretations."[5] Information thus critically affects decisions in two ways: who has what information, and how they and others choose to look at the information they have.

Values

"Most important decision puzzles are so complicated that it is impossible to analyze them completely," Robert D. Behn and James W. Vaupel argue. Furthermore, they contend, "Decisions depend upon judgments—judgments about the nature of the dilemma, the probabilities of events, and the desirability of consequences. Decision making is inherently subjective."[6] Any process that includes some questions while leaving others out, that estimates the likelihood of different outcomes, and especially that weighs preferences for different outcomes is a value-laden process. One important question that decision-making theories must face, therefore, is how such value judgments are to be made.

Furthermore, no public policy decision, no matter how expertly reached, can endure if it does not command political support.[7] As Francis E. Rourke points out, political support for administrative decisions can come from higher levels of the executive branch, from Congress, or from the public.[8] Support from the public, moreover, comes from two sources. An agency's decisions might enjoy a favorable opinion among the general public, what Rourke calls an agency's "mass" public. More important, it might possess support from its "attentive" publics, "groups that have a salient interest in the agency." The two forms of support are not exclusive, and many agencies actively cultivate them both.[9] NASA, for example, works hard to promote the allure of space flight among the general public, while it labors to build support among its contractors for recurring battles on Capitol Hill about financing for its expensive programs.

As important as broad support is, political support from an agency's attentive publics typically is much more crucial. Few private citizens have the resources or the time to follow or comprehend the intricate detail and complex trail that most public policy decisions follow. In most decisions, only those who have the strongest interests are willing to devote the time and money needed to understand and influence the issues. That means, of course, that most difficult administrative decisions are reached within a relatively closed world dominated by those with common and intense interests.[10] It also means that such a closed world can sometimes be corrupted without attracting public notice, as the revelations in 1989 of scandals at the Department of Housing and Urban Development illustrated.

The relatively greater importance of strong support from narrow interests carries with it another dilemma for administrative decision makers. A decision maker who seeks the support of an agency's attentive publics risks sacrificing the broader interests of the public to the narrow stakes of particular interests. In contrast, if the decision maker cultivates only mass public support, he or she risks offending powerful interests that can use their influence to exact a heavy price. In short, every administrative decision maker needs to win political support for decisions, but the way that support is won can raise important problems. Few public decisions are ever stable because the forces that support them constantly change. Most decisions involve carving out boundaries—what is acceptable and what is not, how much is enough and how much is too much. Such boundary setting is an "inherently unstable" process, in which "boundaries are border wars waiting to happen."[11]

The complexity of decision making in bureaucracy has led to many different approaches. In this chapter, we explore four of them and explore how each one deals with the fundamental problems of information and values: (1) the rational approach, which seeks to maximize efficiency; (2) the bargaining approach, which seeks to maximize political support; (3) the participative approach, which seeks to improve decisions by intimately involving those affected by them; and (4) the public-choice approach, which attempts to substitute marketlike forces for other incentives that, to the approach's supporters, distort decisions.

Rational Decision Making

The rational decision-making approach is perhaps *the* classic approach to decision making. It builds on the work of microeconomists (who seek to explain the behavior of individuals and firms) and holds efficiency as the highest value. Proponents of this school argue that the goal of any activity, including governmental programs, is to get the biggest return for any investment. Simply put, they seek the most bang for the buck.

The rational theory fundamentally rests on the systems-theory approach described in chapter 3. The decision maker structures the decision-making problem as a "system" that processes "inputs" to produce "outputs." The decision maker seeks to produce the most output for a given level of inputs or, alternatively, to determine the minimum amount of inputs needed to produce a given amount of output. In short, the decision maker seeks to maximize efficiency.

The systems approach is so simple, its logic so overpowering, that it is easy to understand how it has become a classic. After all, we speak of "computer systems," which are hunks and slivers of silicon, wires, and plastic that process inputs (such as letters typed into a keyboard) into outputs (such as letters and reports and books like this one). Computer analysts strive to improve the system: to make computers work more quickly or more cheaply or do things that could not be done before.

Basic Steps

Rational decision making, according to the basic approach, has five basic steps:

1. *Define goals.* The rational approach starts with a description of a problem to be solved, and an output goal to be achieved. For example, a systems analyst might seek to determine the best way to reduce automobile accident deaths by 10 percent or to reduce air pollution below dangerous limits. This is very different from conventional ways of thinking about government programs, which focus on input measures: numbers of social security checks mailed, miles of highway built, or more dollars added to existing spending. The systems approach concentrates instead on most effectively producing desired outputs. The goals come to analysts through the legislative process.

2. *Identify alternatives.* Once the decision maker has determined the goal, the analyst tries to identify the different ways the goal can be achieved. In the search, the key is to think innovatively about new options that others might never have tried—or even considered.

3. *Calculate the consequences.* The analyst then weighs the alternatives by measuring the costs and benefits of each one. In the strictest form of such analyses, in fact, every cost and benefit is translated into dollar terms. Furthermore, the analyst also considers indirect benefits and costs (often

called *externalities, side effects,* or *spillovers*) that relate to other goals. For example, a highway route that is "best" in terms of the stated transportation goal may destroy parks and increase downtown traffic congestion.

4. *Decide.* Once the analysis is finished, the decision maker chooses the project with the most favorable balance of benefits to costs.

5. *Begin again.* Systems analysis is not a once-and-done process. Instead, analysts see it as an iterative process: a project provides feedback —new information about what works and what does not, as well as consequences (intended and not) of a decision—that then helps the analyst redefine the problem, set new goals, and begin the process again. By continually working to fine tune the system by learning from past mistakes, systems analysis in theory helps decision makers move ever closer to the "best" decisions.

Though the rational approach might seem abstract, it has the appeal of common sense: any sensible person will choose the most rational (and efficient) route to his or her goal. Who, after all, wants to be irrational?[12]

Example: Planning-Programming-Budgeting System

Because of its logic, the rational approach has many followers. As the case of the Planning-Programming-Budgeting System (PPBS) shows, however, the straightforward logic of rational decision making has many variations in practice. Furthermore, the considerable difficulties of *doing* systems analysis can be its undoing.

In 1961, Secretary of Defense Robert McNamara introduced PPBS in the Pentagon.[13] The technique had three phases: (1) planning, in which top-level managers developed five-year strategies for defense activities; (2) programming, in which the strategies were transformed into detailed descriptions of the department's needs, including which weapons systems had to be purchased when; and (3) budgeting, in which officials transformed the program into year-by-year budget requests. The basic idea was to link the annual budgetary process with long-range plans instead of haphazard requests. Furthermore, each branch of the service was to budget by program instead of by organizational unit. The Pentagon, for example, would decide whether the nation's strategic needs required a new jet fighter and, if so, what capabilities it ought to have. Program budgeting, McNamara hoped, would drive down the cost of buying weapons systems by reducing competition among the services for their own individually tailored weapons systems.

President Johnson was so pleased with the results in the Defense Department that he extended it in 1965 to almost all federal civilian departments and agencies. Each agency submitted its budget to the Bureau of the Budget (now the Office of Management and Budget) by program.[14] The program budgets were, in turn, supported by massive memoranda that considered "all relevant outputs, costs, and financing needs" as well as "the benefits and costs of alternative approaches" to solving problems. Each agency also prepared a five-year projection of the agency's future programs and financial requirements. The plans, however, were often "lengthy wish lists of what the agencies would like to spend on their programs if no fiscal constraints were imposed." The connection between PPBS paperwork and what agencies actually planned to do was often amorphous. Since Congress continued to run its appropriations process the old way, the link between PPBS and congressional decisions was fuzzy indeed.[15]

Instead of integrating and improving presidential and congressional decisions on the budget, PPBS produced its own paperwork domain. PPBS finally collapsed under the burden and, in June 1971, the federal government's PPB system ended, when the Office of Management and Budget ceased to require that agencies submit PPBS documents with their conventional budget requests.[16]

In terms of its original objectives, PPBS was a failure. It never was able to transform the base of government planning and link budgets—government's inputs—to its outputs. In foreign governments and nearly all state and local governments that have tried the system, it has produced similar results.[17] Part of PPBS's failure came from budgeters' inability to cope with the system's analytical burdens. More fundamentally, it failed because of a critical design flaw: PPBS was not tailored to the organizational environment in which it had to work. First, PPBS's designers left Congress out of the system, and PPBers "refused to reveal to Congress the studies and information produced by the PPB system ... [though] without information of this kind, the ability of Congress to even ask the right questions concerning program performance is seriously impaired."[18] Second, although PPBS was solely an instrument of the executive branch, even that limited environment was neglected. PPBers were inadequately prepared to neutralize bureaucratic resistance. Any innovation produces such resistance, but PPBers seemed arrogant to many other government officials. Lower organizational units were upset that PPBS appeared to rob them of authority (centralizing it instead in agency heads and the Bureau of the Budget), that it shifted analytical work from agency staffs knowledgeable about the agency's policy area to PPBS technicians skilled in quantifying but unacquainted with the policy area, and that it required an enormous amount of paperwork without discernible impact on decision making.

Nevertheless, PPBS's results were substantial. It brought into the government a number of able analysts, many of whom remained.[19] It acquainted a large number of top executives and career civil servants with a new style of discourse, one that emphasizes clarification of objectives, generation of alternative ways of serving the objectives, and quantification of benefits and costs where such measurement is appropriate. Multiyear projections of program costs are now transmitted to Congress as a regular part of the budgetary process.

The Pentagon, moreover, still actively works on a modified PPB system. Defense officials continue to develop long-range plans, to translate those plans into programs, and to develop the programs into budgets. The way the process works has varied considerably by administration. Republican administrations have tended to vest more authority with the individual services, while Democratic administrations have pulled more authority to the defense secretary. Despite the longevity of the process, however, its results continue to be disappointing. Lawrence J. Korb, former assistant secretary of defense, argues that during the Reagan administration, top officials' approach to PPBS "contributed to a near collapse of rational budgeting in DOD and helped undermine the consensus in this country for a buildup. Indeed, when Weinberger departed the Pentagon in late 1987, the budgeting process was in near chaos." Korb contends that defense planning had "almost no impact on the process," that programming meetings had far too many participants to make meaningful decisions, and that previous decisions never drove final budget decisions.[20]

Appraisal

Because the rational approach to decision making seems so straightforward, it has a large following. Even the most cynical critics of PPBS could scarcely argue against improving the way the federal government formulates its goals and how to achieve them. Still, the rational approach must struggle with several serious problems, dealing with both information and values.

Information. The pure systems approach requires an extraordinary amount of information. Decision makers must consider *all* alternatives to achieving a policy goal. That, of course, is impossible because our wit is not equal to a complete search of possibilities. In fact, to some systems-approach critics, the impossibility of comprehensive analysis itself renders the approach useless. As Charles E. Lindblom, perhaps the method's strongest critic, argues:

> Men have always wanted to fly. Was the ambition to undertake unaided flight, devoid of any strategy for achieving it, ever a useful norm or ideal?

... Achieving impossible feats of synopsis [comprehensive analysis] is a bootless, unproductive ideal.

Moreover, by trying to do the impossible, Lindblom worries, "they fall into worse patterns of analysis and decision."[21] Even the cost, in time, energy, and money, of a nearly comprehensive search is extremely high, and the decision maker driven by comprehensiveness can never be sure what has been left out. The goal itself is impossible, the gaps are rarely known, and the result is an uncharted gap in the analysis whose effects are unknown.[22]

In real life, of course, no one ever tries to be completely comprehensive. Decision makers instead simplify the process: (1) they screen out the silly options and restrict themselves to a few major alternatives; and (2) they stop searching when they come upon a *satisfactory* alternative, even though further search might turn up a better one. James G. March and Herbert A. Simon have called this approach "satisficing."[23]

This realism does not carry us very far, for two reasons. First, most of the calculations required for translating benefits and costs into dollars and cents require value judgments. How much worth should be accorded a life, a child's happiness, a scenic view from the highway, or a pleasing architectural design? Economists in fact have developed mechanisms for pricing even such difficult things as the value of a human life.[24] The very attempt to weigh the value of different items, however, often takes us to extremely difficult (and sometimes bizarre) judgments. As Lewis M. Branscomb writes,

Despite the well-publicized conflict between economic and ecological interests, our appreciation for environmental impact and technology assessment is unique in the world. Where else would (i) a $600-million hydroelectric dam be held up to protect an endangered 3-inch freshwater fish called the snail darter, (ii) a unique butterfly enjoy priority at the end of the main runway of the Los Angeles International Airport, and (iii) the sexual aspirations of a clam threaten the construction of a nuclear power station in New Hampshire?[25]

Second, how do we know when we have found a satisfactory range of alternatives? To study some alternatives and not others is to make a value judgment, yet value-free analysis is the goal of rational decision making. The rational analyst is thus back in the same dilemma: of doing his or her best to guess what alternatives others might have had in mind, or to impose his or her own values on the array of alternatives. Either way, the process for defining standards is vague, and little science remains in "the science of rational decision making." That, in turn, raises new questions about values.

Values. The systems approach depends on a clear statement of goals. Without such a statement, in fact, it quite simply cannot work. The classic literature on rational decision making, however, has little to say about *who* sets goals. Instead, the theory presumes that *some* decision maker will define the objective in the precise form needed for rational decision makers at lower levels to proceed with their tasks. Yet we know that Congress's statements of objectives often lack clarity and consistency, that Congress would fight the president if he attempted to set comprehensive goals, and that executive branch agencies usually get caught between the two. That, in turn, leaves the rational decision maker with two choices: to make his or her own best guess about what Congress, for example, may have intended in passing a law (and risk being told he or she is wrong when, as is likely, someone disagrees); or to apply subjective values to define the goals (and risk undercutting the very objectivity at the core of systems analysis).

Our pluralistic political system constantly formulates and reformulates goals as political majorities shift, as the effectiveness of various interest groups waxes and wanes, as population changes, and as new technologies and new information alter the shape of problems and our capacity to deal with them. The art of assembling majority support, among voters and legislators, for each program typically requires fuzzy goals and vague language. The more precisely objectives are defined, the easier it is for competing parties to disagree with them.

The rational, efficiency-minded approach often works very well for small-scale and technical issues, on which agreement over goals is relatively easy. Should a local government buy or lease its police cars? Which paving material will last the longest? How much of which kind of snow-removal equipment should a city buy? On larger questions, however, the constitutional separation of powers, political realities, bureaucratic dynamics, and rapidity of change in world and domestic conditions give little hope of finding a way to define goals clearly. What is the "best" solution if there is disagreement over what the problem is?

Efficiency is not the only goal we seek. Equality, for example, is often a central objective in public programs. In fact, the economist Arthur M. Okun calls the job of balancing equality and efficiency "the big tradeoff": "We can't have our cake of market efficiency and share it equally."[26] Another economist, Murray Weidenbaum, who served in the Reagan administration as chairman of the Council of Economic Advisers, goes even further. He observes that

> it is possible to develop government investment projects which meet the efficiency criterion (that is, the total benefits exceed the total costs) but

which fail to meet the simplest standards of equity.... Unfortunately, there has been a tendency on the part of some economists to dismiss such "distributional" questions as subjective and political, and hence not within the proper concern of economic analysis.[27]

The rational approach thus has great attraction. It gives an elegant prescription for how the best decisions can be made. In describing the practical policy world, however, it falls short. Its advocates, in fact, often follow "rational" techniques only as long as they help them achieve their own political ends. Moreover, even in the abstract, rational techniques do not tell decision makers where to draw the line short of the impossible task of comprehensiveness. Nor do these techniques solve the fundamental questions of whose values will be used to perform the analysis. Indeed, agreement on goals, as the bargaining approach contends, is the central problem of decision making.

Bargaining

We have earlier taken note of the pluralistic approach to administrative organization (chapter 3), and of the alliances that sometimes develop among an agency, its related congressional committees, and its clientele interest groups (chapter 6). These issues demonstrate how decision making involves conflict, negotiation, persuasion, and individuals with stakes in particular policies and decisions.

The bargaining approach to decision making builds on these concepts to develop a different view of rationality. The approach's proponents, such as Charles E. Lindblom, argue that it is paradoxically most rational to conduct limited analysis and then to bargain out a decision that can attract political support.

Lindblom offers a simple prescription, incrementalism, to analyze public decisions.[28] It is best, he says, to limit analysis to a few alternatives instead of trying to judge them all; to weigh one's values along with the evidence, instead of holding them separate as the rational approach would suggest; and to concentrate on the immediate problems to be solved rather than the broader goals to be achieved. The great goals are almost always beyond reach, especially in the short run, and problems presented in smaller chunks are easier to define, diagnose, and solve. It is, furthermore, easier to build support for a series of incremental changes from the current situation and to correct any errors that might creep in. Decision making is thus essentially value laden.[29] Conflicts are the rule and cannot be resolved by rational analysis. Instead, "partisan mutual adjustment"—the pulling and hauling among decision makers with different views—offers the best hope for the best decisions, supporters of the bargaining approach contend.[30]

In fact, regulatory reformers have developed an explicit bargaining strategy to reduce conflict. Many federal regulations are automatically litigated by interest groups who disagree with what the regulators have written. When new rules are promulgated, lawyers flock to the telephones to report to their offices, and their colleagues rush to file appeals. Endless legal delays thus are the rule, not the exception. To produce better rules and to forestall litigation, the U.S. Environmental Protection Agency holds "regulatory negotiation" sessions involving the various interests potentially affected by new rules. In a series of bargaining sessions, they meet to hammer out a mutually acceptable regulation and, in the process, greatly reduce the chances that the rule will be litigated. While this strategy cannot be used for all rulemaking—even when successful it raises some important problems—regulatory negotiation does reduce conflict and promote quicker, cleaner regulation.[31] More often, of course, the bargaining is much less structured, as the case of the Cuban missile crisis illustrates.

Example: Cuban Missile Crisis

In October 1962, the United States came to the brink of nuclear war with the Soviet Union. American intelligence aircraft discovered that the Soviets had built missile bases in Cuba from which they could have launched nuclear strikes against New York, Washington, D.C., and other important East Coast targets. American experts estimated that war would kill 100 million Americans, more than that number of Russians, and millions more of Europeans. President Kennedy's advisers worried about why the Soviets placed the missiles in Cuba to begin with, and how they could convince the Soviets to remove the weapons.

The President launched a public relations offensive against the Soviets, in which UN ambassador Adlai Stevenson dramatically revealed reconnaissance photos of the bases, asked for an explanation from the Soviet ambassador, and promised to wait for an answer until hell froze over. Meanwhile, President Kennedy's advisers developed several alternatives to deal with the crisis. Military officials planned an attack on the missile bases to wipe them out before they became fully operational. Other advisers suggested a naval blockade to turn back further shipments of the missiles and to give the Soviets a chance to dismantle the missiles before hostilities began. Meanwhile, the administration conducted quiet back-channel diplomacy to try to uncover the Soviet Union's motives and to attempt to defuse the crisis. President Kennedy decided on the blockade, and the nation waited anxiously to see if Soviet freighters bound for Havana would turn around. When they first stopped short of the blockade line and then returned to Soviet ports, tensions eased. Soviet Premier Nikita S. Khrushchev agreed to remove the missiles and never again to deploy such weapons in Cuba; Kennedy in return promised not to invade Cuba and to remove American missiles in Turkey that worried the Soviets. After thirteen days of high tension, from 16 October to 28 October, the crisis ended.[32]

Graham Allison studied the crisis and argued that the events could be understood from three different perspectives. First, in what he christened "Model I," the Cuban missile crisis could be analyzed from a traditional, rational-actor approach. Both the United States and the Soviet Union, by this approach, had unified national positions that guided each side's decisions. Second, he advanced "Model II," based on organizational processes. By this approach, decisions could be understood by analyzing the standard operating procedures of the bureaucracies on both sides. Finally, he proposed "Model III," christened as the bureaucratic-politics perspective. Decisions, by this method, can be understood as "a *resultant* of various bargaining games among players in the national government." By understanding "the perceptions, motivations, positions, power, and maneuvers of the players," one can understand a decision.[33]

This bargaining model helps illuminate the missile crisis. Kennedy, for example, was vulnerable because of the failure of the American-supported Bay of Pigs invasion by Cubans trying to overthrow Cuban leader Fidel Castro in April 1961. Americans had come to believe that communist domination of Cuba constituted a serious threat to American security. Furthermore, the failure of the invasion made Kennedy seem indecisive. Faced with the discovery of missiles in Cuba, the administration, by this perspective, had to act forcefully. Doing nothing or taking a diplomatic approach therefore lost ground to a military response.

Kennedy initially favored what some advisers called a "surgical" air strike, designed to take out the missile launchers without doing more widespread damage. Other participants, however, such as Defense Secretary Robert McNamara, worried deeply that firing shots might spark a nuclear war that would immediately be beyond either side's control. The president's brother, Robert Kennedy, pointedly asked whether the president, if he launched a surprise attack, would become known as an American "Tojo," the Japanese strategist who planned the raid on Pearl Harbor. In fact, as Allison points out, "after these arguments had been stated so strongly, the president scarcely could have followed his initial preference without seeming to become what RFK had condemned."[34]

Three of the president's closest advisers teamed up to press for the blockade: Robert Kennedy, McNamara, and presidential counselor Theodore Sorensen. Meanwhile, military advisers, CIA chief John McCone, and Secretary of State Dean Rusk argued in favor of the air strike. Their position weakened when one of the participants asked how the Soviets would likely respond. The best guess was that the Soviets would strike at American missile bases in Turkey, which would then, under the NATO treaty, compel the United States to attack the Soviet Union. No one found such an event appealing. Finally, military planners began to argue that a "surgical" air strike was impossible and that, to be effective, any military action against the missile launchers would have to be accompanied by a broad-scale attack against all Cuban military installations and, in all likelihood, an invasion.

The decision to establish a blockade, along with the other key decisions of the crisis, thus can be viewed as the result of a bargaining process among the key players. Decisions are, in reality, complex arenas in which decision makers must resolve uncertainties and conflicting preferences. As Allison concludes, "What moves the chess pieces is not simply the reasons that support a course of action, or the routines of organizations that enact an alternative, but the power and skill of proponents and opponents of the action in question."[35] Decisions thus are viewed as the product of bargains. In the bargaining game, the perspective of each player is shaped by the player's position; "where you stand depends on where you sit," the saying goes.[36] Who wins depends on who has the strongest hand and who bargains most effectively.[37]

Appraisal

The bargaining approach has drawn withering fire from its critics, especially among proponents of the rational approach.

Information. Critics contend that the bargaining approach is dangerously incomplete and risks depriving decision makers of important information.[38] The political process, they contend, can be counted on to present decision makers with political opinions, but it is far less useful in identifying which alternatives are likely to be the most efficient. The result, they suggest, is that scarce resources can be wasted. When money is tight, bargaining over public programs might produce common ground only by spreading money among the combatants. One economist, Charles Schultze, acknowledges that "it may, indeed, be necessary to guard against the naïveté of the systems analyst who ignores *political* constraints and believes that efficiency alone produces virtue." But in taking aim at the incrementalists, he concludes, "it is equally necessary to guard against the naïveté of the decision maker who ignores *resource* constraints and believes that virtue alone produces efficiency."[39] It is possible, Schultze argues, to take account of political realities while doing systems analysis.

Lindblom replies that systems analysis cannot be done and argues that his decision-making approach *is* indeed analysis; he merely suggests that limited, successive comparison of alternatives is more successful than attempts at comprehensiveness. The bargaining approach, however, does not really tell the analyst just *how* comprehensive to be, how much analysis to do. Just how large ought an increment to be? How many alternatives should a decision maker consider? The only answer is a circular one. The increments should be small enough and the alternatives few enough to produce political consensus. A decision maker knows that the approach is right if a consensus forms and wrong if it does not. While this might give a useful description of many decisions, it provides a weak guide for officials trying to design a decision-making process.

Values. The bargaining approach is obviously at its strongest in describing how decisions are made and, in particular, how decision makers build political support for their judgments. Indeed, incrementalism grows directly out of enduring American traditions of participation in politics and out of more recent theories of pluralism. Its rooting in this heritage gives the approach extra appeal.

Nevertheless, the role of interests in decision making varies substantially in the government. In some agencies, such as the Agriculture Department or Social Security Administration, relatively broad interests pay careful attention to decisions such as farm price supports or retirement payments. Interest-group pressure is intermittent but occasionally intense. In other agencies, such as the departments of State and Defense, the range of interests is more narrow and public attention is much less intense. For the most part, the partisans at work are those with a direct stake in the decisions, such as military contractors, Defense Department officials, and representatives of other parts of the government. The players and their roles in the bargaining process thus are likely to vary greatly by the type of agency and the nature of its programs. The value of the bargaining approach in resolving decision-making conflicts thus is likely to vary accordingly.

Furthermore, it is often difficult to bargain out differences. When issues are complicated and the interests narrow, it is easy for broader public interests to be submerged. Intense attentive publics can wield heavy influence over decisions before the general public even knows that a major decision is to be made. Well-financed special interests, furthermore, have a large advantage over an agency's general public. They can play a role in framing the decision to begin with, in producing analyses to influence the decision, and in gaining the ears of decision makers at crucial times. Their intimate familiarity with the decisions and the decision makers gives them a strategic advantage that members of the general public can rarely match.

In contrast, especially in foreign policy and national security issues, the range of participants can be very limited and the possibility of bargaining typically evaporates. Indeed, during the Reagan administration, a small group of White House officials conducted a clandestine policy of selling arms to Iran to win the release of American hostages in the Middle East, a policy developed outside regular State and Defense Department channels and without the benefit of expert advice. In many foreign policy cases, top decision makers often work above the alternatives produced by staff at lower levels.[40]

Bargaining thus provides a useful description of how many, but not all, administrative decisions are made. Just as with the rational approach, however, there are important normative problems with bargaining, particularly because not everyone is represented equally around the table, and some interests may not even be invited. Nevertheless, the approach is important for its assertion of the importance of values in decisions and for its stark contrast with the rational model.

Participative Decision Making

Beyond incrementalism is another approach founded even more directly on political democracy: participative decision making, which calls at the most general level for participation by those who will be affected by the decisions. That, however, leaves two ambiguities.

First, what does participation mean? It may mean being *consulted* for advice by someone who has power to make the decision, or it may mean *sharing* decision-making power, as when those affected vote on a proposed decision and the vote settles whether the proposal is adopted or rejected. Second, just who should be entitled to participate in such decision making? Claims to such status can be made by four groups: (1) the employees of the organization making the decision; (2) the persons whom the organization serves or regulates (the clientele); (3) the taxpayers whose pocketbooks the decision will affect; and (4) the whole public, or at least the voting public, of the country. These participants are potentially in conflict. The course of action that any of the groups may recommend can sharply vary from what any other group might choose.

On the surface, the value of such participation seems obvious. Who could object to having the decision-making process enlightened by the view of those who have to live with the decision? The problem, of course, is that each group invokes "democracy" as its own battle cry, sometimes to the exclusion of all other claimants. Furthermore, when one group gains leverage on a decision, such influence often comes only at a cost to other groups.

For example, the poor, especially from black neighborhoods, have for decades sought a greater voice in programs serving them. Residents of middle-class neighborhoods similarly demand a say about new projects, school closings, and other governmental initiatives that seem boons or threats to the quality of life in the immediate environment. Often, in fact, the demand for such participation leads to the "NIMBY" phenomenon: strong pressures to keep potentially objectionable programs "not in my back yard." Federal statutes and administrative regulations require local community or neighborhood participation in decisions about community development, the poverty program, community mental health centers, and other programs. Meanwhile, a host of nongovernmental organizations, most of them newly created for the purpose, have been delegated responsibilities for administering government programs. For example, Congress created the Prospective Payment Advisory Commission to advise the Health Care Financing Administration on rates hospitals should be paid for Medicare cases. Medical professionals dominate the commission, so physicians have a voice in what the federal government pays them. In a number of large cities, likewise, the board of education has decentralized power to elected neighborhood councils.

New techniques for participation evolved so quickly from the 1960s to the 1980s that many have supposed that clientele participation in decision making is a novel idea. In fact, American public administration has had long and rich experience with consultation and shared decisions, especially at the local level. These arrangements have not always been successful, and fewer frustrations would arise if new ventures toward "participatory democracy" and "grass-roots decentralization" took account of the hazards so well marked out by experience.

Example: Federal Level

Federal agencies have long used advisory committees of private citizens in the decision-making process. Most important among these have been industry advisory committees, which have a painful history of troubles over representativeness, secrecy, conflicts of interest, profiteering on privileged information, temptations to violate the antitrust laws, and displacement of the responsible government officials as the real decision makers.

The high-water mark of these industry advisory committees came early in the New Deal when the National Recovery Administration relied heavily on trade associations, first, for the drafting of the nearly 500 codes of fair competition controlling the production and prices of as many industries, and second, for selection of members of the code authorities to which enforcement powers were delegated.[41] During World War II, industry advisory committees proliferated (the War Production Board had a thousand of them, and the Office of Price Administration some 650), and at national and regional levels joint industry-labor-government boards were given decisional power in labor disputes.[42] In the 1950s, the Business Advisory Council of the Department of Commerce attracted such criticism as a privileged big-business channel of influence on administration policy that it was reconstituted as a private organization.[43] Dogging this history of industry advisory committees has been the risk that the government's assembling of representatives of an industry would validate Adam Smith's dictum, "people of the same trade seldom meet together, even for merriment and diversion, but the conversation ends in a conspiracy against the public, or in some contrivance to raise prices."[44]

A second major area of clientele participation through national advisory committees has to do with the allocation of funds for scientific research, including the awarding of research grants and contracts to individual scientists and institutions. The National Science Foundation, National Institutes of Health, and other research-supporting agencies rely heavily on peer review by committees of scientists in the specialized fields. Here again, issues of representativeness, insiders' advantages, and unconscious bias have been raised about clientele participation.[45] During the Carter administration, the number of federal advisory committees was cut by 30 percent, to 816, but critics continued to complain that secrecy afflicted the committees.[46]

Example: Local Level

Over the past fifty years, a variety of national programs have promoted decentralized, grassroots participation by the programs' clients. A few programs, in fact, involve all the program's clients, rather than just representative councils and committees. For example, compulsory marketing quotas and marketing orders for several agricultural commodities can be instituted only by a two-thirds favorable vote in a referendum of all growers of the commodity.[47]

More commonly, federal agencies have relied on local committees whose part-time members were intended to be representative of their communities or neighborhoods. In some programs the local committees were appointed by the president or a federal agency after consultation with the governor, local government officials, or the agency's own field agents. This was true of the 5,500 War Price and Rationing Boards established in World

War II by the Office of Price Administration. And it was true of the some 4,000 local Selective Service Boards that administered the draft during the Vietnam war. Though appointive, each board was meant to be "representative of the community as a whole" (OPA) or "composed of friends and neighbors of the registrant it classifies" (Selective Service).[48]

Farmers and Graziers. The oldest form of local participation in decision making for federal programs comes in the administration of agricultural programs. In what is literally grassroots participation, farmers since 1933 have been elected to serve on committees in 3,000 counties. Members of the three-member committees are chosen either directly by the county's farmers or indirectly by the community committee members. A county committee exercises real power: it "is ultimately responsible for program and administrative policies and decisions at the county level."[49] It establishes individual farms' acreage allotments and marketing quotas for some commodities, administers crop-support loans, provides disaster payments, and supervises government-owned commodity storage facilities. Choosing committee members is often difficult, a problem that spills over into other national programs. In one year's election, for example, the turnout nationally was but 23 percent, and in six major farming states the turnout ranged from 5 to 8 percent.[50] In half the communities of one Illinois county there were more candidates than voters!

The grazing boards in the West, elected by local stockmen, are reminders that clientele participation can magnify self-interest at the expense of public interest, and, indeed, of other special interests. They have effectively made most decisions on the issuance of permits for grazing on public lands. As Grant McConnell pointed out, participation by cattlemen has strengthened the power of the most influential ranchers. Participation in district elections has been low, averaging less than 10 percent in Oregon and Idaho, and the committees have been dominated by the same powerful stockmen for a long time. As a result, "the general [public] interest in conservation of the soil has, on occasion at least, suffered from the pattern of power deriving from the autonomous systems of government of these lands."[51]

City Dwellers. Urban America has wrestled with the same problems without any attentiveness to the lessons of the rural experience. A series of federal programs starting in the mid-1960s required communities to establish citizen committees to help determine how the money should be spent. The mandates began with the 1964 Economic Opportunity Act, which required each local community action program in the War on Poverty to be "developed, conducted, and administered with the maximum feasible participation of the areas and members of the groups served." The 1966 Model Cities Act required that any local plan for rebuilding and revitalizing slum or blighted neighborhoods must provide for "widespread citizen participation" from those neighborhoods. In 1974, the Housing and Community Development Act (which superseded the Model Cities Act, among others) required that any local government applying for community development funds offer "satisfactory assurances" that it had provided citizens with "adequate" information, had held public hearings to learn citizens' views, and had provided citizens a chance to shape the application. If you think the quoted congressional phrases are imprecise, you are right. What is "maximum" or "widespread" or "adequate" participation was left an open question, which led to battles over infusing each term with a specific meaning.

Or consider education. There are approximately 16,000 local school boards around the country. In New York City, there are 32 community school boards, each elected by residents, which have substantial power to run neighborhood schools. As the movement to improve basic education gained steam in the mid-1980s, however, critics began to look seriously at the boards. "The system isn't working, and the reason it isn't working is that the stakes that have become the focus for most of the boards are the jobs involved, not what is happening in the schools and with the kids," said Board of Education president Robert Wagner, Jr. In fact, one *New York Times* headline announced, "School Boards Found Failing to Meet Goals," and its reporter concluded that the school-district system was little more than a collection of "political clubhouses."[52] Turnout for school board elections was consistently less than 10 percent, while patronage loomed over educational issues.[53] Local school boards, more generally, were plagued by apathy and indifference. The turnout for school board elections has never been above 14 percent, and since 1975 has typically been between 7.5 and 9 percent. That has led, in some districts where blacks and Hispanics are in the majority, to boards totally dominated by whites. "A lot of parents are not voting in the school elections because they do not feel connected to the decentralized system," one researcher said. "They do not feel that the local school boards, as they are now constituted, are a good vehicle for positively influencing education."[54]

Appraisal

Since the mid-1970s, as complaints about decentralization have grown and as budgets have gotten tighter, the trend gradually has been to centralize control and put more decision-making responsibility in the hands of elected officials. The trend underlines the recurring dilemmas of participative decision making.

Information. One of the biggest advantages that participative approaches offer is the wealth of information they provide. Few insights into the management of public programs are better than those of the persons who must administer them, and few observers of any program's effects have keener insights than citizens most affected by them. The very wealth of this information is a problem. It typically flows to decision makers as a large, undifferentiated mass, with no easy clues about which information is most important. Too much information can sometimes be as bad as too little.

Values. In sorting through the vast amount of information that the participative approach produces, decision makers must also sort through important value questions. The approach spawns recurring dilemmas:

1. A narrow clientele dedicated to protection of its own self-interest, *or,* at the opposite pole, a broad, mixed clientele with a less-keen interest in the policy.
2. Direct participation in decision making by all persons in the clientele who wish to participate, with the risk of an impossibly large group to deal with, *or* direct participation by those who get appointed or elected to committees, councils, or boards officially assumed to represent the clientele—but that might not be very representative.
3. Formal or informal power given to citizens in making government decisions, with the problem of who looks out for the public interest, *or* simply providing advice (and demands) to public administrators who weigh those views with other considerations and make the actual decisions, with the problem of taking that advice seriously.

The choices are hard, but they carry important implications for responsive and effective policy making. On the one hand, participative decision making led to new public access to government decisions and to the creation of a new cadre of civic leaders. On the other hand, the system created some patronage and new officials seeking to protect their own positions. The record is mixed.[55]

Public Choice

Some microeconomists have developed a different theory to explain how public agencies make decisions (hence the name "public choice").[56] Public-choice theory begins with the bedrock of all economics, the assumption that human beings are rational and seek to maximize whatever is important to them. The most rational thing, says the theory, is to promote one's self-interest. Whether choosing where to live or what car to buy, economists argue, individuals attempt to maximize their utility, the value they derive from their decisions. In the private sector, this makes individuals and corporations competitive and leads to the most efficient distribution of resources.

The public-choice theory argues that public officials, like all other individuals, are self-interested. Their self-interest leads them to avoid risk and to promote their careers. That, in turn, means that they seek to enlarge their programs and increase their budgets. As a result, public-choice economists argue, an organization full of self-interested bureaucrats is likely to produce bigger government that is both inefficient and operating against the public's interest.[57] Bureaucrats' pursuit of self-interest, they contend, helps explain the often disappointing performance of American government.

This argument, in turn, has led proponents of the public-choice school to argue that, wherever possible, governmental functions ought to be turned over to the private sector. In fact, from the Japanese government's sale of the nation's largest airline to Mexico's sale of 250 government-owned corporations, governments around the world have followed the public-choice prescription in privatizing public services. Where this proves impossible, either for practical or for political reasons, public-choice proponents contend that public functions ought to be contracted out to the private sector. The contracting process, they assert, simulates private-sector competition and dilutes the influence of government bureaucrats.[58] As Stuart Butler, one of the movement's strongest voices, put it, privatization is a kind of "political guerrilla warfare" that directs demand away from government provision of services and reduces the demand for budget growth.[59]

The Grace Commission, appointed by President Reagan to study the federal government's management, picked up these themes in the mid-1980s.[60] First, the commission contended, inefficient management gets rewarded with higher appropriations and more staff. Since the current year's budget is usually based on the money spent last year, the incentive is to spend all of the money appropriated whether it is needed or not. There is no incentive to conserve money for return to the Treasury. Second, because government is insulated from competition, it need not respond to changes as, the report alleged, the private sector must. Public agencies can continue on, year after year, administering programs the same way. Finally, powerful constituencies grow up around government programs and protect them from the need to change and adapt. Interest groups often fight change to safeguard their share of government goods and services. As a result, the theory goes, government is not forced to operate efficiently, and nearly everyone involved in the administration of government programs has an interest in keeping it that way.

Example: Banks and Bubbles

The public-choice approach has also led to innovative regulatory strategies. Rather than have government issue rules that require any industry that creates pollution to reduce impurities below a fixed ceiling, regulators can create incentives for industries to reduce pollution more efficiently. The Environmental Protection Agency, for example, set pollution standards for firms. Companies that reduced their pollution below prescribed levels could "bank" their pollution savings for use in future expansion. Other companies, since 1979, have been allowed to establish a "bubble" around all their facilities in an area and decide the cheapest way to reduce overall pollution, rather than have to deal with individual rules applying to each polluting facility. In both pollution banking and bubbles, the strategy is to allow each company's assessment of its self-interest to promote the overall goal of reducing pollution.

In 1980, for example, the first bubble plan approved saved an electric utility $27 million. It substituted high-sulfur coal for low-sulfur coal at one plant, and switched to natural gas from low-sulfur coal at another. The bubble plan not only saved the utility substantial money but reduced emissions. DuPont engineers, furthermore, estimated that a regional bubble for the company's operations could produce an 85 percent reduction in pollution for $14.6 million in costs. If the company reduced each source of pollution by 85 percent, it would have cost more than seven times—$91 million—more.[61]

Appraisal

The public-choice approach to decision making attacks governmental programs with a simple diagnosis—that the self-interest of government officials produces inefficient programs—and with a simple prescription—to turn over as many public programs as possible to the private sector and, when that is impossible, to mimic private-sector competition within the government. The approach, however, leaves significant questions of both information and values unanswered.

Information. The attraction of the public-choice approach to decision making lies in its embrace of the market. Marketlike competition, whether actually in the market or in market-based mechanisms such as contracts, its proponents believe, maximizes efficiency. Decision makers are driven to seek the right information and make the best decisions; if they do not do so, others will outcompete them, and they will lose their jobs. The power of this logic rests on the basic assumption of the bureaucrat as a rational human being: the administrator will single-mindedly pursue things of immediate utility for him or her—personal power, security, and income.

It is hard to argue that any individual does not look to enhance his or her position. Nevertheless, Steven Kelman contends, this account of the operation of the political process is a terrible caricature of reality. "It ignores the ability of ideas to defeat interests, and the role that public spirit plays in motivating the behavior of participants in the political process. The 'public choice' argument is far worse than simply descriptively inaccurate. Achieving good public policy, I believe, requires ... a norm of public spiritedness in the political action—a view that people should not simply be selfish in their political behavior.... The public choice school is part of the assault on this norm."[62]

It is difficult to accept the notion that in administering government programs, government bureaucrats are driven so hard to maximize their own utility that more publicly oriented objectives slip out of sight. Thus, the theory's very simplicity may well be its undoing. Are bureaucratic officials really so single-minded of purpose that there is no room for pride in performance, for striving to meet the goals of legislation, for a sense of public service in the public interest?

Many top administrators could doubtless double or triple their salaries in the private sector, as we saw in the last chapter. A sense of devotion to the public good keeps them working in the public sector. An approach to the public service that starts with a cynical view of public servants is dangerously flawed, especially when used as a prescription for managing government programs. Moreover, some economists, as former chairman of the president's Council of Economic Advisers Murray Weidenbaum contends, have a tendency to dismiss difficult questions as "subjective and political" and thus to define them as outside the proper sphere of rational analysis of efficiency.[63]

The public-choice movement's great attraction is its parsimonious explanation of government problems that dovetails neatly with the antigovernment feeling that grew in the aftermath of Watergate and the conservative philosophy championed by the Reagan administration. Moreover, it offers a neat solution: replace the decisions of government bureaucrats with the allegedly self-correcting influence of the market. Markets, it is argued, eliminate the need for a conscious search for decision-making information, since the self-interested motivations of the participants ensure that relevant data are available. The very parsimony of the explanation, however, greatly oversimplifies the much more interesting problems with which public managers must deal and feeds an unhealthy cynicism about government and the public service. Furthermore, the approach greatly underestimates the tremendous power of public ideas: the notion that some things are good for all of us, and that decision makers seek to achieve those things.[64]

Values. The market analogy, furthermore, suggests that both the goals and the motives of the private sector are identical with those of the public sector. Arguments for privatization, however, sometimes muddle together two very different issues: what government should do, and how government should do it. Most fundamentally, privatization is an argument about *how* the government does things, not what it ought to do.

That, in turn, identifies an important question: what functions are, at their core, *public,* for which government has the basic responsibility? As we said earlier, efficiency is not the only goal that public programs seek, and seeking other important goals, such as equality, typically means making difficult tradeoffs. Some programs are, at their core, public. The deepest debates are usually about ends—what should or should not be public functions—and the public-choice movement's focus on means thus begs the most crucial point. There is, quite simply, a *public* interest in public administration.[65]

Even if we focus solely on means, the public-choice approach is still unsatisfying. Public-choice proponents typically assume that the self-regulating features of the market will solve any problems plaguing public programs. Instruments are not neutral, however, and the long history of government contracts, as well as more recent horror stories in the newspapers, offer ample proof that this is not so.[66]

The point is very simple yet often overlooked: contracts do not administer themselves. Moreover, relying on contracts often replaces one set of values with another. If directly administered government programs must deal with self-interested bureaucrats, contracted-out programs must deal with self-interested proxies, each of which is seeking to maximize its own utility, sometimes at the government's expense. Contracts must themselves be administered to ensure high accountability and performance. The role of government administrators is different, but it does not disappear. As Eli Freedman, Connecticut commissioner of administration, argued, "You can't contract away responsibility to manage."[67] As any defense official facing harsh questions about overpriced weapons could tell, contracting out does not eliminate the government's basic responsibilities. It only changes them. (We discuss this issue more fully in chapter 11.)

The public-choice argument thus leads paradoxically to an important point: there is an irreducible governmental role in shaping government. At the same time, the line between the public and private spheres is not very distinct. The public-choice prescription, therefore, is on the surface an appealing one but a close examination reveals that it is based on an overly simplistic understanding of government administration. It is, in fact, more useful for the problems it raises than for the answers it provides.

Limits on Decision Making

From this discussion, it is clear that no one approach to decision making offers a solution to the problems of making administrative decisions. Each approach has its own special virtues and its own idiosyncratic problems. Every approach, though, shares the fundamental problems of human decision. It is, after all, a collection of human beings who make administrative decisions, and each individual operates in a large organization full of complex pressures, contradictory information, and diverse advice. Even the theories of "satisficing" and incrementalism do not fully take account of the psychological environment in which government executives must operate. James Webb, who served for eight years as administrator of the National Aeronautics and Space Administration, put the problem well:

> Executives within . . . a large-scale endeavor . . . have to work under unusual circumstances and in unusual ways. . . . The executive trained only in . . . traditional principles, able to operate only in accord with them and uncomfortable in their absence, would be of little use and could expect little satisfaction in a large complex endeavor. So too would the executive who has to be psychologically coddled in the fashion that the participative school of management advocates.
>
> In the large-scale endeavor the man himself must also be unusual; he must be knowledgeable in sound management doctrine and practice, but able to do a job without an exact definition of what it is or how it should be done; a man who can work effectively when lines of command crisscross and move in several directions rather than straight up and down; one who can work effectively in an unstable environment and can live with uncertainty and a high degree of personal insecurity; one willing to work for less of a monetary reward than he could insist on elsewhere; one who can blend public and private interests in organized participation for the benefit of both.[68]

Two social psychologists, Irving Janis and Leon Mann, put the point more poignantly. They see the human being "not as a cold fish but as a warm-blooded mammal," one "beset by conflict, doubts, and worry, struggling with incongruous longings, antipathies, and loyalties, and seeking relief by procrastination, rationalizing, or denying responsibility for his own choices."[69] All approaches to decision making share problems: the enormous uncertainty surrounding complex issues, bureaucratic pathologies that distort and block the flow of important information, and recurrent crises that deny the luxury of lengthy consideration.

Uncertainty

It is easy to underestimate how difficult it is for decision makers to know what results their decisions will produce, or even to get good information about what the current state of the world is. Congress, for example, has charged the Federal Reserve with making monetary policy, but it is deceptively difficult even to decide just what "money" is.[70] The Fed has developed several measures of money, variously including cash, checking accounts, savings accounts, and long-term certificates of deposit. These measures have been changed over the years as Americans' banking practices have changed. To make things worse, the supply of money is really only an estimate, subject to constant revision.

Other important economic statistics share the same problems. It often takes months to get good numbers on the growth of the economy or the rate of inflation. What seemed "good" months can sometimes become "bad" months as more data emerge. Furthermore, it is sometimes hard to interpret these numbers. Is high economic growth a sign of a healthy economy or of an inflation that is starting to take off? As one student of economic policy contends, "There are lots of numbers, but little good, firm, reliable information that adequately paints an up-to-date picture of the economy. Even worse, there are very few reliable models about what figures from the past signal for the economy's future."[71]

The complexity of the scientific world raises similar problems. In early 1976, for example, swine flu (a potentially deadly disease that had caused 20 million deaths in an epidemic in the 1920s) threatened to sweep the country. President Ford's scientific advisers, joined by health specialists within the Department of Health, Education, and Welfare, urged him to conduct a major nationwide immunization campaign. The president agreed, and 40 million Americans were vaccinated. The epidemic never came, and thousands of people were injured and some even killed by Guillain-Barré syndrome, a side effect of the vaccine whose link with flu vaccine previously was unknown. HEW Secretary Joseph A. Califano, Jr., during the administration of President Jimmy Carter, pointed out the difficult question the case focused: "How shall top lay officials, who are not themselves expert, deal with fundamental policy questions that are based, in part, on highly technical and complex expert knowledge—especially when that knowledge is speculative, hotly debated, or when 'the facts' are so uncertain?"[72]

With increasing frequency, decision makers must tackle issues on the edge of current knowledge, where experts disagree and the road ahead is uncertain. Indeed, risk is the first cousin to uncertainty, and the costs of being wrong can sometimes be catastrophic (e.g., in judging the risk of exposure to known cancer-causing chemicals).[73] Apart from political pressures, this uncertainty makes any one approach to decision making an inadequate guide. This is all the more true because many decisions, once made, are irreversible, and offer no opportunity for the feedback and correction assumed in both the rational and bargaining approaches.

The swine flu campaign, for example, was a decision that allowed no halfway steps; in the face of the forecast epidemic, President Ford either had to start a national immunization campaign or not. The case recalls the famous, fateful decision by Caesar at the Rubicon, as Plutarch writes:

> [Caesar] wavered much in his mind ... often changed his opinion one way and the other ... discussed the matter with his friends who were about him ... computing how many calamities his passing that river would bring upon mankind and what relation of it would be transmitted to posterity. At last, in a sort of passion, casting aside calculation, and abandoning himself to what might come, and using the proverb frequently in their mouths who enter upon dangerous and bold attempts, "The die is cast," with these words he took the river.[74]

In an age in which a detection system may incorrectly report an enemy's launching of an atomic attack, the few minutes afforded for decision on whether to launch a counterattack permit little computation and calculation, yet the decision is irreversible. The die will have been cast.

Many decisions less momentous for the world are irreversible, or substantially so: drafting a man into military service and assignment to a war zone, denial of a license to practice a profession or operate a business, denial of a loan to prevent bankruptcy of a business or farm, refusal of a pardon to a prisoner scheduled for execution. Decisions often have a stubborn finality for those who suffer loss or risk of life and for those whose livelihoods are impaired. It is often difficult to know what results a decision will produce. The burden of uncertainty weighs all the heavier on decisions that are irreversible.

Information Pathologies

The very structure of bureaucracy, furthermore, can distort the flow of information as it moves upward in the bureaucracy. Not all information collected at the bottom, of course, can be passed along to officials at the top. They would quickly become overwhelmed by paper and uncertain about what is actually happening; therefore, information must be condensed at each bureaucratic level. The process of condensation, however, often leads to filtering. Public officials, not surprisingly, tend to pass along the good news and suppress the bad. At best, this can distort the information flow. At worst, it can completely block early warnings about emerging problems. Furthermore, the official's own professional training can attune him or her more to some kinds of information than others. An engineer, even one who has assumed a general managerial position, still might listen more carefully to engineering problems than to others that might be more pressing.[75]

Sometimes these information pathologies create continuing, nagging problems. In the Peace Corps, one former official discovered, "Training was usually inadequate in language, culture, and technical skills. Volunteers were selected who were not suited to their assignments." But upper-level officials were usually in the dark. He explained that lower-level officials often worked "to prevent information, particularly of an unpleasant character, from rising to the top of the agency, where it may produce results unpleasant to the lower ranks."[76]

Sometimes these pathologies cause disasters. The night before NASA's launch of the space shuttle *Challenger* in January 1986, for example, engineers for one NASA contractor argued furiously that the cold weather predicted for the launch site the next morning could be dangerous. Mid-level NASA managers rejected the advice and refused to pass it on to top launch officials. The engineers proved tragically good prophets, and the shuttle exploded 73 seconds into the flight. Officials with the responsibility for giving the "go" for the launch did not learn about the worries the engineers had expressed that night until the investigation into the disaster began.[77]

Decision makers obviously cannot make good decisions without the right information, so they often create devices to avoid the pathologies. They can rely on outside information, from newspapers to advice from external experts. They can apply a counterbias, by using their past knowledge about information sources to judge the reliability of the facts they receive. They can bypass hierarchical levels and go right to the source. Some management experts, in fact, advocate "management by walking around," getting the manager out from behind the desk and onto the front lines to avoid the "nobody ever tells me anything" problem.[78] They can develop precoded forms that avoid distortion as they move up through the ranks.[79]

Nevertheless, attempts to rid the information chain of these pathologies can paradoxically create new problems:

- ☐ Improvements in incoming information may clog internal channels of information.
- ☐ Increasing the amount of information flow to decision makers may simply overload them, as may attempts to eliminate the fragmented features of decision making.
- ☐ Greater clarity and detail in the wording of decisions may overwhelm implementing officials.[80]

These paradoxes paint a disturbing but very real picture. Administrators are scarcely defenseless, however, for the problem often is not having too little information but too much—and then trying to sort through it all to find the right combination of facts on which to make decisions. In fact, top NASA officials had been earlier informed of the problem that caused the *Challenger* disaster, "but always in a way that didn't communicate the seriousness of the problem," a House committee found.[81] The key to resolving these problems is redundancy, creating multiple sources of feedback that allow decision makers to blend competing pieces of information together into a more coherent picture. That task, however, is often one of the hardest that decision makers must face.

Crisis

Crises often precipitate decisions. The deaths of 119 men in a 1951 mine explosion and of 78 men in a 1968 mine explosion led to passage of the 1952 and 1969 national coal-mine safety acts. Catastrophic floods have time after time broken logjams that had obstructed major changes in national flood-control policy.[82] A 1979 accident in a Pennsylvania nuclear reactor, imperiling the population for miles around, stimulated a fundamental reconsideration of government policy toward the nuclear power industry. The *Challenger* explosion speeded up redesign of the booster rocket and produced plans for a new emergency escape system.[83]

Crises, of course, are not limited to the federal government. Natural disasters such as fires, floods, snowstorms, and earthquakes, as well as accidents such as train wrecks, can put state and local officials just as much on the firing line. All crises share the common pressure of time, an issue rarely considered in the different approaches to decision making. Accounts of decision making in the Cuban missile crisis indicate that the committee advising President Kennedy would probably have recommended a strong military response had its views been required two or three (instead of five) days after discovery of the missile sites. Throughout the crisis, the pressure of time (and the need for secrecy) precluded the group's dipping lower in the bureaucracy for relevant information and advice.[84]

Crises often reverse the order of normal decision-making procedures. If a federal mine inspector finds an "imminent danger" in a coal mine, the inspector may order the mine closed until improvements are made. If the Food and Drug commissioner concludes that a drug presents an immediate danger to the public safety, the commissioner can order it off the market. In both cases the niceties of quasi-judicial hearings to weigh the producers' objections are observed *after* the order's issuance and while it still remains in effect.

Thus, crises upset the normal order of decision making. They make many things difficult: the comprehensive analyses that rational decision making requires, the trial and error of bargaining, the consultation of participative decision making, and the reliance on the private sector of public choice. They accentuate the problems of uncertainty, especially in areas of technological complexity. Most important, they underline an issue of decision making in the public sector not well considered in most approaches: in the end, the public official is responsible for ascertaining and ensuring the public interest, a task that always proves difficult.

Crises can be managed. In the private sector, the manufacturers of Tylenol were widely hailed for their aggressive action in dealing with the poisoning of their capsules. Furthermore, Irving L. Janis argues that "vigilant problem solving" can reduce the risks of crises, as managers aggressively seek to formulate the problem, collect available information, reformulate the situation, and frame the best options.[85] When Governor Richard Thornburgh of Pennsylvania faced the potential of a nuclear disaster during the Three-Mile Island nuclear power plant crisis in 1979, he had to follow precisely these steps in finding his way. Nevertheless, the sudden appearance of the unexpected coupled with high risk for wrong decisions poses enormous problems for decision makers.

Conclusion

We have examined several approaches to administrative decision making: rational analysis, bargaining, participation, and public choice. Though to some measure all these approaches have been put into practice, they all are expressions of theories, full of assumptions, that have tended to harden into dogmas. They also offer, as table 9.1 shows, a wide range of tactics for dealing with the lasting problems of information and values.

The approaches share, though in varying degrees, certain basic defects. We have already noted some oversights, especially uncertainty, information pathologies, and crisis. There are others, too, such as how a problem or a need for a decision is discovered, formulated, and put on the agenda (most

Table 9.1

APPROACHES TO DECISION MAKING

Approach	Information	Values
Rational	Collect comprehensive informa- tion to maximize rationality	Assumed
Bargaining	Intentionally limited	Struggled over
Participative	Acquired through those af- fected by decision	Prominence of value of clients
Public choice	Use self-policing forces of market	Utilize self-interest of players

approaches start with a known and stated problem or need). Furthermore, nondecision—the decision not to decide or the avoidance of an issue altogether, whether conscious or unconscious—often has consequences as great as decisions.

More basic are the tendencies of each of the approaches (1) to exalt a single value, and (2) to neglect to state the conditions necessary for the approach's effective operation and the achievement of that value. The emphasis on a single value is evident in economists' eagerness to increase efficiency through systems analysis, as well as in the incrementalists' commitment to maximizing participation, the participative managers' commitment to full public voice in decisions, and the public choicers' reverence for the virtues of private-sector competition. These are all important values, and indeed that is our point. Because all these values are important, an approach that is single-mindedly designed to achieve only one of these values is inadequate for the reality of the political world.

The second tendency is the failure of an approach's advocates to specify the conditions necessary for their approach to succeed. Sometimes, as in systems analysis, the conditions might not exist in the real world, and the theorists do not explain very well how to adapt their approaches to reality. Often, however, the adaptations may need to be so substantial that the approach will be drained of its essential character. For example, attempts to adapt the rational decision-making approach to take account of the elusiveness of policy goals, the shortage of sufficient quantitative data in many analytic areas, the distortion risked in converting qualitative goals or accomplishments into measurable terms, and the behavior of members of Congress may lead to so truncated a version of the rational approach that it is less useful than, say, the more reality-oriented incremental approach.

It is possible, of course, to identify particular spheres of decision making in each of which one approach is more appropriate than others.[86] This is especially true of the systems analysis, democratic participation, and public-choice approaches. The rational approach, for example, has greater viability in fields with clear objectives, quantitative measures, and minimal political pressures. Yet if we use each for its most appropriate sphere, we are left with the puzzle of how to integrate these distinctive decisional systems into a whole. The budgetary process is governmentwide and involves competition among agencies with different decision-making systems that express different values. Preparation of the president's annual legislative program is a comprehensive planning process that calls for inputs by agencies throughout the government. For the necessary integration, we are apparently left with a choice between the two most comprehensive—the rational and the incremental—or with managing an elusive marriage between the two so as to capture the value of each while avoiding its flaws.

10

Budgeting

Few fields in public administration have been the subject of more turmoil than budgeting. The more federal budget deficits grew, the more immobilized the entire budgetary process seemed to become. Meanwhile, state and local tax limitation acts and referenda deeply cut public programs. Many crosscurrents—economic crises, citizens' growing disillusionment with government spending, and distrust of government institutions—met in the budgetary process, and the problems proved so difficult that often only inaction resulted. Many of President Reagan's budgets were pronounced "DOA" (dead on arrival) when copies arrived on Capitol Hill. Congress, for its part, proved increasingly unable to put together any kind of budget and passed "continuing resolutions" that kept government afloat without tackling the hard questions of setting spending priorities. The continuing resolution passed in 1987 became legendary: It ran to 1,057 pages, weighed 14 pounds, and was accompanied by another 2,239 pages of legislation weighing 29 pounds more.[1]

Budget decisions are important because they shape government programs. They are also important because they focus on two central questions that have recurred throughout history.[2]

First, what should government do? Budgeting is, at its core, about fundamental social decisions on the use of resources. How much should society channel through the government for public purposes, and how much should be left in private hands? And of the resources the government spends, what programs most deserve support? New highways or health programs or weapons or welfare? Budgetary politics is enmeshed in perpetual conflict because of the centrality of these questions in society.

Second, who in government should decide these questions? Throughout the history of the United States, the balance of financial power has shifted between the national and subnational governments, and between the legislature and the executive. The budgetary arena has been the continuing forum for broad policy disputes and pitched battles over not only who should benefit from government programs but also who should decide.

We explore these questions in sorting out the functions and processes of budgeting. We begin with an examination of the lasting economic and political role of the budget. We continue by probing the basic parts of the budgetary process: budget making; budget appropriation; and budget execution. Finally, we conclude by reviewing the relationship between budgetary politics and public administration.

The Role of the Budget

The federal budget has a dual role. Key budgetary decisions are financial, and thus the budget has important economic effects. And because these decisions affect the allocation of resources among competing claimants, the budget has important political effects.

The Economic Role

The very size of the government's financial activity inevitably gives it a strong role in the nation's economy.[3] That role is reciprocal: the budget has enormous impact on the economy, and the economy increasingly has a strong role in shaping the budget.

The Budget's Effect on the Economy. At least since the 1930s, economists and government officials have recognized that government taxation and spending, known as "fiscal" policy, have an important effect on the economy.[4] Many economists and officials, furthermore, have argued that the government can, and therefore should, use the budget to steer the economy: to boost employment, to cut inflation, to improve the nation's balance of trade abroad, and to keep the value of the dollar secure. While the British economist John Maynard Keynes is the intellectual father of this movement, pragmatists within Franklin D. Roosevelt's New Deal were preaching the virtues of "compensatory economics" before Keynes's theory was published.[5] The movement has grown into the cornerstone of macroeconomics —the study of the economy's behavior and of the behavior of broad aggregates such as inflation, employment, and economic growth—and reached its zenith with the "Kennedy tax cut," a huge decrease in income taxes passed in 1964, after the president's assassination, to spur economic growth.[6]

Cycles of economic growth and recession are inevitable, economists tell us. Keynesian economics preaches that the government can use its taxing and spending powers to moderate those cycles, to offset the dangers of too-rapid growth (inflation) and recession (unemployment). A government surplus (more revenues than expenditures) slows economic growth by draining money from the economy. A government deficit pumps money into the economy and promotes economic growth. In good times, the theory suggests, the government ought to run a surplus to keep the economy from expanding too quickly. In bad times, the government ought to run a deficit to keep the economy from becoming too sluggish.

Such economic policymaking is an exclusive province of the federal budget. Constitutional restrictions and sound fiscal management require that state and local budgets be balanced. The federal budget, however, is not like the family budget or even like state and local budgets. The federal government has far greater resources to sustain a deficit over time, and it has the authority to create money and regulate its value, giving it a way to finance deficits that neither families nor state and local governments enjoy. The federal budget has an important effect on the economy, and policymakers have often harnessed it to promote high economic growth and low inflation. The availability of such an instrument, even if it does not always work well, tempts decision makers to use it for electoral advantage.[7]

The Keynesian approach to budgetary policy encountered serious problems during the 1970s and 1980s. Regardless of the theory's economic influence, it has always had a political imbalance: politicians have found it far happier to increase spending and run deficits when the economy dipped than to take the more bitter tax-increase/spending-cut pill when the economy overheated. Especially when a rapid increase in Vietnam war expenditures fueled inflation in the late 1960s, President Johnson and his advisers resisted cutting the president's treasured Great Society social programs and raising taxes to rein in the economy.

Furthermore, economic events undercut the theory's assumption of a relatively simple tradeoff between economic growth and inflation: more of one tended to mean less of the other. During the 1970s, inflation and unemployment both increased to defy the theory and confound policymakers. Budget deficits grew, oil shocks battered the economy, and inflation escalated as policymakers struggled to find new tools for economic management. Traditional Keynesian economics suggested that a budget deficit could help reduce unemployment, while a surplus could cool inflation. It could not cope with simultaneous high inflation and high unemployment. The task of economic management thus fell increasingly to the Federal Reserve, which struggled to deal with stagnant economic growth and inflation, christened "stagflation," and its management of the nation's money supply. As deficits immobilized budgetary policymakers through the Ford, Carter, Reagan, and Bush administrations, the Fed became the only game in town.[8]

The problem reached a crisis during the Carter administration. Under the chairmanship of Paul Volcker, the Federal Reserve Board sharply tightened the money supply to slow inflation. Double-digit inflation fell as interest rates rose to historic levels—more than 20 percent for some short-term investments—and the nation entered the deepest economic decline since the Great Depression of the 1930s.

President Reagan campaigned for office on the platform that the federal budget could be used in a new way to spark economic growth. His "supply side" economics contended that the government could increase both its revenues and the economy's growth paradoxically by cutting taxes: the lower the level of taxes, the more money companies could invest and consumers could spend. The resulting economic growth would increase tax collections. Reagan pushed through Congress a monumental 25 percent individual income tax cut and a virtual elimination of the corporate income tax.[9] The federal deficit nevertheless continued to grow—to a then record $220.7 billion in fiscal year 1986.[10] During the Reagan years, in fact, the national debt more than doubled; in those eight years, the nation accumulated more debt than in its entire history. Although supply siders suggested that the growing deficits were the fault of mismanagement by the Federal Reserve and high spending by congressional Democrats, most experts argued that the huge tax cuts, defense spending increases, and rising outlays for entitlements like social security created the deficit problem. Whatever explanation one believed, the deficit swelled.[11]

The result was unprecedented gridlock. The president's budget came to be taken less seriously and Congress proved unable to pass even routine spending measures. Instead, the participants played budgetary brinkmanship, delaying decisions until the last possible moment in the hope of gaining a tactical advantage over opponents. As the budgetary stakes grew, the process disintegrated into presidential-congressional struggles. In the meantime, more of the job of trying to steer the economy fell from the budget's fiscal policy to the Federal Reserve's monetary policy. The large deficits often left the Fed's policymakers with limited and unpleasant options, but the budgetary process's immobility left little choice.

Far less clear was the effect of two decades of huge deficits on the economy. In the 1980 Republican primary campaign, George Bush charged that Ronald Reagan's supply-side proposal was "voodoo economics" (a charge that Bush was never able to live down). Economists warned that Jimmy Carter's $74 billion deficit in fiscal 1980 was a first step toward financial disaster. Even though that deficit nearly tripled during the Reagan administration, the economy performed surprisingly well: inflation came down and economic growth limped ahead. When the economy slowed during the Bush administration, Bill Clinton's campaign made "It's the economy, stupid!" its watchword. Clinton's promise to boost the economy and cut the deficit took him to the White House.

Most economists agreed that the huge deficits were a dangerous drain on the economy. They suggested that money spent financing the deficits left few resources for private investment (and thus for future growth). They argued that deficits made inflation worse than it would otherwise be. They contended that large deficits would tie the federal government's hands in fighting future recessions, since there would be limited room to increase spending and thus stimulate the economy. Finally, they concluded that deficits over the long run would worsen the nation's international trading position by eroding the value of the dollar. Left unchecked, economists warned, large deficits would "fester, creating problems that become harder and harder to solve."[12] Other economists contended that the deficits actually contributed to the economy's growth and that bringing them down could induce a recession.[13]

Budget deficits, especially over the long run, unquestionably are dangerous. The larger the deficit, the more of the federal budget must be devoted simply to paying interest—14 percent in fiscal year 1994—and that leaves less money for other purposes. Budget deficits also hamstring the political process by giving politicians little maneuvering room. The 1980s, however, also revealed that the economy was far more resilient and adaptable to the stresses of rapid growth in the federal debt than anyone anticipated. Economic growth continued, if sluggishly, and the federal government did manage to make budget decisions, even if in the process decision makers violated most procedural deadlines.

The Economy's Effect on the Budget. If the budget became a less useful tool in managing the economy, the economy's performance became a much more important force in shaping the budget. In general, a strong economy helps lower the budget deficit. Strong economic growth increases tax revenues and decreases expenditures, especially for such need-based programs as unemployment and welfare. The weaker the economy, the larger the deficit; revenues shrink while spending grows. Similarly, inflation increases spending and usually worsens the deficit; while it swells tax collections, it typically pushes spending up even more rapidly, especially for interest payments on the government's debt and cost-of-living increases in social security and other retirement programs. At the state and local levels, these issues have grown as well because, as we saw in chapter 2, retirement and welfare programs coupled with interest payments account for a substantial share of their expenditures.

Budget making for all governments, especially at the federal level, thus has come to depend critically on estimating economic growth, unemployment, inflation, and interest rates. In fiscal year 1995, for example, the Congressional Budget Office estimated that inflation would average 3.1 percent from fiscal year 1996 through 1999; the Clinton administration was less optimistic and estimated inflation at 3.4 percent. CBO, on the other hand, estimated that interest rates would average just .4 percent higher than the Clinton administration's forecasts. By fiscal 1999, CBO said, the deficit would be $43 billion higher than the administration had estimated, and that from 1994 through 1999 the deficit would total $99 billion more.[14] Very, very small differences in economic projects, often well within the range of uncertainty of economic forecasting tools, can produce huge differences in government revenues, spending, and the deficit.

In congressional testimony, Federal Reserve Board chairman Alan Greenspan offered one solution for reducing the federal deficit. Economic studies, he suggested, showed that the government's commonly used cost-of-living measure, the Consumer Price Index (CPI), tended to overestimate inflation by .5 to 1.5 percent. Transforming the CPI to measure inflation more accurately, he suggested, could reduce the federal deficit by $150 billion over five years. Of course, that also meant that federal payments, especially for social security and other retirees, would also decrease. The typical social security recipient might lose $10 per month. Even a hint of such changes in the program quickly brought representatives of senior citizens out to complain that reestimating the CPI would be a breach of faith with retirees.

It follows, therefore, that preparing the budget depends first on forecasting economic performance. It also follows that the temptation to "adjust" these forecasts for partisan purposes grows as deficit politics becomes more heated. As Rudolph G. Penner, former head of the Congressional Budget Office, and Alan J. Abramson, explain,

> Changing a deficit estimate by $10 billion by changing an economic forecast is a minor statistical event. Changing policies sufficiently to alter a deficit estimate by $10 billion is a significant political event. This asymmetry creates an enormous temptation to achieve a given target deficit reduction by adopting optimistic economic assumptions rather than by cutting programs or raising taxes. . . . It is little wonder that the economic forecast adopted by Congress for the purposes of formulating the first budget resolution [Congress's initial vote on the budget] was too optimistic on balance every year in FY 1980–87.[15]

Within the Reagan administration, Office of Management and Budget Director David Stockman became famous for his "rosy scenario": a group of assumptions that no one truly believed but that demonstrated that the promise of supply-side economics could be fulfilled.[16] From fiscal year 1979 to fiscal year 1984, OMB and CBO both often missed the deficit totals by large margins: OMB erred by an average of $34 billion, CBO by an average of $32 billion.[17] As former Citicorp president Walter Wriston put it, "A government budget deficit is the intersection of two wild guesses [on expenditures and revenues] a year from now."[18]

These crosscurrents—the effect of the budget on the economy and the effect of the economy on the budget—have taken on greater importance through the years. The federal budget is far more than a total of the government's expenditures and revenues; it is a statement of the government's relationship with the rest of the economy and of political officials' attempts to influence economic performance. The crosscurrents have, in addition, affected the way the budget is made. The technique and politics of forecasting have taken on a far larger role, and this in turn has opened a new arena in which fundamental budget battles are fought. Finally, the crosscurrents have enhanced the role of the staff members who run the computers that produce the economic estimates.[19]

The Political Role

Budgeting is, of course, much more than the economic decision about how to allocate the nation's wealth on government programs. It embodies fundamental political choices, both about values (which programs get funded and which do not) and institutions, especially the relative sway of the legislative and executive branches of government.

First Steps. Americans have always distrusted public officials with their money. Although there was little question in the republic's first months that the State and War departments would be headed by a single secretary, Congress considered putting the Treasury under the control of a board (so no single person could become too powerful) and putting the board under tight control of Congress (so that the legislative branch could closely oversee how the executive spent money). Although the Constitution clearly granted the executive branch the power to wage war and make treaties, it gave Congress the power to coin money, levy taxes, and appropriate money. Ever since, budgetary politics has been a forum for sharp competition between the president and Congress.[20]

For over a century, federal budgeting was mostly a congressional function. The executive branch's "budget" submitted to Congress, in fact, was little more than the Treasury Department's collection of agency and departmental requests. Congress was the central force in budgeting.

The Rise of Presidential Power. At the beginning of the twentieth century, the Progressive movement increased citizens' concern about the management of government at all levels. Budgetary reform swept state and local government as part of the broader trend toward strengthened executive powers.[21] By the end of World War I, the congressionally dominated system had proved inadequate for managing the federal government's vastly expanded fisc and functions, and the budget-reform movement launched in the states and cities bubbled up to the federal level.

The culmination of this movement was passage in 1921 of the Budget and Accounting Act, which revolutionized federal budgeting. For the first time, the president was to submit an annual budget to Congress. A Bureau of the Budget was created in the Treasury Department (and later moved to the president's own executive office) to assemble and adjust, if necessary, the department's requests to conform with the president's program.[22] Meanwhile, the Treasury Department's auditing functions were transferred to Congress's new General Accounting Office. By gaining the authority to produce his own budget, the president gained leverage: over the executive branch departments and agencies, who first had to bargain with him before having their requests sent to Congress; and over Congress, by submitting the document that framed the terms of debate.

The act thus divided the traditional budget functions into areas of executive and legislative supremacy: budget preparation and execution in the executive branch; budget appropriation and postaudit in the legislative branch; and shared executive-legislative authority over budget control.[23] The division has always been sloppy, but the act nevertheless put the president into a position of preeminence he had not previously known.

Moreover, changing currents within the executive branch enhanced central power, especially during the Reagan administration when the Office of Management and Budget acquired more authority. The Gramm-Rudman-Hollings deficit reduction act, to which we return shortly, required complicated computer projections and tracking of spending patterns. Congressional-presidential budget summits produced other agreements based on a strange vocabulary and complex recordkeeping. As the budgetary process limped along, the short-term bargains that kept it alive required central oversight within the executive branch of each agency's spending patterns, and that in turn enhanced OMB's role. Combined with the Reagan administration's increasing oversight of agencies' information gathering and regulations, which was conducted in OMB, and the president's dislike for details, OMB's power grew significantly during the Reagan era.[24]

The Budget and Accounting Act of 1921 proved a significant advance in presidential power and, in many ways, marks the emergence of the modern presidency. It was the beginning of fifty years of steadily growing presidential dominance over Congress in the budgetary process. While Congress has tried, especially since the mid-1970s, to regain its earlier preeminence in the budgetary process, the president has held the upper hand over most of the twentieth century.[25] These struggles between the branches played themselves out in budget making, budget appropriation, and budget execution. We deal with a related part of the budgetary process, postaudit and control, in chapter 12, "Legislative Control of Administration."

Budget Making

At every level of government, the first step in the budgetary process is preparation of the budget: a set of spending and revenue plans combined in a single document.[26] While the details vary by level of government, the process typically includes both "top-down" and "bottom-up" features.[27]

Budgeting: Top-Down

A government's budget is not simply a collection of agencies' spending requests. Instead, each government's executive—whether mayor, city manager, county administrator, governor, or president—sets broad targets for overall spending and revenues. The spending targets fix a ceiling under which the agencies are expected to stay in preparing their individual budget requests. The ceiling, in turn, is a product of estimates by the executive's budget staff: how expected changes in the economy will affect revenues and expenditures (will the economy's growth bring more tax collection, or its slump put higher demands on welfare?); how demographic changes are likely to affect existing programs (will more school-age children require the school board to hire more teachers?); and how major planned program changes will affect spending (how much money will be required to launch a new defense system?).[28]

At the federal level, preparing the new budget begins almost as soon as the previous one goes to Capitol Hill in late January or early February. During the early spring, the Office of Management and Budget collects information from government agencies about how much money they want for the upcoming fiscal year, both to administer existing programs and to fund new ones. OMB uses these requests to prepare its spending projections, while the Treasury Department prepares estimates of tax revenues. Then staff members from the OMB, the Treasury, and the president's Council of Economic Advisers gather to assemble economic projections for the coming year. This three-part package of spending, revenue, and economic estimates forms the base for the president's first policy decisions on the upcoming budget, which are made in June. The decisions focus on the major "policy streams" in the budget: defense spending (including any new programs to be introduced); domestic spending (especially payments to individuals, such as social security); and the overall effect of the budget on the economy (especially the size of the deficit). The process at the state and local levels is often similar, with the balance among education, highway, and other programs forming the focus.

OMB uses the president's decisions to define policy directives and spending ceilings for the departments and agencies. During the summer, each agency repeats this process internally, from department secretaries to bureau chiefs, from bureau chiefs to division heads, and so on. The agency's package is then assembled, together with supporting documents, and sent to OMB. In the fall and early winter OMB's budget examiners intensively study the departmental requests and hold budget hearings at which the examiners and others closely question departmental representatives. Then an internal OMB "director's review" of staff recommendations culminates in the OMB director's recommendations to the president. Agencies have one final chance to appeal OMB's recommendations as the president makes his final decisions. In some years, in fact, the appeals have stretched into the final days before the budget goes to the printer in early January.[29]

Preparing the federal budget thus begins nearly a full year before the budget is submitted to Congress, more than a year and one-half before the fiscal year begins, and two and one-half years before the fiscal year's end. The long time horizon makes the already difficult economic forecasting job even more difficult—and it makes constant tinkering inevitable. At any given time, administrators must live with three different fiscal years: executing the current fiscal year's budget; defending the next year's requests before Congress; and making budget estimates to submit to OMB for the year after that. Any year's budget battle is thus actually part of interlocking skirmishes reflecting political and economic concerns stretching over many years.[30]

Although the budget game varies by the level of government, the federal processes typically are mirrored at state and local levels. Their message, moreover, is that no program or agency ever starts from scratch. Every budgetary decision is intimately bound up in past experiences, current battles, and future plans.[31]

Budgeting: Bottom-Up

The top-down picture is the big picture, full of worries about the size of the budget deficit, the budget's role in macroeconomic policy, and large-scale policy changes such as the introduction of new defense systems. From the point of view of lower-level administrators, however, the picture is much different.

The central theory (both descriptively and prescriptively) of bottom-up budgeting is *incrementalism,* originally put forth by Aaron Wildavsky and built on the broader incrementalist theories discussed in the last chapter. How much should an agency official request in the budget preparation process? Wildavsky's answer was that officials do, and should, ask for a "fair share" increment over the agency's base. "The base is the general expectation among the participants that programs will be carried on at close to the going level of expenditures," Wildavsky explained. The increments are relatively small increases over the existing base that reflect the agency's share of changes in the budgetary pie.[32]

In budgeting, incrementalism thus has two important implications. First, no one really considers the whole budget. The package is too big for anyone to examine everything, so it is far easier and, Wildavsky argues, more rational to focus on changes. Second, the political battles focus on the size of an agency's increment—and of the increment's size compared with those received by other agencies. Budgeting is a battle fought on the margins, with the sharpest struggles focused on *changes* in the distribution of the government's pie.

Incremental theory, both as a description of how budgeting operates and how agency officials should behave, has dominated the budgeting debate since the first publication of Wildavsky's work in 1964.[33] Many theorists have taken sharp issue with his view, for three reasons. First, incremental budgeting begins with the base, but the meaning of the budget "base" is anything but clear. It can be the current estimate of spending in the previous year, although that estimate constantly changes as Congress acts on the budget and as agencies carry out their programs. It can be the cost of continuing current activities at the same level, which includes increases for inflation and population shifts and decreases for improved productivity. Finally, it can be a spending level set by law, which often can be a different amount from the first two. "OMB actually formulates the base in several ways, which vary substantially over the course of the planning cycle," budget experts explain.[34]

Second, changes from the existing level of spending are not always made in small increments. A study of changes in agency budgets in the U.S. Department of Agriculture from 1946 to 1971, for example, showed that agencies requested budget changes ranging from a decrease (12 percent of the time) to a doubling of their budget (7.3 percent of the time). The average change in budgets from year to year was 11 percent, but some agencies received large cuts, some huge increases. Thus, on the average, budgeting does appear incremental, but the averages hide the rich politics of budgeting: aggressive program managers seeking to build budgets, OMB officials seeking to keep a ceiling on total spending, and presidents and their staffs seeking to pursue new initiatives.[35]

Third, the real focus of budgetary politics is not changes in *agencies'* budgets but changes in their *programs'* budgets. At the agency level, budgets and politics are usually rather stable. "Yet within departmental and agency boundaries (and occasionally between them . . .), there is a constant struggle by program directors, lobbyists, congressmen, state and local politicians, and White House personnel to fund new ideas and to continue the funding of old ones." The competitive success of alternative programs, not changes in the budgets of agencies, occupies budget makers, and in that arena it is the power of policy entrepreneurs who can build the strongest political case for their ideas that makes the difference.[36]

Attempts to Reform Incrementalism. Especially since the mid-1960s, presidents have experimented with different budget reform techniques to secure greater control over budget preparation. Most notable was Lyndon Johnson's Planning-Programming-Budgeting System (PPBS), which we explored in chapter 9. During the Nixon administration, OMB attempted a different strategy, "management by objectives" (MBO). MBO was intended to strengthen the ability of managers to manage. It is addressed to the efficiency with which programs are implemented rather than to grand objectives and choice among major program alternatives. Thus, MBO is both more decentralized and less directly connected to budgeting than PPB. The agency head and his or her principal executives fix on quantified objectives to be attained in the coming year, and they break down each objective into targets for achievement in, say, each quarter year. This is then repeated in turn for each subordinate. While MBO was more a management than a budget strategy, it had clear implications for the allocation of money. Once an agency had its goals defined and factored out among its subunits, the money would naturally follow that path. MBO had a mixed record: in some departments and bureaus it made a significant contribution; in others it failed and was quickly abandoned. As with PPB, there has been "a noticeable disenchantment with MBO as a panacea in the government."[37]

When Jimmy Carter took office in 1977, he brought with him the zero-base budgeting (ZBB) approach he had used as governor of Georgia. ZBB was an assault on incrementalism from a different perspective, but it was not, as the name suggests, budgeting from a zero base. Instead, budgeters began from a certain level of spending (say, 80 percent of current expenditures). They then assembled "decision packages" (consisting of different ways of increasing the level of services) and ranked them. In this way, decision makers could set priorities for spending increases.[38] ZBB seemed attractive at first, but it encouraged agency budget makers to play games with the process (e.g., to rank very low a project they knew would never be cut, in the hope that they could win funding for other programs at the same time). These tactics, combined with ZBB's paperwork burden, ended the tool's reign at the federal level. At the state and local levels, however, many governments continued to find the process a helpful one for making choices in their smaller budgets.[39]

George Bush came to the presidency in 1989 with yet another approach. He campaigned for office promising "no new taxes" and instead said he could balance the budget through a "flexible freeze," in which increases in some programs would be balanced by cuts in others. Almost immediately, however, his flexible freeze encountered deep problems. He announced which programs he wanted to increase, but left it to Congress to decide which programs to cut. Moreover, his plan depended critically on obtaining strong economic growth and low interest rates, but within months of taking office, the Federal Reserve drove interest rates up to stem inflation, and economic growth slowed. His plan to rescue the savings and loan industry promised to cost tens of billions of dollars more than the administration's first estimates. Like other strategies that seem attractive on first blush, President Bush's flexible freeze quickly melted in the political heat of lasting budgetary conflicts. Meanwhile, the National Economic Commission, established in 1987 to develop a nonpartisan approach to resolving the deficit crisis, foundered in 1989 on partisan differences.[40]

In the end, none of these budgetary systems proved the panacea that their sponsors had hoped. Spending continued to grow, and presidential control of the budget was at best only temporarily and marginally improved, until all the players in the budgetary game learned to outwit each system's features. Each system, nevertheless, left behind important features that continue to influence budgeting. The Defense Department continues to use PPB. In MBO-style, many chief executives insist that agencies link their requests with performance data. At the federal level, President Bush directed that a new, limited Management by Objectives system be established to track his key priorities. His fiscal year 1991 budget contains, in fact, a chapter entitled, "Managing by Objectives." Some lower-level governments find ZBB's features attractive. ZBB, furthermore, helped uproot the notion that the budget base was a given. None of these systems, however, proved a magic cure because of the larger political and economic issues in which the budgeting system is enmeshed. At the federal level, furthermore, they all encountered the stark reality of the rise of "uncontrollable" expenditures.

Table 10.1

CONTROLLABILITY OF FEDERAL OUTLAYS,
FISCAL YEAR 1993

Discretionary spending	39%	
Defense		21%
Nondefense		18%
Mandatory spending	47%	
Social security		21%
Medicare		9%
Medicaid		5%
Other		11%
Interest	14%	

SOURCE: Executive Office of the President, *Budget of the United States Government, Fiscal Year 1995* (Washington, D.C.: Government Printing Office, 1994), 235.

The Rise of "Uncontrollables." Perhaps most important, incrementalism has become a weaker explanation over the years because more of the budget has become "uncontrollable." About half the budget consists of mandatory spending (see table 10.1). Federal agencies are required to fund entitlements and other programs according to existing laws. Spending is set by the number of people eligible for the program and the level of spending for each person set in law. In addition, 14 percent of the budget goes for interest on the national debt, which the federal government must pay. That leaves little more than one-third of the budget for discretionary spending. Even here, government officials often have little real discretion. Completion of existing contracts, operation of basic services ranging from federal prisons to the national parks, and other fundamentals account for almost all remaining federal spending.

In preparing the budget, therefore, the president has little room for introducing new programs or even cutting existing ones. More than three-fourths of the budget's spending is mandated by law, and most of the rest is taken up by the expenses of running the government—from paying the salaries of the armed forces to keeping the lights burning in the Capitol and White House—that can scarcely be eliminated.[41] The share of the federal budget over which the president has real authority in any given year is thus extremely small, and getting smaller. Quite naturally, as this share has shrunk, budgetary politics has become more intense.

Furthermore, the growth of payments to individuals and interest on the debt has further reinforced the importance of economic forecasting in preparing the budget. No budget categories are more affected by economic performance than these two, so even small forecasting errors can produce large swings in the budget totals, and thus in the size of of the deficit and the high-stakes politics that swirls around it.[42]

Budget Appropriation

The budget submitted by the president (and by the executives at most other levels of government) is, in the end, only a set of estimates and recommendations. Congress (like legislatures at other levels) makes the effective decisions, for only it can authorize expenditures and determine how revenues shall be obtained.[43]

Because the president and the agencies know that they propose while the Congress disposes, they tailor their requests in two ways. First, the president and agency officials behave according to the "rule of anticipated reactions":[44] they adapt their estimates and recommendations to fit their perceptions of how Congress will react to them. A budget maker who expects Congress to cut the agency's spending by 10 percent might submit a request 15 or 20 percent higher. (Members of Congress, of course, understand this classic ruse, and estimate in turn how much padding has been built into the budget.)

Second, the executive might play a different game by proposing severe cuts from the previous year's levels in certain programs that command strong legislative support. Such cuts conveniently reduce the budget's apparent cost, including the deficit. The executive knows that the legislature will not accept the cuts and thus transfers to legislators the burden of increasing spending. Members of Congress in 1989, for example, greeted President Bush's first budget with enthusiasm until they discovered that he wanted them to decide where the flexible-freeze cuts would have to come. Agencies in turn are famous for occasionally using the "Washington monument ploy": offering their most popular programs (which for the National Park Service is the elevator to the top of the Washington Monument) for cutting, in the full knowledge that legislators will never allow such cuts to take effect. The executive may also propose new taxes that have poor congressional prospects so that he or she can point to a projected decline in the budget deficit or a balanced budget, even though he or she knows that the taxes will never be adopted.[45]

Congressional Budget Decisions

In dealing with these strategies, Congress has often found itself at a disadvantage. During the Nixon administration, when Congress could not muster an effective attack on the president, Nixon won a short-lived power to "impound" funds (i.e., to refrain from spending money Congress had appropriated). President Nixon's use of these powers galvanized his opponents in the 1974 impeachment battle. The federal courts, meanwhile, found impoundment unconstitutional.[46]

Although President Nixon proved unable to force cuts on Congress, he at least "had succeeded in forcing the legislative branch to face up to its own inadequacies," as James L. Sundquist put it.[47] In fact, a 1973 House Rules Committee report argued that "the legislative budget machinery is in disrepair." The committee's report concluded that "the excessive fragmentation of the budget process in Congress makes it difficult for Congress to effectively assess program priorities or to establish overall budget policy."[48]

The Constitution gives Congress the power to spend money, but it does not say what process Congress is to use. By long tradition, Congress had broken the appropriations process into two parts: authorizations, managed by the subject-area committees, such as the Committee on Armed Services and the Committee on Banking, Housing and Urban Affairs; and appropriations, managed by each house's appropriations committee and its thirteen subcommittees. The appropriations committees have long been known as the "guardians of the Treasury."[49] While their colleagues found it easy to authorize new programs, the appropriations committees had a reputation as tight-fisted overseers of government spending. That often led to conflicts between the appropriations and the authorizing committees, but the appropriations committees were king. New programs were nothing without new appropriations.

The Congressional Budget Act of 1974 fundamentally changed all that.[50] It gave Congress more time to work on the budget by pushing the start of the fiscal year forward from 1 July to 1 October. Congress also mandated that the president present a "current services" budget projection. The current services budget is the president's estimate of the cost of continuing all the previous year's programs, at the same level, in the new fiscal year *without policy changes*. Members of Congress thus hoped to separate debate over program changes from continuation of existing programs: that is, to force the president to identify increments, and decrements, in the budget. It also changed the roles of the appropriations and authorization committees by creating new budget committees in each house and a three-part legislative process to accompany them.

1. *Setting the totals.* For the first time, Congress obligated itself to prepare a *legislative* budget: an estimate of total expenditures and revenues (and thus of the deficit). To do the job, the act established a new Committee on the Budget in each house. Early each year, each congressional committee reports to the budget committees about the cost of bills it anticipates passing. The budget committees then revise these requests and combine them into a single resolution that sets estimates of revenues and ceilings on expenditures. Each house then considers the committees' recommendations and passes a concurrent resolution setting binding spending ceilings for each committee. The hope was to avoid the "agglomeration of separate actions and decisions" about which the House Rules Committee complained.

The act also created a new Congressional Budget Office (CBO) to provide staff support to the budget committees and to give Congress a counterweight to the president's Office of Management and Budget. CBO prepares Congress's own economic forecasts, estimates the costs of proposed legislation, and prepares "scorekeeping" reports that compare adopted and pending bills with the targets set in the concurrent resolution. While CBO has struggled with forecasting problems just as much as OMB has, it has reduced Congress's dependence on the executive branch for forecasts of future trends. Put together, the creation of CBO, the budget committees, and the budget resolutions gave Congress a far stronger hand in dealing with the budget—and a larger responsibility for producing solutions to the budget's difficult problems.

2. *Authorizing programs.* Next, the subject-area committees create *authorizations* for programs under their purview. These authorizations, approved by both houses of Congress and signed by the president, can be for one year (including much of the government's routine operations); for several years (including many defense programs); or for permanent programs (including social security), which remain in effect until the basic law is changed. These authorizations set ceilings on the money that Congress can spend on programs or, in the case of permanent authorizations, define the standards by which benefits are to be paid.

3. *Appropriating money.* While authorizations create the programs, appropriations provide the money to fund them. (Congress can authorize a program without providing any appropriations for it, and it often authorizes higher spending than the appropriations it is willing to provide. The reverse, of course, is not true, since appropriations cannot exceed the original authorization.) Like authorizations, appropriations can last for varying lengths of time. The appropriations committees in each house decide how much money should actually be spent by recommending *budget authority* to be enacted by Congress.

This three-part process, however, is one step removed from the bottom line: the revenues the government actually collects, the money it actually spends, and the level of the deficit. The level of revenues and expenditures, as we have seen, depends on economic performance and administrative activity. The congressional budget process fixes budget authority and authorizations, while the money expected to be actually spent, known as *outlays,* is only an estimate of the budget authority that will actually be used in any given year. Estimating outlays is a complicated process. Analysts must determine how much budget authority from past years will be used in a given fiscal year, how much new budget authority will be created and spent, how much previous budget authority will expire at the end of its time limit, and how much budget authority will be carried over into subsequent years. No matter how close a watch Congress keeps on its books, therefore, it has only a loose rein on outlays in any given year, since outlays can vary according to the rate of unemployment or the progress in building a new fighter at an aircraft plant. Hard-fought congressional deficit battles, which revolve around budget authority levels, can be undone when outlay totals do not cooperate—if, for example, economic growth proves sluggish, interest rates rise, or unemployment surges.

Shrinking Power for Authorizers and Appropriators

The rise of the budget committees and intractable budget deficits have greatly reduced the role of the authorization committees. They have become, as one analyst explained, "the forgotten leg" of the three-legged stool (authorizing, appropriations, and budget committees) intended to support the congressional budget process. Long-term authorizations limited the committees' role in annually reviewing programs, and when reviews have occurred, they often have broken down under the pressure of endless debates on amendments to change the programs. Much of what formerly had been the province of the authorization committees shifted to amendments to appropriations bills, but the appropriations committees themselves also found their role reduced. Even less of the budget, furthermore, is subject to annual appropriations because Congress has financed more programs through permanent appropriations.

Within the defense budget, more "black" programs—secret projects hidden from full congressional review—also diminish the appropriators' role. Some of the programs have been not-so-secret new aircraft, like the "stealth fighter" (largely invisible to radar), an artist's conception of which was available for purchase in hobby stores as a plastic model before the air force ever acknowledged its existence. Others have been ultrasecret projects known to few members of Congress. The "black" budget grew from $5.5

billion in fiscal year 1981 to $24.3 billion in fiscal year 1988, in part because the Reagan administration's defense buildup produced many new projects and in part because defense budgeters discovered it was easier to start and build projects under the "black" cover.

Even in the Clinton years, the "black" budget continued to rise, to $28 billion in fiscal year 1995. In fact, in 1995 the ultra-secret National Reconnaissance Agency, charged with operating spy satellites, actually lost $2 billion until CIA auditors found it months later.[51] The entire process, one author wrote, has long been plagued by a "bewildering babble of classified code words and nicknames" that made effective spending control impossible.[52]

Thus, the appropriators' position has shrunk not only because they lost control over spending totals to the budget committees but also because they have control over less of the budget. During the Reagan years, in particular, they lost even more ground in discretionary domestic spending. Such spending decreased from 25 percent of the budget in 1980 to 15 percent in 1991, and this smaller amount was largely committed to pay the day-to-day operating expenses of the federal government.[53]

The shrinking discretionary budget, especially for domestic programs, scarcely reduced congressional demands for new spending, and the appropriators' jobs have been much less fun. Their role has shifted from guardians of the Treasury to arbiters of pork-barrel claims: requests from members for individual projects from new roads to research programs to take back to their districts.[54] That, paradoxically, has subtly increased the appropriators' power. With more competition over less money, their ability to make these decisions has enhanced their position.

If the role of the authorizing and appropriations committees has shrunk, the budget committees have often found themselves hamstrung as well. Congress has often been unable to complete its work on time and has often relied instead on all-in-one "continuing resolutions" that circumvent the Congressional Budget Act's procedures. Continuing resolutions combine all the government's spending decisions into one huge package, sometimes continuing programs at current levels and sometimes incorporating important changes. They often last for short periods of time, sometimes only a matter of hours or days, and typically are the product of rushed congressional debate. The continuing resolutions, ironically, have enhanced the power of some appropriations committee members, since they play the key role in writing these resolutions. Within the continuing resolutions often are buried small but politically valuable programs like appropriations for a national weed center, funds to advertise the benefits of eating fish, and higher limits for government honey loans.[55]

Some committee members have also used the process to hide personal attacks on federal programs. One member, for example, was traveling to Pakistan with his girlfriend, who was a lobbyist and former Miss U.S.A.-World. The Defense Intelligence Agency, which was supplying air transport for the junket refused to allow the girlfriend to accompany the congressman. (DIA rules permit only members of Congress, their staffs, and family members to fly at federal expense.) Two years later, the congressman got even when, in a mad rush toward adjournment, he sneaked into a continuing resolution a provision that took away two aircraft the DIA used to fly ambassadors and their aides. The congressman refused to discuss the ploy, saying, "It just can't help but look like this kind of spoiled congressman with a bloated sense of self-importance trying to get back at someone for not flying his girlfriend around."[56]

Gramm-Rudman-Hollings and Its Successors

The Congressional Budget Act produced some limited successes, especially in forcing Congress to confront the budget as a whole, but those successes proved short-lived until, during the Reagan years, the process broke down completely. President Reagan and the Democratic House squabbled endlessly. Congress, meanwhile, could not meet its deadlines, and the deficit worsened. In 1985, Congress responded by passing the "Balanced Budget and Emergency Deficit Control Act of 1985," more popularly known as the Gramm-Rudman-Hollings Act, after its three congressional sponsors.[57] The law set a five-year schedule for reducing the federal deficit from $220 billion in fiscal year 1986 to zero in fiscal year 1991. If Congress was unable to meet any year's deficit target, automatic across-the-board cuts, called "sequestrations," would be ordered by the General Accounting Office. Half the cuts would come from defense, half from domestic programs. The act exempted many major programs from cuts, however, including interest on the debt, social security, veterans' payments, and welfare. Together these programs totaled about 70 percent of the budget. When the cuts fell, they would fall heavily on defense programs and the "controllable" portion of domestic spending. If the entire budget required a 2.5 percent cut to reach the deficit target, the targeted programs would have to take nearly a 10 percent cut to achieve the necessary savings.

Supporters and detractors alike compared Gramm-Rudman to a "train wreck": a deliberately orchestrated disaster.[58] The bill's supporters hoped that the certainty of automatic cuts would force a more reasoned approach to spending reduction. It was, according to Senator Rudman, "a bad idea whose time has come."[59] Gramm-Rudman was the triumph of what one analyst has called "formula budgeting," the substitution of broad mechanical rules for judgments that prove politically impossible to make.[60]

In early 1986, Congress failed to meet the first year's deficit target, $171.9 billion, and in March, GAO certified the first round of cuts—$11.7 billion. On 7 July 1986, however, the Supreme Court ruled that the Gramm-Rudman act's enforcement provision was unconstitutional.[61] GAO, the Court found, was an agent of Congress and could not constitutionally exercise executive functions, like issuing orders to executive branch agencies about how to make the act's cuts. That left the act toothless until Congress passed a new version in September 1987. The 1987 revision considerably eased the budget-cutting pain of the original act: it limited cuts for the act's first two years (to postpone the painful decisions until after the 1988 presidential election) and delayed until fiscal year 1993 the deadline for eliminating the deficit. To deal with the constitutional issue, it made the Office of Management and Budget, not GAO, responsible for stipulating the cuts required to reach each year's target. (Congressional Democrats originally had balked about giving such power to President Reagan's OMB, but faced with the prospect of no automatic plan at all, they acquiesced. Putting OMB in charge eliminated the constitutional objections to the act.)[62]

Gramm-Rudman thus even more sharply separated the budget's controllables from the uncontrollables (especially entitlement programs) and further reduced the controllables' portion of the budget. It marked three strong currents: No one wanted to tackle entitlement programs, such as social security; without cuts in entitlements, reducing the federal deficit required huge cuts in the rest of the budget that neither the president nor members of Congress could agree on; and without political agreement, only the orchestrated "train wreck" of Gramm-Rudman seemed to offer a hope of reducing the deficit. The GAO pointedly argued that Gramm-Rudman "has accomplished little more than constraining the growth of the deficit."[63] That accomplishment was certainly not trivial. As figure 10.1 shows, it helped rein in the explosive growth of deficits that occurred in the early 1980s. But it did not accomplish what its proponents had hoped: to provide a mechanism for bringing the budget into balance.

Some critics, such as former Congressional Budget Office director Rudolph Penner, were more blunt: "Gramm-Rudman has resulted in only a little bit of real deficit reduction. But that small advantage is overshadowed by the extraordinary dishonesty it has caused by focusing debate on the short run."[64] Because Gramm-Rudman was based on a "snapshot" of the deficit taken near the beginning of the fiscal year, it led to many games that gave the appearance of progress in reducing the deficit that produced no real long-run changes:[65]

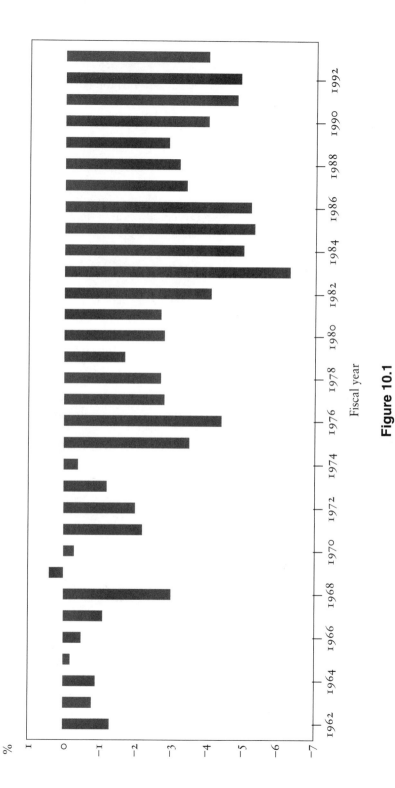

Figure 10.1

FEDERAL BUDGET DEFICIT AS PERCENTAGE OF GROSS DOMESTIC PRODUCT

SOURCE: Congressional Budget Office, *The Economic and Budget Outlook: Fiscal Years 1995–1999* (Washington, D.C.: Government Printing Office, 1994).

1. *Spend the money faster.* If outlays can be shifted into the current fiscal year, they will not be counted against the next year's target. Of course, this tactic only increases the current year's deficit.

2. *Slow down spending.* Spending can be stretched out into future years. This provides the illusion of reducing the deficit while supporting spending increases, but it only increases the cost of federal programs in the long run.

3. *Don't count spending by moving it off budget.* Not all federal spending counts against the Gramm-Rudman targets. Programs that are defined as "off budget" therefore can escape the axe.

4. *Count the same savings over and over.* Congress has cleverly counted the same savings plan several times. Medicare has been a favorite target of repeated plans to save money.

5. *Engage in wishful thinking.* "Planned" savings, such as hoped-for reductions in welfare costs, can reduce the deficit projections without producing any real savings that bring the deficit down in the long term. Overly optimistic economic projections are another form of budgeting by wishful thinking.

Congress tried again in 1990 by passing the Budget Enforcement Act. The act began by separating mandatory spending (including entitlements and interest on the debt) from discretionary spending (defined as programs subject to the annual appropriations process). Congress then broke discretionary spending into three categories: defense (to pay for the military); international (including foreign aid); and domestic (which accounts for the rest). The act set fixed caps for each category of discretionary spending. If the president or Congress want to create new programs or increase spending for existing programs in any of these categories, they have two choices: they can either cut other programs to compensate, or they can find new revenues to pay for the spending. (This provision is known as the pay-as-you-go rule.) This does not mean that Congress cannot enact new programs that increase the deficit, but in practice members of Congress have been reluctant to make any decisions that would make the deficit bigger.[66]

These rather complicated rules proved more successful than the various incarnations of Gramm-Rudman. They focused presidential and congressional attention on where decisions could actually be made in the annual budget process. The pay-as-you-go provision also created a political dynamic that made it hard to propose new programs without somehow finding offsetting cuts, since no one wanted to be held responsible for driving the deficit up even further. These provisions complicated the health-care debate in 1994, as President Clinton struggled to find reforms to produce enough extra revenues to pay for expanding coverage to all citizens. Indeed, the extra complexity this induced made it harder to build support for the program. And when Clinton promoted his $30 billion crime bill the same year, he had to find new money to pay for it. (He found it in the downsizing promised in his "reinventing government" initiative.) The process has not put the deficit in a straitjacket. Since it does not cover either entitlements or interest, which represent more than two-thirds of all federal spending, a huge piece of federal outlays escapes annual review. Moreover, changing economic conditions can change revenues and thus affect the deficit without anyone deciding anything. Nevertheless, the reform has proven painful but important in keeping the deficit from growing larger. Virtually every plan to tackle the deficit has included some version of discretionary spending caps.

Reforming the Budget Process

Growing frustration with what one analyst called a budgetary "ice age," with the process locked in "a frozen mass of spending priorities that no one has really chosen and that no one really likes,"[67] has prompted a host of proposals to reform the budgetary process. Four of them have received particular attention:

1. *Create a biennial budget.* Since Congress persistently misses its budget deadlines, reformers suggest, it would likely do better if its members took a longer view and made the big decisions less often. Both President Clinton's National Performance Review (NPR) and the General Accounting Office recommended switching the federal budget to a two-year cycle. As Vice-President Gore's NPR report concluded: "Biennial budgeting will not make our budget decisions easier, for they are shaped by competing interests and priorities. But it will eliminate an enormous amount of busy work that keeps us from evaluating programs and meeting customer needs."[68] Former CBO director, and Clinton's budget director, Alice Rivlin agreed. "We spend enormous amounts of time going over the same decisions," she notes. "In recent years, there hasn't been time for anything else." Considering the budget only half as often, however, would increase the pressure for supplemental appropriations bills in the interim and would even further increase the budget's dependence on the long-term economic estimates that have already proven so troublesome. The change, moreover, would weaken the congressional oversight that frequently is conducted through annual budget reviews and would transfer more power to the president for deciding how to put two-year plans into effect.[69] As Allen Schick put it, "Congress would still have the power of the purse, but it would hold the strings more loosely."[70] At the state level, ironically, the trend has been toward an-

nual, not biennial, budgeting. Most states switching their budget systems have moved toward annual budgets because of the pressure to keep on top of rapidly changing programmatic and economic conditions.[71]

2. *Create a capital budget.* At state and local levels, budgets typically differentiate spending for current needs, such as police services or professors' salaries, from spending for capital investment, such as highways and bridges, whose benefits stretch into the future. The basic principle is that the costs of programs should be paid by those who benefit from them. Thus, current taxes should pay for current programs, and borrowing (repaid over time from tax revenues) can pay for capital investments. In thirty-seven states, there is a separate capital budget. The GAO has argued that a similar approach at the federal level would encourage investment for the future, better capture the cost of federal loan programs, and focus attention on the whole of the government's financial activities.[72] The problem is that, by creating a capital budget, the government would create a powerful incentive to classify many expenditures, from education to foreign policy, as "investment" for the future and thus pass their costs along to future generations. The distinction between capital and current expenditures is not as clear at the federal level as at state and local levels.

3. *Give the president a line-item veto.* As part of its Contract with America, the House Republican majority in 1995 campaigned hard to provide the president with new veto power over individual line items in the budget. Governors in forty-three states have the power,[73] Republicans since Ronald Reagan had continually insisted. They argued that the president ought to have the same power. After the impoundment battles with Richard Nixon, however, some members of Congress were wary about ceding additional authority to the president.[74] Many Republicans, furthermore, lost their enthusiasm for the change when Republicans took over Congress and faced a Democratic president. Unwilling to vote President Clinton the power for which they had campaigned, they ultimately passed a weak line-item veto in 1996 with the proviso that it not take effect until after the next presidential inauguration.

The line-item veto solution, finally, assumes that the deficit problem stems from congressional spending in excess of the president's requests. Over the Reagan years, when the presidential-congressional disputes were sharpest, the two branches differed relatively little in total spending (although the division between domestic and defense expenditures has often been significant).[75] A federal line-item veto thus probably would not have produced lower deficits, and it would not have attacked the entitlement spending that constitutes so much of the budget. Furthermore, when pressed to identify the programs he would veto if given the chance, President Reagan in 1988 listed $1.5 billion out of a $1 trillion budget. If he had vetoed every one of these programs, many of them pets of individual members of Congress, the $150 billion deficit would have been reduced only marginally. It is unlikely, therefore, that presidents will often use the line-item veto. The likely targets of such vetoes will be not whole programs but individual projects, each of which will be critically important to some member of Congress. Presidents can rarely afford to make enemies, especially since such projects often are crucial to members' votes on other issues important to the president.

4. *Enact a balanced-budget constitutional amendment.* Republicans pursuing the Contract with America were even more enthusiastic in pressing the decades-old case for a constitutional amendment requiring a balanced budget. But in 1995 they proved unable to collect enough votes to pass it, although the proposal was perhaps the most broadly popular of the provisions in the Republican "contract." In fact, since 1975, thirty-two states have passed resolutions calling for such an amendment.[76] Every state but Vermont and Wyoming has a requirement to balance its own budget.[77] Experience at the state level, however, shows that defining "balance" is deceptively difficult. The states, moreover, have shown that budget managers can play many games to produce a short-run balance while hiding persistent deficits. As GAO found, "not all states balance every year, even by the relatively flexible state definitions of balance."[78] A budget balance can be created by shifting programs off budget or expanding guaranteed loans, for example, whose full costs do not show up in the budget.[79] Enforcement of such a constitutional provision raised even more difficult questions. Short of marching the president and Congress off to jail, it was unclear who (but the voters) could seek retribution on whom. And, as Allen Schick reminds us, "the economy often has the last word in determining the fate of presidential and congressional budgets."[80]

Procedure versus Substance. All these proposals share a similar theme: procedural fixes for the budget's substantive problems. "Every reform proposal I have seen so far is really just a way to substitute procedure for substance," argues Senator Mark O. Hatfield (R-Ore.). "We are not going to work our way out of federal deficit difficulties with procedural gimmicks. There is nothing wrong with our present system if we summon the will to make it work. And if we do not have will, no new procedures will work any better." Carol G. Cox, president of the Committee for a Responsible Federal Budget, agreed: "These are not economic problems. They are not analytical problems. They are political problems."[81] Indeed, in 1987 Congress and the president were deadlocked over the budget until the stock market crash galvanized them into action. It was political, not procedural, paralysis that had forestalled action until after the crisis.

This is not to say that process does not matter. As Senator Gramm, one of the Gramm-Rudman engineers, put it, "I submit that procedure produces substance."[82] Neither president nor Congress establishes a process without considering what substance will result; also, negotiations over process often disguise implicit conflicts over substance. When President Reagan and the Democratic Congress agreed on the Gramm-Rudman process, for example, the procedural agreement tacitly recognized that each would contribute half of any deficit reduction—defense spending from the president, domestic programs from Congress.

Back-Door Tactics for Increasing Spending

The peculiar politics of deficit reduction, of course, promoted new tactics to circumvent the budget-cutting process. "The more rigid are the restraints put on the budgeting process, the more is the motive to be imaginative," explains Roy Ash, OMB director in the Nixon administration. "There is no end to the possibilities."[83] To support new programs, some advocates have argued for trust funds, financed with revenues earmarked for particular programs. That way, they contend, the programs would not add to the deficit.[84] Social security is the oldest example of such a program, but more recently highway and mass-transit programs have protected their budgets because they were supported by their own trust funds.

Questions about social security have especially muddled budgetary politics. In 1985, Congress took the social security program "off budget" to protect the program from political tinkering and to insulate it from Gramm-Rudman cuts. (The program since then has been running large and growing surpluses intended to help finance the program for retirees—some of whom are now starting college—well into the twenty-first century.)

Taking the program "off-budget" has insulated its finances from annual budgetary squabbles. In the broader fabric of the federal budget, however, the social security surplus reduces the amount that the federal government must borrow to finance the remaining budget deficit. (The surplus is, in effect, "invested" for the future by buying Treasury securities, the safest of all investments, which helps finance the national debt.) In fiscal year 1993, for example, the deficit in the budget, except for social security, was $301 billion. The social security program ran a $47 billion surplus, which reduced the overall federal deficit to $254 billion.

The social security surplus tends to camouflage the true size of the deficit in the non-social-security portion of the budget. Annual deficit accounting, moreover, hides the long-term problem buried in the social security program. The Bipartisan Commission on Entitlement and Tax Reform found that after 1998, federal spending is projected to increase rapidly as the elderly population increases. By 2012, the commission concluded, "unless appropriate policy changes are made in the interim, projected outlays for entitlements and interest on the national debt will consume all tax revenues collected by the Federal Government."[85] Despite the commission's stark and frightening findings, it could not agree on *any* recommendation to attack the problem. Since its inception in 1935, social security has always had a special place in American politics, but its deep-seated issues coupled with deficit politics have created new budgetary dilemmas.

Furthermore, as the burgeoning deficit has shut off the budget as a source for new programs, Congress has relied more on lending through off-budget entities, such as government corporations and government-sponsored enterprises (which we examined briefly in chapters 2 and 5). Federal loans, both direct and guaranteed loans, increased rapidly. So extensive have the federal government's activities become, in fact, that 88 percent of all housing loans carry the federal government's backing.[86] The attractiveness of hiding programs away from usual budgetary politics is obvious, but many federal lending programs carry three significant problems. First, much of the lending does not carry the government's direct guarantee, so those who lend money to the government for these programs demand higher interest rates. Costs are therefore greater. Second, congressional oversight typically is weak and irregular, so programs financed through such backdoor lending often are not held to the same standard of accountability facing other federal programs.[87] Finally, the potential risk to the government of default by those who have borrowed money is large, but those risks are neither well understood nor well controlled. The expansion of federal programs through lending programs thus carries real danger.

Both Congress and President Bush relied heavily on back-door financing in creating the savings-and-loan bailout in 1989. The savings-and-loan strategy represents what has become a patterned response to financial crises, ranging from the Chrysler Corporation's bailout in the early 1980s to the farm bailout in the middle of the decade. Government borrowing, or government guarantees, offer a way to provide federal support, spend money, and even create new government bureaucracies without seeming to. At the same time, however, they sometimes raise troubling questions about the costs they impose and the control government can exercise over such novel tactics. So long as deficit politics forestalls debate about putting new programs directly on the federal budget, such tactics are likely to continue.

The government has also pursued new programs through the regulatory process. It is tempting to promote new initiatives and transfer their costs to the private sector. The minimum wage, for example, guarantees a floor for workers' pay. Congress has debated similar regulatory initiatives, from requiring employers to provide all employees with health insurance to guaranteeing husbands (as well as wives) time off to care for newborn babies. Whether the government taxes firms and citizens and spends the money to provide services, or simply requires them to use their resources to do the same thing, the effect is the same—except that in one case the program does not show up in the budget and it does not affect the deficit.

Budget battles between the president and Congress are as old as the republic and none of these back-door tactics can avoid that problem. The battles have become more fierce since the mid-1960s, in part because of the mixed-party control of the institutions (with at least the House and often the Senate held by the Democrats and the presidency often held by the Republicans), and in part because of the growth of entitlements and interest on the debt and the steady shrinkage of discretionary spending. The budgetary process embodies these profound struggles: institutional jockeying between the president and Congress over control of the government's business; and substantive debates over the government's relationship to society. No procedural solution will fix the budgetary process unless it embodies a solution to these difficult questions.

Budget Execution

If the legislature rules the budget appropriations phase of budgeting, the executive is overseer of the execution phase. The president's authority derives from his constitutional role as chief executive and commander-in-chief, as well as his constitutional obligation to "take Care that the Laws are faithfully executed." Allen Schick has noted that "much loss of budget control results from executive actions ... but executive practices are a 'dark continent' of Federal budgeting."[88] The budget execution process is a delicate balance between ensuring that a program's legislative goals are served and providing adequate flexibility for administrators to do their work.

Controls on Executive Action

The balance comes from congressional tactics to restrain executive discretion, through both legislative controls and limits on executive impoundment.

Legislative Controls on Execution. In 1950, the House Appropriations Committee established the basic rule governing expenditures by the executive branch. Congressional appropriations constitute "only a ceiling upon the amount" that can be expended for a given activity. "The administrative officials responsible for administration of an activity for which appropriation is made bear the final burden for rendering all necessary service within the smallest amount possible within the ceiling figure fixed by the Congress."[89] In effect, Congress cannot require that an agency spend all money appropriated, because of two practical considerations. First, conditions may change during the fiscal year so that the funds available for a purpose are not all needed. For example, at the local level, a mild winter might mean that most of the snow-removal budget goes unspent. Second, Congress wants to encourage agencies to achieve a program's objectives at less cost wherever possible.

Legislators nevertheless are frustrated by their inability to assure full speed ahead by administrators managing their favorite programs. To reduce the possibility of executive nullification of congressional intent, the enabling legislation sometimes commands (rather than simply authorizes) agencies to implement programs. This, however, neither guarantees that adequate appropriations will be voted nor assures that agencies will spend every dollar appropriated for their programs.

The second concern is exacerbated by the roles of the president and OMB. Most appropriations are made directly to agencies, rather than to the president. In the past, however, an agency sometimes spent its annual appropriation in the first half or three-fourths of the fiscal year and then asked Congress for a supplemental appropriation to avoid closing down the agency.[90] To prevent this, Congress has authorized OMB to apportion to an agency on a quarterly, monthly, or other time-period basis; and to review and revise each apportionment at least quarterly. Congress has forbidden agencies to exceed such apportioned amounts.

Impoundment. In 1974, Congress enacted the Impoundment Control Act to prevent the gross abuse of impoundment authority by the Nixon administration from recurring.[91] All presidents from Franklin D. Roosevelt to Lyndon B. Johnson had claimed and exercised authority to impound: refusal by the president to spend money appropriated by Congress. Their difference from President Nixon lay not in failure to claim presidential power but in their restraint in using that power. Their most controversial impoundments withheld funds for particular weapons systems (a category on which a president might claim some authority as commander-in-chief). Other impoundments partially undid public works legislation, allowing certain projects to proceed while blocking funds for others. A few impoundment actions were justified on deficit-controlling and anti-inflation grounds.

Nixon's impoundments "were unprecedented in their scope and severity," as Louis Fisher, the leading authority on impoundment, put it.[92] The long-range consequences of this conflict during the Nixon administration have been unfortunate. One result has been an effort by Congress to draft authorizing statutes and appropriations acts as narrowly as possible, to deprive the president and agency heads of discretion in implementing programs. Congress increasingly votes, "The Secretary shall . . ." instead of the traditional, "The Secretary is authorized to . . ."

The Impoundment Control Act distinguishes between *rescissions* and *deferrals* of budget authority; the distinction is roughly between permanent and temporary suspension of outlays. When the president proposes to *rescind* budget authority, he must ask Congress to pass a rescission bill or joint resolution. When the president, the OMB director, or a department or agency head proposes to *defer* any budget authority for a specific purpose or project—that is, to delay its availability for a period not extending beyond the end of the fiscal year—the president must inform Congress.[93]

In their first five years, the new procedures produced almost $50 billion in deferrals and $10.3 billion in rescissions. Most deferrals were routine, while the rescissions tended to represent policy disputes between the president and Congress. President Ford tried to use rescissions to cut social programs, while President Carter used rescissions to cut defense spending. In general, however, use of the tool for policy purposes, as opposed to routine administrative reasons, declined steadily. For partisan reasons, a president of the party opposite to that of at least one house of Congress could expect to have little success in overturning many congressional actions; indeed, President Ford lost 90 percent of his proposed rescissions. A president of the same party as the congressional majority has a strong incentive to avoid partisan bickering.[94] During the Reagan years, the forum for settling disputes focused on the congressional budget process, especially the omnibus reconciliation bills as well as continuing resolutions, and the importance of rescissions and deferrals dwindled further.

Management Control

In very different fashion, the flow of money throughout the bureaucracy provides a valuable tool for controlling the implementation of government programs.[95] This flow of money provides several important forms of leverage on administrators' activities. First, the money trail demonstrates who is doing what. While a government official can have substantial impact on citizens without spending a large amount of money (e.g., in regulatory programs), it is very difficult to have impact without spending *any* money. While input measures like money spent do not indicate what output an agency might be producing, they provide a valuable road map to the details of government activity. This tool can be especially important in tracking the activity of third parties, such as contractors or grantees, who produce many government goods and services.

Second, by controlling the flow of money, the executive can control the direction and pace of governmental activity. Managers sometimes presume that everyone within an organization is working toward the same goal only to be surprised later by employees' actions that are grossly out of line with the organization's goals. The flow of money is important symbolically because it signals the goals an organization holds as important. It is important managerially because it helps secure congruence between the broader goals of the organization and the individual goals of workers.

Finally, the flow of money is important for reporting and evaluating an agency's performance. It can help managers identify the "hot spots" that need attention, either because a unit is spending too much money too quickly or, paradoxically, because it is spending very little money. More broadly, it provides important raw materials for program evaluation. By measuring what the money goes for, managers can take a first step toward determining a program's, and thus an agency's, efficiency and effectiveness.

"With rare exceptions," Robert N. Anthony and David W. Young explain, "a management control system is built around a financial structure."[96] This structure, in turn, is constructed with the building blocks of accounts, for functions or agencies, for subunits within those functions or agencies, and on to the individual components of an agency. In most governmental accounting systems, every expenditure is tagged with an account number. Account number 3-45983-6803, for example, might identify precisely the source and use of the money: the first "3" might mean that the money comes from a particular funding source, such as an excise tax on gasoline; the "45983" might mean that the money is allocated to the field unit in charge of repairing roads in the southern part of the state; and the "6803" might mean that the money is going to purchase asphalt patching material. Thus, by using their computers, government managers can monitor the status of all their activities, separated into whatever components they desire.

Weak accounting systems have sometimes cost the government millions of dollars. The Government Accounting Office (GAO), for example, discovered that eighteen federal agencies paid 25 percent of their bills late, costing the government millions of dollars in penalties. Another 25 percent of the bills were paid too early, which meant that the government often had to borrow money, costing the government $350 million annually in lost interest. The Department of Defense, meanwhile, could not account for over $600 million that foreign customers had forwarded to purchase weapons. Many agency accounting systems are "antiquated," the GAO concluded.

"As a result, billions of dollars are not being adequately accounted for, managed or financially controlled."[97]

Different governments operate by different systems, but they all rely on management control systems built on accounts.[98] While the intricacies of such fund accounting often seem boring to those worrying with broad legislative-executive conflicts and the politics of deficit reduction, they provide the ultimate control on the government's money. Management control gives executive branch officials important information about the behavior of those who implement government policies, both within and outside government. Through routine auditing functions, it provides the mechanism for discovering problems and correcting them before they become large. Most important, effective management control provides important leverage over the activities of government officials, contractors, and grantees, and thus improves the chances for effective and efficient provision of public services.

One especially intriguing initiative to improve the connection between budgeting and results, inputs and outputs, is the movement in federal, state, and local governments toward performance management. Governments at all levels have increasingly introduced results-oriented management, built around strategic planning, more carefully to define an organization's goals; performance measurement, to develop clear indicators of program outcomes; and the development of new management systems, especially information and human resource systems, to support the broader movement. Such cities as Sunnyvale, California, have moved to focus management more on results—like the condition of local parks. Oregon launched a long-term effort to define state goals, from success in school to the cleanliness of the environment, and to measure the state's performance against these goals.[99] In 1993, Congress passed the Government Performance and Results Act, which commits the federal government to a decade-long management improvement effort to develop annual strategic plans (before 1988); to prepare annual performance plans (beginning in 1999); and to report annually on actual performance (beginning in 2000). These reforms mirrored even more far-reaching strategies launched in Great Britain, Australia, and New Zealand.

The reforms have sweeping implications. They require radically different skills and approaches for government managers, who must focus much more on outputs (like program outcomes) instead of inputs (like the budget). The information they produce offers greater potential leverage for such central management agencies as OMB, and OMB has been one of the Government Performance and Results Act's most enthusiastic supporters. The evidence both from the American states and from abroad is that performance management is extremely difficult to develop and use. It imposes daunting measurement and management problems. Moreover, legislators have frequently made limited use at best of the great volumes of information such processes produce, in part because finding consensus on what goals ought to be measured is difficult, and in part because legislators often focus much more on attacking problems by passing laws and appropriating money than by overseeing results (as we examine in chapter 12). Nevertheless, the evidence from both foreign and American experiments is that managers often have found results-oriented management useful in focusing agency staff on high-priority goals and for surviving in the increasingly stringent fiscal environment in which they find themselves. The federal government's effort, however, is the largest such experiment in the world, and observers are looking carefully at whether it will offer real promise or will go the way of such previous reforms as PPB, MBO, and ZBB.[100]

Conclusion

Our review of the issues arising in the preparation, appropriation, and execution of government budgets underlines the importance of budgetary decisions: the effect of the budget on the economy; the effect of the economy on the budget; and the use of the budgetary arena for fighting out (if not always resolving) battles between the legislative and executive branches. Most of all, it is the arena that most fundamentally shapes public policy decisions. By putting dollars together with often ambitious, and sometimes conflicting, goals, policymakers provide the resources needed to bring programs to life. While the budgetary process varies greatly at all levels of government, the basic issues remain.

The decision-making models we saw in chapter 9 are complicated enough. This chapter demonstrates that decisions reached and formalized at one stage of a multistage process may be superseded and reshaped by decisions made at later stages by administrators and control agencies. The decision-making process, then, is considerably more complex than is suggested by theories focused on how one person or one organizational unit makes choices among alternatives at a single point in time. *The* decision-making process is also a misnomer, for many such processes operate simultaneously in government. The budget process is only one, even though the allocation of financial resources is basic to all that the government does.

The next question, of course, is how the administrative process acts on those decisions: how it adapts, refines, and sometimes even reshapes the results of the legislative-executive contests. That is the process we call "implementation," and it is to that problem that we next turn.

11

Implementation

Recent well-publicized problems of governmental performance, from over-priced spare parts for the Pentagon to federal housing grant programs riddled with influence peddling, have revived concern about administration. More than a hundred years after Woodrow Wilson's call for the study of administration, his comment that "it is getting harder to *run* a constitution than to frame one" is mirrored in the recognition that it is easier to write laws than to execute them. Concerns about the execution of laws gave birth to a new field of study called *implementation*. Traditional public administration focused on government agencies and sought to understand the way that bureaus operated. More recent implementation studies, by contrast, concentrate on programs and the results they produce. Implementation analysts use many of the traditional approaches of public administration, but by shifting the focus from the agency to the program, they hope to discover why programs' performance so often seems disappointing, and what can be done to manage programs better.

Every citizen—and taxpayer—is entitled to ask straightforward questions about the administration of government programs. Which programs are successful and should be continued? Which are failures and should be ended? What changes make the most difference in improving the efficiency and responsiveness of government programs? Which of these changes can be made by program administrators themselves, and which require action by elected legislators or executives?

Straightforward answers to these questions are disappointingly rare. It is hard even to define what "success" and "failure" are, let alone how to achieve one while avoiding the other. We explore the rocky terrain of implementation in several ways. In this chapter, we consider how to judge a program's success or failure. We study the special implementation problems of administering government programs through the American intergovernmental system, as well as through private contractors. We conclude with a case study that demonstrates that failure is not inevitable, but that success requires great skill in both politics and administration.

Judging Program Success and Failure

This process we call implementation may be, at first, a bit confusing. Is not the entire public administration field about the management of government programs, and thus about implementation? In broad terms, the answer of course is yes. As long as persons have been engaged in the administration of government, they have been worried about implementation. The study of implementation as a discrete process is more recent. In 1973, Jeffrey L. Pressman and Aaron B. Wildavsky sparked great interest in the process—or, as their subtitle, one of the longest in literary history, put it: "How Great Expectations in Washington Are Dashed in Oakland; Or, Why It's Amazing that Federal Programs Work at All, This Being a Saga of the Economic Development Administration as Told by Two Sympathetic Observers Who Seek to Build Morals on a Foundation of Ruined Hopes."[1]

Implementation differs from more traditional approaches to public administration because it focuses narrowly on the "*interaction* between the setting of goals and the actions geared to achieving them," as Pressman and Wildavsky put it. In short, implementation concentrates on the results of administrative action, not just on its process. As their clever subtitle suggests, Pressman and Wildavsky moved to the subject because of their observation that a program's performance so often did not match its promise. The reason, they suggested, was that the "seamless web" of programs tends to become very complex, and the greater the complexity, the greater the chance of failure. Students of implementation see policymaking and policy execution as a web in which each strand depends on all the others.[2]

The studies that followed Pressman and Wildavsky echoed their pessimism. One concludes, "Domestic programs virtually never achieve all that is expected of them."[3] Others see the process as "an uphill battle from start to finish."[4] Some students of implementation look on themselves as physicians seeking to diagnose the many diseases afflicting government programs.[5] The field is the very embodiment of Murphy's Law, "If anything can go wrong, it will." Indeed, the presumption of failure seems endemic to the study of implementation.[6]

What Are "Success" and "Failure"?

To judge whether a program has succeeded or failed, one needs to compare its results with its goals. Implementation analysis thus shares features of the rational analysis model discussed in chapter 9. This obvious comparison, however, is also extremely difficult in practice. Legislative objectives typically are unclear, often are many rather than one, and frequently change over time. In the Johnson administration's War on Poverty, for example, the law required local communities to provide "maximum feasible participation" for the poor in making spending decisions, a policy that produced instead "maximum feasible misunderstanding."[7] Another community development program provided federal grants to local governments. They could spend the money on programs that gave "maximum feasible priority" to programs assisting low- and moderate-income families, or aiding in the prevention of slums and blight, or meeting urgent community development needs.[8] The law, however, did not tell administrators just how strong a priority must be to pass the "maximum feasible" test. It did not define low- and moderate-income families, so it was hard to tell precisely who was eligible. And what constituted an urgent need was anything but clear.

Passing a law in Congress means winning a majority of votes, and the path to coalition building usually is paved with compromises that render goals unclear. One path to such compromises is often to include competing goals in the same law. The result often is prolonged struggles between those who administer and those who are affected by the law.[9]

Goals, finally, can change over time. In New Haven, Connecticut, for example, local officials were administering a youth employment program. A slowdown in building construction made it difficult to place program participants in union jobs, as the officials had planned, so they broadened their goals to include nonunion placements. When they found that sixteen-year-olds in the program were too young to work in some construction jobs, they recruited older participants than first planned. And when the officials discovered that most participants lacked the high school degree that many apprenticeship programs required, the director of the program taught an evening General Education Degree class to help participants qualify.[10]

Goals evolve through the implementation process because administrative reality is always hard to forecast. Unexpected events continually pop up and require administrators to adjust. As one wag put it, "One should expect that the expected can be prevented, but the unexpected should have been expected."[11] Goals also change because their definition is wrapped up inextricably with the ongoing political process. The complex system of American government, with its intricate balance of powers and intergovernmental relations, provides many different points of access to the political process. What a "policy" is can be changed at many points: laws must be interpreted and regulations written by administrators; those interpretations can be challenged in court by those who hold another view; intergovernmental and public-private mechanisms create the possibility of great variation in the way different individuals pursue the same program; and every decision can be challenged somewhere else. Implementation is a continuing game in which every "failure" and "success" sets the stage for the next conflict. Those disappointed by the results of one stage of the policy process can always seek better luck around the process's next turn.[12]

Implementation can thus be understood as the outcome of a continuing, dynamic, often turbulent process in which the many forces of American pluralism struggle to shape administrative action just as they fight over legislative, judicial, and executive decisions.[13] Indeed, implementation is a highly interactive, interdependent process. The more that the public and private sectors of American society are intertwined, the more that all three levels of American federalism become linked, and the more that legislative actions are challenged as agencies write regulations and the regulations are challenged in the courts, then the more implementation depends on a "loosely coupled structure." These continuing interactions shape and reshape policy implementation.[14]

If the goals by which "success" and "failure" are to be judged are so mushy, is there no clear standard for measuring how well a program works? The classical approach is to weigh a program's results against its legislative intent, but, as we have seen, legislative language is a poor benchmark. As the result of compromise, goals are typically vague, multiple, and conflicting. Administrators nevertheless have a legal and ethical obligation to pursue these goals as written, and the courts use legislative goals as standards by which to judge administrative action. The very mushiness of goals, however, introduces two different kinds of discretion into the process: by administrators, in divining what the legislature had in mind; and by courts, in comparing administrators' interpretations with their own judgments about legislative intent.

Thus, in a legal sense, legislative intent supplies the standards for judging a program's success or failure. It does not provide an objective measure, since, as with Rorschach tests, everyone reads into "legislative intent" just what he or she wishes to see. To deal with this quandary, analysts often employ two additional measures for administrative action.

Economists have always argued that *efficiency* is a premier standard for judging action. Whatever a legislature's goals might be, we expect public programs to be run efficiently. What outputs are produced for a given level of inputs? Could a different administrative approach produce more outputs for the same level of inputs (or the same level of output for less input)? Invoking the efficiency standard gives one measure by which to judge implementation.

In addition to efficiency, we also expect programs to be *responsive*.

Does implementation reflect the popular will? And who represents that popular will? Elected officials or those affected by a program? The problem, of course, is that strategies that emphasize efficiency often sacrifice responsiveness. It is costly, for example, to allow those affected by decisions to have a full chance for their opinions to be heard. Efficiency and accountability are tradeoffs; more of one usually means less of the other.[15]

The problem of judging implementation is thus the broader problem of American government: although we all hold the performance of governmental institutions to broad standards of efficiency and responsiveness, many of us have very different ideas about what these standards mean in individual cases. Furthermore, a program's goals are almost always vague. It therefore is often difficult to produce a consistent answer to whether a program succeeds or fails because such judgments vary with the observer. Nevertheless, we seek "successes" over "failures." We want programs that are efficient rather than inefficient, and we want programs to achieve their goals. Even if we cannot agree precisely what these terms mean, they define the overall context in which debate over implementation rages.

Problems of Performance

What factors most make the difference in implementation? If a policymaker desires a particular outcome, what factors affect his or her chances of getting it? Five issues continually resurface:

- ☐ The uncertainty that surrounds programs
- ☐ The resources to get the job done
- ☐ Organizational features that determine how bureaucracies react to problems
- ☐ Leadership that guides bureaucracies through difficult issues
- ☐ Growing interdependence among levels of government, and between government and the private and nonprofit sectors

Uncertainty

Difficult problems may have no known solutions. When that is true, eagerness to meet an obvious need may lead to authorizing the merely plausible, the currently fashionable, or the most powerfully advocated program. The problem, though, is ageless. Elliot Richardson, a member of President Nixon's cabinet, writes:

> Our impatience toward delays in curing social ills reinforces the "don't just stand there, do something" impulse. [This syndrome] encourages . . .

the illusion that we know how to cure alcoholism, treat heroin addiction, and rehabilitate criminal offenders. In fact, we do not. The state of the art in these areas is about where the treatment of fevers was in George Washington's day.[16]

When we undertake to eliminate poverty, provide decent housing for every American family, conquer cancer, make the country's lakes and rivers fishable and swimmable, assure everyone's access to adequate health care, and eliminate discrimination based on race, sex, national origin, age, and physical disability, we express noble hopes that may be dashed because we have not learned how to do these things. As the authors of a study of Medicaid put it, "idealists may frame laws; realists have to administer them."[17]

Even when the uncertainty is technological, formidable challenges often remain. The Soviet nuclear disaster at Chernobyl and the tragic explosion in January 1986 of the space shuttle *Challenger* all too vividly demonstrate the tremendous difficulty of combining complex engineering tasks in never-before-attempted systems. When the problem is social instead of technological, such as with welfare programs, the uncertainty about how to deal with complexity is different and just as troubling.

The difficulty is imperfect knowledge, particularly when the statute directs the agency to solve a new problem or attack an old problem in a new (but unspecified) way. Moreover, administrators' sophistication is often no match for the imagination of average citizens, let alone the skilled specialist. Programs to reduce oversupply of major agricultural crops offered subsidies to farmers for taking some of their acreage out of production. Farmers chose their poorest-yield acres as the ones to lie fallow and stepped up the output of their remaining acres. National goals for curtailing production were not met. The imagination of taxpayers seeking loopholes in the Internal Revenue Service's voluminous regulations is legendary. Even if administrators attempt to anticipate unanticipated consequences of their actions, their judgment can never surpass the inventiveness of thousands, or millions, of clever attorneys, accountants, and other experts who make it their business to find loopholes.

Uncertainty thus often handicaps program implementation. Ever more complex technologies, from space shuttles to nuclear reactors, produce problems that are hard to predict. Interactions between people, and between citizens and their government, are even harder to forecast and influence. We often do not know how to do what we want done, not just in government but in many aspects of an intricate society. Even when we do know, we often do not know how to do it, and these uncertainties hurt the performance of governmental programs.

Inadequate Resources

Resources, both in money and in skilled personnel, are often inadequate for implementing the ambitious programs created by legislatures. Cynics, of course, believe that government is awash with unnecessary bureaucrats, especially at the federal level. Nonetheless, the imbalance between grand objectives and resources for attaining them is amply documented.

Money. When he was secretary of the Department of Health, Education, and Welfare (later split into the Department of Health and Human Services and the Department of Education), Elliot Richardson discovered that the $100 million Congress approved for a new elderly nutrition program would reach only 5 percent of the eligible people, and the Community Health Program only 20 percent of the intended beneficiaries. He asked his staff to estimate the cost in fiscal 1972 of having all the department's programs reach every eligible person. The amount was $250 billion, more than the total federal budget at that time. He writes that "all too often, new legislation merely publicizes a need without creating either the means or the resources for meeting it."[18]

Congress can and often does impose new duties on an agency, expand old ones, and require more elaborate procedures without increasing the agency's appropriations. The president, too, can try to hold back funds or direct an agency to give top priority to a single activity without considering the effects on its full statutory obligations. State and local governments likewise often find that the federal government requires them to meet national guidelines without supplying the money to do so. In mid-1986, for example, officials of St. George, Utah, faced fines up to $25,000 per day for failing to meet federal clean water standards. A new sewage treatment plant they planned would help the city meet the standards. City officials had already spent $100,000 trying to qualify for a federal grant that would fund 75 percent of the plant's $13 million cost. At the same time, the Reagan administration was attempting to eliminate the grant program entirely. "We've been chasing after EPA [Environmental Protection Agency] dollars for years," said Larry Bulloch, St. George's public works director. "It's like a carrot on a string; we just never catch up with it."[19] The gap between a program's goals and its funding is often substantial, a problem that has grown with the federal deficit.

Staff. As we saw in chapter 7, the number of federal employees has lagged behind the growth of population, federal expenditures, and programs to be administered. Even at state and local levels, government responsibilities have outpaced government employment. A staff too small for its responsibilities will be hard pressed to interpret the statute, write and amend regulations, answer correspondence, confer with clientele organizations, disburse money to applicants for a program's benefits, and keep accounts on where the money has gone. Moreover, an understaffed organization will not assign enough of its personnel to monitoring a program's performance or detecting program abuse and fraud.

Organizational Problems

The department or agency in which a program is located has much to do with the program's likelihood of success. Some agencies are extremely friendly toward new programs; others treat them as neglected children. Often, even when a program does not find a hospitable home, no existing department is likely to be more appropriate, or other factors prevent the program's being assigned a better home. In such cases, it is useful to know the hazards—and to know that they can be partially countered by protective measures. Three common organizational arrangements illustrate the problem.

First, it is risky to place regulatory responsibilities in an agency whose primary function is service. Consider the task of promoting industrial development and employment. Many states have regulatory bodies to control industrial activities, and such regulation implies an actual (or potential) adversarial relationship between the government agency and the regulated industry. In contrast, promotion of industrial development requires close and sympathetic collaboration between the agency and its clients. No agency could well serve both goals.

Second, it is risky to place a program in an agency whose staff is unsympathetic to the program.[20] In the early years of the Reagan administration, for example, top officials of the Environmental Protection Agency had a negative attitude toward government regulation of business, and many environmental programs suffered. Furthermore, it is easy to assume that any new program needs an imaginative and vigorous administrative staff and that such vigor is not likely to come from an established old-line department, whose civil servants have been there for years. Yet, as we know, the multiplication of government agencies creates new problems: more conflict between agencies, more need for coordination at the chief executive's level (whether president, governor, county administrator, or mayor), and more centralization of authority in the chief executive's staff.

Third, it is risky to assign related programs to different agencies. The program manager's strategy depends on the strategies and actions of his or her rivals, and bureaucratic objectives tend to replace public policy objectives. In the competition for "customers," the manager may overserve or underregulate the clientele shared with other programs. Classic examples include the competition between the Army Corps of Engineers (in the Defense Department) and the Reclamation Service (in the Interior Department) to build dams, and local governments' shopping around among the four federal agencies (the departments of Agriculture, Commerce, and Housing and Urban Development, as well as the Environmental Protection Agency) that can make sewage-treatment construction grants. In the regulatory arena, three federal agencies oversee banks: the Comptroller of the Currency (in the Treasury Department), the Board of Governors of the Federal Reserve System, and the Federal Deposit Insurance Corporation (both independent regulatory agencies). The result, said one Federal Reserve chairman, is "a jurisdictional tangle that boggles the mind" and fosters "competition in laxity, sometimes to relax constraints, sometimes to delay corrective measures. Agencies sometimes are played off against one another."[21] That tangle complicated efforts in the late 1980s to solve the savings-and-loan crisis.

Leadership

A master of epigrams, Ralph Waldo Emerson, set the theme: "an institution is the lengthened shadow of one man."[22] In the bureaucratic world, an exceptional administrator can make the difference in a program's success. For a generation, the FBI was indeed the "lengthened shadow" of J. Edgar Hoover. The early success of the Peace Corps owed much to the energetic leadership of Sargent Shriver, and James E. Webb managed the nation's remarkable drive to the moon in the 1960s. Bureaucratic entrepreneurs have radically transformed government agencies with the force of their ideas and energy.[23] Such "fixers" are crucial to smoothing out the inevitable problems that emerge in the implementation process.[24]

As James Q. Wilson has pointed out, however, there are not enough of these leaders: "the supply of able, experienced executives is not increasing nearly as fast as the number of problems being addressed by public policy." And, he continued, "the government—at least publicly—seems to act as if the supply of able political executives were infinitely elastic, though people setting up new agencies will often admit privately that they are so frustrated and appalled by the shortage of talent that the only wonder is why disaster is so long in coming."[25]

Programs whose effectiveness depends on individual leaders tend to flag when their leaders depart. The Commerce Department's Economic Development Administration (EDA), previously with a rural emphasis, moved into urban development with a $23 million public works showcase to relieve unemployment in Oakland, California. Eugene P. Foley, characterized as "the enthusiastic, restless and imaginative Assistant Secretary of Commerce who heads EDA," led the change in April 1966. Five months later, Foley resigned, and several key staff people soon left. Without his leadership, the program fell back into the normal channels in Washington, where "its priority and singular importance diminished." Pressman and Wildavsky report, "both Secretary of Commerce Connor and Foley's successor, Ross Davis, felt that the Oakland project was Foley's personal project; they did not share Foley's enthusiasm for a dramatic EDA push in urban areas." The program failed soon afterward.[26]

Dependence on Others

When we think about the implementation of government programs, we tend to think about government officials implementing those programs. It is a fundamental truth of modern public administration, however, that public and private activities are becoming intermingled, "to the point where the dividing line between the federal government's sphere of operations and the rest of the economy has become increasingly blurred, if not eliminated," as economist Murray L. Weidenbaum put it.[27] On the one hand, government has taken an ever increasing role in setting policy for the entire society, from providing subsistence for the poor to setting the terms of competition for industry. On the other hand, the government has come to rely ever more on third parties—other levels of government, nonprofit organizations, and private organizations—to execute programs. Implementation has thus become a complex business of managing interrelationships between government and the many proxies who carry out its programs.[28]

The reasons are varied. The sheer range of governmental activity makes implementation by any single body impossible, so "farming out" of administrative tasks is inevitable. The federal government has decentralized many programs to state and local governments to put them closer to the people and hence make them more responsive. The growing technical complexity of many programs makes it attractive for government to hire contractors to help solve difficult problems.

The interrelationships between government and its proxies are inherently problem filled. It is hard enough for a manager at the top of an agency to control the actions of subordinates at the bottom. It is far harder for the manager to control a program when the details of its implementation rest in the hands of persons not even part of the agency. The more interrelated the public and private sectors have become, with more ambiguous boundaries between "public" and "private" activities, the harder it has become to implement programs efficiently and responsively.

The fundamental problem is that different organizations have different purposes, and the people who work for them naturally pursue different goals. Whenever the government relies on a proxy to produce a service, it faces the task of trying to impose its goals on the often very different objectives of the proxy. The least that can result from such a process is conflict, the most a deflection of the government's goals toward those of its proxy. Two varieties of this strategy raise special problems for implementation: intergovernmental relations, and contracts with the private sector.

Intergovernmental Relations

The national government farms out implementation of many of its programs to state and local governments. The strategy enjoyed a remarkable growth in the 1960s, in particular, as the federal government sought to advance such values as decentralization, local self-government, and neighborhood power. While federal grants once flowed mostly to the states, the expansion of direct federal-local grants in the 1960s made local governments full and direct administrative partners in federal programs. But there's the rub. If intergovernmental programs advance state and local values, what becomes of the federal government's policy goals? In such arm's-length administration, the national government's reach may exceed its grasp. The alternative, arm twisting, is equally unsatisfactory. Autonomous state and local governments may find their own priorities wrenched out of shape as they yield discretion to the federal government. For local governments, sitting at the bottom of the intergovernmental system, the problem is often worse, since they receive intergovernmental aid from both the state and federal governments, and they must try to fit both state and federal goals.

Intergovernmental implementation strategies are of three sorts: grant programs, in which a higher-level government pays lower-level governments to do what it wants done; regulatory programs, sometimes tied to grants and sometimes not, which subtly force changes in governments' behavior; and off-budget programs, such as tax expenditures and loan programs, that provide additional support for governmental goals.

Administration through Grant Programs

As we saw in chapter 2, grants constitute a significant share of government spending. Deficit politics since the late 1970s reduced what had been a very rapid growth in spending for grants, especially at the federal level. Nevertheless, intergovernmental grant programs remain an important part of government action at all levels, both to advance the funding of government's own goals and to lure recipients into a broad range of regulatory programs. In particular, the federal government has used grants to enlist state governments in managing health care for the poor through the Medicaid program, while state grants finance many local education programs.

Federal grants play an important role in the American system. Though "state and local governments have a vital constitutional role in providing government services," as the Office of Management and Budget recognizes, these governments have often lacked the resources—both money and personnel—to do the job. Therefore, as OMB put it, "the Federal Government contributes directly toward that role ... by providing grants, loans, and tax subsidies to States and localities."[29] The federal government uses state and local governments as its administrative agents. As Martha Derthick has written, "the essence of the grant system is that it entails achievement of federal objectives by proxy."[30] The same can be said of state grants to local governments, which use local governments as administrative agents for state programs.

At the high-water mark of federal aid to state and local governments in 1978, there were about 500 grant programs.[31] The Reagan administration began a major effort in the early 1980s to reduce grant spending and to consolidate programs. By 1986, the number of grant programs had dropped to 340, but 85 percent of federal spending was concentrated in only 25 programs.[32] Similar figures for state grants to local governments are notoriously difficult to produce, but most state grants go for aid to local schools.

Grant programs vary in three important ways: by their general function; by their breadth; and by the way in which they are distributed.

Function. About half of all federal grants are, in reality, part of the complex system of government payments to individuals. In administering federal grants, state and local governments have always to some degree been deputies for federal policies, but these payment programs put them more squarely in the role of federal field agents. State governments run federal programs such as Medicaid and child nutrition. Such federal grants for payments to individuals have grown quickly as a share of all federal grants since the mid-1970s, in part because Congress has increased spending for the programs and in part because other programs have suffered cuts. By fiscal year 1993, grants for payments to individuals (dominated by Medicaid) grew to 64 percent of all grants, up from just 35 percent in 1971.

Other federal grants go for capital projects, such as construction of highways and sewage-treatment plants, and account for about 16 percent of all federal grants. Finally, a collection of programs like social services, education, and job training account for the remaining 20 percent of federal grants.[33] The result is a federal grant system that has subtly been undergoing an important change. Federal grants are going proportionately less to help state and local governments fund projects of their own choice and more to administer programs of the federal government's design, especially income transfer programs.

Breadth. Categorized by their functional breadth, federal grants are predominantly of two kinds.[34] *Categorical* grants are for specific, narrowly defined purposes. For example, federal highway grants provide funds to states for road construction. The Environmental Protection Agency awards grants for construction of sewage-treatment plants. *Block* grants, in contrast, are for broad purposes and usually are the result of consolidation of related categorical grants. In fiscal year 1993, categorical grants accounted for 88 percent of all federal grant money, while block grants totaled 10 percent. (General-purpose federal aid, such as grants to the District of Columbia, accounted for the other 2 percent.)[35]

Block grants have long been a favorite of reformers. They reduce red tape by grouping together related programs. They increase the discretion of state and local governments in deciding how to spend the money. Block grants grew rapidly during the early 1970s as part of the Nixon administration's reform efforts. A decade later, the Reagan administration used block grants as part of a strategy to reduce federal aid, especially to local governments. It lured state and local governments into accepting less money by promising they would enjoy more flexibility in spending the money. The administration's commitment to reduced federal interference in state and local affairs, however, soon disappeared into the larger issue of deep cuts in some grant programs. That, in turn, tainted the block-grant strategy. As one intergovernmental analyst pointed out, "What once was regarded by many as a politically neutral technique for simplifying aid management is now likely to be viewed as an instrument of conservative ideology."[36] That turned out to be especially true in the wide-ranging debate over welfare reform and consolidating social service grants into block grants during 1995.

Distributing Funds. Federal funds may be distributed either by *formula* or by *project*. In formula-based programs, statistical procedures determine both who is eligible for money and how much they can receive. The rise of block grants and grants for payments to individuals (mostly Medicaid) has led to a rapid increase in formula-based aid. In fiscal year 1984, the federal government distributed 87 percent of its aid by formula, compared with about two-thirds in fiscal year 1975. Most of these programs were comparatively new: Only 34 of the 142 formula-based programs in fiscal 1984 existed before 1965.[37]

Distribution of funds by project is strikingly different. Each state or local government meeting eligibility requirements may apply for a grant. The applicant describes in detail its proposed project, its capabilities for executing it, and the anticipated benefits to the public. The federal agency then selects the projects that it will fund (within its budgetary limits). Project-based programs thus are competitions that will produce unhappy losers. Project-based programs also have other problems: they impose heavy paperwork burdens on applicants, and they give broad discretion to federal administrators over who actually receives money. They also have less obvious advantages: project-based programs permit concentration of limited federal money where it is thought it will do the most good.

The rise of formula-based programs and the relative decline of project grants reflect earlier criticism about the federal aid system. Critics had complained about the problems of "grantsmanship," in which entrepreneurial local and state administrators exploited the project system for maximum funding.[38] The rapid growth of formula-based grants, however, has changed the site for the fundamental battles over grant distribution: from the administrative to the legislative process, where distribution formulas are enacted in law. The decline in grantsmanship has been replaced by new uncertainties in the formulas. The formulas are often incredibly complex. According to OMB, they involve nearly 500 different statistical factors, from population to income to numbers of special "in-need" groups, many of which are "of questionable accuracy." The formulas have a "bewildering array of mathematical calculations—addition, multiplication, squaring applied without rationale—which all too frequently produce unsatisfactory results that produce an image of poor public administration." Formula-based programs have proliferated, but the data are often stale or inaccurate. Agencies often cannot predict over time what results the formulas will produce, so long-term planning and budgeting at all levels are hamstrung.[39]

Administration through Regulation

The intergovernmental grant system is more than a device for transferring money. Each grant program brings with it a package of regulations and mandates that further spreads federal influence over state and local government activities. The Tenth Amendment of the U.S. Constitution, reserving powers to the states that are not otherwise given to the federal government, prohibits the federal government from directly ordering states to engage in many activities. In the irresistible lure of grants, the federal government has found a way around this impediment: by making the money available, but subject to certain conditions, the federal government can get state and local governments to do what they otherwise might not be inclined to do.[40]

Every program has its own special rules. Potential Medicaid recipients must meet certain income guidelines, and federal highway funds can be spent only on certain kinds of projects. In addition, the federal government has promulgated a remarkable range of crosscutting rules—fifty-nine by one count—that apply across the board to all grant programs.[41] Recipients must, naturally, properly account for how they spend their money, but they must also survey the environmental effects of any program they plan, they must not discriminate in how the money is spent, and they must make projects accessible to the handicapped.

Furthermore, state and local recipients must comply with crossover sanctions: failure to meet one program's standard can produce a punishment in another program. For example, during the energy crisis of the 1970s, Congress forbade the secretary of transportation from approving any highway construction project in a state having a speed limit of more than 55 miles per hour. Since many states, especially in the West, had speed limits of 65 miles per hour on highways, they had the choice of lowering the limits or losing the money.[42] The choice was obvious. From automobile pollution inspection to a minimum twenty-one-year drinking age, such crossover sanctions are a favorite instrument for inducing uniform national standards.[43]

The federal government also sometimes employs a mixed regulatory strategy, called "partial preemption."[44] The federal agency will set standards that state and local governments must follow; for example, legislation mandates minimal water-quality standards. If the subnational government does not meet those standards, the federal government will step in and administer the program itself. Thus, in some states, a program will be run by a state or local official; in others, federal field officials will administer it. For example, the Occupational Safety and Health Administration (OSHA) itself conducts inspections and enforces regulations in thirty states, while only approving and monitoring programs run by twenty state governments. The financial structure of the program can be equally complicated.

These regulations, christened "mandates," became a hot political battle in 1995. Ending mandates without federal funding became a centerpiece of House Speaker Newt Gingrich's Contract with America. Local officials named unfunded mandates as their top problem, over crime, school violence, gangs, and drugs.[45] No one really knows how much such mandates cost. Some analysts have suggested that they amount to somewhere between 2 and 20 percent of state and local budgets.[46] But if the total spending is unclear, the impact on individual governments has been painful. Mayor Hal Conklin of Santa Barbara, California, complained that the city had to shut down all its parks and spend $400,000 to buy new playground equipment to meet the standards of the Americans with Disabilities Act.

The money, he said, was taken out of child-care facilities and after-school programs for disadvantaged youth. "We had to close down a lot of other worthwhile programs in order to meet those particular federal standards which were just passed on without any funding at all," he said.[47] In Rutland, Vermont, the federal Safe Drinking Water Act required local officials to build a $6 million water treatment plant that, in turn, would increase water bills by 240 percent over three years. "We are facing being mandated to spend millions of dollars to achieve efficiencies which no one has shown will be of any benefit to the public health," Mayor Jeff Wennberg complained.[48]

Attacking the mandates was easy. Devising a solution was far tougher. Most reforms would not roll back existing mandates but would only make it harder to impose new ones. Estimating the costs of mandates before they are imposed, however, is an extremely difficult technical problem. Moreover, many interest groups find it far easier to organize in Washington to press for a uniform policy across the country than to fight fifty separate battles in the state capitals. Many businesses worry about trying to accommodate fifty separate sets of laws and standards and find uniform standards much more desirable.

Administration through Off-Budget Programs

In addition to grants (and their related regulations), the federal government uses a complex collection of off-budget strategies to advance its goals. The federal government, for example, allows individuals to deduct local property tax payments from their federal taxable income. The result is a boon to taxpayers, and to local governments. The deductions mean that the federal government shares some of the cost of the local tax and that any tax rate is less painful to taxpayers than it otherwise would be. Exclusions from the federal income tax provide another important form of aid. Those who receive interest from state and local government bonds, for example, do not pay federal income tax on the proceeds. The governments, therefore, do not have to pay as high an interest rate as they otherwise would, and the result is a substantial savings in interest costs.

The federal government also provides credit to state and local governments. It makes direct loans for such projects as rural development and college housing. It also guarantees other loans made to state and local governments. The federal government guarantees private lending for low-rent public housing and Indian services, among others.[49] Implementation through such programs relies on the federal government's creation of incentives, for both governments and citizens. By supporting loans for college dormitories or giving special tax breaks for sports arenas, the federal government has created incentives for action and thus has powerfully influenced the implementation process.

Implementation Problems

Even though we have used intergovernmental strategies during nearly all of American history, implementation problems persist. We examine four of them in this chapter: inequity, fragmentation, functionalism, and lax federal control.[50]

Inequity. Where you live determines what you get so long as state and local governments have the option to participate or not in a grant program, to set standards of eligibility for the program, and to fix the level of benefits the program provides. Many state and local governments refused to participate in some federal programs, such as food stamps and Medicaid, which provide food and medical assistance to the poor, during their early years. More recently, state assistance provided in the Aid for Families with Dependent Children (AFDC) program, the basic welfare program, has varied widely. The grant system thus can exacerbate existing differences in wealth among the states.[51]

Fragmentation. Societal problems rarely respect geographical or programmatic boundaries. Polluted water and dirty air flow across state boundaries. Many metropolitan areas contain over a hundred local governments; the Chicago area has over a thousand. National programs depend for program implementation on state and local governments, each of which has only a piece of a jigsaw puzzle. Furthermore, the multiplicity of federal aid programs, each with its own goals and rules, procedures and forms, creates a maze of great complexity. The rise of block grants has reduced some of this confusion, but less money has at the same time reduced grant recipients' ability to deal with the problems. It is scarcely surprising, therefore, that frustration, impasse, and inconsistency often result.

Functionalism. Delegation, the reliance by the federal government on state and local governments for program implementation, depends heavily on trust. There is more trust when the delegatee speaks the same language as the delegator. Federal program administrators naturally prefer to deal with state and local officials who work in similar agencies, share their values, have the same kind of training, and are responsive to federal objectives. For example, federal, state, and local health agencies develop a common interest in assuring the autonomy of health agencies at all levels. Cutting through the layers of government, therefore, are vertical functional monoliths, each resisting collaboration with other agencies to integrate delivery of related services to the public, and each resisting direction by elected chief executives and their governmentwide coordinating and control agencies.

Lax Federal Control. Federal agencies issue numerous regulations and guidelines, and state and local officials complain about their proliferation. Paradoxically, federal control of state and local implementation is weak. In block-grant programs, such control is intentionally weak because broad discretion is a central federal goal. The federal government may require each state and local government to plan for the use of the grant and to report how the grant was allocated and spent. But it cannot question the money's uses unless the usage clearly violates the law or regulations. In fact, illegal, as well as trivial, uses of block-grant funds may go undetected and unpunished because of federal reliance on self-reporting by recipient governments, inadequate auditing and enforcement staffs, and the overriding commitment to shift decision making downward in the federal system.

Lax federal control extends as well to the categorical-aid programs, so much so that some categorical programs in practice become block grants. Federal agencies usually impose a large number of *procedural* requirements, but they usually exercise only weak control over the *substance* of state and local decision making and the actual achievement of the program's objectives. The principal sanction for performance problems is withholding a grant, a draconian measure rarely invoked. Federal officials otherwise have relatively little leverage. "In our federal system," as Michael Reagan has noted, "no national government can dismiss a state government official."[52]

Even if the federal government did have a good reporting system on the use of funds and effective sanctions for poor performance, it still would be difficult to determine what results the grants produced. Dollars are dollars, one interchangeable with another. A state's or city's money that would have been spent in one program might be replaced with a federal grant, and the freed funds used instead to reduce taxes or increase services in other areas. In effect, the federal grant for one purpose has expanded services in another, a problem known as *fungibility*. Thus the uses and effects of the federal funds often cannot be fully evaluated.

A Cornerstone of Implementation

In a system of delegated administration, much depends on the effectiveness with which the delegator and the delegatee both perform their roles. The deficiencies of the federal government in managing the system are numerous.[53] State and local governments have their own problems. Intergovernmental programs nevertheless have obvious attractions. State and local governments are natural, if sometimes reluctant, administrative partners in federal programs, and by relying on them the federal government promotes the principles of responsive self-government that Americans hold dear.[54] Thus, despite its defects and the strains placed on the intergovernmental system because of budget cuts, this system of delegated administration is here to stay.

Contracting

Contracting in American government is older than the government. In struggling to field his army, George Washington constantly had to deal with provision suppliers seeking a quick profit at the expense of his men.[55]

The federal government obtains a substantial amount of goods and services for its operations through contracts with private companies, research institutions, and individual consultants. Such procurement accounts for 14 percent of federal outlays and 20 million contracts per year. The Department of Defense administers about two-thirds of all money spent by contract, with the Department of Energy and NASA following as the federal government's largest contractees.[56] Federal contracts cover a remarkable range of activities, from purchase of supplies and equipment to services and research and development.

Contracting unquestionably has also grown into a major feature of state and local administration. From road construction to the administration of prisons, from libraries to fire protection, nearly every state and local function has been a target for increased contracting. In La Miranda, California, for example, the city government has only sixty employees. Sixty contractors provide everything from fire and police protection to human services and public works.[57] Minneapolis hired a private organization to manage its schools and linked its pay to performance on educational goals.

The federal government has established a general policy "to rely on competitive private enterprise to supply the commercial and industrial products and services it needs." The government, however, is also committed to perform itself those functions that "are inherently governmental in nature, being ... intimately related to the public interest."[58] This policy leaves enormous room for dispute over what the government should do for itself and what it should get done outside.

Advantages

Reduce Costs. To many of its proponents, the biggest advantage of contracting is saving money. During the Reagan administration, a presidential commission concluded that "privatization" of many goods and services would improve them: to have government *provide* services without *producing them*," that is, by contracting out.[59] In fact, the commission's chairman, J. Peter Grace, concluded that "one of the major inefficiencies in government is that it tries to do everything." By contracting out more services, Grace contended, the government could save $7.4 billion over three years.[60] The degree of cost savings, however, is subject to fierce debate. The Congressional Budget Office much more conservatively estimated in 1987 that greater effort toward contracting out could reduce federal spending by $200 million over five years, a tiny fraction of the Grace Commission's figure.[61] Although figures vary wildly, most analysts agree that contracting out can save money.

Obtain Special Expertise. Contracts enable the government to obtain the services of specialists not on their own staffs. An agency might not have people with the needed skills, or those it has might be fully occupied with their regular duties. For some assignments, the most competent specialists might be outside government either because the pay is better or because they favor the work environment in universities, research institutes, and private companies.

Avoid Red Tape. Contracting out also tends to avoid the bureaucratic syndrome that handicaps large government agencies. The very bureaucratic rules designed to promote fairness, competence, and accountability can prevent quick and effective action on problems. An independent organization can assemble an integrated team to study multidimensional problems; within government, such efforts often encounter all the difficulties of interbureau and interdepartmental cooperation. Many projects, furthermore, are short term, and a contract (with a built-in termination date) avoids the problem of building permanent bureaucratic units for temporary problems.

Contracting is often attractive because contractors' staff members are not counted as government employees and are not subject to regulations governing the civil service. When budget constraints put ceilings on agency size, and when elected officials are sensitive to the problem of "the government bureaucracy," policymakers can minimize bureaucratic growth by contracting out. Government's reach thus can grow larger without its employment increasing. And because contractors are not subject to many government regulations, especially in the hiring, firing, and pay rates of staff, many government managers welcome the opportunity to contract out.

Problems

Despite its advantages, contracting out has problems, some of them the mirror images of the supposed advantages. Most of the problems come down to two questions: How can contractors be selected and their performance be controlled so that the government's objectives are achieved? How can contractors preserve their independence in the face of controls that the government attempts to impose? In short, contracting confronts the same issue of control versus autonomy that we found in our consideration of federal grants.

Choosing Contractors. The organizations with whom the government contracts for goods and services are a varied lot. Some are operated for profit, while others (such as universities) are nonprofit organizations. For some contractors, the government's work is only a fraction of their total activity; others are wholly dependent on government contracts; many that have other income, including universities as well as private firms, find government contract income indispensable to survival. The theory of contracting is that, by opening government programs up to bid, the competition among contractors for the job will drive prices down and keep quality up. Nevertheless, many federal contracts, especially smaller ones, are not awarded through competition. One-third of federal contract dollars are awarded noncompetitively.[62] Large contracts are sometimes so complicated that few concerns can assemble the expertise needed to bid. One of the richest contracts in federal government history, a $4.5 billion competition for a new government telephone system, drew sustained interest from only two groups of bidders—and the contract was so complicated that even AT&T did not tackle the project on its own.[63] Even where there is competition, the government often cannot take full advantage of it. For example, only two American companies are equipped to build submarines. The Pentagon believes that it is in the national interest to keep both companies in the business, so it often splits or alternates contract awards to ensure that strategic firms are kept afloat.

Though the evidence is mixed, the contracting system appears to reward entrepreneurship more than demonstrated competence.[64] Large firms receive new contracts and extensions of old ones despite expensive past failures, lack of staff qualified for the particular projects, and conflicts of interest. Sometimes the agency shows partiality to a firm that is sympathetic to the program, that is unlikely to criticize its implementation, that enjoys past connections with key agency personnel, or that is in a position to facilitate their future careers.

Overspecification. Government contracting, especially for weapons, tends to prescribe "ultra" features to outperform any potential threat or surpass any potential problem. Government naturally wants the best, especially for its fighting men, but the procurement bureaucracy often has a knack for "goldplating" specifications.[65] In *The Pentagon and the Art of War*, Edward N. Luttwak argued that this problem is the result of over-management caused by an oversupply of senior military officers. It produces, he said, "the ultimate case of too many cooks in one kitchen—or rather, of kitchens greatly enlarged to accommodate more cooks around fewer pots."[66] Not surprisingly, as problems change over the life of the contract, so too do contracts' goals—and the problem of measuring results against objectives becomes ever more complex.

Underperformance. The American Federation of State, County, and Municipal Employees (AFSCME), worried that the growth of contracting would cost government employee union members their jobs, compiled an extensive catalog of contract abuses. AFSCME found, for example, that 30 percent of school lunch "meal packs" served by contractors were deficient in basic vitamins. "It would appear that a child eating these meal packs —especially with the usual amount of plate waste—would not be receiving iron and Vitamin A in adequate amounts. Here, it is essentially critical to remember that iron deficiency anemia is the most common of our [nutritional] deficiency diseases." Of thirty-four meals served by one contractor, fourteen were hamburgers, "variously adorned," and eight were hot dogs. Children were served vegetables only six times in a two-month period.[67]

The General Accounting Office surveyed contracts issued by the General Services Administration over three years and found that the government had awarded more than $1 billion in contracts to vendors who repeatedly had failed to meet contract specifications and delivery schedules. Despite the problems, "GSA has continued to do business with repeat poor-performing vendors." GAO found two reasons. First, GSA's managers often had little good information on vendors' past performance. Managers could not avoid poor vendors if they did not know who they were. Second, GSA has not always emphasized product quality in making decisions. "Poor performance on GSA supply contracts has been a long-standing problem," GAO concluded.[68]

Overregulation. Contractors face a bewildering array of regulations with which they must comply. It is not unusual for the attachments to a small contract simply listing all these rules to be longer than the specifications of the contract itself. In military weapons, furthermore, contractors must follow a complex collection of MIL-SPECS (short for military specifications) that prescribe in elaborate detail just how the equipment must perform. The specifications for one military aircraft range over 24,000 documents. One of them, for electronic parts, refers to 235 other documents, which in turn refer to 1,374 more, of which half are more than ten years old. To follow the rules precisely meant installing obsolete components into front-line equipment.[69]

Sanctions. Government officials supervising private contractors have the same problem in imposing sanctions as do their colleagues overseeing federal grants. Cutting off the contract is often more trouble than it is worth and, in the meantime, deprives government of the good or service it needs. When the space shuttle *Challenger* exploded because of a defect in its solid rocket booster, NASA had no other supplier to which it could turn for at least several years. Punishing the contractor, Morton Thiokol, by canceling the booster contract would have grounded the shuttle until a new contractor geared up its operations. Even in more routine services, like garbage collection, governments often have relatively few contractors among whom to choose.

Corruption. The award of rich contracts has always tempted the unscrupulous to make a quick profit at the government's expense. As the AFSCME study put it, "Government contracting and corruption are old friends."[70] In New York state, for example, ten road construction companies were indicted for bid rigging: arranging among themselves who would bid how much on which contracts, which boosted their profits on more than $100 million in contracts over eight years.[71] Corruption in state and local contracts has a rich history. Contractors have long paid government officials kickbacks and bribes to win contracts, and contractors have colluded among themselves to fix bids and share the government's rich contract bounty. More recently, the fuzzier lines between the public and private sectors have increased conflict-of-interest problems, in which government employees steer business to firms that have been in the past—or may be in the future—business connections of theirs. There has been an enormous growth in what some experts call this "new patronage." One Washington interest-group official noted, "The opportunities for misbehavior have increased tremendously as governments have gone to contracting out" as a way to save money.[72] "You make more money rigging bids than robbing banks—more than you could dealing drugs," one federal attorney explained.[73]

Nor are contracting scandals limited to state and local governments. In the Reagan administration, Wedtech, a small Bronx, New York, based tool-and-die manufacturer, used every device at its disposal to acquire more than $250 million in government contracts. The company admitted that it had forged more than $6 million in invoices submitted to the federal government for payment. In addition, federal prosecutors charged, the company's officials used their friendship with top administration officials, including presidential counselor and later Attorney General Edwin Meese, to win contracts. The company eventually went out of business, but not until sixteen people connected with the scandal were indicted, from former White House aide Lyn Nofziger to a member of Congress, Representative Mario Biaggi (D-N.Y.), to the New York regional administrator for the Small Business Administration.[74]

It would be tempting to leap to the cynical conclusion that such corruption is epidemic in government contracting. Of course, it is not. Most contractors are honest and hard working, and most government officials struggle to get the most for the public's tax dollar. The recurring lessons of corruption in contracting, however, emphasize two broader lessons about implementation through contracting. First, contracting is not an automatic, easy solution to the problems of implementing programs directly through government agencies. Instead, it replaces one set of administrative problems with another. Second, to be managed well, contracting requires a sophisticated collection of different administrative tools, which need to be tailored to the special implementation problems of contracting.[75] And it needs incorruptible and highly competent government officials to manage the contracts.

The Government's Dilemma

Implementation is, as we have seen, the study of how laws are executed. That covers all forms of administration, but students of implementation have concentrated particularly on administrative strategies that rely on proxies, that is, on those strategies, such as grants and contracts, in which the end responsibility for the program's results falls outside the bureaucracy that manages the program. Implementation thus is an untidy domain partly because of the variety of organizations that the government enlists through grants and contracts, partly because of the poor fit between the government's cultures and the complex motivations and internal organizational life of the proxies with which it deals, and partly because of the unresolved conflict of demands for accountability and demands for independence.

The government sacrifices much when it opts for implementation through outsiders. It fails to build its own capabilities for doing the work.

Despite the rhetoric of high quality at low price that accompanies proxy federalism and contracting, proxy strategies are sometimes more costly, less effective, and less responsive than work done directly by the government. More critically, by implementing programs through outside agencies instead of through its own bureaucracy, the government has only loose control over grantees and contractors. Often the contracting government agency lacks staff members competent to judge the quality of the contractor's performance.

The fundamental issue is the growing intermingling of federal-state-local and public-private roles in society. As Bruce L.R. Smith put it, "American politics, if once thought to be frozen in too narrow a range of policy debate, now seems to have an agenda of vast scope. The framework of debate has been not simplified, but vastly complicated, by the value cleavages that cut in strange ways through the political landscape."[76] The boundaries have become ever more blurred, especially since World War II. Fewer activities can now be labeled purely "public" or "private." The government has increasingly relied on private agencies to pursue public purposes, while private institutions have increasingly relied on government support for their very life.

The problems of implementation that emerge thus are not the result of failures in government policy and administration but of the growing ambitions of government programs; the increasing interdependence of government and the private sector; and the greater complexity of society itself. When policymaking and implementation stretch across organizational boundaries—public and private, federal, state, and local—it becomes ever harder to reach agreement on what goals ought to be pursued and to collect information about what results are produced.

What Goals?

"Success" sometimes can be changed into "failure" and "failure" into "success." AMTRAK's Metroliner, a high-speed train service introduced into the Northeast corridor in the 1960s, was at first a success. By the late 1970s, though, the trains were running late because of rough roadbeds (the heritage of privately owned railroads). Reconstruction of the roadbeds in the 1980s helped restore the trains' performance, but not without stirring complaints from conservatives who argued that the government had no place in the train business to begin with. Goals can change over time. So can performance and the standards by which we judge performance. Indeed, two observers can look at the same phenomenon and reach very different conclusions. A new highway could be the answer to a business owner's dreams of better access to consumers, while environmentalists could decry the danger the highway poses to a local watershed.

Sometimes programs appear as failures because of "ridiculously high hopes about what might be accomplished with limited funds in a short time," according to former Congressional Budget Office director (and Clinton's budget director) Alice M. Rivlin.[77] As Rivlin explained elsewhere, "current social problems are difficult because they involve conflicts among objectives that almost everyone holds."[78] Different persons in different organizations are likely to hold different views about the same objectives. That raises some serious problems about reaching agreement on how a program should be implemented. Added to this is the government's ultimate difficulty in ensuring that publicly defined objectives remain paramount. One keystone of the problem of implementation thus is the problem of reconciling goals.

What Information?

It likewise is both important and difficult to collect information about what results a program produces. The presidential commission that investigated the 1986 *Challenger* space shuttle disaster, for example, concluded that it was "an accident rooted in history." Even though managers from NASA and Morton Thiokol (the contractor that built the rocket) knew about the problems with the O-rings, gaskets whose failure caused the shuttle's explosion, senior NASA officials did not understand the problem's seriousness. If they had, the commission concluded, "it seems likely that the launch of 51-L [the *Challenger*'s fatal flight] might not have occurred when it did." The problem was due in part to "a propensity of management at Marshall [the space center charged with managing the solid-fuel rockets] to contain potentially serious problems and to attempt to resolve them internally rather than communicate them forward."[79] The relationship between the contractor and its government supervisors prevented key information from reaching top managers.

The information problem is a critical one. Information distortion is a common enough problem in bureaucracies. When information must cross bureaucratic boundaries, the problem intensifies. Organizations often hide information from one another, and the temptation to bury reports of poor performance increases when the cost might be loss of a grant or contract. It is hard to manage implementation effectively when managers do not know precisely what results a program produces.

A Program That Works

It would be easy to surrender to feelings of outrage and futility. Yet some programs work—and work well. Many routine programs are models of remarkable success. Despite all our complaints, the mail does get delivered every day, mostly on time. In Pittsfield, Massachusetts, one postal contractor was legendary for never missing his deliveries, despite blizzards and frigid weather.[80] Federal social security recipients receive their payments on time most of the time, and clients rate the quality of service as high.[81] And despite glaring problems in 1986, NASA's record of achievement in space is remarkable.

Less routine programs also often work well. Notable is a housing rehabilitation program funded by the Department of Housing and Urban Development and administered through a grant to the city of Baltimore—notable especially for its results when compared with other HUD programs enmeshed in Reagan administration era scandals.[82] Local housing officials told HUD that they would renovate 140 public housing units at their Mt. Winans project for 10 percent less than a private contractor would have charged. The program was an exceptionally ambitious one. Baltimore officials planned to hire participants in a low-income job training program to fix up their own apartment complex. For months the project had been vacant, and many rooms had been vandalized. Walls, floors, kitchens, and bathrooms had to be completely redone.

The combination of unskilled workers, run-down public housing, and a job training program seemed the stuff of which implementation failure stories are written. Yet everyone ended up a winner. HUD saved about $250,000 in the project and received quality work—sometimes even better than what a private contractor would have produced. City officials believed that, since many of the trainees were residents in the project, the project was less likely to become run-down in the future, as was the unfortunate case in many public housing neighborhoods. The city's maintenance cost therefore was likely to be less.

The trainees won pride in themselves. As the manager of the Mt. Winans project said, the trainees "feel they've contributed to the community. They're very proud of what they've done." Children can point to the work and say, "Look what mama did." In addition, forty of the city's poor, three-fourths of whom were on welfare, received training in construction skills. Just as important, they developed good work habits. "I loved it from the beginning," said one participant who had been on welfare the previous five years. "As soon as they put a ruler in my hand and let me get my knees dirty, I fell in love with it." When the program ended, city officials were hopeful of placing most of the participants in regular jobs and getting them off welfare.

What accounted for the program's unquestioned success? City officials kept the program's reach within their grasp. The program was small—limited to training only forty to fifty people—and flexible. The community already was close. "It's just like a family," explained the head of a local community organization. Furthermore, city officials won the support of neighborhood leaders. "The key point is the leaders in the community have to be involved, have to want it to work," explained one leader. Community leaders helped recruit the workers and became their biggest cheerleaders when the program started. Program managers made it clear that all the trainees would be given was an opportunity; any rewards would have to be earned by the workers—but when they were, they would belong to the workers.

The program began with a training class on basic skills. Any trainee late for class three times was to be dropped from the program—and nobody was expelled. The trainees were excited at what they learned. "We were so hyped," said one participant. "You feel like someone needs you, wants you." The graduation ceremony ended with everyone in tears. Work on the project was often hot and difficult, and the first buildings went way over budget and schedule. Still, by the time the project was finished, HUD had gotten the public housing units rehabilitated more cheaply than would have been the case with private contractors. The city got a larger supply of quality housing. And the workers got valuable new skills.

There was a darker side to the project. Attrition was high, and one year after the project's start, half the original participants had dropped out, some for attendance or attitude problems, some without giving an excuse, and some to take better-paying private-sector jobs. Wages in the program were low, and some participants lost their welfare and Medicaid benefits. Still, the program was a success, especially when compared with similar training programs that had produced tales of woe. As one participant said, "I didn't think I would graduate. I didn't think I would go that far. I thought it would really be hard.... I'm so happy. I'm so happy." The program succeeded because all participants were able to find common ground in the goals they pursued, and because the information managers needed to correct problems was at hand. The Mt. Winans program thus overcame the twin obstacles that so often doom implementation.

The Importance of Feedback

Effectively steering program implementation depends critically on a manager's obtaining good administrative feedback. The problem, as Herbert Kaufman puts it, is this: "When managers die and go to heaven, they may find themselves in charge of organizations in which subordinates invariably, cheerfully, and fully do as they are bid. Not here on earth."[83] Indeed, noncompliance by subordinates and by an agency's proxies often seems the rule, not the exception. A mismatch between directives and results is frequent. The whole implementation literature is based on this notion, as Pressman and Wildavsky's plaintive subtitle, "How Great Expectations in Washington Are Dashed in Oakland," illustrates.[84]

Furthermore, even though we expect goals and outcomes not to correspond exactly, managers often have a very difficult time discovering the bad news. As we saw in chapter 9, numerous bureaucratic pathologies block and distort the flow of information, especially about problems, from the bottom of an organization (or from outside proxies) to the top. In late 1988, for example, top officials from the Department of Energy and from its predecessor, the Atomic Energy Commission (AEC), denied ever having been told that there were serious safety problems at the department's Savannah River nuclear power plant. The highest officials apparently were unaware that there was a partial meltdown in the plant in 1970, among thirty other accidents.[85]

Administrative Feedback

Such information blockages pose critical problems for implementers. It is unreasonable to expect any manager to get things right the first time, since difficulties inevitably crop up. Indeed, the crucial problem in implementation is not avoiding problems but detecting and solving them. Solving problems is obviously impossible if managers cannot discover them. Therefore, good implementers must develop strategies for obtaining feedback.

Some feedback comes through routine administrative monitoring. Kaufman, for example, identifies five major sources of information about implementation: (1) the trail of paper that programs generate, which can provide valuable clues about performance; (2) personal inspection, which gets supervisors out from behind their desks to see what is happening in the field; (3) personal contacts outside the agency, which can help the administrator bypass internal information problems; (4) investigations, which allow administrators to probe individual problems; and (5) centralization of some services, especially data collection, which can provide early warning about problems.

Unexpected sources of information can also provide valuable feedback. Patterns of complaints by clients can indicate malfunctions at lower bureaucratic levels. Reports by the news media, such as the *New York Times*'s 1988 investigation of the Department of Energy's nuclear power plant problems, can help surface important data. Disaffected employees, sometimes called "whistleblowers," can sometimes produce explosive surprises.[86] For example, the federal False Claims Act, passed in 1863 to penalize contractors who were cheating the army, entitles the government to three times the amount of any overcharges or fraudulent claims. The person who brings the charge to light also is entitled to an award of 15 to 25 percent of the government's award. The prospect of a multimillion-dollar bounty has prompted some employees and former employees of defense contractors to come forward with evidence against their bosses.[87]

Formal Program Evaluation

But this feedback, no matter how useful, at best leaves large gaps. Managers therefore often develop formal systems of evaluation to provide regular, high-quality feedback. "With objective information on the outcomes of programs, wise decisions can be made on budget allocations and program planning. Programs that yield good results will be expanded; those that make poor showings will be abandoned or drastically modified," as Carol H. Weiss argues.[88] Faced with the inevitable paradox of too much or too little information, officials seek regular and reliable feedback through formal evaluation strategies.

Formal evaluation has obvious advantages. Managers can design an evaluation to test precisely what they want and to obtain just the information they need. Moreover, compared with the rest of policy research, the methodology for conducting evaluation research is well accepted and effective.[89] Balancing the potential for such careful experimentation is the risk that, when finished, it will simply collect dust. Careful program evaluation requires controlled experiments and lengthy tests. The political world sometimes cannot tolerate the controls, such as having some groups receive the program while others do not. Most public programs are perceived as benefits, and it is hard to deprive some of the potential advantages for experimental purposes. Furthermore, the long time required to conduct careful research means that results sometimes emerge years after initial interest in new programs—and perhaps years after policy decisions were made. Managers sometimes respond by conducting quick-and-dirty studies that provide useful, if not always fully scientifically valid, feedback. They can also design evaluation strategies that feed more directly into management decisions.[90] But even if evaluations do not directly affect program decisions, they often do affect the intellectual debate over programs by shaping the ideas that structure future decisions. The key, Giandomenico Majone argues, is "to develop methods of assessment that emphasize learning and adaptation rather than expressing summary judgments of pass or fail."[91]

Backward Mapping

Understanding what works how—and what does not—can provide policy-makers with clues about how better to design programs from the beginning.[92] Typically, of course, managers decide what goals they want to accomplish and then define, in increasing detail, the responsibilities of those at each step in the implementation process. Richard F. Elmore calls this "forward mapping," and he argues that it often causes problems because implementers do not control all the factors that affect the process. To correct these problems, he contends, managers ought to begin at the end, where "administrative actions intersect private choices." From there, the manager seeks to understand what will affect that relationship and what kind of behavior the manager desires. The manager then works backward, keeping in mind the constraints at each stage, to plan how best to make sure that the system is structured best to achieve that behavior.[93]

Backward mapping makes a critical point: no part of the policy process works in isolation; to work best, each phase of the process must be integrated with the others. Evaluation can educate managers about what problems implementers can face. Armed with that information, the managers can redesign the implementation process to reduce those risks. More generally, evaluation results can provide valuable feedback to reformulate the goals that drive the process. Evaluation is sometimes dismissed as providing information that is too little, too late. That view misses its true importance. As Majone points out, evaluation is at its best when it promotes adaptation, not when it seeks simple-minded conclusions about success and failure.

Conclusion

The perspective on implementation is thus a mixed one; both hope and despair reflect the current state of opinion. Three considerations may partially shift the balance toward hope.

First, many problems that we view as implementation problems actually reflect far larger issues. What we call "failure" may be the product of goals with which we do not agree and results that we do not like. If implementation is separated out and defined as "program operations," then many "failures" turn out not to be failures in the actual process of implementation but the consequence of poor policy choices, the impossibility of outcomes matching high hopes at a program's conception, and misjudgments in legislative prescriptions of implementation strategies. Sometimes, indeed, the more efficient the implementation of a bad policy, a poor program, or a legislatively mandated faulty strategy, the more conspicuous will be the failure. Implementation "failures" thus often reflect problems in other parts of the policy process.

Second, our principal focus has been on implementation by American *governments*. Wallowing in government failure stories can make it easy to forget that the private sector's record is scarcely clean. Anyone who has ever worked for a private organization can vouch for substantial waste of materials, inefficient ways of processing paper, and problems of bureaucracy that match the public sector's. Millions of automobiles have been recalled for defects, drugs have been introduced that have later been found to be dangerous, computers break down, and other problems in workmanship, services, and materials abound. This is not to compound our misery by suggesting that nothing works anywhere. Instead, it is important to remember that problems of performance are not a purely public-sector problem. Most of the outrageous fraud, waste, and abuse stories in government programs have involved private organizations trying to take advantage of public programs.

Finally, many implementation problems arise out of the increasing complexity of American society and not because of any failing in government itself. The more the boundaries blur—between the public and private sectors, among federal, state, and local governments—the more dependent programs become on the interrelationships of all of these organizations and the more difficult true "success" is to produce.

None of these considerations means that implementation by American governments is what it should be. On the contrary, the evidence is that not only is implementation often unsatisfactory but that its improvement has been neglected—by Congress, by the president, by operating agencies, and by the research community. The first step needed is correction of that neglect.[94]

Part V

Administration in a Democracy

Establishing bureaucracy in a democracy creates two sets of issues. We not only want to see programs managed efficiently and effectively. We also want the process and the result to be responsive and accountable. This section examines the dynamics of bureaucracy's relationship with the larger political system, especially with the legislature and the courts. It concludes with a careful examination of the critical issues surrounding bureaucracy in a democracy and how public administrators can pursue ethical behavior that balances the competing goals of efficiency and accountability.

12

Legislative Control of Administration

Many observers separate the policy process into two parts: the legislature makes policy, and the executive branch implements it. We know, of course, that the legislative and executive roles are far more complex and intertwined than that. At the federal level, the Constitution establishes elaborate checks and balances, not just a separation of powers. Furthermore, as one student of congressional oversight has pointed out, "oversight is in many respects a continuation of preenactment politics."[1] The constitutions of the American states mirror this check-and-balance arrangement, and the varied forms of local government have created related but often even muddier systems.

The Constitution gives Congress a powerful claim to control of administration. The president may be responsible for faithfully executing the laws, but Congress makes them. The bureaucracy is thus a creature of them both. Congress creates the organizational structure within which bureaucrats work. It authorizes their positions and the programs they administer. It appropriates funds to pay for them and retains the right to investigate how they spend the money and run the programs.[2] Congress delegates power to the bureaucracy to administer the law; the president is vested with the faithful execution of the law. Overseeing the bureaucracy is thus as much a congressional prerogative as an executive one.[3] The same is true at the state and local levels.

The relationship between legislature and executive branch agency is very much a reciprocal one, but as we see, it is complicated by the paradox of oversight.

The Paradox of Oversight

As one panel of experts has pointed out, "oversight permeates the activities of Congress."[4] Much of what Congress does, in fact, can be construed as supervision of administrative actions, from the enactment of laws and budgets to committee hearings to program reviews by congressional staff agencies, such as the General Accounting Office. Variations in the level of oversight can be quite remarkable, from investigation of a program's overall performance to probes of the most detailed of program activities. In 1987, the Senate attached eighty-six amendments to a bill authorizing the State Department's budget. Policy questions ranged from the Chinese government's treatment of Tibetan monks to traffic tie-ups caused by long, honking motorcades for foreign dignitaries in Washington.[5]

In fact, critics have blamed congressional "micromanagement" for problems in many defense systems. In 1985, for example, the Pentagon submitted 24,000 pages of documentation to Congress to respond to 458 different reporting requirements established in previous legislation. These reports, Defense officials estimated, had increased 1,000 percent since 1970.[6] Such a penchant for particulars, moreover, imposes a heavy burden on top administrative officials. Former secretaries of state Henry Kissinger and Cyrus Vance, for example, have complained: "Surely there are better ways for the executive and legislative branches to consult than having the secretaries of state and defense spend more than a quarter of their time on repetitive congressional testimony."[7]

Yet there is substantial evidence that control of administration has traditionally ranked low among the priorities of members of Congress. The reelection imperative is all important, and much routine oversight does little to enhance a member's reputation back in his or her district. Passing legislation, taking stands on issues, and tending to constituents' needs through casework dominate members' attention.[8] There rarely are regular procedures for conducting oversight.[9] Members are typically more interested in shaping the immediate future than in investigating what has gone wrong in the past (unless it was so scandalous that an investigation will win wide publicity and be embarrassing to the opposition party). In particular, the difficult task of devising corrective measures to improve administrative organization, procedures, and staffing is unlikely to engage legislators' interest.

This is not a matter of members' concern with the general rather than the particular. Through their staffs, members of Congress devote enormous energy to casework, responding to requests and complaints from constituents, and no work could be more detailed. Most frequently, the constituents want help in getting social security and disability benefits, Medicare reimbursements, admission to a veterans' hospital, and emergency home leave from military service. Although not a direct form of congressional oversight, casework—especially if it reveals patterns of problems—often provides legislators with information on which direct oversight can be conducted. Closely related are legislators' involvement with the approval and progress of projects in their constituency areas—roads, dams, and economic development and social service projects dependent on federal grants and loans.

This suggests the paradox of oversight. While nearly all congressional activities can be considered a form of oversight, such oversight yields little useful information about persistent problems of administrative mismanagement. Suspicion about major failures in implementation, especially if investigation of the failures promises newspaper headlines and time on the evening news, often sparks members' interest. Especially when these problems offer members of Congress a chance to embarrass a president of the opposite party, the taste for oversight often grows.[10] Nevertheless, when oversight occurs, it is more likely to be unsystematic, sporadic, episodic, erratic, haphazard, ad hoc, and on a crisis basis.[11]

Two observers, in fact, have christened this the "fire alarm" style of oversight, in which members of Congress respond to complaints as they arise, instead of "police patrol" oversight, in which they conduct routine patrols at their own initiative. They argue, in fact, that fire-alarm oversight "serves congressmen's interests at little cost" and that it produces oversight that is much more effective. Through periodic interventions sparked by apparent problems, members of Congress can more clearly define the goals they have in mind. Moreover, they contend that responding to problems as they arise is much more likely to detect problems than maintaining a regular police-patrol style.[12] This argument is the subject of much debate, but it demonstrates at the least that congressional oversight of administration is a much more subtle process than the formal check-and-balance system might suggest.

Purposes of Oversight

Even if it is intermittent and ad hoc, oversight nevertheless serves a number of important purposes for members of Congress.[13]

1. *Assure that the intent of Congress is followed.* Members of Congress naturally wish to ensure that administrators' actions are consistent with what Congress intended in passing legislation. That sometimes is hard to determine, of course, because acts of Congress are notorious for their imprecision. Often, in fact, Congress does not determine what it wants until it

sees what it gets. In these cases, oversight provides an opportunity for communicating more clearly, if often informally, to administrators just what results Congress expects.

2. *Investigate instances of fraud, waste, and abuse.* This unholy trinity is a frequent object of congressional investigations. From stories of overpriced hammers purchased by the Pentagon to suggestions of irregularities by contractors serving Indian reservations, allegations of inefficiencies and illegalities often spark oversight.

3. *Collect information.* Since many programs must be reauthorized, congressional oversight gives members of Congress and their staffs the opportunity to obtain basic data that help them determine how laws ought to be changed and which new laws ought to be enacted.

4. *Evaluate program effectiveness.* Oversight can also provide Congress with information about how well a program is performing. This information can help Congress determine how best to improve an agency's effectiveness.

5. *Protect congressional prerogatives.* Members of Congress also sometimes use oversight to protect what they view to be their constitutional rights and privileges from encroachment by the executive branch. The check-and-balance system often breeds boundary-line disputes, and oversight gives members of Congress an opportunity to defend their points of view.

6. *Personal advocacy.* Oversight frequently gives members of Congress their own "bully pulpits" from which to advance programs of interest to them and to attract publicity. Some members of Congress have built their reputations by championing some causes, while others have used televised hearings to promote their careers.

7. *Reverse unpopular actions.* Finally, oversight provides members with leverage to force agencies to reverse unpopular decisions. Through veiled threats and direct confrontation, Congress can signal administrators about what activities are unacceptable and what can be done to address members' concerns.

Congressional oversight occurs through several channels, which we investigate in this chapter: through the work of congressional committees and their staffs; through program reviews conducted by the General Accounting Office; and through the legislative veto and its variants.

Committee Oversight of Administration

Even more than is the case with its legislative work, Congress depends heavily on its committees for monitoring administrative agencies and their implementation of programs.

Indeed, the connection between congressional committees and administrative agencies is one of the most important in government.[14] Committee members and bureaucrats are important to one another. Committee members write the legislation and fund the programs that bureaucrats must implement. The bureaucrats' decisions affect the members' abilities to claim credit for governmental action. It is an exchange relationship: "The ability of each to attain his goals is at least partially dependent on the actions of the other," R. Douglas Arnold writes.[15]

Members of Congress have powerful sanctions, but their use varies. Some committees engage more frequently in oversight, especially those overseeing agencies that must annually receive appropriations. Some committees are far tougher in approving budgets than others. Furthermore, some committees tend to be populated more by members whose goal is constituency service, and in providing that service bureaucrats can build powerful allies. When a committee has a broad national agenda, such as Education or Labor, instead of a narrow constituency focus, oversight can be harsher.[16] Nevertheless, "committees in both houses tend to give more attention to investigations of broad policy questions than to inquiries into agency implementation of programs."[17]

Varieties of Committee Review

Three sets of standing committees have responsibility for legislative review (the official term for legislative oversight). These are the regular legislative committees (usually known as authorizing committees, because they prepare the laws that authorize programs), the appropriations committees, and committees on government operations.

Authorizing committees can initiate, review, and report out bills and resolutions in particular subject-matter areas (e.g., labor, commerce, education, foreign affairs). Each has the oversight responsibility to review the administration of laws within its jurisdiction. While some legislative committees have conducted extensive oversight, overall the tendency is for legislative committees to concentrate more on the passage of new laws than to review the execution of existing ones. Further decreasing the opportunity for oversight is the growth of programs receiving permanent authorizations (as we saw in chapter 10); when program managers do not need to appear regularly to request continuation of their programs, the chances for oversight decrease. Some committees are also moving toward longer reauthorizations to help reduce their workload, but that has also reduced the opportunities for oversight.[18] Furthermore, some legislative committees (and subcommittees) are so amiably disposed toward "their" agencies and programs that they are not eager to initiate penetrating inquiries into possible administrative mismanagement and program ineffectiveness.

Appropriations committees have the most impressive credentials for control of administration. They have prestige, broad scope, power, and competence. Committee members, and especially their staffs, typically command a knowledge of agencies and programs rivaling that of career administrators and surpassing that of political executives. Yet Congress cannot rely mainly on the appropriations committees for the oversight function. The committee members are heavily burdened, they operate under the time pressure of the annual appropriations process, and their focus is on dollar figures and incremental changes from the previous year. The House Appropriations Committee's oversight, a staff member has said, is wide but not deep, whereas legislative committees' oversight is deep but not wide.[19] Moreover, with the rise of the omnibus acts and reconciliation measures discussed in chapter 10, the influence of the appropriations committees, on both budgeting and congressional oversight, has decreased. The committees have responded by adding more "riders"—detailed requirements about how money appropriated for individual programs can be used—but, in general, the effectiveness of the appropriations committees has remained mixed.

The *Senate Committee on Government Affairs* and the *House Committee on Governmental Reform and Oversight* have the broadest responsibility and strongest powers for overseeing administrative activities. Since the early 1800s, Congress has had such committees to reach beyond the usual grasp of legislative and appropriations committees. They are *the* oversight committees of Congress, and their jurisdiction is not constrained by the usual departmental or committee boundaries.[20]

While their potential is great, their performance has fallen short of potential. Both committees have traditionally ranked relatively low in prestige.[21] One consequence is that the members' primary interests lie elsewhere, particularly in the major committees on which they also serve. The committees rarely have adopted any strategy to guide the oversight work, and other congressional committees have jealously guarded their jurisdictions from review. When investigations promise big headlines, other committees are quick to seize the agenda. Both committees have been highly selective and episodic in choice of the administrative activities to be reviewed, generally reflecting the committees' specific areas of legislative jurisdiction (e.g., executive reorganization and intergovernmental relations), reacting to public scandals, or registering the special concerns of leading committee members. They rarely have been able to pursue sustained investigations, however, because they have had only modest funding.[22]

The Need for Information

The problem of congressional control is certainly not a shortage of committees with oversight responsibilities and opportunities. Indeed, the multiplicity of committees and the overlaps among their jurisdictions provide many different avenues for legislative influence on administrative activities. Nevertheless, while Congress's increasingly decentralized system has expanded the points of access and the number of hearings, "it has at the same time weakened the ability of Congress to conduct serious oversight and administrative control." The growing complexity of administrative activities, the difficulty of developing good information about program performance, and the counterbalancing power of interest groups all combine to lessen Congress's direct leverage over the executive branch.[23] Similar phenomena have occurred at the state and local level as well.

Redundancy, in fact, has magnified, not solved, Congress's oversight problem. Changes in the budget process have duplicated the number of reviews to which agencies are subjected and have blurred the responsibilities of each committee. As one Georgetown University study on defense oversight argued, "redundancy in the congressional review process seriously aggravates the oversight problem." The redundant steps mean the "Congress rarely takes conclusive action on any issue," a Senate Armed Services Committee staff report concluded.[24] One estimate is that assistant secretaries must spend as much as 40 percent of their time preparing for congressional testimony and responding to inquiries by members of Congress.[25] Congress's committee structure and operating rules often hinder, not help, oversight of administration.

Congress's effectiveness in monitoring administrative activities depends on its access to information, most of it generated in the executive branch. On the one hand, there are significant barriers to obtaining information about what is happening in the executive branch. On the other hand, legislators typically are awash in data. Effective oversight requires separating the truly useful information from the huge stacks of paper that flood Washington—as well as state capitals and city halls. It truly is a forest-and-the-trees problem: distilling the key issues from the mass of detailed data.

Barriers to Information

Secrecy. Secrecy, particularly in the conduct of foreign affairs, the planning of military strategy and tactics, and the pursuit of intelligence activities, is the most formidable barrier.[26] Few would argue that these matters can be carried on in full view of the public or, for that matter, of the 535 members of Congress. The problem is that under the guise of national security, it is possible for administrators to classify any documents they choose as "top secret," "secret," and "confidential." Classification, once done, is difficult to undo, however trivial or improper the reasons for its having been done. In World War II, for example, documents often received security classifications because that sped their delivery to government offices. In the Defense Department, newspaper clippings have been stamped "secret," and a memorandum urging less use of the "top secret" classification was itself classified top secret.[27]

Forty years later, the Tower Commission, investigating the Reagan administration's elaborate plan to sell arms to Iran, secure the release of Americans held hostage in the Middle East, and divert arms-sale profits to aid the *contras* in Nicaragua, concluded that "concern for preserving the secrecy of the initiative provided an excuse for abandoning sound process."[28] Congressional investigators, furthermore, found that secrecy concerns enormously complicated their probe. Administrative officials argued the need for flexibility in conducting foreign relations and said they had planned to notify Congress after the hostages were out. Senator William S. Cohen (R-Me.) acknowledged that the president needs flexibility, but "flexibility is too often taken as license, and then after the fact it's rationalized as a constitutional power that cannot be diluted or diminished by congressional action." He concluded, "comity is important, but it has to run in two directions on Pennsylvania Avenue."[29]

The problem of security classification has two dimensions. One is the denial to Congress of information that in fact has no national security claim to secrecy or confidentiality. The other is the denial to Congress of information that, though secret or confidential, is essential to Congress's decision making and oversight with respect to the nation's foreign relations, military posture, and intelligence gathering. The typical "solution" has been the furnishing of classified information to only a selected few committees (especially the House and Senate Intelligence Committees) in executive session, to only the chairperson and ranking minority member of such a committee, or to only its pro-Pentagon members. The disclosure that high Reagan administration officials had secretly been using proceeds from arms sales to Iran to fund the administration's Central American program revealed how inadequate such a solution often is. So, too, does the growing share of the Pentagon budget devoted to "black"—that is, secret—programs hidden from all but select members of Congress, as we saw in chapter 10.

Executive Privilege. A second barrier is executive privilege, a prerogative never mentioned in the Constitution but asserted to be inherent in the president's powers. Presidents have claimed that it is akin to the legal doctrine of "privileged communications," such as those between husband and wife, doctor and patient, attorney and client, and priest and parishioner. In the government, the doctrine has most powerfully been invoked to protect the confidentiality of oral and written communication between the president and his White House aides, especially during the Nixon administration's Watergate affair.

Administrative Confidentiality. A third, but lower, barrier to Congress's access to information is "administrative confidentiality." This term covers two distinct practices. One is the protection of private information: individuals' tax returns, completed census forms, possibly derogatory information in investigative agencies' files, and business concerns' trade secrets and financial data. Such information is normally collected by government agencies under pledges of confidentiality. The administrative agencies often resist committee demands for such records. They argue, with considerable force, that abuse of confidentiality could impair the government's ability to obtain full and accurate information.

The other claim to administrative confidentiality relates to drafts, memoranda, and other "internal records" bearing on policies and decisions that may or may not be under serious consideration by an agency. Premature disclosure of such internal records may lead to distorted publicity and public misunderstanding (many memoranda by subordinate staff members make suggestions that will in fact be rejected at higher levels; newspaper headlines, however, may give the impression that the agency is about to adopt the suggestion). Equally important (and paralleling the argument for executive privilege at the presidential level), the possibility that they will have to defend their memoranda before congressional committees may put a chill on those on whom a department head relies for imaginative ideas and frank advice. Congressional committees and their staffs are nevertheless often eager to share in the shaping of agency policies, partly because once such policies are announced they are difficult to reverse.[30]

Other Considerations. Secrecy, executive privilege, and administrative confidentiality are all embroiled in disputes that essentially pit the separation of powers against the check-and-balance system. There remain moral, prudential, and practical considerations. On one side are citizens' stakes in the confidentiality of personal information in government files, the president's and department heads' needs for candid advice from their immediate assistants, the effects of disclosure of unmatured proposals, and the special need for secrecy in matters affecting defense and conduct of foreign affairs. On the other side are the often deplorable results of activities cloaked in secrecy, the people's right to know so that they can participate in democratic government, Congress's responsibilities as creator, empowerer, and financier of agencies and their programs, and Congress's role as investigator and exposer of corrupt, illegal, and unethical behavior in the executive branch. With so many constitutional, moral, prudential, and pragmatic considerations in conflict, no formula, however complex, can provide a solution.

Staff Support

Despite the frequent difficulty of obtaining information, Congress is overwhelmed with information from administrative agencies. A large amount comes in the form of regular reports—annual, quarterly, monthly—that statutes require. This information overload, in fact, is mainly of Congress's own making. The Pentagon reports cited earlier are only one sign of Congress's increasing insistence that administrative agencies provide regular reports on their activities as well as answering detailed intermittent inquiries. The Environmental Protection Agency, for example, must respond to more than 4,000 letters per year from Congress requesting information.[31] In addition, "elaborate public relations programs in some agencies blanket congressional committees with more—and often irrelevant—'information' than they can possibly handle, befogging issues and distorting facts in the process."[32] Congress's informational problem stems partly from a deliberate agency strategy of communications "overkill." More commonly, it reflects the lack of "fit" between congressional interests and the way that information is organized and summarized in administrative agencies. The increasingly scientific and technological character of many fields of governmental activity has further complicated the problem.[33]

For years, Congress dealt with the information problem by vastly increasing the size of its own staff. In a move mirrored in state legislatures around the country, Congress attempted to close the "expertise gap" with the executive branch by three steps: increasing the personal staffs of members; hiring more staff for committees; and strengthening the four staff agencies that serve Congress (the Congressional Research Service, the Congressional Budget Office, the Office of Technology Assessment, and the General Accounting Office, to which we shortly turn).[34] "Committee staffs grew when it became apparent that even specialized committee members needed help if Congress was to get the information required for making informed decisions," Michael J. Malbin argues. "Without its staff, Congress would quickly become the prisoner of its outside sources of information in the executive branch and interest groups."[35]

In just twenty years, from 1965 to 1985, congressional committee staffs tripled. In 1993, the congressional staff totaled 26,784.[36] As part of their takeover of Congress in 1995, the Republicans significantly cut the staff, but it remains large by global standards. The second most heavily staffed legislature in the world, Canada's parliament, had a staff just one-tenth as large.[37]

These staffs have helped members of Congress devote more time to casework for constituents. When a constituent writes to complain about a slow social security check, malfeasance by local grant recipients, or even allegedly abusive treatment by a relative's commanding officer in the military, the letter is assigned to a worker in a member of Congress's office. Congressional mail receives special treatment in government offices. Special, brightly colored "buck slips" are usually stapled to the top; most agencies have quick turnaround times for responses; and the responses are monitored by the agency's congressional liaison unit, to ensure that quick and accurate replies are sent.

Members of Congress and administrators take such letters very seriously, for no one wants to seem indifferent to constituents. There is evidence, however, that such referrals often are not very effective at solving the problems, "since they are usually handled at the same level of the agency (often by the same official) where the complaint arose in the first place." Furthermore, because the complaints are random and extremely detailed, they rarely provide good evidence for overseeing broad administrative issues. Occasionally, patterns of complaints or particularly unusual issues might surface, but evidence of wrongdoing does not often emerge through such casework.[38]

No one seriously supposes that a committee can or should match the expertness of the staffs or agencies under its jurisdiction. Even a moderate expansion of committee staffs could mean multiplication of little congressional bureaucracies, each requiring direction and coordination by the committee or its chairperson, responsibilities for which members of Congress have little time and, often, little talent. In the absence of such control, staff members have been known to go off on their own, harassing agency officials and, in effect, participating in agency decision making; such staff members purport to be representing their committees but in fact may be representing only themselves.

The issue is no longer the quantity of staff assistance but its quality and its effective use and direction by the committees or their chairpersons. One observer notes a shift in committee staff recruitment from experienced civil servants performing as neutral professionals expert in the committees' fields to young lawyers searching for contacts. Staff members innocent of specific subject-matter knowledge but eager to assure publicity for their leader become vigorous entrepreneurs developing innovative ideas for their committees' agendas. But they soon leave for regulatory commissionerships, executive agency posts, candidacy for seats in Congress, or membership in Washington law firms engaged in lobbying.[39] For oversight activities, both neutral professionals and active partisans are needed; the problem is to strike the right balance.

The alternative to the building up of committee staffs is increased reliance on congressional support agencies, including the Congressional Budget Office and the Congressional Research Service. They mostly focus their informational and analytical studies on pending legislative proposals and future policy options, rather than on investigation of administrative operations. Such potential as they have for aiding Congress's oversight activities has not been fully realized, and each receives mixed reviews on its sense of priorities, quality of products, and internal administration. A third support agency, the General Accounting Office, is "Congress's most valuable oversight support agency" in the opinion of the Senate Committee on Governmental Affairs. Ernest S. Griffith, the former director of what is now the Congressional Research Service, goes further, "the General Accounting Office is the finest instrument in any nation in the world to serve as watchdog over a bureaucracy and enable its parliament or legislature to keep it under control—if GAO wills to do so."[40] We examine it in the next section.

The General Accounting Office

In 1921 Congress transferred the government's auditing functions from the Treasury Department, where they had been based since 1789, to a new General Accounting Office.[41] GAO is headed by the comptroller general of the United States, who is appointed by the president with the advice and consent of the Senate. Congress wanted to ensure that the GAO was protected from interference by the executive branch, so the comptroller general holds a fifteen-year term (the longest in the government, except for the lifetime appointment of federal judges) and can be removed only by a joint resolution of Congress or by impeachment.

GAO exercises functions with both executive and legislative roots. It performs legislative branch duties by auditing the expenditures of executive branch agencies. It performs executive branch duties by approving agencies' payments and settling their accounts. This ambiguous position has been a source of continuing controversy. During the Reagan administration, the Competition in Contracting Act of 1984 gave GAO the power to halt a contract under dispute. President Reagan objected to this power, and Attorney General William French Smith instructed executive branch agencies not to comply with the provision. A federal district judge ruled Smith's action illegal, and Congress backed up the decision by withholding all funds for the attorney general's office until he agreed to go along with the law. Smith's successor, Edwin Meese III, backed down. Meanwhile, a federal appeals court agreed with Congress and held that GAO was a "hybrid agency" that could exercise such executive functions as reviewing contracts before their execution. As we saw in chapter 10, however, the Supreme Court in 1986 held, in *Bowsher* v. *Synar,* that the comptroller general was an agent of Congress and thus could not constitutionally exercise executive budget-cutting powers.[42] Thus, GAO is a hybrid whose constitutional position is a very vague one.

Era of Detailed Control

Two major provisions in the 1921 Budget and Accounting Act's definition of GAO's powers created the basis for much of this friction.[43] One reads, "The Comptroller General shall prescribe the forms, systems, and procedure for ... accounting in the several departments and establishments, and for the administrative examination of fiscal officers' accounts and claims against the United States." This meant that the government's accounting systems could be designed primarily with the GAO's needs in mind and without attention to the accounting needs of the operating departments, the Treasury Department, and the budget bureau. GAO's external-control needs could be met at the expense of the executive branch's internal-control needs.

The second major provision reads: "All claims and demands whatever by the Government of the United States or against it, and all accounts whatever in which the Government of the United States is concerned, either as debtor or creditor, shall be settled and adjusted in the General Accounting Office." This appeared to mean (and was so interpreted by the first comptroller general) that no financial transaction of the government could legally be completed until specifically approved by the GAO. Agency officials continued to spend money for goods and services, but the vouchers for all transactions were transported from all over the world to Washington for review by the GAO. If it disapproved any expenditure, the public official who approved the expenditure would, by law, be personally responsible for the difference.[44] The risk of such personal liability was so threatening that spending officers often asked the GAO for advance opinions, and the GAO increasingly preaudited expenditures before they were made. As a result, the GAO not only delayed actions but became less an after-the-fact auditor than an active participant in the very transactions it was supposed later to audit.

For the first fifteen years, the comptroller general cherished his "watch-dog of the Treasury" role. He usually interpreted grants of spending power narrowly and statutory restrictions broadly. *Interpreted* is the key word here, and one that is often overlooked in discussions of external control. Statutory provisions, as we observed earlier, are often open to varying interpretations, and their meaning depends on who has the last word.[45] Lawyers from an agency and the Treasury might interpret a provision one way and, in case of doubt, obtain an official opinion from the attorney general. The comptroller general, however, does not accept the attorney general's rulings as binding. If the GAO disallows an expenditure as "contrary to law," the ruling stands unless the executive branch carries the dispute to court. Giving the last word to an external-control official can, and did, open opportunities for hamstringing of programs with which the comptroller general is unsympathetic.[46]

Reorientation

Remarkable changes have taken place in recent decades. Although the GAO still has power to, and does, audit some individual transactions, the GAO has come to emphasize the strengthening of agencies' internal audit and control systems, whose effectiveness in turn relieves the GAO of the need to audit every transaction. Instead, it can concentrate on programs that are important in financial terms and those that have provoked criticism or congressional interest. The GAO, in short, has moved from cost accounting to program auditing, from examining the money trail to measuring program performance. Its reports on cost overruns in weapons procurement have often created sensations. In more routine audits of agencies the GAO uses statistical sampling and other strategies to test the effectiveness of internal control systems, thus again removing itself from the burden of second-guessing every transaction. Most audits are done "on site"—that is, in the agencies and their field offices—so freight-car loads of vouchers need no longer be shipped to the GAO in Washington. These and other changes have reduced the GAO staff from 15,000 in 1946 to 4,400 today.

The GAO has moved far toward becoming an all-purpose, external-control agent. Former Comptroller General Elmer B. Staats observed that governmental auditing "no longer is a function concerned primarily with financial operations. Instead, governmental auditing now is also concerned with whether governmental organizations are achieving the purpose for which programs are authorized and funds are made available, are doing so economically and efficiently, and are complying with applicable laws and regulations."[47] Legislation enacted during the 1970s emphasized that the GAO "shall review and evaluate the *results* of Government programs and activities."[48] The GAO's reviews are remarkable for both their detail and their variety, as a sample of reports shows:

- □ "Women in the Military: Impact of Proposed Legislation to Open More Combat Support Positions and Units to Women"
- □ "Land Exchange: Problems with Fee System for Resorts Operating on Forest Service Lands"
- □ "Highways: How State Agencies Adopt New Pavement Technologies"
- □ "Seafood Safety: Seriousness of Problems and Efforts to Protect Customers"
- □ "AIDS Education: Reaching Populations at Higher Risk"

After the past several presidential elections, moreover, the GAO has released a transition series, providing advice to members of Congress and newly elected presidents on topics ranging from the budget deficit and the public service to NASA and national defense.

The GAO, therefore, occupies a powerful position. It is a direct congressional agent exercising delegated control authority over administrative agencies. In addition, it has a substantial, skilled investigative and analytical staff that aids congressional committees in their oversight of agency performance and sometimes conducts reviews on its own initiative.

It has two handicaps, neither of them irremediable.[49] The first is its "green eyeshade" image, created partly by its past and partly by the preponderance of accountants, particularly at executive levels. (Until the switch to program auditing, many of its employees in fact wore the green eyeshades then fashionable among bookkeepers.) But the staff pattern has been shifting, with recruitment of business and public administration specialists, economists and other social scientists, engineers, and computer and information specialists. The second handicap is the time required for investigation and completion of audits and other studies. This stems largely from GAO's commitment to accuracy, thoroughness, and objectivity, but the result is that its reports often lack timeliness for Congress's agenda. Nevertheless, the GAO's "blue cover" reports—and their handy "tear sheets" that summarize key findings—are staples at congressional hearings and in news reports of government activities. GAO's computer experts provided much of the data used to track down the secret financial transfers used by Reagan aide Oliver North to channel arms sale profits to Central American guerrillas. The GAO's influence, moreover, has spilled over into the states, where many legislatures have established their own "mini-GAOs" to conduct evaluations of state programs.

Criticisms

GAO's aggressive expansion of its mission, however, stimulated substantial criticism, especially about its objectivity and impartiality, even among the agency's staunchest friends. A 1994 report by the National Academy of Public Administration (NAPA), commissioned by key congressional committees, found several important problems.[50] First, NAPA found that GAO's mission had become "broader and more diverse than appropriate for the government's central audit and evaluation agency" and that it had gone "beyond its core purpose, skills, and resources." NAPA recommended that GAO focus more on the root causes of problems and that it strengthen its core expertise. It suggested that GAO be cautious about being drawn into problems of policy analysis development, even if requested by members of Congress. Second, although GAO responds to congressional inquiries, it has focused its work through an internal strategic planning process invisible to those (including members of Congress and their staffs) outside it. NAPA recommended that GAO be far more open in planning where it would focus its energy. Third, NAPA found that GAO's work was often uneven in quality. Fourth, NAPA found a conflict between GAO's traditionally adversarial audits and its emerging role as a source of management analysis and technical assistance to agencies.

Finally, congressional requests have "increasingly embroiled GAO in political and policy controversy, threatening its impartial role and institutional staffing." As a result,

> Increasingly adversarial relationships between congressional and executive entities in the last 20 years and intra-Congress rivalries make it hard for GAO to produce objective work—and to be perceived as doing so. Any use of GAO that erodes perceptions of its fairness and objectivity reduces its usefulness.

NAPA recommended that Congress be more careful about the problems into which it draws GAO, that GAO avoid a "gotcha" approach in its reports, and that GAO work harder to create a nonpartisan environment for its work.

In part, the study criticized GAO for moving too far beyond its resources and capacity. In part, it criticized Congress for drawing GAO into political issues that undermined its long-cultivated aura of impartiality. But most of all, the report pointed to the need to redefine GAO, its processes, its staff, and its mission. GAO had moved beyond its earlier eras into a new one that sometimes remained ill defined. The evolution from financial and process control to broader analysis, evaluation, and management support proved an uneasy one for GAO, and it struggled in the mid-1990s to find a new balance.

The Legislative Veto

A final form of congressional control of administration, one under even more vigorous debate, is the legislative veto. Members of Congress have long been unhappy simply to review administrative actions after the fact. They hungered for a mechanism to participate in administrative decision making and stop proposed administrative actions with which they disagreed. In search of a way of nullifying an impending executive decision or action before it could take effect, Congress developed extremely complex legislative veto provisions.

The legislative veto has over time taken four forms: (1) a one-house veto, in which either the Senate or the House of Representatives adopts a resolution disapproving of an executive action; (2) a two-house veto, in which both houses pass such a resolution; (3) a committee veto, in which a committee of either house (sometimes of both houses) vetoes an action; and (4) a veto by the chairman of a congressional committee.[51]

Early Forms

The device dates from the 1930 when Herbert Hoover wanted authority to reorganize the government without having to submit each plan to Congress for advance approval. Congress, unwilling to make such a broad grant of authority, instead allowed Hoover to issue executive orders for reorganization. The orders would take effect within sixty days, unless either house voted to disapprove the order. Through congressional creation of the legislative veto, Louis Fisher explains, Hoover "could, in effect, 'make law' without obtaining the approval of Congress."[52] Congress continued to renew the president's reorganization authority, with some lapses and revisions.

The legislative veto proved a very popular congressional strategy in fields other than reorganization because, as Fisher points out, it provided "a simple quid pro quo that allowed the executive branch to make law without any legislative action but gave Congress the right to recapture control without having to pass another public law."[53] By the spring of 1983, there were 207 legislative veto provisions in 126 statutes. Vetoes were applied to emergency oil supplies, railroads, financial aid to New York City, electoral finance, arms sales to the Mideast, export controls, standby gasoline rationing, and all regulations of the Federal Trade Commission.[54] Important versions of the legislative veto emerged particularly during the 1970s, largely in response to Congress's anger at Richard Nixon's exercise of power.

When Nixon asserted the right to commit American troops as a presidential power, Congress responded by passing the War Powers Resolution of 1973. The resolution requires the president to notify Congress within forty-eight hours of sending troops into hostilities. Congress has sixty days to declare war or extend the sixty-day period. Otherwise, the president is required to remove the troops. A year later, Congress acted to restrain the president's power over government spending. Nixon had refused to spend money Congress had appropriated, an action that Congress believed threatened its power of the purse. The Impoundment Control Act of 1974 stipulated that, if the president temporarily decided to withhold spending (through a "deferral"), either house of Congress could veto the decision and force him to spend the money. If the president wanted permanent spending cuts, he would have to ask Congress's permission (by passing a "rescission").[55]

Legislative committees used the legislative veto's logic to expand their own powers over administrative acts through a variety of formal and informal arrangements. Some statutes explicitly delegated veto authority to committees; many required formal approval of the proposed executive action by the relevant committees in both houses. Other statutes prohibited the appropriations committees from including funds in their bills for any projects or contracts without the prior approval of the relevant legislative committees.

Chadha and Its Aftermath

In 1983, however, the Supreme Court struck down the legislative veto as unconstitutional. The Court ruled in *Immigration and Naturalization Service* v. *Chadha* that legislative vetoes violated the Constitution's separation-of-powers provisions. Congress's role was to pass legislation and present it to the president for his signature. Congress might find the legislative veto a convenient and efficient way to oversee executive action, but the veto nevertheless violated the checks and balances of the Constitution, the Court held. As Chief Justice Warren Burger wrote in the Court's opinion, "To preserve those checks, and maintain the separation of powers, the carefully defined limits on the power of each Branch must not be eroded."[56] As dissenting Justice Byron White pointed out, the Court in one blow invalidated more laws than in its entire history.[57]

While some legislative veto supporters vigorously contested the Court's ruling,[58] the decision's tough language appeared at first to put an end to the legislative veto. The device, however, proved too convenient an instrument of legislative influence—and its forms were far too varied—for the decision to bury it. "Executive officials still want substantial latitude in administering delegated authority; legislators still insist on maintaining control without having to pass another law," Fisher explains. In fact, by the end of

1988, five years after the *Chadha* decision, Congress had created more than 140 new legislative vetoes. Many new statutes included "report and wait" provisions, in which Congress gave administrators discretion to take some actions, such as reprogramming funds or issuing regulations, but required that the actions not take effect for a specified period, such as thirty or sixty days. The waiting period gives Congress the opportunity to voice disagreements or take even stronger action before the administrators act. Other laws contain provisions that Congress must pass a joint resolution, which to be effective must be signed by the president, before the administrative action is taken.[59] The provisions ranged from a requirement for prior approval of Environmental Protection Agency construction grants to a stipulation for advance authorization of funds for the Secret Service.[60]

The legislative veto persists because it offers useful flexibility to both the Congress and the president. A 1987 case illustrated its utility. For years, foreign-aid bills had carried a legislative veto: "None of the funds made available by this Act may be obligated under an appropriation account to which they were not appropriated without the prior written approval of the Committees on Appropriations." The provision allowed foreign-aid administrators to transfer money among accounts, provided they first got the Appropriation Committees' approval. In 1987, however, the Reagan administration's director of the Office of Management and Budget, James C. Miller III, decided to challenge the provision as unconstitutional, because of the *Chadha* decision. Miller's action provoked bipartisan anger on Capitol Hill. The key subcommittee chairman said that Miller's announcement "means we don't have an accommodation anymore, so the hell with it." Members of Congress resolved to remove the flexibility and to force administrators to spend the money just as they had appropriated it. OMB then staged a retreat, realizing, as Fisher puts it, "that it had shot itself in the foot."[61]

The legislative veto and its post-*Chadha* variants thus serve mutually useful purposes. They provide administrators with broader discretion and allow members of Congress to intervene selectively in decisions with which they might not agree. Rarely does an agency risk the displeasure of the committee by proceeding despite such objections.[62] Informal consultations, furthermore, provide other mechanisms for congressional review. Executive branch officials usually consult with congressional committees before making sensitive decisions, especially about construction projects, real estate transactions, purchase-contract awards, and closing of federal facilities. Normally, committee members refer each such proposed action to the member of Congress from the affected district and the senators from the affected state to assure that they do not object.[63]

Conclusion

Legislative control of administration is based on the sound proposition that legislators, not just executives, have a legitimate concern with seeing to it "that the laws be faithfully executed." Legislators can by law fix the objectives and methods of implementing the programs they authorize, determine the funding of each program, and organize and reorganize agencies. They can limit the life span of program authorizations and appropriations. Through committees and accounting offices, such as the GAO, they can make their own investigations of agency performance. The circle is completed by legislative alteration of enabling statutes, appropriations, and organizations so as to make agencies' future performance conform more closely to congressional intent.

As Christopher H. Foreman, Jr., following a study of congressional oversight of regulatory policies, has observed:

> Oversight emerges as a sometimes painful, inevitably self-interested process of consultation and second-guessing that reasonably well keeps administration sensitive to the concerns of persons and groups affected by or attentive to regulatory policy. As a system for monitoring agency decision making and adherence to approved procedure—that is, as a set of mechanisms for enforcing accountability regarding agency behavior and policy choice—oversight succeeds.

While the process is often confusing, with muddled jurisdictional boundaries and uncertain leverage, the whole entourage comprises "an intricate and impressive system of screens or 'fire alarms.' "[64] It is a system that defies easy description or rational organization, but the intricate relationships nevertheless provide an impressive range of information and leverage, both formal and informal, for legislative influence on administrative activities. It is also a system in which members of Congress can transmit signals—sometimes blunt, sometimes subtle—about their expectations of administrators' actions.

We have discovered two major problems. One is the limited degree of interest and moderate capability that Congress, as well as legislatures at other levels, brings to its oversight responsibilities.[65] Oversight is at best intermittent, and sustained congressional attention to major administrative issues is rare. The other problem is the danger that legislators (especially in committees and subcommittees) will intrude excessively into the executive function, sometimes to promote their own self-interest.[66] Legislators should not—for reasons of both constitutional comity and administrative efficiency—so confuse their roles as to become, in effect, coadministrators of agencies and programs. A long-time chairman of the House Naval Affairs Committee, for example, was dubbed "the Secretary of the Navy." The involvement of judges in administration raises similar issues, and we turn to these next.

13

Regulation and the Courts

All governments regulate the behavior of individuals and organizations. The primary objective is to change the way that private individuals and corporations behave when pursuit of their self-interest is likely to harm others—consumers, competitors, suppliers, distributors, workers, and members of future generations.[1] A secondary, but vitally important, objective is to regulate how government agencies and their employees go about their administrative tasks, particularly those that involve regulation of private behavior. In the pursuit of both objectives, three features are central. One is the source of regulatory authority, namely, legislation that vests administrative discretion in agencies and specifies the limits of such discretion and the conditions governing how it shall be exercised. A second is the resources that Congress and the president make available to the agencies for performance of their regulatory responsibilities. The first and the second features are often not in harmony. That is, Congress may expand an agency's responsibilities without increasing its appropriations, and the president may impose limits on staff size that impair the agency's effectiveness. A third feature is the interplay between, on the one hand, responsibility for regulating private behavior and, on the other hand, the rules that Congress, the president, and the courts establish for regulating agencies' and employees' behavior. Those rules, admirably intended to keep regulators accountable and responsive and so to assure a government of laws and not of men, can be so complex that regulatory decisions get entangled in red tape and their issuance gets delayed for years. All three features, "delegation of legislative power," adequacy of resources, and regulatory procedure, occupy much of our attention in this chapter.

The range of regulation of private behavior is very wide. At one extreme are speed limits and stoplights, at the other extreme, restriction of entry into a business or profession and regulation of prices and wages. Regulation is old as well as wide. The Constitution in 1789 gave Congress the power "to promote the progress of science and useful arts by securing for limited times to authors and inventors the exclusive right to their respective writings and discoveries."[2] This book is protected against plagiarism by a certificate issued by the Copyright Office of the United States, which administers a statute based on that provision. In 1988, administering a statute under the same constitutional clause, the Patent and Trademark Office awarded the world's first animal-invention patent to Harvard University, whose scientists had transformed a mouse through genetic manipulation.[3]

What private behaviors are appropriate for regulation is a major focus of policy disputes. That question concerns the wisdom of the legislative branch, which is beyond the confines of this book. Our focus is on the administration of regulatory laws. Nevertheless, enacted regulatory programs, especially the newer ones, remain the subjects of lively political controversy. This affects their administration. A regulatory agency has a relatively serene environment in pursuing its goals if the regulatory policy enjoys wide public support or acquiescence by the regulated interests. When public support is slight or so diffused that it cannot be mobilized, and when the regulated interests are opposed and well organized, the agency confronts a hostile environment that threatens its program and perhaps the agency's very existence.[4] An airlines regulatory program that protected established airlines against the entry of new competitors survived for decades with industry support. In contrast, pollution-control programs that add to the costs of doing business are resisted by many affected companies.

The public's opinion of regulation is ambivalent. At a general level, it is hostile. Almost two-thirds of those surveyed who have an opinion say that government regulation of business usually does more harm than good, and over 40 percent say that there is too much government regulation of the economy. Those views do not carry over to attitudes toward specific regulatory programs. Asked about two major areas, 90 percent say there should be more or about the same amount of regulation of workers' health and safety, as do 90 percent about regulation of the environment.[5]

As both the general and the policy-specific opinions are from nationwide samples, they miss a third element of agencies' and programs' need for support. Strong reactions greet regulatory initiatives that may adversely affect particular regions, communities, and industries, causing increased costs, loss of competitive advantage, and unemployment. Such reactions are vigorously communicated to senators and representatives from the affected areas, and the initiating agency may need to moderate its regulation in order to maintain congressional support. Prudence may take over even if the proposed regulation is in accord with the letter of the law. Such caution was more needed in earlier decades. Support for regulation of industry was diffuse, and advocacy organizations (such as those for environmental protection) lacked staying power and the capacity to mobilize resources against weakening of statutory programs by implementing agencies. This has changed so that agencies cannot readily cave in to industry and localized pressures without offending so-called public-interest groups and their congressional allies.

"The uniqueness of the American approach to regulation," writes David Vogel, "is the one finding on which every cross-national study of regulation is in agreement." In explaining this, he anticipates much of what we treat in this chapter:

> The American system of regulation is distinctive in the degree of oversight exercised by the judiciary and the national legislature, in the formality of its rulemaking and enforcement process, in its reliance on prosecution, in the amount of information made available to the public, and in the extent of the opportunities provided for participation by nonindustry constituencies.... The restrictions the United States has placed on corporate conduct affecting public health, safety, and amenity are at least as strict as and in many cases stricter than those adopted by other capitalist nations. As a result, in no other nation have the relations between the regulated and the regulators been so consistently strained.[6]

The Regulatory Task

Regulatory agencies vary in the kinds of regulation they administer.[7] They operate under both vague and highly specific statutory mandates. They are more expert in their particular fields than Congress, the president's office, and the courts, all of which play major roles in regulation. Yet on many matters the uncertainties of the nation's scientific and technological knowledge set limits to their expertness.

Kinds of Regulations

Government regulation is conventionally defined as composed of *economic* regulation and *social* regulation. The expansion of economic regulation began in the states; in the federal government it dates from 1887 when the Interstate Commerce Commission was established to regulate the railroads.[8] This was the dominant form of regulation until the 1960s. Its characteristic activities were two. One set sought to assure competition by preventing monopolies and unfair methods of competition (including deception of consumers). These "antitrust laws" embraced all industries where such evils might appear and were administered by the Justice Department and the

Federal Trade Commission. The other set of activities, confined to particular industries, focused primarily on two issues: *entry* to the business (by issuance or denial of "certificates of convenience and necessity," which are licenses to do business and serve certain routes or areas), and *prices* (by fixing maximum and in some cases minimum rates to be charged).[9] The responsibility was usually lodged in independent regulatory commissions in federal and state governments. Each commission had a single industry or a handful of related industries as its clientele, and it was likely to fall under domination by those supposed to be regulated. In the absence of effective consumer organization, the "capture" phenomenon was a major concern, with no remedy in sight.[10]

Social regulation, though appearing early in this century (as with child labor and food and drug regulation), grew enormously in the 1960s and 1970s. It focuses on the quality of life through such activities as protection of the environment, protection of workers' health and safety, assurance of the safety and quality of consumer products, and prohibition of discrimination on grounds of race, color, sex, age, or disability. Responsibility for achieving social regulation is mostly lodged not in independent commissions but in bureaus within departments or, as with the Environmental Protection Agency (EPA), in a single-headed agency outside a department. Such bureaus' and agencies' jurisdictions are not confined to single industries but cover all industries where threats to health, safety, fair employment, and the environment may occur. Though social regulation is addressed to the quality of life rather than economic imperfections of the market, it also has market effects. It reduces a business firm's freedom to act purely in its self-interest and often adds to the costs of the firm, thus affecting its profit margin.

Defense of the government's intervention rests on the economic concept of *externalities,* sometimes called spillover effects. If a paper mill discharges pollutants into a river, downstream communities must pay the costs of cleaning up the river or purifying their intake to assure drinking water for their citizens. And downstream swimmers, fishers, and boaters pay the price in pleasures forgone. The pollution practice reduces manufacturing costs and so is rational behavior for the company. But the costs—financial, aesthetic, and other—exported to people downstream are high. Economists would compare the manufacturer's savings and the downstream costs, and if the latter were high enough, would find justification for restricting the paper mill's discharges, thus adding to its costs of doing business. Such regulation would compel the company to internalize the externalities.[11] The externalities approach has wide applicability. For example, a company's freedom to market unsafe drugs, foods, or toys and an employer's freedom to endanger workers' health and safety are limited by government because of the social costs of such free enterprise.

Economic regulation and social regulation are not two sides of a single coin. In the political world, at least, they are two distinct coins. Otherwise, it would be hard to explain what happened in the late 1970s and in the 1980s. Economic deregulation occurred, while social regulation expanded. The government retreated from extensive regulation of trucking, airlines, telecommunication, and financial services.[12] At the same time, the environment, workers' health and safety, and consumers' products gained more elaborate protections at first under Carter and then despite Reagan's contrary pressures. In both developments, Congress and the judiciary were major actors, while the departures from past patterns aroused varying degrees of support from the agencies affected.

Though the categories of economic and social programs help us to avoid thinking of regulation as an undifferentiated collection of activities, each category in turn disguises important differences among regulatory programs and agencies. Some agencies, such as the Food and Drug Administration, are required by law to act immediately when a food or drug on the market is found to cause death or serious disease; any procedural niceties must follow, rather than precede, an order to remove the product from merchants' shelves. Some programs simply require disclosure of information. Examples are cigarette labels' highlighting the health hazards of smoking and factories' annual reports of the use of toxic chemicals in the workplace and in the surrounding community.[13] A piquant case turns on whether the front panel (not the small-print list of ingredients) on frozen pizza boxes must disclose the presence of a cheese substitute; the FDA requires such display on all pizzas without meat toppings, while the Department of Agriculture, with jurisdiction over meat-topped pizzas, requires it only if the substitute is over 90 percent of the cheese topping.[14]

Agencies vary in their choice between performance standards (e.g., maximum permitted emission of pollutants), which let companies choose methods of compliance, and technological specifications (e.g., requiring installation of "scrubbers" in electric utilities' smokestacks to reduce pollution).[15] Some agencies adversely affect regulated companies when they announce the bringing of charges or the initiation of hearings; the effect is like that of an indictment that besmirches an official or a private person despite the presumption of innocence until proven guilty. Consumers' preferences may be influenced by some agencies' press releases, such as those listing cigarette brands by tar content, automobiles by fuel consumption per mile, and airlines' percentage of on-time arrivals. Some agencies have large staffs of inspectors visiting industrial plants, restaurants, nursing homes, and other locations to detect violations of laws and regulations and to order compliance;[16] other agencies (or the same ones if inspectional staffs are too limited) rely on companies' self-reporting of workers' accidents and health impairments, though owners' incentives for accurate reporting are slight.[17]

The range of variation is barely suggested by these examples. They suffice to indicate that the styles of regulatory administration do not fit comfortably in one category or a few broad categories. A persistent problem, then, is how the governmental system can accommodate the variations while giving effective force to general principles about citizens' rights, fair procedures, and institutional arrangements for control of bureaucratic organizations. Congress tends to legislate by program and by agency, thus differentiating as it deems appropriate. In its broader legislation, however, it conflates the many programs and agencies, as do both the courts and the president in devising controls over the regulatory system.

State and Local Regulations

Though we focus our discussion on the national government, regulation is a major activity of state and local governments. Their regulatory work is of two kinds. One is substantially autonomous, without involvement of the national government. State governments have public utility commissions controlling intrastate rates and services, banking departments regulating state-chartered banks, "lemon laws" imposing disclosure and warranties requirements on used-car dealers, minimum-wage and antidiscrimination laws, bottle deposit and recycling laws, and health and safety laws and regulations that cover a wide range of enterprises—from factory conditions to nursing homes to restaurants and saloons to farmers' use of pesticides. The states, not the federal government, regulate insurance companies, despite their countrywide operations. Local governments also regulate broadly, sharing in assurance of health and safety protections and the honesty of weights and measures (e.g., grocery scales and gas pumps). They administer land-use zoning, which seeks to control the location, structural features, and uses of buildings.

About 800 occupations are regulated in this country, 20 of them in every state (from attorneys, physicians, and pharmacists to barbers, cosmetologists, and real estate agents).[18] Over half the states regulate funeral directors, chauffeurs, milk samplers, plumbers, and hearing-aid dealers, to cite only a few of this group. Typically, entry to the professions and some other occupations is restricted by licensing laws, often lobbied for by professionals' associations and administered by substantially autonomous licensing boards whose members are effectively nominated by the associations. Though rationalized as social regulation, to protect the health and safety of consumers of such services, the licensing systems tend to be economic regulation, limiting competition by restricting entry.

The second regulatory role of state and local governments is administration of national regulatory programs.[19] Congress has the power to preempt much state regulatory activity, displacing it by programs executed directly by federal officials. But in many cases it has chosen the alternative of partial preemption.[20] In such fields as environmental protection, occupational safety and health, meat and poultry inspection, and energy regulation, "partial preemption centralizes policy formulation, but it shares policy implementation with the states."[21] In this arrangement, the national government decides on regulatory standards, and each state government may (1) choose to administer those prescribed standards; or (2) create and administer its own standards, provided they are at least as stringent as those of the federal government. If a state fits neither situation, the appropriate national agency directly administers its national program within the state. In fact, a state may switch around. In mid-1987, California terminated its occupational safety and health enforcement program, thereby shifting enforcement to direct national administration by OSHA; two years later, though, California was seeking OSHA's permission to have its own program, including resumption of enforcement responsibility.[22] Partial preemption is now a prominent part of the regulatory system. It allows some adaptation to local circumstances and lets individual state governments choose their roles in a regulatory system. It has the advantage of permitting a state to have more rigorous standards than those of the national laws and regulations; full national preemption would not permit this. It has the disadvantage of all farming-out of the implementation of national policies—the weakness of federal sanctions over "third-party" noncompliance with national directives.[23]

Statutory Mandates

Economic regulation and social regulation sharply differ in the content of legislative mandates. At both national and state levels, the economic regulation statutes have vested broad discretion in regulatory agencies. Licenses to enter a business field are to be issued to serve "the public interest, convenience, or necessity," and rates to be fixed are to be "just and reasonable"; the Federal Trade Commission is to eliminate "unfair methods of competition" and "deceptive practices."

Congress's social regulation statutes, although they also contain broad phrases,[24] are remarkably detailed. The most famous specific provision is the Delaney Clause in the Food, Drug, and Cosmetic Act. After generally requiring the Food and Drug Administration to approve only substances that are "safe," the clause provides that no food additive, color additive, or drug for food animals "shall be deemed to be safe if it is found to induce cancer when ingested by man or animal, or . . . , after tests which are appropriate for the evaluation of the safety of [noningested] additives, to induce cancer in man and animal."[25] The plain meaning is that once an additive has been found to induce cancer in animals the FDA must ban it despite any finding that humans who ingest or apply the additive face no significant risk—and regardless of costs to manufacturers and merchants. Though the FDA has tried to chip away at the absolute standard (e.g., when human risk is rated at one in a million or less), courts have insisted on compliance with the statute.[26] Curiously, though, when the Food and Drug Administration obeyed the law by banning saccharin, a sugar substitute (after earlier banning cyclamates), Congress responded to diabetics' and industries' pressures by enacting a series of moratoriums on the ban.

Many other statutory details stemmed from Congress's intent to protect the newer regulatory agencies from capture by the regulated industries and from enfeeblement by the Nixon, Ford, and Reagan administrations. For example, social regulation statutes name specific air and water pollutants on which EPA must act. The most innovative practice is congressional setting of deadlines for agency accomplishment of statutory objectives. The 1972 amendments to the Federal Water Pollution Control Act directed that navigable waters were to become fishable and swimmable by 1983 and that all discharge of pollutants into navigable waters was to be eliminated by 1985; the best practicable control technologies were to be in place by 1977 and the best available technologies by 1983, phrases that substantially limit EPA's considering the costs to the regulated interests. In 1984, Congress set over two dozen specific statutory deadlines for EPA regulation of the management and disposal of currently generated hazardous waste.[27] In all, the laws for EPA contain thirty-eight mandatory deadlines for issuance of rules and regulations, and thirty-six deadlines for studies, guidelines, and reports.[28] Though Congress has extended many deadlines, their action-forcing is law until amendment occurs, and so they offer a peg on which environmental and other groups can hang a court case against the agency. They also are a spur to action even when achievement falls short of meeting a deadline.

Expertness

Whether an independent regulatory commission or a single-headed agency has regulatory responsibility, the important defining characteristics are much the same.[29] Both are headed by presidential appointees who have reason to be attentive to presidential policy preferences. The distinctive features of a regulatory agency, compared with the president's office, Congress, and the judiciary, are its specialization on a limited field of private behavior (an industry, a social problem, or their conjunction) and the expertness of its staffs. The two features are mutually reinforcing. Over time, the concentration on a limited agenda of concerns builds experience with what works and what does not in the assigned field, a kind of expertness unmatched by other would-be interveners in the agency's business. This, however, is not all to the good. A specialized agency may develop a myopia that blocks from view the relation of its initiatives to those already taken or being contemplated by other agencies. And it may discount unduly the president's office's interest in a consistent direction of public policy that reflects the president's perceived electoral mandate. The passage of time may harden an agency's commitment to one way of achieving statutory goals and to one set of procedures for obtaining input from affected interests. Such commitment may be powerfully reinforced by the agency's most influential clientele, whether regulated interest or public interest group or professional association.

The expertness of regulatory agencies is an important assumption, not least because courts have long cited it as a reason for their deferring to the agencies' judgments. The assumption has validity for most agencies' staffs. The largest regulatory agency, the Environmental Protection Agency, has about 14,000 employees, distributed among offices concerned with regulating air pollution, water pollution, solid waste, hazardous waste, toxic substances, radiation, and pesticides, together with others concerned with policy analysis, research, enforcement, and other legal matters. Scientists, engineers, economists, lawyers, and other professional specialists abound. The dynamics of intragency conflicts among these specialists tends to counteract the danger of adherence to a time-established orthodoxy of approach.[30]

The oddity of the expertness assumption is that it overlooks noncareerists in higher positions, though they determine their agencies' agendas and make key decisions. Members of independent regulatory commissions are political appointees, many of whom have no background in their commission's field of activity. The single-headed EPA has thirteen presidential appointees and fourteen noncareerist members of the Senior Executive Service. Some have gotten into trouble. In the Reagan administration, the head of the agency resigned under pressure after promising a gasoline refinery that she would not enforce lead-content regulations the company was violating; the head of her hazardous waste cleanup was imprisoned for lying to Congress about involvement of her former employing company in a case she was handling.[31] More significant than the incidents that caused their departure was the fact that the president had chosen them, and others as well, to minimize regulation's impact on private enterprise. Foxes in the chicken coop can nullify the expertness assumption.

When Congress knows what it wants, it wants it sooner rather than later. But in most social regulation, this rarely takes account of the uncertainties of science and technology. What we do not know can hurt us. And in many regulatory programs, experts lack firm knowledge of causes, consequences, and remedies. Part of the problem is time: there are scores, sometimes hundreds, of suspected pollutants in the air and water, and of cancer-causing and other unhealthful and unsafe elements in the workplace. Not all can be researched and their threats appraised in a few years.[32] Often the scientific community lacks answers. Similarly, the technologies for eliminating or lessening known threats may be elusive, and newly developed technologies make earlier decisions obsolete.

Cost-benefit analysis has come to play a large role in regulatory programs. This is largely attributable to the increased influence of economists in the government and recent administrations' commitment to reducing regulatory burdens on industry. Too, there is an appeal to the basic proposition that a proposed government regulation should demonstrably result in greater benefits than costs. On its face, this is a striving for certainty. Some statutes require consideration of costs; others rate some evils so great that they should be eliminated or reduced regardless of cost. The president's office has strongly pressed cost-benefit analysis on agencies and used such analysis in reviewing proposed actions. Cost-benefit analysis, however, is itself beset with uncertainties. The calculations are quantitative, but some costs and especially some benefits are difficult to express in dollar terms. What is the value of a human life? What is the value of an unspoiled national park or forest; of a Grand Canyon view free of noisy, low-flying airplanes; of fishable and swimmable streams; of nondiscriminatory employment?[33] Translation of these into dollar figures has what Justice Holmes called, in another connection, "delusive exactitude." Given such imprecision, cost-benefit numbers can be skewed to serve political objectives.

Risk assessment has taken its place alongside cost-benefit analysis as a presumably expert approach to regulation. We all are constantly exposed to risks. Some risks are more serious than others, and some persons are more exposed than others. Yet some risks are a necessary cost of progress, even of progress toward greater safety.[34] Which risks should government try to eliminate or diminish, and which leave unregulated? As with cost-benefit analysis, measurements and tradeoffs are supposed to provide answers. Adequate reporting systems should tell us which industries and occupations have the highest rates of worker injuries and deaths, how many children are strangled by crib toys or hurt by lawn darts. With ingenuity, we can compare risks. Such efforts suggest, for example, that (1) traveling the same route by automobile as by a scheduled airline increases the likelihood of death by seventy times; and (2) death is as probable from one chest X-ray, a thousand-mile scheduled air flight, and living for fifty years within five miles of a nuclear reactor. A nagging problem, though, is that the public's perception of relative degrees of risk does not fit the risk assessments by agencies' expert staffs. The agendas of both the Environmental Protection Agency and the Consumer Product Safety Commission have given priority to citizens' concerns rather than to their staffs' top risk-rated concerns.[35]

A social regulation agency, expert though it may be, is caught between detailed statutory mandates, including often unrealistic deadlines for action, and the uncertainties stemming from inadequate scientific, technological, and economic knowledge. Progress may be possible, but failure to meet expectations is virtually certain. Congress's response tends to be an odd mix of greater specification of mandates and postponement of previously mandated deadlines.

Regulatory Procedure

The Fifth and Fourteenth amendments to the Constitution prohibit the national government and the states (including their local governments) from depriving any person of life, liberty, or property without due process of law. The language is interpreted to treat corporations as "persons" and deprivation of property as including governmental denial of the opportunity to earn a fair return from prudent management of the property. Historically, the courts have used the provisions in two ways. One is the obvious one of requiring fair procedures before a deprivation action. The other, used against statutes as well as regulatory orders, is not procedural but substantive: a deprivation of property or of a fair return on it had in itself to be "reasonable" in the eyes of the courts, a test that often failed when conservative judges considered progressive legislation and rate-fixing orders of regulatory commissions. The courts have largely abandoned a directly substantive approach, though sometimes achieving it camouflaged as a procedural question.[36] In the case of regulatory administration, the courts usually avoid reference to the constitutional amendments and instead accept statutorily prescribed procedures as adequate or cite due process as a general concept and add requirements the courts deem needed to preserve their own reviewing functions.

The procedures agencies must use vary according to whether they are making a rule (applicable to a whole industry or to all industries) or deciding an individual case (e.g., resulting in an order applying to a single company or person). These two categories are roughly analogous to a legislative body's committee hearings preceding enactment of a statute and a court's adjudication of an ordinary case between two parties (one of whom, of course, may be the government or an agency). The legislative and judicial analogies have affected ideas of what procedures should be required. Rulemaking, therefore, calls for less formal and elaborate procedures than administrative adjudication.

Congress's prescriptions for rulemaking and adjudicative procedures for a particular agency are found in two sources. One is the Administrative Procedure Act of 1946 (APA) as amended by the Freedom of Information Act and the Government in the Sunshine Act.[37] The APA has general application. The other is the organic statute establishing the agency and assigning its functions, together with other statutes on individual programs. The two sources are intertwined, as some APA provisions depend on what agency-specific statutes actually say.[38]

Rulemaking

Delegation of legislative powers to administrative agencies is an accepted feature of our political system. It was not always so. The Constitution says, "All legislative Powers herein granted shall be vested in a Congress of the United States." In 1935, the Supreme Court held two New Deal measures unconstitutional as violative of this provision. Neither before nor since, though, has the Court nullified a statute for this reason.[39]

Unless the agency's statutes require a formal procedure (courtlike hearings), the APA imposes apparently modest requirements on rulemaking; so much is this the case that the activity is called "informal rulemaking" because it is not courtlike. An agency contemplating issuance of a rule must (1) publish a notice of its proposed rulemaking in the *Federal Register,* which is the daily journal containing all rules and notices affecting the public;[40] (2) give interested parties an opportunity to submit *written* data, views, or arguments; and (3) after consideration of the relevant material presented, publish the final rule, together with a "concise general statement" of the basis and purpose of the rule.[41] The APA does not require oral hearings and opportunity for cross-examination of witnesses (key elements of adjudicative procedure) in rulemaking unless an agency's particular statutes prescribe them.

Agencies' extensive use of rulemaking is a relatively recent development. Most economic regulation agencies preferred to proceed on a case-by-case basis of adjudication. This mode was criticized because it ignored the need for development and statement of general policies on which industry could rely. Further, because of changes in commission membership, it led to discontinuity and contradiction in such policies as could be inferred from individual decisions. Social regulation agencies, facing known evils that needed prompt correction throughout society (e.g., asbestos in the workplace, schools, and other public places), could not address their problems by the creeping pace of case-to-case actions. So they chose to regulate by general rules. Voluntary compliance would achieve the principal objectives. The formal case-to-case method could then be limited to cases of violation of the rules.

Judicial Review of Rulemaking. The APA provides for judicial review of an agency action challenged by a person (or corporation) claiming legal wrong, adverse effect, or grievance.[42] A court thus invoked is, in addition to protecting constitutional rights, to hold unlawful an agency action that it finds "arbitrary, capricious, an abuse of discretion, or otherwise not in accordance with law." These phrases, as they bear on rulemaking, actually restrict judicial review of rules and contrast with the standard for review of individual adjudicative decisions by agencies. They manifest a concern that bureaucracy should not run amok, a different concern from one that invites a court to decide whether on its view of the evidence an agency's adjudicative decision was substantially correct.

Most cases involving rulemaking challenge agencies' actions. But inaction is also a problem. The APA enables a court to "compel agency action unlawfully withheld or unreasonably delayed." This has enabled consumers, environmentalists, and safety-minded citizens and groups to use courts to bring pressure on foot-dragging agencies to meet their rulemaking responsibilities. The opportunity arises especially when Congress has included clear mandates and set calendar deadlines in program-specific statutes.[43]

The courts confront a difficult problem in reviewing informal rules. They need, they say, a record of the agency's rulemaking in order to have something to review—even to test for arbitrariness and the rest. Because oral hearing and cross-examination of witnesses are not required by statute, rulemaking fails to produce the kind of record with which courts are familiar. The rulemaking "record" includes the mass of written comments received, often a huge collection that includes significant and trivial comments. Courts want that record, massive though it is. They also want to know how the agency reacted to each "significant" objection to the proposed rule. The result is a considerable burden on a regulatory process intended to be informal. It goes well beyond the agency's obligation to provide a concise general statement of the basis and purpose of a rule. Once in possession of the record of evidence, the courts are tempted to look at agency failure to deal satisfactorily with one or another significant objection as a sign of arbitrariness. Their range of tolerance is then likely to vary, depending on whether a court does or does not choose to emphasize, and defer to, the expertness of the regulatory agency.

Administrative Adjudication

Enforcement of rules depends heavily on voluntary compliance and, when that does not occur, on negotiations and compromises (such as extensions of deadlines for compliance) with regulated companies. The extent to which these account for regulation's effectiveness is generally underestimated. They are, on their face, independent of formal procedural requirements, but occur in a climate of expectations, built on past events, about regulated companies' chances of winning in agency adjudication or in court reviews. In another way, though, the frequency of their use reflects the burdens of formalized approaches. An agency eager to achieve its objectives will prefer negotiation and compromise to get substantial compliance over the alternative of long-drawn-out, lawyer-dominated hearings and appeals through the court system.

Agency adjudication occurs when the agency cites an alleged violator or the latter protests an agency order. The APA's adjudicatory requirements apply when an agency's statutes require that issuance of an order (other than a rule) be "determined on the record after opportunity for an agency hearing." Most such statutes require this (but agencies vary in emphasis on orders or on rulemaking). The consequence is that proceedings must be much like those of a court. Most proceedings are presided over by intendedly impartial "administrative law judges," who number over a thousand.[44] They are appointed by the agencies with approval of the Office of Personnel Management. Their tenure and compensation, the latter "independently of agency recommendations or ratings," are determined by the OPM and the Merit Systems Protection Board. Proceedings before such judges include oral hearings and cross-examination of witnesses and are fully recorded along with documentary evidence. Usually the administrative law judge makes findings and an "initial decision" that is final unless appealed to the head(s) of the agency. Alternatively, the agency's head can make the decision after receiving the administrative law judge's recommended decision.[45]

Judicial Review of Adjudicative Decisions. In reviewing agencies' adjudicative decisions, the courts have two foci. One is procedure. The courts disallow decisions reached without conformity to the APA's and other statutes' procedural requirements. More broadly, the courts sometimes invoke the general concept of "due process." Second, the courts decide, in accord with the APA, whether on examining the whole record they find an agency's "action, findings, and conclusions . . . unsupported by substantial evidence." Some statutes make the test more rigorous than that of the APA.

Courts' Regulation of the Regulators

Courts regulate the regulatory system in many ways. Often, as we have indicated, this occurs through appeals from agency rules and specific decisions. Sometimes it is through suits filed against agencies to require them to issue rules mandated or implied in statutes. Sometimes an agency sues a company seeking to punish noncompliance with a rule or order and to get a court order requiring compliance. Apart from these agency-involvement suits are suits between private parties, with a corporation as defendant charged with violation of a statute or rule.

Consider a set of simultaneous cases in the regulation of asbestos, all of them in the metropolitan area of New York City. In November 1987 about 200 employees sued the Consolidated Edison Company seeking millions of dollars in damages because of asbestos exposure. (Asbestos is a harmful air pollutant that can cause cancer and lung disease, though the effects may not appear for many years.) In January 1988 the EPA filed a civil suit against Consolidated Edison seeking civil penalties of over $1 million and a court order requiring the company's full compliance with the Clean Air Act; the violations charged were failure to follow prescribed asbestos-removal procedures and failure to inform EPA fully and promptly of the removal operations. A few days earlier, the government filed a criminal suit against officials of twenty-three companies removing asbestos materials; they were charged with bribing a federal inspector to overlook violations of federal regulations.[46] Here are three suits—a civil suit for damages brought by private citizens, a civil suit brought by the government, and a criminal suit brought by the government. None is an appeal from an agency, though all relate to EPA and its regulations.

In the judicial landscape thus apparently opened up by the several avenues of access, a barrier must first be surmounted. This is the question of who has "standing to sue" under what circumstances. That legal question suggests a practical question: who can afford the costs of litigation?

Liberalization or contraction of access to the courts leads to a more fundamental issue: how interventionist should courts be in reviewing regulatory agencies' policy-making and enforcement activities? Here two sets of considerations need assessment. One is the difference between the judicial system and the administrative system in which regulatory agencies operate.

The other is the array of values that we want reflected in the regulation of private affairs that are colored with public concern. How we balance these has much to do with the balance we prefer between the regulatory agencies and the courts.

Access to the Courts

Doctrines governing the right to sue have wavered, so we must take account of both their expansion and their contraction. Many statutes on particular program areas specifically provide an opportunity for judicial review of agency actions. In addition, the Administrative Procedure Act of 1946 has a blanket authorization: "A person suffering legal wrong because of agency action, or adversely affected or aggrieved by agency action within the meaning of a relevant statute, is entitled to judicial review thereof." This apparently wide-open invitation is qualified, however, for it does not apply if "(1) statutes preclude judicial review; or (2) agency action is committed to agency discretion by law." Nor does it apply to persons who, though unhappy about an agency decision, are held not to have suffered a "legal wrong." Until 1989, Congress made the Veterans Administration's denials of claims under the Veterans' Benefit Act unreviewable by the federal courts.[47] In sum, despite generous judicial interpretations of the main provision of the APA, access for aggrieved persons is not so broad as it seems at first reading.

Class-Action Suits. Recourse to a class-action suit has proved important for a class of citizens most of whom have suffered so small a monetary loss that it is not worthwhile for each to hire a lawyer for representation in legal proceedings, though the damage to the whole class of affected individuals (and the profit to a corporation) may amount to millions of dollars. This is a private lawsuit for money damages and is usually brought against a private person or corporation. Though the active plaintiff is typically only one or a few of the persons damaged (presumably sufficiently indignant and well-off to afford the lawyer), the suit is brought on behalf of all the affected individuals. Class-action suits matter to us because the plaintiffs often claim damages on the ground that the defendant has violated statutes or rules. A class-action suit, therefore, may complement government agencies' efforts to enforce the law or, indeed, substitute for such efforts when agencies neglect their responsibilities. As in other kinds of damage suits (automobile injury cases, for example), the defendant often prefers to settle out of court rather than risk the court's (especially a jury's) making of a generous award. Defendant corporations are inclined to regard class-action suits as "legalized blackmail," but they and others in the same business are also likely to mend their ways so as to conform to statutes and avoid future class-action suits.

In the early 1970s, class-action suits were gaining popularity as a way for otherwise helpless citizens to deter corporate damage to their interests and indirectly to spur agency enforcement of statutes protective of those interests. Then, a 1974 Supreme Court decision held that the plaintiff could not seek damages for himself and the other 6 million persons in his "class" unless he first notified all the more than 2 million persons whose names were known.[48] Giving this notice would have cost him $225,000, though his own damage claim was for only $70. With such a notification requirement, few will venture a class-action suit, even though its claims might rest on violations of antitrust and security statutes (as in this case) or of other laws protective of the public. In 1988, an appeals court required the National Wildlife Federation, in challenging the Interior Department's strip-mining regulations, to spend tens of thousands of dollars obtaining 1300 pages of affidavits from members to establish standing.[49] In this area, as in some others, the courts' decisions are so inconsistent that a pattern is scarcely discernible. The most dramatic class-action suit was against seven corporations on behalf of over 15,000 named persons who had severe illnesses or whose children suffered birth defects that they claimed resulted from exposure to a herbicide, Agent Orange, used by the army during the Vietnam war. In 1985 the case was ended by the largest tort-case settlement in history, $180 million plus interest.[50]

Private Attorneys General. Individuals and organizations may cast themselves in the role of "private attorneys general." Such suits are not for money damages. Instead, they seek to compel a government agency or a corporation to do or cease doing something that affects a major public interest or group—the environment, consumers, and the like. The two principal legal issues in recent years have been (1) standing to sue, and (2) payment of plaintiffs' legal fees.

To have standing to sue, the traditional rule is that the plaintiff must show that a "legal wrong" is involved. That is, he or she must plausibly claim to have individually suffered a wrong protected against by the Constitution, the statutes, or the common law. The APA states this traditional rule and extends standing to any person "adversely affected or aggrieved within the meaning of a relevant statute." Interpretation of this provision was liberalized in the 1960s and early 1970s. The adverse effect or grievance may be recreational, environmental, or aesthetic, rather than only economic or physical.[51] Agency-specific legislation, beginning in the 1970s, has often authorized any person to sue administrators for taking unauthorized action or for failing to perform nondiscretionary duties (such as those mandated by law). And in the liberalization period, the courts often found an implied, even if not statutory, right to redress.

The role of private attorneys general has been assumed by a number of old and new organizations and by private attorneys. The National Association for the Advancement of Colored People and the American Civil Liberties Union long ago discovered the value of lawsuits to establish and protect constitutional rights, whether administrative actions or legislative enactments. Other action groups have sprung up or have shifted to the lawsuit strategy. Illustrative are the Ralph Nader organizations, Consumers Union, the Natural Resources Defense Council, the Environmental Defense Fund, and the Sierra Club. Apart from such major organizations, local and ad hoc sets of people have won the right to challenge administrative agencies' actions. The Federal Power Commission was sued by the Scenic Hudson Preservation Conference (which the commission characterized as "birdwatchers, nature fakers, and militant enemies of progress") over the agency's licensing of the Storm King power plant on the Hudson River. A group of George Washington University Law School students was granted standing to challenge an Interstate Commerce Commission decision raising freight rates; the rise, they claimed, would discourage shipment of recyclable goods and result in more timber cutting and more environmental pollution, some of it in the Washington-area national parks that the students used.

In the later 1970s and in the 1980s, however, the Supreme Court narrowed the scope of standing to sue, looking to specific statutes for authorization of suits by individuals or groups "indirectly" affected by agency actions under those statutes.

Tort Liability of Governments and Officials. A tort action is a civil suit seeking money damages for harm allegedly done to the plaintiff by the defendant.[52] The majority of tort actions in America arise out of automobile accidents.[53] They also are used extensively against manufacturers of products claimed to be dangerous or health impairing and against employers of workers exposed to conditions hazardous to life or health. From 1976 to 1986, asbestos suits accounted for 60 percent of the growth in product-liability tort cases in federal courts.[54] Product-liability and working-condition suits supplement or substitute for governments' direct regulation.

The tort liability of governments and their officials has evolved through a tangled history and will continue to evolve.[55] Simplistically summarized, the federal and state governments cannot be sued for torts without their consent ("The king can do no wrong"), but their officials and employees can be sued. Many qualifications apply to such a statement. The doctrines governing liability of officials apply not only to those in the usual regulatory fields but to those outside them as well. Schoolteachers, policemen, and FBI and narcotics agents are frequent targets of tort suits.

Governments can waive their sovereign immunity by consenting to be sued. The Federal Torts Claims Act of 1946 provided a partial waiver, permitting a damage suit against the government for personal injury, death, or property damage caused by the "negligent or wrongful act or omission" of any federal employee acting within the scope of his or her employment.[56] The statutory qualifications and exceptions severely narrow this apparent waiver. Most notably, the government is not liable for an act or omission when the government employee is "exercising due care, in the execution of a statute or regulation, whether or not such statute or regulation be valid," or when he or she is performing or failing to perform "a discretionary function or duty on the part of a federal agency or an employee . . . whether or not the discretion involved be abused."[57]

In the 1960s, courts accorded federal officials absolute immunity from tort actions when performing duties committed by law to their control or supervision.[58] In the 1970s, the Supreme Court made a sharp turn by holding officials liable for violation of constitutional rights if they knew or reasonably should have known that they were violating them.[59] It is presumed that an official should know the rights protected by the Constitution. The presumption has been criticized on grounds that every such right has been and continues to be interpreted through court decisions, which an official cannot be expected to have mastered. In 1988, the Supreme Court held that federal employees could be held personally liable for damages caused by negligent performance or omission of nondiscretionary conduct (as, in this case, negligence in handling and storing hazardous material). Congress responded by passing a statute that makes the government, rather than the employee, the defendant in such suits.[60]

State governments, under the Eleventh Amendment, are immune from damage suits in federal courts. Local governments are not immune. State and local officials are liable under an 1871 Act that provided, "Every person who, under color of any statute [or] regulation . . . of any State, subjects . . . any citizen . . . to the deprivation of any rights, privileges, or immunities secured by the Constitution and laws, shall be liable to the party injured in an action at law."[61] The provision is known as Section 1983 (from its location in the U.S. Code). From 1961 on, the federal courts experienced a great increase in Section 1983 tort actions, consistently with the Supreme Court's narrowing of officials' defenses. The principal defense is now lack of knowledge or presumptive knowledge of relevant provisions of the Constitution and laws.

Tort law's evolution cannot be understood without awareness of the dilemma expressed in many court opinions. On the one hand are citizens' rights to receive monetary compensation for damages done them by over-zealous, negligent, or malicious government officials and employees, plus the virtue of deterrence that such court victories will exert on other "bu-reaucrats." On the other hand is the need for prompt and effective adminis-trative action in executing laws and regulations, a need that entails a con-siderable scope for discretionary judgment. The deterrent effect, a virtue as some see it, also invites officials to avoid risks and even disobey superiors' orders (for such orders are no shield against personal liability). The result, then, could be a serious debilitation of the administrative system and of its responsibility for achieving legislative objectives. The solution, it appears, is abandonment of the immunity of governments for torts and the substantial freeing of officials and employees from personal liability. That, though, im-plies that agencies will have administrative systems strong enough to con-trol the behavior of subordinate officials and employees. Readers of this book may have doubts about attainment of this rigorous a disciplinary en-vironment, given the long hierarchical distance between agency heads and "street-level bureaucrats"[62] and the need for delegation of discretionary powers.

Costs of Litigation. The professional talent for pursuing cases in the public interest has been provided by private attorneys, acting alone or in groups, as well as by attorneys on the staffs of major organizations. Social conscience and a tradition of legal aid for the poor are incentives for law-yers. But few lawyers can afford to be without professional incomes. There-fore, a critical condition for maintenance of public-interest law is money to cover plaintiffs' legal expenses. In 1975, the Supreme Court ruled that fed-eral courts could not award attorneys' fees to successful public-interest plaintiffs (at the expense of the defendants) unless this was authorized by the statute under which the suit was brought. Some statutes, especially civil rights and environmental ones, do permit such fee recovery, but they gener-ally call for "appropriate amounts." Since 1980, the Equal Access to Justice Act authorizes courts to award "reasonable fees and expenses of attorneys" who win suits for individuals, corporations, or organizations of modest net worth, or with few employees, or with tax-exempt status as nonprofits.[63] The fees are to be based on prevailing market rates but may not exceed $75 per hour unless the court finds a higher fee justified by increase in the cost of living or by the limited availability of qualified attorneys for the suit. This leaves the courts with considerable discretion. One standard might be the prevailing levels in the community (often $150 to $200 an hour), without a statutory ceiling. In the late 1980s, however, the Reagan Justice Department and some judges moved toward restrictive awards; the Justice Department proposed that fees be the equivalent of its own staff attorneys' salaries (though private attorneys pay for secretaries, office supplies, and other overhead expenses, as civil servants do not, and though civil servants' salaries are well below those in the private sector).[64] The movement continued in the 1990s with further efforts to limit damages.

Systems and Values

More fundamental than details of judicial oversight of regulatory agencies are the contrasts between the judicial and administrative systems and the clash of values between individual rights and the urgency of achieving public policy objectives.

The Judicial and Administrative Systems. In regulatory administration, courts and agencies make strange partners. The two institutions have different traditions and are staffed with dissimilar kinds of people.[65] Courts are passive, depending on parties to bring cases before them. Because of that and because their jurisdiction is broad, they hear in sequence cases that have no discernible connection, many of them unrelated to governmental regulation. With few exceptions (the federal district and appeals courts in the District of Columbia), they can claim expertness neither in regulation generally nor in particular regulatory programs. The judges lack expert supporting staffs, and instead rely on evidence and analysis offered by lawyers for the two sides.

The most significant characteristic of judicial involvement in the regulatory field is a court's focus on the single case before it. The issue is the reasonableness of a single agency decision that was made at a single point in time and affected a single individual, corporation, or group. True, the issue of reasonableness is placed in a setting of legal doctrine and precedents. But how the particular agency decision fits in the agency's full responsibility for achieving program objectives with limited funds and staff is largely ignored. Instead, a court may require budgetary and staff emphasis on the program in the case before it, without considering that this subtracts from the resources supporting an agency's other programs.

Most agencies are active, initiating the achievement of public objectives by developing an agenda of priorities that balances their resources against relative opportunities for a significant impact. They make decisions through time, linking each one with others in an effort to assure coherence both in technical foundations and in program effectiveness. With that agenda and continuity of focus their staffs engage in fact gathering, analysis, and consultation of interested persons and organizations, all as a basis for the issuance or nonissuance of regulatory rules and orders. In sharp contrast to the courts, agencies specialize in their assigned subjects and have career staffs expert in economics, science, and engineering, as well as law. Except for agency lawyers, the judges and agency staff members march to different drummers.[66] It would be a wonder if the two sides kept in step.

The recent trend appears to be toward mutual accommodation.[67] Two strong thrusts have characterized the accommodation. First, the courts have pressed the agencies to widen the participation of interested citizens and groups in the formulation of rules,[68] and, though less clearly, have widened access to the courts for such interested parties. Second, the courts have tended to "make law," attributing intentions to Congress that are not apparent in the language of statutes.[69] The agencies tend to regard these thrusts as helpful. Increased participation favored environmental and other "public interest" groups whose efforts supported the agencies' missions. And in giving statutory weight to program activities not clearly specified in statutes the courts expanded the jurisdictions of the agencies. Shep Melnick reports, "While complaining about some decisions, EPA officials generally credit the courts with improving the agency's competence and programs."[70] Reconciliation of the two systems has also advanced because of what Jerry Mashaw characterizes as the Supreme Court's "significant retrenchment from its procedurally interventionist posture in the early 1970s."[71]

Values: Conflict or Harmony? Essentially, three values are involved in regulatory administration: procedural fairness, substantive correctness of decisions, and achievement of public policy goals. No dissent is likely to the proposition that the process leading up to agency issuance (or nonissuance) of a rule or individual order should be fair. It is tempting for courts to say, "Why can't administrative agencies be more like us?" The question applies principally to agencies' adjudicative procedures, though courts have had this wish in mind too in imposing requirements on the making of general rules despite its classic analogy to legislative, rather than judicial, procedure. For agency adjudication, the APA and many agency-specific statutes, as we have seen, support the courts' view, requiring notice, oral hearings, and cross-examination of witnesses. To be sure, these are less rigorous than in ordinary court cases. Nonetheless, they are enough alike that lawyers play the leading roles, paperwork mounts, and tactics of delay are practiced by companies facing regulatory action.

The second value is not procedural, but substantive: the correctness of the decision reached. Theoretically, what our system should assure is a "correct" decision, and if the agency does not make one, the court should.

But neither agency nor court can assure that its decision is correct, particularly in matters plagued by scientific and technological uncertainties. In both the agency subsystem and the court system there are opportunities for appeal to higher levels. But even in the judicial branch there is no certainty that the highest court's decision is correct. At best, then, the objective is to limit error to a low, but not zero, tolerance level. Judges' self-restraint, reinforced by deference to agency expertise, permits agency discretion to operate in accord with this objective.

In the judicial system itself, the determination of what conclusion the evidence warrants is left to lay juries or trial-court judges (with exceptions to be noted). A basic distinction is made between questions of fact and questions of law. In jury trials, the jury decides questions of fact and the judge determines questions of law. In appellate cases, the appeals court respects the trial court's findings of fact and decides only contested points of law. If these models were followed in regulatory affairs, an agency might be analogized to a trial court jury or, when appeals are made directly from the agency to a federal court of appeals (as many are), the agency might be treated as a trial court is. That is, the agency's findings of fact would be unreviewable. But that leaves questions of law, and here complications arise.

Many issues turn out to be such a mixture of fact and law that a court cannot decide the legal question without also deciding a factual question. Courts have historically often capitalized on this by substituting their judgment for that of lower courts, treating as a question of law whether the evidence was sufficient to support the lower decision. Their doctrines have varied on whether they were merely looking to determine if there was *substantial* evidence on the winning side to warrant the decision or they were completely second-guessing the lower court by *weighing* the evidence on both sides. In the latter situation, disagreement about the preponderance of evidence sufficed to warrant overturning of the lower decision. In reviewing agency decisions, the courts have applied the substantial-evidence test, but they take "a hard look" and, in the case of agency adjudication, look at the whole record (as the APA requires) rather than at just the parts on the winning side.

The third value is achievement of public policy objectives. Here lurks a danger that two very different institutions—judicial and administrative—will find their traditional modes of operation at loggerheads. Excessive formalization of procedure can tie administrative regulation in knots, causing delay, absorbing budgetary and staff resources, increasing red tape, and inviting passivity in agency pursuit of policy goals. Some agencies react to the risk of judicial reversal by adopting even more cumbersome procedures than courts are likely to demand. Some seek to demonstrate the substantial-ity of evidence for a decision with massive accumulations of documents. Even in rulemaking, the courts' insistence that an agency respond to every "significant" objection filed by individuals, groups, and companies imposes a burden likely to be exaggerated by agencies' uncertainty as to which objections the courts might think "significant." Meantime, the agency is charged by Congress with implementing programs fully and expeditiously, an assignment whose shortfalls expose the agency to congressional retribution.

The tasks of some agencies are enormous, their very size making fully courtlike procedures inappropriate. An extreme example lies outside the regulatory field. Initial claims for disability benefits from the Social Security Administration number over a million per year. In a typical year 250,000 denials of initial benefits were appealed for reconsideration, denials at this stage led to 150,000 requests for hearings before administrative law judges, 25,000 were then appealed to the Appeals Council, and 10,000 cases were taken to federal district courts.[72] The SSA figures alone are comparable to the total load of the federal judicial system, where in 1987 district courts acted on 279,000 cases, courts of appeals on 36,000, and the Supreme Court on 4,340.[73]

The three values—fair procedures, sound decisions, and policy achievement—are both interlinked and in conflict. What is important is to avoid lifting any one to absolute status, though each invites such treatment. Fairness in regulatory procedure may be enough to obviate the need for independent court review of the correctness of the decision reached. Relaxation of claims that regulatory procedure must substantially mimic that of courts may suffice to enable effective implementation of policy objectives. The formula under which the values are reconciled has come to be the doctrine of court deferral to agencies' expertness. This is not an ideal formula, for courts will differ on how much deferral is appropriate, how expert particular agencies are, and whether a particular decision rests substantially on expertness rather than on other considerations. In these circumstances it is no wonder that judicial doctrines on regulatory matters continue to evolve and reflect changing patterns of judicial appointments.

Presidential Regulation of the Regulators

Presidents seek to control regulatory agencies, insisting that they are part of the executive branch and as such must be accountable to the president. Otherwise, goes the argument, their policymaking, via rules and regulations under broad delegations from Congress, would flout the democratic system of our government. The argument rests on three concepts: the need for coordination lest agencies contradict or duplicate one another; the need for consistency with the president's policy agenda; and the need for economy and efficiency, responsibilities of the president as chief administrator. These concepts are all familiar from earlier chapters of this book.

A few elements of the existing pattern are clear. The president's case has greater bearing on fully executive branch agencies—departments and their bureaus—than on the ambiguously situated independent regulatory commissions. Over both groups the president has powers to appoint top officials, to set budgetary estimates in his annual budget proposal, and to set personnel ceilings on their staffs' size. In the fully executive branch agencies, he can remove top officials. These powers might seem sufficient to give leverage over regulatory zeal or feebleness.[74] But presidents seek greater influence on specific regulatory decisions. Presidential initiatives for such detailed control have focused on executive branch agencies, whose tasks are social regulation, generally exempting the commissions, most of whom are engaged in economic regulation.

The focus is on rulemaking. A president who directly or through immediate aides sought to intervene in an agency's adjudicative decision making would provoke an outcry politically negating any gain sought. Indeed, even intervention in rulemaking arouses controversy, particularly if it amounts to an effort to ignore program-specific statutory instructions to the agency or to negate the APA's and courts' procedural standards for rulemaking.

The Review System

The Nixon, Ford, Carter, Bush, and Clinton administrations all established processes for central review of agencies' proposed significant regulations and required agencies to prepare analyses of their impact. Yet the processes vested no power in central authorities to interfere with an agency's discretion in reaching a decision. The Reagan administration went much further. Its executive orders, effective until changed, require, first, that agencies prepare and submit to OMB for review a cost-benefit analysis on each proposed major rule and, to the extent permitted by law, not act unless benefits exceed costs to society, net benefits are at a maximum, and among alternative approaches the one with the least net cost to society is chosen. No agency may publish a notice of proposed rulemaking until OMB review is concluded, nor may it publish a final rule until the OMB director has communicated any views and the agency has responded. Second, they require each agency annually to prepare and submit to OMB a regulatory program detailing every significant agency regulatory action (later defined as a "rule") "planned or underway," explaining, among other things, how they are consistent "with the Administration's policies and priorities." Any proposed regulatory action not included in the earlier regulatory program or materially different from an action described in that program must be submitted to the OMB for review and, except for cases of statutory or judicial deadlines and emergency situations, must be deferred until completion of that review. In the case of both the regulatory program and proposed actions later contemplated, the OMB director may return agency submissions for reconsideration.[75]

The "regulatory management" process thus established provoked much friction.[76] The OMB gained review authority not only over the final stages of rulemaking but as well over such early stages as initiation of research studies meant to contribute to agency consideration of whether or not to start rulemaking proceedings.[77] Delays of months and years characterized some reviews. The small review staff, in the OMB's Office of Information and Regulatory Affairs, consisted of persons trained in economics, business administration, and law, often young and with scant prior knowledge of the agency programs they oversaw. Understandably, agencies' expert staffs chafed at the sometimes nitpicking objections and the revisions imposed. The OMB consulted industry representatives (a practice sharply reduced by the Bush administration) and communicated with agency officials, often by telephone, without such contacts or their substance being reflected in the rulemaking record. And, because of the deregulatory policy of the president, some abandonments, delays, and revisions of proposed rules displaced the agencies' informed and preferred use of their congressionally mandated responsibilities.[78]

Despite the defects in practice under the Reagan administration, the major independent study of the system recommends "that regulatory management be accepted as an essential element of presidential management, within such limits and with such exceptions as may be established by law." The study panel proposed that "Congress establish by law the basic elements of the regulatory management system,"[79] including "decision rules" (such as how costs and benefits would be identified and evaluated) and decide, agency by agency, whether independent regulatory commissions should be included in the process.[80] The movement led to new proposals, by congressional Republicans in particular, to subject proposed rules to benefit-cost regulation. That, they hoped, would slow the flood of regulations.

Conclusion

The regulation of the behavior of private individuals and corporations to protect others from harm is a central responsibility of government. Its scope and methods are disputed issues of public policy. However those issues are resolved, there is no doubt that some discretion must be vested in regulatory agencies and that discretion is subject to abuse. Legislatures, courts, and chief executives all seek to reduce opportunities for such abuse. Yet, in using this control authority, they often seek to advance their own policy preferences or to impose regulatory procedures that, intentionally or not, impede regulatory effectiveness.

The balance between effective and ineffective regulation shifts from time to time, largely reflecting public opinion, elections, and appointments and attitudes of administrators and judges. As we move toward 2000, signs of a shift toward effective regulation are visible, most clearly in the field of environmental protection and workers' health and safety. Yet signs of success have scarcely protected regulatory agencies from political attack. They suffered some of the biggest cuts by congressional Republicans in 1995.

Administrative discretion is tolerable only when not misused, and there lies a major problem. One student of the legal aspects of public administration puts it this way: "Just how we ensure that the public interest is served and that administrative power is not abused is the problem of administrative responsibility. . . . [While] the formal legal constraints have received the most attention . . . there is a risk that excessive concern with avoiding suits will cause us to ignore many aspects of the responsibility question of equal or greater significance."[81] We address those ignored aspects in the final chapter.

14

Conclusion

We return to the theme of bureaucratic responsibility stated at the outset of this book. Nothing is more basic in a constitutional, democratic system. But how such responsibility is to be defined and how it is to be achieved are more problematic than glib rhetoric indicates. "Bureaucrat bashing" achieves nothing but officials' resentment, demoralization, and reluctance to take initiatives. Demands by "experts" in the bureaucracy to act on their own views of what is best for their segments of public policy do not fit our understanding of the democratic system. Finding the proper balance is not easy.

Bureaucratic responsibility has two elements. One is accountability: faithful obedience to the law, to higher officials' directions, and to standards of efficiency and economy. The other is ethical behavior: adherence to moral standards and avoidance even of the *appearance* of unethical actions. The two elements overlap and are generally compatible, but not always. Morality may call for disobedience to superiors or reporting of superiors' unethical behavior to *their* superiors, to legislators, or to the public. So differences between bureaucratic accountability of the usual type and bureaucratic ethics becloud our undertaking.

The problem we face has troubled the American republic since the beginning. Alexander Hamilton chose a notorious speculator to be second in command at the Treasury Department. The $200,000 he appropriated for his private use was never repaid.[1]

Bureaucratic Accountability

A constitutional system of government entails the subordination of bureaucrats to mandates and constraints of the Constitution and laws, as interpreted by the courts, and to hierarchical superiors in the executive branch. A democratic system of government entails the subordination of bureaucrats to the people and their elected representatives, both legislative and executive. Indisputable though these propositions are, their elaboration in theory and their realization in practice are beset with difficulties. Bureaucratic accountability has engaged our attention at many points in this book, especially in the chapters on legislative and judicial control.

Theoretical Approaches

The problem has been formulated at the theoretical level in a variety of ways. One is the legal-formal doctrine we stated in chapter 1: Bureaucrats' authority is delegated authority, delegated by the legislative body and/or the chief executive to agency heads and by them through the hierarchy to subunits and their employees. In this approach "the emphasis falls on the strict obedience of the individual bureaucrat to hierarchy, the orders of superiors, and the explicit laws, regulations, and procedures that these superiors and other legitimate political authorities establish."[2] Though this formula needs elaboration to embrace real-world conditions, it is the most basic way of relating administration to the constitutional, democratic system.

A second approach is to see democracy and efficiency as two values that are in conflict.[3] Democracy has been defended not as the most efficient system but as the only way for the people to rule, using the majority principle (coupled with minority rights, including those protecting a minority's efforts to become the majority). Absent strong party discipline, policy decisions emerge from an untidy process of interest-group pressures, shifting legislative coalitions, responsiveness to legislators' particularistic desires to accommodate their electoral constituencies, and the president's (and his appointees') attentiveness to the groups electing him and his party's legislators. Advocacy and compromise are the hallmarks of the political process. Administration, in contrast, has aspired to efficiency. The merit system of staffing, the rise of professions with expert knowledge, and the complexity of fields now engaged in by government all reinforce the capability and the need for efficiency. Indeed, administrative efficiency is popularly demanded, its absence a ground for claiming frustration of democratically enacted policies. Given the contrasting values of democracy and efficiency, together with the strikingly different skills and incentives of persons on both sides of the fence, reconciliation seems remote.

A third approach takes into account the first two approaches and seeks reconciliation by way of a mutual dependency in which each side has resources that the other seeks.[4] For example, as we saw in chapter 9, bureaucrats have a superior amount of information about their programs, processes, and results, and those seeking to control bureaucracies need information of this kind in order to pursue an effective strategy of intervention. Bureaucrats otherwise disposed to withhold information can be induced to share it because they gain something: well-informed controllers will be less likely to make disruptive and misguided interventions.[5] In sum, an exchange relation, not unlike a market, exists between administrators and their controllers.

Two other approaches downplay the control problem. One emphasizes the representativeness of the people making up the bureaucracy.[6] As we saw in chapter 8, the American higher public service is a representative elite; the occupations of its members' fathers substantially match those of fathers of members of Congress. More broadly, the whole civil service is highly representative of the American population in terms of class origins and other characteristics. On this basis it can be argued that a representative bureaucracy presents no threat to democracy and, in fact, can be vested with substantial discretion.

The other approach that lessens concern about controls emphasizes the fragmentation of the bureaucracy. We have many bureaucracies, not a single, comprehensive bureaucracy. Agencies' jurisdictions overlap, agencies are alert to opportunities to take the initiative when others fail to act; they are active resisters to trespass by sister agencies; significant decisions require clearance procedures both among agencies and among a single agency's bureaus and specialized staffs. Even at the elite level, the Senior Executive Service is not a single corps of administrators but a loose assemblage of agency-based officials. Groups of career employees within a single agency may go public with attacks on political heads' departures from norms treasured by the careerists. For example, in 1982, over a hundred lawyers in the Justice Department's civil rights division signed a letter that attacked the department's asking the Supreme Court to let racially discriminating private schools get the same tax exemption given other educational institutions; and in 1989, about fifty career lawyers criticized the department's urging the Court to reverse its abortion-right decision.[7] Competition among agencies, their subordinate units, and distinctive sets of officials, it is argued, provides an in-built protection against ill-considered administrative actions.

Experience, however, teaches that neither a representative nor a fragmented bureaucracy obviates the need for a system of bureaucratic accountability to external controllers.

Complications

Theorists commonly hypothecate *a* controller and *a* bureaucrat or agency. But that is not what American government offers. Controllers are many.

Congress, the president, and the judiciary are all controllers. Each, in turn, branches out into components and appendages. So, too, bureaucrats and agencies are many. Controls appropriate for one may not be appropriate for others.

Congress is the House of Representatives and the Senate, whose dynamics sharply contrast. Each does much of its work, including "oversight" (i.e., control), through committees and subcommittees. Each is aided in control work by congressional staff and by institutions such as the General Accounting Office. Individual senators and representatives engage extensively in "casework," intervening in agencies on behalf of individual constituents who have sought such help. All these actors proceed largely independently of one another in control activities—in contrast to the joint efforts required for enactment of legislation.[8]

The president is one man, but his efforts to control the bureaucracy must largely be delegated to others—his White House staff, the Office of Management and Budget, and his political appointees in the departments and agencies. Hierarchy produces a tidier universe than that in Congress, but disagreements among his controllers may confuse control efforts, as when OMB and an agency's political head come into conflict.

The judiciary consists of many parts, all with control responsibilities when invoked. It, too, has the neatness of a hierarchy, but this can be misleading, certainly in the short run. Federal district courts may decide similar cases differently, often involving the same agency and statute; so may courts of appeal. If a case in this set reaches the Supreme Court, the differences may be resolved, but pending such an outcome, an agency may face different control mandates from different courts in different areas of the country.

The multiplicity of controllers and controls vastly complicates the task of assuring effective control of bureaucracy. Conflicting mandates from different controllers force bureaucrats to make choices without authoritative guidance. When the president and Congress or one of its houses are of different parties, which is most of the time, the priorities pressed on agencies are bound to differ.[9] Similarly, and of great importance, legislative mandates unsupported by adequate appropriations force bureaucrats to fail to execute the law faithfully, as they must choose which mandates to obey fully, which to follow at low speed, and which to neglect. Both conflicting mandates and underfinanced mandates invite bureaucrats to use their own discretion without clear guidance—the very phenomenon that control is intended to avoid.

Agencies' differences introduce further complications. We have seen that agencies have different cultures. Judith Gruber has proposed that major differences in agencies' technologies and external environments indicate whether control should focus on agency procedures or on the substance of agency decisions, whether dense control would unduly shrink an agency's needed flexibility, and whether controllers are likely to issue contradictory restraints.[10] Different kinds of tasks also pose different risks.

The fact is that administration suffers as much from a very elaborate set of controls as from an inadequacy of controls to identify and correct significant deviations from sound practice. Effective execution of policies and programs requires room for administrative discretion, else strict conformity to red-tape requirements displaces positive efforts to achieve policy and program objectives.[11]

Control Systems

Control can be both positive and negative. Legislative and judicial attention to rules not issued or programs not begun can energize a sluggish agency; other attention can constrain an overly exuberant one. Sins of omission as well as sins of commission are subject to investigation, criticism, instructions, and sanctions. The principal focus of control, though, is on discovering bureaucratic errors and requiring their correction—a largely negative approach. The negative note tends to become dominant for other reasons as well. First, sins of commission are more easily seen—and criticized—than sins of omission. Second, an external-control body (such as Congress) can more easily specify actions to be corrected than impose a strategy to be followed. Our discussion accordingly gives primary, though not exclusive, attention to the negative aspect of external control: the correction of bureaucratic behavior deemed by external controllers not to be in the public interest.

We could more easily solve the problem of control if we assumed that maximization of control is a desirable objective. Strict guidelines, carefully supervised, could give unambiguous guidelines to administrators. In fact, we would not want such control. Administrators in such a system would have to work in a pervasive climate of distrust, which would demoralize those on whom we depend for achievement of public programs. In many cases, moreover, sound administration requires the exercise of professional judgment. How likely is it that the drug thalidomide or the addition of cyclamates to food will cause deformities in humans?[12] How can a dangerous chemical dump best be cleaned?

Excessive controls can disrupt consistent administration and produce inequities. Excessive controls multiply requirements for review of proposed decisions, increase red tape, and delay action. So much energy can be spent attempting to control administrative activities, in fact, that little time or money is left to do the job at hand. Excessive controls, therefore, may dull administration's responsiveness to its public. Peter Self, a British scholar, has put it succinctly: "The tensions between the requirements of responsibility or 'accountability' and those of effective executive action can reasonably be described as *the* classic dilemma of public administration."[13]

Discretion is inevitable in administrative action, as we saw in earlier chapters. No legislature could ever specify all the factors that administrators must weigh in making decisions. Even if they could, the necessity of reaching legislative compromise typically produces vague, sometimes even conflicting, guidance. Not all circumstances are the same, and good administration requires adapting general policies to special needs. Hence, effective administration always entails discretion. Still, there must be controls to ensure that the legislative intent is met. Because controls are necessary, we must take stock of the elements of control, even though we know that external controls themselves are imperfect.[14]

Elements of Control. Systems of control have at least four elements: voluntary compliance, standard setting, monitoring, and sanctions.

The foundation of control is *voluntary compliance.* Even though people are not angels, most people most of the time voluntarily comply with most of the significant constraints on their behavior. They do so for a variety of reasons, ranging from moral standards, through indifferent acquiescence, to self-interest. Or, as Max Weber stressed, they do so because they believe in the legitimacy of the system of authority. Were it unrealistic to rely on substantial voluntary compliance, the scope and intensity of control systems would be unbearable.

Two purposes are served by *standard setting.* One is to inform individuals what behavior is expected; to put it negatively, individuals need to know what will be regarded as violations of expectations and, hence, subject to sanctions. The other purpose is to identify the appropriate concerns of control agencies—and to restrict them to these concerns, for control agencies themselves need to be controlled.

Some standards are obvious. Few people should need to be told that "stealing violates expectations," although petty crimes—from taking government office supplies home to misappropriating government photocopy machines to duplicate favorite recipes—are often epidemic. At the other extreme are standards so numerous and detailed that an individual cannot be expected to know all that apply to any given role. The process for paying contractors, for example, can occupy thick manuals. A front-line administrator is unlikely to consult the regulations and instead usually depends on people such as agency lawyers, procurement specialists, and masters of accounting regulations to raise a red flag about potential problems.

Observance of standards, however, can become mechanical and trivial. Nearly everyone has had experience in dealing with administrators so obsessed with the proper completion of forms and procedures that the basic mission of public service becomes lost. Standards can range from basic rules set in the Constitution and statutes, to codes of ethics that attempt to define precisely what integrity means. The key for administrators is to ensure that overattentiveness to details does not displace genuine dedication to their positive obligations as public servants.

Any system of control must have *monitoring* of whether the standards are met. Sometimes an administrator's intended action must be approved by superiors (including controllers) before it is effective. Sometimes such an action must "incubate," that is, lie in a congressional committee for, say, sixty days before it becomes final; meantime, committee members may (or may not) seek to persuade the agency to abort the action. Other forms of monitoring call for reviewing actions already completed. For example, monitors often conduct postaudits of financial transactions and review the error rate in payments to welfare clients. The auditors can criticize any improprieties found and demand that the administrative agency mend its ways in the future. External-control systems are largely based on this retrospective approach; they review actions taken in the past and seek to alter future behavior.

Monitoring may be comprehensive or selective.[15] It is tempting to believe that all errors should be identified and, if possible, corrected. Sometimes, however, monitoring can cost more (in money, in time, in focus on trivia, and in morale of those monitored) than the money saved. Administrators thus use selective monitoring of three kinds. The first is reactive: monitors investigate complaints (by citizens, members of the press, congressional committees, or employees) about mismanagement or illegal actions, such as bribery or fraudulent claims.[16] The second is sampling—examining, say, every fifth case or examining all of an agency's units' cases in one out of five years. The objective naturally shifts from correction of individual errors to identification of those agencies or units that have so poor a *pattern* of actions that a systemic change is needed. The third kind of selection calls for concentrated monitoring of those agencies, programs, or sets of officials most prone to illegal or otherwise deviant behavior. The awarding of government contracts is one such field. The granting, withholding, suspension, and termination of licenses constitute another. Within such broad fields, intensive attention may be given those particular settings where government officials must frequently deal with types of private citizens, business firms, or labor organizations notorious for earthy rather than ethical habits of behavior. Risk of abuse of discretion also characterizes the work of inspectors (of buildings, factories, mines, restaurants, etc.). As with "street-level bureaucrats" (policemen, social workers, et al.), effective control is problematic.[17]

Finally, a control system needs *sanctions* or it will lose its credibility. The problems, though, are substantial. Often the punishment may not fit the crime. The delicate task is to devise sanctions strong enough to be taken seriously by administrators but not so strong as to disrupt an agency's mission, so strong as never to be invoked, or so strong as to require rarely met standards of proof. These problems all plague enforcement of federal ethics laws.[18]

If a federal agency or one of its officials offends Congress, and Congress responds with a sharp budget cut, important public services may be curtailed. In contrast, available sanctions may be too mild, too slowly applied, or misdirected to serve as adequate punishment or deterrent. An agency may simply ignore a legislative investigation whose only product is a critical report. Higher officials may escape punishment for having encouraged (but not explicitly commanded) behavior by subordinates subjected to criminal prosecution; the irony is that a subordinate, such as Oliver North of the NSC staff, may escape conviction on major charges because, it seems, a jury concluded he was doing what his superiors wanted.[19]

Interrelations. The control system of a large organization in fact embraces many different control systems. Their interrelations present troublesome problems at both the analytical and the practical levels. We consider first the relations between external and internal controls and then the relations among external controls themselves.

The more effective an agency's system of internal control, the less external control is needed. Nevertheless, agencies can sometimes use a highly developed internal-control system to resist external control. It can not only justify relaxation of external controls but also can suppress or distort information desired by external-control agencies. An agency with a tight control system may be tempted to discipline any public-spirited, "whistleblowing" employee who reports agency improprieties to a congressional committee, government auditors, or the press. In the Defense Department, for example, A. Ernest Fitzgerald waged a battle against his Pentagon superiors for more than a decade. In 1969, he charged at a congressional hearing that the air force had underestimated the cost of its new C-5A jet transport by half. President Nixon responded, "I want that sonofabitch fired," and the Pentagon eventually obliged. Fitzgerald battled for years to regain his job, and the federal courts finally ordered him reinstated during the Reagan administration.[20]

Whistleblowing, it should be understood, has two manifestations: (1) it may be used by an employee genuinely motivated to expose wrongdoing, or (2) it may be used maliciously and groundlessly by an employee to embarrass a superior against whom he or she has a grudge, or even to protect against a warranted personnel action—such as dismissal, low performance rating, or disallowance of promotion or a salary increase—by alleging the action is really reprisal for whistleblowing. In the Whistleblower Protection Act of 1989, Congress concluded that the balance should be so struck as to encourage and protect whistleblowers.[21] It made the Office of Special Counsel (previously attached to the Merit Systems Protection Board) a distinct agency whose primary role, it says, "is to protect employees, especially whistleblowers, from prohibited personnel practices." The special counsel has two primary functions. One is to pursue investigation by his office and by the relevant agency of any information an employee "reasonably believes evidences a violation of any law, rule, or regulation; or ... gross mismanagement, a gross waste of funds, an abuse of authority, or a substantial and specific danger to public health or safety." The second function, shared partly with the Merit Systems Protection Board, is to protect any whistleblower who has been or is likely to be punished by an agency's personnel action for his disclosure of agency error. The burden is put on the agency to counter a whistleblower's allegation of such treatment. Corrective action may be ordered "if the Special Counsel has demonstrated that a disclosure ... was a contributing factor in the personnel action which was taken" unless "the agency demonstrates by clear and convincing evidence that it would have taken the same personnel action in the absence of such disclosure." The substantial gap between "a contributing factor" and "clear and convincing evidence" works to the whistleblower's advantage. Despite these efforts, whistleblowers continue to have difficulty with the system. Although the share of federal employees willing to report problems had increased, so too did the number of employees reporting reprisals or threats of reprisals for identifying problems.[22] In fact, many whistleblowers are frustrated with the process.[23]

The external-internal distinction can be an overly mechanical one. No external-control agency can replace an agency's own *internal* controls. Moreover, external-control systems often depend on information collected by an agency's own internal system, illustrated best by the work of the inspectors general established by statute and appointed by the president in twenty-six departments and agencies.[24] Their audits and investigative reports go to Congress as well as to their agency heads. Finally, both external and internal controllers often share the same kinds of employees (such as accountants, lawyers, or personnel specialists); the professional goals and values they share create common bonds that sometimes encourage but sometimes restrain harsh investigation. Internal and external controllers can become mutually supportive, enmeshed in a network whose communication lines facilitate cooperation.

How can we ensure that the external controllers will do their job vigorously and pursue their mission uncorrupted? How can we guarantee that they will not try to transform their power into improper dominance over those they control? And how can we make sure that the multiple external controllers do not send conflicting messages? The Roman satirist Juvenal asked the pivotal question two millennia ago: "Who is to watch the watchers?"[25] The American setting presents two partial answers. One is *independence*, making each control agency autonomous and insulated from those individuals and forces that might corrupt or restrain it. The other is *redundancy*, multiplying the control agencies and giving them overlapping functions.

Independence is a favorite prescription for assuring integrity, or at least for protecting it from the pressures of those who might seek to compromise it. By design, the legislative and judicial branches, both major instruments for controlling administration, are constitutionally separate from the executive branch. By statutory provision, the General Accounting Office, Congress's principal control agency, is "independent of the executive departments."

The situation is not so clear with executive agencies that perform control functions over other agencies and their officials and employees. The attorney general is responsible for enforcing the laws by criminal prosecutions and civil suits. But the attorney general and other top officials in the Justice Department are political appointees, and the attorney general is often a political intimate and adviser of the president. During the 1987 investigation of the Reagan administration's secret aid to the *contras* in Nicaragua, members of Congress suggested that Attorney General Edwin Meese's long friendship with the president created a conflict of interest that prevented him from investigating the case energetically enough.

Similar problems arose during the Watergate scandals in the early 1970s; in fact, Nixon's attorney general was among those eventually convicted. Congress in 1978 created procedures for a court to appoint from time to time a special prosecutor, later renamed "independent counsel," to investigate charges against high governmental officials.

Redundancy, a more sophisticated prescription than independence, promises safety in numbers and overlapping jurisdictions.[26] Although one control agency may become corrupt or ineffectual, several control agencies with overlapping functions increase the probability that problems will be detected and solved. If one agency flags in effort, another may move into the neglected areas. This is more important when a long term of office or other insulation from outside pressure precludes early invigoration of the laggard control agency. Furthermore, competition among control agencies may itself stimulate alertness and vigor in all of them.

Redundancy, however, is not without problems. If several control agencies make conflicting demands, a department's confused effort to comply with them all may reduce not only performance but control.[27] Yet, when any of several control agencies might assume jurisdiction over an especially troublesome case, each may await another's move—and in the end, nothing may happen. Redundancy can be an illusory protection if the several control agencies are responsive to the same superior; watchdogs might all stop barking at their common master's command. Finally, redundancy has the one obvious cost: duplication of oversight is expensive, and at some point the costs overwhelm the advantages produced.

Control Objectives. While the elements of a control system are the same whatever the objectives sought, the techniques vary considerably. One useful distinction is among fiscal accountability, process accountability, and program accountability.[28] Fiscal accountability is the most traditional and, even today, the most pervasive. By studying the records of financial transactions, a controller can discover ordinary corruption, insist that expenditures be legally made, and ensure that the legislature maintain its power of the purse. Review of financial records is the key tool that investigators use in uncovering and prosecuting kickbacks in contracts and abuse of welfare programs. Following "the money trail" was a critical element in exposing both the Watergate and Iran-*contra* scandals.

Process accountability is concerned with *how* agencies perform their tasks. While the meanings of efficiency, economy, and procedural fairness are often disputed, most observers can recognize large disparities. Outcomes such as discrimination in government employment or waste in road construction will lead any careful observer to look for procedural irregularities and their cures.

Program accountability is the newest and most difficult objective of control systems. Government funds and procedures are merely means to ends, and efficiency is not the same as effectiveness. Program accountability focuses on results: Is the program achieving its legislatively defined purpose? Program analyses, like those produced by the General Accounting Office and similar oversight agencies at the state level, are designed to bring heat, as well as light, to bear on agencies that are ineffective. Standards, however, are elusive, for intended results are rarely clear and operating programs often have unanticipated consequences, some beneficial and some not. Furthermore, finding a way to measure agencies' achievement in relation to the resources at their disposal is often difficult.

Who Is to Be Controlled? A final complication is the variety of people and organizations on which control systems focus. "Control of the bureaucracy" is an oversimplification. The vast range of government by proxy extends the government bureaucracy into the private and nonprofit sectors, as we saw in chapter 11. The issue, of course, is not whether these proxies ought to produce responsive, efficient, and effective government services. Instead, the problem is how government officials can induce proxies to produce such results. Penetrating the complexities of these institutions is difficult. Congress cannot find its way through the confused array of state, local, private, and semiprivate implementers of its statutes (particularly as many such implementers are uncooperative with congressional inquiries). Federal auditors confront accounting systems ill designed to disentangle federally sponsored activities from private or distinctively local activities performed by the same organizations. The problems multiply themselves over again when state and local governments delegate tasks to proxies. Yet, as partnerships (federal-state-local and public-private) expand, the senior governmental partners need some kind of protection against the hazard of every partnership—that one partner may waste the assets of both.

Solution?

Clearly, our problem is not readily resolved. A possible escape starts with two elements: the legal-formal doctrine of accountability and the necessity of administrative discretion within the bounds of a modified version of the doctrine. Administrators would adhere to the original doctrine so far as that is possible. When the possibility of strict adherence is weakened by conflicting mandates or inadequate resources, administrators would (1) use their best judgment to discover the controllers' primary intent, and (2) consult with the controllers in an effort to resolve uncertainties about choices that need to be made among the mandates.[29]

This is no magic formula. Because controllers may be several, they may not agree on priorities an agency should observe. When a congressional statute conflicts with a president's desire to weaken its administration, an agency head, appointed by the president, must choose which to obey; to make the obvious choice, faithfully executing the law, may simply result in his or her displacement by an appointee more amenable to the president's wishes. When a court orders actions that divert an agency's funds from its other responsibilities, no recourse is normally possible.[30] And when an agency head seeks clarification of priorities among conflicting or under-financed legislative mandates, there is no "Congress" to be talked to, only a congressional committee or its chairman whose interpretation may not conform to the view of Congress as a whole.

The real-world situation, it turns out, leaves administrators responsible for resolving uncertainties that remain when a control system is in place. Their use of their discretion depends heavily on their internal compasses—a matter of character, devotion to the public service, and respect for faithful execution of the law. When serious conflict among controllers occurs, administrators face a conflict of loyalties and a choice of "voice" or "exit." If they choose voice, they remain in their positions fighting for their perception of which mandate should prevail (and they risk dismissal). If they choose exit, they resign, possibly with a public attack on the controller whose mandate they condemn.[31]

The qualities an administrator needs in order to exercise his discretion responsibly are personal qualities, reinforced often by socialization in the public service, the examples of peers, and the standards of his professional specialty. One vital quality is a regard for ethics. The government's efforts to assure ethical behavior is a further development of bureaucratic responsibility. Here, again, as was argued long ago, it is unclear how much can be accomplished by formal prescriptions and control mechanisms and how much must depend on what we have called "the inner compasses" of persons entrusted with public responsibilities.[32]

Ethics

The public service demands a higher standard of ethics than that prevailing in some of the occupations from which political appointees come.[33] As Calvin Mackenzie has written:

> At one time or another in their work lives, most business leaders have found jobs in their own companies for family members or friends, have entered into contracts with firms in which they had a financial interest, or have accepted substantial gifts from people with whom they regularly do business.... When public officials engage in similar activities, however, they break the law.[34]

That fact requires screening of prospective appointees, monitoring of their behavior in the government, and restricting of their activities after they leave the government. The Ethics in Government Act of 1978 was intended to incorporate such protective measures; it also established an Office of

Government Ethics, headed by a presidential appointee, and agency ethics officers to oversee the enforcement of the restrictions.[35]

Scandals in the 1980s, together with indications that overly strict requirements were deterring able persons from accepting government appointments, led to reform efforts. A 1988 bill passed by Congress was pocket-vetoed by President Reagan. One of President Bush's first acts was the appointment of a commission on ethics-law reform, whose recommendations he largely followed in a proposal to Congress.[36] The Ethics Reform Act of 1989 altered earlier requirements, but without significantly easing them.[37] The central problem remains: how to balance ethics-assuring measures against the need to attract talented persons to government service.

Screening Prospective Appointees

As president-elect, George Bush "heard about talented men and women who, though perfectly honest, declined to come to serve in government out of fear—fear of the sheer complexity of Federal ethics laws, fear that a simple, honest mistake could lead to a public nightmare."[38] The screening requirements of the 1989 act are among the most intimidating. The financial disclosure requirements apply to everyone at or above GS-16 or at comparable pay rates in the Executive Schedule, the Senior Executive Service, the Foreign Service, and other categories. Prospective appointees must fill out a financial disclosure report that a major study characterizes as "a pale, green monstrosity . . . a daunting, confusing, excessively detailed hurdle that few presidential appointees are able to negotiate successfully on the first attempt."[39] Each person must report his or her income for the preceding calendar year, including the amount and source of each item of $200 or more, except that each item of income from dividends, rents, interest, and capital gains is reported as in one of eight categories (not more than $1,000; $1,000 to $2,500; . . . over $1 million), rather than in exact amounts. Seven categories (starting with up to $15,000) apply to each purchase or sale of real estate, stocks, or bonds and to debts of over $1,000. Similarly property and investment assets (except for assets over which the appointee has no control) must be reported. The report must also include roughly comparable information on income and property transactions of spouses and dependent children. All this information is made available to the public, including news media.

These requirements add up to overkill in the effort to assure that an appointee's personal finances make improbable a potential conflict of interest. A $200 item of income or $1,000 of property is unlikely to affect an executive's decisions. And the intricate placing of income items and property holdings in each of a number of categories adds complexity without enhancing detection of the possibility of conflicts of interest.

Prospective appointees with investments deemed suspect on conflict-of-interest grounds have several options. They can sell such assets, paying large capital-gains taxes on the year's thus-swollen income. The Bush ethics commission reported, "Although divestiture of assets is the simplest, most direct, and most effective method of eliminating conflicts of interest, the tax burden attributable to capital gains on divested assets is a significant disincentive to divestiture. The tax laws are consequently a significant disincentive to the acceptance of high level policy-making positions in the government.[40] Two major alternatives to divestiture are to have assets in (or move assets into) a blind trust or a widely held investment fund.[41] The investment fund became an alternative in 1989. In its absence 32 percent of Reagan's first-term appointees had to sell stocks or other assets, and 12 percent created blind trusts.[42]

An appointee may avoid such major options by two methods. He or she may file a "recusal" statement promising not to participate in decisions affecting assets owned (e.g., stock in companies regulated by the agency). Among Reagan's first-term appointees 17 percent executed recusal statements.[43] Alternatively an appointee may request a waiver from the employing agency (e.g., because the investment is deemed too small to bias decision making).

Confusion is rife. Some appointees need prodding to rid themselves of assets, income, and corporate board memberships that suggest conflict of interest; this may result from recent tightening of standards, especially about avoidance of the appearance (as distinguished from the actuality) of a conflict. Others earnestly seeking to avoid such appearance go well beyond the law's requirements. Still others opt for recusal so broad as to cut them out of much of the decision making normally expected in their positions.

The FBI conducts a full field investigation of every person under consideration for presidential appointment; this typically involves over thirty interviews with friends, neighbors, and associates of the candidate, and takes from two to more than eight weeks. The focus is mostly on criminal law violations, national loyalty, drug use, sexual practices, and other behavior observed or heard about by those interviewed. The FBI reports merely its raw findings, gossip and all. Even so, disqualifying behaviors are missed. The delays could be reduced and the benefits of the process enhanced if greater resources were put into the operation, especially at peak appointments periods; if the focus were more on substantive qualifications for the particular positions; if findings were digested rather than served up raw; and if the scope of investigation varied with the importance of the positions.[44] Traditionally, the FBI reports were treated as secret, accessible only to the president and a few White House officials. In 1989, however, senators' pressure led the Bush administration to share with them the FBI's huge file on John G. Tower; its contents contributed to the Senate's refusal to confirm Tower's appointment as secretary of defense.

Monitoring On-the-Job Behavior

All higher executive branch officials must file financial-disclosure reports each year covering financial details of the previous calendar year. They are subject to review and challenge by agency ethics officers and by the Office of Government Ethics, though their reviews have sometimes been inadequate.[45]

All federal employees are forbidden to take any action that might result in or even create the appearance of (1) using public office for private gain; (2) giving preferential treatment to any person; (3) impeding government efficiency or economy; (4) losing complete independence or impartiality; (5) making a government decision outside official channels; or (6) affecting adversely the confidence of the public in the integrity of the government. Some violative actions are specified, and violators are subject to civil and criminal penalties (e.g., fines of $10,000 or two years in prison or both, for seeking or receiving bribes in return for being influenced in performance of any official act). Violations, however, need to be discovered and reported for enforcement to occur.

Some restrictions are galling to executive branch employees. None of an employee's meals, refreshments, travel, or entertainment may be paid for by anyone who is seeking official action from or doing business with the agency, or whose activities are regulated by the agency or may be substantially affected by the employee's performance or nonperformance of official duties. These are gifts and, so, forbidden. Though regulations may provide for reasonable exceptions, employees are confused about how to conduct their relations with their agency's clientele.[46] Given the gap between government employees' and business executives', private lawyers', and lobbyists' incomes, it seems that shared-cost meals must be in modest restaurants.

State and local governments vary in the extent of restrictive legislation and enforcement provisions, and in the prevalence of conflicts of interest. In an FBI "sting" operation, 105 of 106 offers of bribes to suspected municipal officials in the State of New York were accepted; the 106th was rejected as too small.[47] Elsewhere, locally elected officials with purchasing and contract-award authority can fall into a pattern of soliciting and accepting kickbacks from suppliers and contractors. In Oklahoma, federal courts convicted 175 of the 231 elected county officials for such practices, and in Mississippi a similar wave of convictions occurred.[48] A striking feature of all three settings is that the FBI, federal prosecutors, and federal courts, not their state and local counterparts, investigated, sued, and convicted.

Postgovernment Activities

The severe constrictions on prospective and in-place appointees are matched by restrictions on what they can do after leaving the government. Again, a prudent forward look may deter acceptance of a government position. The statutory constraints, including their duration, vary according to the former employee's responsibilities and rank while on the job. (1) No former government employee may ever represent another party or try to exert influence for him before the government on a matter (such as cases or contracts) in which the former employee participated personally and substantially. (2) He may not do so for two years after leaving a government position on any matter that fell under his official responsibility in his final year, even if it was dealt with by subordinates rather than by himself. (3) Still more broadly, for one year after ending government service, no former *senior* official (at GS-17 or above) may, on behalf of another person, try to influence official action by his former agency (regardless of whether he was involved in or responsible for related matters). (4) Finally, for the one-year period, no former *very senior* official (cabinet-level official, or Executive Schedule II official in the Executive Office of the President) may similarly try to influence any Executive Schedule official, whatever his or her agency. Criminal and civil penalties are applicable to violations.[49]

None of these closes the "revolving door" through which departing officials get jobs at corporations with which they dealt while in government.[50] But a 1988 law substantially closed that door for Defense Department and NASA procurement officials. It provided that those who have participated in conducting a federal procurement or have approved award or alteration of a procurement contract may for two years after such work neither participate in any way as an agent of a contractor in related contract negotiations with the government nor participate personally and substantially for the contractor in performance of any contract for such procurement.[51] The law's implementation was ineffective and Congress twice suspended its application because of its adverse effect on Defense Department recruitment and retention of procurement officials.[52]

These provisions are aimed, first, at keeping government employees from switching sides. They are also aimed at providing a cooling-off period during which former employees cannot take advantage of friendships and acquaintances formed on the job to influence agencies' decision making. Lawyers and prospective lobbyists may find these postgovernment constraints on their normal activities a deterrent to acceptance of public-service positions, as may able candidates unwilling to disqualify themselves from future private-sector employment opportunities. About 12,000 former Defense Department employees work for defense contractors; a third of them had responsibilities at the department for the defense contractors that became their employers, including a fifth who worked for a defense contractor on the same project that they worked on at the department.[53]

The need for preventing former officials from converting their public service to private gain is demonstrated by a number of prominent cases of alleged conversion. In December 1987, Michael K. Deaver, a close friend and former deputy chief of staff to President Reagan, was convicted of lying to a grand jury and a congressional committee about his lobbying White House and other officials for clients paying $250,000 or more a year. In June 1989, the conviction of Lyn Nofziger, the former White House political adviser to Reagan, for violation of postemployment lobbying prohibitions, was overturned on appeal because of an ambiguity in the ethics law.[54] No law prohibited former Secretary of the Interior James Watt from receiving $300,000 for holding a half-hour meeting with his former colleague, Samuel R. Pierce, Jr., secretary of housing and urban development, and making eight telephone calls to HUD on behalf of government subsidizing of a developer's low-income housing project.[55]

About half the states have revolving-door laws, some of them covering local as well as state government employees. But in the absence or weakness of such laws and local ordinances, anything goes.[56]

The Dilemma

Treating the ethics of public officials as something to be assured through preemployment disqualifications and prohibition of unethical actions is a negative approach heavily colored by a distrust of human nature. Public officials whose integrity has been unquestionable did not achieve that reputation by assuming that they could do anything not specifically forbidden by law. As one of Wilfrid Sheed's characters says, "I don't know, maybe you have to take up decency early, like the violin."[57] Perhaps recruiters of political executives should put character high on the list of qualifications for appointment. That is not the same as trying to discover, through FBI investigations and other inquiries, whether a candidate's past has any smirches that would politically embarrass the administration if they became public.

Yet, candidates and holders of high-level government appointments are many, and among them will be some of doubtful character.[58] To keep them from office, or from unethical behavior in office, auxiliary precautions may be needed. In another connection, James Madison wrote:

It may be a reflection on human nature, that such devices should be necessary to controul the abuses of government. But what is government itself but the greatest of all reflections on human nature? ... In framing a government which is to be administered by men over men, the great difficulty lies in this: You must first enable the government to controul the governed; and in the next place, oblige it to controul itself. A dependence on the people is no doubt the primary controul on the government; but experience has taught mankind the necessity of auxiliary precautions.[59]

The difficulties with the precautions now in place are that they are too detailed and burdensome, that they subject the many honorable men and women to the same complexities for entry to the public service as they do the few tainted candidates, and that they unquestionably reduce the pool of able persons who are willing to be recruited. As Aaron Wildavsky puts it, "We are trying so hard to prevent evil that we are making it difficult for good people to do well in and for our government."[60] Reforms are needed that will moderate the barriers without sacrificing protection of the public interest.

On the latter concern, a special prosecutor in a postemployment lobbying case advised Congress that "the present [1978] Ethics in Government Act is essentially unenforceable, and its protection of the public is illusory." The act, he said, is full of "murky definitions and meaningless exemptions which have converted the law into a quagmire of potential reasonable doubt."[61] Despite the act's existence, a historian concludes that "the Reagan administration compiled the worst record of conflict-of-interest allegations and scandals since the Eisenhower administration."[62]

The Public Service

In the end, we come back to the recruitment and retention of individuals dedicated to public service, respectful of its call for bureaucratic accountability and ethical behavior, and both knowledgeable about and committed to the constitutional, democratic system. Instilling of such values is a societal task, dependent on communication by family, schools, and the peers in one's generation. The Volcker Commission found the task poorly attended to by educational institutions at all levels.[63] An oddity is that, though a "me-first" college generation is being succeeded by a generation much engaged in community service while in college, career choices continue to be heavily weighted by aspirations for wealth. In 1987, 76 percent of college freshmen said it is "important to be well-off financially," an increase from 41 percent in 1966.[64] "Of the 10 percent of all college seniors who earn a

3.5 grade average, only 2 percent enter public service. Among college seniors belonging to the major academic honor societies, less than 5 percent look with favor on a government career, while over a third are hoping to work for a large corporation."[65] The contrast with European civil service recruitment is striking.

If American governments are to recruit and retain a fair share of the nation's talent, much needs to be done. The most obvious need is for them to offer salaries reasonably, even if not fully, competitive with employment opportunities in the private sector. Colleges and universities bear a special responsibility for encouraging education for the public service and offering undergraduate and graduate curricula that enrich students' capabilities for governmental careers.[66] Those capabilities include more than in the past. Public administration is no longer primarily the direct execution of governmental programs. Much of it now is administration by proxy, the delegation to and supervision of activities by third parties—state and local governments, profit-oriented corporations, and nonprofit organizations. This calls for a degree of sophistication and a continuing awareness that government is different, with obligations that eclipse those of the nongovernmental agents whose energies it enlists.

The government needs to provide incentives and opportunities that invite the ablest citizens to join and delight in public service. Few of them can then fail to welcome the challenge to help "to form a more perfect union, establish justice, insure domestic tranquility, provide for the common defense, and secure the blessings of liberty to ourselves and our posterity."[67] Animated by such opportunities, they will recognize that the public service, as President Bush said, is "the highest and noblest calling."[68]

Notes

1. Introduction (pp. 1–24)

1. See, for example, *A Centennial History of the American Administrative State,* ed. Ralph Clark Chandler (New York: Free Press, 1987); John A. Rohr, *To Run a Constitution: The Legitimacy of the Administrative State* (Lawrence: University Press of Kansas, 1986); Lawrence C. Dodd and Richard L. Schott, *Congress and the Administrative State* (New York: Wiley, 1979); Emmette S. Redford, *Democracy and the Administrative State* (New York: Oxford University Press, 1969). The term was perhaps first used in Dwight Waldo, *The Administrative State* (New York: Ronald Press, 1948; rev. ed., New York: Holmes and Meier, 1984).

2. See chapter 7 for a comparison of governments' percentages of their countries' total workforces.

3. At the French Chamber of Accounts, field administrators placed their financial records on a brown woolen cloth, *la bure,* which covered the table where they faced the king's auditors. The room came to be called the *bureau.*

4. Honoré de Balzac, *Les Employés.* English translations carry various titles (e.g., *The Civil Service, Bureaucracy,* and *The Government Clerks*).

5. These and other meanings are fully analyzed in Martin Albrow, *Bureaucracy* (New York: Holt, Rinehart, and Winston, 1971).

6. Herbert Kaufman, *Red Tape: Its Origins, Uses, and Abuses* (Washington, D.C.: Brookings Institution, 1977).

7. Nikolai I. Ryzhkov, speaking to the seventeenth Communist Party Congress, quoted in Philip Taubman, "Soviet Premier, in Congress Talk, Criticizes Economy," *New York Times,* 4 March 1986; Zhao Ziyang (later named general secretary of China's Communist Party), quoted in Edward A Gargan, "More Change Due in China's Economy," *New York Times,* 26 October 1987.

8. For a well-documented and well-argued case explaining and defending bureaucracy, see Charles T. Goodsell, *The Case for Bureaucracy: A Public Administration Polemic,* 3d ed. (Chatham, N.J.: Chatham House, 1994).

9. The respective figures are $1.1 trillion and $2.8 trillion. Office of Management and Budget, *The Budget of the United States Government: Fiscal Year 1990* (Washington, D.C.: Government Printing Office, 1989), 10–9; "The Forbes Sales 500," *Forbes* 141 (25 April 1988): 136.

10. For example, the government subsidizes tobacco growers and promotes foreign sales of tobacco, but requires dangerous-to-health messages on tobacco packages and advertisements in the United States.

11. For a thorough exploration of the definitional problem, see A. Dunsire, *Administration: The Word and the Science* (New York: Wiley, 1973).

12. Dwight Waldo, *The Study of Public Administration* (Garden City, N.Y.: Doubleday, 1955), 5–6; and Herbert A. Simon, *Administrative Behavior* (New York: Macmillan, 1947; 3d ed., New York: Free Press, 1976), 72–73. How one ascertains what the goals are and relates rational action to them is a difficult problem, recognized by both Waldo and Simon, as is the nonrational dimension of human behavior.

13. We later take note of legislative bodies' and courts' rivalry with the chief executive over the direction and control of administrative agencies.

14. Anthony King, in "Executives," *Handbook of Political Science,* 9 vols., ed. Fred I. Greenstein and Nelson W. Polsby (Reading, Mass.: Addison-Wesley, 1975), 5:181.

15. For a review of these arguments, see Harold F. Gortner, Julianne Mahler, and Jeanne Bell Nicholson, *Organization Theory: A Public Perspective* (Chicago: Dorsey Press, 1987), 16; and Gary L. Wamsley and Mayer N. Zald, *The Political Economy of Public Organizations: A Critique and Approach to the Study of Public Administration* (Bloomington: Indiana University Press, 1973), 4.

16. Douglas Yates, Jr., *The Politics of Management* (San Francisco: Jossey-Bass, 1985), 7.

17. Barry Bozeman, *All Organizations Are Public: Bridging Public and Private Organization Theories* (San Francisco: Jossey-Bass, 1987), 83–85.

18. William A. Robson, "The Managing of Organizations," *Public Administration* (London) 44 (Autumn 1966): 276.

19. Dwight Waldo, *The Enterprise of Public Administration: A Summary View* (Novato, Calif.: Chandler and Sharp, 1980), 164. Compare Bozeman, *All Organizations Are Public,* 5; and Hal G. Rainey, Robert W. Backoff, and Charles H. Levine, "Comparing Public and Private Organizations," *Public Administration Review* 36 (March/April 1976): 234.

20. See Graham T. Allison, Jr., "Public and Private Management: Are They Fundamentally Alike in All Unimportant Respects?" in *Current Issues in Public Administration,* 3d ed., ed. Frederick S. Lane (New York: St. Martin's Press, 1986), 184–200.

21. Some theorists, for example, argue that the distinction is based on who benefits; public agencies are those whose prime beneficiary is the public. See Peter M. Blau and W. Richard Scott, *Formal Organizations: A Comparative Approach* (San Francisco: Chandler, 1962), 42–43.

Others have argued that they are distinctive because of who owns and funds them; public agencies are those "owned" by the state. See Wamsley and Zald, *The Political Economy of Public Organization,* 8.

22. Gortner, Mahler, and Nicholson, *Organization Theory,* 26.

23. These distinctions are based on comparisons developed by John T. Dunlop and summarized in Allison, "Public and Private Management," 17–18. See also Ralph Clark Chandler, "Epilogue," in Chandler, *A Centennial History,* 580–86; and Rainey, Backoff, and Levine, "Comparing Public and Private Organizations."

24. Anthony Downs, *Inside Bureaucracy* (Boston: Little, Brown, 1967), 30.

25. See Marver H. Bernstein, *The Job of the Federal Government Executive* (Washington, D.C.: Brookings Institution, 1958), 26–28; James W. Fesler et al., *Industrial Mobilization for War* (Washington, D.C.: Government Printing Office, 1947), 971–72. The "goldfish-bowl" phenomenon applies specifically to the United States, rather than to public administration everywhere. See Harold L. Wilensky, *Organizational Intelligence* (New York: Basic Books, 1967), 116–18.

26. Wallace Sayre, "The Unhappy Bureaucrats: Views Ironic, Helpful, Indignant," *Public Administration Review* 10 (Summer 1958): 245.

27. "Evolving Needs in the Preparation of Future Leaders for the Federal Service," address before the National Association of Schools of Public Affairs and Administration, 3 May 1974, 13–15. Processed.

28. Statutes do specify criteria (e.g., no criminal record and liquor store location not near a school), but they offer no guides to choice among the numerous applicants who meet these simple criteria.

29. So, too, must politically appointed agency officials.

30. See *Revitalizing Federal Management: Managers and Their Overburdened Systems: A Panel Report* (Washington, D.C.: National Academy of Public Administration, 1983).

31. For the variety of approaches, see *Public Administration: The State of the Discipline,* ed. Naomi B. Lynn and Aaron Wildavsky (Chatham, N.J.: Chatham House, 1990); and Chandler, *A Centennial History.*

32. Dwight Waldo, "Politics and Administration: On Thinking about a Complex Relationship," in Chandler, *A Centennial History,* 89–112, at 96–104.

33. See Frank J. Goodnow, *Politics and Administration* (New York: Macmillan, 1900). Wilson is discussed later in this chapter.

34. Nicholas Henry, "The Emergence of Public Administration as a Field of Study," in Chandler, *A Centennial History,* 37–85. See also *American Public Administration: Past, Present, and Future,* ed. Frederick C. Mosher (University: University of Alabama Press, 1975).

35. Luther Gulick, "Time and Public Administration," *Public Administration Review* 47 (January/February 1987): 115–19.

36. Carl J. Friedrich, *Man and His Government* (New York: McGraw-Hill, 1963), 464–83.

The remarkable and lasting innovations in British and French administrative institutions and methods in the twelfth to fourteenth centuries are treated in James W. Fesler, "The Presence of the Administrative Past," in *American Public Administration: Patterns of the Past,* ed. James W. Fesler (Washington, D.C.: American Society for Public Administration, 1982), 1–27, at 3–16. A comprehensive administrative history, much broader than its title, is Carolyn Webber and Aaron Wildavsky, *A History of Taxation and Expenditure in the Western World* (New York: Simon and Schuster, 1986).

37. Alexis de Tocqueville, *Democracy in America* (New York: Knopf, 1945), 1:211–12; paperback edition (New York: Vintage Books, 1954), 1:219–20.

38. All quotations of Woodrow Wilson are from his "The Study of Administration," *Political Science Quarterly* 2 (June 1887), as reprinted in the *Political Science Quarterly* 56 (December 1941): 481–506. As the first scholarly article urging attention to public administration, it is often described as "seminal"; however, the article was not widely read until its reprinting in 1941. For a full canvass of Wilson's significance, see *Politics and Administration: Woodrow Wilson and American Public Administration,* ed. Jack Rabin and James S. Bowman (New York: Marcel Dekker, 1984); Daniel W. Martin, "The Fading Legacy of Woodrow Wilson," *Public Administration Review* 48 (March/April 1988): 631–36.

39. Ferrel Heady, "Comparative Public Administration in the United States," in Chandler, *A Centennial History,* 477–508, at 496. See also Robert C. Fried, "Comparative Public Administration: The Search for Theories," in Lynn and Wildavsky, *Public Administration,* 318–44. The literature, however, grows. See Ferrel Heady, *Public Administration: A Comparative Perspective,* 3d ed. (New York: Marcel Dekker, 1984); Joel D. Aberbach, Robert D. Putnam, and Bert A. Rockman, *Bureaucrats and Politicians in Western Democracies* (Cambridge: Harvard University Press, 1981); B. Guy Peters, *The Politics of Bureaucracy: A Comparative Perspective,* 3d ed. (New York: Longman, 1989); Ezra Suleiman, ed., *Bureaucrats and Policy Making: A Comparative Overview* (New York: Holmes and Meier, 1984); Donald C. Rowat, ed., *Public Administration in Developed Democracies: A Comparative Study* (New York: Marcel Dekker, 1988).

40. Fesler, *American Public Administration.* An excellent starting point is Stephen Skowronek, *Building a New American State: The Expansion of National Administrative Capacities, 1877–1920* (New York: Cambridge University Press, 1982).

41. The list is not exhaustive. See James G. March, "How We Talk and How We Act: Administrative Theory and Administrative Life," in *Leadership and Organization Culture: New Perspectives on Administrative Theory and Practice,* ed. Thomas J. Sergiovanni and John E. Corbally (Urbana: University of Illinois Press, 1984, 1986), 18–35, esp. 21.

42. For a broad critique, see Charles Perrow, *Complex Organizations,* 3d ed. (New York: Random House, 1986).

43. The concept of overlays is presented in James M. Pfiffner and Frank R. Sherwood, *Administrative Organization* (Englewood Cliffs, N.J.: Prentice Hall, 1960), 16–32. They propose a basic sheet portraying the formal structure of authority, with five overlays: sociometric ("contacts people have with each other because of personal attraction"); functional (arising out of "the relationships created by technical experts" and the authority they exercise "because of their superior knowledge and skills"); decisional; power; and communication.

44. *Organization* is a confusing term. Conventionally it has meant only admin-

istrative structure, in effect its architectural design. An *organization,* however, refers to a whole enterprise, whether a government agency, a business corporation, a non-profit enterprise or one of their subordinate units, such as a bureau or division, and so to any aspect of it, structural or not. In recent literature the word *organization* has largely displaced *administration*—that is, *organization theory* and *organizational behavior* commonly substitute for *administrative theory* and *administrative behavior.*

2. What Government Does (pp. 27–42)

1. See Seymour Martin Lipset and William Schneider, *The Confidence Gap: Business, Labor, and Government in the Public Mind,* rev. ed. (Baltimore: Johns Hopkins University Press, 1987), 1; Karlyn H. Keene and Everett C. Ladd, "What the Public Says," *Government Executive,* January 1988, 14; and *Washington Post,* 3 November 1991.

2. Lipset and Schneider, *Confidence Gap,* 378, 380.

3. Ibid., 380.

4. John 7:24, quoted by Frederick C. Mosher and Orville F. Poland, *The Costs of American Governments: Facts, Trends, Myths* (New York: Dodd, Mead, 1964), 1.

5. Robert Pear, "U.S. Pensions Found to Lift Many of Poor," *New York Times,* 28 December 1988, A1.

6. *Wall Street Journal,* 17 March 1989, A1.

7. Office of Management and Budget, *Budget of the United States Government: Fiscal Year 1990, Special Analyses* (Washington, D.C.: Government Printing Office, 1989), F-1.

8. Robin Toner, "Pollsters See a Silent Storm That Swept Away Democrats," *New York Times,* 16 November 1994, A13. Budget figures from Congressional Budget Office, *The Economic and Budget Outlook: Fiscal Years 1995–1999* (Washington, D.C.: Government Printing Office, 1994).

9. U.S. Bureau of the Census, *Government Finances in 1986–87* (Washington, D.C.: Government Printing Office, 1988), 12–13.

10. Ibid., 23. The national average is 41.2 percent of expenditures by the states and 58.8 percent by local governments.

11. For the classic exposition of the "marble cake" argument, see Morton Grodzins, *The American System: A New View of Government in the United States,* ed. Daniel J. Elazar (Chicago: Rand McNally, 1966).

12. Christopher C. Hood, *The Tools of Government* (Chatham, N.J.: Chatham House, 1983), 2. For other examples of the "tools" approach to public administration, see Donald F. Kettl, *Government by Proxy: (Mis?)Managing Federal Programs* (Washington, D.C.: CQ Press, 1988); and Lester M. Salamon, ed., *Beyond Privatization: The Tools of Government Action* (Washington, D.C.: Urban Institute, 1989).

13. Congressional Budget Office, *An Analysis of the President's Budgetary Proposals for FY 1995* (Washington, D.C.: Congressional Budget Office, 1994), 43.

14. Frederick C. Mosher, "The Changing Responsibilities and Tactics of the

Federal Government," *Public Administration Review* 40 (November/December 1980): 541–48, esp. 542.

15. Donald Haider, "Grants as a Tool of Public Policy," in Salamon, *Beyond Privatization,* 93.

16. Office of Management and Budget, *Budget of the United States Government, Fiscal Year 1995* (Washington, D.C.: Government Printing Office, 1994), 77. Figures are outlay equivalents for FY 1995.

17. The dominance of the federal government in setting tax expenditures is increased because most state and local income taxes rely on federal law to define income and basic deductions.

18. Both the Reagan and Bush administrations argued strongly for "enterprise zones," in which economically blighted areas would be selected for special government aid, including relaxed regulations and favorable tax treatment, to encourage economic growth.

19. For a review of tax expenditures, see Stanley S. Surrey and Paul R. McDaniel, *Tax Expenditures* (Cambridge: Harvard University Press, 1985); John F. Witte, *The Politics and Development of the Federal Income Tax* (Madison: University of Wisconsin Press, 1985); and Paul R. McDaniel, "Tax Expenditures as Tools of Government Action," in Salamon, *Beyond Privatization,* 167–96.

20. Lester M. Salamon, "Rethinking Public Management: Third-Party Government and the Changing Forms of Government Action," *Public Policy* 29 (Summer 1981): 260.

21. Ted Kolderie, "The Two Different Concepts of Privatization," *Public Administration Review* 46 (July/August 1986): 285–91.

3. Organization Theory: Foundations (pp. 45–67)

1. The text's statement is not descriptive of all actual reorganizations. Though usually meant to establish a long-lasting structure, a reorganization's design is often affected by considerations of the competence, incompetence, or potential opposition of current incumbents of key positions.

2. Daniel Katz and Robert L. Kahn, *The Social Psychology of Organizations,* 2d ed. (New York: Wiley, 1978), 188, 196. Note, however, the caveat: "Role expectations are by no means restricted to the job description as it might be given by the head of the organization or prepared by some specialist in personnel, although these individuals are likely to be influential members of the role set of many persons in the organization" (p. 190).

3. We are here merely laying the ground for the structural approach to governmental administration. For more substantial analysis of the complex issue of authority, see, for example, Carl J. Friedrich, *Man and His Government* (New York: McGraw-Hill, 1963); and Charles E. Lindblom, *Politics and Markets* (New York: Basic Books, 1977), 17–32.

4. Luther Gulick, "Notes on the Theory of Organization," in *Papers on the Science of Administration,* ed. L. Gulick and L. Urwick (New York: Institute of Public Administration, 1937), 1–45. For an attack on that essay, see Herbert Simon, *Ad-*

ministrative Behavior (New York: Macmillan, 1947, and later editions), 20–44. For reviews of the controversy, see Alan A. Altshuler, "The Study of Administration," in *The Politics of the Federal Bureaucracy,* 2d ed., ed. Alan A. Altshuler and Norman C. Thomas (New York: Harper & Row, 1977), 2–17; Vincent Ostrom, *The Intellectual Crisis in Public Administration* (University: University of Alabama Press, 1973), 36–47; Brian R. Fry, *Mastering Public Administration: From Max Weber to Dwight Waldo* (Chatham, N.J.: Chatham House, 1989), 73–97; Thomas H. Hammond, "In Defense of Luther Gulick's 'Notes on the Theory of Organization,'" *Public Administration* (London) 58 (Summer 1990).

5. Gulick, "Theory of Organization," 31.

6. Weber's views became accessible to American readers lacking command of the German language through two translations of portions of his works, which appeared in 1946 and 1947 and were reprinted in the following paperback editions: *From Max Weber: Essays in Sociology,* trans. and ed. H.H. Gerth and C. Wright Mills (New York: Oxford University Press, 1958), and *The Theory of Social and Economic Organization,* trans. A.M. Henderson and Talcott Parsons (New York: Free Press, 1964).

7. Weber, *Social and Economic Organization,* 328.

8. Weber, *From Max Weber,* 209.

9. Weber, *Social and Economic Organization,* 330.

10. Ibid., 333.

11. Ibid., 337.

12. Weber, *From Max Weber,* 196–97.

13. Ibid., 228.

14. The most frequent criticism of his rational-legal bureaucratic model is that there is an unacknowledged conflict between the hierarchic authority Weber emphasizes and the specialized, professional knowledge and technical competence he also recognizes, and which, he fails to note, gives "authority" to subordinates having such specialized competence. Talcott Parsons explains Weber's neglect of professional authority and his emphasis on hierarchy as "a healthy reaction against the common utopianism" that "tends to minimize the significance of authority, coercive power, and physical force in human affairs." Parsons's introduction to Weber, *Social and Economic Organization,* 56, 58–60n.

15. Systems theory and its organizational derivatives are more fully treated in Katz and Kahn, *Social Psychology of Organizations,* 17–34; and Chadwick J. Haberstroh, "Organization Design and Systems Analysis," in *Handbook of Organizations,* ed. James G. March (Chicago: Rand McNally, 1965), 1171–1211.

16. An alternative is to treat the department, its pressure groups, and Congress's agricultural committees as a "system."

17. General systems theory allows for the "nesting" of smaller systems in medium-scale systems and the latter in still more comprehensive systems. Nevertheless, *organizational* systems theorists neglect the executive branch. Instead, they identify the department or a bureau as *the* organization or system, perhaps because its size makes it the closest analog to a business corporation, perhaps because its behavior makes it the closest analog to a biological organism facing the challenge of survival

in a threatening environment.

18. Talcott Parsons, "Suggestions for a Sociological Approach to the Theory of Organizations," *Administrative Science Quarterly* 1 (June and September 1956): 64. (Emphasis in original.)

19. For a trenchant argument that an organization's survival is the lucky result of natural selection processes, rather than of efforts to achieve that objective, see Herbert Kaufman, *Time, Chance, and Organizations: Natural Selection in a Perilous Environment* (Chatham, N.J.: Chatham House, 1985).

20. Sir Eric (later Lord) Ashby, *Technology and the Academics* (New York: Macmillan, 1958), 67–68.

21. President-elect Nixon, announcing his choice of cabinet members, quoted in *Congressional Quarterly Weekly Report* 26 (13 December 1968): 3263.

22. President Nixon's Message to Congress, 25 March 1971, in Office of Management and Budget, Executive Office of the President, *Papers Relating to the President's Departmental Reorganization Program* (Washington, D.C.: Government Printing Office, March 1971), 7.

23. The 1973 official statement of purpose and functions (since revised) was ridiculously disingenuous: "The Department of Agriculture (USDA) is directed by law to acquire and diffuse useful information on agricultural subjects in the most general and comprehensive sense. *To accomplish this purpose,* the Department functions in the areas of research, education, conservation, marketing, regulatory work, agricultural adjustment, surplus disposal, and rural development" (emphasis added). *United States Government Manual 1973/74* (Washington, D.C.: Government Printing Office, 1973), 94.

24. Systems theories vary in attentiveness to authority. For a work that does incorporate authority and its hierarchical structuring in a systems framework, see Katz and Kahn, *Social Psychology of Organizations,* esp. 199–222.

25. Frederick Winslow Taylor, *The Principles of Scientific Management* (New York: Harper & Brothers, 1911; Harper & Row, 1947; Norton, 1967). See Fry, *Mastering Public Administration,* 47–72.

26. Taylor unfortunately wrote that because of "the grinding monotony" of the work, "one of the first requirements for a man who is fit to handle pig iron as a regular occupation is that he shall be so stupid and so phlegmatic that he more nearly resembles in his mental make-up the ox than any other type." Taylor, *Principles of Scientific Management,* 59; see also 61–62.

27. An early canvass of this literature is in James G. March and Herbert Simon, *Organizations* (New York: Wiley, 1957), although puzzlingly, the findings were not brought to bear on the book's later concerns with organizational structure and processes.

28. The earliest significant research moving from traditional managerial analyses to concern with the human behavior of workers was conducted in the late 1920s and the 1930s at the Hawthorne Works of the Western Electric Company. For reports of the research and reappraisals of the findings, see George C. Homans, *The Human Group* (New York: Harcourt Brace Jovanovich, 1950); and H.M. Persons, "What Happened at Hawthorne?" *Science* 183 (8 March 1974): 922–32.

29. "Group members tend to feel better satisfied under moderate degrees of structure than under overly structured or totally unstructured situations. But they prefer too much structure over none at all. Groups tend to be more productive and more cohesive in structured rather than unstructured situations. Formal structure does not necessarily block satisfaction of needs for autonomy and self-actualization. Some degree of structure is necessary for the satisfaction of follower needs." Bernard M. Bass, *Stogdill's Handbook of Leadership: A Survey of Theory and Research,* revised and expanded ed. (New York: Free Press, 1981), 588–89.

30. Edwin A. Locke, "The Nature and Causes of Job Satisfaction," in *Handbook of Industrial and Organizational Psychology,* ed. Marvin D. Dunnette (Chicago: Rand McNally, 1976), 1297–1349, at 1332. As Locke points out, the human relationists' causal arrow may point the wrong way; that is, high productivity may be a cause of high satisfaction.

31. Chris Argyris, "Being Human and Being Organized," *Transaction* 1 (July 1964): 5. See also his "Some Limits of Rational Man Organization Theory," *Public Administration Review* (33 May–June 1973): 253–67, esp. 253–54, 263–65.

32. For a full description and critique of the human relations model, see Charles Perrow, *Complex Organizations,* 3d ed. (New York: Random House, 1986), 79–118. See also H. Roy Kaplan and Curt Tausky, "Humanism in Organizations: A Critical Appraisal," *Public Administration Review* 37 (March–April 1977): 171–80.

33. Douglas McGregor, *The Human Side of Enterprise* (New York: McGraw-Hill, 1960), 33–57.

34. Lawrence B. Mohr, *Explaining Organizational Behavior: The Limits and Possibilities of Theory and Research* (San Francisco: Jossey-Bass, 1982), 125–53; Bass, *Stogdill's Handbook of Leadership,* passim.

35. Abraham H. Maslow, "The Superior Person," *Transaction* 1 (May 1964): 12–13. For a major test of "the participation hypothesis" in public administration, see *Government Reorganizations: Cases and Commentary,* ed. Frederick C. Mosher (Indianapolis: Bobbs-Merrill, 1967).

36. Kurt W. Back, *Beyond Words: The Story of Sensitivity Training and the Encounter Movement,* 2d ed. (New Brunswick, N.J.: Transaction Books, 1987); American Psychiatric Association Task Force on Recent Developments in the Use of Small Groups, *Encounter Groups and Psychiatry* (Washington, D.C.: American Psychiatric Association, 1970). The latter report says, "the term 'encounter group' ... is far more prevalent in the west; in the east, 'sensitivity' group or 'T-group' is more often used" (p. 7).

37. Bass, *Stogdill's Handbook of Leadership,* 560–65.

38. The fault was neglect of a common problem. A single individual with an innovative approach often finds no support from peers or superiors accustomed to the organization's standard mode of operation, and eventually conforms to that mode rather than fight for reform.

39. The OD approach is fully presented and appraised in Robert T. Golembiewski, *Humanizing Public Organizations* (Mt. Airy, Md.: Lomond, 1985).

40. Michael H. Harmon, "Organization Development in the State Department: A Case Study of the ACORD Program," in Commission on the Organization of the

Government for the Conduct of Foreign Policy, *Appendices* (Washington, D.C.: Government Printing Office, 1975), 6:65. The same point is made in Donald P. Warwick, *A Theory of Public Bureaucracy: Politics, Personality, and Organization in the State Department* (Cambridge: Harvard University Press, 1975), 228.

41. Harmon, "Organization Development in the State Department," 77.

42. Ibid., 76. The ideological elements of the human relations school were prominent in the "New Public Administration" movement in the late 1960s. *Toward a New Public Administration,* ed. Frank Marini (Scranton, Pa.: Chandler, 1971); and *Public Administration in a Time of Turbulence,* ed. Dwight Waldo (Scranton, Pa.: Chandler, 1971). For retrospective views, see *Public Administration Review* 49 (March/April 1989): 95–225, esp. H. George Frederickson, "Minnowbrook II: Changing Epochs of Public Administration," 95–100.

43. Among the many writings illustrative of the pluralistic approach to public administration, three classics are David B. Truman, *The Governmental Process,* 2d ed. (New York: Knopf, 1971), esp. 395–478; J. Leiper Freeman, *The Political Process: Executive Bureau—Legislative Committee Relations,* rev. ed. (New York: Random House, 1965); and Francis E. Rourke, *Bureaucracy, Politics, and Public Policy,* 3d ed. (Boston: Little, Brown, 1984).

44. Rourke, *Bureaucracy, Politics, and Public Policy.*

45. A good introduction is J. Steven Ott, *The Organizational Culture Perspective* (Chicago: Dorsey Press, 1989). See also Edgar H. Schein, *Organizational Culture and Leadership* (San Francisco: Jossey-Bass, 1987); and Michel Crozier, *The Bureaucratic Phenomenon* (Chicago: University of Chicago Press, 1964).

46. Spatial relations are rarely treated in the literature. For a valuable exception, see Frederick C. Mosher, *A Tale of Two Agencies: A Comparative Analysis of the General Accounting Office and the Office of Management and Budget* (Baton Rouge: Louisiana State University Press, 1984), 87–98. The whole book usefully contrasts the organizational cultures of the two agencies.

47. Harold Seidman and Robert Gilmour, *Politics, Position, and Power: From the Positive to the Regulatory State,* 4th ed. (New York: Oxford University Press, 1986), 167. See pp. 166–94 on "The Executive Establishment, Culture and Personality."

48. Donald F. Kettl, *Leadership at the Fed* (New Haven: Yale University Press, 1986). The dominance issue is treated at pp. 30–32 and 85–88.

49. Herbert Kaufman, *The Forest Ranger: A Study in Administrative Behavior* (Baltimore: Johns Hopkins University Press, 1960).

50. Frederick C. Mosher, "The Changing Responsibilities and Tactics of the Federal Government," in *American Public Administration: Patterns of the Past,* ed. James W. Fesler (Washington, D.C.: American Society for Public Administration, 1982), 198–212; quoted passage at 201. See also Lester H. Salamon, "Rethinking Public Management: Third-Party Government and the Changing Forms of Government Action," *Public Policy* 29 (Summer 1981): 259–78.

51. Donald F. Kettl, *Government by Proxy: (Mis?)Managing Federal Programs* (Washington, D.C.: CQ Press, 1988).

52. See, for example, Howard Aldrich and David A. Whettan, "Organization-

Sets, Action-Sets, and Networks: Making the Most of Simplicity, in *Handbook of Organizational Design,* vol. 1, *Adapting Organizations to Their Environments,* ed. Paul C. Nystrom and William H. Starbuck (New York: Oxford University Press, 1981), 385–408; W.W. Powell, "Neither Market nor Hierarchy: Network Forms of Organization," in *Research in Organizational Behavior,* ed. B. Staw and L.L. Cummings (Greenwich, Conn.: JAI Press, 1990), 295–336; Robert Agranoff, "Human Services Integration: Past and Present Challenges in Public Administration," *Public Administration Review* 51 (1991): 533–42; H. Brinton Milward and Keith G. Provan, "Services Integration and Outcome Effectiveness: An Empirical Test of an Implicit Theory," paper presented at the 1993 annual conference of the Association for Public Policy Analysis and Management; Fritz W. Scharpf, "Coordination in Hierarchies and Networks," in *Games in Hierarchies and Networks: Analytical and Empirical Approaches to the Study of Governance and Institutions,* ed. Fritz W. Scharpf (Boulder, Colo.: Westview Press, 1993), 125–65; Eugene Bardach, "Generic Models in the Study of Public Management," paper presented at the 1993 conference of the Association for Public Policy Analysis and Management.

53. Eugene Bardach, "But Can Networks Produce," paper prepared for the conference on "Network Analysis and Innovations in Public Programs," La Follette Institute of Public Affairs, University of Wisconsin–Madison, Madison, 1994, 2.

54. For a comprehensive review of theories we have discussed, and many more (reinforcing the impression of disparity), see Jeffrey Pfeffer, "Organizations and Organization Theory," in *Handbook of Social Psychology,* ed. Gardner Lindzey and Elliot Aronson (New York: Random House, 1985), 1:379–435.

4. Organization Theory: Strategies and Tactics for Administration Reform (pp. 68–87)

1. Portions of this chapter were originally presented at a conference in Brisbane, Australia, sponsored by the Australian Fulbright Symposium on Public Sector Reform. The conference, "New Ideas, Better Government," was held on 23–24 June 1994 and was organized by the Griffith University Centre for Australian Public Sector Management. We are grateful to the conference organizers, Glyn Davis and Patrick Weller, for their support of the research and for their permission to use the material developed for the conference in this chapter.

2. Organization for Economic Cooperation and Development, *Public Management Developments: Survey 1993* (Paris: OECD, 1993).

3. Roy Bahl, *Financing State and Local Governments in the 1980s* (New York: Oxford University Press, 1984), 184–85.

4. Irene Rubin, *The Politics of Public Budgeting: Getting and Spending, Borrowing and Balancing,* 2d ed. (Chatham, N.J.: Chatham House, 1993), 51–52.

5. J. Richard Aronson and John Hilley, *Financing State and Local Governments,* 4th ed. (Washington, D.C.: Brookings Institution, 1986), 223–24.

6. See Bahl, *Financing State and Local Government.*

7. E.S. Savas, *Privatizing the Public Sector: How to Shrink Government* (Chatham, N.J.: Chatham House, 1982), 16–17.

8. President's Private Sector Survey on Cost Control (Grace Commission), *A Report to the President* (Washington, D.C.: Government Printing Office, 1984), II-1.

9. Charles Goodsell, "The Grace Commission: Seeking Efficiency for the Whole People," *Public Administration Review* 44 (May/June 1984): 196–204.

10. David Osborne and Ted Gaebler, *Reinventing Government: How the Entrepreneurial Spirit Is Transforming the Public Sector, from Schoolhouse to Statehouse, City Hall to the Pentagon* (Reading, Mass.: Addison-Wesley, 1993).

11. Al Gore, *From Red Tape to Results: Creating a Government That Works Better and Costs Less* (Washington, D.C.: Government Printing Office, 1993), iii–iv.

12. General Accounting Office, *Federal Employment: The Results to Date of the Fiscal Year 1994 Buyouts at Non-Defense Agencies*, GGD-94-214, September 1994.

13. Jack Germond and Jules Witcover, "A Political Elixir for the President," *National Journal*, 11 September 1993, 2211.

14. Gallup Organization, CNN/*USA Today* poll, September 1993 wave.

15. Osborne and Gaebler, *Reinventing Government.*

16. William Niskanen, *Bureaucracy and Representative Government* (Chicago: Aldine Atherton, 1971); Savas, *Privatizing the Public Sector;* and André Blais and Stéphane Dion, *The Budget-Maximizing Bureaucrat: Appraisals and Evidence* (Pittsburgh: University of Pittsburgh Press, 1991).

17. Donald F. Kettl, *Sharing Power: Public Governance and Private Markets* (Washington, D.C.: Brookings Institution, 1993).

18. Michael Hammer and James Champy, *Reengineering the Corporation: A Manifesto for Business Revolution* (New York: HarperBusiness, 1993).

19. J. Mechling, "Reengineering Part of Your Game Plan? A Guide for Public Managers," *Governing* 7 (February 1994), 41–52; Russell M. Linden, *Seamless Government: A Practical Guide to Re-Engineering in the Public Sector* (San Francisco: Jossey-Bass, 1994); and Sharon L. Caudle, *Reengineering for Results* (Washington, D.C.: National Academy of Public Administration, 1994).

20. Hammer and Champy, *Reengineering the Corporation,* 2, 3.

21. Ibid., 47–49.

22. Mechling, "Reengineering."

23. General Accounting Office, *Management Reforms: Examples of Public and Private Innovations to Improve Service Delivery* AIMD/GGD-94-90BR (1994), 37–38.

24. Frederickson, "Painting Bull's Eyes Around Bullet Holes." *Governing* 5 (October 1992): 13.

25. Ronald C. Moe, Edward Davis, Frederick Pauls, and Harold Relyea, "Analysis of the Budget and Management Proposals in the Report of the National Performance Review," Congressional Research Service, Washington, D.C., 21 September 1993, 4. Photocopied.

26. Henri Fayol, *General and Industrial Management* (London: Pitman and Sons, 1925).

27. L. Urwick, "The Function of Administration," in *Papers on the Science of Administration,* ed. Luther Gulick and L. Urwick (New York: Institute of Public Ad-

ministration, 1937), 124.

28. Luther Gulick, "The Theory of Organization," in ibid., 25.

29. Michael M. Harmon and Richard T. Mayer, *Organization Theory for Public Administration* (Boston: Little, Brown, 1986), 42–47.

30. James Q. Wilson, *Bureaucracy: What Government Agencies Do and Why They Do It,* (New York: Basic Books, 1989), 163.

31. For an excellent survey, see James L. Perry, ed. *Handbook of Public Administration* (San Francisco: Jossey-Bass, 1989).

32. Hammer and Champy, *Reengineering the Corporation,* 6.

33. Gore, *From Red Tape to Results,* 94.

34. Mechling, "Reengineering," 50.

35. See W. Edwards Deming, *Out of Crisis* (Cambridge, Mass.: Massachusetts Institute of Technology Center for Advanced Engineering Study, 1986); and Rafael Aguayo, *Dr. Deming: The American Who Taught the Japanese about Quality* (New York: Simon and Schuster, 1990).

36. Aguayo, *Dr. Deming,* 19.

37. Bill Creech, *The Five Pillars of TQM: How to Make Total Quality Management Work for You* (New York: Dutton, 1994), 27, 54.

38. Steven Cohen and Ronald Brand, *Total Quality Management in Government: A Practical Guide for the Real World* (San Francisco: Jossey-Bass, 1993).

39. Creech, *The Five Pillars of TQM,* 78.

40. Cohen and Brand, *Total Quality Management in Government,* 175–97.

41. Ibid., 197.

42. Peter M. Senge, *The Fifth Discipline: The Art and Practice of the Learning Organization* (New York: Doubleday, 1990); and Donald F. Kettl, "Learning Organizations and Managing the Unknown," in *Rethinking Public Personnel Systems,* ed. Patricia W. Ingraham and Barbara S. Romzek (San Francisco: Jossey-Bass, 1994), 19–40.

43. H. Metcalf and L. Urwick, *Dynamic Administration: The Collected Papers of Mary Parker Follett* (New York: Harper & Brothers, 1942).

44. Abraham Maslow, "A Theory of Human Motivation," *Psychological Review* 50 (July 1943): 370–96.

45. See, for example, Michael Barzelay with Babak J. Armajani, *Breaking Through Bureaucracy: A New Vision for Managing in Government* (Berkeley: University of California Press, 1992); and Harry P. Hatry and John J. Kirlin, "An Assessment of the Oregon Benchmarks: A Report to the Oregon Progress Board," June 1994. Mimeo.

46. For two excellent surveys of administrative issues around the world, see Randall Baker, ed., *Comparative Public Management: Putting U.S. Public Policy and Implementation in Context* (New York: Praeger, 1994); and B. Guy Peters, *The Politics of Bureaucracy,* 3d ed. (New York: Longman, 1989). The Organization of Economic Cooperation and Development also publishes regular updated on reforms in public administration. See OECD, *Public Management Developments: Survey 1993* (Paris, OECD, 1993).

47. OECD, *Public Management Developments: Survey 1993.*

48. For a study of the Australian reforms, see Task Force on Management Improvement, *The Australian Public Service Reformed: An Evaluation of a Decade of Management Reform* (Canberra: Australian Government Publishing Service, 1992).

49. For an early survey, see Donald F. Kettl and John J. DiIulio, Jr., eds., *Inside the Reinvention Machine: Appraising the National Performance Review* (Washington, D.C.: Brookings Institution, 1995).

5. The Executive Branch (pp. 88–110)

1. Rufus E. Miles, "The Origin and Meaning of Miles' Law," *Public Administration Review* 38 (September–October 1978): 399–403.

2. This proposition is persuasively demonstrated in Thomas H. Hammond, "Agenda Control, Organizational Structure, and Bureaucratic Politics," *American Political Science Review* 30 (May 1986): 379–420.

3. A temporary commission advocated taking the Federal Aviation Administration out of the Department of Transportation for this and other reasons; the airlines and the Air Line Pilots Association supported the proposal. Laura Parker and Martha M. Hamilton, "Major Overhaul of Airline Regulation Urged," *Washington Post,* 19 April 1988. The FAA has three-fourths of the department's employees.

4. For organizational history, to 1922, see Lloyd M. Short, *The Development of National Administrative Organization in the United States* (Baltimore: Johns Hopkins University Press, 1923).

5. The War Department is here treated as the antecedent of the Department of Defense, established in 1949; the War Department included naval concerns until establishment of the Navy Department in 1798.

6. Three of these six were substantially conversions to departmental status of the previously established Federal Security Agency (1939), Housing and Home Finance Agency (1947), and Veterans Administration (1930).
For the latest two departmental creations, see Beryl A. Radin and Willis D. Hawley, *The Politics of Federal Reorganization: Creating the U.S. Department of Education* (New York: Pergamon Press, 1988); Terrel H. Bell [first secretary of education], *The Thirteenth Man: A Reagan Cabinet Memoir* (New York: Free Press/ Macmillan, 1987); and *Evaluation of Proposals to Establish a Department of Veterans Affairs* (Washington, D.C.: National Academy of Public Administration, 1988).

7. See "The Independent Status of the Regulatory Commissions," in U.S. Senate Committee on Governmental Affairs, *Study on Federal Regulation,* vol. 5, *Regulatory Organization* (Washington, D.C.: Government Printing Office, 1977), 25–81.

8. The restriction on the president's removal power was upheld in *Humphrey's Executor* v. *United States,* 295 U.S. 602 (1935). The Supreme Court characterized the Federal Trade Commission as "wholly disconnected from the executive department" and, rather, "an agency of the legislative and judicial departments," one that Congress intended to be "independent of executive authority, except in its selection, and free to exercise its judgment without the leave or hindrance of any other official or any department of Government."

9. U.S. Senate Committee on Governmental Affairs, *Organization of Federal*

Executive Departments and Agencies (Washington, D.C.: Government Printing Office, 1990). The averages exclude the untypical Nuclear Regulatory Commission.

10. Commodity Futures Trading Commission, Consumer Product Safety Commission, Federal Communications Commission, Federal Energy Regulatory Commission (in the Energy Department), Federal Maritime Commission, Federal Reserve System (Board of Governors), Federal Trade Commission, Interstate Commerce Commission, National Labor Relations Board, Nuclear Regulatory Commission, Securities and Exchange Commission.

11. For an insightful account of how deregulation came about, see Martha Derthick and Paul J. Quirk, *The Politics of Deregulation* (Washington, D.C.: Brookings Institution, 1985).

12. Donald F. Kettl, *Leadership at the Fed* (New Haven: Yale University Press, 1986), 1.

13. William E. Brigman, "The Executive Branch and the Independent Regulatory Agencies," *Presidential Studies Quarterly* 11 (Spring 1981): 244–61; David M. Welborn, *Governance of Federal Regulatory Agencies* (Knoxville: University of Tennessee Press, 1977).

14. The chairman appoints and supervises the staff, distributes the workload, and allocates funds. Often several fellow commissioners are patronage appointees, content to follow the chairman's lead. For a disheartening assessment of the quality of appointments from 1949 to 1974 (especially to the Federal Communications Commission and Federal Trade Commission), see U.S. Senate Committee on Commerce, *Appointments to the Regulatory Agencies* (Washington, D.C.: Government Printing Office, 1976).

15. It was not always thus. In 1937 the Brownlow Committee characterized the regulatory commissions as "a headless 'fourth branch' of the Government, a haphazard deposit of irresponsible agencies and uncoordinated powers." President's Committee on Administrative Management, *Report with Special Studies* (Washington, D.C.: Government Printing Office, 1937), 40.

16. Kettl, *Leadership at the Fed*, 205–6.

17. Because no accepted definition of government corporations exists, counts differ. The figures cited are respectively from Ronald C. Moe, *Administering Public Functions at the Margin of Government: The Case of Federal Corporations*, Report No. 83-236 GOV, processed (Washington, D.C.: Congressional Research Service, 1 December 1983); and General Accounting Office, *Congress Should Consider Revising Basic Corporate Control Laws* (Washington, D.C.: Government Printing Office, 1983). Both reports are valuable reviews of the status and problems of government corporations.

18. Interstate, state, and local government corporations numbered at least 7000 in 1978, and they too were multiplying. Annmarie Hauck Walsh, *The Public's Business: The Politics and Practices of Government Corporations* (Cambridge, Mass.: MIT Press, 1978), 6.

19. For "government-sponsored enterprises," which borrow and lend money (often so unbusinesslike as to have authority to lend only to those turned down by private lending institutions), see Office of Management and Budget, *Budget of the*

United States Government, Fiscal Year 1991 (Washington, D.C.: Government Printing Office, 1990), 229–46.

20. U.S. Bureau of the Census, *Statistical Abstract of the United States: 1994* (Washington, D.C.: Government Printing Office, 1994), 347.

21. Problems of the functional and areal systems are explored in James W. Fesler, "The Basic Theoretical Question: How to Relate Area and Function," in *The Administration of the New Federalism,* ed. Leigh E. Grosenick (Washington, D.C.: American Society for Public Administration, 1973), 4–14.

22. In France, as elsewhere, functional pressures by central departments force departures from the model, followed periodically by efforts to reestablish its purity.

23. John Mudd, *Neighborhood Services: Making Big Cities Work* (New Haven: Yale University Press, 1984).

24. The general problem is reviewed in James W. Fesler, *Area and Administration* (University: University of Alabama Press, 1949, 1964).

25. For fifty years, interagency boards have existed in major cities, but they have been poorly supported from Washington and rarely addressed problems of program coordination. See General Accounting Office, *Federal Executive Boards Contribute to Improved Field Management but Future Is Uncertain* (Washington, D.C.: Government Printing Office, 1984).

26. For a vivid account, see "Turf Wars in the Federal Bureaucracy," *Newsweek,* 10 April 1989, 24–26. For much of the 1980s, coordination of the war on drugs was under the National Drug Enforcement Policy Board, but it was ineffective in dealing with interagency disputes. A drug "czar" was appointed in 1989.

27. Advisory Commission on Intergovernmental Relations, *Improving Federal Grants Management* (Washington, D.C.: Government Printing Office, 1977), 181–99; James L. Sundquist, *Making Federalism Work* (Washington, D.C.: Brookings Institution, 1969), 272–75.

28. President's Task Force on Government Organization, "The Organization and Management of Great Society Programs," 15 June 1967, 8. Processed. Available at the Lyndon B. Johnson Presidential Library, University of Texas, Austin.

29. Advisory Commission on Intergovernmental Relations, *The Question of State Government Capability,* prepared by Mavis Reeves (Washington, D.C.: ACIR, 1985), 130–33.

30. Constitution of the United States, Article II; *Myers v. United States,* 272 U.S. 52 (1926), as modified for quasi-judicial officers by *Humphrey's Executor* (1935) and by *Weiner v. United States,* 357 U.S. 349 (1958).

31. See Peri E. Arnold, *Making the Managerial Presidency: Comprehensive Reorganization Planning, 1905–1980* (Princeton, N.J.: Princeton University Press, 1986), 361–64; and, more generally, Richard P. Nathan, *The Administrative Presidency* (New York: Wiley, 1983); and Colin Campbell, *Managing the Presidency: Carter, Reagan, and the Search for Executive Harmony* (Pittsburgh: University of Pittsburgh Press, 1986).

32. *Leadership in Jeopardy: The Fraying of the Presidential Appointments System* (Washington, D.C.: National Academy of Public Administration, 1985), 4–5.

33. A notable exception was Edwin Meese, III, counselor to President Reagan

and later attorney general, who, as chairman of the Cabinet Council on Management and Administration, devoted energy to management reforms.

34. President's Committee on Administrative Management, *Report with Special Studies,* iv (Washington, D.C.: Government Printing Office, 1987), 40.

35. Herbert Emmerich, *Federal Organization and Administrative Management* (University: University of Alabama Press, 1971), 199; U.S. Bureau of the Census, *Statistical Abstract of the United States: 1994* (Washington, D.C.: Government Printing Office, 1994), 346. Here and later in this section, official data are presented; however, their accuracy has often been questioned. For the varying counts, see John Hart, *The Presidential Branch,* 2d ed. (Chatham, N.J.: Chatham House, 1995), 42–46, 112–25; Gary King and Lyn Ragsdale, *The Elusive Executive* (Washington, D.C.: CQ Press, 1990), tables 4.1 and 4.2; Office of Personnel Management, *Employment and Trends;* and Office of Administration, Executive Office of the President, "Aggregate Report on Personnel Pursuant to Title 3, *U.S. Code of Federal Regulations,* sec. 113 (annual). Processed.

36. General Accounting Office, *Personnel Practices: Detailing of Federal Employees to the White House* (July 1987) and *Personnel Practices: Federal Employees Detailed from DOD to the White House* (March 1988) (Washington, D.C.: Government Printing Office, 1987 and 1988).

37. Thomas E. Cronin, "The Swelling of the Presidency: Can Anyone Reverse the Tide?" in *American Government: Readings and Cases,* 9th ed., ed. Peter Woll (Boston: Little, Brown, 1984), 345–60.

38. President's Committee on Administrative Management, *Report with Special Studies,* 5.

39. Samuel Kernell, "The Creed and Reality of Modern White House Management," in *Chief of Staff: Twenty-Five Years of Managing the Presidency,* ed. Samuel Kernell and Samuel L. Popkin (Berkeley: University of California Press, 1986), 193–222.

40. For a full and admiring description of the White House staff, see Bradley H. Patterson, Jr., *The Ring of Power: The White House Staff and Its Expanding Role in Government* (New York: Basic Books, 1988).

41. Greg Schneiders, "My Turn: Goodbye to All That," *Newsweek,* 24 September 1979, 23. Cf. "Even when working a seventy-hour week the President does not see most of his White House Office staff, or most of his Cabinet." Carter devoted a third of his time to seeing *senior* staff members and a sixth to seeing cabinet and other officials. Richard Rose, *The Postmodern President: The White House Meets the World* (Chatham, N.J.: Chatham House, 1988), 151–52.

42. Kernell and Popkin, *Chief of Staff,* 229–31.

43. *The Executive Presidency: Federal Management for the 1990s* (Washington, D.C.: National Academy of Public Administration, 1988), 7. Former President Ford and Carter's domestic policy chief, Stuart Eizenstat, have also proposed a permanent secretariat.

44. Ibid., 6. See also Stephen Hess, *Organizing the Presidency,* 2d ed. (Washington, D.C.: Brookings Institution, 1988), 172–74.

45. Samuel Kernell, "The Evolution of the White House Staff," in *Can the Government Govern?* ed. John E. Chubb and Paul E. Peterson (Washington, D.C.:

Brookings Institution, 1989), 235.

46. U.S. Bureau of the Census, *Statistical Abstract of the United States: 1994* 346.

47. Because the Trade Representative's Office has operational functions inappropriate to the advisory staff role of EOP agencies, proposals recur for its absorption in the Department of Commerce or in a new Department of International Trade and Industry.

48. The best comprehensive review of the OMB is U.S. Senate Committee on Governmental Affairs, *Office of Management and Budget: Evolving Roles and Future Issues* (February 1986), 99th Cong., 2d. sess., S. Rpt. 99–134 (Washington, D.C.: Government Printing Office, 1986). For its and the Budget Bureau's history, see also Larry Berman, *The Office of Management and Budget and the Presidency, 1921–1979* (Princeton, N.J.: Princeton University Press, 1979); and Frederick C. Mosher, *A Tale of Two Agencies: A Comparative Analysis of the General Accounting Office and the Office of Management and Budget* (Baton Rouge: Louisiana State University Press, 1984).

49. Presidents vary in their involvement in the budgetary process. Those who, like Nixon and Reagan, dislike the conflictive atmosphere surrounding personal arbitration of appeals by agency heads from the budget director, delegate the responsibility to others.

50. Hugh Heclo, "OMB and the Presidency—The Problem of 'Neutral Competence,'" *Public Interest* 38 (Winter 1975): 80–98.

51. This will seem unimportant only to those who have not observed the frequency with which "new" ideas are enthusiastically advanced and acted on by newly recruited high officials who are unaware that the same idea, or a near-analog, was earlier introduced and failed.

52. Hugh Heclo, *A Government of Strangers: Executive Politics in Washington* (Washington, D.C.: Brookings Institution, 1977), 80–81.

53. See David A. Stockman, *The Triumph of Politics: The Inside Story of the Reagan Revolution* (New York: Harper & Row, 1986; paperback ed., New York: Avon Books, 1987).

54. Ronald C. Moe, "Assessment of Organizational Policy and Planning Function in OMB," in U.S. Senate Committee on Governmental Affairs, *Office of Management and Budget,* 147–67, at 163. See also General Accounting Office, *Managing the Government: Revised Approach Could Improve OMB's Effectiveness* (Washington, D.C.: Government Printing Office, 1989).

55. *Revitalizing Federal Management: Managers and Their Overburdened Systems* (Washington, D.C.: National Academy of Public Administration, 1983), 10–13. Opponents argue that such an office would lack the power over agencies that inclusion in OMB confers.

56. Office of Management and Budget, Memorandum, 94–96, 1 March 1994.

57. See Alan Dean, Dwight Ink, and Harold Seidman, "OMB's 'M' Fading Away," *Government Executive* 26 (June 1994): 62–64.

58. 50 *U.S Code* 401. Reorganization Plan No. 4 of 1949 placed the NSC in the Executive Office of the President.

59. Attendance was expanded by President Reagan to include the attorney general, secretary of the treasury, director of OMB, and chief delegate to the United Nations.

60. For details on the interagency committee structure and national security advisers' conceptions of their role before and after the Iran-*contra* scandal of 1985–86, see Robert C. McFarlane, Richard Saunders, and Thomas C. Shull, "The National Security Council: Organization for Policy Making," in *The Presidency and National Security Policy,* ed. G. Gordon Hoxie et al. (New York: Center for the Study of the Presidency, 1984), 261–73; and Colin L. Powell, "The NSC System in the Last Two Years of the Reagan Administration" in *The Presidency in Transition,* ed. James P. Pfiffner and R. Gordon Hoxie et al. (New York: Center for the Study of the Presidency, 1989), 204–18. McFarlane and Powell were national security advisers. The Bush administration simplified the interagency committee structure. Bernard Weinraub, "Bush Backs Plan to Enhance Role of Security Staff," *New York Times,* 2 February 1989.

61. Patterson, *Ring of Power,* 340.

62. Bert Rockman, "America's Departments of State: Irregular and Regular Syndromes of Policy Making," *American Political Science Review* 75 (December 1981): 911–27.

63. The NSC staff's organizational status is ambiguous. Fifteen staff members are special assistants to the president, thus bringing them within the White House Office. Nine of these assistants head staff units (e.g., Asian Affairs, African Affairs, Defense Policy, Intelligence Programs). *The Capital Source,* Spring 1996, 11–12.

64. Curiously, Lieutenant Colonel Oliver North, the major figure in illegal, covert operations, "served under four national security advisers in five years and found that the almost annual change in leadership and continual turnover in the staff was an advantage to him. Former and current members of the council's staff say he served as the institutional memory of the National Security Council, providing a continuity that made him almost indispensable." Keith Schneider, "North's Record: A Wide Role in a Host of Sensitive Projects," *New York Times,* 3 January 1987.

65. *Report of the Congressional Committees Investigating the Iran-Contra Affair . . . ,* 100th Congress, 1st sess., Union Calendar No. 277, S. Rpt. 100–216, H. Rpt. 100–433 (Washington, D.C.: Government Printing Office, 1987).

66. Reorganization Plan No. 2, and Message of the President, in 5 *U.S. Code of Federal Regulations* (1982 ed.), Appendix 1129–32.

67. The experience of President Ford's most active council is related by its executive secretary, Roger B. Porter, *Presidential Decision Making: The Economic Policy Board* (New York: Cambridge University Press, 1980). Few of the other cabinet councils were more than marginally active. James P. Pfiffner, "White House Staff Versus the Cabinet: Centripetal and Centrifugal Roles," *Presidential Studies Quarterly* 16 (Fall 1986): 666–90, at 682–83. Reagan had seven cabinet councils in his first term. Collectively they held nearly 500 meetings. Ralph C. Bledsoe, "Policy Management in the Reagan Administration," in Pfiffner and Hoxie, *Presidency in Transition,* 54–61, at 59.

68. See, on Reagan's and earlier domestic policy offices and councils, Margaret Jane Wyszomirski, "The Role of a Presidential Office for Domestic Policy: Three Models and Four Cases," in *The Presidency and Public Policy Making,* ed. George C. Edwards et al. (Pittsburgh: University of Pittsburgh Press, 1985), 130–50.

69. The office was created by Nixon; under Carter, staff members were assigned for labor, business, consumers, women, the elderly, Jews, Hispanics, white ethnic Catholics, Vietnam veterans, and gays. John P. Burke, "The Institutional Presidency," in *The Presidency and the Political System,* 2d ed., ed. Michael Nelson (Washington, D.C.: CQ Press, 1988), 355–77, at 364.

6. Organization Problems (pp. 111–32)

1. Jack H. Knott and Gary J. Miller, *Reforming Bureaucracy: The Politics of Institutional Choice* (Englewood Cliffs, N.J.: Prentice Hall, 1987), 274.

2. Herbert Kaufman, "Emerging Doctrines of Public Administration," *American Political Science Review* 50 (December 1956): 1059–73. He assigns their relative dominance historically in this sequence: representativeness, neutral competence, and executive leadership.

3. Federal Regulation Study Team, *Federal Energy Regulation: An Organizational Study,* April 1974 (Washington, D.C.: Government Printing Office, 1974), appendix D, D1–2.

4. Ibid., D2.

5. The bias appears most clearly in members of the human relations "school" of thought (reviewed in chapter 3). But when leaders of that school acquire experience as heads of organizations, their views change. See Douglas McGregor, "On Leadership," in *Leadership and Motivation: Essays of Douglas McGregor,* ed. Warren G. Bennis and Edgar N. Schein (Cambridge, Mass.: MIT Press, 1966), 66–70; and Warren G. Bennis, *The Leaning Ivory Tower* (San Francisco: Jossey-Bass, 1973). McGregor was president of Antioch College from 1948 to 1954, and Bennis was provost and vice-president of the University of Buffalo from 1967 to 1971 and president of the University of Cincinnati from 1971 to 1977.

6. E.S. Turner, *The Court of St. James's* (London: Michael Joseph, 1959), 305–6.

7. Note that the issue is whether to organize by clientele (industry) or by purpose or, perhaps, process (promotion, regulation).

8. Doubts exist that the Nuclear Regulatory Commission adequately protects the public's health and safety, perhaps because it focuses on a single industry, or because many AEC staff members were transferred to the NRC, or both.

9. *United States Government Organization Manual, 1977/78,* 312.

10. President's Task Force on Government Organization, "The Organization and Management of Great Society Programs," 15 June 1967, 5 (original emphasis omitted). Processed. Available at the Lyndon B. Johnson Presidential Library, University of Texas, Austin.

11. The concept of core activities is akin to the concept of "organizational essence" in Morton H. Halperin, *Bureaucratic Politics and Foreign Policy* (Washing-

ton, D.C.: Brookings Institution, 1974), 28–40. He soundly argues that an organization must vigorously protect its organizational core or essence. But the intensity of border warfare among domestic departments seems to contradict his view that an organization is "often" or "sometimes" indifferent to and inclined to push out functions that are not of the essence.

12. Todd S. Purdom, "Scuba Feud Pits Idled Bravest Against Prideful Finest," *New York Times,* 5 May 1988; and Ari L. Goldman, "New Rules Set for Handling Emergencies, *New York Times,* 5 July 1990.

13. Ironically, though the lead-agency formula does not work well in the federal government, that government often requires use of it by state governments in programs financed with federal grants-in-aid.

14. See Allen Schick, "The Coordination Option," in *Federal Reorganization: What Have We Learned?* ed. Peter Szanton (Chatham, N.J.: Chatham House, 1981), 85–113, esp. 95–99.

15. William J. Lynn, "The Wars Within: The Joint Military Structure and Its Critics," in *Reorganizing America's Defense: Leadership in War and Peace,* ed. Robert J. Art, Vincent Davis, and Samuel P. Huntington (Washington, D.C.: Pergamon-Brassey's, 1985), 168–204, esp. 174–83.

16. Both deficiencies are well documented and analyzed in U.S. Senate, Committee on Armed Services, *Defense Organization: The Need for Change: Staff Report,* 99th Cong., 1st sess., 16 October 1985, S. Rpt. 99–86 (Washington, D.C.: Government Printing Office), 157–79 (re Joint Chiefs), and 302–24 (re Unified Commands). Note that the Unified Command problem (the individual armed services vs. the regional commanders) is an example of the function-area conflict we have earlier examined.

17. *The National Military Command Structure: Report,* prepared by Richard C. Steadman, July 1978 (Washington, D.C.: Department of Defense, 1978), 52, 55.

18. President's Commission on Defense Management (chaired by David Packard), *A Quest for Excellence: Final Report to the President,* June 1986 (Washington, D.C.: Government Printing Office, 1986) 35–37; Department of Defense Reorganization Act of 1986, 100 U.S. Statutes 1005.

19. For details on interagency strife in narcotics control, see W. John Moore, "No Quick Fix," *National Journal* 20 (21 November 1987): 2954–59; "Turf Wars in the Federal Bureaucracy," *Newsweek,* 20 April 1989, 4–6.

20. 102 U.S. Statutes 4181. The czar is formally the director of National Drug Control Policy.

21. Sandra Panem, *The AIDS Bureaucracy* (Cambridge: Harvard University Press, 1988).

22. See Jean Blondel, *The Organization of Governments: A Comparative Analysis of Governmental Structures* (Beverly Hills, Calif.: Sage, 1982).

23. *Strengthening the U.S.-Soviet Communications Process to Reduce the Risks of Misunderstandings and Conflicts: A Report by a Panel* (Washington, D.C.: National Academy of Public Administration, 1987), 39–40. The panel favors establishing a bureau of Soviet and East European Affairs, headed by an assistant secretary. For other State Department organizational-reform proposals, see Christopher Madi-

son, "Avoiding the Ax," *National Journal* 20 (16 January 1988): 118–22.

24. For one of the most ambitious reorganizations, see *After a Decade: A Progress Report on Organization and Management of the Florida State Department of Health and Rehabilitative Services* (Washington, D.C.: National Academy of Public Administration, 1986). For a penetrating critique of such reorganizations and of milder efforts at horizontal coordination, see Janet A. Weiss, "Substance vs. Symbol in Administrative Reform: The Case of Human Services Coordination," *Policy Analysis* 7 (Winter 1981): 21–45. A full bibliography is in General Accounting Office, *Welfare Simplification: Projects to Coordinate Services for Low-Income Families,* August 1986 (Washington, D.C.: Government Printing Office, 1986), 50–61.

25. Staff units, in the broader meaning of *staff,* are numerous. Of all bureaus and group-of-bureau units in the executive departments (excluding Defense) in 1973, 58 percent were line, 38 percent staff, and 4 percent mixed line and staff units. Herbert Kaufman, *Are Government Organizations Immortal?* (Washington, D.C.: Brookings Institution, 1976), 38–39. Since 1973, department heads' staff aides have multiplied, leading to the same kind of complaints as are raised about White House aides.

26. Commission on the Organization of the Government for the Conduct of Foreign Policy, Report (Washington, D.C.: Government Printing Office, 1975), 32–33. (Emphasis in original.)

27. The second point does not apply fully to staff *aides,* as their time perspectives are often shortened by heavy involvement in helping their superior deal with immediate crises. In practice, staff *units* risk being diverted to shortrange tasks either by their superior's urgent requests or by their own desire to prove "useful"; such diversion leaves long-range analysis untended to—a neglect that may be costly.

28. Robert T. Golembiewski, *Organizing Men and Power: Patterns of Behavior and Line-Staff Models* (Chicago: Rand McNally, 1967), 62. Pages 60–89 provide the definitive analysis of the tensions between line and staff-auxiliary-control activities.

29. For a striking example, demonstrating the high stakes in such commonplace auxiliary activities, see Herbert Kaufman, *The UN Publications Board,* Inter-University Case Program, Case No. 11 (Washington, D.C., 1952; currently distributed by the Inter-University Case Program, Syracuse, N.Y.).

30. For verification, readers in universities should consult faculty members in science departments.

31. A major problem is the vast number of regulations and review requirements imposed by auxiliary units on program administrators. The best assessment of this is *Revitalizing Federal Management: Managers and Their Overburdened Systems* (Washington, D.C.: National Academy of Public Administration, 1983).

32. For major critiques of the "neutral competence" approach, see Knott and Miller, *Reforming Bureaucracy;* and *Organizing Governance and Governing Organizations,* ed. Colin Campbell and B. Guy Peters (Pittsburgh: University of Pittsburgh Press, 1988). See also Harold Seidman and Robert Gilmour, *Politics, Position, and Power: From the Positive to the Regulatory State,* 4th ed. (New York: Oxford University Press, 1986); James G. March and Johan P. Olsen, "Organizing Political Life: What Administrative Reorganization Tells Us about Government," *American*

Political Science Review 77 (June 1983): 281–96; and Terry M. Moe, "The Politics of Bureaucratic Structure," *Can the Government Govern?* ed. John E. Chubb and Paul E. Peterson (Washington, D.C.: Brookings Institution, 1989), 267–329.

33. *Immigration and Naturalization Service v. Chadha,* 462 U.S. 919 (1983). See Barbara Hinkson Craig, *Chadha: The Story of an Epic Constitutional Struggle* (New York: Oxford University Press, 1987; paper ed., Berkeley: University of California Press, 1990).

34. 98 U.S. Statutes 3192 (8 November 1984). The president cannot use this method to propose creating a new agency outside a department or existing agency.

35. Herbert Kaufman, *Are Government Organizations Immortal?* 24, 42. From 1939 to 1973, presidents submitted 109 plans and Congress permitted 86 to go into effect. A number were notable and some created new agencies. Office of Management and Budget, "President's Reorganization Authority," April 1977, appendix 3, p. 4 (processed); Harvey C. Mansfield, "Executive Reorganization: Thirty Years of Experience," *Public Administration Review* 29 (July–August 1969): 332–45; reprinted in *American Public Administration: Patterns of the Past,* ed. James W. Fesler (Washington, D.C.: American Society for Public Administration, 1982), 215–35.

36. Ease of adoption varies greatly. Some bureaus and their functions have proved immovable in face of a long history of recommendations for transfer (e.g., the Forest Service and the civil works functions of the Army Corps of Engineers, both proposed for transfer to the Interior Department, the major locus for natural resource bureaus and functions).

37. The exceptions are Kennedy and Ford, with short tenures, and Reagan. For a full account and analysis of presidential reorganization efforts, see Peri E. Arnold, *Making the Managerial Presidency: Comprehensive Reorganization Planning, 1905–1980* (Princeton, N.J.: Princeton University Press, 1986).

38. Nixon's ambitious plan (described below) failed to win congressional support and then the Watergate scandal exhausted his political capital. In 1967–68 Johnson, losing his political capital because of the Vietnam war, neither allowed publication nor advocated adoption of recommendations of the President's (Heineman) Task Force on Government Organization.

39. Others, however, led to later reforms. See James W. Fesler, "The Brownlow Committee Fifty Years Later," *Public Administration Review* 47 (July/August 1987): 291–96.

40. See Ronald C. Moe, *The Hoover Commissions Revisited* (Boulder, Colo.: Westview Press, 1982).

41. Herbert Emmerich, *Federal Organization and Administrative Management* (University: University of Alabama Press, 1971), 127.

42. Office of Management and Budget, *Papers Relating to the President's Departmental Reorganization Program,* March 1971 (Washington, D.C.: Government Printing Office, 1971). See also the revised edition of February 1972.

43. Frustrated by Congress's failure to act, Nixon set out in 1973 to do by fiat what Congress would not let him do by law. Four cabinet members were additionally given White House posts as counselors to the president, each with powers over

the existing departments in the fields of the proposed departments. In May 1973, with Watergate unraveling, Nixon abandoned this scheme of "supersecretaries."

44. The major success claimed was reform of the civil service, but this was mostly nonorganizational.

45. Reagan supported creation of the Department of Veterans' Affairs, but its success in Congress was already assured.

46. The success of Reagan's strategy is assessed in *The Reagan Legacy: Promise and Performance,* ed. Charles O. Jones (Chatham, N.J.: Chatham House, 1988), esp. chaps. 1 and 4.

47. James K. Conant, "In the Shadow of Wilson and Brownlow: Executive Branch Reorganization in the States, 1965 to 1987," *Public Administration Review* 48 (September/October 1988): 892–902. One state, Iowa, reorganized in 1985–86.

48. March and Olsen, "Organizing Political Life," 288, 292.

49. See Herbert Kaufman, *The Limits of Organizational Change* (University: University of Alabama Press, 1971); and idem, *Are Government Organizations Immortal?*

50. For a classic analysis of the expansive tendencies, see Matthew Holden, Jr., "'Imperialism' in Bureaucracy," *American Political Science Review* 60 (December 1966): 943–51.

51. Craig W. Thomas, "Reorganizing Public Organizations: Alternatives, Objectives, and Evidence," *Journal of Public Administration and Theory* 3 (1993): 457–86.

7. The Civil Service (pp. 135–78)

1. Associated Press dispatch, *New Haven Register,* 18 July 1969; 5 *U.S. Code of Federal Regulations,* 5546, 5547.

2. Most large, private-sector organizations also have classification systems, though they are usually less rigid than those in civil service systems.

3. U.S. Bureau of the Census, *Statistical Abstract of the United States: 1994* (Washington, D.C.: Government Printing Office, 1994), 318. Official sources vary in these and other employee statistics, depending on the time of year the counts are made and on whether a count records only full-time employees, both full-time and part-time employees, or full-time equivalent employees (i.e., with part-time employment collapsed to full-time equivalence).

4. Council of Economic Advisers, *Economic Report of the President,* 1994 (Washington, D.C.: Government Printing Office, 1994), 318–19.

5. Office of Management and Budget, *Special Analyses,* 1-13. Government-wide changes mask significant details. According to another source, between 1977 and 1987 the federal civilian workforce increased 191,000 (7 percent), but the big gains were in the Postal Service, 151,000 (23 percent); Defense, 76,000 (8 percent); and the Veterans Administration, 21,000 (9 percent). Major losers were Health and Human Services, down 26,400 (–16.8 percent) and Agriculture, Transportation, and Interior, from –11,000 to –22,000 (–14 to –18 percent). Congressional Budget Office, *Federal Civilian Employment* (Washington, D.C.: Government Printing Office,

1987), 27.

6. Computed from data in U.S. Bureau of the Census, *Government Finances in 1987–88* (Washington, D.C.: Government Printing Office, 1990), table 2.

7. Actually less, as severance pay, retirement pensions, and unemployment compensation would add to outlays. For analysis of a 2 percent cut, see Congressional Budget Office, *Reducing the Deficit: Spending and Revenue Options: A Report . . . —Part II* (Washington, D.C.: Government Printing Office, 1989), 299–301.

8. Public Law 95-454, approved 13 October 1978, 92 Stat. 1111. The Equal Employment Opportunity Commission has a limited role. The Office of Special Counsel, charged with investigating civil service abuses, was originally associated with the Merit Systems Protection Board; in 1989 Congress made it an independent agency.

9. 5 *U.S. Code of Federal Regulations.*

10. Joseph B. Wright, deputy director of OMB, in John D.R. Cole, "Joe Wright on Reform '88," *Bureaucrat* 12 (Summer 1983): 7–11.

11. *Revitalizing Federal Management: Managers and Their Overburdened Systems: A Panel Report* (Washington, D.C.: National Academy of Public Administration, November 1983), 37–40. The panel adds a caveat that program managers need to be trained for exercise of this hitherto withheld role.

12. *Leadership for America: Rebuilding the Public Service,* Report of the National (Volcker) Commission on the Public Service and Task Force Reports (Lexington, Mass.: Lexington Books, 1990), 144; Bernard Rosen, "Crises in the U.S. Civil Service," *Public Administration Review* 46 (May/June 1986): 207–14, at 209.

13. *Leadership for America,* 40. See also General Accounting Office, *Managing Human Resources: Greater OPM Leadership Needed to Address Critical Challenges* (Washington, D.C., 1989), and, more broadly, *The Public Service: Issues Affecting Its Quality, Effectiveness, Integrity, and Stewardship* (Washington, D.C., 1989); and see Merit Systems Protection Board, *U.S. Office of Personnel Management and the Merit System: A Retrospective Assessment* (Washington, D.C., 1989).

14. U.S. Bureau of the Census, *Statistical Abstract of the United States: 1994* 348.

15. Among these are the Executive Schedule (mostly for political appointees), the Senior Executive Service, and the Foreign Service, all parts of the higher public service, the subject of the following chapter.

16. A similar problem occurs in state and local governments. In the New York City school system "a teacher reaches maximum pay after 15 years and can only be promoted by moving to an administrative post." Report of the Commission on the Year 2000, quoted in Jane Perlez, "Reviving Education System: A Call for Radical Changes," *New York Times,* 1 July 1987.

17. Though the Congressional Budget Office "found that grade distribution in the federal government was top-heavy relative to that in the private sector," it discovered "nearly identical . . . work force distribution by pay levels." Congressional Budget Office, *Reducing Grades of the General Schedule Work Force* (Washington, D.C.: Government Printing Office, 1984), 12–13. For a broad-gauged appraisal of the classification system, including recent use of simplified, multioccupational

guides, see Merit Systems Protection Board, *OPM's Classification and Qualification Systems* (Washington, D.C.: Government Printing Office, 1989).

18. An agency sometimes gives narrowly specialized features to a job description to elude competitive appointment standards, knowing that, with not more than three persons in the country who can qualify, it will be able to appoint its preferred candidate. Central personnel agencies have difficulty distinguishing such cases from legitimate ones.

19. 5 *U.S. Code of Federal Regulations* 5104.

20. General Accounting Office, *Federal Personnel: Observations on the Navy's Personnel Management Demonstration Project* (Washington, D.C.: Government Printing Office, 1988).

21. *Leadership for America,* 290 (Task Force Report).

22. Ibid., 95.

23. 5 *U.S. Code of Federal Regulations* 3304(a). The substance and much of the language date from the Pendleton Civil Service Act of 1883.

24. Office of Personnel Management, *Federal Civilian Workforce Statistics: Employment and Trends as of January 1989* (Washington, D.C.: Government Printing Office, 1989), 80. Some "excepted services" (e.g., the Postal Service and the Tennessee Valley Authority) have their own merit systems and are included in the four-fifths figure.

25. Merit Systems Protection Board, *Delegation and Decentralization: Personnel Management Simplification Efforts in the Federal Government* (Washington, D.C.: Government Printing Office, 1989), 8.

26. Lana Stein, "Merit Systems and Political Influence: The Case of Local Government," *Public Administration Review* 47 (May/June 1987): 263–71, at 267.

27. The five-point bonus is for any veteran who served on active duty in the armed forces during wartime or a military campaign, or who served on active duty in peacetime between 1955 and 1976. The ten-point bonus is for any veteran with a service-connected disability who served on active duty during wartime or peacetime. Spouses, widows and widowers, and mothers of veterans are entitled to preference under stated circumstances. 5 *U.S. Code of Federal Regulations* 2108, 3309; 5 *U.S. Code of Federal Regulations* 332.401.

28. Merit Systems Protection Board, *Delegation and Decentralization,* 9–11.

29. 5 *U.S. Code of Federal Regulations* 2108, 3309–16. See also the current edition of Office of Personnel Management, *Veterans' Preference in Federal Employment: Opportunities in the Federal Service* (Washington, D.C.: Government Printing Office).

30. Office of Personnel Management, *Federal Workforce Statistics as of January 1989,* 72.

31. Sharon R. Cohany, "Labor Force Status of Vietnam-Era Veterans," *Monthly Labor Review* 110 (February 1987): 11–16, at 15.

32. An alternative would be to permit a veteran to use his preference only once, rather than several times.

33. The Equal Employment Opportunity Commission is authorized to act on complaints appealed by individual applicants and employees from denials by federal

agencies and state and local governments, and can invoke courts' intervention when necessary.

34. Message of the President, accompanying Reorganization Plan No. 1 of 1978 (23 February 1978), 42 *U.S. Code of Federal Regulations* 2000(e)(4).

35. 5 *U.S. Code of Federal Regulations* 7201.

36. Gregory B. Lewis, "Equal Employment Opportunity and the Early Career in Federal Employment," *Review of Public Personnel Administration* 6 (Summer 1986): 1–18.

37. *Civil Service 2000* (Washington, D.C.: Office of Personnel Administration, 1988), 19.

38. Although all eligible applicants took the same written test, its several parts measured different abilities, and those passing the test were certified for specific positions according to the relative importance of the different abilities measured.

39. Of those taking the 1976 examination, 87 percent were white and 11 percent were black. Of those passing, 95 percent were white and 3 percent black. Half of the white examinees passed, 9 percent with a score of 90 or above. Of the black examinees, only 4 percent passed, 0.6 percent with 90 or above scores. U.S. Comptroller General, *Federal Employment Examinations: Do They Achieve Equal Opportunity and Merit Principle Goals?* (Washington, D.C: Government Printing Office, 1979), 11.

See also U.S. Merit Systems Protection Board, *A Question of Equity: Women and the Glass Ceiling* (Washington, D.C.: Government Printing Office, 1992).

40. 5 *U.S. Code of Federal Regulations*, sec. 6.2.

41. For these and related data and assessments, see Merit Systems Protection Board, *In Search of Merit: Hiring Entry-Level Federal Employees* (Washington, D.C.: Government Printing Office, 1987).

42. OPM's oversight of agency *examining* activities is "more than adequate," but half of the government's personnel specialists judge ineffective its monitoring of agency *personnel systems* to detect abuses. Merit Systems Protection Board, *Delegation and Decentralization*, 13, 25.

43. See *Leadership for America*, 148–51 (Task Force Reports), for appraisal of these programs and additional proposals for improving recruitment of college graduates.

44. George Bush, statement issued 5 October 1988; "Remarks of the President to the Career Members of the Senior Executive Service," 26 January 1989. Reprinted in *Bureaucrat* 18 (Spring 1989): 3.

45. See Merit Systems Protection Board, *Attracting College Graduates to the Federal Government: A View of College Recruiting* (Washington, D.C.: Government Printing Office, 1988); *Leadership for America*, Report, 3–4, 24; and Task Force Reports, 84–88.

46. Constance Horner, OPM director, as quoted in Judith Havemann, "U.S. Plans New System for Hiring," *Washington Post*, 23 June 1988. Ms. Horner announced a new student-recruitment program, but its realization depended on its appeal to her successor under the Bush administration. See Office of Personnel Management, "New Program to Fill GS-5 and GS-7 Entry-Level Jobs," 23 June 1988.

Processed.

47. Judith Havemann, "Taking the Guesswork and Chance Out of Hiring," *Washington Post National Weekly Edition,* 30 April to 6 May 1990; Merit Systems Protection Board, *Attracting and Selecting Quality Applicants for Federal Employment* (Washington, D.C.: Government Printing Office, 1990).

48. See Patricia W. Ingraham, *The Foundation of Merit* (Baltimore: Johns Hopkins University Press, 1995).

49. National Advisory Council on the Public Service, *Ensuring the Highest Quality National Public Service* (Washington, D.C.: National Advisory Council on the Public Service, 1993), 20.

50. Carolyn Ban and Norma Riccucci, "Personnel Systems and Labor Relations: Steps toward a Quiet Revitalization," in *Revitalizing State and Local Public Service: Strengthening Performance, Accountability, and Citizen Confidence,* ed. Frank J. Thompson (San Francisco: Jossey-Bass, 1993), 83.

51. Office of Personnel Management, *Federal Civilian Workforce Statistics: Employment and Trends as of January 1990* (Washington, D.C.: Government Printing Office, 1990), 73.

52. Congressional Budget Office, *Employee Turnover in the Federal Government* (Washington, D.C.: Government Printing Office, 1986). The "technical adjustments" take into account different federal and private workforces' blue- and white-collar proportions, age distributions, etc.

53. This confines attention to the supervisor's evidence and is an easier test than support by "a preponderance of evidence," which involves weighing both the supervisor's and employee's evidence and is required in all other employee appeals cases.

54. When the employee is a female or member of a minority, the supervisor risks the complications of demonstrating that his charges are not a mask for discriminatory treatment.

55. 5 *U.S. Code of Federal Regulations* 351.201 to 351.1005. For the 1986 changes in OPM regulations (incorporated in our text), see Merit Systems Protection Board, *Reduction in Force: The Evolving Ground Rules* (Washington, D.C.: Government Printing Office, 1987).

56. 5 *U.S. Code of Federal Regulations* 536.01. Such employees get only half of any pay increase for their new grades until the grade's pay catches up.

57. General Accounting Office, *Retrenchment and Redirection at the Office of Personnel Management* (Washington, D.C.: Government Printing Office, 1983), 11–14.

58. 97 U.S. Statutes 65, sec. 101; 100 U.S. Statutes 514.

59. The exodus will mount slowly, as few pre-1984 employees have opted for inclusion in the new system.

60. General Accounting Office, *Federal Employment: The Results to Date of the FY 1994 Buyouts at Non-Defense Agencies* T-GGD-94-214, 22 September 1994, 4–5.

61. For an analysis of the economics of workforce reduction, see Congressional Budget Office, *Reducing the Size of the Federal Civilian Work Force* (Washington,

D.C.: Government Printing Office, 1993).

62. One study found that clerk-typists and secretaries, with small pay gaps compared to private salaries, had high quit rates, while chemists, accountants, and engineers, with large pay gaps, had low quit rates. General Accounting Office, *Federal Workforce: Pay, Recruitment, and Retention of Federal Employees* (Washington, D.C.: Government Printing Office, 1987), 2–3. For more comprehensive occupational analysis of voluntary separations, see Congressional Budget Office, *Employee Turnover*, 6–8.

63. For a comparison of government and private-sector employees' evaluation of a number of such job features, see Michael P. Smith and Steven L. Nock, "Social Class and the Quality of Work Life in Public and Private Organizations," *Journal of Social Issues* 30 (1980): 59–75; and Barry Bozeman, *All Organizations Are Public: Bridging Public and Private Organizational Theories* (San Francisco: Jossey-Bass, 1987), 15–23. Federal workers' appraisals are surveyed in Merit Systems Protection Board, *Federal Personnel Policies and Practices: Perspectives from the Workplace* (Washington, D.C.: Government Printing Office, 1987).

64. The pay agent is currently the OMB and OPM directors and the secretary of labor. See U.S. President's Pay Agent, *Comparability of the Federal Statutory Pay System with Private Enterprise Pay Rates* (annual). Processed.

65. Provisions referred to in this and the following paragraph are codified in 5 *U.S. Code of Federal Regulations* 5301-8.

66. A minor exception: About 160,000 white-collar positions (many of them in engineering occupations) receive higher pay than the statutory pay rates to reduce staffing problems caused by major occupational and locality pay discrepancies with the private sector. Tom Shoop, "Wage Wars," *Government Executive* 22 (June 1990): 40–48, at 41.

67. General Accounting Office, *Federal Pay: Changes to the Methods of Comparing Federal and Private Sector Salaries* (Washington, D.C.: Government Printing Office, 1987). For revisions by the Bureau of Labor Statistics, see also John D. Morton, "BLS Prepares to Broaden Scope of Its White-Collar Pay Survey," *Monthly Labor Review* 110 (March 1987): 3–7.

68. Congressional Budget Office, *Reducing the Deficit: Spending and Revenue Options* (Washington, D.C.: Government Printing Office, 1987), 184; Richard E. Schumann, "State and Local Government Pay Increases Outpace Five-Year Rise in Private Industry," *Monthly Labor Review* 110 (February 1987): 18–20. The five-year (1981–86) state and local "outpace" phenomenon compensated for a 1975–81 lag, so that "by 1986 the relative rates of pay in the two sectors were about what they were in 1975."

69. Terry W. Culler, "Most Federal Workers Need Only Be Competent," *Wall Street Journal*, 21 May 1986.

70. General Accounting Office, *Recruitment and Retention: Inadequate Federal Pay Cited as Primary Problem by Agency Officials*, GGD-90-117, September 1990, 3.

71. General Accounting Office, *Federal Pay: Comparisons with the Private Sector by Job and Locality* (Washington, D.C.: Government Printing Office, 1990),

54-55, 62; and *Managing Human Resources,* 23-25.

72. *Leadership for America,* 38. About 40,000 GS employees are already covered by special rates for particular occupations. See also the Commission's Task Force Reports, 231-33, 236.

73. The leading case, that of Washington State, is assessed in Peter T. Kilborn, "Wage Gap Between Sexes Is Cut in Test, but at a Price," *New York Times,* 31 May 1990. For Minnesota and Oregon, see Sara M. Evans and Barbara J. Nelson, *Comparable Worth and the Paradox of Technocratic Reform* (Chicago: University of Chicago Press, 1989). See also Joan Acker, *Doing Comparable Worth: Gender, Class, and Pay Equity* (Philadelphia: Temple University Press, 1989); Steven R. Rhoads, *Incomparable Worth: Pay Equity Meets the Market* (New York: Cambridge University Press, 1993); Elaine Sorensen, *Comparable Worth: Is It a Worthy Policy?* (Princeton: Princeton University Press, 1994); and Michael W. McCann, *Rights at Work: Pay Equity Reform and the Politics of Legal Mobilization* (Chicago: University of Chicago Press, 1994).

74. Some receive "quality step increases," moving to the next step faster than the calendar would dictate.

75. We draw on General Accounting Office, *Pay for Performance: Implementation of the Performance Management and Recognition System* (Washington, D.C.: Government Printing Office, 1987); and Merit Systems Protection Board, *Performance Management and Recognition System: Linking Pay to Performance* (Washington, D.C.: Government Printing Office, 1987). The system's deficiencies remained in 1989; General Accounting Office, *Pay for Performance: Interim Report on the Performance Management and Recognition System* (Washington, D.C.: Government Printing Office, 1989).

76. 5 *U.S. Code of Federal Regulations* 5401-10.

77. If already in the upper two-thirds of the positions' salary range, the top-rated group get a full-step increase but those in the next two rating levels only a half or a third of that. Employees at a grade's maximum rate, of course, get no increase.

78. 5 *U.S. Code of Federal Regulations* 4301-5.

79. College students and faculty members will recognize a parallel to pressures for inflation of course grades.

80. For a thorough coverage of the issues, see Richard B. Freeman and Casey Ichniowski, eds., *When Public Sector Workers Organize* (Chicago: University of Chicago Press, 1988).

81. U.S. Bureau of the Census, *Statistical Abstract: 1994,* table 683.

82. Sar A. Levitan and Frank Gallo, "Can Employee Associations Negotiate New Growth?" *Monthly Labor Review* 112 (July 1989): 5-14, at 8 and 10.

83. The representation percentage is not the same as membership in unions; unions may "represent" unorganized as well as organized workers (as explained below).

84. Leonard Buder, "Walkout Is Hobbling Schools in New York," *New York Times,* 24 February 1977.

85. Quoted in Frank Swoboda, "AFGE's Optimistic Organizer," *Washington Post,* 21 January 1988.

86. Victor Gotbaum, cited by Martin Tolchin, "Union Bargaining Power and Municipal Financial Trouble in a Strong Union Town," *New York Times,* 9 June 1975.

87. Joel M. Douglas, "State Civil Service and Collective Bargaining Systems," *Public Administration Review* 52 (January/February 1992): 162–71.

88. Quoted in National Academy of Public Administration, *Leading People in Change: Empowerment, Commitment, Accountability* (Washington, D.C.: National Academy, 1993), 10.

89. David T. Stanley, *Managing Local Government under Union Pressure* (Washington, D.C.: Brookings Institution, 1972), passim.

90. Ibid., 89–111; Steven M. Goldschmidt and Leland E. Stuart, "The Extent and Impact of Educational Policy Bargaining," *Industrial and Labor Relations Review* 39 (April 1986): 350–60.

91. 92 U.S. Statutes 1191–1217; 5 *U.S. Code of Federal Regulations* 7101–35.

92. "Appropriateness" turns on whether the proposed unit "will ensure a clear and identifiable community of interest among the employees in the unit and will promote effective dealings with, and efficiency of operations of, the agency involved."

93. Office of Personnel Management, *Union Recognition in the Federal Government* (Washington, D.C.: Government Printing Office, 1987), table A; Judith Havemann, "Federal Labor-Relations Marred by Increasing Strife," *Washington Post,* 31 May 1987.

94. For the Federal Labor Relations Authority's interpretations of "compelling need" and "procedures," see Sar Levitan and Alexandra Noden, *Working for the Sovereign: Employee Relations in the Federal Government* (Baltimore: Johns Hopkins University Press, 1983), 36–40, and annual reports of the FLRA.

95. Executive Order 12564, 15 September 1986. For its implementation, see General Accounting Office, *Drug Testing: Federal Agency Plans for Testing Employees* (Washington, D.C.: Government Printing Office, 1989); and *Drug Testing: Action by Certain Agencies When Employees Test Positive for Illegal Drugs* (Washington, D.C.: Government Printing Office, 1990).

96. *National Treasury Employees* v. *Von Raab,* 109 Supreme Court Reporter 1384 (1989).

97. The relation is a matter of dispute. For technical discussion, see "The Cause of AIDS," *Science* 242 (18 November 1988): 997–98.

98. Richard L. Berke, "State Department to Begin AIDS Testing," *New York Times,* 29 November 1986.

99. The phrase recurs in a succession of bills passed by the House of Representatives to amend the Hatch Act, discussed later.

100. 5 *U.S. Code of Federal Regulations* 7324-27. For specifically permissible activities and prohibited activities, see 5 *U.S. Code of Federal Regulations* 733.111 to 733.122. Exceptions to the ban exist (1) for nonpartisan elections and with regard to questions (such as constitutional amendments and referenda) not specifically identified with a national or state political party; and (2) in certain local communities near Washington and elsewhere (designated by OPM) where federal employees

are a majority of voters. OPM restricts activity in such communities' partisan elections to candidacy as, or advocacy or opposition to, an independent candidate.

101. Those free of the restrictions are the president and vice-president, aides paid from appropriations for the president's office, heads and assistant heads of executive departments, and officers who are appointed by the president, by and with the advice and consent of the Senate, and who determine policies to be pursued by the United States.

102. *United Public Workers v. Mitchell,* 330 U.S. 75 (1947).

103. *United States Civil Service Commission* v. *National Association of Letter Carriers, AFL-CIO* 413 U.S. 548 (1973).

104. What was taking "an active part in political management or in political campaigns" gained sufficient specificity by a 1940 amendment that incorporated the activities that the Civil Service Commission had prohibited in about 3,000 decisions made under civil service rules between 1907 and 1940.

105. Richard Berke, "Senate Upholds Veto of Bill on U.S. Workers in Politics," *New York Times,* 22 June 1990.

106. Kenneth J. Cooper, "Many Hatch Act Curbs on Politics Are Lifted," *Washington Post,* 22 September 1993, A1.

107. 427 U.S. 347 (1976).

108. 445 U.S. 507 (1980).

109. For a criticism of the two cases, see Kenneth J. Meier, "Ode to Patronage: A Critical Analysis of Two Recent Supreme Court Decisions," *Public Administration Review* 41 (September/October 1981): 558–63.

110. Case No. 88-1872 (21 June 1990); Linda Greenhouse, "Court Widens Curb on Patronage in Jobs for Most Public Workers," *New York Times,* 22 June 1990.

111. In contrast, the city of Chicago's Democratic administration substantially ended its patronage hiring system when it settled federal court suits by signing a consent decree. For an excellent review, see Anne Freedman, "Doing Battle with the Patronage Army: Politics, Courts, and Personnel Administration in Chicago," *Public Administration Review* 48 (September/October 1988): 847–59.

112. Ronald N. Johnson and Gary D. Libecap, *The Federal Civil Service System and the Problem of Bureaucracy* (Chicago: University of Chicago Press, 1994).

8. The Higher Public Service (pp. 179–213)

1. *Fairness for Our Public Servants,* Report of the 1989 Commission on Executive, Legislative and Judicial Salaries, 15 December 1988 (Washington, D.C.: Government Printing Office, 1988), 8–9. Other counts of Executive Schedule officials report 500 and 683: President's Commission on Compensation of Career Federal Executives, *Report,* 26 February 1988 (Washington, D.C.: Government Printing Office, 1988), chart 1; *Leadership for America: Rebuilding the Public Service,* Report of the National [Volcker] Commission on the Public Service and Task Force Reports (Lexington, Mass.: Lexington Books, 1990), 17. Executive Schedule positions are listed in 5 *U.S. Code of Federal Regulations* 5312–17 and "Note."

2. Patricia W. Ingraham, "Building Bridges or Burning Them? The President, the Appointees, and the Bureaucracy," *Public Administration Review* 47 (September/October 1987): 425–35, at 428. The group hold Schedule C positions, which involve policymaking roles or confidential relations with their chiefs. The limited subgroup at GS-13 to GS-15 are more than all of President Ford's Schedule C employees at grades 1 to 15.

3. Joel D. Aberbach, Robert D. Putnam, and Bert A. Rockman, *Bureaucrats and Politicians in Western Democracies* (Cambridge: Harvard University Press, 1981), table 3-3, pt. B, at 55.

4. Ibid., table 3-1, at 48–49.

5. General Accounting Office, *Senior Executive Service: Executives' Perspectives on Their Federal Service* (Washington, D.C.: Government Printing Office, 1988), 35–36.

6. Unless otherwise noted, data on European administrative elites are from James W. Fesler, "The Higher Public Service in Western Europe," in *A Centennial History of the American Administrative State,* ed. Ralph Clark Chandler (New York: Free Press, 1987), 509–39, and sources cited therein.

7. Aberbach, Putnam, and Rockman, *Bureaucrats and Politicians,* table 3-2, at 52. France's practice is deceptive. Though it recruits to its elite corps a number of graduates in engineering and science from the Polytechnic School, they in fact are generalists, not specialists, and have a strong base in the humanities.

8. Richard Rose, "The Political Status of Higher Civil Servants in Britain," in *Bureaucrats and Policy Making: A Comparative Overview,* ed. Ezra N. Suleiman (New York: Holmes and Meier, 1984), 136–73, at 145. Aberbach et al. give a 40 percent figure.

9. Aberbach, Putnam, and Rockman, *Bureaucrats and Politicians,* table 3-2, at 52.

10. General Accounting Office, *Evaluation of Proposals to Alter the Structure of the Senior Executive Service* (Washington, D.C.: Government Printing Office, 1985), 24.

11. Frederick C. Mosher, *Democracy and the Public Service,* 2d ed. (New York: Oxford University Press, 1982), 110–42. For tensions among professionals in the Environmental Protection Agency, see R. Shep Melnick, *Regulation and the Courts: The Clean Air Act* (Washington, D.C.: Brookings Institution, 1985), 255–61. A comprehensive treatment of the various professions in the public service (including city management) is the symposium, edited by Mosher and Richard J. Stillman, Jr., "The Professions in Government," *Public Administration Review* 37 (November/December 1977): 631–50, and *Public Administration Review* 38 (March/April 1978): 105–50.

12. United Kingdom, *The Civil Service,* vol. 1, *Report of the Fulton Committee, 1966–68;* Cmd. 3638 (London: Her Majesty's Stationery Office, 1968), 11.

13. Rufus E. Miles, Jr., "Rethinking Some Premises of the Senior Executive Service," in *Improving the Accountability and Performance of Government,* ed. Bruce L.R. Smith and James D. Carroll (Washington, D.C.: Brookings Institution, 1982), 35–60.

14. Compare foreign elite entrance in the 20s age group to the U.S. Senior Executive Service, where no careerist is under 35 years old, and only 17 percent are younger than 45 (including the 3.2 percent less than 40).

15. The two American elite services also apply an "up-or-out" policy, under which members who fail to be promoted at a specified career stage are separated from the service. As the number of vacant higher posts is limited, and varies from year to year, the service may lose some able persons.

16. Civil Service Commission, Bureau of Executive Personnel, *Executive Personnel in the Federal Service,* November 1977 (Washington, D.C.: Government Printing Office, 1978), 35.

17. General Accounting Office, *Senior Executive Service: Executives' Perspectives, 38, 51.* But two-thirds had 20 or more years of federal service (p. 37).

18. We have interpreted "higher levels" strictly (i.e., at Executive Schedule levels, in the Senior Executive Service, at GS-16 to GS-18, or serving in the White House, or serving as ambassadors and ministers). About 1,650 persons are political appointees under Schedule C ("positions of a confidential or policy-determining character") at GS-15 and below; as noted earlier, about 1,000 of them are at GS-13 to 15.

19. On Nixon and Reagan, see Richard P. Nathan, *The Administrative Presidency* (New York: Wiley, 1983).

20. Terry M. Moe, "The Politicized Presidency," in *The New Direction in American Politics,* ed. John E. Chubb and Paul E. Peterson (Washington, D.C.: Brookings Institution, 1985), 235–71.

21. *Leadership for America,* 17. For other counts and thoughtful analyses, see Linda L. Fisher, "Fifty Years of Presidential Appointments," in *The In-and-Outers: Presidential Appointees and Transient Government in Washington,* ed. G. Calvin Mackenzie (Baltimore: Johns Hopkins University Press, 1987), 1–29; Ingraham, "Building Bridges"; G. Calvin Mackenzie, *The Politics of Presidential Appointments* (New York: Free Press, 1981); and Thomas P. Murphy, Donald E. Nuechterlein, and Ronald J. Stupak, *Inside the Bureaucracy: The View from the Assistant Secretary's Desk* (Boulder, Colo.: Westview Press, 1978).

22. Paul C. Light, "How Thick Is Government?" *American Enterprise* 5 (November/December 1994): 60–61. See also the book based on his study, *Thickening Government: Federal Hierarchy and the Diffusion of Accountability* (Washington, D.C.: Brookings Institution, 1995).

23. Ronald I. Spiers, "Remarks," 14 November 1986, in *Perspectives on the Public Management Challenge* (Washington, D.C.: National Academy of Public Administration, 1987), 25–35; and data as of 20 May 1987, furnished by the State Department; Elaine Sciolino, "Friends as Ambassadors: How Many Is Too Many?" *New York Times,* 7 November 1989; "Bush's Ambassadors: Rewarding the Faithful," *Government Executive* 21 (August 1989), 51. As of 1987 the last eight ambassadors to Austria were a lawyer, an investor, a builder, a business executive, a real estate developer, a former personal secretary to President Reagan, a cosmetics magnate, and an editor. David Binder, "Grunwald's Delicate Deliberations on Austria," *New York Times,* 19 August 1987. For the memoirs of one of these, see Helene von

Damm, *At Reagan's Side* (New York: Doubleday, 1989).

24. Seven of Bush's ambassadors appointed through October 1989 had contributed over $100,000 each to the Republican Party's 1988 campaign; several others had been campaign officials. Sciolino, "Friends and Ambassadors."

25. Expendability is impaired when, as often, a political appointee is the darling of a congressional committee or interest group or both.

26. *Strengthening the U.S.-Soviet Communications Process to Reduce the Risks of Misunderstandings and Conflicts: A Report by a Panel* (Washington, D.C.: National Academy of Public Administration, 1987), 5, 7. In 1987 only two U.S. officials comparable in status to the Soviet officials cited had had high-level experience with the Soviets prior to 1981. Ibid., 7. In 1990 the new USSR ambassador had served in the United States nearly twenty years, six at the United Nations and thirteen at the USSR embassy. Clifford Krauss, "Moscow's New Ambassador An Old Hand in Washington," *New York Times*, 29 May 1990.

27. Richard Bernstein, "The UN versus the U.S.," *New York Times Magazine*, 22 January 1984, 18ff, at 26, 68.

28. For qualifications needed to perform well in one set of political posts, see John H. Trattner, *The Prune Book: The 100 Toughest Management and Policy-Making Jobs in Washington* (Lanham, Md.: Madison Books, 1988).

29. G. Calvin Mackenzie, "Appointing Mr. (or Ms.) Right," *Government Executive* 22 (April 1990): 30–35; the transitions exclude Johnson's and Ford's rises from the vice-presidency. Cf. Burt Solomon, "Bush's Laggard Appointment Pace ... May Not Matter All That Much," *National Journal* 21 (2 December 1989): 2952–53. Through 1989 and often beyond, the Consumer Products Safety Commission lacked a quorum; only four of eighteen top Energy Department officials were in place, as was true of six of eleven assistant secretaries of Labor; the Census Bureau's director had not been appointed though the 1990 census was soon to start; and in HHS the headships of the National Institutes of Health, Food and Drug Administration, and the Health Care Financing Administration were unfilled.

30. Partisan and some other obligations (e.g., to large campaign contributors) are deflected by appointments to boards, commissions, and committees, and invitations to White House galas for foreign dignitaries.

31. James W. Fesler, "Politics, Policy and Bureaucracy at the Top," *Annals of the American Academy of Political and Social Science* 466 (March 1983): 27 and citations there.

32. Philip H. Burch, Jr., *Elites in American History: The New Deal to the Carter Administration* (New York: Holmes and Meier, 1980), 374–75. Though Burch includes Supreme Court and some ambassadorial appointees in his database, they are too few to affect the figures we cite.

33. Ralph Nader, in Ronald Brownstein and Nina Easton, *Reagan's Ruling Class*, updated ed. (New York: Pantheon, 1983), xv.

34. From 1953 to 1976, 55 percent of the initial appointees and 85 percent of replacement appointees had had such experience. James J. Best, "Presidential Cabinet Appointments: 1953–1976," *Presidential Studies Quarterly* 11 (Winter 1981): 62–66.

35. This and later paragraphs draw on Fesler, "Politics, Policy, and Bureaucracy," 23–41, and sources there cited.

36. See Becky Norton Dunlop, "The Role of the White House Office of Presidential Personnel," in *Steering the Elephant: How Washington Works,* ed. Robert Rector and Michael Sanara (New York: Universe Books, 1987), 145–55. Ms. Dunlop was deputy director of the Reagan Office of Presidential Personnel.

37. Fisher, "Fifty Years of Presidential Appointments," 9.

38. *Leadership in Jeopardy: The Fraying of the Presidential Appointments System,* November 1985 (Washington, D.C.: National Academy of Public Administration, 1985), 19. For details, see Fisher, "Fifty Years of Presidential Appointments," 14–21. Note that (*a*) these do not include nonpresidential political appointments, where experience is even less; and (*b*) because the count includes appointments throughout the life of an administration, promotions and transfers from one political post to another are counted in the "with government experience" category.

39. For informative analyses of political officials who had such capability, see *Leadership and Innovation: A Biographical Perspective on Entrepreneurs in Government,* ed. Jameson W. Doig and Erwin C. Hargrove (Baltimore: Johns Hopkins University Press, 1987).

40. Two examples within one month: (*a*) the chairman of the Securities and Exchange Commission forced the resignation of the noncareer head of SEC's important New York office after a number of careerists on her staff threatened to resign if she stayed; (*b*) the president and chief executive officer of a subordinate unit of the Federal Home Loan Bank Board was demoted for lack of managerial ability (though she retained her remarkable salary of $250,000) and was later dismissed. "New York Office's Head Resigns from SEC," *New York Times,* 30 September 1987; Robert D. Hershey, Jr., "U.S. Demotes Top-Paid Official," *New York Times,* 16 October 1987, and Nathaniel C. Nash, "Hot Seat for Asset Agency's Chief," *New York Times,* 29 February 1988.

41. A third set of appointees may have contradictory policy priorities. President Bush appointed an outstanding environmentalist to head the Environmental Protection Administration, but chose advocates of natural-resource exploitation elsewhere (e.g., with authority over the U.S. Forest Service, National Park Service, and public lands).

42. *Leadership in Jeopardy,* 4–5. Regulatory commissioners, who have fixed terms and are removable only "for cause," are excluded from the figures we use. The figures measure tenure in specific positions; appointees' median service within the same agency was 3 years, and within the government 4.3 years.

For details, see Fisher, "Fifty Years of Presidential Appointments," 21–26; Carl Brauer, "Tenure, Turnover, and Postgovernment Employment Trends of Presidential Appointees," in Mackenzie, *The In-and-Outers,* 174–94; and Trattner, *Prune Book.* See also General Accounting Office, *Political Appointees: Turnover Rates in Executive Schedule Positions Requiring Senate Confirmation* GGD-94-115 FS, April 1994.

43. "Heavy Turnover," *National Journal* 19 (18 April 1987): 919.

44. Robert Thalon Hall, quoted in Brauer, "Tenure, Turnover, and Postgovernment Employment," 178–79.

45. General Accounting Office, *Department of Labor: Assessment of Management Improvement Efforts* (Washington, D.C.: Government Printing Office, 1986).

46. General Accounting Office, *Social Security Administration: Stable Leadership and Better Management Needed to Improve Effectiveness* (Washington, D.C.: Government Printing Office, 1987), 3.

47. Hugh Heclo, *A Government of Strangers: Executive Politics in Washington* (Washington, D.C.: Brookings Institution, 1972), 158 and passim.

48. For an entertaining fictional account of the comparable interplay between a British minister and his ministry's permanent secretary, see *The Complete Yes Minister: The Diaries of a Cabinet Minister by the Right Hon. James Hacker MP*, ed. Jonathan Lynn and Anton Jay (Topsfield, Mass.: Salem House, 1987).

49. HHS (including SSA) data from Robert Pear, "Many Policy Jobs Vacant on Eve of Second Term," *New York Times,* 14 January 1985. In 1987, when five Central American countries proposed a regional peace plan, the United States had ambassadors in only two of those countries; lesser-ranked diplomats represented the United States in the other three. Neil A. Lewis, "U.S. Envoys Told to Convey Doubt over Latin Plan," *New York Times,* 18 August 1987. The president's special envoy for Central America had also resigned.

50. General Accounting Office, *Temporary Appointments: Extended Temporary Appointments to Positions Requiring Senate Confirmation* (Washington, D.C.: Government Printing Office, 1986), appendix 1.

51. Fisher, "Fifty Years of Presidential Appointments," 26–27.

52. Judith Havemann, "Vacancies Abound in Top U.S. Jobs," *Washington Post,* 15 February 1988.

53. Article II, sec. 2.

54. U.S. House Committee on Post Office and Civil Service, *United States Government Policy Positions,* 65–77.

55. *Leadership in Jeopardy,* 18.

56. Fisher, "Fifty Years of Presidential Appointments," 2.

57. Frederick V. Malek, *Washington's Hidden Tragedy* (New York: Macmillan, 1978), 102–3.

58. *Leadership for America,* Task Force Report, 7.

59. "Allocated positions" are those that OPM has authorized agencies to establish and fill; they outnumber actual appointees by about 1,000. Noncareerists, therefore, can exceed 10 percent of SES members. They have not done so. Noncareerists (excluding "limited term" appointees) were 8.4 percent of allocated positions in 1986 and, then and in 1987, 9.8 percent of filled positions.

60. General Accounting Office, *Federal Employees,* 11 and passim.

61. U.S. Senate Governmental Affairs Committee, *Politicization of the Career Senior Executive Service, 1980 to 1986,* Majority Staff Analysis (August 1987), 2, 8–9. Processed.

62. 5 *U.S. Code of Federal Regulations* 3132(b).

63. *The Government's Managers: Report of the Twentieth Century Fund Task Force on the Senior Executive Service* (New York: Priority Press, 1987), 8–9, 63–64.

64. Computed from OPM data, table 7.2, *The Politics of the Administrative*

Process (Chatham, N.J.: Chatham House, 1991), 160.

65. *The Government's Managers,* 13.

66. For appraisal of a career executive, over half the members of the performance review board must be career appointees. Some doubt that this assures objectivity, for this majority is often only a bare one and the board's chairman is usually a political appointee, often the supervisor of one or more careerists on the board.

67. 92 U.S. Statutes 1168. The act's numbering of items has been omitted.

68. Comptroller General Charles A. Bowsher, House Subcommittee on Civil Service, *Senior Executive Service: Hearings,* 98th Cong., 7 November 1983 to 13 April 1984, 18. See also General Accounting Office, *An Assessment of SES Performance Appraisal Systems* (Washington, D.C.: Government Printing Office, 1984).

69. 92 U.S. Statutes 1165.

70. 92 U.S. Statutes 1175.

71. Public Law 101-94, "Ethics in Government Act," sec. 506, 30 November 1989.

72. 5 *U.S. Code of Federal Regulations* 534.403. An alternative ceiling, if larger, is 15 percent of the average annual rates of basic pay to career SES appointees.

73. General Accounting Office, *Senior Executive Service: Reasons Why Career Members Left in Fiscal Year 1985* (Washington, D.C.: Government Printing Office, 1987), 8, 15, 16. See also Merit Systems Protection Board, *The Senior Executive Service: Views of Former Federal Executives* (Washington, D.C.: Government Printing Office, 1989), 17–19.

74. General Accounting Office, *Senior Executive Service: Executives' Perspectives on Their Federal Service* (Washington, D.C.: Government Printing Office, 1988), 12. Many in SES had expected bonuses to supplement their actual base pay, which by statute cannot exceed the amount for Executive Schedule IV.

75. Quoted in *Leadership for America,* Task Force Reports, 143.

76. Comptroller General Bowsher, in U.S. House Committee on Civil Service, *Senior Executive Service,* 20 and 43.

77. U.S. House of Representatives, Subcommittee on Civil Service, Committee on Post Office and Civil Service, "Staff Report on Awards and Ranks to Career Members of the Senior Executive Service," 1 July 1987. Processed. For a summary and commentary, see Rebecca B. Allen, "Executive Bonuses," *Government Executive 19* (September 1987): 58–63.

78. U.S. House of Representatives, Subcommittee on Civil Service, "Staff Report on Awards and Ranks," 30.

79. *Leadership for America,* Task Force Reports, 142.

80. Ibid., 193–96.

81. James E. Colvard, OPM deputy director, cited in Judith Havemann, "Management Training: A Mixed Bag in Quality and Performance," *Washington Post,* 2 September 1987.

82. General Accounting Office, *Senior Executive Service: Agencies' Use of the Candidate Development Program* (Washington, D.C.: Government Printing Office, 1986), 12–15, and *Senior Executive Service: Training and Development of Senior*

Executives (Washington, D.C.: Government Printing Office, 1989), 21, 25.

83. Frank P. Sherwood, "FEI's Next 25 Years," *Bureaucrat* 16 (Summer 1987): 31–36; Susan Kellam, "Bringing FEI Back," *Government Executive* 21 (August 1989): 24–27. The Federal Executive Institute Alumni Association publishes annually the results of a survey of its members' assessments of their government experience and various aspects of the higher career service. See, for example, *FEIAA Executive Summary*, no. 215 (May 1996), for the 1995 survey.

84. General Accounting Office, *Senior Executive Service: The Extent to Which SES Members Have Used the Sabbatical Program* (Washington, D.C.: Government Printing Office, 1988), 3.

85. Cf., though, Merit Systems Protection Board, *The Senior Executive Service: Views*, 1, 13, 34–35 (items 42f, 42j, 42l). On noncareerists' conversions to career status, see General Accounting Office, *Federal Employees: Appointees Converted to Career Positions, October through December 1988* (Washington, D.C.: Government Printing Office, 1988), appendix VI (1987 and 1988 totals), and General Accounting Office, *Federal Employees: Supplemental Information on Appointees Converted to Career Positions* (Washington, D.C.: Government Printing Office, 1989).

However, two opportunities for political weighting have been capitalized on: (1) the Carter and Reagan administrations together raised the number of noncareerist Schedule C positions at GS-15 and below from less than 1,000 to 1,600; (2) as earlier noted, some subunits substantially exceed the 25 percent limit on noncareer SES appointees that applies to the whole of its department or major agency (balanced, of course, by lower percentages in other subunits).

86. Joel D. Aberbach and Bert A. Rockman, "From Nixon's Problem to Reagan's Achievement—The Federal Executive Reexamined," in *Looking Back on the Reagan Presidency*, ed. Larry Berman (Baltimore: Johns Hopkins University Press, 1990), table 1.

87. Ibid., table 4. Corresponding figures for Reagan's lower group of SES careerists were 29 and 20.

88. General Accounting Office, *Senior Executive Service: Reasons Why Career Members Left*, 8. "Great, very great, and moderate importance" ratings were 60 percent for top management and 53 percent for political appointees. For 1983–88 departures, see Merit Systems Protection Board, *The Senior Executive Service: Views*. This rarely distinguishes careerists' from noncareerists' views, but see pp. 20–21 for careerists' ratings of noncareerists.

89. General Accounting Office, *Senior Executive Service: Reasons Why Career Members Left*, 2, 42.

90. General Accounting Office, *Senior Executive Service: Executives' Perspectives*, 2, 12, 18, 62. Cf. *FEIAA Executive Summary*, no. 215, reporting that, in October 1995, 46 percent of respondents expressing opinions would encourage young people to begin a federal career and 54 percent would not.

91. A variation on this is the Volcker Commission's recommendation that "to recognize the importance of management as a distinctive skill, the President should create a separate track within the Senior Executive Service for generalist managers." *Leadership for America*, 44.

92. General Accounting Office, *Evaluation of Proposals to Alter the Structure of the Senior Executive Service* (Washington, D.C.: Government Printing Office, 1985); *The Government's Managers*, 7–8, 51.

93. Frank P. Sherwood and Lee J. Breyer, "Executive Personnel Systems in the States," *Public Administration Review* 47 (September/October 1987): 410–16.

94. Stephen Labaton, "The SEC's Top Cop Moves On," *New York Times*, 21 May 1989.

95. Brauer, "Tenure, Turnover, and Postgovernment Employment," 184–87.

96. James P. Pfiffner, "Political Appointees and Career Executives: The Democracy-Bureaucracy Nexus in the Third Century," *Public Administration Review* 47 (January/February 1987): 61. Cf. Merit Systems Protection Board, *The Senior Executive Service: Views*, 21 (table 4).

97. Elliot L. Richardson, "Civil Servants: Why Not the Best?" *Wall Street Journal*, 20 November 1987. In the Nixon period he was undersecretary of state and then headed the Health, Education, and Welfare, Defense, and Justice departments. Under Ford he was ambassador to the Court of St. James and secretary of commerce. Under Carter, he was ambassador-at-large.

98. Quoted in Clyde H. Farnsworth, "Commerce Department: Good Will and Progress Mark a Brief Tenure," *Washington Post*, 29 November 1988.

99. *Leadership in Jeopardy*, 23–24.

100. Brauer, "Tenure, Turnover, and Postgovernment Employment," 181.

101. John W. Macy, Bruce Adams, and J. Jackson Walters, *America's Unelected Government: Appointing the President's Team* (Cambridge, Mass.: Ballinger, 1983), 82.

102. General Accounting Office, *Senior Executive Service: Answers to Selected Salary-Related Questions* (Washington, D.C.: Government Printing Office, 1987).

103. Philip M. Boffey, "Scientists Do Not Live by Patriotism Alone," *New York Times*, 14 December 1987. In 1988 an NIH presidential appointee, the director of the National Institute of Cancer for over eight years, left for the Memorial Sloan-Kettering Cancer Center with an estimated salary increase to as much as $400,000 from a government salary of about $90,000. The NIH director called him "one of the truly great directors of any institute in the history of NIH, . . . an extraordinary leader who will be very tough to replace." Boffey, "Top U.S. Cancer Official Going to Sloan-Kettering," *New York Times*, 12 August 1988.

104. Milt Freudenheim, "Doctors' Concern: Fixing Prices and Price Fixing," *New York Times*, 18 December 1988.

105. Anthony Fauci (director of the National Institute of Allergy and Infectious Diseases), "The Salary Squeeze," *Washington Post*, 14 November 1988.

106. At all governmental levels there are also some curiosities of pay, often because some agencies are autonomous and self-financing enterprises. Though the chairman of the Federal Reserve Board gets $89,500 under the Executive Schedule, the president of the New York Federal Reserve Bank gets $170,800. The president of a subordinate unit of the Federal Home Loan Bank Board had a salary of $250,000, which continued after she was demoted for lack of managerial ability, until eventually dismissed. The TVA pays $335,000 to its director of nuclear power

under a contract arrangement. The director of the New York Port Authority is paid $170,000. See General Accounting Office, *Federal Pay: Executive-Salaries in Government-Related Banking Organizations* (Washington, D.C.: Government Printing Office, 1987); *New York Times,* 16 October, 7 December, and 25 May 1987.

107. *The Municipal Yearbook: 1989* (Washington, D.C.: International City Management Association, 1989), table 1/4; Elizabeth Kolbert, "Parking Chief Named to Head Fire Department," *New York Times,* 21 October 1987; "Pay Increases for Officials," *New York Times,* 18 December 1986; *The Book of the States: 1988–89* ed., vol. 27 (Lexington, Ky.: Council of State Governments, 1988), table 2.11.

108. *Fairness for Our Public Servants,* 1; see chart 2.

109. In 1986, however, California voters defeated a measure limiting the governor's pay to $80,000 and all other employees to $64,000. The latter provision would have reduced the pay of almost 7,000 top managers, professors, doctors, judges, and others.

110. 99 U.S. Statutes 1322. Before this 1985 amendment of the Federal Salary Act, disapproval could be by resolution of either the House or the Senate. This had fallen victim to the Supreme Court's decision invalidating "congressional vetoes" that deprived the president of his constitutional right to approve or veto legislation. *Immigration and Naturalization Service* v. *Chadha* 462 U.S. 919 (1983). A joint resolution must be submitted to the president.

111. Public Law 101-94, sec. 701 (i).

112. Rose, "The Political Status of Higher Civil Servants," 152.

113. *Leadership for America,* 37. This was conditioned on Congress's failure, using the old system, to restore 1969 levels of purchasing power, a 50 percent increase staged 25 percent in 1989 and 25 percent in 1991.

114. *Weekly Compilation of Presidential Documents* 25 (10 July 1989): 1041–43; Public Law 101-94, sec. 701 (i).

9. Decision Making (pp. 217–49)

1. Herbert A. Simon, *Administrative Behavior: A Study of Decision-Making Processes in Administrative Organization,* 3d ed. (New York: Free Press, 1945, 1976).

A few years earlier, Chester I. Barnard also argued the importance of decision making. See *The Functions of the Executive* (Cambridge: Harvard University Press, 1938). Simon's work, however, has proved more influential.

2. See, for example, Charles E. Lindblom and David K. Cohen, *Usable Knowledge: Social Science and Social Problem Solving* (New Haven: Yale University Press, 1979).

3. Max Weber, "Bureaucracy," in *From Max Weber: Essays in Sociology,* trans. and ed. H.H. Gerth and C. Wright Mills (New York: Oxford University Press, 1946), 196–244. Francis E. Rourke more generally discusses this point in *Bureaucracy, Politics, and Public Policy,* 3d ed. (Boston: Little, Brown, 1984).

4. See, for example, Don K. Price, "The Scientific Establishment," *Proceedings*

of the *American Philosophical Society 106* (June 1962): 235–45; and idem, *The Scientific Estate* (Cambridge: Harvard University Press, 1965). The Congressional Research Service has assembled a useful collection of readings on the role of science in decision making. See U.S. House of Representatives, Committee on Science and Technology, *Expertise and Democratic Decisionmaking: A Reader,* Science Policy Study, Background Rpt. No. 7, prepared by the Congressional Research Service, 99th Cong., 2d sess., 1986.

5. Deborah A. Stone, *Policy Paradox and Political Reason* (Glenview, Ill.: Scott, Foresman, 1988), 21.

6. Robert D. Behn and James W. Vaupel, *Quick Analysis for Busy Decision Makers* (New York: Basic Books, 1982), 19, 20.

7. See Charles O. Jones, *An Introduction to the Study of Public Policy,* 3d ed. (Monterey, Calif.: Brooks/Cole, 1984), esp. chap. 6.

8. Rourke, *Bureaucracy, Politics, and Public Policy,* 49.

9. Ibid., 50.

10. This follows Hugh Heclo's argument in "Issue Networks and the Executive Establishment," in *The New American Political System,* ed. Anthony King (Washington, D.C.: American Enterprise Institute, 1978), 87–124.

11. Stone, *Policy Paradox and Political Reason,* 309.

12. Donald W. Taylor, "Decision Making and Problem Solving," in *Handbook of Organizations,* ed. James G. March (Chicago: Rand McNally, 1965), 70.

13. For sympathetic accounts of PPBS in the Department of Defense, written by those in charge of its application, see Charles J. Hitch, *Decision Making for Defense* (Berkeley: University of California Press, 1965); and Alain C. Enthoven and K. Wayne Smith, *How Much Is Enough? Shaping the Defense Program, 1961–1969* (New York: Harper & Row, 1971). Compare James R. Schlesinger, "Uses and Abuses of Analysis," in U.S. Senate, Committee on Government Operations, *Planning, Programming, Budgeting: Inquiry,* 91st Cong., 2d sess., 1970, 125–36; and Blue Ribbon Defense Panel (Gilbert W. Fitzhugh, chairman), *Report to the President and the Secretary of Defense on the Department of Defense* (Washington, D.C.: Government Printing Office, 1970), 112–18, which reports, "the PPBS does not contribute significantly to the decision-making process for consideration of programs which center on major weapons systems" (p. 114).

14. U.S. Bureau of the Budget, *Bulletin No. 68-9,* 12 April 1968. All descriptive, but no evaluative quotations are from this text.

15. Jack W. Carlson (assistant director for program evaluation, Bureau of the Budget), "The Status and Next Steps for Planning, Programming, and Budgeting," in U.S. Congress, Joint Economic Committee, *The Analysis and Evaluation of Public Expenditures: The PPB System,* 91st Cong., 1st sess., 1969, 2:613–34; and his testimony in U.S. Congress, Joint Economic Committee, *Economic Analysis and the Efficiency of Government,* Hearings, 91st Cong., 2d sess., 1970, pt. 3, 694–706.

16. For the leading analysis of why PPB failed, see Allen Schick, "A Death in the Bureaucracy: The Demise of Federal PPB," *Public Administration Review 33* (March/April 1973): 146–56.

17. Allen Schick, *Budget Innovation in the States* (Washington, D.C.: Brook-

ings Institution, 1971); Aaron Wildavsky, *Budgeting: A Comparative Theory of Budgetary Processes* (Boston: Little, Brown, 1975), 335–52; Jack Rabin, "State and Local PPBS," in *Public Budgeting and Finance,* 2d ed., ed. Robert T. Golembiewski and Jack Rabin (Itasca, Ill.: Peacock, 1975), 427–47.

The most searching critiques of PPBS's inherent defects are in Aaron Wildavsky, *The New Politics of the Budgetary Process* (Glenview, Ill.: Scott, Foresman, 1987), 416–20; and idem, *The Revolt Against the Masses* (New York: Basic Books, 1971); and Leonard Merewitz and Stephen H. Sosnick, *The Budget's New Clothes: A Critique of Planning-Programming-Budgeting and Benefit-Cost Analysis* (Chicago: Markham, 1971). See also Ida R. Hoos, *Systems Analysis in Public Policy: A Critique* (Berkeley: University of California Press, 1972).

18. U.S. Congress, Joint Economic Committee, *Economic Analysis and the Efficiency of Government,* Report, 91st Cong., 2d sess., 9 February 1970, 9.

19. For an illuminating study of these and other analysts (mostly oriented to economics), see Arnold J. Meltsner, *Policy Analysts in the Bureaucracy* (Berkeley: University of California Press, 1976).

20. Lawrence J. Korb, "Ordeal of PPBS in the Pentagon," *Bureaucrat* 17 (Fall 1988): 19–21.

21. Charles E. Lindblom, "Still Muddling, Not Yet Through," *Public Administration Review* 39 (November/December 1979): 518. As we see shortly, Lindblom himself has been subjected to vigorous counterattack.

22. To make matters worse, "rational decision makers" never use all the information they get, yet continue to seek even more. See Martha S. Feldman and James G. March, "Information in Organizations and Signal and Symbol," *Administrative Science Quarterly* 26 (1981): 171–86.

23. James G. March and Herbert A. Simon, *Organizations* (New York: Wiley, 1958), 140–41.

24. See Steven E. Rhoads, ed., *Valuing Life: Public Policy Dilemmas* (Boulder, Colo.: Westview Press, 1980).

25. Lewis M. Branscomb, "Science in the White House: A New Start," *Science* 196 (20 May 1977): 848–52. To protect the snail darters, a court injunction enforcing the Endangered Species Act held up an almost completed $120 million TVA water project. *Tennessee Valley Authority* v. *Hill,* 437 U.S. 153 (1978). Congress then established a review commission to grant exemptions from the act, but the commission refused to exempt the TVA project. In 1979, Congress itself voted the exemption.

26. Arthur M. Okun, *Equality and Efficiency: The Big Tradeoff* (Washington, D.C.: Brookings Institution, 1975), 2.

27. Murray Weidenbaum, *The Modern Public Sector* (New York: Basic Books, 1969), 178.

28. The most persuasive and comprehensive descriptions and defenses of the incremental decision-making model are by Charles E. Lindblom. A good, brief statement is his "The Science of 'Muddling Through,'" *Public Administration Review* 19 (Spring 1959): 79–88. The model is further elaborated in *The Intelligence of Democracy: Decision Making through Mutual Adjustment* (New York: Free Press,

1965); *Politics and Markets: The World's Political-Economic Systems* (New York: Basic Books, 1977), 314–24; and *The Policy-Making Process,* 2d ed. (Englewood Cliffs, N.J.: Prentice Hall, 1980). He responds to criticisms of the model in "Still Muddling, Not Yet Through."

29. The incremental approach, moreover, has not been limited to politics. For applications to business decision making, see James Brian Quinn, "Strategic Change: 'Logical Incrementalism,'" *Sloan Management Review,* Fall 1978, 7–21; "Strategic Goals: Process and Politics," *Sloan Management Review,* Fall 1977, 21–37; and "Managing Strategic Change," *Sloan Management Review,* Summer 1980, 3–20, in which he promotes Lindblom's "muddling-through" approach.

30. The bargaining model has also spun off several related procedures, most notably the "garbage can" approach. In this approach, participants dump problems and solutions into a garbage can. Decisions are not made but rather "occur," in response to many ambiguous values and objectives. See Michael Cohen, James March, and Johan Olsen, "A Garbage Can Model of Organizational Choice," *Administrative Science Quarterly* 17 (March 1972): 1–25.

31. See *National Journal,* 15 November 1986, 2767; Philip J. Harter, "Negotiating Regulations: A Cure for Malaise," *Georgetown Law Journal* 71 (October 1982): 1–118; Henry J. Perritt, Jr., "Negotiated Rulemaking in Practice," *Journal of Policy Analysis and Management* 5 (Spring 1986): 482–95; and Daniel J. Fiorino and Chris Kirtz, "Breaking Down Walls: Negotiated Rulemaking at EPA," *Temple Environmental Law and Technical Journal* 4 (1985): 40.

32. Robert Kennedy's dramatic first-person memoir of the crisis, *Thirteen Days* (New York: Norton, 1969), provides a detailed description of the events. For an analytical version, see Graham T. Allison, *Essence of Decision: Explaining the Cuban Missile Crisis* (Boston: Little, Brown, 1971), from which the discussion that follows is drawn. In particular, see chap. 6.

33. Allison, *Essence of Decision,* 6.

34. Ibid., 203.

35. Ibid., 145.

36. The aphorism is credited to Rufus Miles and is often known as "Miles's Law." See Rufus E. Miles, "The Origin and Meaning of Miles' Law," *Public Administration Review* 38 (September/October 1978): 399–403. See also Allison, *Essence of Decision,* 176.

37. For another case study of bargaining in decision making, see the study by two *Wall Street Journal* reporters of the passage of the tax reform act of 1986: Jeffrey H. Birnbaum and Alan S. Murray, *Showdown at Gucci Gulch: Lawmaking, Lobbyists, and the Unlikely Triumph of Tax Reform* (New York: Random House, 1987).

38. See Charles L. Schultze, *The Politics and Economics of Public Spending* (Washington, D.C.: Brookings Institution, 1968).

39. Ibid., 76. (Emphasis in original.)

40. For a thoughtful treatment of this and related matters, see Alexander L. George, "The Case for Multiple Advocacy in Making Foreign Policy," *American Political Science Review* 66 (September 1972): 751–85; and his *Decisionmaking in For-*

eign Policy: The Effective Use of Information and Advice (Boulder, Colo.: Westview Press, 1980).

41. Leonard S. Lyon and others, *The National Recovery Administration* (Washington, D.C.: Brookings Institution, 1935).

42. Edythe W. First, *Industry and Labor Advisory Committees in The National Defense Advisory Commission and the Office of Production Management, May 1940 to January 1942* (Washington, D.C.: Civilian Production Administration, 1946); selected portions appear in *Public Administration: Readings and Documents,* ed. Felix A. Nigro (New York: Holt, 1951), 406–26. See also Harvey C. Mansfield, *A Short History of OPA* (Washington, D.C.: Government Printing Office, 1948), 311; and Allan R. Richards, *War Labor Boards in the Field* (Chapel Hill: University of North Carolina Press, 1953).

43. Grant McConnell, *Private Power and American Democracy* (New York: Knopf, 1966), 276–79. For a more recent look at the role of interest groups in decision making, see Jeffrey M. Berry, *The Interest Group Society* (Boston: Little, Brown, 1984).

44. Adam Smith, *The Wealth of Nations,* Everyman's ed. (London: Dent, 1910), 1:117.

45. See National Academy of Sciences (Committee on the Utilization of Young Scientists and Engineers in Advisory Services to Government, National Research Council), The Science Committee, *Report* and (separately) *Appendixes* (Washington, D.C.: National Academy of Sciences, 1972); and Thane Gustafson, "The Controversy over Peer Review," *Science* 190 (12 December 1975): 1060–66.

46. "The President's War on Advisory Committees," *National Journal,* 12 May 1979, 800; U.S. Comptroller General, *Better Evaluations Needed to Weed Out Useless Federal Advisory Committees* (Washington, D.C.: General Accounting Office, 1977); Kit Gage and Samuel S. Epstein, "The Federal Advisory Committee System: An Assessment," *Environmental Law Reporter* 7 (February 1977): 50, 101–12; and Henry Steck, "Private Influence on Environmental Policy: The Case of the National Industrial Pollution Control Council," *Environmental Law Reporter* 5 (Winter 1975): 241–48.

47. An illuminating case study is Don F. Hadwiger and Ross B. Talbot, *Pressures and Protests: The Kennedy Farm Program and the Wheat Referendum of 1963* (San Francisco: Chandler, 1965).

48. Imogene H. Putnam, *Volunteers in OPA,* issued by Office of Price Administration, U.S. Office of Temporary Controls (Washington, D.C.: Government Printing Office, 1947); James W. Davis and Kenneth M. Dolbeare, *Little Groups of Neighbors: The Selective Service System* (Chicago: Markham, 1968). Membership of OPA's local boards totaled 125,000; Selective Service Boards, 17,000.

49. Agricultural Stabilization and Conservation Service, U.S. Department of Agriculture, Programs and Services (Washington, D.C.: Information Division, Agricultural Stabilization and Conservation Service, 1977), 17. See also the service's "Farmer Committee Administration of Agricultural Programs" (Washington, D.C., 1975).

50. U.S. Department of Agriculture, *Review of the Farmer Committee System:*

Report of the Study Committee (Washington, D.C.: Agricultural Stabilization and Conservation Service, U.S. Department of Agriculture, 1962), pt. 4, 132.

51. McConnell, *Private Power and American Democracy,* 207, 210–11.

52. *New York Times,* 5 December 1988, B1.

53. *New York Times,* 16 December 1986, B8.

54. *New York Times,* 16 February 1989, B6.

55. The most comprehensive survey, covering 269 case studies of decentralization in urban areas, is Robert K. Yin and Douglas Yates, *Street-Level Governments* (Lexington, Mass.: Lexington Books, 1975). For private interest groups' participation in national and state administration, McConnell, *Private Power and American Democracy* is the classic source.

56. "Microeconomists" deal with decision making by individuals and organizations; "macroeconomists," in contrast, study the broad economy of society, including governmental finance.

57. For the roots of the theory, see Anthony Downs, *An Economic Theory of Democracy* (New York: Harper & Row, 1957); James M. Buchanan and Gordon Tullock, *The Calculus of Consent* (Ann Arbor: University of Michigan Press, 1962); Gordon Tullock, *The Politics of Bureaucracy* (Washington, D.C.: Public Affairs Press, 1965); Anthony Downs, *Inside Bureaucracy* (Boston: Little, Brown, 1967); and William A. Niskanen, *Bureaucracy and Representative Government* (Chicago: Aldine-Atherton, 1971).

58. For a discussion, see the "Symposium on Privatization," *International Review of Administrative Sciences* 54 (December 1988): 501–83.

59. Stuart Butler, *Privatizing Federal Spending* (New York: Universe Books, 1985), 58, 166.

60. President's Private Sector Survey on Cost Control (Grace Commission), *Report on Privatization* (Washington, D.C.: Government Printing Office, 1983), vii. See also Butler, *Privatizing Public Spending;* and E.S. Savas, *Privatization: The Key to Better Government* (Chatham, N.J.: Chatham House, 1987).

61. This discussion draws on Steven E. Rhoads, *The Economist's View of the World: Government, Markets, and Public Policy* (Cambridge, England: Cambridge University Press, 1985), 44–50; and Joseph E. Stiglitz, *Economics of the Public Sector* (New York: Norton, 1986), chap. 8.

62. Steven Kelman, "'Public Choice' and Public Spirit," *Public Interest,* no. 87 (Spring 1987): 81.

63. Weidenbaum, *The Modern Public Sector, 178.* More broadly, compare Rhoads, *The Economist's View of the World.*

64. See Robert B. Reich, ed., *The Power of Public Ideas* (Cambridge, Mass.: Ballinger, 1988).

65. See Ted Kolderie, "The Two Different Concepts of Privatization," *Public Administration Review* 46 (July/August 1986): 285–91; Ronald C. Moe, "Exploring the Limits of Privatization," *Public Administration Review* 47 (November/December 1987): 453–60; and James W. Fesler, "The State and Its Study: The Whole and Its Parts," *PS* 21 (Fall 1988): 891–901.

66. The American Federation of State, County, and Municipal Employees, for

example, compiled a lengthy collection of stories illustrating that privatization-as-contracting often breeds its own problems. American Federation of State, County, and Municipal Employees, *Passing the Bucks* (Washington, D.C.: AFSCME, 1983); and *When Public Services Go Private: Not Always Better, Not Always Honest, There May Be a Better Way* (Washington, D.C.: AFSCME, 1987).

67. Speech to Spring Meeting, National Academy of Public Administration, Washington, D.C., 6 June 1986.

68. James E. Webb, *Space Age Management: The Large-Scale Approach* (New York: McGraw-Hill, 1969), 136–37.

69. Irving L. Janis and Leon Mann, *Decision Making: A Psychological Analysis of Conflict, Choice, and Commitment* (New York: Free Press, 1977), 15.

70. See Donald F. Kettl, *Leadership at the Fed* (New Haven: Yale University Press, 1986), 7–8.

71. Ibid., 7.

72. Richard E. Neustadt and Harvey V. Fineberg, *The Swine Flu Affair: Decision-Making on a Slippery Disease* (Washington, D.C.: Government Printing Office, 1978), iv.

73. *Science*, 236 (17 April 1987): 267–300, contains a useful symposium on the problems of risk and uncertainty in public policy. See R. Wilson and E.A.C. Crouch, "Risk Assessment and Comparisons: An Introduction"; B.N. Ames, R. Magaw, and L.S. Gold, "Ranking Possible Carcinogenic Hazards"; P. Slovic, "Perception of Risk"; M. Russell and M. Gruber, "Risk Assessment in Environmental Policy Making"; L.B. Lave, "Health and Safety Risk Analyses: Information for Better Decisions"; and D. Okrent, "The Safety Goals of the U.S. Nuclear Regulatory Commission."

74. Plutarch, *The Lives of the Noble Grecians and Romans* (New York: Modern Library, n.d.), 874.

75. See Peter M. Blau and W. Richard Scott, *Formal Organizations* (San Francisco: Chandler, 1962); Tullock, *The Politics of Bureaucracy*, 137–41; Downs, *Inside Bureaucracy*, chap. 10; Harold L. Wilensky, *Organizational Intelligence* (New York: Basic Books, 1967), chap. 3; and Brian W. Hogwood and B. Guy Peters, *The Pathology of Public Policy* (Oxford: Oxford University Press, 1985), chap. 4.

76. Charles Peters, "From Ouagadougou to Cape Canaveral: Why the Bad News Doesn't Travel Up," *Washington Monthly*, April 1986, 27.

77. See Presidential Commission on the Space Shuttle Challenger Accident [Rogers Commission], *Report to the President* (Washington, D.C.: Government Printing Office, 1986).

78. Thomas J. Peters and Robert H. Waterman, Jr., *In Search of Excellence* (New York: Warner Books, 1982).

79. See Downs, *Inside Bureaucracy*, 118–27, for a discussion of antidistortion factors.

80. Hogwood and Peters, *The Pathology of Public Policy*, 85.

81. U.S. House of Representatives, Committee on Science and Technology, *Investigation of the Challenger Accident*, Report, 99th Cong., 2d sess., 1986, 172.

82. U.S. Senate, Report No. 91-411, *Federal Coal Mine Health and Safety Act*

of 1969, 91st Cong., 1st sess., 17 September 1969, 5–6; Henry C. Hart, "Crisis, Community, and Consent in Water Politics," *Law and Contemporary Problems* 22 (Summer 1957): 510–37.

83. Rogers Commission, *Report to the President.*

84. All rational (in the broad sense) models assume that crisis decisions made under severe time pressures are usually worse than those affording more time for data assemblage, specialists' advice, and deliberation. For the view that "a 'hasty' decision made under pressure may on average be better than a less urgent one," see Wilensky, *Organizational Intelligence,* 75–77. A full treatment of decision-making behavior under stress of crisis and shortness of time is provided by Janis and Mann, *Decision Making,* 45–67.

85. Irving L. Janis, *Crucial Decisions: Leadership in Policymaking and Crisis Management* (New York: Free Press, 1989).

86. See Amitai Etzioni, "Mixed Scanning: A Third Approach to Decision-Making," *Public Administration Review* 27 (December 1967): 385–92.

10. Budgeting (pp. 250–83)

1. See Joseph White, "The Continuing Resolution: A Crazy Way to Govern?" *Brookings Review* 6 (Summer 1988): 28.

2. For a broad look at the history of budgeting, see Carolyn Webber and Aaron Wildavsky, *A History of Taxation and Expenditures in the Western World* (New York: Simon and Schuster, 1986). On what questions a theory of budgeting must answer, see V.O. Key, Jr., "The Lack of a Budgetary Theory," *American Political Science Review* 34 (December 1940): 1237–40; and Verne Lewis, "Toward a Theory of Budgeting," *Public Administration Review* 12 (Winter 1952): 42–54.

3. See, for example, Herbert Stein, *Governing the $5 Trillion Economy* (New York: Basic Books, 1989).

4. The word "fiscal" is Old French in origin and appears to have roots in the Latin word for "treasury" or for "basket," which put together sum up the topic well.

5. Keynes is best known for *The General Theory of Employment, Interest, and Money* (New York: Harcourt Brace Jovanovich, 1964; originally published in 1936). On compensatory economics in the Roosevelt administration, see Donald F. Kettl, "Marriner Eccles and Leadership in the Federal Reserve System," in *Leadership and Innovation: A Biographical Perspective on Entrepreneurs in Government,* ed. Jameson W. Doig and Erwin C. Hargrove (Baltimore: Johns Hopkins University Press, 1987), 318–42.

6. See Herbert Stein, *The Fiscal Revolution in America* (Chicago: University of Chicago Press, 1969); and James E. Alt and K. Alec Chrystal, *Political Economics* (Berkeley: University of California Press, 1983), 54–77.

7. See Edward R. Tufte, *Political Control of the Economy* (Princeton, N.J.: Princeton University Press, 1978).

8. The Federal Reserve operates through three principal policy tools: fixing reserve requirements that banks must hold against deposits (the higher the reserves

required, the less money banks can lend out, and thus the higher interest rates become and the more economic growth is slowed); setting the discount rate (the rate at which the Fed lends to banks, which then affects interest rates across the nation); and managing open-market operations (in which the Fed purchases government securities to increase the money supply—thus lowering interest rates and fueling economic growth—and buys securities to decrease the money supply—thus raising interest rates and slowing economic growth).

The classic treatment of the history of monetary policy is Milton Friedman and Anna Jacobson Schwartz, *A Monetary History of the United States, 1867–1960* (Princeton, N.J.: Princeton University Press, 1963). For a favorable account of the Volcker era, see Donald F. Kettl, *Leadership at the Fed* (New Haven: Yale University Press, 1986), chap. 7. William Greider, in *Secrets of the Temple: How the Federal Reserve Runs the Country* (New York: Simon and Schuster, 1987), takes a far more critical view.

9. Congress increased corporate taxes once again while cutting individual taxes in the 1986 tax reform act. See Jeffrey H. Birnbaum and Alan S. Murray, *Showdown at Gucci Gulch: Lawmakers, Lobbyists, and the Unlikely Triumph of Tax Reform* (New York: Random House, 1987).

10. The "fiscal year" is a government's budget year. The federal fiscal year begins on 1 October and runs through the following 30 September. Fiscal years are numbered according to the year in which they end; the fiscal year ending 30 September 1992, for example, is known as FY 1992.

11. For a sympathetic look at supply-side economics, see Paul Craig Roberts, *The Supply-Side Revolution: An Insider's Account of Policymaking in Washington* (Cambridge: Harvard University Press, 1984). David Stockman gives an unsympathetic insider's account in *The Triumph of Politics* (New York: Harper & Row, 1986). For an analysis of the debate, see Herbert Stein, *Presidential Economics: The Making of Economic Policy from Roosevelt to Reagan and Beyond* (New York: Simon and Schuster, 1984).

12. Lester Thurow, "Budget Deficits," in Daniel Bell and Lester Thurow, *The Deficits: How Big? How Long? How Dangerous?* (New York: New York University Press, 1985), 140. See also Benjamin M. Friedman, *Day of Reckoning: The Consequences of American Economic Policy* (New York: Vintage Books, 1989).

13. Robert Eisner, "The Federal Deficit: How Does It Matter?" *Science* 237 (25 September 1987): 1577–82. See also his *How Real Is the Federal Deficit?* (New York: Free Press, 1986).

14. Congressional Budget Office, *An Analysis of the President's Budgetary Proposals for Fiscal Year 1995* (Washington, D.C.: Government Printing Office, 1994), 24–28.

15. Rudolph G. Penner and Alan J. Abramson, *Broken Purse Strings: Congressional Budgeting, 1974–88* (Washington, D.C.: Urban Institute Press, 1989), 99.

16. Stockman, *Triumph of Politics*, 98.

17. David C. Grinnell, "Implications of Uncertainty in Economic Forecasting Under Gramm-Rudman-Hollings: Options for Congressional Response" (Washington, D.C.: Congressional Research Service of the Library of Congress, 8 August

1986), 23. A General Accounting Office report concluded that neither CBO nor GAO had been less accurate than the other, or for that matter, than private-sector forecasters. See General Accounting Office, *Budget Reductions for Fiscal Year 1986, Report to the President and Congress Under the Balanced Budget and Emergency Deficit Control Act of 1985,* January 1986 (Washington, D.C.: Government Printing Office, 1986), appendix B, 37 ff.

18. *Wall Street Journal,* 21 August 1986, 22.

19. An excellent survey of the federal budget process is Allen Schick, *The Federal Budget: Politics, Policy, Process* (Washington, D.C.: Brookings Institution, 1995).

20. For a history of these issues, see Leonard D. White, *The Federalists* (New York: Macmillan, 1956), 116–27; Frederick C. Mosher, *A Tale of Two Agencies: A Comparative Analysis of the General Accounting Office and the Office of Management and Budget* (Baton Rouge: Louisiana State University Press, 1984), 13–34; and Jerry L. McCaffery, "The Development of Public Budgeting in the United States," in *A Centennial History of the American Administrative State,* ed. Ralph Clark Chandler (New York: Free Press, 1987), 345–77.

21. See William F. Willoughby, *The Movement for Budgetary Reform in the States* (New York: Appleton, 1918).

22. In the wake of the Brownlow Committee's report (1937), the Bureau of the Budget was transferred from the Treasury Department to the newly established Executive Office of the President.

23. Mosher, *Tale of Two Agencies,* 32.

24. See David G. Mathiasen, "The Evolution of OMB," *Public Budgeting and Finance* 8 (Autumn 1988): 3–14; and Peter M. Benda and Charles H. Levine, "Reagan and the Bureaucracy: The Bequest, the Promise, and the Legacy," in *The Reagan Legacy: Promise and Performance,* ed. Charles O. Jones (Chatham, N.J.: Chatham House, 1988), 102–42.

25. See Howard E. Shuman, *Politics and the Budget: The Struggle between the President and the Congress* (Englewood Cliffs, N.J.: Prentice Hall, 1984).

26. The federal budget is a two-inch-thick volume, the size of a large city's telephone directory, printed on very thin paper with tiny type. The task of publishing such a huge volume of information, in the quantities needed by members of Congress, the press, and interested members of the general public, preoccupies the Government Printing Office for more than a month each year. Copies of the budget are available at nearly all college and university libraries, usually in the government documents section.

27. See Lance T. LeLoup, "From Microbudgeting to Macrobudgeting: Evolution in Theory and Practice," in *New Directions in Budget Theory,* ed. Irene S. Rubin (Albany: State University of New York Press, 1988), 19–42.

28. On forecasting, see, for example Larry D. Schroeder, "Forecasting Revenues and Expenditures," in *Management Policies in Local Government Finance,* ed. J. Richard Aronson and Eli Schwartz (Washington, D.C.: International City Management Association, 1981), 66–90; on the problems of forecasting the federal budget, see "Uncertainty and Bias in Budget Projections," in U.S. Congressional

Budget Office, *The Economic and Budget Outlook: An Update* (Washington, D.C.: Government Printing Office, 1987), 63–86.

29. See David C. Mowery, Mark S. Kamlet, and John P. Crecine, "Presidential Management of Budgetary and Fiscal Policymaking," *Political Science Quarterly* 95 (Fall 1980): 395–425. For a broader examination of budgeting that includes state and local issues, see Irene S. Rubin, *The Politics of Public Budgeting,* 3d ed. (Chatham, N.J.: Chatham House, 1997).

30. H. Douglas Arnold argues, for example, that congressional decisions may be used "partly as rewards for past support, partly as payments for support during the current year, and partly to create a favorable climate for future years." Arnold, *Congress and the Bureaucracy: A Theory of Influence* (New Haven: Yale University Press, 1979), 56.

31. For a look at the problems posed by the annual budget process, see Naomi Caiden, "The Myth of the Annual Budget," *Public Administration Review* 42 (November/December 1982): 516–23.

32. Aaron Wildavsky, *The New Politics of the Budgetary Process* (Glenview, Ill: Scott, Foresman, 1988), 83.

33. Wildavsky's work received support at the federal level by Otto A. Davis, M.A.H. Dempster, and Aaron Wildavsky, "A Theory of the Budgetary Process," *American Political Science Review* 60 (September 1966): 529–47; and at the state level by Ira Sharkansky, "Agency Requests, Gubernatorial Support and Budget Success in State Legislatures," *American Political Science Review* 62 (December 1968): 1220–31. In his later work, Wildavsky moved away from incrementalism. For a discussion, see Irene Rubin, "Aaron Wildavsky and the Demise of Incrementalism," *Public Administration Review* 49 (January/February 1989): 78–81.

34. Mark S. Kamlet and David C. Mowery, "The Budgetary Base in Federal Resource Allocation," *American Journal of Political Science* 24 (November 1980): 804 and, more generally, 808–10. For another criticism of incrementalism, see Allen Schick, "Incremental Budgeting in a Decremental Age," *Policy Sciences* 16 (1983): 1–25.

35. Lance T. LeLoup and William B. Moreland, "Agency Strategies and Executive Review: The Hidden Politics of Budgeting," *Public Administration Review* 38 (May/June 1978): 232–39; see also Peter B. Natchez and Irwin C. Bupp, "Policy and Priority in the Budgetary Process," *American Political Science Review* 67 (September 1973): 951–63.

36. Natchez and Bupp, "Policy and Priority in the Budgetary Process," 956 and, more generally, 951–63. On the role of entrepreneurs in building support for their programs, see *Leadership and Innovation: A Biographical Perspective on Entrepreneurs in Government,* ed. Jameson W. Doig and Erwin Hargrove (Baltimore: Johns Hopkins University Press, 1987).

37. Frank B. Sherwood and William J. Page, Jr., "MBO and Public Management," *Public Administration Review* 36 (January/February 1976): 11. The Office of Management and Budget agrees. See Clifford W. Graves and Stefan A. Halper, "Federal Program Evaluation: The Perspective from OMB," in U.S. Senate, Committee on Government Operations, *Legislative Oversight and Program Evaluation,*

committee print, 94th Cong., 2d sess., 1976, 266–67. The MBO experience is perceptively analyzed in James A. Swiss, "Implementing Federal Programs: Administrative Systems and Organization Effectiveness" (Ph.D. dissertation, Yale University, 1976). See also Richard Rose, *Managing Presidential Objectives* (New York: Free Press, 1976).

38. Peter A. Pyrrh introduced the system at Texas Instruments and helped Carter install it in Georgia. See *Zero-Base Budgeting: A Practical Tool for Evaluating Expenses* (New York: Wiley, 1973). More broadly, see "Forum: ZBB Revisited," *Bureaucrat* 7 (Spring 1978): 3–70; Thomas P. Lauth, "Zero-Base Budgeting in Georgia State Government: Myth and Reality," *Public Administration Review* 38 (September/October 1978): 420–30; and George Samuel Minmier, *An Evaluation of the Zero-Base Budgeting System in Governmental Institutions* (Atlanta: School of Business Administration, Georgia State University, 1975), excerpted in U.S. Senate, Committee on Government Operations, Subcommittee on Intergovernmental Relations, *Compendium of Materials on Zero-base Budgeting,* committee print, 95th Cong., 1st sess., 1977.

39. Stanley B. Botner discusses the spread of PPB, MBO, and ZBB, among other tools, in "The Use of Budgeting/Management Tools by State Governments," *Public Administration Review* 45 (September/October 1985): 616–20.

40. See *Report of the National Economic Commission* (Washington, D.C.: Government Printing Office, 1989). Both Republican and Democratic members of the commission did concur on the need to protect the social security trust fund for future retirees, but they could not agree on a plan for doing so.

41. Legislative formulas, furthermore, can make budgetary giants out of what were once intended to be small and relatively insignificant programs. See Martha Derthick, *Uncontrollable Spending for Social Services Grants* (Washington, D.C.: Brookings Institution, 1975).

42. A further challenge to incrementalism—and a different source of "uncontrollable" spending—is increased judicial intervention into budgeting through mandated spending. See Jeffrey D. Straussman, "Courts and Public Purse Strings: Have Portraits of Budgeting Missed Something?" *Public Administration Review* 46 (July/August 1986): 345–51.

43. For an analysis of how congressional and presidential policies have differed, see Mark S. Kamlet and David C. Mowery, "Influences on Executive and Congressional Budgetary Priorities, 1955–1981," *American Political Science Review* 81 (March 1987): 155–78.

44. Carl J. Friedrich, *Man and His Government* (New York: McGraw-Hill, 1963), 199–215.

45. For a catalog of the many strategies used in the budget game, see Wildavsky, *Politics of the Budgetary Process,* 21–62.

46. See Richard P. Nathan, *The Administrative Presidency* (New York: Wiley, 1983), 51–56.

47. James L. Sundquist, "Congress as Public Administrator," in Chandler, *Centennial History of the American Administrative State,* 275.

48. U.S. Congress, House of Representatives, Committee on Rules, *Budget and*

Impoundment Control Act of 1973: Report, House Rpt. No. 93-658, 93d Cong., 1st sess., 1973, 21–22.

49. See Richard F. Fenno, Jr., *The Power of the Purse: Appropriations Politics in Congress* (Boston: Little, Brown, 1966).

50. Congressional Budget and Impoundment Control Act of 1974, Public Law 93-344. For an analysis of the act's effects on Congress, see Dennis S. Ippolito, *Congressional Spending* (Ithaca, N.Y.: Cornell University Press, 1981); and Allen Schick, *Congress and Money: Budgeting, Spending, and Taxes* (Washington, D.C.: Urban Institute Press, 1980).

51. Tim Weiner, "$28 Billion Spying Budget Is Made Public by Mistake," *New York Times,* 5 November 1994, 7; idem, "A Secret Agency's Secret Budgets Yield 'Lost' Billions, Officials Say," *New York Times,* 30 January 1996, A1.

52. David C. Morrison, "Truth Elusive in 'Black' Maze," *National Journal,* 10 October 1987, 2552.

53. Lawrence J. Haas, "Blame the Appropriators, *National Journal,* 8 August 1987, 2027; and OMB, *Budget, Fiscal Year 1991,* 271.

54. See Schick, *Congress and Money,* 415–81.

55. The "gimmicks" include purposely underfunding entitlements and then tacking on new programs to the inevitable supplemental appropriations bill, and squeezing some spending into different fiscal years to reduce the deficit temporarily. Ibid., 2025, 2028. See also Gary Klott, "Your Taxes at Work: A National Weed Center, an Ad Drive on Fish," *New York Times,* 26 May 1987, B4.

56. Steven Engelberg, "A Congressman, a Plane Ride and the Budget," *New York Times,* 4 January 1988, sec. 1, 1.

57. Public Law 99-177. The sponsors were Senators Phil Gramm (R-Tex.), Warren R. Rudman (R-N.H.), and Ernest F. Hollings (D-S.C.).

58. In public discussion, "Gramm-Rudman-Hollings" proved too long a label and was quickly shortened to "Gramm-Rudman"; to Senator Ernest Hollings's chagrin, wags suggested that a cut had to be made somewhere.

59. *Congressional Quarterly Almanac, 1985* (Washington, D.C.: CQ Press, 1986), 459.

60. Eric A. Hanushek, "Formula Budgeting: The Economics and Analytics of Fiscal Policy Under Rules," *Journal of Policy Analysis and Management* 6 (Fall 1986): 3.

61. *Bowsher* v. *Synar,* 106 Supreme Court Reporter 3181 (1986).

62. The 1987 revision also gave the president more latitude in determining among the budget accounts where the cuts would fall.

63. General Accounting Office, *The Budget Deficit* (Washington, D.C.: Government Printing Office, 1988), 5. See also GAO's *Deficit Reductions for Fiscal Year 1989: Compliance with the Balanced Budget and Emergency Deficit Control Act of 1985* (Washington, D.C.: Government Printing Office, 1988).

64. *New York Times,* 30 April 1989, sec. 3, 1.

65. These tactics are outlined by Peter Milius, "Cooked Books," *Washington Post,* 24 April 1989: A11.

66. For an analysis of these provisions, see Schick, *Federal Budget,* 39–41; and

Nicholas A. Masters, *The Congressional Budget Process: 1974–1993,* U.S. House of Representatives, Committee on the Budget, committee print, 103d Cong., 1st sess., 1994.

67. Jonathan Rauch, "The Fiscal Ice Age," *National Journal,* 10 January 1987, 58. For an appraisal of the process, see Donald F. Kettl, *Deficit Politics* (New York: Macmillan, 1992); Wildavsky, *Politics of the Budgetary Process;* Schick, *Congress and Money;* Allen Schick, ed., *Making Economic Policy in Congress* (Washington, D.C.: American Enterprise Institute, 1983); and Allen Schick, *The Capacity to Budget* (Washington, D.C.: Urban Institute Press, 1990).

68. Al Gore, *From Red Tape to Results: Creating a Government That Works Better and Costs Less* (Washington, D.C.: Government Printing Office, 1993), 17. See also the statement of Susan J. Irving, U.S. General Accounting Office, before U.S. House of Representatives, Committee on Rules, *Budget Process: Some Reforms Offer Promise,* T-AIMD-94-86, 2 March 1994.

69. Congress experimented with a two-year budget in December 1987 when it negotiated with the White House a continuing resolution that set a two-year plan for meeting the Gramm-Rudman spending ceilings.

70. Schick, *Federal Budget,* 201.

71. Jonathan Rauch, "Biennial Budgeting Taking Root," *National Journal,* 27 September 1986, 2318–19; and General Accounting Office, *Budget Issues: Current Status and Recent Trends of State Biennial and Annual Budgeting* (Washington, D.C.: Government Printing Office, 1987), 2.

72. Statement of Frederick D. Wolf, General Accounting Office, "Capital Budgeting for the Federal Government," before the Subcommittee on Public Works and Transportation, Committee on Public Works and Transportation, House of Representatives (Washington, D.C.: General Accounting Office, 1987).

73. The debate over line-item vetoes predates the Constitution. See, for example, Forrest McDonald, "Line-Item Veto: Older Than Constitution," *Wall Street Journal,* 7 March 1988, 16. The Constitution of the Confederate States of America, moreover, provided President Jefferson Davis with a line-item veto as well as a six-year term.

74. Ronald C. Moe argues that experiences in the states have limited applicability to the federal government and that "practices found useful at one level may produce just the opposite effect if employed at the other level." The line-item veto might, moreover, cause more damage in the relations among the principal branches of government than any financial advantages it might produce. See *Prospects for the Item Veto at the Federal Level: Lessons from the States* (Washington, D.C.: National Academy of Public Administration, 1988). See also U.S. House of Representatives, Committee on the Budget, *The Line-Item Veto: An Appraisal,* committee print, 98th Cong., 2d sess., 1984.

75. As Allen Schick argues, "variances between the two budgets [presidential and congressional] are often due to differing economic and technical assumptions rather than to policy disagreements." "The Evolution of Congressional Budgeting," in *Crisis in the Budget Process: Exercising Political Choice,* ed. Allen Schick (Washington, D.C.: American Enterprise Institute, 1986), 19.

76. General Accounting Office, *Balanced Budget Requirements: State Experiences and Implications for the Federal Government,* AFMD-93-58BR, March 1993, 1.

77. Ibid. See also National Association of State Budget Officers, "State Balanced Budget Requirements: Provisions and Practice," Washington, D.C., 24 June 1992. Photocopied.

78. Ibid., 2.

79. For two different arguments for a constitutional amendment, see Aaron Wildavsky, *How to Limit Government Spending* (Berkeley: University of California Press, 1980); and Milton and Rose Friedman, "Constitutional Amendment to Limit the Growth of Spending," in *Control of Federal Spending,* ed. C. Lowell Harriss (New York: Proceedings of the Academy of Political Science, 1985), 132–36.

At the state level, it is far more difficult to define what a government's fiscal status is—and balanced-budget requirements often induce governments to discover imaginative devices for shifting unpleasant news to future fiscal years. See Robert B. Albritton and Ellen M. Dran, "Balanced Budgets and State Surpluses," *Public Administration Review* 47 (March/April 1987): 143–52.

State and local spending limitations have sometimes produced unexpected, and unsatisfactory, results. See Terry Schwardon, ed., *California and the American Tax Revolt: Proposition 13 Five Years Later* (Berkeley: University of California Press, 1984); and Elaine B. Sharp and David Elkins, "The Impact of Fiscal Limitation: A Tale of Seven Cities," *Public Administration Review* 47 (September/October 1987): 385–92.

80. Schick, *Federal Budget,* 198.

81. Lawrence J. Haas, "If All Else Fails, Reform," *National Journal,* 4 July 1987, 1713.

82. Lawrence J. Haas, "An Open Window for Budget Reforms," *National Journal,* 23 May 1987, 1362.

83. Quoted in Jeffrey H. Birnbaum, "As Lawmakers Devise Ways to Trim Deficit, Backdoor Projects Rise," *Wall Street Journal,* 19 November 1987, 1, 7.

84. Many taxes hide under the umbrella of "user charges." See Jonathan Rauch, "Swing Toward Spending," *National Journal,* 18 April 1987, 926. For an exploration of the basic issues, see E.S. Savas, *Privatization: The Key to Better Government* (Chatham, N.J.: Chatham House, 1987).

85. Bipartisan Commission on Entitlement and Tax Reform, *Interim Report to the President* (Washington, D.C.: The Commission, 1994), 6.

86. OMB, *Budget, Fiscal Year 1991,* 229, 233.

87. For a look at federal guaranteed loan programs for student aid, see Donald F. Kettl, *Government by Proxy: (Mis?)Managing Federal Programs* (Washington, D.C.: CQ Press, 1988), chap. 5. See also Herman B. Leonard, *Checks Unbalanced: The Quiet Side of Federal Spending* (New York: Basic Books, 1986); Hanushek, "Formula Budgeting," 15; and Ronald C. Moe and Thomas H. Stanton, "Government-Sponsored Enterprises as Federal Instrumentalities: Reconciling Private Management with Public Accountability," *Public Administration Review* 49 (July/August 1989): 321–29.

88. U.S. House of Representatives, Committee on the Budget, *Congressional Control of Expenditures,* Report prepared by Allen Schick, committee print, 95th Cong. 1st sess., 1977, 126.

89. U.S. House of Representatives, Committee on Appropriations, *General Appropriations Bill, 1951,* Report, 74th Cong., 1st sess., 1950, 9.

90. Members of Congress were outraged one year when the Post Office, having spent about $400 million in each of the first three quarters of the fiscal year, had only $9 million left for the final quarter and sought a supplemental appropriation from Congress. See Louis Fisher, *Presidential Spending Power* (Princeton, N.J.: Princeton University Press, 1975), 155.

91. The Impoundment Control Act is Title X of the Congressional Budget and Impoundment Control Act of 1974.

92. Fisher, *Presidential Spending Power,* 176. See 147–201 for a detailed analysis of presidential impoundment. We have drawn heavily on this account for this discussion.

93. If the budget authority was provided for only one fiscal year, however, withholding of funds is regarded as a rescission, not a referral.

94. Schick, *Congress and Money,* 403–6.

95. This discussion draws on Robert N. Anthony and David W. Young, *Management Control in Nonprofit Organizations,* 4th ed. (Homewood, Ill.: Irwin, 1988), esp. 3–49.

96. Ibid., 21. Emphasis in the original omitted.

97. U.S. Comptroller General, *Financial Integrity Act: Continuing Efforts Needed to Improve Internal Control and Accounting Systems* (Washington, D.C.: General Accounting Office, 1987). See also these other GAO reports: *Financial Management: Examples of Weaknesses* (Washington, D.C.: General Accounting Office, 1988); and *Managing the Cost of Government: Building an Effective Financial Management Structure* (Washington, D.C.: General Accounting Office, 1985).

98. For an examination of these issues, see Leo Herbert, Larry N. Killough, and Alan Walter Steiss, *Governmental Accounting and Control* (Monterey, Calif.: Brooks/Cole, 1984); and Leon E. Hay, *Accounting for Governmental and Nonprofit Entities,* 8th ed. (Homewood, Ill.: Irwin, 1989).

99. For example, see Oregon Progress Board, *Oregon Benchmarks: Standards for Measuring Statewide Progress and Institutional Performance* (Salem: Oregon Progress Board, 1994).

100. See, for example, General Accounting Office, *Managing for Results: State Experiences Provide Insights for Federal Management Reforms,* GGD-95-22, December 1994; and John J. DiIulio et al., *Performance Measures for the Criminal Justice System* (Washington, D.C.: Bureau of Justice Statistics, 1993).

11. Implementation (pp. 284–315)

1. Jeffrey L. Pressman and Aaron B. Wildavsky, *Implementation* (Berkeley: University of California Press, 1973). They cite their debt to an earlier work on implementation by Martha Derthick, *New Towns In-Town* (Washington, D.C.: Urban

Institute, 1972).

2. Ibid., xv.

3. Randall B. Ripley and Grace A. Franklin, *Policy Implementation and Bureaucracy,* 2d ed. (Chicago: Dorsey Press, 1986), 2.

4. Daniel A. Mazmanian and Paul A. Sabatier, *Implementation and Public Policy* (Glenview, Ill.: Scott, Foresman, 1983), 277. See also Eugene Bardach, *The Implementation Game: What Happens After a Bill Becomes a Law* (Cambridge, Mass.: MIT Press, 1977).

5. Brian H. Hogwood and B. Guy Peters, *The Pathology of Public Policy* (Oxford: Clarendon Press, 1985).

6. For a spirited rebuttal to the literature of failure, see Sar A. Levitan and Robert Taggart, *The Promise of Greatness* (Cambridge: Harvard University Press, 1976). See also Henry J. Aaron, *Politics and the Professors: The Great Society in Perspective* (Washington, D.C.: Brookings Institution, 1978); Robert H. Haveman, ed., *A Decade of Federal Antipoverty Programs: Achievements, Failures, and Lessons* (New York: Academic Press, 1977); and Malcolm L. Goggin, Ann O'M. Bowman, James P. Lester, and Laurence J. O'Toole, *Implementation Theory and Practice: Toward a Third Generation* (Glenview, Ill.: Scott, Foresman/Little, Brown, 1990).

7. See Daniel P. Moynihan, *Maximum Feasible Misunderstanding: Community Action in the War on Poverty* (New York: Free Press, 1970).

8. Housing and Community Development Act of 1974, 88 U.S. Statutes 633.

9. Ripley and Franklin, *Policy Implementation and Bureaucracy,* 22–23.

10. Martin A. Levin and Barbara Ferman, *The Political Hand: Policy Implementation and Youth Employment Programs* (New York: Pergamon Press, 1985), 72–73.

11. Norman R. Augustine, *Augustine's Laws* (New York: Viking, 1986), 313.

12. Stephen Percy, *Disability, Civil Rights, and Public Policy: The Politics of Implementation* (University: University of Alabama Press, 1990).

13. See Giandomenico Majone and Aaron Wildavsky, "Implementation as Evolution," in Jeffrey L. Pressman and Aaron Wildavsky, *Implementation,* 3d ed. (Berkeley: University of California Press, 1984), 163–80.

14. Paul Berman, "The Study of Macro- and Micro-Implementation," *Public Policy* 26 (Spring 1978): 165.

15. See Arthur M. Okun, *Equality and Efficiency: The Big Tradeoff* (Washington, D.C.: Brookings Institution, 1975).

16. Elliot Richardson, *The Creative Balance* (New York: Holt, Rinehart and Winston, 1976), 128.

17. Robert Stevens and Rosemary Stevens, *Welfare Medicine in America: A Study of Medicaid* (New York: Free Press, 1974), 73.

18. Richardson, *Creative Balance,* 130, 132–34.

19. W. John Moore, "Mandates Without Money," *National Journal,* 4 October 1986, 2366.

20. See Mazmanian and Sabatier, *Implementation and Public Policy,* 24.

21. Quoted in Louis M. Kohlmeier, "Banking Reform Chances Grow Dim-

mer," *National Journal,* 20 September 1975, 1341.

22. Ralph Waldo Emerson, "Self-Reliance," in Emerson, *Essays* (Boston: Houghton Mifflin, 1865, 1876, 1883), 62.

23. See Jameson W. Doig and Erwin C. Hargrove, eds., *Leadership and Innovation* (Baltimore: Johns Hopkins University Press, 1987); and John Kingdon, *Agendas, Alternatives, and Public Policies* (Boston: Little, Brown, 1984), 129–30.

24. Bardach, *Implementation Game,* 274–75. See also Levin and Ferman, *Political Hand,* 5.

25. James Q. Wilson, "The Bureaucracy Problem," *Public Interest,* no. 6 (Spring 1967): 7. See also his *Bureaucracy: What Government Agencies Do and Why They Do It* (New York: Basic Books, 1989).

26. Pressman and Wildavsky, *Implementation,* 1, 31, 48, 100. All quotations come from this source.

27. Murray L. Weidenbaum, *The Modern Public Sector: New Ways of Doing the Government's Business* (New York: Basic Books, 1969), 4. See also Bruce L.R. Smith, "Changing Public-Private Sector Relations: A Look at the United States," *Annals of the American Academy of Political and Social Sciences* 466 (March 1983): 149–64.

28. See Lester M. Salamon, "Rethinking Public Management: Third-Party Government and the Changing Forms of Government Action," *Public Policy* 29 (1981): 255–75; and Donald F. Kettl, *Government by Proxy: (Mis?)Managing Federal Programs* (Washington, D.C.: CQ Press, 1988).

29. Office of Management and Budget [OMB], *Budget of the United States Government, Fiscal Year 1988: Special Analyses* (Washington, D.C.: Government Printing Office, 1987), H-1.

30. Martha Derthick, *The Influence of Federal Grants: Public Assistance in Massachusetts* (Cambridge: Harvard University Press, 1970), 197.

31. Advisory Commission on Intergovernmental Relations, *A Catalog of Federal Grant-in-Aid Programs to State and Local Governments: Grants Funded FY 1978* (Washington, D.C.: Government Printing Office, 1979).

32. OMB, *Budget, Fiscal Year 1988: Special Analyses,* H-25.

33. OMB, *Budget, Fiscal Year 1988: Special Analyses,* H-23; and *Budget, Fiscal Year 1991,* A-303.

34. A third variety, general-purpose grants, virtually ended in 1986 when Congress failed to reauthorize General Revenue Sharing, which provided nearly strings-free aid to all state and general-purpose local governments. A few general-purpose grants remain, such as federal payments to the District of Columbia, but general-purpose aid is now a relatively insignificant part of the intergovernmental landscape.

35. U.S. Advisory Commission on Intergovernmental Relations, *Characteristics of Federal Grant-in-Aid Programs to State and Local Governments: Grants Funded FY 1993* (Washington, D.C.: Government Printing Office, 1994), 7.

36. David R. Beam, "New Federalism, Old Realities: The Reagan Administration and Intergovernmental Reform," in *The Reagan Presidency and the Governing of America,* ed. Lester M. Salamon and Michael S. Lund (Washington, D.C.: Urban Institute, 1985), 427.

37. General Accounting Office, *Grant Formulas: A Catalog of Federal Aid to States and Localities* (Washington, D.C.: Government Printing Office, 1987), 12.

38. See General Accounting Office, *Fundamental Changes Are Needed in Federal Assistance to State and Local Governments* (Washington, D.C.: Government Printing Office, 1975), 12.

39. GAO, *Grant Formulas,* 13.

40. See, for example, Donald F. Kettl, *The Regulation of American Federalism* (Baltimore: Johns Hopkins University Press, 1987); Advisory Commission on Intergovernmental Relations, *Regulatory Federalism: Policy, Process, Impact and Reform* (Washington, D.C.: Government Printing Office, 1984); and Edward I. Koch, "The Mandate Millstone," *Public Interest,* no. 61 (Fall 1980): 42–57.

41. OMB, *Managing Federal Assistance in the 1980's* (Washington, D.C.: Government Printing Office, 1980), 20–26.

42. Congress reversed itself in 1996 and allowed states to increase the speed limit back to 65 miles per hour.

43. Another regulatory strategy, "partial preemption," establishes federal standards but allows states to adopt their own standards if they are at least as tough.

44. For an examination, see Joseph F. Zimmerman, *Federal Preemption: The Silent Revolution* (Ames: Iowa State University Press, 1991).

45. John M. Goshko, "Unfunded Mandates Top Cities' List of Problems," *Washington Post,* 19 January 1995, A13.

46. Bruce D. McDowell, "Federally Induced Costs: Mandate Relief Comes of Age," *Intergovernmental Perspective,* Summer–Fall, 1994, 21.

47. Rochelle L. Stanfield, "Thanks a Lot for Nothing, Washington," *National Journal,* 26 March 1994, 726–27.

48. Margaret Kriz, "Cleaner Than Clean?" *National Journal,* 23 April 1994, 947.

49. OMB, *Budget, Fiscal Year 1990: Special Analyses,* H-41-42.

50. For a full review of administrative problems of the grant system, see Advisory Commission on Intergovernmental Relations, *Improving Federal Grants Management* (Washington, D.C.: Government Printing Office, 1977).

51. See Martha Derthick, *Uncontrollable Spending for Social Services Grants* (Washington, D.C.: Brookings Institution, 1975).

52. Michael D. Reagan, "Accountability and Independence in Federal Grants-in-Aid," in *The New Political Economy: The Public Use of the Private Sector,* ed. Bruce L.R. Smith (New York: Wiley, 1975), 206.

53. See National Governors' Conference, *Federal Roadblocks to Efficient State Government,* 2 vols. (Washington, D.C.: Government Printing Office, 1976, 1977); and Advisory Commission on Intergovernmental Relations, *Improving Federal Grants Management.*

54. Robert P. Stoker, *Reluctant Partners: Implementing Federal Policy* (Pittsburgh: University of Pittsburgh Press, 1991).

55. See John D. Hanrahan, *Government by Contract* (New York: Norton, 1983), esp. chap. 3.

56. Federal Procurement Data Center, *Federal Procurement Data System*

Standard Report: Fiscal Year 1993 Fourth Quarter (Washington, D.C.: Government Printing Office, 1994).

57. *National Journal,* 1 March 1986, 504. See also Harry P. Hatry, *A Review of Private Approaches for Delivery of Public Services* (Washington, D.C.: Urban Institute Press, 1983); and Philip E. Fixler, Jr., Robert W. Poole, Jr., and Lynn Scarlett, *Privatization 1987: Second Annual Report on Privatization* (Santa Monica, Calif.: Reason Foundation, 1988).

58. OMB, Circular No. A-76 revised, 29 March 1979.

59. President's Private Sector Survey on Cost Control, *Report on Privatization* (Washington, D.C.: Government Printing Office, 1983), i. Compare President's Commission on Privatization, *Privatization: Toward More Effective Government* (Washington, D.C.: Government Printing Office, 1988).

60. J. Peter Grace, *Burning Money: The Waste of Your Tax Dollars* (New York: Macmillan, 1984), 175.

61. Congressional Budget Office, *Contracting Out: Potential for Reducing Federal Costs* (Washington, D.C.: Government Printing Office, 1987), vii–ix.

62. General Services Administration, Federal Procurement Data Center, *Federal Procurement Data System: Fiscal Year 1993* (Washington, D.C.: Government Printing Office, 1994), 13.

63. Steve Coll and Judith Havemann, "Dispute Threatens U.S. Phone Contract," *Washington Post,* 31 July 1987, B1. See also Donald F. Kettl, *Sharing Power: Public Governance and Private Markets* (Washington, D.C.: Brookings Institution, 1993), chap. 4.

64. For scathing critiques, see Garry Brewer, *Politicians, Bureaucrats, and the Consultant* (New York: Basic Books, 1973); Daniel Guttman and Barry Wilner, *The Shadow Government: The Government's Multi-Billion-Dollar Giveaway of Its Decision-Making Powers to Private Management Consultants, "Experts," and Think Tanks* (New York: Pantheon, 1976); and Hanrahan, *Government by Contract.* For a broad look at the evidence, see John D. Donahue, *The Privatization Decision: Public Ends, Private Means* (New York: Basic Books, 1989).

65. U.S. Congress, Senate, Armed Services Committee, *Defense Organization: The Need for Change,* staff report, 99th Cong., 1st sess., 1985, 558. For one example, see Nick Kotz, *Wild Blue Yonder: Money, Politics, and the B-1 Bomber* (New York: Pantheon, 1988).

66. Edward R. Luttwak, *The Pentagon and the Art of the War* (New York: Simon and Schuster, 1984), 184.

67. American Federation of State, County, and Municipal Employees, *Passing the Bucks* (Washington, D.C.: AFSCME, 1983), 38.

68. General Accounting Office, *General Services Administration: Actions Needed to Stop Buying Supplies from Poor-Performing Vendors,* GGD-93-34, January 1993, 2, 4.

69. *New York Times,* 15 June 1986, sec. 3, 4.

70. AFSCME, *Passing the Bucks,* 69.

71. Selwyn Raab, "U.S. Indicts Ten Road Contractors on Bids," *New York Times,* 26 June 1987, B1.

72. W. John Moore, "Grass-Roots Graft," *National Journal,* 1 August 1987, 1963, 1966.

73. AFSCME, *Passing the Bucks,* 69–70.

74. Josh Barbanel, "Wedtech: Rise and Fall of a Well-Connected Bronx Company," *New York Times,* 19 January 1987, B1; George Lardner, Jr., "Wedtech Going Out of Business," *Washington Post,* 25 July 1987, A5.

75. Effective contracting out requires careful management. For a discussion of this problem, see John A. Rehfuss, *Contracting Out in Government: A Guide to Working with Outside Contractors to Supply Public Services* (San Francisco: Jossey-Bass, 1989).

76. Bruce L.R. Smith, "Changing Public-Private Sector Relations, 152.

77. Alice M. Rivlin, "Social Policy: Alternate Strategies for the Federal Government," Woytinsky Lecture, Department of Economics and Public Policy, University of Michigan, Ann Arbor, 1973, 10–11. For a vigorous, well-documented argument that the Great Society programs "had a massive, overwhelmingly beneficial impact," see Levitan and Taggart, *Promise of Greatness.* Most writers do not share this view.

78. Alice M. Rivlin, "Why Can't We Get Things Done," *Brookings Bulletin* 9 (Spring 1972): 6.

79. Presidential Commission on the Space Shuttle *Challenger* Accident, *Report to the President* (Washington, D.C.: Government Printing Office, 1986), 103.

80. "'Never Missed a Day or a Delivery,'" *Washington Post,* 28 December 1987, A5.

81. U.S. Comptroller General, *Social Security: Clients Still Rate Quality of Service High* (Washington, D.C.: General Accounting Office, 1987).

82. This discussion, including questions, is drawn from Kitty Krause, "Hammers and Nails in Mt. Winans," *Washington Monthly* 18 (April 1986): 21–26.

83. Herbert Kaufman, *Administrative Feedback: Monitoring Subordinates' Behavior* (Washington, D.C.: Brookings Institution, 1973), 2.

84. Pressman and Wildavsky, *Implementation.*

85. Keith Schneider, "Ex-Nuclear Aides Deny Being Told of Plant Mishaps," *New York Times,* 5 October 1988, A26.

86. Kaufman, *Administrative Feedback,* chap. 3. See also Myron Peretz Glazer and Penina Migdal Glazer, *The Whistleblowers: Exposing Corruption in Government and Industry* (New York: Basic Books, 1989).

87. James Hirsch, "Singer Case Whistle-Blower Says Decision Was Difficult," *New York Times,* 16 March 1989, D1.

88. Carol H. Weiss, *Evaluation Research: Methods of Assessing Program Effectiveness* (Englewood Cliffs, N.J.: Prentice Hall, 1972), 2.

89. See, for example, ibid.; Donald T. Campbell and Julian C. Stanley, *Experimental and Quasi-Experimental Designs for Research* (Chicago: Rand McNally, 1966); and Joseph S. Wholey, Harry P. Hatry, and Kathryn E. Newcomer, eds., *Handbook of Practical Program Evaluation* (San Francisco: Jossey-Bass, 1994).

90. See Harry P. Hatry, Richard E. Winnie, and Donald M. Fisk, *Practical Program Evaluation for State and Local Governments,* 2d ed. (Washington, D.C.: Ur-

ban Institute Press, 1981); and Joseph S. Wholey, Kathryn E. Newcomer, and Associates, *Improving Government Performance: Evaluation Strategies for Strengthening Public Agencies and Programs* (San Francisco: Jossey-Bass, 1989).

91. See Giandomenico Majone, "Policy Analysis and Public Deliberation," in *The Power of Public Ideas,* ed. Robert B. Reich (Cambridge, Mass.: Ballinger, 1988), 173.

92. See, for example, Stephen H. Linder and B. Guy Peters, "From Social Theory to Policy Design," *Journal of Public Policy* 4 (1984): 237–59.

93. Richard F. Elmore, "Backward Mapping: Implementation Research and Policy Decisions," in Walter Williams and others, *Studying Implementation: Methodological and Administrative Issues* (Chatham, N.J.: Chatham House, 1982), 21, and, more generally, 18–35.

94. For one effort, see James D. Carroll, "Public Administration in the Third Century of the Constitution: Supply-Side Management, Privatization, or Public Investment?" *Public Administration Review* 47 (January/February 1987): 106–14.

12. Legislative Control of Administration (pp. 319–39)

1. Christopher H. Foreman, Jr., *Signals from the Hill: Congressional Oversight and the Challenge of Social Regulation* (New Haven: Yale University Press, 1988), 12. For a thorough and careful look at oversight, see Joel D. Aberbach, *Keeping a Watchful Eye: The Politics of Congressional Oversight* (Washington, D.C.: Brookings Institution, 1990).

2. See Richard E. Neustadt, "Politicians and Bureaucrats," in *The Congress and America's Future,* 2d ed., ed. David B. Truman (Englewood Cliffs, N.J.: Prentice Hall, 1973), 119.

3. For a history of congressional-administrative relations, see James L. Sundquist, "Congress as Public Administrator," in *A Centennial History of American Public Administration,* ed. Ralph Clark Chandler (New York: Free Press, 1987), 261–89.

4. National Academy of Public Administration, *Congressional Oversight of Regulatory Agencies: The Need to Strike a Balance and Focus on Performance* (Washington, D.C.: National Academy of Public Administration, 1988), 1.

5. Nathaniel C. Nash, "Telling State Dept. How to Run Foreign Policy . . . ," *New York Times,* 12 October 1987.

6. J. Ronald Fox with James L. Field, *The Defense Management Challenge: Weapons Acquisition* (Boston: Harvard Business School Press, 1988), 76. See also David C. Hendrickson, *Reforming Defense: The State of American Civil-Military Relations* (Baltimore: Johns Hopkins University Press, 1988), 30–34. More broadly, see Louis Fisher, "Micromanagement by Congress: Reality and Mythology," in *The Fettered Presidency: Legal Constraints on the Executive Branch,* ed. L. Gordon Crovitz and Jeremy A. Rabkin (Washington, D.C.: American Enterprise Institute, 1989), 139–57.

7. Henry Kissinger and Cyrus Vance, "Bipartisan Objectives for American Foreign Policy," *Foreign Affairs* 66 (Summer 1988): 901.

8. See David R. Mayhew, *Congress: The Electoral Connection* (New Haven: Yale University Press, 1974).

9. See Seymour Scher, "Conditions for Legislative Control," *Journal of Politics* 25 (August 1963): 526–51.

10. Ibid., 527.

11. These and similar terms are scattered throughout U.S. Senate, Committee on Government Operations, *Study on Federal Regulation,* vol. 2, *Congressional Oversight of Regulatory Agencies,* committee print, 95th Cong., 1st sess., 1977. Despite the restrictive title, this volume is one of the best reviews of performance and problems of oversight of both regulatory and nonregulatory agencies by both the House and the Senate. See also National Academy of Public Administration, *Congressional Oversight of Regulatory Agencies,* which reached similar conclusions.

12. Mathew D. McCubbins and Thomas Schwartz, "Congressional Oversight Overlooked: Police Patrols versus Fire Alarms," *American Journal of Political Science* 28 (Fall 1984): 169, 172.

13. This list comes from National Academy of Public Administration, *Congressional Oversight of Regulatory Agencies,* 7–9.

14. See Hugh Heclo, "Issue Networks and the Executive Establishment," in *The New Political System,* ed. Anthony King (Washington, D.C.: American Enterprise Institute, 1978), 87–124.

15. R. Douglas Arnold, *Congress and the Bureaucracy: A Theory of Influence* (New Haven: Yale University Press, 1979), 35.

16. Ibid., 67–68.

17. Lawrence C. Dodd and Richard L. Schott, *Congress and the Administrative State* (New York: Wiley, 1979), 170. More generally, see Morris S. Ogul, *Congress Oversees the Bureaucracy: Studies in Legislative Supervision* (Pittsburgh: University of Pittsburgh Press, 1976).

18. National Academy of Public Administration, *Congressional Oversight of Regulatory Agencies,* 9.

19. See Foreman, *Signals from the Hill,* chap. 4.

20. Dodd and Schott, *Congress and the Administrative State,* 166.

21. On the basis of members' shifts to and from other committees prior to 1973, the House Government Operations Committee ranked eighteenth in prestige among the twenty standing committees, and its Senate counterpart ranked thirteenth among the sixteen standing committees. See Leroy N. Rieselbach, *Congressional Politics* (New York: McGraw-Hill, 1973), 60–61n.

22. Dodd and Schott, *Congress and the Administrative State,* 168.

23. Ibid., 173–84.

24. U.S. Senate, Committee on Armed Services, Staff Report, *Defense Organization: The Need for Change,* committee print, 99th Cong., 1st sess., 1985, 581–82. The Georgetown University study is quoted in this report.

25. Thomas P. Murphy, "Political Executive Roles, Policymaking, and Interface with the Career Bureaucracy," *Bureaucrat* 6 (Summer 1977): 107.

26. For one interest group's discussion of these issues, see Stephen L. Katz, *Government: Decisions without Democracy* (Washington, D.C.: People for the

American Way, 1987).

27. Improper classification and other issues are reviewed in U.S. House of Representatives, Committee on Government Operations, *Executive Classification of Information . . . Third Report,* House Rpt. 93–221, 1973.

28. Summary of the board's findings by Edmund S. Muskie, in John Tower, Edmund Muskie, and Brent Scowcroft, *The Tower Commission Report* (New York: Bantam Books, 1987), xvii.

29. Christopher Madison, "Flexibility v. Congress's Right to Know," *National Journal,* 4 July 1987, 1727.

30. In 1972, both the Justice Department and the White House refused to furnish the draft of Executive Order 11753 (on classification of documents!) to the House Committee on Government Operations, arguing that it was only a working draft; this occurred after a newspaper's disclosure of details of the draft. See U.S. House Committee on Government Operations, *Executive Classification of Information . . . Third Report,* 53.

31. National Academy of Public Administration, *Congressional Oversight of Regulatory Agencies,* 24.

32. Frederick C. Mosher and others, *Watergate: Its Implications for Responsible Government* (New York: Basic Books, 1974), 115.

33. Excellent treatments of earlier congressional efforts to cope with scientific and technological issues are Thomas P. Jahnige, "The Congressional Committee System and the Oversight Process: Congress and NASA," *Western Political Quarterly* 21 (June 1968): 227–39; and U.S. House, Committee on Science and Aeronautics, Subcommittee on Science, Research, and Development, *Technological Information for Congress,* 92d Cong., 1st sess., 1971.

34. Francis E. Rourke, "Bureaucracy in the American Constitutional Order," *Political Science Quarterly* 102 (Summer 1978): 217–32.

35. Michael J. Malbin, *Unelected Representatives: Congressional Staff and the Future of Representative Government* (New York: Basic Books, 1979), 5. On the role of staffs in helping with congressional casework, see Morris P. Fiorina, *Congress: Keystone of the Washington Establishment* (New Haven: Yale University Press, 1977). See also Harrison W. Fox and Susan Webb Hammond, *Congressional Staffs: The Invisible Force in American Lawmaking* (New York: Free Press, 1977).

36. Norman J. Ornstein, Thomas E. Mann, Michael J. Malbin, Allen Schick, and John B. Bibby, *Vital Statistics on Congress* (Washington, D.C.: American Enterprise Institute, 1984), 121; and Richard E. Cohen, "The Hill People," *National Journal* 19 (16 May 1987): 1171; and congressional sources.

37. Malbin, *Unelected Representatives,* 10.

38. Dodd and Schott, *Congress and the Administrative State,* 270–71.

39. Michael J. Malbin, "Congressional Control of Committee Staffs: Who's in Charge Here?" *Public Interest,* no. 47 (Spring 1977): 16–40. For a full treatment of committee, personal, and legislative-agency staffs, see Fox and Hammond, *Congressional Staffs.*

40. U.S. Senate Committee on Government Operations, *Study on Federal Regulation,* 2:71; Ernest S. Griffith, in U.S. Senate, Commission on the Operation of the

Senate, *Congressional Support Agencies,* 126.

41. For a study of the history, development, and role of the General Accounting Office, see Frederick C. Mosher, *The GAO: The Quest for Accountability in American Government* (Boulder, Colo.: Westview Press, 1979).

42. See Louis Fisher, *The Politics of Shared Power: Congress and the Executive,* 2d ed. (Washington, D.C.: CQ Press, 1987), 125–29; and *Bowsher v. Synar,* 106 Supreme Court Reporter 3181 (1986).

43. Budget and Accounting Act of 1921, Secs. 309, 305 (31 *U.S. Code* 49, 71).

44. These officials could then attempt to collect disallowed payments from the recipients; failing that, they might seek passage of congressional acts reimbursing them. In the 1940s, about a million federal employees paid almost $2 million annually to insurance companies to cover any liabilities for disallowed payments of public funds. Finally, in 1955, Congress authorized agencies themselves to purchase blanket surety bonds for their employees. See U.S. Senate, Committee on Government Operations, *Financial Management in the Federal Government,* 92d Cong., 1st sess., 1971, 2:233–38.

45. Nicely illustrative of the point, as well as of auditors' petty tendency to question common-sense judgments of ambassadors and other officials, are the case studies in Gerald C. Schulsinger, *The General Accounting Office: Two Glimpses,* Inter-University Case No. 35 (Syracuse, N.Y.: Inter-University Case Program, 1956). For a full set of case studies illustrating past and current practice, see *Cases in Accountability: The Work of the GAO,* ed. Erasmus H. Kloman (Boulder, Colo.: Westview Press, 1979).

46. See the classic study, Harvey C. Mansfield, *The Comptroller General* (New Haven: Yale University Press, 1939).

47. General Accounting Office, *Standards for Audit of Governmental Organizations, Programs, Activities & Functions* (Washington, D.C.: Government Printing Office, 1973), i.

48. Congressional Budget Act of 1974, 88. Stat. 326; 31 *U.S. Code of Federal Regulations* 1154. (Emphasis added.)

49. These and other problems are treated by Joseph Pois and Ernest S. Griffith in U.S. Senate, Commission on Operation of the Senate, *Congressional Support Agencies,* 31–54, 126–33; Joseph Pois, "Trends in General Accounting Office Audits," and Ira Sharkansky, "The Politics of Auditing," in Smith, *The New Political Economy,* 245–318; and John T. Rourke, "The GAO: An Evolving Role," *Public Administration Review* 38 (September–October 1978): 453–57. A full history and analysis is Mosher, *The GAO.*

50. National Academy of Public Administration, *The Roles, Mission, and Operation of the U.S. General Accounting Office* (Washington, D.C.: National Academy of Public Administration, 1994), esp. i–ix.

51. For an analysis of the legislative veto, see Fisher, *Politics of Shared Power,* 94–104; Fisher, *Constitutional Conflicts Between Congress and the President;* Commission on Federal Paperwork, *Rulemaking* (Washington, D.C.: Government Printing Office, 1977), 59–79, 101–10; U.S. Congress, House of Representatives, Committee on Rules, *Studies on the Legislative Veto,* 96th Cong., 2d sess., 1980; John R.

Bolton, *The Legislative Veto: Unseparating the Powers* (Washington, D.C.: American Enterprise Institute, 1977); and Robert J. Spitzer, *The Presidential Veto: Touchstone of the American Presidency* (Albany: SUNY Press, 1988).

52. Fisher, *Politics of Shared Power*, 95.

53. Fisher, "Micromanagement by Congress," 147.

54. Sundquist, "Congress as Public Administrator," 281.

55. For an analysis, see Fisher, *Politics of Shared Power*, 86–89, 108–9.

56. *Immigration and Naturalization Service* v. *Chadha*, 462 U.S. 919, 957–58.

57. For a case study of *Chadha*, see Barbara H. Craig, *Chadha: The Story of an Epic Constitutional Struggle* (New York: Oxford University Press, 1988).

58. Some scholars vigorously objected to the Court's ruling. See, for example, Louis Fisher, "The Administrative World of *Chadha* and *Bowsher*," *Public Administration Review* 47 (May/June 1987): 213–20.

59. National Academy of Public Administration, *Congressional Oversight of Regulatory Agencies*, 12.

60. The estimate of the number of vetoes comes from Fisher's ongoing study of the legislative veto. See also Louis Fisher and James Saturno, *Legislative Vetoes Enacted After Chadha* (Washington, D.C.: Congressional Research Service, 28 April 1987).

61. The story is told in Fisher, "Micromanagement by Congress," 148–49. Congressional hearings after the *Chadha* decision provided useful insights into its effects. See U.S. House of Representatives, *Legislative Veto After Chadha, Hearings*, 98th Cong., 2d sess., 1984.

62. Joseph P. Harris puts the point more strongly: "if the committee objects to the proposed action, the departments invariably suspend action or modify the plans to meet the wishes of the committee." Harris, *Congressional Control of Administration* (Washington, D.C.: Brookings Institution, 1964), 233. For an example, see Donald F. Kettl, *The Regulation of American Federalism* (Baltimore: Johns Hopkins University Press, 1987), 143–46.

63. See Michael W. Kirst, *Government without Passing Laws: Congress' Nonstatutory Techniques for Appropriations Control* (Chapel Hill: University of North Carolina Press, 1969).

64. Foreman, *Signals from the Hill*, 6, 7. See also McCubbins and Schwartz, "Congressional Oversight Overlooked."

65. Complicating Congress's role is the era of divided government, with different parties in control of Congress and the presidency, for nearly all of the post—Vietnam period. See James L. Sundquist, "Needed: A Political Theory for the New Era of Coalition Government in the United States," *Political Science Quarterly* 103 (Winter 1988–89): 613–35.

66. Judith H. Gruber, *Controlling Bureaucracies: Dilemmas in Democratic Governance* (Berkeley: University of California Press, 1987), 57.

13. Regulation and the Courts (pp. 340–66)

1. Another object, often disputed, is reducing adults' freedom to harm them-

selves, as by smoking cigarettes, using narcotics, neglecting to use automobile safety belts, or buying excessively risky stocks and bonds. Regulation may be aimed at manufacturers and distributors (on the "harming others" premise), but often merely requires full disclosure of the risks, leaving citizens free to endanger their health, safety, or money.

2. Article I, sec. 8 (8). The current statute permits "fair use" by others of copyrighted material; the term's reach is judicially determined in individual cases.

3. Keith Schneider, "Biotechnology Advances Make Life Hard for Patent Office," *New York Times,* 17 April 1988.

4. For a more developed analysis, see *The Politics of Regulation,* ed. James Q. Wilson (New York: Basic Books, 1980), 364–72.

5. The response "too much regulation," though the largest category, needs qualification, as 24 percent say "not enough" and 35 percent say "about the right amount," a total of 59 percent. Our figures exclude the "Don't know" and "Not sure" responses, which were 11 percent in both cases. Survey results from the mid-1930s to the present have been remarkably consistent on the issue. See Seymour Martin Lipset and William Schneider, *The Confidence Gap: Business, Labor, and Government in the Public Mind,* rev. ed. (Baltimore: Johns Hopkins University Press, 1987), 221–56. See also Karlyn H. Keene and Everett C. Ladd, "Government as Villain: Has the Era Ended?—What the Public Says," *Government Executive* 20 (January 1988): 11–16, at 15 (reporting 1987 surveys by the Gallup Organization and NBC News/*Wall Street Journal*).

6. David Vogel, *National Styles of Regulation: Environmental Policy in Great Britain and the United States* (Ithaca, N.Y.: Cornell University Press, 1986), 267.

7. The best guide to each regulatory agency's activities, including problems encountered, is the *Federal Regulatory Directory,* 5th ed. (Washington, D.C.: Congressional Quarterly, 1986). More generally, see its section on the regulatory process at 1–77.

8. For the development of ICC railroad regulation to 1920, see Stephen Skowronek, *Building a New American State: The Expansion of National Administrative Capacities, 1877–1920* (New York: Cambridge University Press, 1982), 248–84.

9. A third issue addressed concerned safety and standards of service.

10. The classic work on the capture phenomenon is Marver H. Bernstein, *Regulating Business by Independent Commission* (Princeton, N.J.: Princeton University Press, 1955).

11. Our treatment draws on Michael D. Reagan, *Regulation: The Politics of Policy* (Boston: Little, Brown, 1987), 38–40.

12. For an insightful account and analysis of the deregulation movement, see Martha Derthick and Paul Quirk, *The Politics of Deregulation* (Washington, D.C.: Brookings Institution, 1985).

13. Even such seemingly moderate regulations may meet vigorous opposition from the affected industries. See A. Lee Fritschler, *Smoking and Politics,* 4th ed. (Englewood Cliffs, N.J.: Prentice Hall, 1989). Sometimes, though, industries welcome federal disclosure requirements, either because, as in the case of chemicals,

they displace confusing state and local regulations with a uniform national standard or because they enlighten responsible corporations on reprehensible practices of which they had been unaware. On worker and community "right-to-know" laws, see Margaret E. Kriz, "Fuming Over Fumes," *National Journal,* 26 November 1988, 3006–9.

14. General Accounting Office, *Food Marketing: Frozen Pizza Cheese—Representative of Broader Food Labeling Issues* (Washington, D.C.: Government Printing Office, 1988).

15. For a vivid account of EPA's regulation of coal-burning plants, see Bruce A. Ackerman and William T. Hassler, *Clean Coal/Dirty Air or How the Clean Air Act Became a Multibillion-Dollar Bail-Out for High-Sulfur Coal Producers and What Should Be Done about It* (New Haven: Yale University Press, 1981).

16. Regulatory inspectors' roles and performance are a major subject of Eugene Bardach and Robert A. Kagan, *Going by the Book: The Problem of Regulatory Unreasonableness,* a Twentieth Century Fund report (Philadelphia: Temple University Press, 1982).

17. See General Accounting Office, *Occupational Safety & Health: Assuring Accuracy in Employer Injury and Illness Records* (Washington, D.C.: Government Printing Office, 1988).

18. See Reagan, *Regulation,* 203–4; and Kenneth J. Meier, *Regulation: Politics, Bureaucracy, and Economics* (New York: St. Martin's Press, 1985), esp. 175–201 on occupational licensing.

19. See, especially, Reagan, *Regulation,* 178–202; Donald F. Kettl, *The Regulation of American Federalism* (Baton Rouge: Louisiana State University Press, 1983); and Advisory Commission on Intergovernmental Relations, *Regulatory Federalism: Policy, Process, Impact and Reform* (Washington, D.C.: Government Printing Office, 1984).

20. Advisory Commission on Intergovernmental Relations, *Regulatory Federalism,* 9–10, 82–88.

21. Ibid., 82.

22. The state had to convince OSHA that its program would assure workers' safety and health through appropriate legislation and standard setting and enforcement procedures, adequate funding, and a sufficient number of competent enforcement personnel. General Accounting Office, *Occupational Safety and Health: California's Resumption of Enforcement Responsibility in the Private Sector* (Washington, D.C.: Government Printing Office, 1989).

23. However, individuals claiming entitlement to benefits under federal statutes that a state fails to provide may sue to obtain the benefits for themselves and others with like entitlements. *Maine v. Thiboutot,* 448 U.S. 1 (1979).

24. EPA is to promulgate such regulations for treatment and disposal of "hazardous wastes ... as may be necessary to protect human health and the environment"; the secretary of labor is directed "to the extent feasible" to eliminate worker exposure to toxic substances capable of causing health impairment; the Consumer Products Safety Commission is "to protect the public against unreasonable risks of injury associated with consumer products."

25. 21 *U.S. Code of Federal Regulations* sec. 348, 360b, 576.

26. *Public Citizen* v. *Young,* 831 F.2d [Federal Circuit Court for the District of Columbia, 1987] 1108. The FDA's revisionary efforts and the court's decision are fully treated in Richard A. Merrill, "FDA's Implementation of the Delaney Clause: Repudiation of Congressional Choice or Reasoned Adaptation to Scientific Progress?" *Yale Journal on Regulation* 5 (Winter 1988): 1–88.

27. Reagan, *Regulation,* 96–97.

28. Lee M. Thomas, EPA administrator, address to the National Academy of Public Administration, 6 June 1986. Cf., on EPA's and other agencies' deadlines, *Congressional Oversight of Regulatory Agencies: The Need to Strike a Balance and Focus on Performance* (Washington, D.C.: National Academy of Public Administration, 1988), 20.

29. For the weakening of the independence of "independent regulatory commissions," see chap. 4.

30. See R. Shep Melnick, *Regulation and the Courts: The Case of the Clean Air Act* (Washington, D.C.: Brookings Institution, 1983), 38–43, 258–61; and William F. West, "The Growth of Internal Conflict in Administrative Regulation," *Public Administration Review* 48 (July/August 1988): 773–82.

31. "Scandals, Etc., From A to Z," *National Journal,* 14 January 1984, 92–93.

32. Cancer research depends mostly on mice and rats, whose morbidity is not a sure guide to humans' susceptibility. Human experience is scantily documented (though one in four Americans is estimated to have been exposed to carcinogens at work), partly because effects may occur decades after carcinogen exposure. For scientists' disagreements over the effect on lungs of ozone (the key ingredient in smog), see "Clean Air? Don't Hold Your Breath," *Science* 244 (5 May 1989): 517–20.

33. For a detailed critique, see Reagan, *Regulation,* 123–31.

34. One of many provocative points made by Aaron Wildavsky, *Searching for Safety* (New Brunswick, N.J.: Transaction, 1988). The risk-assessment literature is large. Entry to it and the issues may be pursued through Wildavsky; Charles Perrow, *Normal Accidents: Living with High-Risk Technologies* (New York: Basic Books, 1984); and Leroy C. Gould et al., *Perceptions of Technological Risks and Benefits* (New York: Russell Sage Foundation, 1988).

35. Peter Passell, "Life's Risks: Balancing Fear Against Reality of Statistics," *New York Times,* 8 May 1989, and "Making a Risky Life Bearable: Better Data, Clearer Choices," *New York Times,* 8 and 9 May 1989; Adam Clymer, "Polls Show Contrasts in How Public and EPA View Environment," *New York Times,* 22 May 1989; Cathy Marie Johnson, "New Agencies: What They Do and Why They Do It—The Case of the Consumer Product Safety Commission," paper prepared for the 84th Annual Meeting of the American Political Science Association, 1–4 September 1988.

36. For an argument that courts have moved to substantive review of regulatory agencies' actions, see Martin Shapiro, "The Supreme Court's 'Return' to Economic Regulation," in *Studies in American Political Development* (New Haven: Yale University Press, 1986), 1:91–141; and idem, *Who Guards the Guardians? Judicial Control of Administration* (Athens: University of Georgia Press, 1988).

37. 5 *U.S. Code of Federal Regulations,* 551–59; and 702–6 (judicial review).

38. For example, the APA's adjudicative requirements apply only if the agency's statutes require that its cases must "be determined on the record after opportunity for an agency hearing."

39. For a review of the delegation issue's development, see Louis Fisher, *Conflicts between Congress and the President* (Princeton, N.J.: Princeton University Press, 1985), 99–139; and Theodore J. Lowi, *The End of Liberalism: The Second Republic of the United States,* 2d ed. (New York: Norton, 1979), the latter a spirited critique of "the end of the rule of law." We should note that courts tend to interpret narrowly a statute that otherwise would be vulnerable to the constitutional attack.

40. See Office of the Federal Register, National Archives and Records Administration, *The Federal Register: What It Is and How to Use It,* rev. ed. (Washington, D.C.: Government Printing Office, 1985).

41. In addition, an interested party has the right to petition an agency for issuance, amendment, or repeal of a rule.

42. The APA's provisions about judicial review do not apply "to the extent that ... agency action is committed to agency discretion by law." The Supreme Court held this to be "a very narrow exception, ... applicable in those rare instances where 'statutes are drawn in such broad terms that in a given case there is no law to apply' " [quoting the Senate Report on the APA]. *Citizens to Preserve Overton Park, Inc.* v. *Volpe,* 401 U.S. 402 (1971).

43. For the problems associated with the "statutory duty" concept, see Shapiro, *Who Guards the Guardians?* 115–24.

44. 5 *U.S. Code of Federal Regulations* 3105, 5372, 7521. Before 1978, their titles were "hearing officers." About 700 are in the Social Security Administration; for SSA pressures on their impartiality, see Martin Tolchin, "Judges Who Decide Social Security Claims Say Agency Goads Them to Deny Benefits," and "Are Judge and Agency Too Close for Justice?" *New York Times,* 8 January and 5 February 1989.

45. The agency head(s) may also bypass these arrangements by holding the hearings and making the decision. Given the volume of cases and the time required for hearings, this is unusual.

46. Leonard Buder, "U.S. Is Suing Con Edison Over Asbestos," *New York Times,* 8 January 1988.

47. The VA (now a cabinet department) had a well-developed, informal process, including internal appeals, in which veterans were to be given the benefit of every doubt. Veterans' organizations (whose staff members represent veterans in the claims process) opposed the 1988 change of the statute. Lawyers favored change, along with repeal of a statutory limitation on their fees to $10 per case. See also Jerry Mashaw, *Due Process in the Administrative State* (New Haven: Yale University Press, 1985), 264–67, where he called the VA "the most competent and humane social services agency since King Solomon sat to dispense charity and justice to his adoring subjects."

48. *Eisen* v. *Carlyle & Jacquelin,* 417 U.S. 156 (1974).

49. Rochelle L. Stanfield, "Out-Standing in Court," *National Journal* 20 (13 February 1988): 388–91. The case, *National Wildlife Federation* v. *Hodel* (earlier

titled *In Re: Permanent Surface Mining Regulation Litigation),* was pending in the Federal Court of Appeals for the District of Columbia. The case had been in the courts since 1979(!).

50. See Peter H. Schuck, *Agent Orange on Trial: Mass Toxic Disasters in the Courts* (Cambridge: Harvard University Press, 1986). In 1989, the Department of Veterans' Affairs abided by, instead of appealing, a federal court decision that could result in government payments to up to 35,000 veterans who claimed disabilities from Agent Orange. Charles Mohr, "U.S. Not Appealing Agent Orange Case," *New York Times,* 12 May 1989.

51. *Data Processing Service Organizations* v. *Camp,* 397 U.S. 150 (1970). This propounded the "zone of interests" doctrine: even if a plaintiff cannot tie his claimed injury directly to a particular statutory or constitutional provision, the suit may proceed if the plaintiff's interest is "arguably within the zone of interests to be protected or regulated by the statute or constitutional guarantee in question." Ibid., 151–52.

52. Suits claiming breach of contracts are excluded from the torts category.

53. Whence comes the image of "ambulance chasing" lawyers. A recent development is the rise of tort actions against physicians and hospitals, leading to expensive liability insurance policies, which contribute to the rise in medical costs for patients.

54. General Accounting Office, *Product Liability: Extent of "Litigation Explosion" in Federal Courts Questioned* (Washington, D.C.: Government Printing Office, 1988).

55. For the history, see Phillip J. Cooper, *Public Law and Public Administration,* 2d ed. (Englewood Cliffs, N.J.: Prentice Hall, 1988), 363–89. An admirable review, with proposals for increasing governments' liability, is Peter H. Schuck, *Suing Government: Citizen Remedies for Official Wrongs* (New Haven: Yale University Press, 1983). Our treatment draws extensively on this work and on Jerry L. Mashaw and Richard A. Merrill, *Administrative Law* (St. Paul: West, 1992), 783–843. See also Jeremy Rabkin, "Where the Lines Have Held: Tort Claims Against the Federal Government," in *New Directions in Liability Law: Proceedings of the Academy of Political Science* 37, no. 1, ed. Walter Olson (New York: Academy of Political Science, 1988), 112–25.

56. 28 *U.S. Code of Federal Regulations* 1346, 2674, 2680. A 1974 amendment specified tort liability for assault, battery, false imprisonment, false arrest, abuse of process, and malicious prosecution by federal "investigative or law enforcement officials." Ibid., sec. 2680 (h).

57. Other significant limitations are (*a*) that the government is liable only to the extent that a private individual would be liable under the relevant state's law (though some government actions have no private counterpart); and (*b*) that the government is not liable for interest prior to judgment or for punitive damages (as distinguished from merely compensatory damages), for both of which a private defendant might be liable.

58. The leading case is *Barr* v. *Matteo,* 360 U.S. 564 (1959).

59. *Bivens* v. *Six Unknown Named Agents of the Federal Bureau of Narcotics,*

403 U.S. 388 (1971), and *Wood* v. *Strickland,* 420 U.S. 308 (1975). Curiously, absolute immunity continues to protect judges, administrative law judges, and prosecutors from tort actions (though not from criminal prosecution). The Supreme Court's reasoning, seemingly serving the self-interest of its branch's members and associates, has been criticized as indistinguishable from the reasoning that would ensure executive officials' riskless exercise of discretionary judgment.

60. *Westfall* v. *Erwin,* 108 Supreme Court Reporter 580 (1988). Federal Employee Liability and Tort Compensation Act, 102 U.S. Statutes 4563. The key question becomes whether the employee was acting "within the scope" of his or her official duties, not whether the duties were discretionary or non-discretionary.

61. 42 *U.S. Code of Federal Regulations* 1983.

62. See Michael Lipsky, *Street-Level Bureaucracy: The Dilemmas of the Individual in Public Services* (New York: Russell Sage Foundation, 1980).

63. 94 U.S. Statutes 2325. For later amendments, see 28 *U.S. Code of Federal Regulations* 2412. Net worth of an individual must be under $2 million and of a corporation or organization under $7 million. Number of employees (an alternative basis) may not exceed 500.

64. For a critique of fee recovery, see Grover Rees III, "Foul Play in 'Public Interest' Litigation: The Joy of Attorneys' Fees," *Regulation,* January/February 1985, 19–55.

65. For further development of the contrasts, see Donald L. Horowitz, *The Courts and Social Policy* (Washington, D.C.: Brookings Institution, 1977).

66. So do agency lawyers and those in the Department of Justice, which claims (not always successfully) a monopoly of litigating authority. For the conflicting attitudes, see Donald L. Horowitz, *The Jurocracy: Government Lawyers, Agency Programs, and Judicial Decisions* (Lexington, Mass.: Lexington Books, 1977). For agency lawyers' attributes and incentives, see Eve Spangler, *Lawyers for Hire* (New Haven: Yale University Press, 1986), 107–43.

67. See Phillip J. Cooper, "Conflict or Constructive Tension: The Changing Relationship of Judges and Administrators," *Public Administration Review* 45 (Special Issue, November 1985): 643–52.

68. The classic analysis of the courts' emphasis on wide participation in agency proceedings is Richard B. Stewart, "The Reformation of American Administrative Law," *Harvard Law Review* 88 (June 1975): 1667–1813.

69. The courts derive such intentions from the legislative history of a statute. For an argument that this has unhappily magnified the role of congressional subcommittees and their staffs, which compile the legislative history (reports, floor statements, and hearings), see R. Shep Melnick, "The Politics of Partnership," *Public Administration Review* 45 (Special Issue, November 1985): 651–60.

70. Melnick, *Regulation and the Courts,* 379. Melnick's book is an admirable review of the throes of developing policies in a court-monitored setting.

71. Mashaw, *Due Process,* 160–61. The shifting attitudes are well traced and appraised in this work. For greater detail, see Mashaw and Merrill, *Administrative Law.*

72. Jerry L. Mashaw, *Bureaucratic Justice: Managing Social Security Disability*

Claims (New Haven: Yale University Press, 1983), 18. In 1988 the SSA was losing 50 percent of appeals (disability and other types) within the agency and in the courts. Irvin Molotsky, "Plan to Curb Benefit Appeals Is Rejected," *New York Times,* 4 December 1988.

73. Chief Justice Rehnquist's annual report, quoted in "Rehnquist Taking Stock of the Federal Judiciary," *New York Times,* 6 January 1988.

74. Two studies argue from data that Reagan's extraordinary use of these powers and presidentially initiated regulatory review did not diminish significantly the agencies' vigor in enforcing regulatory statutes. B. Dan Wood, "Principals, Bureaucrats, and Responsiveness in Clean Air Enforcements," *American Political Science Review* 82 (March 1988): 213–34; William J. Pielsticker, "Presidential Control of Administrative Rule Making: Its Potential and Its Limits," paper delivered at the 1988 Annual Meeting of the American Political Science Association, Washington, D.C., 1–4 September 1988.

75. Executive Orders 12,291, 3 *U.S. Code of Federal Regulations* (1981 compilation) and 12,498, ibid. (1985 compilation).

76. Major assessments are Morton Rosenberg, "Regulatory Management," in U.S. Senate Committee on Governmental Affairs, *Office of Management and Budget: Evolving Roles and Future Issues,* 98th Cong., 2d sess., Senate print 99–134 (February 1986), 185–233; *Presidential Management of Rulemaking in Regulatory Agencies: A Report by a Panel of the National Academy of Public Administration* (Washington, D.C.: National Academy of Public Administration, January 1987); and Pielsticker, "Presidential Control of Administrative Rule Making." See also General Accounting Office, *Regulatory Review: Information on OMB's Review Process* (Washington, D.C.: Government Printing Office, 1989).

77. This is reinforced by OMB's power, under the Paperwork Act of 1980, to review and disapprove agencies' proposals to collect information. But the Supreme Court overturned OMB's use of the Act to block agencies' regulations that require private parties such as employers to disclose information (e.g., exposure to hazardous substances) to other private parties such as employees. *Dole* v. *U.S. Steelworkers of America,* 110 Supreme Court Reporter 929 (1990).

78. The president's 5 January 1985 memorandum to agencies said, "This review will not interfere with the exercise of authority committed by statute to heads of agencies," and the executive orders formalize this. But practice did not conform; OMB even ignored statutory deadlines applying to agency actions.

79. The system was instituted by President Reagan without specific statutory authorization, though he claimed to be acting "by the authority vested in me as President by the Constitution and laws of the United States."

80. *Presidential Management of Rulemaking,* vii and passim.

81. Cooper, *Public Law and Public Administration,* 398–99.

14. Conclusion (pp. 367–86)

1. *Responses of the Presidents to Charges of Misconduct,* ed. C. Vann Woodward (New York: Dell, 1974), 9.

2. John P. Burke, *Bureaucratic Responsibility* (Baltimore: Johns Hopkins University Press, 1986), 10. He claims, too boldly it appears, that "one of the essential claims of formal legalism is that bureaucrats should have no discretion in either making or implementing policy" (p. 11). A close analogy to the formal-legal concept is the legal doctrine of principal-agent relations, which allows for the agent to use discretion on behalf of his principal's interests.

3. See Douglas Yates, *Bureaucratic Democracy: The Search for Democracy and Efficiency in American Government* (Cambridge: Harvard University Press, 1982), esp. 8–61; and Arthur M. Okun, *Equality and Efficiency: The Big Tradeoff* (Washington, D.C.: Brookings Institution, 1975).

4. Judith E. Gruber, *Controlling Bureaucracies: Dilemmas in Democratic Governance* (Berkeley: University of California Press, 1987), esp. 202–14.

5. This is not guaranteed. As noted in chapter 13, the Office of Management and Budget's requirement that regulatory agencies submit proposed studies and regulations for OMB review resulted during the Reagan administration in OMB rejection of some important regulatory initiatives closely attuned to statutory mandates.

6. Norton Long, "Bureaucracy and Constitutionalism," *American Political Science Review* 46 (September 1952): 814. Cf. Samuel Krislov and David H. Rosenbloom, *Representative Bureaucracy and the American Political System* (New York: Praeger, 1981).

7. Michael Wines, "Justice Department Lawyers Assail Anti-Abortion Effort," *New York Times,* 26 March 1989.

8. For perceptive analyses, see William F. West and Joseph Cooper, "Legislative Influence v. Presidential Dominance: Competing Models of Bureaucratic Control," *Political Science Quarterly* 104, no. 4 (1989–90): 581–606; and Christopher H. Foreman, Jr., *Signals from the Hill: Congressional Oversight and the Challenge of Social Regulation* (New Haven: Yale University Press, 1988).

9. For two-thirds of the time between 1955 and 1990, the government was divided between the parties. For the implications of this for the "party government" theory, see James L. Sundquist, "Needed: A Political Theory for the New Era of Coalition Government in the United States," *Political Science Quarterly* 103 (Fall 1988): 613–35.

10. Gruber, *Controlling Bureaucracies,* 121–48.

11. Bernard Rosen, *Holding Government Bureaucracies Accountable* (New York: Praeger, 1982); *Revitalizing Federal Management: Managers and Their Overburdened Systems,* A Panel Report of the National Academy of Public Administration (Washington, D.C.: National Academy of Public Administration, 1983).

12. Very likely. See Burke, *Bureaucratic Responsibility,* 7 and 152. However, his chapter 8 cautions against overreliance on professional expertise.

13. Peter Self, *Administrative Theories and Politics* (London: Allen and Unwin, 1972), 277–78. (Emphasis in original.)

14. "The need for operative ideas on how to make accountability a reality under modern conditions is urgent, but it must be admitted that there is a remarkable dearth of such ideas despite great dissatisfaction with the present state of affairs and with the older … notions of accountability." *The Dilemma of Accountability in*

Modern Government, ed. Bruce L.R. Smith and D.C. Hague (New York: St. Martin's Press, 1971), 28.

15. See chapter 11's discussion of "The Importance of Feedback."

16. For the prevalence and the inadequacy of this approach to internal control, see U.S. Comptroller General, *Federal Agencies Can and Should Do More to Combat Fraud in Government Programs* (Washington, D.C.: Government Printing Office, 1978); and Jerome B. McKinney and Michael Johnston, eds., *Fraud, Waste, and Abuse in Government: Causes, Consequences, and Cures* (Philadelphia: Institute for the Study of Human Issues, 1986).

17. Michael Lipsky, *Street-Level Bureaucracy* (New York: Russell Sage Foundation, 1980).

18. *Serve with Honor: Report of the President's Commission on Federal Ethics Law Reform,* March 1989 (Washington, D.C.: Government Printing Office, 1989), 104–8. Most violations are felonies, punishable by up to two years' imprisonment and a fine of up to $250,000. The commission proposed and the 1989 Ethics Reform Act added civil penalties and injunctive relief.

19. The "Eichmann Defense" (a Nazi's plea that I was not guilty because I was only doing what my superiors told me to do) is inadmissible in this country as a defense against a criminal charge. In the North case, the federal district judge so instructed the jury. The jury, however, ignored the instructions, and the judge's mild sentence rested on North's having done what his superiors wanted. Later, North's superior, Admiral John Poindexter, was convicted of lying to Congress.

20. James Coates and Michael Kilian, *Heavy Losses: The Dangerous Decline of American Defense* (New York: Viking, 1985), 103; A. Ernest Fitzgerald, *The Pentagonists: An Insider's View of Waste, Mismanagement, and Fraud in Defense Spending* (Boston: Houghton Mifflin, 1989). For a broader coverage, see Myron Peretz Glazer and Penina Migdal Glazer, *The Whistleblowers: Exposing Corruption in Government and Industry* (New York: Basic Books, 1989).

21. Public Law 101-12, 10 April 1989.

22. U.S. Merit Systems Protection Board, *Whistleblowing in the Federal Government: An Update* (Washington, D.C.: Government Printing Office, 1993).

23. General Accounting Office, *Whistleblower Protection: Reasons for Whistleblower Complainants' Dissatisfaction Need to Be Explored,* GGD-94-21, November 1993.

24. Inspector General Act of 1978, Public Law 95-452. An additional thirty-two inspectors general are appointed by heads of other agencies. See General Accounting Office, *Inspectors General: Information on Vacancies and Previous Experience* (Washington, D.C.: Government Printing Office, 1990); Eileen Siedman, "Toothless Junk-Yard Dogs?" *Bureaucrat* 18 (Winter 1989–90): 6–8; and Sherman Funk and Eileen Siedman, "Are Inspectors General Toothless Junk-Yard Dogs?" *Bureaucrat* 19 (Spring 1990): 7–8.

25. "Quis custodiet ipsos custodes?" Juvenal, *Satires,* line 347. Our free translation communicates more immediately and less ambiguously than the standard translations, such as "Who will be guarding the guards?" "Who is to keep guard over the guards?" and "Who will watch the Warders"—particularly as Juvenal's

point is distrust of the eunuchs guarding a man's mistresses.

26. The classic argument for redundancy in administrative organization and process is Martin Landau, "Redundancy, Rationality, and the Problem of Duplication and Overlap," *Public Administration Review* 29 (July–August 1969): 346–58.

27. For example, until the 1950s, the General Accounting Office, the Treasury Department, and the Bureau of the Budget separately prescribed the kinds of information that agencies' accounting systems had to produce.

28. Smith and Hague, *Dilemma of Accountability*, 29.

29. We should not be interpreted as going so far as one scholar: "Bureaucrats ought not determine which of several competing demands they should follow, nor should they themselves 'scale down' impossibly high expectations. They should, however, refuse to be 'passed the buck,' and they should encourage higher authorities to make proper decisions." And "Bureaucrats incur responsibilities to make sure that policy makers provide the resources necessary to their policy tasks." Burke, *Bureaucratic Responsibility*, 51, 82.

30. If the court claims to interpret a statute (not the Constitution), the agency may seek congressional amendment of the law, but is unlikely to succeed unless a major issue is at stake.

31. Albert O. Hirschman, *Exit, Voice, and Loyalty: Responses to Decline in Firms, Organizations, and States* (Cambridge: Harvard University Press, 1970). Popular commentaries generally exaggerate the ease of conscience-driven exit. A civil servant with a family to support is deterred by the prospect of the immediate ending of his income and uncertainties about timely employment in the private sector. In contrast, most high political appointees, with established reputations and extensive contacts in the private sector, can exit to prompt employment at higher salaries. Consider, too, that an attack by a resigning official is usually only a one-day media event.

32. See Carl J. Friedrich, "Public Policy and the Nature of Administrative Responsibility," in *Public Policy*, ed. Carl J. Friedrich and E.S. Mason (Cambridge: Harvard University Press, 1940), 3–24; and Herman Finer, "Administrative Responsibility in Democratic Government," *Public Administration Review* 1 (Summer 1941): 335–50.

33. Ethical breakdowns in the 1980s partly account for growth of the literature about governmental ethics. See John A. Rohr, *Ethics for Bureaucrats: An Essay on Law and Values*, 2d ed. (New York: Marcel Dekker, 1989); James S. Bowman and Frederick A. Elliston, eds., *Ethics, Government, and Public Policy: A Reference Guide* (Westport, Conn.: Greenwood Press, 1988); Robert N. Roberts, *White House Ethics: The History of the Politics of Conflict of Interest Regulation* (Westport, Conn.: Greenwood Press, 1988).

34. G. Calvin Mackenzie, " 'If You Want to Play, You've Got to Pay': Ethics Regulation and the Presidential Appointments System, 1964–1984," in *The In-and-Outers: Presidential Appointees and Transient Government in Washington*, ed. G. Calvin Mackenzie (Baltimore: Johns Hopkins University Press, 1987), 77.

35. Appraisal of the Office of Government Ethics has varied from a congressman's saying it functioned "like a toothless terrier on Valium" to a view that it has

done a creditable job, given its tiny staff (27 persons in 1988; later increased). Clifford D. May, "Office of Government Ethics: Taking Lots of Heat from and about Meese," *New York Times,* 8 July 1987; Government Accounting Office, *Ethics: Office of Government Ethics' Policy Development Role (1988),* and *The Public Service: Issues Affecting Its Quality, Effectiveness, Integrity, and Stewardship* (Washington, D.C.: Government Printing Office, 1989), 49.

36. *To Serve with Honor: Report of the President's Commission on Federal Ethics Law Reform,* March 1989 (Washington, D.C.: Government Printing Office, 1989); *Weekly Compilation of Presidential Documents* 25 (12 April 1989): 525–34. See also Executive Order 12674, 12 April 1989, ibid., 526–28.

37. Public Law 101–94, 30 November 1989. The act did extend most ethics requirements to the legislative and judicial branches, with some adaptation to institutional differences.

38. "Remarks to the American Society of Newspaper Editors," 12 April 1989, in *Weekly Compilation,* 531–34, at 532.

39. *Leadership in Jeopardy: The Fraying of the Presidential Appointments System* (Washington, D.C.: National Academy of Public Administration, 1985), 13.

40. *To Serve with Honor,* 25.

41. Such a fund may be a mutual fund, regulated investment company, pension or deferred compensation plan, or other investment fund, provided the fund is publicly traded or the fund's assets are widely diversfied and, in either case, the appointee has no control over the fund's handling of assets.

42. Mackenzie, "If You Want to Play," 85–86.

43. Ibid.

44. *Leadership in Jeopardy,* 11–12. Currently, the report notes, "candidate for Assistant Secretary of Agriculture for Rural Development requires the same kind of background investigation as a candidate for Secretary of Defense."

45. General Accounting Office, *Ethics Enforcement: Filing and Review of the Attorney General's Financial Disclosure Report* (Washington, D.C.: Government Printing Office, 1987).

46. For example, an annual financial disclosure report need only list gifts from each source that aggregate $250 or more. An intendedly clarifying, but confusing, document: Inspector General, Department of Defense, *Defense Ethics: A Standards of Conduct Guide for DoD Employees* (Washington, D.C.: Government Printing Office, 1989).

47. Ralph Blumenthal, "Public Officials Around the State Accepted 105 of 106 Bribes Offered, the FBI Says," *New York Times,* 12 August 1987. New York City was in 1986–87 beset with corruption problems. See "Tangled Strands: Anatomy of the New York City Scandals," *New York Times,* 23 March 1987. For the state government's 1987 ethics law's operation, see Elizabeth Kolbert, "Once-Feared, Albany Ethics Law Leaves Mainly Annoyance," *New York Times,* 3 September 1989.

48. Ronald Smothers, "Political Graft Charges Mounting in Mississippi," *New York Times,* 20 October 1987.

49. 18 *U.S. Code of Federal Regulations* 207.

50. An awkward problem for these is the criminal code's ban on participating

in matters in the government that would affect the financial interests of a company with which they are negotiating for employment. A solution chosen by some is to announce their intention to resign months before their resignation, expecting that by the latter date they will have on hand several offers about which they can negotiate.

51. 102 U.S. Statutes 4065; 10 *U.S. Code of Federal Regulations* 2397 b and c.

52. General Accounting Office, *DOD Revolving Door: Few Are Restricted from Post-DOD Employment and Reporting Has Some Gaps* (Washington, D.C.: Government Printing Office, 1990); Andrew Rosenthal, "Worry on Government Recruiting Prompts Vote to Delay Ethics Law," and "House, Like Senate, Votes to Delay Ethics Law," *New York Times,* 13 and 16 May 1989.

53. General Accounting Office, *DOD Revolving Door: Post-DOD Employment May Raise Concerns* (Washington, D.C.: Government Printing Office, 1987).

54. "Deaver Abandons Appeals on Convictions for Perjury," *New York Times,* 5 February 1989. His sentence was a $100,000 fine and 1,500 hours of community service, editorially criticized as "a slap on the wrist." "Justice Blinked for Michael Deaver," *New York Times,* 28 September 1988; Martin Tolchin, "Court Overturns Guilty Verdict in Nofziger Case," *New York Times,* 28 June 1989. The later 1989 Ethics Reform Act precludes defense claims like Nofziger's.

55. Philip Shenon, "Watt Details Role for $400,000 Fees," *New York Times,* 10 June 1989. The 1989 Ethics Reform Act bans former Cabinet members' lobbying of presidential appointees for a year after departure form office. Disclosure of Watt's profiting by influence peddling began a broad-ranging congressional exposure of scandals at HUD in the Reagan administration. In addition to its top appointees' favoring former political officials, HUD so neglected supervision of private escrow agents ("proxies" used by HUD in sales of foreclosed properties) that one such agent stole $5.7 million, diverting much to charity; federal investigators dubbed her "Robin HUD." Jason DeParle, " 'Robin HUD' Given a Stiff Sentence," *New York Times,* 23 June 1990.

56. Neal R. Peirce, "Locals, Too, Exit through the Revolving Door," *National Journal* 18 (21 June 1986): 1556.

57. Quoted in review of Wilfrid Sheed, *The Boys of Winter* (New York: Knopf, 1987), *New York Times Book Review,* 2 August 1987.

58. One account says that in six years, "more than 100 members of the Reagan Administration have had ethical or legal charges leveled against them. That number is without precedent." "Morality Among the Supply-Siders," *Time* 129 (25 July 1987): 18–20, at 18. Individual cases are detailed there and in "Scandals, Etc., From A to Z," *National Journal* 13 (14 January 1984): 92–93. A list of 242 alleged violators of ethics in the Reagan period was issued on 30 March 1988 by Patricia Schroeder, chairwoman of the House Subcommittee on Civil Service; some allegations, of course, are unfounded.

59. No. 51 of *The Federalist Papers,* ed. Jacob E. Cooke (Middletown, Conn.: Wesleyan University Press, 1961), 349. Madison was here justifying the system of checks and balances.

60. Aaron Wildavsky, "Ubiquitous Anomie: Public Service in an Era of Ideological Dissensus," *Public Administration Review* 48 (July/August 1988): 753–55, at

754.

61. Whitney North Seymour, Jr., quoted in Martin Tolchin, "Deaver Prosecutor Asks Tougher Conflict Laws," *New York Times,* 19 December 1987. Seymour sued Deaver for perjury, rather than for Ethics Act postemployment lobbying, because the Office of Government Ethics, using its discretionary authority, had designated nine units of the Executive Office as separate agencies, so none that Deaver contacted, other than the White House itself, was "his" former agency. See General Accounting Office, *Ethics Regulations: Compartmentalization of Agencies Under the Ethics in Government Act* (Washington, D.C.: Government Printing Office, 1987), 13–17. The 1989 Ethics Reform Act precludes the office's compartmentalization of the Executive Office.

62. Carl M. Brauer, *Presidential Transitions: Eisenhower through Reagan* (New York: Oxford University Press, 1986), 232. A *New York Times* editorial (3 January 1988) even said that "President Reagan presides over one of the most corrupt administrations ever. . . . Precise comparisons to the Grant, Harding and Nixon Administrations aren't possible or necessary. The Reagan Administration rivals them all." See also "The Reagan Swamp," *New York Times,* 26 June 1989.

63. *Leadership for America: Rebuilding the Public Service,* Report of the National Commission on the Public Service (Lexington, Mass.: Lexington Books, 1989), 25, and Task Force Reports, 178–79, 199.

64. Ibid., Task Force Reports, 177.

65. Derek Bok, " 'A Daring and Complicated Strategy,' " *Harvard Magazine,* May–June 1989, 47–58, at 49. President Bok was chairman of the Volcker Commission's task force on education and training.

66. Ibid; and *Leadership for America,* Task Force Reports, 185–91. Bok's article, his annual presidential report for 1987–88, provides an appreciative and critical review of Harvard's John F. Kennedy School of Government.

67. Preamble to the Constitution of the United States.

68. "Remarks to the Members of the Senior Executive Service," 26 January 1989, *Weekly Compilation of Presidential Documents* 25, 117–19.

List of Acronyms

ACLU	American Civil Liberties Union
ACWA	Administrative Careers with America
AEC	Atomic Energy Commission
AFDC	Aid to Families with Dependent Children
AFSCME	American Federation of State, County, and Municipal Employees
AIDS	Acquired Immune Deficiency Syndrome
AMTRAK	National Railroad Passenger Corporation
APA	Administrative Procedure Act
BOB	Bureau of the Budget
CBO	Congressional Budget Office
CEA	Council of Economic Advisors
CEQ	Council on Environmental Quality
CFR	Code of Federal Regulations
CPI	Consumer Price Index
CPSC	Cosumer Product Safety Commission
DIA	Defense Intelligence Agency
DOD	Department of Defense
DOE	Department of Energy
DOEd	Department of Education
DOT	Department of Transportation
EDA	Economic Development Administration
EEOC	Equal Employment Opportunity Commission
EOP	Executive Office of the President
EPA	Enviromental Protection Agency
FBI	Federal Bureau of Investigation
FDA	Federal Drug Administration
FDIC	Federal Deposit Insurance Corporation
Fed	Federal Reserve Board

FEI	Federal Executive Institute
FLRA	Federal Labor Relations Authority
FPC	Federal Power Commission
FTC	Federal Trade Commission
GAO	General Accounting Office
GDP	Gross domestic product
GRH	Gramm-Rudman-Hollings Act
GS	General Schedule of Classification and Pay
HCFA	Health Care Financing Administration
HEW	Department of Health, Education, and Welfare
HHS	Department of Health and Human Services
HUD	Department of Housing and Urban Development
ICC	Interstate Commerce Commission
IRS	Internal Revenue Service
MBO	Management by Objectives
MSPB	Merit System Production Board
NAACP	National Association for the Advancement of Colored People
NAPA	National Academy of Public Administration
NASA	National Aeronautics and Space Administration
NCSL	National Council of State Legislatures
NEA	National Education Association
NIH	National Institutes of Health
NIMBY	"Not in my back yard"
NPR	National Performance Review
NRA	National Recovery Administration
NRDC	National Resources Defense Council
NSC	National Security Council
NSF	National Science Foundation
OASDI	Old Age, Survivors, and Disability Insurance
OD	Organization Development
OECD	Organization of Economic Cooperation and Development
OGE	Office of Government Ethics
OMB	Office of Management and Budget
OPA	Office of Price Administration
OPM	Office of Personnel Management
OSHA	Occupational Safety and Health Administration
OTA	Office of Technology Assessment
PACE	Professional and Administrative Career Examination
PPBS	Planning-Programming-Budgeting System
RIF	Reductions in force

SEC	Securities and Exchange Commission
SES	Senior Executive Service
SSA	Social Security Administration
TQM	Total Quality Management
TVA	Tennessee Valley Authority
USCG	U.S. Coast Guard
USDA	U.S. Department of Agriculture
USPS	U.S. Postal Service
VA	Veterans Administration
ZBB	Zero-base budgeting

Index of Names

Index of Subjects

About the Authors

JAMES W. FESLER is the Alfred Cowles Professor Emeritus of Government at Yale University. He was born in Duluth, Minnesota, graduated from the University of Minnesota, and received his doctorate from Harvard University. He taught at the University of North Carolina before joining the Yale faculty.

He has served as vice-president of the American Political Science Association, editor-in-chief of the *Public Administration Review,* and associate editor of the *American Political Science Review.* He received the Dwight Waldo Award of the American Society for Public Administration "for distinguished contributions to the professional literature of public administration," and the John Gaus Award of the American Political Science Association for "a lifetime of exemplary scholarship in the joint tradition of political science and public administration."

His books include *Area and Administration; The Independence of State Regulatory Agencies; Public Administration;* and, as editor and co-author, *Industrial Mobilization for War* (the official history of the War Production Board); *The 50 States and Their Local Governments;* and *American Public Administration: Patterns of the Past.*

He has served on the staffs of the President's (Brownlow) Committee on Administrative Management and the War Production Board, and as a consultant to federal agencies and the United Nations. He has also been a member of the New Haven Redevelopment Agency's governing board and of the Connecticut Governor's Committee on the Structure of State Government.

DONALD F. KETTL previously taught at Columbia University, the University of Virginia, and Vanderbilt University before joining the faculty at the University of Wisconsin, where he is Professor in the Department of Political Science and in the Robert M. La Follette Institute of Public Affairs. He is the author of several books, including *Inside the Reinvention*

Machine with John J. DiIulio, Jr.; *Deficit Politics: Public Budgeting in Institutional and Historical Context; Government by Proxy: (Mis?)Managing Federal Programs; Leadership at the Fed;* and *The Regulation of American Federalism;* and many articles. He has served as a consultant to the U.S. Food and Drug Administration, the Federal National Mortgage Association, the National Commission on the Public Service, the Securities and Exchange Commission, and the U.S. Department of the Treasury.